TO BATTLE

The Formation and History of the 14th Galician Waffen-SS Division

Of all the 'foreign' Waffen-SS divisions, the 14th has arguably maintained a higher public profile and continued to attract more attention in the UK, USA, Canada, Russia, Ukraine and Poland than any other.

Drawing extensively upon a wide variety of sources, the author details the abortive history of German/Ukrainian relations during the first half of the twentieth century which preceded the formation of the Galician Division in the spring of 1943.

Set firmly within the political context of the time, this work demonstrates that from the outset both German and Ukrainian architects of the Division sought to exploit the formation for their own conflicting agendas.

The author gives a careful assessment of the Division's military engagements and explains the reasons for its defeat at the Battle of Brody, emphasising how the military initiative and vast material superiority of the Red Army led to its virtual destruction during the Soviet summer offensive of 1944.

The book concludes with the cessation of hostilities, when the Division, despite being the focus of Stalin's attention, escaped the forced repatriation operations undertaken by the Western Allies in the immediate post-war period.

Michael J. Melnyk

Michael J. Melnyk is a 38-year-old son of a veteran of the 14th Galician Division who has been engaged in researching this unit for over 15 years. In the process he has travelled to several different countries in Europe, as well as to Canada and the USA, interviewing veterans and visiting numerous historical archives and institutions collecting material. Over this period, he has become a recognised international authority on the subject and in this capacity he is often consulted by national and international newspapers and has been interviewed for numerous radio programmes, as well taking part in television documentaries. He is currently engaged preparing a new book.

Cover photograph credits

Front cover Neuhammer, 14 April 1944, Waffen-Untersturmführer Dyhdalewysch with his NCOs from the 3rd Company Pioneer Battalion.

Rear cover (clockwise, reading from top left) Grave of Waffen-Untersturm-führer Bohdan Sobolewsky of Kampfgruppe Beyersdorff, who shot himself just before the unit's departure upon learning members of his company had illegally appropriated food from the local inhabitants; Sverkha on the Buh river. Action against partisans. A machine-gun group from Kampfgruppe Beyersdorff at the ready; L'viv, 18 July 1943, before the university building mounted Ukrainian Cossacks carrying a flag of the Ukrainian national colours (blue and yellow) parade before the assembled dignitaries; March 1944 – SS-Brigade- führer und Generalmajor der Waffen-SS Freitag inspects the Division at Neuhammer prior to the bestowal of awards.

I0869363

TO BATTLE

The Formation and History of the 14th Galician Waffen-SS Division

Michael James Melnyk

HELION & COMPANY

Dedicated to the memory of my father, Petro Igor Melnyk

Helion & Company Limited
26 Willow Road
Solihull
West Midlands
B91 1UE
England
Tel. 0121 705 3393
Fax 0121 711 4075
Email: publishing@helion.co.uk
Website: http://www.helion.co.uk

Originally published by Helion & Company Limited 2002. Reprinted in paperback 2007.

Designed and typeset by Bookcraft Ltd, Stroud, Gloucestershire
Cover design by Michael Melnyk
Printed by Henry Ling Ltd, Dorchester, Dorset

ISBN 978 1 874622 19 2

British Library Cataloguing-in-Publication Data.
A catalogue record for this book is available from the British Library.

The author is interested in hearing from any readers with their comments and criticism, especially veterans and anyone possessing additional material relating to this unit. Please contact him via the publishers.

CONTENTS

5

6

7

8

9

10

APPENDICES

LIST OF MAPS

(With the exception of the sketch maps prepared and sent to the author by W. D. Heike, the remaining maps were prepared by the author).

ACKNOWLEDGEMENTS

To mention by name all those who contributed to the preparation of this study would be an arduous task, and while they are no less deserving, for the sake of brevity I have elected to limit my thanks to the few to whom I owe a special debt of gratitude.

I would like to offer my sincere and heartfelt thanks to Roman Kolisnyk, Eugene Shypailo, Roman Hawrylak, and Marian Hajva, who are the respective representatives of the The Brotherhood of Former Combatants in Canada and the USA, and The Association of Ukrainian Former Combatants in Great Britain.

Similarly, I would like to extend my appreciation in equal measure to; Roman Cholkan, Prof. Roman Drazniowsky, Michael Duskursky, Ihor Fedyk, Wolf-Dietrich Heike, *Frau* Käthe Heike, Roman Herasymowych, Jaroslav Hnatkiv, Orest Horodysky, Mychailo Klymchuk and his son Andrej, Bohdan Kutny, Jaroslav Kunysky, Stephan Sadiwsky, Myroslav Scharko, Eugene Shypailo, Dr Wasyl Sirskyj, Dr Ostap Sokolsky, Orest Slupchynskyj, Dr Vasyl Veryha and Constantine Zelenko all of whom generously took the time and trouble to supply useful material and help me resolve some very difficult and often contentious issues.

Acknowledgements are also due to Sean Claxton, David Daynes, Rick Goodwin, Julian Hendy, Andrew Hook, Martin Kirby, Iago Krusel, Trevor Markworth, Mrs Rakowbowchuk, Steve Tyas, and Steve Rawluk, whose encouragement and contributions in various capacities greatly facilitated and expedited the completion of this work. The remarkable computer skills of Andrew Keys, who came to my rescue on many occasions from the perils of technology, also merit a special mention.

David M. Glantz very kindly provided me with a copy of his translation of the Soviet General Staff Study of the L'vov-Sandomierz Operation, which proved to be an invaluable source of information, as did the excellent *Offiziereliste der Waffen-SS*, compiled over the course of many years by John P. Moore. For the numerous translations, I was fortunate to have the assistance of Roman Hawrylak, whose expertise and knowledge of the German language I cannot overestimate, while Klemen Luzar made available much useful data pertaining to the Division's activities in Slovenia.

A great deal of credit for the successful completion of this book belongs to Roman Kolisnyk for his industrious work on my behalf and for his inexhaustible patience, unflagging enthusiasm, wise counsel and constant encouragement. Throughout the many years that I was engaged on this project, we exchanged a huge amount of material in addition to which I received over one hundred and seventy letters from him which bears witness to the measure of his assistance.

The assistance of the respective staffs at the National Archives in Washington D.C., the Imperial War Museum, London, the Ukrainian Research and Documentation Centre, Toronto, and Giles Bennett at the Institut für Zeitgeschichte, München, was also much appreciated.

A special thanks to my mother Rose Melnyk, not least for her secretarial skills, my ever suffering companion Julie Schofield who shared many of the trials and tribulations associated with this work, for her understanding, and our first son, Myron Oskar Schofield Melnyk, for inspiration.

Several authorities read the entire manuscript in various draft forms and added either to the content, or made numerous incisive criticisms, corrections, amendments and additions. Any errors or omissions that remain in the text in spite of their efforts are solely my own responsibility.

Norwich, England, 2002

NOTES ON SOURCES AND STYLE

LIST OF ABBREVIATIONS

See also glossary at rear of book for abbreviations relating to military terms.

AA	Author's Archive
ABFC	Archives of the Brotherhood of Former Combatants
APL	Archiwum Panstwowe w Lublinie
BA-KO	Bundesarchiv, Koblenz (When this work was almost complete, the German military archive at Koblenz transferred all its Third Reich material to the new archive established in Germany at Berlin-Lichterfelde. The files deposited here retained their original references.)
BA-MA	Bundesarchiv-Militärarchiv, Freiberg im Breisgau
IWM	Imperial War Museum, London
NA	National Archives, Washington D.C., USA
PRO	Public Record Office, Kew, London
SUAP	Statni ustredni archiv v Praze
USHMMA	US Holocaust Memorial Museum Archives

SOURCES

This study is based predominantly on original source materials, namely documents, manuscripts, unpublished memoirs and papers given to, or prepared at the request of, the author. Other sources include questionnaires, six volumes of personal correspondence, spanning more than twelve years, and the tape recordings and extensive notes of the interviews conducted with veterans of the Division. These have been supplemented by previously published materials, reference to which can be found in the bibliography.

Documents pertaining to the formation and organisation of the Galician Division (i.e. covering the period from March 1943-June 1944) can be found at the Imperial War Museum, Lambeth, London, in the Enemy Document Section [EDS], in particular the 'Papers of the Reichsführer SS', or so-called 'Himmler File'. Documents from this file are numbered H/10/1-H/10/81. At the time of writing these have subsequently been transferred, along with similar items, to the museum's site at Duxford and are available to researchers on request.

To obtain the necessary supplementary material for the Division's wartime existence (from July 1944 until May 1945) I consulted several additional sources. The National Archives, 8601 Adelphi Road, College Park, Maryland 20740–6001, Washington D.C., USA, holds further documentation on microfilms T175 roll 74 (for the most part this material consists of duplicates of the Himmler papers H/10/1–81 referred to above), T175–94, T175–70 and T175–141. The alphabetically indexed SS Officer files (reference A3343-SSO, Surnames A-F are on rolls 001–231: names G-Q are on rolls 001A–399A: names R-W (part) can be found on rolls 001B–251B and the remainder on rolls 001C–026C. Together they form a complete series of 909 rolls with no duplication of names. The originals, held at the Berlin Document Centre, were invaluable for establishing accurate details of the antecedents of key personalities and individual officers. Other miscellaneous items such as a copy of the audio recording of Himmler's speech made to the Division's officer corps at Neuhammer on 16 May 1944, can be found in the Select Audio-visual Records, Captured German Sound Recordings, Record Group 242 – Item 206.

For the Battle of Brody from the German perspective, I made extensive use of the twenty-seven page report by General Lange, the commander of *Korpsabteilung* C which led the breakout attempt. Other after-action reports, submitted by the participating regular army units, are grouped together on Microfilms T78, rolls 139 and 142. Similar reports can be found in the Records of German Field Commands: Divisions, T315 – rolls 2147 (*Abwickstab* 349. I.D.) and 2152 (*Abwickstab* 361. I.D.) respectively. Despite extensive efforts, it was impossible to locate the Galician Division's own post-battle reports prepared by its staff. Most of the information pertaining to the involvement of the Red Army units was drawn from the manuscript entitled *L'vov-Sandomierz 1944, The Soviet*

General Staff Study. It provides excellent background on all Soviet tactical and strategic planning, as well as detailed accounts of all phases of the operation.

Some exceptionally rare and hitherto unused information, relevant to the Division from the last weeks of the war, recently came to light. It was obtained following the declassification by the Public Records Office, Kew, London, of decrypted Enigma German *Polizei*/Waffen-SS radio transmissions.

The Brotherhood of Former Combatants also kindly placed its considerable archive at my disposal and supplied many rare and unique items of special interest that would otherwise have been unobtainable.

A number of documents were also acquired from the Bundesarchiv-Militärarchiv Freiberg, (in particular file N/756/170 referred to as the 'Sammlung Vopersal'), the Bundesarchiv Koblenz, the Berlin Document Centre, the Holdings of the US Holocaust Memorial Museum Archives and from archives in Munich, L'viv, Kiev and Prague. Lastly, individual documents as well as personal papers such as award and promotion certificates, citations and *Soldbuchs*. Other items of this nature, with few exceptions, were acquired directly from veterans of the Division or their immediate families.

A full reference to the provenance of each document has been indicated accordingly in the footnotes to the text. For the purposes of authentication, several hitherto unpublished documents have been reproduced in their entirety.

The extensive personal accounts that I have incorporated within the text should be judged on their own merits. The validity of their inclusion is as questionable as their accuracy. However, I chose to do so as I felt it would add an extra dimension to what could so easily be a dry study. When such quotations appear I have selected those from veterans who kept diaries, or whose testimony it was in many instances possible to corroborate. Moreover, with the exception of occasional grammatical changes, they appear verbatim without alteration or change.

Interviews are indicated by name, date and location. Questionnaires are quoted by their numbers, which follow numerical sequence (i.e. Q12) and the surname of the individual involved. In a very few instances contributors have requested anonymity which I have respected.

There are two principle sources of photographic material featured in this book. The first is the Archives of the Brotherhood of Former Combatants, whose unrivalled collection is meticulously and carefully administered by Bohdan Maciw. The second is the author's private collection. Collated over many years, these items came directly from veterans of the Division, and from other sources as far apart as England, Sweden, USA, Canada, Germany and Poland.

Several of the pictures selected for inclusion appear to have been altered. These were originally published in various wartime newspapers, including the Division's own journals. The prints had first been subjected to artistic treatment, by adding lines or shading in order to accentuate certain features, as was the fashion at the time. In such cases the author is often in possession of the original captioned prints and occasionally original editions of the newspapers in which they were first published. I am satisfied that nothing of importance has been obliterated or added.

With regard to previously published materials, Wolf Dietrich Heike's memoir is an indispensable companion to anyone wishing to acquaint him/herself with the subject. He was the Division's former Ia (Operations Officer) from January 1944, until capitulation in May 1945. His duties included assisting directly with all matters pertaining to its organisation, training and tactical command. In that capacity his knowledge, of all military matters pertaining to the Division, was unsurpassed. However, some background to the publication of his memoirs is necessary.

They were originally written from memory, in 1947, whilst still in British internment. Without the aid of supplementary documentation, except for his field diary entries and some maps, the manuscript of his memoirs lay untouched for over twenty years. Having come to light, it was passed to the executive of the Brotherhood of Former Combatants in the USA, who decided to publish it in Ukrainian. To extend the historical content, footnotes, photographs and maps were added.

Because of the success of that edition, it was felt that a German publication would be appropriate. Heike made some minor changes to the text. Then, in 1973, the German edition appeared under the title *Sie wollten die Freiheit: Die Geschichte der Ukrainischen Division 1943–1945*.

Finally, The Brotherhood decided to translate the work into English. 1988 saw the emergence of *The Ukrainian Division "Galicia", 1943–45, A Memoir*. With reference to the English translation that was made directly from the Ukrainian, a word of caution is necessary. The memoir contains several significant errata as the result of the translator having no military knowledge or background. In spite of this minor reservation, Heike's testimony has been utilised extensively.

Other works have not addressed the subject matter in sufficient depth so that their authors, despite their proficiency in Slavic tongues, have often unwittingly perpetuated important mistakes. Those I have attempted to rectify. Similarly, I have made little use of the many Soviet, and to a lesser extent Polish, publications. Many were the products of propaganda specialists. In the main these are tendentious, careless in details and tend to suffer from a lack of appreciation of the 'rules of evidence.' Together with often rabid accusations this means that, in my opinion, their credibility is greatly undermined.

Adhering to current academic practice this book makes extensive use of notes. In the case of documentary evidence, they are included to allow the reader to verify the information from the source to which he/she is referred. Similarly, the suffix 'author's archive' is not intended to suggest exclusive rights to valuable information, or material evidence, but occurs as the consequence of my personal ownership of the said items.

For the greater part, German technical terms, titles and ranks have been retained. On the first occasion when such words appear, a literal translation is given in brackets. Translations and definitions for all of these terms can also be found in the glossary.

Readers will also note the discrepancy between the various titles used to describe the Division. This is because the title by which it was known underwent several changes during its existence. In this book, I have therefore referred to it as 'The Galician Division'/the 'Division' or by part or all of the title by which it was officially known at that time (such as the SS-Freiwilligen-Division *Galizien*, or '14. Waffen Grenadier Division der SS [*Ukrainische* Nr. 1]'). Other variations of the title occasionally appear in some of the documents quoted verbatim, for example '14. SS Division '*Galizien*', (a description used by Slovenian authors). Although these are colloquial titles, they have been reproduced exactly as they appear in the original documentation, for purposes of authenticity. Similarly, while he held the post of Governor of Galicia, reference is made to Governor Wächter. However, after that post became redundant in August 1944, reference is made simply to Dr Wächter.

This work is by no means claimed to be a definitive history, or even to be free from errors, for which the indulgence of the reader is sought. As it is the author hopes that this study will add a worthwhile contribution to the history of the Division.

Introduction

Of all the SS Divisions, the '14. *Galizische SS-Freiwilligen* Division' or '1st Division of the Ukrainian National Army' as it became in the last weeks of the war, has arguably maintained a higher public profile and continued to attract more media attention in Great Britain, the USA, Canada, Russia, Ukraine and Poland than any other. This is partly because of its wartime activities and those of its affiliated units which have led to unsubstantiated allegations of war crimes and of equal import, because of its exclusion from the forced repatriation operations involving over 2 million people undertaken by the victorious Western Allies in the immediate post war period.

This study follows the fate of this Division composed of Galician Ukrainians, under the auspices of the Waffen-SS, documenting its origins, formation and military engagements. It concludes with Germany's capitulation in May 1945, when the great majority of its soldiers entered British internment, only to find themselves facing Stalin's demand for their repatriation.

Brought together by their mutual enemy, Soviet Communism, from the outset, both the German and Ukrainian architects of the Division sought to exploit it for their own respective and diametrically opposed agendas. In the case of the Germans, it was to bolster their rapidly weakening war machine whose objective was imperialist conquest; for the Ukrainians, the nucleus of an independent army – an indispensable prerequisite in the creation of a sovereign state.

However as a military force, from its inception, the Galician Division's ability to fulfil its potential was critically compromised by a constant dearth of suitably trained Ukrainian officers and NCOs caused by the absence of an indigenous army during the inter-war period. Appointed in their place were mostly unsuitable German personnel who not only knew nothing and cared even less for any projected political role the formation might have had, but brought with them the excess baggage of Nazi ideology with its anti-Slav beliefs. This fundamental flaw was compounded when the inexperienced Division was deployed at a sector of the front earmarked to bear the brunt of a massive Soviet summer offensive. Here, despite being well trained and equipped to the highest standards for a contemporary *Waffen-Grenadier* Division, in consequence of the strategic initiative and vast material superiority of the Red Army, from any objective viewpoint it could only have suffered devastating losses.

For the populations of the western world whose perception of Communism has always been remote and who have come to take their liberty and independence for granted, it is easy to question the wisdom of the western Ukrainians who thought that they could use this unit as a vehicle to achieve their own ends. For many veterans of the '14. *Galizische SS-Freiwilligen* Division' who harboured this belief, the sum legacy of their sacrifices on the altar of independence was not, ultimately, to be a free sovereign Ukrainian state, but rather exile from their homeland, a permanent scar in the form of a tattoo of their blood group under their left armpit, and an undeserved 'pro Nazi' stigma which came from having served in a Waffen-SS division.

However, there are indications that old prejudices and the ignorance of the real motives of many of those who fought in German uniform, are finally beginning to be re-evaluated.

Armed collaboration with the Germans during the German/Soviet conflict by the Galician Ukrainians was not a unique phenomenon. Other populations of the occupied eastern territories, including Latvians, Estonians, as well as tens of thousands of Russians (General Vlasov's Army and Cossacks) fought at their side. At the same time, the Netherlands, Denmark, France, Spain, Norway, Italy, and Belgium, amongst other western European nations, also provided soldiers for the regular German army or Waffen-SS to fight against Soviet Communism, even though their respective populations had never been subjected to the rule of Stalin, whose crimes equalled if not surpassed those of the leader of Nazi Germany. Until the recent dissolution of the Soviet Union, the eastern Europeans, amongst them the Galician Ukrainians, had been afforded little opportunity to explain their actions. If this study contributes to the gradual process of revising the often obsolete perceptions of why they chose to act as they did, its purpose will have been well served.

1

Why Germany?

From 1918, Germany played an active role in the Sisyphean-like quest of the Ukrainian people to achieve and sustain autonomy. With borders distant enough to pose no immediate threat to their political aspirations, many politically articulate Ukrainians regarded Germany as a natural ally against their two traditional enemies, Russia and Poland, whose long-standing dominant positions in Europe, Germany was keen to undermine. On the other hand, the respective attitudes that German governments cultivated and maintained towards the Ukrainians which led to military co-operation and in WWII, the creation of the 14th Galician Division and the Ukrainian National Army, was never more than a manifestation of self-interest dictated by tactical necessity, political expediency or sheer opportunism.

The first significant co-operation between the two countries occurred towards the end of the First World War. At the outbreak of the war the territory of Ukraine was divided between two empires. Galicia,[1] Bukovina, and Ruthenia[2] were part of the Austro-Hungarian Empire, Galicia being the largest province of that empire.[3] The remainder of Ukraine was popularly known as Greater Ukraine, then part of the Russian Empire. In November 1917, in the aftermath of the collapse of Imperial Russia, the Bolsheviks seized power in Russia. Meanwhile, the Ukrainians established their own government, known as the Central Rada,[4] in the Ukrainian capital Kiev. Having initially recognised Central Rada's authority, the Bolsheviks quickly became dissatisfied and attempted to assert their control in Ukraine. However, they found little support, and in December 1917 the Red Army marched on Kiev. This Russian incursion into Ukrainian territory led to an outbreak of hostilities and an unconditional declaration of Ukrainian independence by the Central Rada, made in Kiev on 22 January 1918.[5]

Eighteen days later, on 9 February 1918, when defeat at the hands of the Bolsheviks was imminent, the Ukrainian government signed the peace treaty of Brest Litovsk[6] with the Central Powers (Germany, Austria, Turkey and Bulgaria). Under the terms of the treaty Germany, which had endured years of blockade and faced famine, agreed to the recognition of the Ukrainian Peoples Republic (UNR-*Ukrainska Narodna Respublyka*). They also agreed to the provision of military aid to the Central Rada, enabling them to fight Lenin's Bolshevik forces. In return there would be deliveries of large quantities of grain and agricultural products. Consequently, between 19 February and 29 April 1918, with Ukrainian approval, an 800,000 strong German/Austrian army, under the overall command of Field Marshal Hermann von Eichhorn, entered Ukraine and began their offensive against the Bolshevik occupied lands.

This alliance between Germany and Ukraine deteriorated quickly. The Ukrainian government procrastinated in fulfilling the terms of the treaty, partly because the Germans insisted on interfering in its internal affairs and partly because it lacked the administrative apparatus with which to collect the promised food supplies. In response, the commander in chief of the German army in Ukraine, Field Marshal Eichhorn instituted a series of draconian measures to ensure that deliveries continued. On 6 April 1918, he issued an order reversing the Rada's land nationalisation policies, to force the recalcitrant peasants to sow their fields and on the 25th of the same month he formally proclaimed martial law.[7] Finally, on 29 April 1918, in Kiev, a German-backed coup d'état was carried out against the Central Rada, and a new pro-German regime installed under Pavlo Skoropadskyj, who was made Hetman (Headman) of Ukraine and given German financial and administrative assistance.

The *Hetman* government lasted eight months. During that time, executive power was exercised by the German authorities. They redoubled their efforts to extract badly needed foodstuffs and to exploit Ukraine economically. Crops were brutally and arbitrarily expropriated from the Ukrainian peasants. Hundreds of thousands of tons of *chornozem,* the famous fertile black topsoil, was exported to Germany in continuous rail transports.[8]

Widespread disillusionment with Skoropadskyj's government, and its subservient pro-German policies, led to the outbreak of a series of peasant uprisings. The culmination was a series of assassinations, including that of Field

Marshal von Eichhorn.[9] Thereafter, the position of Skoropadskyj's government continued to become increasingly untenable, especially after the collapse of Germany, in November 1918. The collapse deprived the *Hetman* of German support. Eventually, on 14 December 1918,[10] the regime was overthrown. Symon Petlura and Colonel Evhen Konovalets led a combined force of Ukrainian regular army units and armed insurgents. In its place the regime of the Directory of the UNR assumed temporary power.[11]

Galicia and Unification

At the end of the First World War in November 1918, the Ukrainian population of Galicia, which had enjoyed a considerable amount of autonomy during one hundred and fifty years of Austrian rule, found themselves in a situation in many ways analogous with that of their compatriots from Greater Ukraine. With the disintegration of the Austro-Hungarian Empire, two peripheral border areas of Ukrainian territory, Bessarabia and Ruthenia, were annexed by Romania and Czechoslovakia. Meanwhile, the Ukrainians in Galicia, who had developed a highly distinct national consciousness, immediately established the West Ukrainian Peoples Republic. From the outset it was intended that the republic would unite with the larger Ukrainian state. The newly independent Ukrainian state adopted the Trident[12] as its national insignia. The act of unification and proclamation was formally made on 22 January 1919, in Kiev, in a symbolic demonstration of sovereignty.

The idealistic and non-aggressive policies of the socialist government of the Ukrainian Republic resulted in the demobilising of the greater part of the Ukrainian army. That left the republic vulnerable. With a greatly diminished force at its disposal, and without German military aid, it was unable to withstand the constant pressure exerted on it by Russia and Poland, both of which attempted to reclaim their lost territory. In March 1921, at the Treaty of Riga, Ukraine was split once again and left to the mercy of its historic adversaries. The entente sanctioned the annexation of Galicia and Western Volhynia by Poland, as a 'bulwark against Bolshevism'. It consigned 6 million Ukrainians to Polish rule. 4.5 million were in Galicia. Meanwhile, the Russian Bolsheviks occupied the larger part of Ukraine with its 41.9 million inhabitants.

Those Ukrainians who found themselves forcibly integrated into the Soviet Union, were subjected to a campaign of brutal persecution, unleashed by Stalin, over the next twenty years. In 1932 to 1933, under Stalin's orders, in order to consolidate the Soviet power base, 120,000 soldiers of the Red Army, *Komsomol* (*Kommunisticheskii soiuz molodezhi*), Communist Youth members and Communist party activists were sent into Ukraine. They had to crush the peasants who resisted Stalin's collectivisation programme, which he carried out regardless of the consequences.[13] The outcome was genocide on an unprecedented scale, and the largest premeditated artificial famine in history. During it, in excess of 7 million Ukrainian peasants were estimated to have died.[14] Stalin's reign of terror continued unabated, with the mass purges of 1937 and 1938 that followed in the wake of the famine. The purges resulted in the liquidation, wholesale deportation and forced exile of hundreds of thousands of Ukrainian intellectuals, writers, and artists whose patriotism was even so much as suspected. Simultaneously, to ensure complete assimilation, churches, some dating from the eleventh century, historical monuments, art and literary works denoting Ukrainian culture and identity, were targeted and systematically destroyed as 'objects incompatible with Communist ideology'.

Similarly, on a smaller scale, the Polish government in Galicia began a forceful 'Polonization' of the Ukrainian populace then under its rule. Galicia was officially renamed Little Eastern Poland. Polish settlers were introduced[15] and anti-Ukrainian policies maintained throughout the 1920s, which promoted active and widespread social and political discrimination against the Ukrainian and other minority populations.

Ukrainian political parties, through their representation in the Polish parliament (*Sejm*), led opposition to the severity of the Polish regime officially but unsuccessfully. There was opposition too from an underground Ukrainian military organisation, *Ukrainska Viis'kova Organizatsia,* the UVO. They were the society of veterans of the Ukrainian Armies of 1918 to 1920. After 1929, opposition came from the 'Organisation of Ukrainian Nationalists', the OUN. They were formed in Vienna from leaders of the disparate nationalist elements. During the interwar period, they had fled either from Bolshevik or Polish persecution, and were living in exile in Germany and Austria.[16] The organisation, headed by a former colonel of the Ukrainian Army, Evhen Konovalets, became the focus of the struggle for the restoration of a united Ukrainian state, and hence of anti-Polish activities in Galicia. The Polish government subsequently arrested hundreds of prominent Ukrainian political, civic and cultural figures. They were subjected to beatings, and dispatched to a concentration camp established at Bereza Kartuzka.[17] In turn, the OUN urged the Ukrainians resident in Galicia to resist the occupation policies and carry out sabotage. Such behaviour was branded as 'disloyalty to the Polish government'. It acted as a catalyst for an infamous pacification programme initiated in retaliation.[18] For each 'atrocity' committed by the Ukrainian revolutionary organisations the Interior Minister, General Pieracki, threatened that Poland would continue to punish the entire population. The policy was based on the principle of collective responsibility.

Germany was still in the ascendancy as a major world power, and shared a mutual anti-Polish sentiment with Konovalets. He led the OUN until his assassination by a Soviet agent in May 1938. He had cultivated and maintained links with institutions such as the German army, the *Reichswehr*, and in particular the German military intelligence service, the *Abwehr*.[19]

In exchange for providing intelligence information about the Polish government, the nationalists received supplementary funds[20] to finance OUN operations and military training. They intended to exploit that funding, in order to attain their political objectives by military force, as soon as the circumstances were conducive. From 1935, the *Abwehr* had been headed by Admiral Wilhelm Canaris, and operated with a fair degree of autonomy in its pursuit of German national interests. However its policies did not reflect those of the governing National Socialists. More importantly, it had no influence on Hitler's political ambitions.

This was clearly demonstrated when, on 15 March 1939, taking advantage of the break up of Czechoslovakia, Monsignor Voloshyn proclaimed the independence of the remote region of Ruthenia to be under the protection of the Reich. For that purpose a locally raised nationalist militia of 15,000 men was formed. They were known as the *Carpathian Sich* and were organised with the assistance of the OUN. Since German benevolence towards Ukrainian nationalism was at that time tactically conditional, and dependent on an expedient foreign policy, the anticipated support from Berlin failed to materialise. Instead Hitler, who regarded the friendship of Hungary to be of greater importance, backed Hungarian claims to the territory and made no move to support the small republic. The Magyars crushed them within a week.[21]

Disappointed, but undeterred, the OUN continued to sustain its orientation towards Germany as the only power opposed to the European status quo. Hence, in the summer of 1939, the *Abwehr* was able to create a formation known as the Nationalist Military Detachments (*Viis'kovi viddily natsionalistiv*) to facilitate the advance of the German troops in the planned invasion of Poland. Initially, the unit was formed in Austria from members of the OUN living in Germany, and from former soldiers of the *Carpathian Sich* who had been released from Hungarian internment in June 1939. The formation, although organised by Colonel Roman Sushko,[22] was commanded by a German Colonel, Erwin Stolze. It comprised two under-strength infantry battalions with a combined strength of approximately 600 men, and operated under the name of *Bergbauern-Hilfe* (BBH Mountain Peasant Helpers).

The nationalists' expectations were raised on 1 September 1939, when without any formal declaration of war, the German army invaded Poland. Three weeks later the Ukrainian detachment crossed the former Czech-Polish border. They started to advance through the Lemko region, disrupting communications and promoting dissension behind Polish lines. The unit successfully carried out its task.[23] Shortly after, however, the Germans were forced to intervene. They demobilised the unit and returned it to German-occupied Poland, known as the *Generalgouvernement*. Then, with characteristic duplicity, Hitler handed over Galicia to the Soviet Union. That was in accordance with the Molotov-Ribbentrop pact[24] a secret treaty signed on 23 August. It brought together the two, hitherto bitterly antagonistic regimes, with a declaration of non-aggression, friendship and co-operation.[25] The treaty also contained a secret protocol that divided Eastern Europe into two distinct spheres of influence. To appease Stalin, Hitler ceded to the Soviets territory that included Bukovina, Bessarabia, Volhynia, Western Belorussia and Galicia. All those were to be in return for the remainder of Poland and part of Lithuania. At that time Belorussia and Galicia were occupied by Poland.

Once again, the illusion of German assistance in the nationalist cause was temporarily shattered. With the Hitler-Stalin pact in force, the German government's support for the Ukrainian nationalist organisations in the

Generalgouvernement was allowed to lapse. But worse was yet to come. Henceforth, Stalin's policies of extermination, repression, and deportation were now extended to Galicia. The official justification for the Nazi-Soviet dismemberment of Poland, and subsequent Soviet occupation of Galicia, had been 'a desire to aid the oppressed minorities', notably the Ukrainians and Belorussians. This justification was reflected in the initial stages of the occupation. During it the Soviets directed oppressive measures primarily against the wealthier land owning Polish ruling classes, but also Polish and Ukrainian civil servants, and other undesirable elements.

As a gesture of goodwill some minor cultural and social reforms were permitted.[26] However, those were accompanied by severe political and religious repression. Through the tentacles of his security apparatus, Stalin rapidly inaugurated a campaign of mass arrests and deportations of the western Ukrainian intelligentsia, who were the leading force in the national movement in Galicia. During the next twenty-one months of occupation, an estimated 400,000 Ukrainians[27] were classified as hostile or disloyal elements. They were imprisoned, deported or executed, thus firmly establishing Stalin as the arch-enemy of the Ukrainians.

The remaining political activists in Galicia were centred round the underground network of the OUN. Its leadership still clung to the conviction that an alliance with Germany, the only power capable and possibly willing to challenge the USSR, could potentially offer liberation from Soviet oppression. The leaders believed that there were long-term possibilities for the realisation of their own agenda, i.e. the re-establishment of an independent state. This, they believed, would come about with German aid if war should break out between Germany and the Soviet Union on a quid pro quo basis. They believed that the OUN would mobilise Ukrainian support for the German army in a war against the Soviet Union. In return they counted on German recognition of an independent Ukraine. They were mistaken. Therefore, to escape the widespread Soviet persecution, large numbers of people, including approximately 30,000[28] Ukrainians, fled to the comparative sanctuary of the German occupied *Generalgouvernement*.

There, the cadres of the OUN revolutionaries, whose numbers were swelled by the influx of political refugees escaping from the Soviet Union, continued to exist.[29] The already strained German-Ukrainian relations were further exacerbated after a split occurred within the OUN in February 1940. At that time the activist wing, under Stephan Bandera, disassociated themselves from the moderates under Andrij Melnyk. From then on there were two rival wings, OUN-B and OUN-M. The *Abwehr* objected to the split and urged reconciliation. They clandestinely recruited from both factions but principally from the stronger and more radical OUN-B wing.

In April 1941, with the *Abwehr's* approval, two battalions[30] were enlisted by the military department of the OUN. They were code-named *Nachtigall*[31] and *Roland*.[32] Formed without the knowledge of the Nazi leadership, the two battalions were suitably camouflaged as State Labour Units within the *Reichsarbeitsdienst* (RAD) so as not to arouse suspicion from Germany's Soviet ally. The *Abwehr* trained *Roland* in Saubersdorf near Vienna, and *Nachtigall* in Neuhammer, Silesia. In the event of a German-Soviet war, both units were intended to precede the main German attack and organise provocative coups in Ukraine. They would prompt Ukrainians serving in the Red Army to desert, and attract Ukrainians to German military service. For the Ukrainians the two battalions were regarded as the embryo of a future Ukrainian Army and a vehicle for their future policies.

To ensure their full co-operation, the *Abwehr* made a number of concessions. They recognised Ukrainian national identity, guaranteed the units a degree of independence, and ensured that they would defend Ukrainian interests. It was agreed that both units were to be used exclusively against the Soviets, that neither would be required to swear an oath to Hitler, but both would swear allegiance instead to Ukraine, the OUN and its leader.[33]

While *Nachtigall* and *Roland* underwent their training with the German military intelligence the *Reichsführer-SS*, Heinrich Himmler, rejected an opportunity to utilise Ukrainians in a similar capacity within the emerging SS establishment. *SS-Gruppenführer* Gottlob Christian Berger, the recruitment chief of the Waffen-SS, as the result of wartime mobilisation had instigated a rapid expansion programme for the Waffen-SS[34] in order to create an army that would rival the Wehrmacht. By the spring of 1941, in preparation for the imminent conflict with the Soviet Union, its strength stood at four full divisions and one brigade. It included the first major non-German formation to be raised. It was the so-called 5th *Wiking* Division. It consisted of Flemish, Dutch, Danish and Norwegian volunteers, with German commanders and cadres.[35] On 28 April 1941, Berger had written to the

Reichsführer with a suggestion that would allow 679[36] Ukrainians, the majority of whom could speak German, and whom he had had at his disposal for a year, to undergo combat training. That was with a view to having a group of soldiers, available to the SS, who would be conversant in Ukrainian. Himmler, who was not prepared to compromise what was still a racially elite Germanic fighting force, replied in the negative via his secretary Dr Rudolph Brandt:

> Berlin, 31 April 1941
>
> "Dear *Gruppenführer*!
> I have informed the *Reichsführer-SS* of your letter dated 28.4.1941 regarding the Ukrainians.
> The *Reichsführer-SS* is not willing at this stage to take any action regarding the combat training of these men."[37]

The anticipated conflict for which *Nachtigall* and *Roland* had been preparing was constantly drawing closer. Finally, by mid–1941, Hitler was confident enough to dispense with the German-Soviet pact. Convinced that German technical superiority, and the political weakness of the Soviet regime would guarantee a swift victory,[38] he now sought a convenient justification to turn on his ally. He claimed that the Soviet Union was preparing to attack Germany, and used Stalin's seizure of the Baltic States, northern Bukovina and the attack on Finland as a pretext. On Sunday 22 June 1941, at 3.15am, the lead elements of the German Wehrmacht crossed the Soviet frontier. Thus started what, according to Hitler's political testimony *Mein Kampf*,[39] was an ideological crusade. In it the racially superior Aryans, i.e. those of Germanic descent, were destined to eliminate the *Untermensch* or Sub-humans,[40] i.e. Slavic peoples such as Ukrainians, and establish a New Order in Europe.

Drang Nach Osten (Eastward expansion)

Codenamed Operation Barbarossa, the German attack started with three army groups, North, Centre and South, attacking simultaneously, on a front stretching from the Baltic Sea to the Carpathian Mountains. They met with vast and immediate success. The Red Army, crippled by the Stalinist purges of the 1930s, offered little resistance. They frequently conducted haphazard and uncoordinated offensives that resulted in the loss of entire armies, and hundreds of thousands of prisoners being taken.

Accompanying the German forces were the military units formed by both factions of the OUN. *Roland* advanced with Romanian forces into Southern Bessarabia. *Nachtigall* was attached to Army Group South, and entered Galicia. They crossed the Soviet frontier on 21 June[41] with a written authority for their convoy to take precedence over all units.[42] Their presence amid the vanguard of the German troops boosted civilian morale. The *Pokhidni hrupy*,[43] i.e. expeditionary civilian groups also organised by the OUN, consisted mostly of students. Their aim was to increase awareness amongst the populace of their Ukrainian heritage.[44] They too were part of the vanguard, and they further strengthened the arguments of those who advocated active co-operation with Germany. Ultimately they believed that it would present the Ukrainians with an opportunity to win their independence. Consequently, ignorant of Hitler's true intentions, and also of Nazi racial ideology, many welcomed the Germans and placed great hopes in them as their liberators from Soviet oppression.[45]

During the first week of the invasion, the speed of the German advance into Galicia and western Belorussia caught the Soviets by surprise. Throughout Galicia, immediately prior to the departure of the Soviet civil authorities, and as part of Stalin's 'Scorched Earth' policy, the panic-stricken and suspicious NKVD (Soviet secret police) conducted last minute arrests and deportations of thousands of arbitrarily chosen civilians. Branded as being anti-Russian, or anti-Communist, they were herded eastwards, destined for Siberian Gulags.[46]

In Sambir, Zolochiv, Stanyslaviv, Chortkiv, Ternopil, and every major city or town near the border, the advancing German units found the bodies of those, who in their haste, the NKVD had been unable to evacuate.[47] The first German units, including the *Nachtigall* battalion, entered the Galician capital of L'viv on 30 June 1941, at 5.00am.[48] There they found that the three main prisons, Brygidky, Yaniwska and Lontsky, were hardly to be distinguished from abattoirs. They were surrounded by terrified relatives, and found "the air full of the stench of decomposing bodies."[49] In the basement cells and courtyard of the Lontsky prison alone, the Germans discovered over 2,300 tortured and mutilated corpses, mostly of Ukrainians.[50] The criminal actions of the NKVD, and memories of the occupation of 1939–41, further reinforced the hatred felt by the overwhelming majority of the population towards the Soviets. Later, Galician Ukrainians were encouraged to co-operate with the Germans, when the Soviets were poised to occupy Galicia once again.

The Spectre of Ukrainian Nationalism

Immediately upon the arrival of *Nachtigall* in L'viv,[51] while German forces in the city were still relatively small, the OUN-B seized the initiative by acting to realise its political plans. Intending to present the German authorities with a fait accompli, Jaroslav Stetsko called a meeting at the Prosvita hall. There, before a hastily collected assembly of Ukrainians and a few Germans,[52] a declaration of an independent Ukrainian state was made in the name of the OUN faction, led by Stepan Bandera. To lend it authority, a statement of support was obtained from Metropolitan Sheptyskyj,[53] the head of the Uniate Church. Shortly thereafter Stetsko broadcast the proclamation from the city's radio station.

To all intents and purposes it appeared that, with German assistance, the Ukrainian nationalists had successfully realised their goal. The initial German reaction was encouraging, as that unexpected event had caught the authorities in Berlin by surprise. Failing to grasp that a direct challenge to German supremacy was involved, they were slow to respond. The German military command in L'viv made no immediate attempt to prevent the proclamation. They allowed the state administration, established by Stetsko, to operate relatively unhindered for the next few days. Then they sought to take advantage of the situation by distributing phonograph recordings of the proclamation. These were to be played through loudspeakers, at the frontline, to encourage Ukrainians serving in the Red Army to desert.[54]

The nationalists were so confident of the Germans accepting the fait accompli, and of gaining their support in the war against the Soviet Union, that Stetsko sent the following letter, dated 3 July 1941, to Hitler in Berlin:

> Ukrainian Government Lemberg, 3 July 1941
> To His Excellency the Führer and Reichschancellor
> Berlin
>
> Your Excellency!
>
> Full of sincere gratitude and admiration for your heroic army, which has now won new glory on the battlefields in conflict with Europe's greatest enemy, Muscovite Bolshevism, we send to you, the great leader, in the name of the Ukrainian people and its government, which has organised itself in liberated Lemberg [L'viv], hearty congratulations for crowning the struggle with final victory. The victory of German arms will give you the opportunity to extend your projected construction of a new Europe to its eastern part. In this way you have also enabled the Ukrainian people to play its part in the realisation of this great plan, as one of the fully-fledged, free members of the European family of nations, in its Ukrainian sovereign state.
>
> For the Ukrainian Government
> Jaroslav Stetsko – Head[55]

The German authorities finally realised the significance of the declaration. On the same day, they summoned the leading members of a newly formed Ukrainian National Committee,[56] including Stepan Bandera, to an enquiry that took place in Cracow. A special commission headed by Under-Secretary of the Third Reich, Kundt, pointed out that, contrary to Ukrainian pronouncements, the Germans were not allies of the Ukrainians, but rather conquerors of the Soviet Russian regions. He announced that only the German Wehrmacht and the Führer, who conquered this land, had the right to form a government.[57] In response, Bandera stated there had been no agreement with the German authorities regarding the proclamation of an independent Ukrainian National state. Neither did he appeal to them for permission, as "the OUN was the only organisation that led the struggle for an autonomous independent and free Ukraine and was therefore entitled to form a government."[58]

The results of such a confrontation were inevitable. After some initial hesitation, caused by an expected uprising behind Soviet lines,[59] the Germans promptly dissolved Stetsko's state administration and demanded the withdrawal of the proclamation. When they refused to do so, Bandera and Stetsko were deported to Berlin, and placed under house arrest for two months.[60]

Nachtigall, under whose protection the embryonic state had been announced, had continued to advance through Ternopil and on to Vinnycia. It was then given two weeks' rest in Juzvyn, where news of the events in L'viv caught up with it. A former member of the battalion recalled:

> '[In Juzvyn] we were informed about the arrests of our leader S. Bandera and Premier Y. Stetsko. We immediately filed a protest stating that we would refuse to fight with them [the Germans] unless they agreed to 1) release these men, and 2) reinstate Ukraine's proclamation of independence.'[61]

Fearing a mutiny, *Nachtigall* was disarmed in early August 1941. Along with *Roland*, the Chief of the *Abwehr* Admiral Canaris ordered them to be withdrawn from the Eastern Front.[62] After discharging the dissenting element, the remaining recruits of the two battalions were transported to Frankfurt-an-der-Oder where they were combined and formed into *Schützmannschaft* 201.[63] In spite of the failure of their national hopes, all but 14 men were prepared to commit themselves to another year of service with the Wehrmacht.

Stetsko's new Ukrainian state had lasted nine days. However, the ramifications of the event were extensive, even if they were not immediately apparent to the Ukrainians. They had not yet perceived that the political principles and racial beliefs, of the 'New Order' that the Nazis were planning, were fundamentally and irreconcilably opposed to Ukrainian aspirations and objectives.

Firstly, it marked the beginning of a rift between the Germans and the OUN-B that eventually ended in open opposition. The OUN-M felt that, through its actions, the Bandera faction had brought its misfortune on itself. They had not experienced the same kind of confrontation, and still hoped to reach the goal of a sovereign Ukrainian state, by evolutionary means, and through close conformity with the Germans. Consequently, it continued to assign many of its adherents as interpreters with regular Wehrmacht units. They supported the local administration in eastern Ukraine, where they continued to promote the nationalist cause.

Secondly, it reinforced Hitler's conviction that under no circumstances should Germany attempt to enlist the mass support of Ukrainians, and other Slavic peoples, in the war against the Soviet Union. Hitler believed that arming them would only serve to create a potential threat to the planned German hegemony over Europe. As a result, on 6 July, when the OUN-M sent a statement to Hitler via the offices of *Abwehrstelle* II/Cracow, calling for the creation of an Ukrainian Army to be used in conjunction with the German Wehrmacht, and for extensive German Ukrainian co-operation, the letter remained unanswered.[64]

On the same day *Oberst* Alfred Bisanz,[65] a former lieutenant colonel in the Ukrainian Galician Army (UHA), and adviser for Ukrainian affairs, in the population and social welfare department of the *Generalgouvernement* in Cracow, reported to his superiors in Berlin. He told them that generals Myhailo Omelianovych-Pavlenko and Mykola Kapustianskyj, together with colonels Roman Sushko, Hnat Stefaniv, Petro Diachenko and Captain Myhailo Khronoviat had expressed an interest in establishing an Ukrainian military unit within the German Army.[66] Those representatives of the Ukrainian veterans organisations who had created The General Council of Combatants (a central organisation that would provide the nucleus of an administration for a national Army[67]), despatched a missive to Hitler. They requested that the Ukrainians be permitted to join the German sponsored legions of Europe, in the fight against Bolshevism.[68] That, and other similar appeals,[69] also went unheeded.

Thirdly, it presented Hitler with an added impetus to separate Galicia from the rest of Ukraine, i.e. to defeat the activities of the Ukrainian nationalists whose centre he correctly adjudged to be L'viv in Galicia, and not Kiev. These considerations led to the pivotal decisions taken at the conference at Angerburg in July 1941.

Conference at Angerburg (16 July 1941)

The repercussions of the proclamation by OUN-B had not died down when, on 16 July 1941, less than one month after the invasion had begun Hitler assembled his chief minions. Göring, Lammers, Keitel, Bormann and the party ideologue Alfred Rosenberg[70] met at Angerburg, in East Prussia, for a conference. It was there that Hitler revealed his plans for the fate, and future administration, of the occupied eastern territories.[71] The consequences of the decisions taken at the conference guaranteed that for the duration of the war, hopes of close German/Ukrainian relations were fated to be stillborn.

Recognising the strategic importance of Ukraine's location as a theatre of operations vital for a successful maintenance of the German Eastern Front, Hitler quickly identified it as "the most important region for the next three years."[72] Rosenberg's proposal envisaged the splitting up of the former Soviet Union into its component ethnic parts, with all races granted the status of independent republics under German protection.[73] The idea was brushed aside by Hitler, who unequivocally rejected the idea of a sovereign Ukraine. Ukraine was not to be a semi-autonomous ally, but rather a colonial country without political or civil rights, in the same way that India had been for the British. The great expanses of this vassal state, were designated as *Lebensraum* (living space), to be colonised by Aryan peasants and farmers of Germanic descent. Hitler further directed that, initially, the implementation of the policy of colonisation had to be carried out in such a way that an external appearance of a policy of liberation of the Ukrainian people would be maintained.

Since Hitler associated the 'right to bear arms' as having political significance, he went on to state that the creation of a military power west of the Urals was out of the question, even if it was necessary to fight for a hundred years.[74] Mindful of recent events and mistrustful of their nationalist ambitions, Hitler emphasised that there should be no basis for any military co-operation with Ukrainians and other *Ostvölker* (eastern people[75]):

> 'It must always remain a cast iron principle that none but the Germans shall be allowed to bear arms. Even when it might seem expedient to summon foreign peoples to arms, one day it would prove our absolute and irretrievable undoing. Only the German must be permitted to bear arms, not the Slav, nor the Czech, nor the Cossack, nor the Ukrainian.'[76]

Finally, Ukrainian nationalist aspirations received a further setback, when Hitler announced that Galicia was to be separated from the bulk of Ukraine. Galicia would be added as a fifth district[77] of the *Generalgouvernement*, because of its former status as a province of the Austro-Hungarian Empire.[78] The land between the Dnestr and Buh (Bug) rivers, known as Transnistria, together with Bukovina and Bessarabia, was given to Romania. The remainder of Ukrainian territory was to become the *Reichkommisariat Ukraine* and would be administered by Eric Koch. He was the notoriously brutal *Gauleiter* of East Prussia, and leading apostle of the *Untermensch* policy, whom Hitler then appointed as *Reichskommissar*.[79] Hitler directed that Koch's single objective was to muster and extract Ukraine's abundance of natural resources.[80] These would become an indispensable source of supply for German war industry. Meanwhile, the subhuman Ukrainian population, fit only for slavery, would provide an enormous pool of slave labour for the Third Reich.

The Galician Fulcrum

The events of the previous weeks had by no means put an end to Ukrainian expectations, nor to their willingness to co-operate with the Germans. Indeed, throughout the summer months of 1941 the Wehrmacht continued to make spectacular gains. They surged deeper and deeper into the Soviet Union and seized vast tracts of territory that could not be controlled without indigenous help. In order to do so, the German occupation forces which were far less numerous than the Soviets had been, enlisted anti-Communist Ukrainians into *Hilfpolizei* units, *Schutzmannschaft* (*Schuma*)[81] or *Werkschutz* battalions,[82] and other support formations.[83] These units were affiliated to and under the jurisdiction of the police authorities. They were utilised for auxiliary and mundane security duties, but generally not in frontline combatant roles. Although heavily infiltrated by both factions of the OUN, who ultimately intended to use them as the basis for a national revolutionary army, few had Ukrainian officers[84] and therefore were unable to directly promote Ukrainian interests.

At the same time, the civilian population was becoming directly acquainted with the reality of the New Europe that the Germans were advocating. Its inherent features were, firstly, of racial discrimination, which relegated all those classified as non-Aryan, to the status of second-class citizens.[85] Secondly, there was colonisation via a programme involving the extensive re-settlement of Germans. Thirdly, there was economic exploitation to support the German war effort.[86] Above all, the hated *kolkhozes* (collective farms) were retained. The results of such myopic policies dampened the hopes of the Ukrainians, especially those in the *Reichskommissariat Ukraine* who experienced some of the worst excesses of Nazi racist policies.[87]

By comparison, the regime in Galicia that had been officially incorporated into the *Generalgouvernement* on 1 August 1941,[88] under *General-governor* Dr Hans Frank, was incomparably less severe for the Ukrainians. They were seen to have benefited from the influence of submission to Austrian rule, for 150 years, prior to 1918. One reason was that, unlike *Reichkommisar* Koch, *General-governor* Frank permitted the Ukrainians in Galicia, some official representation before the German authorities, through the Ukrainian Central Committee [UCC].[89] It was a central, non-political organisation originally established the previous year in Cracow, to provide social welfare and humanitarian assistance,[90] as well as cultural activities, for the Ukrainian population in the *Generalgouvernement*.[91]

Headed by the well-known and respected Professor Volodymyr Kubijovych, who was assisted by his first deputy Kost Pankivskyj, the committee's potential was however retarded by the man whom Frank appointed as the first Governor of Galicia. He was *General der Polizei* Dr Karl Lasch[92] who personified the low calibre of officialdom employed in the Nazi administration of the occupied eastern territories.[93] Like *Reichskommissar* Koch, Lasch too regarded Galicia solely as an object of economic exploitation and as a labour reservoir. It therefore came as no surprise that, under his governorship, the numerous petitions and protests presented by the committee were repeatedly ignored. The petitions requested the curbing of the worst abuses, perpetrated on the local civilian population by the German occupational forces and administrative authorities, in view of the detrimental impact they were having.[94] Similarly, requests to re-open cultural and educational institutions were refused.[95]

Moreover, in September 1941, to prevent the rapid and extensive spread of the nascent Ukrainian National independence movement, the Germans struck at the cadres of the OUN throughout Galicia and the *Reichskommissariat Ukraine*. Thousands of OUN-B, who were thought to have posed the more serious threat, and later OUN-M members too, were arrested. They were deported to concentration camps and prisons, or secretly liquidated.[96] Among them were Bandera and Stetsko who had both been under house arrest in Berlin. They were confined to the political bunker of the Sachsenhausen concentration camp on 15 September 1941, where they were to remain until their release three years later.

Some argued that these measures were only temporary and would improve in time. Others consoled themselves with the knowledge that the German/Soviet war would be a protracted one. Sooner or later the Germans would have no alternative but to accept the Ukrainians and other eastern peoples, as equal partners, if they were to have any hope of winning the war.

In November 1941, with the hopes of a swift German victory diminishing day by day, elements of the German administration in Galicia took it upon themselves to implement a local initiative. They wanted to recruit racially suitable, German speaking volunteers, as replacements for frontline Waffen-SS formations. Knowing of the Ukrainians' burning desire for an autonomous military formation, the spurious rumour was circulated that an Ukrainian Army was about to be created. From those who stepped forward, approximately 2,000 of the best men, having Germanic racial characteristics, were selected.[97] Mostly they came from the regions of Podilla, Pokuttia, and the Carpathian Mountains. Among them was the cousin of the deputy head of the UCC, Kost Pankivskyj.[98] They were later dispersed within various Waffen-SS formations, including the 1st SS-Motor Brigade and SS-Regiment[99] at the front.[100] One of them gave an account of his experiences:

'In late 1941 I was in Berezhany [Ternopil Oblast] when I noticed several hundred young men assembled in four rows. Amongst them I recognised some from my village. I enquired what was going on and was told that they were volunteering for the 'Ukrainian Army.' I stepped into the second or third row and joined them. A group of 4 or 5 tall and impressive looking German officers, all wearing combat decorations, appeared. They began the inspection walking along the rows of volunteers. I was selected by an officer and told to climb up on the stage where I was examined by a medical commission and then told to return home. I heard nothing more until mid-January 1942, when I received a letter telling me to report to L'viv where I joined eleven others who were called up. *Oberst* Alfred Bisanz made a speech to us in Ukrainian. He said that we had been selected by the Germans as a sample, that we would be observed closely and should behave properly because we would eventually become officers of the Ukrainian Army. Recruit training for my group of eleven men took place at Heidelager. We were then sent the city of Zhytomyr and from there I was despatched to the 1st SS-Motor Brigade for three months' front experience before I was to have been sent to officers' school.'[101]

In practical terms the enlistment of 2,000 men, into combat units fighting on the Eastern Front, was inconsequential. It did however help establish a precedent, in that Ukrainian nationals were recruited, albeit without official sanction, nor the knowledge, of the central German authorities in Berlin and in the *Generalgouvernement*. They were utilised in frontline formations, and in combatant roles, for more than eight months before the Waffen-SS officially extended its recruitment to encompass eastern nationals. It also gave some indication to the authorities in Galicia of the amount of support that such a venture would engender, in the event of it being repeated in earnest.

By 1942 it was rapidly becoming evident to the Germans that they had lost the sympathy of the Ukrainian people. That was because of the general course of their occupation policies, in particular the routine systematic evacuations, in order to secure forced labour for work in the Reich.[102] Even more alarming was the growing number of disaffected Ukrainian youth who were turning to active opposition. They had begun to establish armed camps, in the Ukrainian forests, and in the marshlands of Polissya province, under the command of Taras Bulba.[103]

That marked the beginning of the Ukrainian underground nationalist partisan movement or UPA (*Ukrainska Povstanska Armiya*).[104] From October 1942 they were led by Roman Shukhevych, under the pseudonym Taras Chuprynka. Following the dissolution of *Schuma* Battalion 201, *Roland-Nachtigall*, and the imprisonment of its officer corps, Taras escaped. He succeeded in fighting his way through to the insurgents, whereupon he assumed command. The UPA immediately conducted a series of military operations, aimed principally at the German administration. In turn, the Germans retaliated in characteristic fashion by conducting punitive operations against the partisan units, and by arresting civilians.

Under such inauspicious circumstances, and until there was a fundamental revision of the German regime, there was to be no solid basis for any large scale German/Ukrainian military co-operation in the war against their mutual enemy, Soviet Communism. When the situation demanded change, it was not in the *Reichkommisariat Ukraine* but rather in Galicia, where the first remedial steps were taken to rectify the damage that had already been done.

Governor Wächter

The first sign that augured an impending change was the arrest and subsequent dismissal of Governor Lasch, in November 1941, for extensive black market activities.[105] Lasch's successor was the former Governor of Cracow, *SS-Brigadeführer* Dr Otto Gustav Freiherr[106] von-Wächter[107] who took office on 1 January 1942. He determined to follow a more enlightened policy in the province.

Otto Wächter was born in Vienna and came from a family with a long-standing military tradition. His father, General Josef Freiherr von Wächter, a *Sudetendeutscher* (German hailing from the Sudetenland), had commanded troops of the Austro-Hungarian Army deployed in Galicia, during the First World War. Later he had been appointed to the post of *General und Minister fur Heerwesen* (Military Affairs). A loyal Nazi Party member since 1923, Governor Wächter was a lawyer by profession.[108] Following his assignment to *SS-Oberabschnitts Ost* (SS Main District East), on 1 October 1942,[109] he brought direct experience of German administration, to the *Generalgouvernement*. Described in his personal SS officer file as being 'very intelligent',[110] he was a perceptive administrator, with far reaching political ambitions. He believed, for reasons of expediency, that Galicia with its

Austrian influence, should have its German culture restored and its population, especially the nationalist Ukrainian youth, turned into an active component of German interests.[111] His disposition in this respect is succinctly summarised by his former personal assistant, Dr Heinz Georg Neumann who on this issue later recalled, "Although we liked the Poles much more, we [i.e. Wächter's administration] favoured the Ukrainians because of political expediency. Wächter therefore tried to carry out as much as possible the old tradition of Austrian policy in Galicia."[112]

In contrast to both his predecessor and his immediate superior, *General-governor* Frank,[113] Governor Wächter recognised that the German political course towards the Ukrainians had been inconsistent. He understood that the administration policies of racial discrimination, brute force and coercion had not only deprived Germany of substantial material assistance, but had successfully alienated large sections of the hitherto friendly population.

At a session of the governor and the heads of departments in Cracow, he expanded on this theme. He emphasised the dangers inherent in the German political approach towards the Ukrainians in Galicia, which he described as extraordinarily confused. Then he drew attention to the urgent need for German propaganda to assume a unified and consistent political policy, if Ukrainians were to be won over into co-operating with Germany:

> '... A German radio station in Königsberg ended each transmission with the cry 'Hail, free Ukraine'. Should an Ukrainian say this openly in Lemberg [L'viv] then he would be arrested. This utter confusion in the official German approach, is intolerable. ... If an absolutely consistent and positive position regarding Ukraine is not taken soon, dire consequences will result.'[114]

To overcome the growing hostility, and to facilitate his desire to harness the population of Galicia to serve German needs, Governor Wächter strove to grant the favoured elements more freedom, and to obtain a positive resolution of some of the most unpopular German policies. In one prominent example he publicly voiced his opposition to the resettlement of Germans in Eastern Europe during the war, which he believed "would reduce economic production". Such statements in the Nazi occupied east, inevitably brought him into conflict with other senior members of the administration in the *Generalgouvernement*. On that occasion it was HSSPf. (*Höhere SS-und Polizeiführer*, Senior SS and Police Commander) *SS-Obergruppenführer* Friedrich Wilhelm Krüger who, as *Reichskommissar* for the establishment of the German *Volkstum,* i.e. ethnicity, was responsible for implementing the resettlement programme. In a five-page letter to Wächter, after emphasising that he was Wächter's senior in both age and rank, Krüger reminded him that his recent public pronouncements on the issue were in direct confrontation to the policies of the *Reichsführer-SS* Himmler. He added that wearing the uniform of an *SS-Brigadeführer* has "certain responsibilities". Giving vent to his frustration, Krüger wrote in this respect "I am firstly an SS man whilst you are a politician."[115]

The vehement disagreement over that issue, and growing antipathy between the two men, was only resolved following the personal intervention of Himmler who was in charge of all racial re-settlement arrangements. Himmler flew to L'viv on 17 August 1942 to discuss the matter. While so doing, Himmler offered Wächter the option of relocating to his hometown of Vienna. Wächter duly declined, preferring to remain as Governor of Galicia.[116]

In that capacity, notwithstanding occasional interference from his superiors, but through the simultaneous introduction of a number of long-term initiatives, Wächter endeavoured to promote a greater degree of co-operation between the occupying Germans and the Ukrainians. Foremost, was a successful attempt to integrate the maximum number of Ukrainians in Galicia into all but the highest level administrative posts in areas of local government. The tactic was complemented, by removing many aggressively anti-Ukrainian bureaucrats from his command. He selected as principal aides for the key posts in his administration[117] all those who entertained guarded pro-Ukrainian sentiments, notably *Oberst* Alfred Bisanz, Dr Otto Bauer,[118] and Dr Ludwig Losacker.[119]

In late 1942, encouraged by the success of his policies in Galicia, and accompanied by select members of his administration, Governor Wächter visited the *Reichskommissariat Ukraine.*[120] He wanted to witness at first hand, and in operation, the effect of Koch's policies of repression and subjugation. On his return in December 1942, prompted by what he had seen, he sent a secret ten-page letter to Martin Bormann[121] in the *Führerhauptquartier* (Führer Headquarters) in Berlin. In it he pointed out the serious mistakes made in the handling of the Ukrainians, and the far-reaching ramifications with regard to the overall conduct of the war against the Soviet Union.

> 'With growing concern' – began Dr. Wächter – 'I am observing the rise of some danger areas, which will, if we are unable to eliminate them, give rise to unforeseeable consequences. The Bolsheviks have done useful preparatory work for us. In their own country they are hated and regarded as oppressors. The German soldier is greeted with grateful hearts as a liberator of the enslaved native population. It has probably never been the case that a people have, during the fulfilment of their historical mission, met with such favourable psychological conditions, as we have found in the Soviet Union. Even if we only provide some relief for the population there, in contrast to the terror of the Soviet regime, then we will win them to our side. Unfortunately we are not doing this. The resistance of our enemy in the east hardens in the same degree, as the population in the Soviet Union loses its enthusiasm regarding the German liberation and feels disappointment and defeat with respect to the German measures ... *We are dependent on the co-operation of the Ukrainians.*' [Author's emphasis]

Governor Wächter continued his harsh criticism of the German agrarian policy in Ukraine, especially the decision to retain the hated collective farms. He pointed out that the proper treatment of the Ukrainian population of Galicia had resulted in many successes. He stressed that success could also be achieved in the *Reichskommissariat Ukraine* if those responsible, i.e. Koch and his administration, were dismissed. He assumed that they were unable to follow any promising avenue of co-operation with the Ukrainians. "If we show the Ukrainian" wrote Governor Wächter in conclusion, "a task and a place in the battle for the New Order of Europe, then the vast majority of the Ukrainian population will unite on our side and make the battle of the Reich into its own."[122]

Not surprisingly, the letter made no impact on Hitler, who allowed Koch to retain his office in Ukraine, and continued to support his policies, partly out of his comradeship for the *Alt Parteikämpfer* (old party fighters).

Notwithstanding Wächter's nonconformism, *Reichsführer-SS* Heinrich Himmler remained tolerant towards 'his obedient servant'.[123] He recognised him as a valuable and important asset, as well as a counterbalance to Hans Frank who was constantly at loggerheads with the SS and *Polizei* (police) in the *Generalgouvernement*. When *HSSPf.* Krüger sent a telex to Himmler on 25 February 1943, asking whether *SS-Brigadeführer* Dr Wächter should be inducted into service in the Waffen-SS according to the directive for all SS members who were civil servants in the *Generalgouvernement* born in 1901,[124] Himmler refused. His telex reply of the same day read: "The *Reichsführer-SS* has decided that *SS-Brigadeführer* Dr Wächter is not to be released for service at the front with the Waffen-SS."[125]

The decision to retain his services soon paid dividends. Governor Wächter had already determined to capitalise on the strong anti-Communist feeling, which was one of the intrinsic characteristics of Ukrainian nationalist movement in Galicia, in order to support the rapidly worsening German war effort.

Ersatz Aryans

Despite Hitler's explicit edict to the contrary, the utilisation of anti-Communist elements among the population of the Soviet Union had become common practice, from the very start of the campaign. The impact of the savage Soviet policies, on the majority of the countries that had been incorporated into the Soviet Union, engendered a fanatical hatred of Soviet Communism among their respective populations. An increasing number of Wehrmacht generals and German government officials, who had adopted a less doctrinaire attitude towards Nazi racial and political policies in the occupied eastern territories, sought to take advantage of that predilection. However, as long as the majority of the Nazi hierarchy espoused the *Untermensch* thesis, and while the Axis forces still held the strategic initiative, those who advocated a radical change in approach were unable to make any significant headway.

By late 1942 and early 1943, the situation had altered dramatically as the Axis advance was stopped. The Western Allies seized the initiative. They inflicted staggering losses on the Axis forces, in terms of manpower that could not be made good. In the west, the British and American forces had gained significant successes in Africa. In the east, the German Sixth Army, of some 300,000 men, had reached Stalingrad on the banks of the river Volga.

They were eventually encircled and the pitiful remnants forced to surrender in January 1943. The loss of strategic initiative, combined with an acute shortage of manpower and increasing partisan activity in the occupied territories, compelled elements of the Nazi leadership to partially revise and dilute its racist ideology.

Less bound by Nazi dogma, the Wehrmacht had already begun, clandestinely at first and then openly, to encourage recruitment from among anti-Communist, non-Russian Soviet prisoners and deserters, to bolster its exhausted reserve. By the end of 1942 a number of separate eastern legions had been raised. They were composed of Caucasians, Georgians, Turkomen, Cossacks, Uzbeks, Arabs, Belorussians, Armenians, Kazakhs, Crimean Tatars and Ukrainians who were recruited by the simple expedient of consolidating those serving in *Schuma* Battalions.[126] In the case of the latter, a majority were, or were supposed to have been, organised in the Ukrainian liberation (UVV, *Ukrainske vyzvol'ne vijsko*) a title adopted by the Wehrmacht propaganda department. Thousands deserted to the nationalist partisans, because they could not reconcile their consciences to carrying out the tasks set them by the Germans. The orders often involved setting fire to villages of their own people, and shooting unarmed civilians.

However it should be stressed, that the eventual formation of those legions was not accompanied by any form of political recognition or concession. The Nazi leadership still adamantly refused to make such concessions.

Following the example of the Wehrmacht, the Waffen-SS was obliged to begin a tactical retreat from ideological conformity, in order to supplement the urgently needed replacements for its depleted frontline divisions. Under those circumstances, and prompted by *SS-Gruppenführer* Berger, the term 'Germanic' had already been extended by the *Reichsführer-SS* Himmler. It included the inhabitants of ethnically German areas, the so-called *Volksdeutsch* or ethnic Germans, i.e. those who were not citizens of the German Reich but were German in language and culture. Consequently, Romanians, Hungarians, Bulgarians, and Slovaks, among others, found themselves being drafted, en masse, into Waffen-SS divisions as replacements. That principal of Germanic influence, and the influx of increasing numbers of foreigners, changed the profile of the Waffen-SS. It paved the way for preparations being made for the raising of Waffen-SS divisions from the inhabitants of the Baltic States of Latvia and Estonia. Himmler saw them as heirs to the colonisation of the Teutonic Knights.

Governor Wächter knew that even in the absence of the critical political dimension it had still been possible to recruit Ukrainians into armed service. By the spring of 1943, approximately 4,000 Ukrainians from the Galician region were serving in Polizei and guard units (*Wachformationen*) created by various local authorities (*Dienststellen*).[127] Such developments, and the success of the previous recruitment action in Galicia in November 1941, in which *Oberst* Bisanz had been instrumental, provided the seed of the idea for more extensive German/ Ukrainian co-operation. Governor Wächter determined to elevate that to new heights.

On Christmas Eve 1942, in a letter to the *Reichsführer*, he sought a personal meeting. There, at last, he could present his ambitious plans. He would emphasise that his administration policies had created a potential opportunity. His policies could be translated into securing the active military co-operation of the Ukrainians in the fight against the Soviet Union. Co-operation would be secured by setting up a SS formation in Galicia.[128]

In his reply, dated 18 January 1943, Himmler acknowledged Wächter's achievements and gave notice of his intention to visit L'viv:

> 18 January 1943
>
> Dear party comrade Wächter!
>
> My sincere thanks for your letter dated 24.12.1942 and also for the beautiful picture from Lemberg.
>
> I am definitely intending to visit Lemberg during the first part of the year and [will] then discuss many things with you. Most importantly, at the end of 1942 I would like to affirm one thing: Galicia remained peaceful and orderly. It is greatly due to your efforts and it is not in the least due to your harmonious work with the efficient Katzmann.[129] To say impartially, this is the result of the co-operation of the administration with the SS and *Polizei* in your district.
>
> Heil Hitler!
> Yours H. Himmler[130]

The 1st Cossack Volunteer Division, known as the 'Bluecoats'.

Shortly before their retreat, the Soviet OGPU (forerunner to the NKVD) slaughtered the inmates of the prisons in the major Ukrainian cities and towns. This picture shows Ukrainians look for relatives amongst the 2300 bodies found in L'viv on 30 June 1941.

Two pictures from the same sequence. General-governor *Hans Frank accompanied by Governor Wächter and members of his Galician administration, accepts the traditional Ukrainian greeting of bread and salt from M. Khronoviat in his capacity as a representative of the Military Board, during a visit to Drohobych, 20 June 1943, to inspect volunteers for the Galician Division. Left to right, Wächter (wearing white shirt), Otto Bauer his deputy (behind and to the left of Wächter, adjusting glasses), Khronoviat (front right, with back to camera in dark suit), Hans Frank,* SS-Gruppenführer *Gerret Korsemann.*

A second picture taken on the same occasion.

2

Opening Moves

Himmler's preserved meeting notes record that, on 2 March 1943,[1] Governor Wächter travelled to meet the *Reichsführer-SS* in Hochwald, East Prussia. There Himmler had established his field HQ in his train. The recorded agenda for the meeting shows it took place only one month after the momentous German defeat at Stalingrad. It included some of the more pressing problems in Galicia such as Jews, administration breakdowns, the re-settlement of German *Volksdeutscher* and partisan groups.[2]

Whilst discussing those issues at length, Dr Wächter set out some of his long term political ideas based on a retroactive plan for a new administrative structure of the *Generalgouvernement*. Essentially, they envisaged the unification of the two districts of Cracow and Lemberg, i.e. Galicia, into one 'Greater Galician District' the *Grossdistrikt Galizien*, and the merger of the districts of Radom, Warsaw and Lublin into two districts. One of those would include the Polish Congress area west of the Vistula, and the other would cover the territories east of the Vistula. Finally, one would be restricted separately to the city-district of Warsaw. As well as the predicted simplification of the administration, the plan contained a political concept. It would allow for the possibility of treating the Polish population in the new districts, especially in rural areas, according to their degree of loyalty, while simultaneously granting more freedom to those resident in Galicia. Moreover, it would afford the opportunity of applying the policy of suppression to the Polish Congress and Warsaw areas only. Those areas represented the principal centres of resistance and unrest. It was hoped to achieve the disintegration of the solidarity of the Polish resistance movement.[3]

Hoping to win his approbation, Wächter also entreated Himmler finally to consent to the temporary cessation of resettlement of racial Germans in Galicia, while the war was still in progress. He wanted to re-introduce private ownership of land in the province.[4] Governor Wächter was confident that the goodwill that would be generated by these two initiatives would be of crucial importance, but only if the Ukrainian population was to support another major scheme which involved organising a German sponsored Division[5] from Galician Ukrainians. Such a formation, he argued, would help to cripple the growing Ukrainian underground partisan movement [UPA], which at that time was operating against both the Soviets and the Germans, by conscripting the young Ukrainian men into controlled military service. In addition to the propaganda advantages, it would also raise much needed additional manpower for the strengthening of the Eastern Front, by exploiting the Ukrainian hatred of Bolshevism. It would utilise the services of thousands of forced labourers, who had been sent to the Reich, but who often practised sabotage and managed to escape.

Wächter was also fully cognisant of the fact that, if the enterprise were successful, it would be good currency that could potentially win over Himmler to support his long-term political plans. Himmler expressed an interest in the basic concept, provided it met with the Führer's approval. He was aware of the already overstretched state of the resources of his organisation, and made the explicit proviso that the population of Galicia shared the burden of providing the required matériel.

Two days after the meeting, on 4 March 1943, together with a secret letter to Himmler, Governor Wächter submitted the draft text of a planned call to arms. It would be made to the population of Galicia on the occasion of the promulgation of the proposed division. Essentially, the text of Wächter's appeal was contrived to convince the Ukrainians in Galicia that, in recognition of their achievements and "continued pressure to allow them to fight" (sic.), Hitler had finally given his approval to the formation of the *SS-Freiwilligen-Division 'Galizien'*. Additionally, the draft appeal called on the Galician youth to fight to defend their homes, and families, against the Bolshevik enemy, and for a "just New Order in Europe." It also sought to give the impression that service in the division was a privilege, by indicating that applications of volunteers whose fathers had served in the Austro-Hungarian Army, would be given preferential treatment.

In the covering letter Wächter suggested that, should Himmler authorise the call to arms, he would then make the necessary preparations, via preparatory discussions with Ukrainian representatives, that would ensure a favourable reception from the Galician people for the idea of raising the SS Volunteer Division 'Galicia'. He concluded by saying that, if Himmler's basic approval was forthcoming, he could then begin the technical execution. It would be in agreement with *SS-Gruppenführer* Berger (head of the SS Main Office) and *SS-Obergruppenführer und General der Polizei* Krüger[6] in his capacity as the HSSPf. in the *Generalgouvernement (Höhere SS-und Polizei Führer Ost* und *Staatssekretär* im *Generalgouvernement*).[7]

Pre-empting official sanction for the project, in late March and early April, *Oberst* Bisanz had picked up where he left off. He had already widely disseminated the news in L'viv about the formation of a 'Ukrainian Army'. He had begun conversations with individual veterans and, according to Kubijovych, tried to induce the men to volunteer in the, as yet non-existent, formation.[8]

Cognisant of the promising response, on 20 March Governor Wächter went to see *SS-Gruppenführer* Berger. He left written plans delineating his long-term political proposals, in detail, to be passed on to Himmler. Berger duly passed the plans to Himmler's secretary, *SS-Obersturmbannführer* Dr Brandt, with a covering letter that revealed there would be no difficulty in raising the required manpower for a planned *'Polizei Schützen Regiment Galizien'*:[9]

Regarding: New District Divisions in the *Generalgouvernement*
Enclosures: 2
20 March 1943
Secret!

Dear Doctor!

SS-Brigadeführer Freiherr von Wächter has visited me today and has left the enclosed plans with a letter. I assume that the *Reichsführer-SS* has spoken to *SS-Brigadeführer* Wächter with regard to this, and I wish to provide a short briefing.

By 15 April a commission will leave here for Lemberg. 12,000 pre-trained [*vorausgebildete*[10]] Ukrainians selected predominantly from the population of the mountain villages, will be presented to us for the formation of the *Polizei Schützen* Regiment '*Galizien*'. Of these 3,000 plus, 500 will be selected.

Heil Hitler!
G. Berger
SS-Gruppenführer.[11]

Along with his principal aides, Governor Wächter wanted to gain a better view of the sentiments of the Ukrainian population. To do this, he began to discuss the use of Galician Ukrainians in a combatant role, during private meetings with the two chief spokesmen of the Ukrainian Central Committee, Professor Kubijovych and his deputy Dr Pankivskyj. As Governor, Wächter lacked the necessary authority the discussions and commitments at that stage were vague. Nevertheless, he felt encouraged that, notwithstanding their experiences with the German occupation policies, the Ukrainians were still prepared to support the formation of a military unit that would fight against the Soviets. But that would be in return for ultimate political recognition. In fact, independent of Wächter's proposal, Kubijovych had already broached, in a letter to General-governor Frank, the idea of raising a volunteer Ukrainian military unit on the territory of the *Generalgouvernement*. It would join forces with the Germans against their mutual enemy. The letter remained unanswered.[12]

With positive signs from the Ukrainian representatives, Governor Wächter felt compelled to write again to Himmler and Krüger on 24 March 1943. This time the letter concerned his proposed modification of German agricultural policy in favour of private ownership. Wächter deduced that the introduction of new legislation, favouring privatisation, would be welcomed by the Galician Ukrainians. It would also serve as an added incentive to help cultivate a wider basis of support for his appeal for volunteers, especially among the predominantly peasant population.[13]

Himmler addressed both the issue of re-privatisation, and the formation of a military unit, in a secret letter to Wächter dated 28 March 1943, which read:

Feldkommandostelle
28 March 1943
Secret!

Dear party comrade Wächter,

I confirm the receipt of your letter dated 4.3.1943. The Führer has approved of the formation of the *SS-Freiwilligen-Division 'Galicia'* in principle. In my opinion we should proceed in stages, as follows.

After the cultivation of the fields has been completed in the spring, all the farmers who have delivered their quotas in an exemplary and irreproachable fashion in 1941 and 1942, and who have cultivated their fields in the spring of the years 1942 and 1943, to our complete satisfaction, will be reprivatised in recognition of their achievement.

Those farmers who have not made regular quota deliveries and generally those who are not up to the mark and are lazy, by reason of their insufficient performance, will not be reprivatised. Shortly after that, your summons will be issued to the able-bodied youth of Galicia. I enclose it with a few suggested corrections.

In my mind, these men will not be organised in *Polizei* battalions but a whole horse-drawn Grenadier Division. As I discussed with you the horses, supply wagons or carts, as well as winter clothing, are all to be provided from the ranks of the population and craftsman of the *Distrikt* Galicia. We will, of course, pay the valid rates for the articles supplied.

I would ask you to discuss these questions further with *SS-Obergruppenführer* Krüger and *SS-Gruppenführer* Berger. The staff for the medical examinations will be sent to you in good time. There will have to be more discussions as to the place where the division is to be set up. It is a question that can be answered one way or another. The division can either be set up on a training area in the *Altreich* (Old Reich) or in the garrisons of Galicia itself. From the general impression I have at the moment, I would prefer a training area in the *Altreich*.

I have read your proclamation to the population of Galicia. I think it is very good.

Heil Hitler!
Signed H. Himmler[14]

In a second letter, with the same date, Himmler gave his approval for the limitation of the colonisation policy for the duration of the war, "in view of the political and military situation."[15]

Dr Wächter, who correctly assessed the significance and potential impact of the re-privatisation measures,[16] hastened to send Himmler a telegram dated 3 April 1943. It requested that, in order successfully to augment the recruitment drive, the re-privatisation should take place without Himmler's demand for prior concessions. In support of that request Wächter pointed out that it would be interpreted as an anti-Bolshevik move. He insisted that it was imperative, for propaganda reasons, to introduce such an initiative in order to win the support, and active participation, of the Galician population as part of the anti-Bolshevik defence front (*Antibolschewistische Abwehrfront*).[17] On that issue Himmler raised no further objections and accepted the reprivatisation plan without qualification.

The Ukrainian Response

Having received Himmler's conditional consent to the raising of a military unit from Galicia, to the re-privatisation scheme, and to the limitation of the resettlement programme, Wächter's discussions with Ukrainian representatives assumed new dimensions.

Both factions of the OUN, i.e. OUN Bandera and OUN Melnyk having been consulted, refused to co-operate in the formation of a division.[18] On 3 April 1943, Governor Wächter and his vice governor, Dr Otto

Bauer, had further confidential discussions with Professor Kubijovych, the chief Ukrainian spokesman, in his capacity as the head of the UCC.

During those discussions, Kubijovych mentioned the issue of the desire of Ukrainians to fight, alongside the Germans, against the Bolsheviks. He warned against undertaking a recruiting drive without a firm political basis of support in the Ukrainian community.[19] At the same time, Wächter revealed to Kubijovych that, in terms of future Ukrainian political developments, only very limited concessions could be made. That was because of the opposition of certain individuals among the Nazi hierarchy, including some of Hitler's close associates. For that reason the Ukrainians should not expect to receive any immediate political benefits from volunteering for the Division. It was to have a regional, i.e. Galician, and not a national, i.e. Ukrainian, character. Wächter did however emphasise that its performance in battle would be of the utmost importance. The greater its success in that respect, the greater the amount of political leverage the Ukrainians would have in dealing with the Germans. In addition, he stressed that since only native Germans could be drafted into regular Wehrmacht units, the Galician Division, like those made up of ethnic Germans, would be an integral part of the Waffen-SS.

To make those conditions more palatable, and to win official Ukrainian backing, Dr Wächter stated that the UCC was to act as the principal representative for the proposed Division before German and Ukrainian authorities. He announced that a Military Board would be established. It was to be led by Kubijovych. It would oversee recruitment and assist families and dependants of the volunteers. He also promised that the Division would have an evenly divided German/ Ukrainian officer corps. He said that some political prisoners, i.e. members of the OUN, would be released from prisons and concentration camps. Finally, knowing that the influence of the Church was of critical importance, in gaining the support of a deeply religious population, Governor Wächter agreed that Ukrainian priests would be attached to the Division.

In the event of those inducements failing to satisfy Ukrainian expectations, Wächter warned Kubijovych that, "Certain consequences would follow for the Ukrainians if a move to raise a division was resisted, as the Germans would form such a formation whether the Ukrainians acquiesced and agreed to co-operate or not."[20]

Towards a *Polizei* Division

After broaching the preliminary issues with Ukrainian representatives, and in compliance with Himmler's instruction, Governor Wächter discussed the organisational problems of the formation of the envisaged *Polizei* Division (*Polizei Schützen Division*) with *SS-Obergruppenführer* Krüger of the HSSPf., on 4 April 1943. Two days later on 6 April 1943, he met for the second time with *SS-Gruppenführer* Gottlob Berger. In a secret letter to Himmler, dated 6 April 1943, Berger, who fully expected that because of the serious shortages of training instructors and ordnance within the Waffen-SS establishment the unit was to be raised under the auspices of the *Ordnungspolizei,* reported briefly on the developments. He indicated that the enlistment commission (*Annahmekommission*) for the Division was already in operation and that the appropriate arrangements had been made:

> 6 April 1943
>
> *Reichsführer*!
>
> *SS-Brigadeführer* Freiherr von Wächter visited me again today. We agreed that he would approach the Ukrainian population of Galicia with a large-scale call to arms. On the 30.3.1943 the enlistment commission for this new Ukrainian *SS-Polizei-Schützen-Division*, came into operation. The necessary agreements have been made with *SS-Gruf.* Winkelmann[21] of the head office (*Hauptamt*) of the *Ordnungspolizei*. *SS-Brigf.* von Wächter will make sure that we receive the necessary horses from the country. The outcome (of these events) will be reported.
>
> G. Berger
> *SS-Gruppenführer*[22]

Himmler, however, continued to demur. He hesitated to confirm his endorsement for the formation of the Division. However, the exigencies of war had resulted in reduced racial requirements to such an extent that the

Waffen-SS, which represented the combat element of his empire, were accepting recruits from ethnic groups who by no stretch of the imagination could be considered as Germanic.[23] He had already voiced his scepticism about the wisdom of such a venture. As a result of petitioning by one of his best generals, Felix Steiner,[24] who wanted to utilise the help of Ukrainians in the war against the Soviet Union by granting them autonomy to win their support. Himmler had retorted, "Do not forget that in 1918 these splendid Ukrainians murdered Field-Marshal von Eichhorn."[25] His officials were concerned that the new proposed formation would become an instrument for the Ukrainian nationalists, as the Ukrainians themselves intended.[26] On 10 April 1943, his office sent the following telex to Governor Wächter:

> 10 April 1943
>
> *Brigadeführer*!
> *SS-Gruppenführer* Berger has reported that you recently visited him and discussed the canvassing and your call to arms with him. The *Reichsführer-SS* requests that you move slowly with regard to the canvassing and do not yet issue the call to arms. You will receive further information either from *SS-Gruppenführer* Berger or myself next week.
>
> Heil Hitler!
> Signed Brandt
> *SS-Obersturmbannführer*[27]

Ignoring the warning, Governor Wächter convened a conference in L'viv on Monday 12 April 1943. He invited nine locally active SS, *Polizei*, propaganda department and Nazi party officials,[28] to work out a detailed plan covering the practicalities associated with the organisation of the formation. The conference endorsed a number of key decisions, which Himmler was to be required to ratify, as recorded in the minutes of the meeting which have been preserved.[29] These included:

- The title *SS-Freiwilligen Division Galician* or *Freiwilligen Division Galician* was to be adopted for the proposed formation at Wächter's suggestion. It was agreed however that although *Polizei* ranks were to be used and the personnel and material costs were to be carried by the *Ordnungspolizei* the inclusion of the word *Polizei* in the title, would be avoided on political-psychological grounds.
- Its members would wear a field-grey uniform with a shield on the right upper arm, similar to those of the other European volunteer formations, depicting a traditional Galician emblem – "but nothing symbolic of Ukraine or Ukrainian national aspirations."
- The Division was to be a horse-drawn infantry unit, with weapons and equipment similar to that of any German infantry division. 2–3,000 draft horses, with the necessary harnesses and carts, would be furnished by the Galician population, who would share with Germany the costs of other equipment and training. It was to have 600 officers, 50 doctors and 20 veterinarians. According to estimates, there would be available 300 Ukrainian officers from the Austro-Hungarian Army, about 100 officers from the Polish army, and an unknown number from the Ukrainian intelligentsia who had served in the Polish army, but who for political reasons had not been commissioned.
- In the case of the latter, after three months of service at the front they could be sent to officers' schools. The majority of officers from the Ukrainian Galician army had also served in the Austro-Hungarian army. In addition, 2,000 non-commissioned officers would be required. They would be drawn from former members of the Polish and Austro-Hungarian armies. For the positions of company administrators (*Spiess*), former members of the Austro-Hungarian army were to be appointed as they already had command of both languages. Three hundred NCOs from the Netherlands, plus a further three hundred NCOs from Oranienburg were available for cadre personnel, along with a regular battalion for the planned *Polizeiregiment Galizien*.[30]
- The minimum height requirement for recruits would be reduced to 1.65 m to accommodate the "lower quality human resources," while those born between the years 1908 and 1925 inclusive would be admitted

for voluntary registration. The conference noted that special attention should be paid to canvassing among those currently being called up for *Baudienst* (construction service) while "the voluntary principle should be fundamentally adhered to in every case."

- For recruitment purposes a civilian Military Board (*Wehrausschuss*) was to be established. It was to be made up of officers of the former Austro-Hungarian and Ukrainian armies, in conjunction with representatives of the Ukrainian Central Committee (*Hauptauschuss*). Its main concern was to be recruitment activity, to be carried out in consultation with German *Polizei* and administrative authorities.

The conference ended by establishing a timetable for the recruitment activities and associated festivities. It would begin with a ceremonial declaration, in L'viv on 28 April 1943, to be attended by county and district chiefs, representatives of the Wehrmacht, the *Polizei*, the Military Board, the UCC, and the Greek-Catholic priesthood.[31]

Governor Wächter had continued with his preparatory measures, in defiance of the instruction from Himmler's office to hold his preparations in abeyance. Wächter knew that the inauguration of his programme was dependent on Himmler's consent, which he did not yet have. To avoid jeopardising his plan, he dispatched a telex to Himmler reporting his recent discussions, with various Nazi functionaries, concerning the technical details of the raising of the SS-Division *Galicia*. At the same time he endeavoured to appease Himmler by informing him that a full report of recent events would be forwarded to him, via the Chief of the *Ordnungspolizei*, Kurt Daluege, who would be in Cracow on 14 April. Diplomatically, he hastened to add that the starting date for the campaign, i.e. the call up, would be immediately followed by propaganda evaluation. The date had not been decided, but 28 April had been considered. He also repeated his request to be allowed to make a final report to the *Reichsführer*, in person, as there "was still a fundamental political question to resolve."[32]

A Waffen-SS Division

While Wächter waited for Himmler's permission to proceed with his plans, Himmler spelled out in no uncertain terms that he regarded the 'Galician Division' not as a *Polizei* formation, but as a combat unit to be raised under the auspices of the Waffen-SS. Instead, distinct *Polizei* regiments were to be raised from 10,000 men, for anti-partisan and security duties.[33] In what capacity an individual would be permitted to serve, would be determined by the religious group to which he belonged. Only the favoured Greek-Catholic Ukrainians from Galicia were to recruited into the Galician Division, while the Ukrainians from the Lublin District, who were members of the Greek-Orthodox Church, were to be utilised for the separate *Polizei* regiments.

To clarify this, Himmler's office sent telex messages dated 13 April 1943, to both Wächter and *SS-Obergruppenfuhrer* Krüger, which stated unequivocally that, "The *Ordnungspolizei* has nothing to do with the Galician division."[34]

The following day, on Himmler's instructions, the Chief of the *Ordnungspolizei, SS-Obergruppenführer und Generaloberst der Polizei* Kurt Daluege, sent a letter to *SS-Gruppenführer und Generalleutnant der Polizei*, Otto Winkelmann, in which he reiterated the same point. He further elucidated on the reason for Himmler's desire to exclude nationalist elements, under all circumstances, from the formation:

> 14 April 1943
>
> To *Generalleutnant* Winkelmann
>
> I have spoken with the *Reichsführer-SS* about the mythical *Polizei-Schützen-Division*. The *Reichsführer-SS* knows nothing of this division and neither does he know of it by its former title. In addition he issues a new order which will contain the following:
>
> A frontline division shall be created for the Waffen-SS and by the Waffen-SS, which will consist of the Greek-Catholic Ukrainians and probably will be called the 'Galician Division,' for these Ukrainians come from Galicia.
>
> The remaining Ukrainians in the *Generalgouvernement*, including those from the Lublin district, are Greek-Orthodox. These will be made available for the establishment of *Polizei* regiments with some German leadership, or for the establishment of 3 battalions comprised solely of these Ukrainians. The use of

> National Ukrainian intelligence groups,[35] i.e. Bandera, is absolutely out of the question. The *Reichsführer-SS* forbids this fundamentally. He still recalls very clearly the time during the war of 1917–1918, where the German authorities attempted to create an independent Ukraine. The result was that the leading circle – to which Bandera and a great number of his followers belonged[36] – showed their recognition and gratitude by the shooting of German officers and men. I would like to see *SS-Gruppenführer* Berger ascertain as quickly as possible the sizes of the two groups of Ukrainians in the *Generalgouvernement*, (i.e. the Greek Catholics of Galicia and the Greek Orthodox of Lublin) [… .][37]

On 16 April, in a letter to Himmler, HSSPf. Krüger sought to clarify the latest edict, in view of the respective concerns expressed by Berger and Governor Wächter. In the case of the former, Krüger said that Berger had informed him that the Waffen-SS was not in a position to provide the required training staff for the formation of the *Freiwilligen Division 'Galizien'*.

In the latter case, Krüger wrote, Governor Wächter was "of the opinion that the setting up of the *Polizei* Regiments in the Lublin district with the powers of the *Ordnungspolizei*, prior to the formation of the *Freiwilligen Division 'Galizien'*, would not serve the political purpose that was originally intended." Krüger ended the letter by stating that "In order to comply with the order of the *Reichsführer-SS* the formation of the *Freiwilligen Division 'Galizien'* would have to be provisionally postponed."[38]

Himmler's office responded by immediately sending a telex to Wächter, on the same day, instructing him that the *Reichsführer* was not ready to approve a specific date for further discussions regarding the matter of the *SS-Freiwilligen Division 'Galizien'*. He was therefore to wait with all plans for the official launch.[39]

Thus, for the second time in one week, in view of the issues that needed to be resolved, Himmler made a belated attempt to delay Wächter's programme which was rapidly gathering pace. Governor Wächter remained undeterred by Himmler's insistence on creating distinct *Polizei* units, and continued to lobby him to accede to his plan. For added support he turned to *SS-Gruppenführer* Berger, knowing that he was an enthusiastic supporter of the Division and that he also enjoyed the close confidence of the *Reichsführer*. In a telegram to Himmler dated 16 April 1943, Berger exhorted him to permit the call to arms to take place on schedule. At the same time, he repeated his warning that the Waffen-SS establishment did not have the available resources to train and equip a Division, and that the segregation of Ukrainians by religious denomination was an impractical proposition:

> 16 April 1943
> Regarding: *Galizien* Division
>
> *Reichsführer*
>
> In line with orders, I have put myself in contact with those involved [with the *Galizien* Division] and in doing so have discovered the following:
>
> 1. The preparations for the formation of the division have commenced. *Brigadeführer* Wächter has in view of the urgency, driven things ahead to such an extent that by 20.4.43[40] the entire population of Galicia will await a call to arms. In view of the severe political unrest, that has at the moment also affected the whole [General] *Gouvernement*, it is possible that the cessation of canvassing for the Division would strengthen resistance activities and would significantly support enemy propaganda.
>
> 2. According to *Brigadeführer* Wächter's communications at least 10,000 men are available at the shortest notice. I fear that the *Führungshauptamt* [SS Main Operations Office] has neither the necessary instructors nor the necessary weapons for training. If it is to become a division of the Waffen-SS, then I venture to suggest, that the existing training cadres (*Ausbildungskadres*) be included, if only temporarily, into the Waffen-SS. I request a rapid decision by the *Reichsführer-SS*.
>
> 3. There are several areas in which Catholic Orthodox and Greek Orthodox populations are very mixed. Separation of men into Waffen-SS and *Polizei* is therefore not really possible.
>
> Signed *SS-Gruppenführer* Berger.[41]

Three days later, on 19 April 1943, Wächter notified Grothmann, Himmler's office chief, by telex that *SS-Gruppenführer* Berger had confirmed the campaign could be started. In light of that he intended to make the call to arms with a *festakt*, i.e. a celebratory decree, on 28 April as proposed.[42] Thereafter he would begin conducting intensive propaganda throughout Galicia with the assistance of the Military Board.[43]

In the face of Berger's arguments and Wächter's persistence, Himmler finally relented, and made no further attempt to prevent the call to arms from going ahead as planned.

The Conflicts of Co-operation

While Himmler was still deliberating, Professor Kubijovych took the opportunity to assemble a select number of prominent Ukrainians at a meeting in L'viv on 18 April 1943. They were to discuss official participation in the creation of a division and he solicited their comments.[44] Among those in attendance were members of various military veterans' organisations who supported the concept, regional chairmen of the UCC, and members of the newly formed Military Board.

Despite previous setbacks, Kubijovych argued that co-operation with the Germans to that end was as much in the Ukrainian interest as it was in the Germans' since it afforded an opportunity to form a large disciplined Ukrainian military force. In the event of a German defeat, followed by a period of turmoil, as had been the case at the end of WWI, such a force would be an invaluable asset for the re-assertion of an independent state. In that way the German army would become a school that would train, arm and equip the Ukrainian youth for a future army. Ukrainians could thus achieve political recognition and become an accepted political factor in the eyes of the outside world. Kubijovych pointed out that this was especially important since the Germans, without using Ukrainian intermediaries, were already recruiting Ukrainians into various formations that were in no way connected with Ukrainian political objectives.[45]

After a lengthy debate, but still with a few reservations, the conference agreed to co-operate with Wächter's proposal and officially endorse the undertaking. As well as the reasons outlined above, the conference acknowledged that active co-operation would enable the Ukrainians to optimise their influence on the German policy in Galicia, and to a certain extent in the *Reichkommissariat* Ukraine, and keep them informed of any new German initiatives. It was also agreed that, as a precondition for the active Ukrainian participation, a number of requests, formulated as a result of previous discussions would be put forward as a condition of consent.[46] Foremost among those were:

1. The Division would be used exclusively against the Bolsheviks.
2. Its name and markings would be Ukrainian.
3. Its officers would be Ukrainians (attached German officers to act as liaisons with German high command staff).
4. The Division would be provided with religious ministration from Ukrainian priests.
5. The Division would be attached to the Wehrmacht (that is the *Heer* or regular army).
6. The Division would be considered as the first unit in the creation of the Ukrainian National Army into which it would be eventually incorporated.
7. All Ukrainian political prisoners, in German prisons and concentration camps would be released under a general amnesty – including the former officers of *Nachtigall.*
8. All other Ukrainian military units would be dissolved.
9. The Division would be a fully motorised unit possessing a full range of weapons including tanks.
10. Forced labourers who fled from Germany would be granted amnesty.[47]

The requests made by the Ukrainians to the German authorities were not arranged or presented in order of priority, which Governor Wächter was quick to exploit. Only two points, numbers 1 and 4, which coincided with previous German pronouncements, were actually accepted. It was agreed that the unit, when formed, would not be obliged to fight on the Western Front against the Americans and the British, but exclusively against Ukraine's historical enemy, Russia,[48] and that the Division would have its own Catholic chaplains to serve the spiritual needs of its soldiers.

Points 7 and 10 were also partially complied with. Some Ukrainian political prisoners, but by no means all, were released from German prisons and concentration camps, while the amnesty for forced labourers who had escaped was only applicable if they registered as volunteers. With regard to the appointment of Ukrainian officers in point 3, Wächter offered a compromise, and agreed that the Division would have a balanced German/Ukrainian officer corps. In every other respect, requests which suggested Ukrainian political aspirations, or which would have assured that the Division had a distinctive and outwardly perceptible Ukrainian character, were rejected out of hand. That even extended as far as symbolic gestures, such as the use of the national emblem, the Trident, which was not permitted. Instead, at the suggestion of *Oberst* Bisanz,[49] it was to be the regional Galician symbol consisting of a golden lion, on a blue background, standing on its hind legs, with three crowns, two above its head and one beneath the hind legs.[50] The full extent of the failure of the Ukrainian negotiators did not, however, become apparent until after the Division had actually been formed. By that time Governor Wächter had reneged on his promise that Professor Kubijovych would head the Military Board. Instead, he appointed one of his senior administrators, a German Galician, *Oberst* Bisanz, in his place.

Had the Ukrainians who negotiated the terms for the Galician Division not overestimated German strength, and failed to appreciate how great German dependency on outside help had become, they might at least have obtained a favourable compromise on some of their requests, as did other nationalities in similar circumstances.[51] Instead, by allowing them to be categorically rejected, the Ukrainian leaders took a gamble by sacrificing short-term form for long-term substance.

Thus, in the final analysis, even before the Division's formation had been officially announced, both sides had diametrically opposed objectives in supporting its creation. In the words of one former veteran, "The Germans had their objectives and we had ours."[52]

Wächter's Position – Germany First

From his earliest discussions with Ukrainian representatives Governor Wächter had been aware that the rationale behind their support for the Division was based exclusively on their own long-term national aspirations. Wächter, in line with his own agenda, had already rejected most of the proposals put forward by the Military Board. He also issued two documents intended to make certain that the Division would ultimately serve German interests rather than those of the Ukrainian nationalists.

Prepared in advance of the proclamation, he issued a secret circular letter dated 28 April 1943. It was sent to all local authorities, containing detailed instructions concerning the ambitious recruitment that was about to commence. In his seven-page letter, Wächter stated that a Recruitment Commission (*Werbekommission*) for the Division would be set up for every district, to be presided over by the *Kreishauptmann* of the *Landkommissar*. They would work in close co-operation with his representative body within the Ukrainian population, i.e. the Military Board (*Wehrausschuss Galizien*). Wächter stressed that these commissions were to actively support and further the propaganda activities of the Military Board. It was to be seen as an independent body in order to maintain the illusion of an equal German/Ukrainian partnership. Also it would avoid giving the impression that it was "simply an organ of the German authorities or that it was bound by the decisions of the Ukrainian auxiliary committees and delegations."

Regarding the procedures, special mention was made indicating that in order to maximise the influence of the clergy and teachers, every consideration was to be given to their utilisation in recruitment activities. As for the actual recruits, to overcome the anticipated difficulties in securing the 20,000[53] fully-fit men needed for the formation of a division, and as an added incentive that would make enlistment a more attractive proposition, the document contained a directive. It said that Ukrainians who had escaped from forced labour could be granted an amnesty, but only if they registered, by 1 June 1943, as volunteers in the *SS-Schützen-Division 'Galizien'*. Wächter also stated that, as a matter of principle, service in the Division, enlistment into which was to be limited exclusively to volunteers of Ukrainian origin currently resident in Galicia, would take precedence over all other types of employment.[54]

Within the instructions he once again drew particular attention to the fact that the use of coercion, or even moral pressure, to obtain volunteers was forbidden. He believed that would "destroy the political aim of the undertaking." Lastly, for propaganda purposes, permission was granted to fly blue and yellow flags, in the Ukrainian national colours, alongside the swastika flag (*Hakenkreuzflagge*). In closing, attention was drawn to the fact that the use of the Ukrainian Trident was not to be encouraged. Instead the regional symbol of the Galician lion was to be employed wherever possible.[55]

To cover all eventualities the circular letter was accompanied by confidential directives for the Recruiting Commissions, that reiterated several of the points in Wächter's circular.[56] Secret directives included guidelines for the German speakers within the commissions themselves. The orators' guidelines were not to be seen by Ukrainian members of the commissions and were to be destroyed after the contents had been memorised. The guidelines advised speakers "not to address Ukrainians as allies or give the impression that the Germans are dependent on their help". Speakers were further instructed with regard to the key issue of political rights. Reference to the Galician Ukrainians aspirations for a greater Ukrainian state were to be avoided, or if it was absolutely necessary, it was to be made clear that fulfilment of these desires was dependant on the consequences of the new formation proving its worth in battle, and not as a precondition to its existence.[57] (see Appendix I).

3

Proclamation and Propaganda: 28 April 1943

As planned, and with the contingency measures in force, the formation of the Division was promulgated on 28 April 1943. There were staged rallies in all the larger cities and towns throughout Galicia in accordance with the predetermined timetable.

The centrepiece of the official launch was an elaborate ceremony in L'viv.[1] There in the Statthalterpalais, the festivities were opened by Vice Governor Dr Bauer. In his opening address he greeted all those present, i.e. envoys of the German administration, the Nazi party, the Wehrmacht, the *Polizei*, officers and former ranking servicemen of the Austro-Hungarian Army and the Ukrainian Galician Army. Among those in attendance were two Ukrainian representatives who were specifically singled out by Dr Bauer. Professor Volodymyr Kubijovych was president of the Ukrainian Central Committee, and General Victor Kurmanovych was a former commander of the Ukrainian Galician Army. He was described by Dr Bauer as "a general whose service to the Ukrainian people deserves the highest praise."

Governor Wächter then took the floor. He issued a proclamation, on behalf of the Germans, during which he emphasised Galicia's Germanic links by announcing, that "Since Galicia had belonged to Germany for the past 150 years, Hitler placed a special importance on bringing Galicia back into the lap of Great Germany." He then read his appeal to the population for volunteers to the *SS-Freiwilligen-Division 'Galizien'*.

He praised the behaviour of the population and promised special privileges to those who enlisted, and to the young men of Galicia who were fit for military service. Since the Bolshevik oppressors were driven out by the victorious struggle of the German soldier, the population of Galicia had shown its gratitude in many ways. The Galician farmer had worked hard and conscientiously and contributed to the feeding of Europe. In the German Reich, an army of Galician men and women were working in agriculture and industry to produce bread and weapons for victory. He continued:

> 'Time and time again, the Galician people have also expressed the wish to participate in the struggle of the Reich, with weapons in their hands. In recognition of the achievements of the Galician people, the Führer has now given in to this pressure to allow them to fight, and has given his approval to the formation of the *SS-Freiwilligen-Division 'Galicia'*.
>
> 'Every member of this *Freiwilligen-Division* will be placed on an equal footing with the German soldier in equipment, pay, rations and maintenance arrangements for his family. Priests of their confession and nation will attend to pastoral care.
>
> 'Applications of volunteers whose fathers served in the Austrian army will be given preferential treatment. Youth of Galicia, you are thus entitled and called upon to participate in the struggle against the deadly Bolshevik enemy. The struggle is for religion and native country, for family and homeland, the struggle for a just new order for a victorious young Europe. For centuries you stood on the side of Europe against the marauding Orient, prove yourselves now in this hour of destiny.'[2]

Governor Wächter was followed by Dr Ludwig Losacker, Minister of the Interior of the *Generalgouvernement*. He read the manifesto on behalf of *General-governor* Frank. It was addressed to the population of Galicia. In his manifesto, full of typical Nazi hyperbole, Frank declared "that the time had come to commit the residents of the *Generalgouvernement* to the gigantic struggle against Bolshevism in order to partake in the undying combat glory of the European people. They had to win to ensure prosperity, and seize the opportunity to enjoy the benefits of European Culture."

Like Wächter, Frank stressed that the Division would be formed in accordance with the voluntary principle. He emphasised that the volunteers would enjoy legal equality with the German soldiers in terms of insurance for their immediate families.[3] Significantly, so as not to encourage any form of nationalism, neither Wächter nor Frank mentioned fighting for a free democratic and independent Ukrainian state.

Next to speak was Professor Kubijovych who, on behalf of the Ukrainian delegation, addressed the gathering in somewhat more reserved tones:[4]

> 'Today, for Ukrainians in Galicia, is a very historical day, because by today's Act of State one of the most coveted wishes of the Ukrainian people is realised – to fight against Bolshevism with weapons in our hands. This wish, expressed on many occasions since 22 June 1941, has been the conviction not only of the leaders but also of the whole nation, that Bolshevism is our greatest enemy. It brings to us not only material and spiritual ruin but also the death of the nation. Fate predestined our people to be the first to settle the score with Bolshevism. This seeking of justice lasted for twenty-five years, at first in military fight, in clandestine contest in all areas of human existence. When the Führer on the historical day of 22 June called upon all nations of Europe to the final struggle against Bolshevism, the decision for us was clear.
>
> This wish was the result of the deeper conviction, that it is our duty not to stay neutral in the great fight for building the new European order, and what we can do for the victory of the new Europe. On these principles were based our active role in the co-operation with the German government. We did everything that was possible. I have mentioned the voluntary departure of hundreds of thousands of workers to Germany. Their conscientious contribution of quotas, the collection of winter clothing for the German armed forces, their large donations of money for military purposes show their readiness. The creative work of members of our society in our workshops, plants, offices and government institutions aim for our victory. The public relations work of our intelligentsia evokes the understanding of war's necessities in wide sections of the population. We are glad that you, Governor Wächter, as the highest representative of the German government in Galicia, speak out words of recognition for this share of labour. A special pleasure for us, is the news that the highest authorities of the German state have also acknowledged our efforts.
>
> The highest authorisation, to form the Rifle Division of the SS from the Ukrainians of Galicia, is for us a recognition, and at the same time, an honour.
>
> We realise the great meaning of this highest decision for our people. Therefore, we want to ensure that it will be the best. The formation of the Galician-Ukrainian division within the framework of the SS, is for us not only a distinction, but our responsibility that we will continue to [support] and maintain this active decision, in co-operation with the German state organisations, until the victorious end of the war. I ask you, Governor, to accept our assurances that we will fulfil our responsibilities.
>
> This historic day was made possible by the conditions in our land created under your leadership, Governor Wächter. Based on these conditions you took the initiative to create a worthy opportunity for the Ukrainians of Galicia, to fight arm in arm with the heroic German soldiers of the Army and the Waffen-SS against Bolshevism, your and our deadly enemy.
>
> We thank you from our heart. Of course we ought to thank the Great Führer of the united Europe for recognising our participation in the war, that he approved your initiative and agreed to the creation of the Galicia Division.'[5]

To foster the impression of the solidarity of Ukrainian support for the formation of the Division, Myhailo Khronoviat[6] also made a speech along the same lines, on behalf of the military veterans' organisations.

The Church – the First Open Breach

Immediately after the speeches, Governor Wächter, who had already taken great care to cultivate the active co-operation of the Church, proceeded with his entourage to the Cathedral of St George. There he had astutely arranged for a divine service to be held, presided over by Reverend Dr Joseph Slipyj. The sermon was read by Reverend Dr Wasyl Laba. He was head of the department of religious affairs, was on the Military Board, and refused to pay lip service to the German propaganda theme of fighting for a 'New Europe'. He openly declared that the Ukrainians should view the formation of the Division as the first step in the re-establishment of an Ukrainian army:

> 'The German government, with the permission of the Führer of the German people, has granted the Galician Ukrainians permission to set up their own volunteer Division of riflemen. On this day of celebration, the Ukrainian people's army is resurrected. The Sich Riflemen return to join the Ukrainian people's army, to restore the link that was severed twenty years ago. At this decisive time we receive from the German government the weapons that will let us join forces with the renowned German army and its allies, to take part in the battle against Bolshevism.'[7]

Public statements of that nature were certain to be seen by the Nazis as being deliberately antagonistic, especially as they were entirely contrary to their declared aims. Consequently, from that moment on, the role of the Church in connection with the Division, was regarded with great suspicion by some senior members of the SS organisation. Subsequently, the activities of the priests who actually enlisted were closely monitored.

Evidence of the seriousness with which the Germans viewed the influence of the priests is confirmed by the measures taken to ensure that audio recordings were made of Reverend Dr Laba's sermon. Those were then forwarded, via the propaganda department, to Himmler's office[8] who passed them on to Berger.[9] The instructions were to have the recordings translated, and returned to Himmler's office for evaluation, complete with a written transcript.

Having complied with the request, Berger sent them back with a covering letter in which he acknowledged the reason for concern. But he indicated that there was no immediate cause for alarm as the necessary steps would be taken to rectify the problem, if need be, commenting, "There are certain dangerous expressions included (in the text) but we will remove this rather sore tooth."[10]

As the culmination of the festivities in L'viv on 28 April, the first concrete step in the organisation of the Division was taken when Governor Wächter officially confirmed the membership of the Military Board, headed by *Oberst* Alfred Bisanz.[11] The executive consisted of Andrij Palii, Osyp Navrotskyj, Severyn Beigert, Reverend Dr Vasyl Laba, Myhailo Kushnir, Volodymyr Bilozor, Myhailo Khronoviat, Ivan Rudnytskyj, Stefan Volynets, Evhen Pyndus, Lubomyr Makarushka, Yurij Krokhmaliuk, and Zenon Zelenyi.

Governor Wächter considered the Military Board to be a civilian organisation that was to function as an intermediary between the German authorities and the Galician population. As it would serve as a useful propaganda tool, to assist in the procurement of volunteers, he sought to limit its authority and independence. That was reflected both in the appointment of *Oberst* Bisanz, a German Galician rather than an Ukrainian, as its chairman. The accompanying statutes took the form of a twelve-page booklet. It was in bilingual German/Ukrainian text, entitled *Satzungen des Wehrausschusses Galizien*.[12] The statutes not only defined the purpose vaguely, but also stated that the Military Board was to act in an auxiliary capacity under Wächter's personal direction, or that of the head of the relevant authority, and with the agreement of the *SS-und Polizeiführer*.[13]

Recruitment and Conscription: Everyone to the Division

Immediately after the ceremony in L'viv, on Wächter's instructions, an intensive recruitment campaign was conducted across the whole of the province of Galicia, under the slogan, 'Everyone to the Division'. The campaign was orchestrated by the local German authorities, in conjunction with the Military Board, the Ukrainian Central Committee, and the subordinate local branches of both organisations in the rural areas. The Recruitment Commissions, whose remit had already been clearly established in its confidential operational directives dated 28 April 1943, undertook the practical work. Amongst other things, it was stipulated that each commission had to work in two places every day. It had to utilise town and village heads, priests and teachers as widely as possible and it had to enlist only Ukrainians from Galicia.[14]

Only those who had received prison sentences of five years and over were to be automatically debarred from enlisting. Exceptions could be made, where sentences had been pronounced under the Polish or Soviet authorities, when a letter of permission could be sent to the Governor through the Military Board. Lastly, the directives contained a tell-tale portent for the seemingly arbitrary enlistment which was to follow, stating that "*detailed examinations of the volunteers would not have to be done by the Recruitment Commissions as such examinations would slow down the recruitment process. However, attention should be turned to visible diseases or mental instabilities.*"[15] [Author's emphasis] In effect, the directives gave the commissions carte blanche to enrol almost anybody. That was precisely what they later did.

As part of the widely publicised recruitment drive posters, displayed under, 'A Call from the Governor', leaflets and other propaganda matériels advertising the Division, were liberally distributed throughout Galicia. The German propaganda machinery ensured that popular newspapers in the *Generalgouvernement* carried detailed coverage of the official proclamation of 28 April. In the following weeks numerous articles were featured promoting the Division.[16] Like the rest of the recruitment propaganda, they deliberately avoided the suggestion that the Division would be fighting for Hitler and the Third Reich, because of the known political sentiments of the population. Instead, appeals were made for the "active participation of the Galician Ukrainian people in the European fight for freedom against the Soviet Union"[17] and "to fight for a New Europe in order to earn a proper place among the nations fighting for a New Europe".

To complement the publicity, individual members of the Military Board visited the larger towns and regional centres in the region to address public meetings and gatherings to urge young men to volunteer.[18] The most popular themes repeated in their speeches were:

- An Ukrainian military force trained for modern warfare could have a decisive influence in the political re-shaping of eastern Europe.
- Fighting to defend the Ukrainian fatherland, the natural rights of the Ukrainian people, for the national culture, and for the entire European culture.
- The failure of the European Entente of 1918–1920, testified that there was only one nation capable of conquering the USSR, namely Germany.
- Taking up arms as a continuation of Ukrainian martial tradition, particularly that set of the *Sichovi Striltsi*[19] of the Ukrainian Galician army.
- Fighting together with the German army against the deadliest enemy of Ukraine, 'Bolshevism', and the ruin, famine, exile, torture and murder it brought.
- Avenging the innocent blood of brothers tortured in camps in Siberia and of the millions killed by forced collectivisation.

Among those most supportive of the enterprise were the politically articulate Ukrainians, especially those from urban areas. They were receptive to public statements that the Division would be an Ukrainian military force that could have a decisive influence in the political re-shaping of eastern Europe. They believed that its establishment would strengthen the Ukrainian position in Galicia and could ultimately serve to change German policy toward Ukraine. Likewise they regarded it as the potential nucleus of a future national army that would fight for the liberation of their homeland and, in the aftermath of the war, serve a free and independent Ukraine.[20]

At every opportunity nationalistic sentiments of that type, were propagated by individual Ukrainian speakers who were involved with recruitment.[21] Such arguments provided the inspiration for those highly motivated and nationally conscious individuals[22]. Many of them were university students or graduates from secondary schools. They formed the majority of those who volunteered in the initial period of the recruitment.[23] One student recalled:

> 'I attended a student meeting where the speaker was Mr Khronoviat. The main argument was that now there is a real chance to get our hands on some military arms and equipment, to get military training, one of the best, and to be ready (for the time) when both superpowers would weaken to the point of chaos. Ukraine's independence can only be achieved with weapons in our hands. As the first Division we were to become the nucleus of an Ukrainian army.'[24]

Most rallied to the calls of the Military Board and enlisted of their own volition. In a short letter to his parents, a second year student at the L'viv polytechnic institute gave his reasons for doing so:

L'viv, 6 May 1943

Dear Father and Mother,

I have joined the Division. I trust that you will not object to it, but I have followed my conscience. I want to fulfil my duty to my people. What the outcome will be is unknown, but the moment has arrived and if we lose it, we shouldn't call ourselves a nation.

Around us [i.e. in L'viv] huge displays took place. The Poles are getting mad. When I get home next week I will tell you everything. Yurko must remain home after I leave and has to take my place. He must repress his eagerness to join the army because he is too young and not too healthy ...

Your ever loving Evhen.[25]

Recruitment of high school and university students was aided by teachers and college principals. Like the Ukrainian clergy, many openly supported the concept of the Division as a future Ukrainian force. Teachers urged their pupils to enrol, some before they had completed their studies.[26] Reporting on the developments of the recruiting campaign, the newspaper *Stanislaviske Slovo* of 23 May 1943, drew attention to the growing numbers of students enlisting and cited several examples of those who did so under the guidance of their college or school principals.[27]

The leadership of the VSUM, the *Vykhovni Spilnoty Ukrainskoi Molodi*, who were the wartime successors to the *Plast*[28] Ukrainian Youth Association, was also generally supportive of the Division and encouraged its members to join up. This organisation was similar to the British Boy Scout movement and was divided into three age groups. 7–12 years old (junior), 12–18 years (core group), and 18–30 years (senior). It was a uniformed, apolitical, national organisation within Galicia, that had no direct affiliation with any political party or movement. Highly patriotic, its members numbering thousands, frequently took part in organised outdoor pursuits and sporting activities, and were regarded as something of an elite amongst the Ukrainian youth. Between their enlistment in May 1943, and their call up in July, many members of this popular movement took part in recruitment rallies. In fact their presence was a significant contributory factor in persuading many others to join up.[29]

Those who were politically aware felt it to be their patriotic duty to volunteer. Others, with bitter memories of the Soviet occupation of 1939–41,[30] received the appeals of the Military Board and the other recruiting agencies to fight against "Bolshevism, the deadliest enemy of Ukraine", and to defend the Ukrainian fatherland, enthusiastically. Although by the spring of 1943, the Galician Ukrainians had no sympathy for the Germans, the majority hated the Soviets even more. They had experienced the mass deportations, and savage policies, inflicted on them during their twenty-one months of occupation. The incentive for joining was not therefore belief in a German victory, but rather fear of the disastrous consequences in the event of a German defeat. Encouraged by declarations that the Division would fight only on the Eastern Front, against the Soviets, and supported by both the Church[31] and the former veterans, especially those of 1917–1921, many of whom also signed up, they too signed up in their thousands.

Other Ukrainians enlisted voluntarily via a more circuitous route. They were men who, at the time of the announcement of the Division's formation, were already serving in various *Schuma* or *Werkschutz* battalions, and other units scattered throughout the German armed forces. Many were in non-combatant roles as *Hilfswilliger* (*Hiwis*) or helpers, in unarmed auxiliary capacities such as interpreters, guides, cooks, orderlies, tailors etc. The applications of such 'experienced' men were often regarded favourably as they had already undergone at least some basic training. The first opportunity to enlist in an Ukrainian formation that offered some kind of national identity was an attractive proposition. It provided sufficient incentive for them to join in its formative stages.[32] Ivan Nyzchka was one such man, who described his enlistment as follows:

'I was serving with the Luftwaffe as a helper and put in charge of a group of Red Army prisoners. Our job was to make smoke screens for anti-aircraft batteries. We were stationed in Heidebeck where American and British planes would make daylight raids every other day. In the spring of 1943 I was allowed seven days'

> home leave to attend my grandfather's funeral. When I arrived home I saw a poster advertising the Division and I made up my mind to join. When I returned to my unit I notified the German officer in charge that I wanted to join a Ukrainian unit with its own uniforms and insignia. By May 1943, the arrangements had been made and I left to join the Division.'[33]

Throughout the recruitment campaign the Ukrainian intelligentsia, who were connected with the Military Board and Ukrainian Central Committee exerted themselves, in order to maximise their influence. Anxious to attract as many volunteers as possible, a new tactic was adopted whereby to set an example to the impressionable Ukrainian youth, individual members of both organisations themselves volunteered. That symbolic action, by some of the leading members of the intelligentsia in Galicia, was in reality little more than a token gesture, a propaganda exercise designed to demonstrate mass support for the Division. Unlike those who followed their example, most of the prominent figures who volunteered including Professor Kubijovych, actually avoided having to serve. They had their individual cases appealed by local branches of the Central Committee, whereupon most were classified as being *unabkoemmlich*, i.e. indispensable for the local administration, and were subsequently discharged.[34]

Rifle or Spade?

Effective propaganda, and successive inducements, convinced increasing numbers of Ukrainian youths, motivated to a greater or lesser extent by idealism, to report to the enlistment commissions. Force of circumstance compelled others to do the same. Some Ukrainians, out of fear of being drafted into *Arbeitsdienst*, i.e. forced labour in German agriculture or industry, volunteered for the Division instead.

> 'There were three choices, work in Germany, join the Division or wait for the Russians and be conscripted into the Soviet Army to fight and die for the hated Stalin and his regime, or be sent to Siberia.'[35]

Earlier, in his appeal to the population of Galicia, Governor Wächter had proclaimed that, "An army of Galician workers had shown their gratitude after their liberation by working in the factories and fields to produce weapons and food for victory". The reality of the situation was somewhat different. Often, young Ukrainian males, after being summoned by the German Labour Offices (*Arbeitsamter*) and given a medical examination, had a choice. They could report for registration for the Division, whereupon full security would be provided for their families, and they would be automatically exempted from all other duties. Alternatively, they could be sent to serve in the *Baudienst*, i.e. the construction service and forced labour. Living conditions and treatment for the forced labourers were notoriously bad. Thus many of those who escaped took advantage of Wächter's amnesty for forced labourers, and enrolled.

It should also be noted that despite Wächter's earlier pronouncements that the voluntary aspect would be respected in every case, and that the use of compulsion was forbidden, steps were taken by the German authorities to ensure the avoidance of failure of the recruitment programme. Those steps included circulating a list, to all the recruitment commissions, of those categories of men who were due for compulsory registration and who were therefore obliged to register for a preliminary medical examination. Thus from the outset, there were those for whom the term 'volunteer' was not applicable. Those who were required to report were:

- All those born in the years 1920 to 1925 (i.e. those aged 18–23 years)
- All non-commissioned officers, up to the age of 40 years, who had served in any army whatsoever.
- All officers, and those cadets who have graduated from military academies but have not yet obtained a commission, as well as military officials up to the age of 45 years.
- Doctors and veterinary surgeons up to the age of 45 years.

In the case of university students near the end of their courses, the obligation to register was deferred, until their completion.[36]

Even the mandatory requirement for former officers, NCOs and professionals, such as doctors and veterinary surgeons to report for enlistment was insufficient to guarantee that the required numbers would be available. To try and find the prescribed quotas of officers and NCOs, a circular was sent out on 1 July 1943, to all replacements bureaux (*SS-Ergänzungsstellen*) in Germany, asking for the names of any former Ukrainian officers and NCOs. Six bureaux were also asked for lists of doctors.[37]

In some cases suitable officer candidates were not released from their employment by the German authorities while other highly qualified men refused to serve, mainly on political grounds.[38] Of those who did enlist, a majority had served with the Austro-Hungarian Army of 1914[39] and then with the UHA. An examination of their personal files reveals that others had been in the Russian Imperial Army, the Army of the Ukrainian National Republic (UNR) 1918–1920, the Polish, Soviet, Czech, and even Romanian armies, while a minority had served with various German Wehrmacht formations from 1939. In the case of the former officers of the Austro-Hungarian Army, having enlisted, many were subsequently released because of their advanced age[40] and poor physical condition.

The situation for NCOs was only marginally better than for officers. Veterans of other armies were available, especially from the Polish Army. However, it quickly became apparent that, as a direct consequence of foreign occupation of Galicia during the inter-war period, which had prevented the maintenance of an indigenous army, as with the officers, the required number of NCOs could simply not be found. Most would therefore have to be trained from scratch. The inability to provide a sufficient number of trained Ukrainian officers and NCOs would not only continue to vex the Division's organisers throughout its existence, but would ultimately compromise its military prowess.

The recruitment of medical doctors was another problematical area. Working in conjunction with the Ukrainian medical association, Dr Volodymyr Bilozor who headed the health department of the Military Board, issued a special appeal for doctors to sign up. But he met with only limited success:

> 'As doctors from the general hospital in Peremyshl, myself and two colleagues responded to the appeal of the *Viys'kova Uprava* (Military Board) because of the need of professional people such as physicians.'[41]

Unlike their German counterparts the Ukrainian doctors were not given officer rank automatically. First they were required to undergo three months of basic training, as enlisted men, before being given a non-commissioned rank. Full officer rank was to have been given pending completion of courses at German medical academies.[42] In practical terms, the German policy of treating the Ukrainian doctors as enlisted men did little to frustrate Dr Bilozor's efforts to recruit qualified medical personnel. The same decisive considerations for enlisting into the Division were just as applicable to professionals as they were to the rank and file, if not more so. One later wrote:

> 'Some of us doctors, in anticipation of a compulsory draft or, sooner rather than later, going underground and facing a total hopelessness in the Insurgents' army, were more inclined to join the ranks of a regular military unit in which the chances of simple physical survival appeared to be somewhat better.'[43]

Eventually by 4 June 1943, 161 doctors had reported for duty. Most were unsuitable because of their age, and were subsequently rejected. Ultimately only 32 remained in service with the Division.[44]

The recruitment of priests presented a different kind of problem that was singled out by the German authorities as being worthy of special attention. There was a widely held view among high-ranking members of the SS establishment that the Catholic clergy, who would serve as chaplains in the Division, were potentially subversive elements.

This was clearly evident in a letter to Himmler, dated 28 June 1943, from the *Chef der Sicherheitspolizei und des SD, SS-Obergruppenführer* Dr Ernst Kaltenbrunner. In it he expressed his concern about the numerous voluntary applications of Greek-Catholic priests which had already been received for the *SS-Schützen Division 'Galizien'*. In his letter Kaltenbrunner stated, that even if the applications were attributed to the enthusiasm the Galicians were showing for the formation of the Division, the deployment of the Greek-Catholic priests as soldiers within it, and thus at the Eastern Front, could hardly be described as safe. They would clearly be serving Schepticky's (sic.) long-standing goal, to "open up the east for the aims of the Vatican." In light of that Kaltenbrunner requested a decision as to how the voluntary applications of Greek-Catholic priests be dealt with.[45]

Himmler's office replied with the following letter to *SS-Obergruppenführer* Dr Kaltenbrunner:

16 July 1943

Obergruppenführer!

Your letter of 28.6.1943 in which you draw attention to the admission of Greek-Catholic priests to the *SS-Schützen-Division* and the danger this implies was submitted to the *Reichsführer-SS*. I can inform you that the *Reichsführer-SS* wants to exploit the influence of the priests. The best plan would probably be for *SS-Obergruppenführer* Berger to ask the Metropolitan to come and see him, and make it clear to him that as long as the influence of the priests on the troops is good, they can stay. If, however, they start to agitate, they will be removed, in which case the Metropolitan will bear the full blame. The *Reichsführer-SS* is of the opinion that in this way the admission of the priests into the *SS-Schützen-'Galizien'* can be used to our advantage".[46]

Berger later reported to Himmler that, because of ill health, the Metropolitan Sheptyskyj had been prevented from attending the conference that Himmler had instructed him to arrange. Instead Sheptyskyj had sent his representative Dr Laba.[47] At the meeting Berger was already cognisant of Dr Laba's attitude and nationalist sentiments, from having examined the transcript of his sermon of the 28 April. He took the opportunity to informally apprise Reverend Dr Laba "of his duties and those of his clergymen, making him particularly aware of the magnitude of the concession by the *Reichsführer-SS*, in allowing clergymen to be made available to this division." Laba answered by diplomatically suggesting that he would personally select the clergymen who would serve in the Division, of whom there were to be 12 in total,[48] and gave his word of honour, that "he would do everything to ensure that this experiment for the Galician Division is successful".[49]

While Berger contented himself that having confronted Reverend Dr Laba personally with Himmler's ultimatum, the Church would in future tow the line, Himmler demanded that the position be spelt out even more unequivocally. In a letter dated 31 July, his office instructed Berger to make it clear, at his next meeting with the Metropolitan Sheptyskyj, that Himmler would not tolerate any encouragement of Ukrainian nationalism. "The *Reichsführer-SS* has no sympathy for even the smallest of experiments involving the creation of an Ukrainian national state".[50]

Sources of Opposition

During the campaign, opposition to the Division came from a number of sources and for a variety of reasons. Not surprisingly, the main German antagonist in this respect was *Reichskommissar* Koch who as soon as training commenced claimed that most of its men were deserting to the partisans.[51] A number of lesser officials and functionaries belonging to the *Polizei* establishment, and the civilian administration, protested on similar lines.

Within the Galician population there were also those who objected to the Division, principally because of the brutal nature of the German regime in Galicia. They pointed to the indiscriminate confiscation of foodstuffs and livestock, and the mass seizures of Ukrainian youth for forced labour in Germany. Others disapproved of the Division being subordinated to the Waffen-SS and its regional nomenclature. They questioned why the Division should wear German uniform, and not an Ukrainian one with Ukrainian insignia, i.e. the Trident.

As was expected, a further source of opposition emanated from both the Communist and Polish underground movements. Because of traditional animosities, they viewed the formation of an armed Ukrainian military unit as a potentially threatening development. In both cases their respective channels were used to spread anti-Division propaganda, via leaflets.[52] Occasionally they perpetrated acts of violence against members of the Division or their families.[53] Moreover, in some instances Polish officials, in the lower levels of administration, did their best to sabotage the activities of the Military Board. However, in the main their efforts produced negligible results.[54]

The most significant opposition came from elements within the OUN-B Bandera faction[55]. From 1941 they had rebuilt its organisation around the UPA and continued to exercise a major influence over a large portion of the population, especially the young in rural areas.

Some amongst the OUN-B leadership, including General Roman Shukhevych, eventually favoured the formation of an armed military unit, as an opportunity for young Ukrainian nationalists to obtain a good military training. However the majority, including Colonel Klym Savur and General Leonid Stupnyckyj, initially adopted an anti-Division stance and called for a boycott of recruitment. The essence of their opposition stemmed from their own previous experiences with the Germans. They argued that having exploited Ukraine economically, the Germans now sought to take advantage of the physical strength of the nation by using Ukrainians as cannon-fodder. They believed that the existence of the Division would result in a loss of prestige for the idea of an Ukrainian state.[56]

The gist of their objections was outlined in *Buleten* (Bulletin) of the Organisation of Ukrainian Nationalists. This read:

> 1. For what should they [the volunteers] fight?
>
> The Germans are in a desperate situation. Regardless of their violent methods and colonial policies towards the population in the occupied territories they are helpless. They have suffered heavy losses. By creating the [Galician] Division they want to weaken the active underground. Should the soldiers of the Division fight for the hated new Europe? The Germans will be in the commanding positions and will do what they want. Furthermore they are again dividing the Ukrainian nation into eastern Ukraine and Galicia. Nevertheless the German wagon rolls into an abyss. The Germans have eliminated every trace of the political commitments as far as the Division is concerned. It will be a purely colonial unit."
>
> 2. Who are the supporters of the Division?
>
> Peasantry is against it. The greater part of the intelligentsia has the common sense not to participate. There are a bunch of 'activists' who support the Division because:
> (a) Bolshevism will occupy the whole of Europe, therefore we have to fight it.
> (b) The Division will be the kernel for the creation of the Ukrainian National Army.
> (c) The situation may be repeated as it was after WWI.
>
> These criteria are nonsensical. The Division will be under the control of the Waffen-SS and they will do what they please. Only the wild dreamers might believe in the arguments of these supporters.[57]

To counter the UPA's anti-Division activities, both the Military Board and the German authorities held further public meetings. They appealed to Ukrainians to resist the radical elements that would mislead them.[58]

The attitude of the OUN-B leadership gradually became more ambivalent as the recruitment campaign progressed. After several conferences and consultations on the issue of co-operation with the Division's formation, a compromise was eventually reached between those who supported and those who opposed it. The UPA command decided to oppose the concept of the Division as the natural successor of the *Sichovi Striltsi*[59] and of the Ukrainian Galician Army. It was an analogy that was often drawn in the public announcements, by members of the Military Board and local recruiting agents. At the same time, following a secret meeting in October 1943, between a representative of the Military Board and Roman Shukhevych, the UPA agreed that the boycott of recruitment would be lifted. They proceeded to order whole groups of men to join to receive proper army training.[60] As this otherwise would have been impossible to obtain, this consideration often proved to be the decisive factor that lead many to enlist:

> 'I was imprisoned by the Germans for attending military training conducted by the OUN. Here I witnessed and endured the atrocities committed by the German guards. When I was released it took me a year to regain the fifty pounds that I had lost during my imprisonment. The time came that I had to make a decision, join the partisans, wait for the Red Army to draft me, or volunteer for the Division. I chose the latter. We got the best training in modern warfare and three square meals a day, things that I wouldn't have got in the UPA.'[61]

Among those who received personal orders, from General Shukhevych, to join and act as contact officers between the Division and the OUN, were some high profile members of the UPA such as Bohdan Pidhayny, Myroslav Maleckyj and Swiatoslav Lewytzkyj. They were sent to the Division to exercise some influence and form a

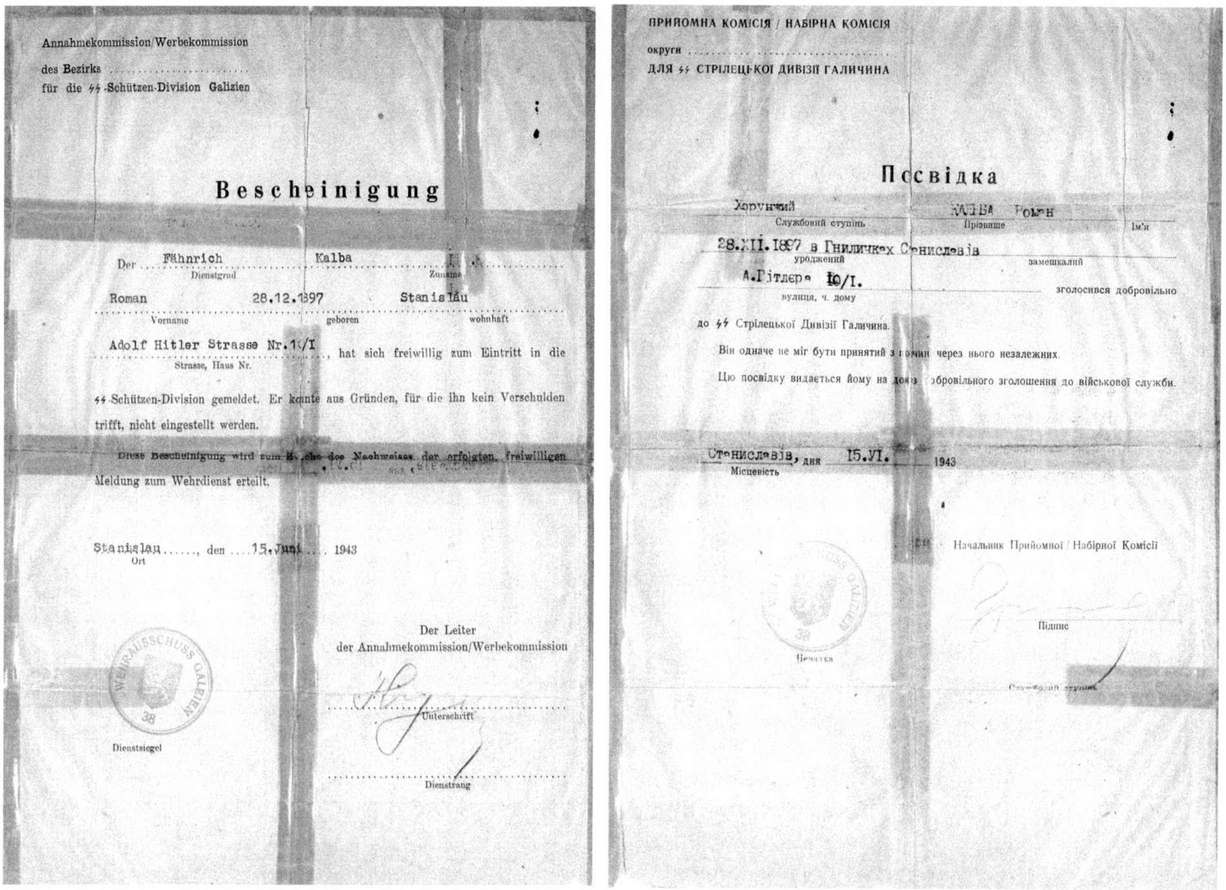
Annahmekommission/Werbekommission
des Bezirks ....
für die SS-Schützen-Division Galizien

Bescheinigung

Der Fähnrich (Dienstgrad) Kalba (Zuname)
Roman (Vorname) 28.12.1897 (geboren) Stanislau (wohnhaft)
Adolf Hitler Strasse Nr.10/I (Strasse, Haus Nr.), hat sich freiwillig zum Eintritt in die SS-Schützen-Division gemeldet. Er konnte aus Gründen, für die ihn kein Verschulden trifft, nicht eingestellt werden.
Diese Bescheinigung wird zum Nachweis der erfolgten, freiwilligen Meldung zum Wehrdienst erteilt.

Stanislau (Ort), den 15.Juni 1943

Der Leiter
der Annahmekommission/Werbekommission
Unterschrift
Dienstrang
Dienstsiegel

ПРИЙОМНА КОМІСІЯ / НАБІРНА КОМІСІЯ
округи ....
ДЛЯ SS СТРІЛЕЦЬКОЇ ДИВІЗІЇ ГАЛИЧИНА

Посвідка

Хорунжий (Службовий ступінь) Калба (Прізвище) Роман (Ім'я)
28.XII.1897 в Гниличках (уроджений) Станиславів (замешкалий)
А.Гітлера 10/I. (вулиця, ч. дому) зголосився добровільно
до SS Стрілецької Дивізії Галичина.
Він одначе не міг бути принятий з причин через нього незалежних.
Цю посвідку видається йому на доказ добровільного зголошення до військової служби.

Станиславів (Місцевість), дня 15.VI. 1943

Начальник Прийомної / Набірної Комісії
Підпис
Печатка
Службовий ступінь

Call-up notice for SS-Schützen-Division Galizien *issued by the* Wehrausschuss Galizien *to Roman Kalba, in both German and Ukrainian.*

political structure.[62] According to Pidhayny, Shukhevych's plan was to ensure that at least one out of every seven Ukrainian soldiers became a member of OUN.[63]

In summary, the young Ukrainian males who volunteered for service in the 'Galician Division', during the spring and summer of 1943, did so for a mixture of reasons. On the one hand, it appeared that the majority who volunteered had already run the gauntlet of the active opposition forces, and did so out of patriotism. However, prevailing circumstances dictated that, even in the early stages of recruitment, the hard core nationalist element was partly diluted, and compromised, by those who were compelled to join out of necessity. Their convictions and priorities lay elsewhere. Idealists and patriots, pragmatists and opportunists, all registered as volunteers. The respective numbers in each category will never be known.

Enlistment Figures: Fact and Fiction

Irrespective of the methods employed, and the mixed motives of those who enlisted, in numerical terms recruitment to the Division appeared to be a resounding success. However, it was carried out against a backdrop of active German resistance to Ukrainian nationalism and unity.

Within two weeks of the start of the campaign, HSSPf. *SS-Obergruppenführer* Krüger sent a telex to Berger. In it he said that Governor Wächter had reported that by 8 May 1943, the number of registrations had reached 32,000. Of those over 26,000 had been provisionally accepted by the recruiting commissions. Somewhat nonplussed by this unexpected response, Krüger went on to ask Berger, in view of the numbers coming forward, "What should the total strength of the *SS-Schützen-Division 'Galizien'* be?"[64]

By 14 May, the figure had risen to 38,569.[65] Soon after, a delighted Wächter, who had previously thought that because of the large number of men, who had already been drafted for labour, it would be difficult to obtain

20,000 volunteers[66] dispatched two telegrams to Himmler. He informed him that 40,000 men had enrolled[67]. He invited Himmler to visit Galicia to witness for himself the reception the Division was getting.[68]

As the recruitment drive continued throughout May, and the number of registrations increased steadily, the early indications suggested that although support differed considerably from region to region, it was exceeding all expectations. As well as a genuine enthusiasm, a combination of nationalist zeal, persuasive tactics, a fear of the return of the hated Soviets, and a mandatory requirement for certain categories to register all contributed to the early success. The organisers also contrived to maintain the momentum by extending the campaign from Galicia to other areas of the *Generalgouvernement,* including the neighbouring provincial centres of the districts of Cracow and later Lublin.[69]

Frequent mention was also made of Kolomyia,[70] the region that provided the second highest number of volunteers. There, on 16 May, Ukrainians were registered and the following week, on Sunday 23 May, a rally and liturgy were held on the fields near the river Prut.[71] To guarantee that attendance was satisfactory, transportation to Kolomyia from the surrounding area, by bus and train, was provided free of charge. The itinerary, for what turned out to be a cold and rainy day, included a march of veterans from 'The War of Liberation' (1918–1920) followed by a meeting at the Kolomyia stadium. The day culminated in a speech, delivered personally by *SS-Brigadeführer* Dr Wächter, to the assembled crowd.[72] The event became something of a showpiece for the recruiting agencies and featured prominently in a colour propaganda film made specifically for that purpose.[73]

A report on enlistment, prepared by the Military Board, disclosed that by 25 May 1943, 67,210 had registered[74]. Four days later, on 29 May, and still less than five weeks after the campaign had begun, a total of 73,159 men had signed up in the districts of Galicia and Cracow.[75]

The culmination of the first stage of the programme came about when, on 2 June 1943, according to the figures compiled by the Military Board, a total of 81,999 had registered. 52,875 had been provisionally accepted, and 29,124 had been rejected out of hand, even before they had been called to a medical commission[76] (see Appendix II). The reason for the high number of rejects can be traced directly to the instruction given to the recruitment commissions. It stated that they were not to undertake detailed examinations of the volunteers. They had to exclude only those with visible diseases or mental instabilities. In that way they were allowed to resort to indiscriminate registration, irrespective of eligibility. Thereby thousands, who were mostly too old for service, were near retirement age, or were medically unfit, were mobilised. That was done in order to boost the number of registrations for propaganda purposes.[77]

On 3 June 1943, Berger conveyed the news of the preliminary results to the *Reichsführer*, in a secret progress report. Conspicuously failing to expand on the massive discrepancy between the total number of registrations and the percentage that had been provisionally accepted, Berger was nevertheless still encouraged by the potential that resulted from access to the remaining reservoir of manpower. In one of the other major issues broached in the report, Berger stated that he concurred with Wächter's view. He urged the abandonment of the policy of simultaneous recruitment of Ukrainians into Polizei units, and into the Division:

> 3 June 1943
>
> *Reichsführer*!
>
> The number of voluntary registrations for the Legion[78] *Galizien* has risen to approximately 80,000. Of these approximately 50,000 have been provisionally accepted. Of those 50,000, 13,000 have been examined half of these are k.v. [suitable for combat use] and may be enlisted. Consequently, one may expect after final completion of the examinations, a total of approximately 25,000 suitable individuals measuring at least 165cm.
>
> I have become convinced that my original plan, to enlist for both the Division and *Polizei* simultaneously, can for political reasons, not be pursued. It was not previously known to me that approximately 4,000 Ukrainians from the Galician region are to be found in the *Polizei* and *Wachformationen* (guard units) created by various local authorities (*Dienststellen*). Uniformity, in pay and benefits for surviving relatives, has not as yet been established. Undesirable political consequences are therefore to be expected. As far as the Ukrainian population is concerned, these 4,000 men do however count as *Polizei*, despite the fact that we have no

influence whatsoever over this. Hence the decision against [enlisting] the *Polizei*. Apparently the plan was to enlist 10,000 of these volunteers into *Polizei* formations for deployment in fighting against partisans. *SS-Brigadeführer* von Wächter does not consider this viable. After apprising myself of the situation I have to agree with him. I may refer in this matter to the attached special report.

Since the formation of the Division is at the moment not possible for the known reasons, but since slower progress would cause civil unrest, I venture to suggest the following:

1. The registered officers and NCOs will, after confirmation with the *SS-Führungshauptamt*, be enlisted as soon as possible in retraining courses, and will form the foundation for the planned Division.
2. The Head Office of the *Ordnungspolizei*, which has at its disposal, the required number of officers and NCOs (*Führer* and *Unterführer*) for the training, and which can also provide the necessary weapons, will temporarily transfer training units (*Ausbildungskommandos*) to the Waffen-SS. These units would later be returned to the Head Office of the *Ordnungspolizei*, and will be available for the training of the *Polizei* formations that may be created after the formation of the Division.

In the interim, I will make available to the Head Office of the *Ordnungspolizei* approx. 1,500 recruits – suitable for combat use in the SS and the army, born 1908 and 1909. *Polizei* training for a small fraction of this ethnic group may at a later date become particularly important.

It is possible, if we were to reduce the minimum height to 160cm, to create a second Division from the Galician region. Most important of all is that the Legion exists prior to the enlistment for the *Polizei*. After deployment at the front, this Division may be used without difficulty in combating partisans.

I request further orders. The Head of the *SS-Führungshauptamtes* will receive a copy of this suggestion.

Signed G. Berger *SS-Gruppenführer*[79]

The enormity of the problem with the rejects became even more apparent, once the screening process of those who had been called before the medical commission had started in earnest. The main reason for this, as Berger had recognised, was the application of the SS's own stringent physical criteria, especially the minimum height requirement of 165cm. To emphasise the impact, Berger notified Himmler that by 21 June the number of those registered, who had been medically examined, had risen to 26,436 men, of whom only 3,281 were classified as suitable for service in the Division. While 10,281 were deemed suitable for the army, 12,874 were considered completely unsuitable for military service. 7,139 were rejected because of the minimum height requirement of 165cm.[80]

Berger's initial optimism began to evaporate. Access to the remaining suitable manpower was rapidly eroded by intensive competition from other agencies, both civilian and military. All were looking to meet their own manpower needs from the local population. To apprise him of the difficulties that he was facing, and to make certain that the *Reichsführer* had not fallen victim to the propaganda figures, which continued to boast that '80,000 men were available for the Division', on 2 July, Berger sent him the following telex:

Secret! Urgent! 2.7.43 to the *Reichsführer-SS und Chef der Deutschen Polizei*

Regarding draft status in Galicia, as incorrect numbers have apparently been quoted to the *Reichsführer-SS*, I wish to report accurately. At our disposal are:

300 officers (including those born 1890)
1,300 NCOs
800 high school graduates
48 medical doctors
20,270 men – of which 3,670 fall into the height range 160–164cm.

We can expect at least 700, most likely 800, men from the first action, thus around 28,000[81] will be available. In addition to these comes a guard battalion (*Wachbataillon*) in Debica of about 800 men, who urgently request inclusion, as they were after all the first and would now be disadvantaged if they are not included as part of the Division.

> In the interim at least 10,000 volunteers suitable for us have been secured for work in the Reich. Neither the governor [Wächter] nor I were able to intervene as a direct order from the Führer was shown. If we wait too long then by the 1 October 1943, more than 20,000 men will no longer be available, even fewer [will be available] when the *Oberkommando der Luftwaffe* [Luftwaffe high command] attempts to take some of these men into the Reich by illegal means for anti-aircraft duties.
>
> *Der chef des SS-Hauptamtes,*
> Signed G. Berger *SS-Obergruppenführer*[82]

Just how unfounded the euphoria over the impressive numbers that had responded to the call to arms, became evident when the final results of the first phase of the recruitment programme were announced at a general meeting of the district representatives of the Military Board, held on 30 October 1943. By that time, responsibility for control and supervision of recruitment had been taken over by a purely German organisation formed as a counterpart to the Military Board and known as the *Ergänzungsamt der Waffen-SS, Ergänzungsstelle Warthe (XX1),* Nebenstelle.*[83] The organisation, headed by *SS-Hauptsturmführer* Dr Karl Schulze, successfully transformed the Military Board, as Wächter had intended. It became a mere auxiliary body concerned only with propaganda and liaison related activities with the Ukrainian population.[84] At the meeting, Dr Schulze gave a detailed report concerning the results of the enlistment programme based on information collected by the Military Board and his own *Ergänzungsamt der Waffen-SS* including the following breakdown of the registrations:

Volunteered/Registered	80,000
Called before the medical commissions	53,000
Reported to medical commissions	42,000
Accepted	27,000
Reclaimed (appealed for release)	1,400
Received induction notice	25,600
Called up for service	19,047
Actually reported	13,245
Released from training camps as sick	1,487
In training	11,578
Due to be called up Nov 1–13	6,150

A sober analysis of the figures revealed that of 80,000 men, only 27,000 were passed as medically fit. Of those, the best 11,578 reported for, and actually began, their training. With the exception of 6,150 who were due for call-up in November, 62,272 men were unable or unwilling to serve.[85] As well as those rejected on medical grounds, the report also highlighted the problem of the large number of draft dodgers who signed the enlistment forms and received the summons but declined to report to the drafting boards. Dr Schulze attributed this phenomenon to the fact that the Ukrainians were unwilling to serve in an SS formation, and to the great influence of the OUN on the young, who preferred to serve in UPA.[86]

Recruiting poster for the Galician Division. The text reads "Join the ranks of the SS Rifle Division Galicia for the defence of your homeland in armed fellowship with the best soldiers in the world!"

Recruiting poster for the Galician Division. The text reads "Volunteer for SS Rifle Division Galicia! You are guarding your homeland in armed fellowship with the best soldiers in the world!"

Window display in the bookshop of the Scientific Shevchenko Society, L'viv, encouraging enlistment into the Galician Division.

Peremyshl, 28 April 1943. Gathering place for the recruiting campaign.

May 1943. Volunteers report to recruitment commissions and receive enlistment forms.

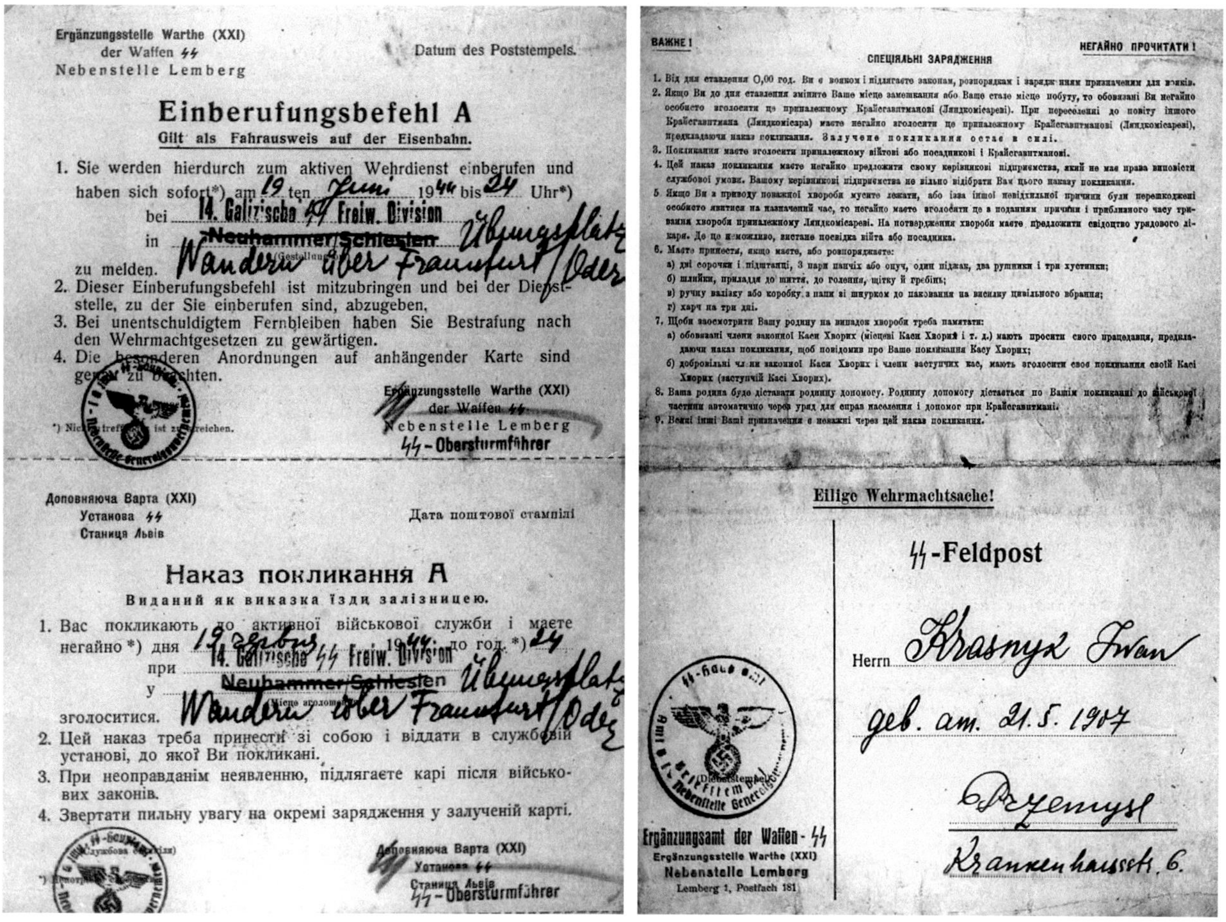

Ergänzungsstelle Warthe (XXI)
der Waffen ϟϟ
Nebenstelle Lemberg

Datum des Poststempels.

Einberufungsbefehl A

Gilt als Fahrausweis auf der Eisenbahn.

1. Sie werden hierdurch zum aktiven Wehrdienst einberufen und haben sich sofort*) am 19 ten Juni 1944 bis 24 Uhr*) bei 14. Galiz'sche ϟϟ Freiw. Division in ~~Neuhammer/Schlesien~~ Übungsplatz Wandern über Frankfurt/Oder zu melden.
2. Dieser Einberufungsbefehl ist mitzubringen und bei der Dienststelle, zu der Sie einberufen sind, abzugeben.
3. Bei unentschuldigtem Fernbleiben haben Sie Bestrafung nach den Wehrmachtgesetzen zu gewärtigen.
4. Die besonderen Anordnungen auf anhängender Karte sind genau zu beachten.

Ergänzungsstelle Warthe (XXI)
der Waffen ϟϟ
Nebenstelle Lemberg
ϟϟ-Obersturmführer

Доповняюча Варта (XXI)
Установа ϟϟ
Станиця Львів

Дата поштової стампілі

Наказ покликання А

Виданий як виказка їзди залізницею.

1. Вас покликають до активної військової служби і маєте негайно *) дня 19 червня 1944 до год. *) 24 при 14. Galiz'sche ϟϟ Freiw. Division у ~~Neuhammer/Schlesien~~ Übungsplatz Wandern über Frankfurt/Oder зголоситися.
2. Цей наказ треба принести зі собою і віддати в службовій установі, до якої Ви покликані.
3. При неоправданім неявленню, підлягаете карі після військових законів.
4. Звертати пильну увагу на окремі зарядження у залученій карті.

Доповняюча Варта (XXI)
Установа ϟϟ
Станиця Львів
ϟϟ-Оберштурмфюрер

ВАЖНЕ! НЕГАЙНО ПРОЧИТАТИ!

СПЕЦІЯЛЬНІ ЗАРЯДЖЕННЯ

1. Від дня ставлення 0,00 год. Ви є вояком і підлягаєте законам, розпорядкам і зарядженням призначеним для вояків.
2. Якщо Ви до дня ставлення змінитe Ваше місце замешкання або Ваше стале місце побуту, то обовязані Ви негайно особисто зголосити це приналежному Крайсгавптманові (Ляндкомісареві). При переселенні до повіту іншого Крайсгавптмана (Ляндкомісара) маєте негайно зголосити це приналежному Крайсгавптманові (Ляндкомісареві), предкладаючи наказ покликання. Залучене покликання остає в силі.
3. Покликання маєте зголосити приналежному війтові або посадникові і Крайсгавптманові.
4. Цей наказ покликання маєте негайно предложити своєму керівникові підприємства, який не має права виповісти службової умови. Вашому керівникові підприємства не вільно відібрати Вам цього наказу покликання.
5. Якщо Ви з приводу поважної хвороби мусите лежати, або ізза іншої невідхильної причини були перешкоджені особисто явитися на назначений час, то негайно маєте зголосити це з поданням причини і приблизного часу тривання хвороби приналежному Ляндкомісареві. На потвердження хвороби маєте предложити свідоцтво урядового лікаря. Де це неможливо, вистане посвідка війта або посадника.
6. Маєте принести, якщо маєте, або розпоряджаєте:
   а) дві сорочки і підштанці, 3 пари панчіх або онуч, один піджак, два рушники і три хустинки;
   б) шлийки, приладдя до шиття, до голення, щітку й гребінь;
   в) ручну валізку або коробку з папи зі шнурком до паковання на висилку цивільного вбрання;
   г) харч на три дні.
7. Щоби заосмотрити Вашу родину на випадок хвороби треба памятати:
   а) обовязані члени законної Каси Хворих (місцеві Каси Хворих і т. д.) мають просити свого працедавця, предкладаючи наказ покликання, щоб повідомив про Ваше покликання Касу Хворих;
   б) добровільні члени законної Каси Хворих і члени заступчих кас, мають зголосити своє покликання своїй Касі Хворих (заступчій Касі Хворих).
8. Ваша родина буде діставати родинну допомогу. Родинну допомогу дістається по Вашім покликанні до військової частини автоматично через уряд для справ населення і допомог при Крайсгавптмані.
9. Всякі інші Ваші призначення є неважні через цей наказ покликання.

Eilige Wehrmachtsache!

ϟϟ-Feldpost

Herrn Krasnyk Iwan
geb. am. 21.5.1907
Przemysl
Krankenhausstr. 6.

Ergänzungsamt der Waffen-ϟϟ
Ergänzungsstelle Warthe (XXI)
Nebenstelle Lemberg
Lemberg 1, Postfach 181

Call-up notification for Iwan Krasnyk: the text is translated below.

SS-Feldpost
Mr Krasnyk, Iwan
Date of birth 21.5.1907
Peremyshl,
Krankenhaus Strasse 6

Ergänzungsstelle Warthe (XXI) der Waffen-SS *Lemberg (L'viv)*
Order to report to the Division type 'A'
Valid also as a train pass

1. *You are ordered to active duty in the* Wehrdienst *(army service) and must appear immediately on *) 19th June 1944 within 24 hours*) at 14* Galizische SS Freiw. *Division training camp at [Neuhammer/Schlesien – deleted] Wandern near Frankfurt/Oder.*
2. *You should bring this order with you and return it to the* Dienststelle *(authority).*
3. *For an unauthorised non-appearance (*Fernbleiben*) you will be punished according to military law (*Wehrmachtgesetzen*).*
4. *You are responsible for the points listed on this card.*

Ergänzugsstelle Warthe (XXI) der Waffen-SS *Lemberg, Signed* SS-Obersturmführer *[signature illegible].*

1. *From the date appearing (0,00 hour) you are a soldier and fall under military rule.*
2. *If you change address or move to another location you must personally immediately report to the* Kreishauptmann *or* Landkommissar *and show him this order to report. Should you move to another district you must report immediately.*
3. *You must show this order to report to the village elder or official in your community and the* Kreishauptmann
4. *You must report at work to show this order to report to your employer who has no right to change your working agreement and is not allowed to take this order away from you.*
5. *If you are not able to appear personally because you are bedridden due to a serious illness, you must report immediately to the* Landkommissar *with an appropriate certificate from a government-appointed medical doctor. In case of unavailability, the certificate from the village elder will be acceptable.*
6. *You are obliged to bring with you (if available)*
   (a) Two shirts, underwear, three pairs of socks, one jacket, two towels and three handkerchiefs
   (b) Braces, sewing kit, shaving kit, brush and comb
   (c) One suitcase or strong box, wrapping paper and string for shipping home your civilian clothing
   (d) Food supplies for three days
7. *To provide medical needs for your family in case of an illness you must remember:*
   (a) Advise your employer of your enlistment and to notify the 'social services'
   (b) Advise private insurance
8. *Your family will receive medical allowance. Family allowance will be automatically forwarded through government agencies located at the* Kreishauptamt.
9. *Under this order all previous orders are nullified.*

Hans Frank (left) and Alfred Bisanz (right) at a recruitment rally in Stanyslaviv, 1943.

Kolomyia provided the second greatest number of volunteers. Here, SS-Brigadeführer *Wächter addresses a carefully staged recruitment rally at Kolomyia Stadium 23 May 1943.*

May 1943. Having registered, recruits await their turn for a medical examination.

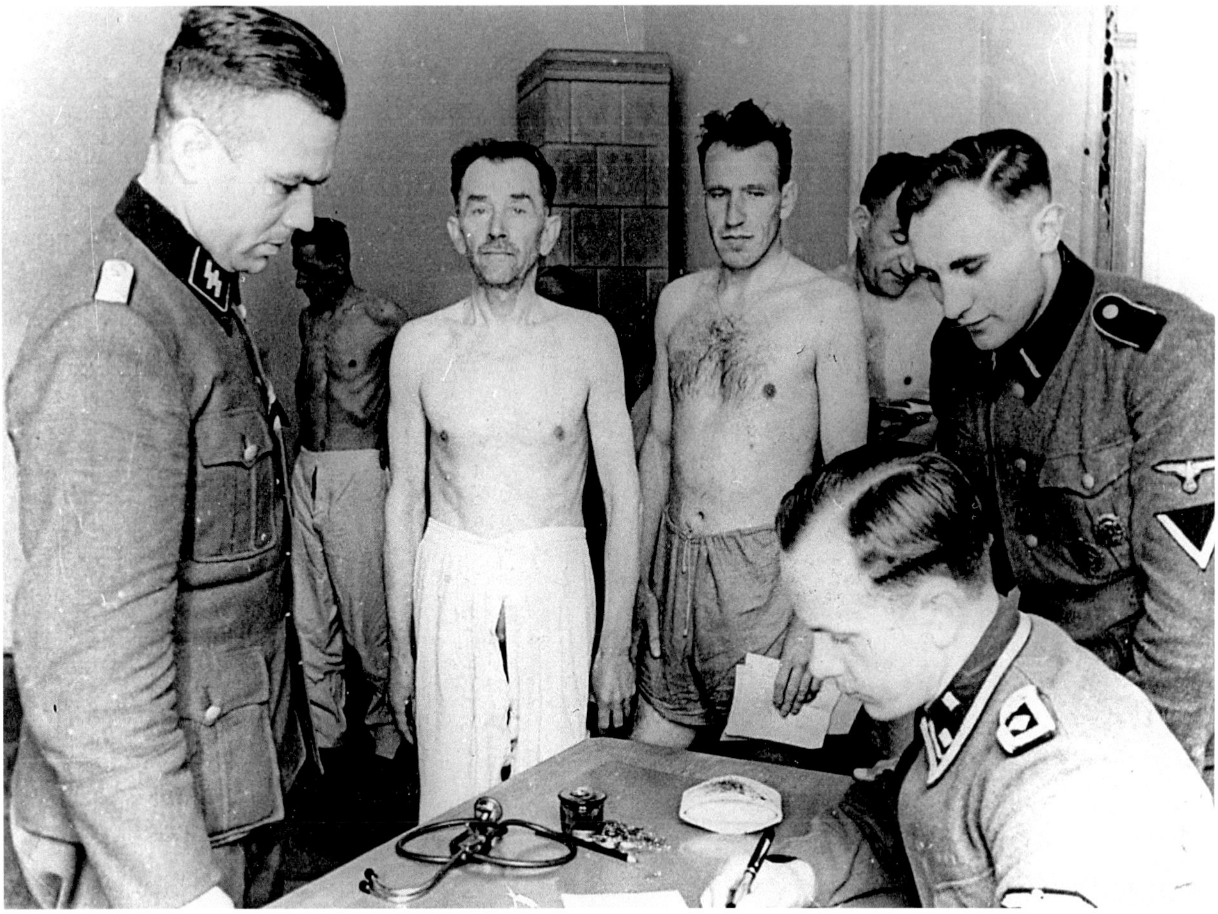

May 1943. Volunteers undergo a thorough medical by German staff. The advanced age (50+) of many of the recruits is evident from the next man waiting to be examined.

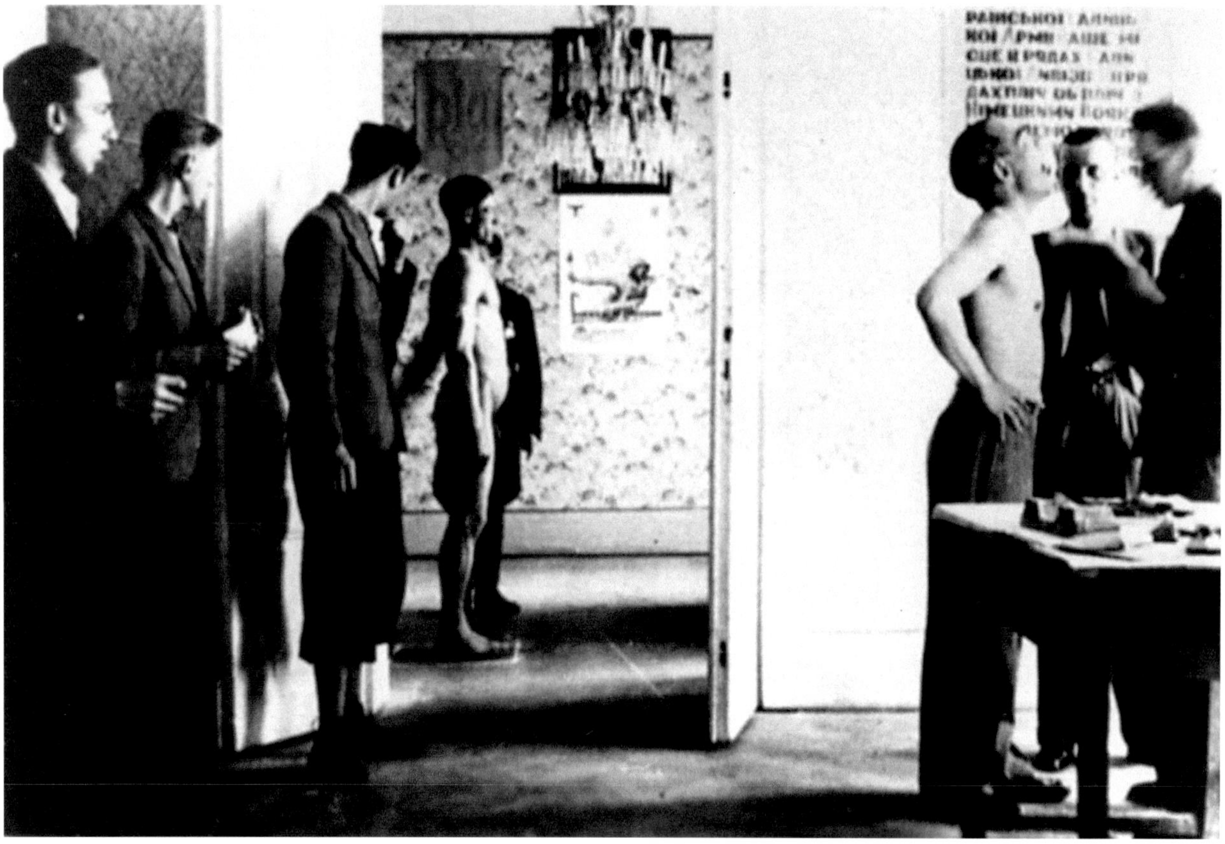

One group of recruits who underwent their medical examinations in Drohobych, which took place 11–19 May 1943.

Parade before the university building in L'viv, 18 July 1943. Centre, Governor Wächter, on his left (wearing dark suit and glasses) Prof. Volodymyr Kubiiovych, on his left (standing at the front also in dark suit) Oberst *Alfred Bisanz, with members of the Military Board.*

L'viv, 18 July 1943. Before the university building mounted Ukrainian Cossacks carrying a flag of the Ukrainian national colours (blue and yellow) parade before the assembled dignitaries.

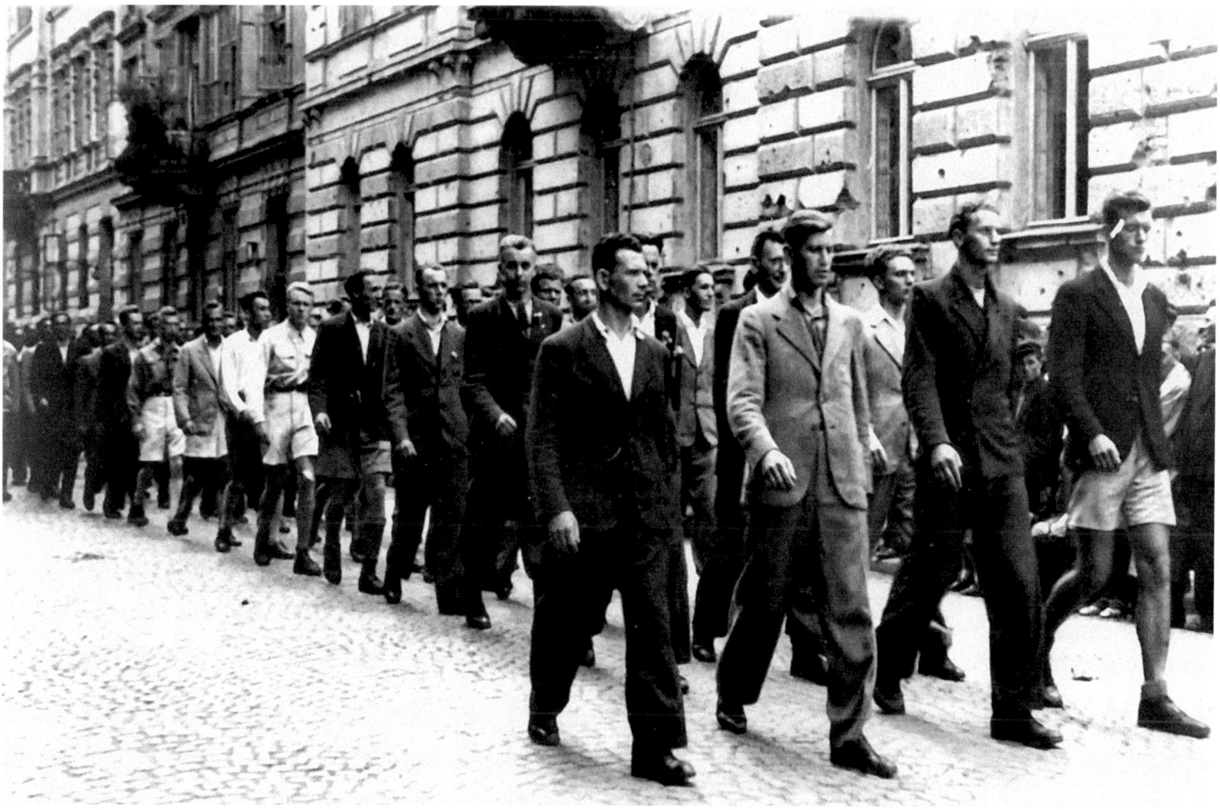

L'viv, 18 July 1943. Parade of the first group of volunteers in L'viv. Towards the rear of the column, wearing light coloured shirts and shorts, are members of Plast Kurin Peredovi. *Fifth from the front (wearing white shirt and shorts), Oleksander Podolynskyj.*

L'viv, 18 July 1943. Governor Wächter (second right) and members of the military and civil administration in Galicia take the salute of the volunteers.

L'viv, 18 July 1943. Members of the Military Board were given prominent positions amongst those in attendance.

18 July 1943. The first group of volunteers for the Galician Division assembles outside the Opera House in L'viv. A crowd of some 50,000 gathered to witness their farewell.

Governor Wächter (left), Bauer (centre), with Rev. Laba, L'viv. Wächter took great care to cultivate the support of the church during the formation of the Division.

Official rally in Stanyslaviv, to mark the departure of the first batch of recruits.

Volunteers departing for the training camps pose with members of their families before leaving. Although officially discouraged by the German authorities, the Ukrainian national symbol of the trident featured prominently amongst the chalk markings drawn onto the sides of the freight cars.

25 July 1943, L'viv. Volunteers from the village of Kobaky, Kosiv region, wait to board trains.

Ціна числа 20 грошів.

ЛЬВІВСЬКІ ВІСТІ

ЩОДЕННИК ДЛЯ ДИСТРИКТУ ГАЛИЧИНИ

Рік III. | Львів, четвер, 29 липня 1943 р. | Ч. 169 (589)

„Найжахливіший державний злочин"

БУКАРЕШТ, 28 липня. (—) Румунський журналіст Попович описує свої враження з Винниці на сторінках часопису „Курентул" і пише м. ін. таке:

„Як воєнний кореспондент румунської армії, бачив я в Совєтській Росії багато страхіть. Проте над масовою могилою у Винниці пройшла мене дрож. Цим разом не можна навести ніяких аргументів війни та переворотів, як відтяжних моментів. Большевики перевели ці вбивства ще в часі миру на особах власних громадян. Після Катину, місцем найстрашнішого державного злочину у світовій історії являється Винниця, де вбито майже 10.000 українців і багато румунів.

В БОЛЬОНІЇ ТАКОЖ ЗНИЩЕНО БАГАТО КУЛЬТУРНИХ ПАМ'ЯТОК

РИМ, 28 липня. (—) Після Риму також у Больонії бомби аліянтів понищили неоцінені культурні пам'ятники. Налет розпочався в суботу, в год. 9-ій 50 хвилин ранку і тривав до 12-ої години 30 хвилин пополудні. Особливо в центрі міста понищено або важко пошкоджено багато будинків, головним чином житлових. Частинно зруйновано величаву будівлю Паляццо д'Аккурсіо. Важко поцілено також Базиліку Св. Франка, одну з найкращих будівельних пам'яток XIV-го століття. Завалилася передня стіна Базиліки. Зовсім зруйновано славний готель Брун, важко пошкоджено міську лікарню та

Від'їзд на вишкіл

Добровольці-кандидати на старшин СС Стрілецької Дивізії Галичина у вікні вагону на залізничому двірці у Львові.

(Фот.: Роман Тиляєський)

Приклад гідний наслідування

Львів, 28 липня. Підчас воєнного лихоліття справи хліборобської продукції і прохарчування — одні з найважніших. І тому треба докладати всіх зусиль у тому ці в ділянці хліборобської продукції, що посередньо чи безпосередньо впливають на її успішний розвиток — тільки бажані.

З другого боку це давно

Edition of the daily publication L'viv News *of 29 July 1943, showing pictures of the first batch of recruits leaving L'viv for training. The picture – reproduced separately to the side – shows members of Kurin* Peredovi *in Plast uniforms. From left front: Myroslav Scharko, Roman Hawrylak, Bohdan Tschajkiwskyj, (back) not known, Jaroslav Havrych, Roman Olesnyskyj.*

4

The Raising of the Division

Taking his cue from the information and figures for specific categories, provided by Berger in his telex of 2 July 1943, Himmler issued a secret circular order on 5 July 1943, effective on 15 July. It gave directions as to the first call up of 4,448 men to the Galician Division. Determined to retain as much manpower as possible, the document also decreed that a further 12,000 men were to be enlisted for the Galician *SS-Freiwilligen* Regiments 4 to 8, and not as originally specified, according to their religious denomination.

Der Reichsführer-SS
Feldkommandostelle 5 July 1943

Tgb. Nr. 35/88/43g
RF/Bn
SECRET

The following sections of the *SS-Freiwilligen-Division* will be called up by 15 July 1943:

1. 300 officers and 48 doctors on courses in the Reich
2. 1,300 NCOs and 800 high school diploma holders for NCO training
3. 2,000 for the *Wachbataillon* (guard battalion) Heidelager, which will thereby be expanded into the 1st *SS-Freiwilligen-Grenadier-Regiment.*

This will result in a call up of 4,448 officers, NCOs, and troops, to the *SS-Freiwilligen-Division*, by 15.7.1943. In addition 12,000 men will be called up during July, for the formation of the Galician *SS-Freiwilligen* Regiments 4 to 8. These are to be taken predominantly from the 10,000 men allocated for labour use in the Reich, and from those in the height range 160cm to 164cm.

Signed Himmler[1]

On 18 July 1943, three days after the call up became effective, the departure of the first transport of 740 men for service in the Galician Division, took place from L'viv. As it was intended to form the foundation of the Division around those already qualified as officers and NCOs[2], the first batch of recruits included both. There were also high school graduates and university students, many of whom were designated as suitable officer/NCO candidates. To mark the departure, more than 50,000 people, including both local German and Ukrainian dignitaries, representatives of military, religious and civil authorities, gathered to attend a "Festive Farewell of the first call up of officers, NCOs and riflemen to the *SS Schützen Division Galicia.*" A circular notice published by the Military Board announced the following itinerary for the event:

Sunday 18 July 1943
8 – 9am Special field Mass to bless the volunteers,
9 – 10am March to assembly of the volunteers by the opera house to hear Governor Wächter's farewell speech.
10 – 11am Grand parade before the L'viv opera house
11 – 12am March past before the old parliament house
12 noon – A delegation to visit Metropolitan Sheptysky[3]

After hearing addresses by Governor Wächter, Bisanz, Pankivsky[4], other German luminaries, and a representative of those who had enlisted[5], the recruits paraded through the city streets carrying placards and banners.

'The Ukrainian citizens of L'viv greeted us enthusiastically throwing flowers as we marched by. The general excitement and enthusiastic approval displayed by the populace towards us, dispelled the last doubts about our rationale for going to the notorious SS to obtain badly need training and armaments."[6]

When the festivities had ended the men proceeded to Chernovetsky railway station where at 3.00pm they boarded freight cars[7]. On the sides were various German military emblems. Some of the volunteers added Ukrainian nationalistic symbols. They wrote slogans such as 'L'viv – Kiev – free Ukraine' which reflected their motives for enlisting. According to the instructions that each man had been given on his enrolment, the volunteers carried with them provisions to last for three days. Where possible each had 1 packet of undergarments, 1 sewing kit, 1 knife, a watch and writing equipment.[8]

In the late afternoon of 18 July 1943, the transport left L'viv. They were destined for a transit camp at Brno (Brunn) in Bohemia-Moravia, and arrived early on the morning of 19 July. There, situated in an elevated location, the Waffen-SS had established a large, military training complex called *Kuhberg* (Kaserne). The *SS-Pz.Gren.Ausb.u.E.Btl. 10* (*SS-Panzergrenadier* Training and Replacement Battalion 10) was based at Brno. For administrative purposes the Ukrainian recruits were temporarily attached to that unit, and the Battalion 10 designation subsequently appeared on their *Erkennungsmarke*, i.e. identity tags.[9]

On the first day at Brno, each recruit was required to write a *Lebenslauf* (Lifecourse), before being given a medical examination. In the following days the men were issued with field-grey Waffen-SS uniforms[10] and other military equipment from the camps supply store.[11] Thereafter they were formed into three companies in which they underwent a general introduction to military service. 500 recruits formed the 1st and 2nd companies. 240 former officers, who had qualified while serving in a variety of armies including the Austrian, Ukrainian, Polish, Romanian, Czechoslovak and Soviet armies, became the 3rd Company.[12] As would be expected, the former officers were considerably older than the recruits. The age of those who had been in the Austrian army was generally between 45 and 55 years.

However, the stay at Brno was to be a short one. Within two weeks of their arrival the SS-FHA issued a document, dated 30 July 1943, that set out the organisational details of the SS *Freiw.* Div. *'Galizien'*. It officially confirmed that its formation was to commence at the SS troop training area Heidelager[13] (SS-Tr. Ub. Pl. Heidelager).[14] A former Polish cavalry training ground which had been allocated to the SS for training purposes, it was situated near Debica (Dembitsa), in the *Generalgouvernement* between Cracow and L'viv, (see Appendix III) and was commanded by *SS-Brigadeführer* Bernhard Voss.

Two days later on 1 August 1943, at 2.00pm, the Ukrainians left the camp at Brno. Already segregated in respect of their arm of service, some 240 former officers of the 3rd Company were sent on refresher courses and for further training. They went to various camps, according to their qualifications and the Division's requirements.[15] The remaining officers, along with the 500 recruits, were redirected to Heidelager.[16] There they joined their countrymen who had been sent there directly.[17] They were then incorporated into an SS-Special Purpose Training Battalion (*SS-Ausbildungs-Battalion z.b.V*).[18] Although referred to as a 'training battalion' the unit, commanded by *SS-Sturmbannführer* Bernhard Bartelt,[19] actually consisted of a staff company and twelve training companies numbered 1–12,[20] i.e. 9 infantry companies and 3 heavy weapons companies.[21] There was a combined strength of approximately 3,600 men[22] which made it closer to the size of an infantry regiment. It was this unit and not *Wachbataillon Heidelager*, as originally intended, that formed the nucleus of the Division.

A Question of Semantics

News of the, apparently, enormous success of the recruitment campaign, was welcomed by Governor Wächter and other proponents of the Division. They saw it as being a positive step towards bigger and more ambitious plans. A letter addressed to the *Staatssekretär* (*SS-Obergruppenführer* Krüger) read:

> 'The formation of the *SS-Schützendivision* in Galicia has been achieved with surprising speed. To date 80,000 men have volunteered. If the call up to join the Waffen-SS is reinforced with that intensive propaganda aimed at the Ukrainians, then we could, judging by the current position, easily make even more extensive plans. These would result in a measurable reduction of the number of German troops deployed in the east, and a saving of German blood in the battle against Bolshevism.
>
> 'The propaganda campaign is especially important, in view of the fact that the Ukrainian nationalist partisan leader, Taras Bulba, occasionally attempts to get able-bodied young Ukrainians to join the partisans.

The cost of the campaign totals DM 125,000 a figure that does not seem high, when considering the success expected, in view of our previous findings.'[23]

At the same time the inflated enlistment figures aroused considerable suspicion among the Division's opponents. Once again they seized the opportunity to voice their misgivings about the reliability of the formation. They claimed that "these individuals have the same purpose as in 1918, where they accepted weapons only to turn them against the Germans at the appropriate time."[24] Moreover there was a disturbing tendency, among both the Ukrainian population and the new recruits, to perceive the Division, and refer to it, as 'Ukrainian' and not 'Galician'.

To counter that, on 30 June 1943, Himmler sent *SS-Sturmbannführer* d'Alquen, commander of the *SS-Kriegsberichters* (SS war correspondents) the following telex:

'In writing about the Galicia Division the words 'The Ukrainian Lion' were used. The word 'Ukrainian' is forbidden, now and for all time. I direct that only the term 'Galician' should be used.'

Signed H. Himmler.[25]

That limited order, directed at the SS war correspondents, did not however satisfy the Division's most ardent opposition. Among them, were the HSSPf. *Ukraine und Russland-Süd, SS-Obergruppenführer und General der Polizei* Hans Prützmann,[26] who called for a far more comprehensive order. In a letter to the *Reichsführer-SS* dated 8 July 1943, Prützmann wrote:

'I am taking the liberty to send you the enclosed comment of the *Gebietskommisar* of Gorochow. Since, unfortunately, even in the press of the General-Government (sic.), reference is frequently made to the 'Ukrainian SS-Div', I would be grateful for an order from the *Reichsführer* designating the division in Galicia as *Galizische Division* and forbidding the use of the term Ukrainian entirely.'[27]

Himmler needed no prompting to accommodate Prützmann's request. He was determined to stamp out the nationalist spirit once and for all. Six days later, on 14 July 1943, he issued an order. It was circulated to "All Department Heads", as well as to *SS-Sturmbannführer* Bartelt and his training staff, at Heidelager where the Galician Division was to be raised, and where the members of the *SS-Ausbildungs-Battalion z.b.V*, were already in training. It read:

'When mentioning the Galician Division I forbid all future mention of an Ukrainian Division or of Ukrainian nationhood.'[28]

Opponents of the Division received that order with great satisfaction. For its supporters, especially Governor Wächter, the order and its implications caused a great deal of consternation. In reply Wächter, at whose suggestion the title *Galizien* had been incorporated into its title in the first place,[29] wrote a lengthy secret report, dated 30 July. In it he attempted to convince Himmler that it would be advisable for all parties concerned to have the order rescinded.

The memorandum opened by drawing attention to the fact that the term 'Galicia' described a geographical and territorial concept, not the mixed Galician population of Germans, Poles and Ukrainians. Governor Wächter then stressed that any attempt to merge Ukrainians and Poles into 'Galicians' contradicted German literature on the subject. It also contradicted the previous policy of the German authorities who recognised, and officially appointed, Ukrainian committees, delegations, *Polizei* and newspapers. But they knew it would also encourage pan-slavonic tendencies.

Wächter maintained that it was necessary to make a distinction, not only because the Ukrainians, like the Poles, were unique in both language and culture, but also in view of the guidelines issued by Himmler. Those stated that the Division was open only to the Ukrainians of Galicia and not to the Poles. He concluded that in the interests of gaining 10,000 reliable SS men, and ensuring that the population of Galicia continued to serve the interests of the Reich, the respecting of an Ukrainian racial identity was imperative in order to sustain the morale of the population. It was also imperative that a plentiful harvest should be gathered, and the supply routes secured for the German armies fighting on the Eastern Front[30] (see Appendix IV).

Himmler, for whom anything with even undertones of Ukrainian nationalism was anathema, remained unmoved by Wächter's dialectics and refused to be drawn on a subject which he did not consider was open for discussion.

As there had been no response, a second letter dated 5 August 1943, reiterating all the main points of Wächter's arguments, was sent to Himmler. Almost certainly it was sent at Wächter's instigation. The author voiced the opinion that Himmler's insistence on making the title 'Galician' obligatory would offend the national pride of the Ukrainians who had responded enthusiastically to the call up for the formation of the *SS-Schützendivision Galicia*. Furthermore, it could potentially endanger the whole undertaking and provide propaganda for the Division's critics, especially the Bolsheviks and the Bandera adherents.

To assuage Himmler's fear that permitting the Division to be known as 'Ukrainian' would in any way be tantamount to sanctioning the idea of an Ukrainian national state, the letter continued:

> 'Despite the fact that all organisations of the Ukrainian population of Galicia work under the title 'Ukrainian', this has so far only established ethnic origins, and has been in no way connected with thoughts of an independent Ukrainian state or any possibilities of a united-Ukrainian (Gross-Ukrainian) future. In my opinion the concept 'Ukrainian' is of similar value in the *SS-Schützendivision 'Galizien'*. All call-ups to Ukrainians called to the Division, have been geared towards their planned deployment, not for Ukraine or Ukrainian culture, but rather as the contribution of the Ukrainian ethnic group in the battle to defend against Bolshevism and for a new Europe.'

The writer, who was obviously familiar with Wächter's earlier submission, added that similar considerations applied to the Reichsführer's instruction that the Ukrainians in the *Generalgouvernement* should be known as 'Ruthens'. That title, the letter explained, was given to the Galician Ukrainians by the Poles and Hungarians of the Austro-Hungarian Empire to accuse them of representing 'Russophillic', i.e. Russia friendly elements. Its re-introduction would be taken to mean that the Ukrainians of Galicia were regarded as pro-Soviet. The letter ended by saying that refusing to call the Division 'Ukrainian' would have an adverse effect on the morale of its predominantly Ukrainian soldiers, and may even encourage some to go over to the Soviet side.[31]

Confronted twice by much the same arguments, Himmler still had no intention of rescinding his order. He remained intolerant of any manifestation that so much as hinted at the concept of Ukrainian nationalism, even when it was reduced to little more than a question of semantics. Exasperated by Wächter's insistence on pressing the issue, he responded with a circular letter. In it Himmler emphasised Wächter's inconsistencies. Finally and unequivocally, he used them to reject Wächter's long-term political ideas for the new administrative structure of the *Generalgouvernement* that five months previously he had submitted for endorsement.

> 11 August 1943
> *Feldkommandostelle*
> Secret
>
> Dear Wächter!
>
> I confirm receipt of your letter of 30 July 1943. I do not understand you. Your whole idea, of once again uniting the former kingdom (Kronland) of Galicia, breaks down completely in your explanation.
>
> I am surprised that your views have changed so suddenly. The word 'Galician' could be insisted upon under the 150 year tradition, in which case your desire to unite the former Kingdom of Galicia within its old borders, would be justified and realistic, as would your desire for preferential treatment over other parts of the country. Alternatively, and this is new to me, you are of the opinion that this term, i.e. 'Galician', is not enforceable, in which case there is obviously no realistic basis for your desires. In the case of the latter, I believe that any unification of the present Governments of Galicia and of Cracow would be fundamentally wrong even in its most abstract form.

It being my region, I will stand by my order. It is enough that in your area the Galician intelligentsia takes it for granted that we have left them the university of Lemberg, but they, ungrateful and unprincipled, as is the Slav, send out their emissaries into the entire Russian Ukraine to incite.

It goes without saying that if Galicians should refer to themselves as Ukrainians, I will not punish them for this, but I will not let this force me to refer to them as anything other than Galicians.

Heil Hitler!
Yours
Signed H. Himmler.[32]

Although Wächter hastened to refute the claim concerning the Galician intelligentsia, and to reassure Himmler of his sincerity and readiness to carry out his commands, Himmler refused to repeal his order.[33] As a sign of his displeasure, he denied Wächter the opportunity to report to him in person. Wächter had been eager to do so.[34]

Thus the Division's regional identification remained, with all its unfortunate connotations. When its title was finally changed to 'Ukrainian' on 12 November 1944, as noted by the Liaison Officer of the SS to the OKH in the *Verordnungsblatt der Waffen-SS*[35] neither Galicia, nor any other part of Ukraine, was in German hands. Nor were they ever likely to be again.

SS-Ausbildungs Battalion *z.b.V.*

By early August 1943, the first contingent of Ukrainians had begun their basic training at Heidelager as members of the *SS-Ausbildungungs-Battalion z.b.V.* They were under the supervision of experienced German and Austrian Waffen-SS instructors who were temporarily assigned to the unit.[36] The guidelines issued for the daily timetable for an intensive and arduous programme that lasted until the end of October, specified the inclusion of the following; *Heerwesen* (military affairs), *Waffenlehre* (weapons training), *and Taktik* (tactics).[37]

Together they covered all aspects of combat training and included the use and handling of light infantry weapons such as rifles, small arms, hand grenades and light machine-guns. For the heavy weapons companies, i.e. numbers 4, 8 and 12, that was extended to cover heavy machine-guns and 8.1cm mortars. There were exercises in close combat, night fighting and anti-tank combat. Also included were target practice, lectures on legal matters and conduct on the battlefield, field orientation (map and compass reading). There was training in attack and retreat, as well as the ubiquitous drill, and field marches of up to 30/40 kms at a time.

The former Ukrainian officers did not participate directly, but were instead allocated to individual training companies where they acted as observers.[38]

No sooner had training begun than difficulties arose on linguistic grounds. The organisers of the Division, both German and Ukrainian had failed to take them into account. An instruction originating from the *SS-Hauptamt* (SS Head Office) directed that the language used for the issuing of orders for the 'Galician Division' was to be German.[39] The language of command was to be Ukrainian.[40] In practice, that was ignored. Both orders and commands were given in German. Among themselves the Ukrainians continued to converse in their native language. The former Ukrainian officers and NCOs, in particular those who had served in the Austro-Hungarian army, usually had a good grasp of the German language. However, as a rule, the enlisted men did not. To overcome the problem, some German instructors were obliged to use interpreters in their training companies, to convey the required skills both practical and theoretical. On occasion that proved to be both difficult and time consuming. Many of the frictions that later arose between the German and Ukrainian personnel, on national or political grounds, were compounded by the language barrier. It was never successfully addressed and remained a barrier throughout the Division's existence.

The majority of the first contingent of enlisted men, 90% aged between 18 and 30 years,[41] had not received any military training prior to enlistment. However, according to their SS-instructors, they were "open minded and eager to learn"[42] and often excelled in technical training.

The difficulties of adjusting to the discipline and harsh routine of life in the German army demanded considerable strength and resilience. To a large extent they were offset by the high degree of enthusiasm and commitment

Double-page photo spread from the Stuttgarter Illustrierte *Nr. 45, 10 November 1943, depicting life in the Galician Division.*

which prevailed amongst the majority of the recruits. Motivated by their strong patriotism, and their belief that they had volunteered for a division that would eventually become the nucleus of a future Ukrainian army, they weathered tough treatment at the hands of instructors determined to put them through their paces.

Alongside the physical demands, the recruits had to cope with an additional factor, that of frequent verbal abuse. Some of the instructors quickly gained notoriety amongst the Ukrainians.

> 'The commander of our platoon [1 platoon/3rd Company] was *SS-Oberscharführer* Hennicke and the drill sergeant was *SS-Unterscharführer* Eichenberg. The soul of the whole company was the executive non-com, *SS-Stabsscharführer* Brandscheidt, popularly called 'Spiess'. He was the embodiment of all the best 'virtues' characteristic to all German drill sergeants. He was always ill-tempered, excelled in yelling, abusing and insulting and was always trying hard to persecute and abuse us. For example on Sundays our duties were lighter and there was a Holy Mass that we could attend if we wanted to. One Sunday, 'Spiess' mustered the whole company and said "Heute ist Sonntag, und Ihr habt Dienstfrei. Ihr koennt zum Bad gehen oder zum Gottesdienst, Ich weiss nicht was dreckiger, ist Ihre Seelen oder Ihre Aersche." (Today is Sunday and you are free from regular duties and can go either to the bath or to Holy Mass. I don't know which is dirtier in your case, your soul or your arse.)'[43]

Official complaints about the use of foul language did bring about some improvement but, more often than not, elicited the response, "You are treated the same as Germans – get used to it."[44]

For the minority who had formerly been members of either the Polish or Red Army, the hardships of basic training were somewhat mitigated by their experiences while serving with those armies. Those with less

До історії Стрілецької Дивізії „ГАЛИЧИНА“

Формування СС. Стрілецької Дивізії

Вже здавен-давна були мешканці цього простору, що його займає Галичина, хоробрим народом. Хоробро й відважно боролися вони цілі десятиліття й терпіли за свою батьківщину.

Твердо й завзято видержали вони роки повні терпіння під советським пануванням з вірою у краще майбутнє. І коли прийшло звільнення завдяки німецьким військам, як радувався тоді кожний, як радо хотів кожний боротися по боці німецьких військ проти зненавидженого відвічного ворога. Одначе треба було спершу виконати інші завдання, завдання мирної відбудови. З цілою віддaністю розв'язав український ремісник, передусім український селянин Галичини, ці завдання. Він видержав успішно пробу.

І це було не останньою з причин, що Фюрер вволив часто повторюваному бажанню українців Галичини втягнути його боєздатних мужчин в ряди активного бойового фронту. 28. квітня ц. р. покликано до життя ƒƒ Стрілецьку Дивізію „Галичина“. Створено комісії для перегляду тисячів добровольців усіх станів і звань, у містечках і селах відбулися збори, що являлися єдиним свого роду виявом віри українців Галичини.

Добровольці прощаються із своїми селами й містечками, щоб піти до своїх вишкільних таборів. З цілим серцем виконують вони там свій обов'язок, щоб колись, як добрі вояки, бути сильними бойовиками для своєї гарної батьківщини.

Ми утривалили тут ці дні в образах. Хай вони будуть для тих, що при тому були, тривалим спогадом. А для тих, що стояли осторонь, можуть вони бути заохотою, щоб піти в сліди своїх товаришів, вступити в сірі ряди, що під знам'ям золотого льва хоронять і захищають батьківщину.

З В'ЯЗНИЦІ ГПУ ДО ГАЛИЦЬКОЇ ДИВІЗІЇ

Він один із перших зголосився до ƒƒ Стрілецької Дивізії Галичина. Велике і гарне явище. Прямо й одверто гляділи його голубі очі, коли ми зустріли його в канцелярії Військової Управи. Нам цікаво дещо ближче про нього довідатися. Він радо сам інформує нас. Два роки працював в німецькій галицькій колонії. Це було перед вибухом нім.-поль. війни. Мило згадує цю працю. І було видно, що був вдоволений цею працею. Але скоро прийшов кінець, бо прийшли большевики. З гордістю показує нам карту прийняття. Ми глядимо на нього ...

... тюрмі НКВД. Там мене скатували, і сліди цього остали на мені. Але незалежно від цього, мушу дістатися до Дивізії. Чи розумієте, що мушу бути юнаком?

Я один із нечисленних, що живий вийшов із мурів смерти. Це було жахливе. Ревізії і переслухання чергувалися зі собою. Ті, що мучили нас, були переважно жиди. Замітне, що вони не виступали публично при арештуваннях. Але за те в тюрмах були жорстокі. Катування вони переводили з очевидним почуттям помсти. Духові і фізичні тортури, які я перебув з товаришами ...

ДО ЗБРОЄЗДАТНОЇ МОЛОДІ ГАЛИЧИНИ!

ƒƒ Стрілецька Дивізія ГАЛИЧИНА

Губернатор Вехтер промовляє.

Уважаю себе тепер щасливим, що буду могти воювати з цею світовою чумою. Хто пережив те, що я, то знає, що большевизм не є тільки небезпекою для його батьківщини; далі, не тільки для Німеччини чи европейських народів, але для цілого світу. Він є знищенням кожної культури, цього найбільшого скарбу людства ...

Ставай же поруч та борись!

Горить земля, клекочуть дні боями,
Нове життя крізь гуркіт, смерть та дим,
Крокує переможно над краями,
Проклятими раніш усім живим.

Ще світ не знав таких боїв суворих,
Ще не було таких кривавих втрат;
Але ж попереду людського щастя зорі,
Й у боротьбі нема шляхів назад.

Тепер, коли в кривавому змаганні,
Лише мечем вирішують права —
Чи може бути в нас якесь вагання,
А замість дії — мрії та слова!?

Нам з Заходу у поміч вийшла сила,
Що з нею шлях до звільнення одкривсь —
Єдиний шлях то — Україні милій...
Ставай же поруч та борись!

Леонід Чміль.

(„Український Доброволець“ № 11, 24. VII. 1943)

Добровольці йдуть до Набірної Комісії

Сотня співаючи, йде на площу вправ у стрільниці.

Добровольці при вишколі

Перед стрілянням треба кріса наоливити.

Машиновий кріс у становищі. Кулі мусять влучати. Стрілець і влучає докладно.

Перед обідом — їдунка й руки мусять бути чисті.

„Збірка до обіду!“

З важким кулеметом у полі на становищі.

ПРИСЯГА ПЕРШИХ ДОБРОВОЛЬЦІВ У ГАЙДЕЛЯҐЕРІ

Почесна сотня вмашировує на майдан.

Губернатор ƒƒ-Бріґаденфюрер Др. О. Вехтер, ƒƒ-Бріґаденфюрер Фосс і Командант вишколу переходять перед фронтом добровольців готових до присяги

З прапором вперед!

Хор добровольців співає підчас польової Служби Божої, перед присягою

Three pages from a special edition of the weekly Divisional newspaper Do Peremohy *('To Victory') entitled 'We Are Going Into Battle' (*My idemo v biy*), 38 (39) depicting:*

(a) Dr Wächter and recruitment material

(b) Ukrainian recruits undergoing training at Heidelager

(c) The oath-taking ceremony, 29 August 1943

conventional experience that had been gained while active as partisans in the Ukrainian insurgent army, i.e. "Men from the forest" as the Germans called them, often had the least difficulty in adapting:

> 'Before we joined the Division we had heard about 'SS training' and we were terrified. It wasn't easy – but we got almost every Sunday off, we had warm comfortable barracks, hot food and ample weapons and equipment. When we were in the UPA we lived in the forest, using any weapons we could find, always short of food and always on the move day and night with no time to rest.'[45]

A tendency to practise with live ammunition, to acclimatise the soldiers to frontline conditions, also led to a number of training accidents. The most common injuries ranged from cuts and sprains, to broken limbs, and wounds from bullets or shrapnel[46]. Occasionally there were even fatalities. Even the most experienced German officers were able to learn much from their Ukrainian counterparts who, even without the advantage of recent technical training, "proved superior in the use of terrain, camouflage, rapid trench digging, building of temporary shelters, establishment of camps and the like".[47]

Since the *SS-Hauptamt* insisted that, as well as physical training, some form of ideological indoctrination should be given, there was an addition to combat exercises and drill. The Ukrainian recruits at Heidelager also received two hours, each week, of political education known as *weltanschauung,* i.e. 'world perception'. Without so much as a hint of irony, these sessions were considered to be an integral part of all lessons[48]. Inevitably they focused on the invincibility of the Third Reich, and on various aspects of National Socialist ideology,[49] subjects with which the Ukrainians had nothing in common and about which they could not have cared less.

> 'Political education consisted of lectures by the company commander once a week, lasting about two hours. The whole company sat down comfortably in the shade of the trees and he talked, usually about the situation at the front and how the Führer would take care of everything. Our interpreter translated very loosely. It was a farce. Nobody cared what he said. Most dozed off.'[50]

To demonstrate their own patriotic convictions, despite official prohibition, alongside the Galician lion the Ukrainians displayed their national symbol, the Trident. In almost every barrack that they occupied, they placed it in flowerbeds and stone mosaics outside their quarters. It was much to the irritation of the extreme National Socialists amongst the Germans.[51] In that way the training continued throughout the first few weeks, in the field, on the ranges and in the class room. As a reward for out-performing his peers, and as an added incentive, in exceptional circumstances a recruit could be granted leave and a travel permit to visit his family in Ukraine.[52]

Towards the end of August a medical team arrived at the camp and began tattooing the Ukrainian recruits with their blood group under the left arm. The practice, unique to the Waffen-SS and *Fallschirmjäger* (Parachute) formations, was developed to assist with blood transfusions in the event of a wound being received in combat.

On Sunday, 29 August 1943, the members of the *SS-Ausbildungs* Battalion *z.b.V* were sworn in at Heidelager.[53] Governor Wächter, the camp commander *SS-Brigadeführer* Voss, and members of both the Military Board and the UCC, attended the ceremony along with some civilian guests. It took place in a clearing in the woods and began with a field service (*Feldgottesdienst*) presided over by Reverend Dr Laba and accompanied by the choir.[54] Following that the individual companies were paraded in service dress and steel helmets and formed into three sides of a hollow square. On the fourth side of the square facing the assembled recruits, was a decorated podium, in front of which were 3 mortars, 2 heavy machine-guns and 21 stacked rifles. A German NCO, acting as ensign and carrying the Reich's war flag, took his place directly opposite the podium. 4 members of the battalion, representing their comrades, placed their hands on the flag. In the presence of the battalion commander, *SS-Sturmbannführer* Bartelt, and senior members of his training staff, the Ukrainian soldiers repeated the text of a special form of oath, authorised for the Division, in German:

> 'I swear before God this holy oath, that in the battle against Bolshevism, I will give absolute obedience to the commander in chief of the German Armed Forces Adolf Hitler, and as a brave soldier I will always be prepared to lay down my life for this oath.'[55]

Governor Wächter gave a short speech. Then, together with *SS-Brigadeführer* Voss and *SS-Sturmbannführer* Bartelt, he conducted an inspection of the uniformed ranks. The event was recorded in a special brochure, published in newspaper format, entitled 'We Are Going Into Battle' (*My idemo v biy*).[56] When the official ceremony had finished, to mark the occasion a *Kameradschaftfest* (festive celebration) took place. It began with a programme of entertainment. The highlight was a performance by the popular 'Merry L'viv' dance and theatre troupe. They were making the first of what would eventually be several visits to the Division.[57]

Once the formality of the oath had taken place, 133 former Ukrainian officers,[58] who had remained with the recruits as observers, and had passed an internal commission for verification of officers' abilities,[59] left Heidelager on 30 August 1943. They left for an eight-week officer re-training course at the officer school at Prosetschnitz (Leschan).[60] Their return to the Division in late 1943 was scheduled to coincide with the next phase of its organisation.

Heidelager was an open camp. That meant that every Sunday civilians, from nearby Galicia, arrived by the trainload to visit the soldiers. The camp had few sports and recreational facilities apart from a football pitch.[61] The weekly visits were therefore eagerly anticipated by the men, who were able to supplement their meagre food rations with the ample supplies of food and alcohol brought by their visitors. Contact with friends and relatives also brought news of German defeats at the front, and of German misdeeds in Galicia. Those had a negative affect on morale, a development that the camp authorities were anxious to discourage.

Heidelager's proximity to Galicia, and the easy access into the training site, were also exploited by the OUN/UPA. They were able to spread their own propaganda, and maintain regular contact with their own cadre within the Division, without any difficulty. The influence of the OUN, especially the Bandera faction and the UPA, with its increasingly anti-German activities, was a serious concern for the Germans. They were well aware that the overwhelming majority of the Ukrainian recruits supported the OUN and its agenda for Ukrainian independence. The desertions that began to take place, and the loss of quantities of equipment and weapons, were directly attributed to the influence of the UPA.[62] To remedy the situation the Germans sought to restrict access to the camp. They issued a prohibition against civilians in the camp compound. However, it had little effect, as the soldiers simply began to meet their relatives in the nearby woods, and at Kochanivka station near Debica. An attempt to dissuade visitors, by spreading a rumour that a typhoid epidemic had broken out in the camp, also met with failure for similar reasons.[63]

Finally, plans were made to relocate the Division to a training-ground in Germany. The necessary space was there in which to conduct exercises involving the whole unit. There were also better quarters and conditions. The actual transfer had to be delayed for several weeks because a suitable ground was not available. During that time the visitors continued to be a major problem.

In September 1943, further personnel arrived at Heidelager and were incorporated into 2nd and 5th companies.[64] According to the battalion's staff roster, on the 27 September, the appointments were:

Btl. CO: *SS-Stubaf.* Bernhard Bartelt
Btl. Adj.: *SS-Ustuf.* Artur Preuss
Btl. Orderly officer: Unoccupied
Btl. supplies officer: *SS-Ostuf.* Alfred Paul
Btl. doctor: *SS-Ostuf.* Datley Körber
Btl. medical officer: *SS-Ustuf.* Erich Schmidt
Dental surgeon: *SS-Ustuf.* Kurt-Heinz Neumann
Officer resp. for ideological instruction: *SS-Ustuf.* Werner Urlen
1st Company Commander: *SS-Ostuf.* Adolf Hofmann
2nd Company Commander: Unoccupied (vice CO) *SS-Ustuf.* Friedrich Frommelt
3rd Company Commander: *SS-Hauptstuf.* Kurt Wawrzik
4th Company Commander: *SS-Ostuf.* Joachim von Glan
5th Company Commander: Unoccupied (vice CO) *SS-Ustuf.* Karl Hoffrichter

6th Company Commander: *SS-Ostuf.* Olaf Pedersen
7th Company Commander: *SS-Hauptstuf.* Heinz Müller
8th Company Commander: *SS-Ostuf.* Richard Bitzer
9th Company Commander: Unoccupied (vice CO) *SS-Ostuf.* A. Graf zu Dohna
10th Company Commander: *SS-Ostuf.* Paul Baldauf
11th Company Commander: *SS-Hauptstuf.* Johannes Kleinow[65]
12th Company Commander: Unoccupied (vice CO) *SS-Ustuf.* H. Schneller[66]

A 'strength' report for the *SS-Ausbildungs Batl. z.b.V.* indicated that as of 19 October, a total of 3,368 men comprising 160 officers and 3,208 recruits, among them 1,139[67] high school graduates and university students, were undergoing training at Heidelager.[68]

In the following weeks the number of Ukrainians enlisting for service in either the Division or one of the *Polizei* regiments, continued to increase. There was a constant flow of new recruits, so that by the end of October, in a letter to Himmler dated 30 October, Governor Wächter was able to refer to "the Galician units in which almost 13,000 men were presently under arms."[69]

On the same date, the '1st Galician Officers' retraining Course' for the older Ukrainian officers at Leschan came to an end[70]. A confidential report followed, along with suggestions for employment for each graduate. It was prepared by the school commander and forwarded to the Division's command at Heidelager. Of those who completed the course, 11 participants were classified as capable of commanding battalions and received the rank of *Waffen-Hauptsturmführer.*[71] 53 were deemed suitable to command companies and were ranked as *Waffen-Obersturmführer.* 29 were capable of commanding platoons and ranked as *Waffen-Untersturmführer.* 8 participants received the non-commissioned officer rank of *Oberscharführer.*[72]

Returning to Heidelager to assist with training, in some cases these older Ukrainian officers, many of whom lacked the continuity of military tradition, were treated with open scorn. They became objects of ridicule amongst the young German trainers and NCOs,[73] a development that was partly self-inflicted. One of their number wrote:

> 'Men came to the Division Galicia as officers of various former armies. Not only did they forget their military profession but they had also changed in character. They had forgotten the behaviour of an officer, the camaraderie and the obligation of duties. It was no wonder that in such a gathering of various men, you could always find those who wished they were not there at all. As soon as the screw had tightened one could see the reluctance of some to accept their new environment. Now they used all kinds of excuses just to avoid their duties.'[74]

In his memoirs, while evaluating his seniors, one of the younger generation of Ukrainian officer aspirants also acknowledged the positive influence of their presence:

> 'For the first time I encountered older Ukrainian officers who came to the Division having been sent to Bohemia for short refresher re-training. They were for the most part officers from the First World War mostly in their fifties and with few exceptions, had twenty years of civilian life behind them. As far as military bearing and appearance is concerned they compared unfavourably with their German counterparts who had in their immediate past, years of military duty and excellent training. In such a short time the Ukrainian officers did not succeed in acquiring or returning to the smart bearing and gloss so typical of officers in all European armies – especially the German army. Their difficulties were compounded especially amongst those who had served in Petlura's army, by a lack of knowledge of the German language and thus their usefulness was limited. The Divisional command assigned them mainly to the Training and Reserve Regiment.
>
> 'There were however brilliant exceptions – mainly those who had served in the Polish Army and had spent the inter-war years on active duty. Among them were highly qualified officers such as Palienko, and Pobihushtschyi.[75] However, the sole presence of Ukrainian officers was of tremendous importance to the ordinary enlisted men. They understood our boys and gave them some fatherly love and concern which was

highly appreciated by Ukrainian soldiers in foreign uniforms and was a welcome relief and counterbalance against the brutal Prussian discipline.'[76]

At the same time, the first contingent of Ukrainians finally completed their basic training. Following that, 600 officer and 200 NCO candidates were sent to various schools, or specialist *Waffenschulen,* for further training.[77] The mandatory requirement was waived that all NCO and officer candidates should have had recent combat experience in that instance, because of the urgent need for officers in the Division.[78] A further 100 recruits were incorporated into the 12th *MG-Lehrkompanie* (12th heavy machine-gun training company). That was unofficially a non-commissioned officers' training company in which the recruits undertook short-term NCO courses without leaving the Division.[79]

The NCO courses such as those for infantry held at Radolfzell and Lauenburg in East Prussia, lasted four months. They were held in various camps throughout the Reich and the occupied territories. The principle specialist training grounds for the Ukrainian recruits included:

Glau bei Trebbin : *SS-Artillerieschule* I
Beneschau (Bohemia) : *SS-Artillerieschule* II
Metz (Lorraine) : *Nachrichtenschule*
Prosetschnitz (Bohemia) : *SS-Panz.Gren.Schule Lehrgang* I
Teinitz (Bohemia) (*Panzergrenadier*) : *SS-Panz.Gren.Schule Lehrgang* II
Graz Rosenberggurtel (Austria) : Jursiaische Arzte
Bussum (Netherlands) : 3 *Panz.Jag.Ausb.Abtl.* 2
Pikowitz (Bohemia) : *SS-Pion.Ausb.Btl II.Komp.* 3
Warschau (*Generalgouvernement*) : *SS-Kavallerie-Ausb. u. Ers. Btl.*
Breslau-Lissa 4 (A) : *Inf. Gesch. Ausb. u. Ers. Btl.* 1
Hilversum (Netherlands) : 1. *Panz.Ausb.Abtl.* 2
Nurnberg II Zug (SS barracks) : *SS-W-E-Regt*
München : *SS-Flak Ausb. u. Ers. Btl*
Heidenheim-Brenz : *Gal. SS-Freiw.Ers.Btl.*
Oranienburg-Berlin : *Dolmetscher Schule der Waffen-SS*[80]

Within those establishments specialised instruction was given. For example, the 54 recruits selected for service in the Division's SS Pioneer Battalion were sent to Pikowitz in Bohemia. There, the demanding schedule included route marching and laying and disabling mines, as well as construction of bridges (temporary and permanent) with varying capacities of up to 60 tons in weight. There was also machine gun and rifle range practice, training with explosives, demolition and use of flame-throwers.[81] The difficulty of the courses far surpassed the instruction given at Heidelager, as one NCO candidate recalled:

'Our basic training lasted some three months. Some of us were assigned to the Division, which started to assume its proper structure, and some were sent to non-commissioned officers' schools. I was assigned to the Lauenburg school in Pomerania near Gdansk (Danzig). This school had a reputation of being the toughest in the system of the Waffen-SS. The school at Lauenburg was in several nice brick buildings that, we found out later, housed a lunatic asylum before the war. This school, as its successor, could be viewed as an appropriate continuation of the 'lunacy' that had gone on before. If our training at Heidelager was tough, then this was tougher tenfold. We were chased around like a pack of dogs, yelled at, abused and insulted in an appropriate way, so that we could learn how to do it to others when we returned to our Division.'[82]

On completion of these courses all those qualified as NCOs returned to the Division in March 1944. There they were assigned as commanders of squads or platoons. Before the Division departed for the front, in June 1944, some 200 of the men were selected for officer training by company or battalion commanders. That lasted a further four months, for platoon commanders, or five months, including an additional company commander course. Those were held at *SS-Waffen-Junkerschulen* (SS officer schools) at Kienschlag, near Prague, Arolsen, Braunschweig, Klagenfurt, Beneschau, Hradischko and Posen-Treskau.[83]

The standards at all those schools, for Germans and non-Germans alike, were very high. That was reflected in the large numbers who failed the exams, or were dismissed from the courses for a variety of reasons. The figures for the five-month officer-training course at the *SS-Junkerschule* at Braunschweig in Posen-Treskau were typical. From the original group of about 200 Ukrainian candidates who started the course, only 86 completed it.[84]

In the interim, because of the prevailing shortage of suitable training officers, of NCOs and weapons allocated to the Galician division at Heidelager, a large proportion of the newly enlisted personnel who arrived at the camp in the late autumn months had to be re-assigned. They were sent to regular army reserve units, based at different locations throughout the Reich.[85] For example, on 26 November 1943, one group of 380 Galician volunteers was despatched to Gren. *Ersatz* Regt. 34 at Koblenz, where they received their basic recruit training.[86]

The Structure of the Division

The organisational core of the 'Galician Division' was already beginning to take shape under the Austrian anti-partisan specialist *SS-Brigadeführer* und *Generalmajor der Waffen-SS* Walter Schimana[87]. Himmler had appointed him to oversee its formation. Three infantry regiments numbered 1, 2 and 3, each with three battalions, formed the backbone of the Division. They were each supported by an artillery battalion with the same numerical prefix. In addition they had various support elements and services which were already in their formative stages.[88] The basic structure did however undergo some modification at an early stage, in response to an order issued by the SS-FHA and signed by *SS-Obergruppenführer* Juttner, dated 22 September 1943.

It directed that the *Freiw.* Div. *'Galizien'* was to be reorganised as a new 1944 type infantry division.[89] That involved detaching the third battalion of each of the three infantry regiments to provide a field replacement battalion (14th *Feld Ersatz Bataillon*) and a Füsilier Battalion.[90] In the case of the latter, the battalion accepted only volunteers. They were subsequently sent for training to a Wehrmacht ground at Eschweiler, near Aachen in Germany. Interestingly, whilst at that camp those recruits were permitted to wear Wehrmacht uniforms only. Divisional SS uniforms could be worn only on Sundays and holidays.[91]

During that period the Division's title also changed, following a decision by the SS-FHA to re-number all Waffen-SS divisions, and their component infantry regiments, according to the sequence in which they had been raised. Consequently the '14', which had preceded the formations title almost from the beginning, became official. The formation was thus re-titled. From '*SS-Freiw. Div. Galizien*' it became '*14 Galizisches SS-Freiw. Div.*'.[92] Likewise, in the coming weeks its infantry regiments were renumbered as follows:

*SS-Freiw.*Gren.Rgt 1 became *SS-Freiw.*Gren.Rgt.29
*SS-Freiw.*Gren.Rgt 2 became *SS-Freiw.*Gren.Rgt.30
*SS-Freiw.*Gren.Rgt 3 became *SS-Freiw.*Gren.Rgt.31[93]

During the initial stages of the Division's organisation, German personnel in command positions were restricted to the general staff[94]. In compliance with the agreement, all three embryonic infantry regiments were commanded by Ukrainians. The first regiment, 29, was commanded by *Waffen-Sturmbannführer* Evhen Pobihushtschyi, the second, 30, by *Waffen-Hauptsturmführer* Borys and the third, 31, by *Waffen-Hauptsturmführer* Stepan Kotyl.[95] Additionally the Pioneer Battalion,[96] the Artillery Regiment[97] and the Signals *Abteilung*,[98] were also commanded by Ukrainians.

Galizische SS-Freiwilligen Regimenter 4–8

From 14 April 1943, Himmler had issued instructions that, in addition to the Galician Division which was to be a combat unit recruited from the Greek Catholic population of Galicia, separate *Polizei* regiments were to be set up from the Greek Orthodox Ukrainians from the Lublin district.[99] Ignoring objections from both Wächter and Berger,[100] Himmler proceeded to issue an order, dated 24 June 1943, to all relevant authorities. It stated that, from the Galician volunteers, 12,000 were to be designated for the building of five *'Polizei-Schützen-Regimenter'*. They were to be armed and supplied by the central bureau of the Waffen-SS (*SS Führungshauptamt*) in conjunction with the HSSPf. Ukraine and the *Ordnungspolizei* (*Orpo*), whose chief was also responsible for providing the regiments with 500 officers and NCOs. Knowing that the Ukrainians were reluctant to serve in *Polizei* units of any kind, the order stated that these *SS-Polizei-Schützen-Regimente,* "for psychological and political reasons, will be designated *Galizisches SS-Freiwilligen Regimenter* with the numbers 4–8". That meant they were to be consecutive to the original numbers of the three regiments of the Galician Division.[101] Four days later, to resolve the necessary preparatory measures, a circular order was issued, by *Oberst* Hans Flade,[102] a senior official within the head office of the *Ordnungspolizei*. It announced that a meeting would be held on Monday 28 June 1943, to discuss the formation of the five *Galizischen* Regiments as ordered by the *Reichsführer.*[103]

Himmler had already been forced to abandon his original plan of inducting Greek Orthodox Ukrainians into the *Polizei* regiments.[104] He therefore ordered that the recruits for those units were, instead, to be taken predominantly from the 10,000 men allocated for labour use in the Reich. Others were taken from those who were 160–164cm tall and hence deemed unsuitable for service in the Galician Division.[105]

Although a revised directive had been issued, the new specifications were still not adhered to. Firstly, the selection process advocated by Himmler, based on the minimum height requirement or potential non-suitability for the Division, appeared largely to have been ignored. The requisite personnel were simply taken from the initial wave of recruits for the Galician Division, especially from the cities of Peremyshl, Yaroslav and Sianok. This understandably caused resentment among the recruits who had enlisted to fight the Soviets, and not for *Polizei* and anti-partisan duties.

Secondly, contrary to Himmler's instruction, only four of the intended five regiments were actually fully formed. Their total combined strength amounted to approximately 6,500, or half the number originally intended. The 8th Regiment was to have been raised in Maastricht on the basis of personnel from the *Pol. Waffenschule IV*, but it was never fully developed.

The remaining four regiments which were made up of three battalions, consisting of four companies,[106] were trained as separate units at several training grounds under the control of the *Orpo*. Despite their temporary secondment to the *Orpo*, the recruits were issued with standard field-grey Waffen-SS uniforms. On these the majority wore either no collar patches (*Kragenspiegel*) at all, blank collar patches, the same collar patch and armshield depicting the Galician lion as their counterparts in the Galician Division[107] or, in a few instances, the SS lightning runes. In the case of the latter they were soon replaced with blank insignia.[108]

Galizischen SS-Freiwilligen Regiment 4 had a strength of 1,264[109] men. From 20 July 1943, it was commanded by *Major der Schutzpolizei* Siegfried Binz,[110] an experienced and hardened *Polizei* officer. Binz's service record indicated that prior to his appointment as commander of the *Gal. SS-Freiw.* Rgt. 4, he had previously commanded *Polizei* Batl. 307. It took part in a number of anti-partisan actions in *Weissruthenien* (White Russia) in the rear of the Army Group.[111] The 4th Regiment underwent training in the area of Zabern (Alsace), region of France. Its headquarters, along with the I Battalion, were based at Zabern. II Battalion was at Saaralben (Saarbrücken) and the III Battalion was at a Luftwaffe training-ground at Fernschweiler, near Trier.[112] The chaplain (*Feldgeistlicher*) assigned to the unit was Joseph Karpynskyj. According to an order dated 5 July 1943, its German cadre were to be drawn primarily from the *Polizei* Training Regiment at Oranienburg.[113]

The same order, quoted above, specified that the staff and I Battalion of *Galizischen SS Freiwilligen* Regiment 5 were to be raised in the *Generalgouvernement* at the *Ordnungspolizei* training camp at Adlershorst, near Gotenhafen. The II Battalion was at the *Ordnungspolizei* camp at Thorn, and the III Battalion at the former resettlement camp at Kösslin. The Regiment had a strength of 1,372 men[114] and was commanded by *SS-Obersturmbannführer und Oberst der Schutzpolizei* Franz Lechthaler. He was another experienced *Polizei* officer. As a member of *Polizeibataillon* 11 in 1941–42 he had, like Binz, participated directly in similar 'pacification actions' in the occupied eastern territories. In the post war period he was successfully prosecuted.[115] The German training and administrative cadre for this regiment were drawn primarily from the *Polizei-Schutz* Regiment 32.[116] Wsewolod Durbak was its chaplain.

Galizischen SS-Freiwilligen Regiment 6 had a strength of 1,800[117] and was commanded by *Oberstleutnant der Gendarmerie* Kuhn. The recruits from this regiment came mainly from the areas of L'viv and Peremyshl. As of 6 August 1943, the strength and location of its three battalions were:

Regimental staff:
I Battalion consisting of 700 recruits in training at Sudauen
II Battalion consisting of 550 recruits in training at Fichtenwalde
III Battalion consisting of 550 recruits in training at Grajewo[118]

In November 1943, the Regiment underwent additional training at Pau and Tarbes, in western France, at the foot of the Pyrenees. The regimental chaplain was Johann Holojda.

Galizischen SS-Freiwilligen Regiment 7 was also formed and trained in south-western France. The Regiment's staff, along with the I and III battalions, were based at Salies de Bearn near Bayonne, and the II Battalion at Orthez.[119] Commanded by *Oberstleutnant der Sicherheitspolizei* Heinrich Huber,[120] it had a strength of 1,671 men. The chaplain serving with the Regiment was Danylo Kowaluk.[121]

According to the *Reichsrangliste der Offiziere der Schutzpolizei und Gendarmerie, Oberstleutnant der Schutzpolizei* Wilhelm Schwertschlager[122] was appointed commander of the planned 8th Regiment as of 1 October 1943, until 13 January 1944.[123] In his report to the Military Board on 30 October 1943, Dr Schulze stated that the strength of this unit was 1,573 men. Notwithstanding this, and the existence of a complete list of staff appointments[124] it is unlikely that the regiment ever existed, except on paper. The personnel who were to have been assigned to it, including 12 officers (see Appendix V), 118 NCOs and 3 doctors,[125] were later allocated to other *Polizei* units instead.[126]

Galizisches SS-Freiwilligen-Ersatz-Bataillon was established at Heidenheim as a reserve battalion for regiments 4–8. Commanded by *Major der Sicherheitspolizei* Paul Kärnbach, it consisted of a staff, staff company, signals platoon, engineer platoon, 1st and 2nd rifle companies, and 4th heavy weapons company (with machine-gun and mortar platoons).[127]

The personnel of both the 4th and 5th regiments were given basic infantry training throughout the autumn of 1943. That included instruction, based on operations, as part of a small combat group. They were trained in fighting in the immediate proximity of a built up area, safeguarding road, rail, communication and waterway centres, and the seizing and securing of industrial and signal installations.

The 6th and 7th regiments underwent the same standard basic light infantry training as the recruits inducted directly into the 'Galician Division'. However, according to one veteran, this was not as rigid.[128] In respect of the 7th Regiment that appears to have been partly because most of its officers and NCOs were *Volksdeutsch Polizei* personnel from Silesia and Warthe. Few were frontline veterans.[129]

Like their counterparts in the Galician Division proper, the families of those enlisted into each of the Galician *Polizei* Regiments were entitled to social assistance. That responsibility was transferred to the Waffen-SS as of 21 December 1943.[130]

The creation of the additional regiments, and their temporary secondment to the *Orpo* for training purposes, meant that the *Orpo* effectively exercised complete control over them. Later that facilitated the deployment of two of the regiments, the 4th and 5th for security duties. That violated the spirit of the understanding between Governor Wächter and the Galician representatives, that Ukrainians would only be used in frontline combat formations on the Eastern Front. It was a breach of faith on the part of the Germans that was indicative of the reality behind the facade of a German/Ukrainian partnership. Despite appearances, the Nazi hierarchy had in no way fundamentally revised their attitude towards the Ukrainians. Significantly, with the exception of one or two NCOs, the entire officer and NCO cadres of both regiments were exclusively German,[131] presaging future developments within the Galician Division itself.

Fritz Freitag

On 22 October 1943, as the Galician Division was entering its next phase of structural organisation, *SS-Brigadeführer und Generalmajor der Waffen-SS* Schimana received notification from Himmler. He was to be transferred to a new post as the HSSPf. in Greece, with effect from 9 November 1943.[132] As a replacement, Himmler selected a man whom he believed to be eminently suitable. *SS-Oberführer* Fritz Julius Gottfried Freitag[133] commanded the Division from 20 October until the end of the war.[134]

Approximately four weeks after his appointment had become effective, on 19 November 1943, a special two-day visit to L'viv was arranged. The itinerary included a tour of the sights of the city and an evening visit to the opera house to watch two acts of 'Hamlet' by Schekspir [sic.]. During the play, Governor Wächter and the Military Board endeavoured to give Freitag further background information regarding the Division, its long-term goals, and the role and function of the Military Board in relation to it.[135]

An ardent National Socialist, described by his Operations Officer as "a petty bureaucrat who made life unpleasant for all those around him",[136] Freitag was a highly ambitious man who had risen up through the ranks of the German *Polizei* establishment. Documents in his personal SS officer file show that at the beginning of the German invasion of the Soviet Union in June 1941, he was serving with the command staff of the *Reichsführer-SS*. After that he held the post of Ia (Operations Officer) with the 1st SS Motorised *Infanterie* Brigade. That unit, like the 2nd SS Motorised *Infanterie* Brigade and the 1st SS *Kavallerie* Brigade operated separately or alongside the notorious *Einsatzgruppen* under the direct command of Himmler.[137] Charged with similar 'special tasks',[138] they were used for the pacification of rear areas of the rapidly advancing German Army. As Operations Officer, with the rank of *Oberstleutnant*, Freitag was responsible for producing daily activity reports on the units' actions for submission directly to the *Reichsführer-SS*. The contents of these reports reveal clear evidence of the nature of its assignment. It was to do with little more than the ruthless subjugation of the localities in which it operated. In a typical entry dated 24 August 1941, Freitag diligently reported 114 prisoners taken, 283 Jews shot,[139] and a haul of captured booty amounting to only 2 guns, 3 heavy and 6 light machine-guns.[140]

During the course of the next two years he was rewarded for his dedication to duty. According to his service record, at some point Freitag held positions with 8th *SS-Kavallerie-Division 'Florian Geyer'*,[141] 2nd SS *Infanterie* Brigade, the SS-FHA, briefly with the Latvian *SS-Freiw.* Legion, and as a regimental commander with the 4th *SS-Polizei Panzergrenadier* Division.[142]

Like his predecessor *SS-Brigadeführer* Schimana, *SS-Oberführer* Freitag was also a product of the *Ordnungspolizei*. However, as a regimental commander in frontline formations deployed on the Eastern Front, he had gained a substantial amount of combat experience,[143] and a sound technical knowledge of military tactics. Those military attributes would later be of great benefit to the Division. They contributed significantly to helping it develop into a disciplined, powerful and effective battle-ready unit. As later events would prove however, Freitag was not suited to the command of a Division that consisted of non-German nationals, i.e. Ukrainians, with whom he had no direct contact[144] and whose psychology he made no attempt to understand.[145] He adopted negative and sometimes hostile attitudes towards the Ukrainians. That, together with his personality quirks, his volatile character and inflexible Prussian approach, ensured that his appointment as Divisional commander was a serious error.[146]

At the time of Freitag's appointment in November 1943, the Division consisted of 6,000 Ukrainians[147]. It had reached a critical juncture in its development. The immediate and most important task that confronted him was to supervise the completion of its formation, and also the establishment of its infrastructure. By now the first of the Ukrainian officers and NCOs who had not been discharged from service by various verification commissions, had returned from their retraining courses. Some had old ranks reinstated, and some had lower ranks to that which they previously held. They sought appropriate command postings.

Unfortunately, Freitag ignored the long-term potential diplomatic role of the 'Galician Division', as envisaged by Governor Wächter. Although Wächter had promised a balanced officer corps, it was apparent that the necessary numbers of Ukrainian officers who had undergone recent tactical training, in all departments, were simply not available. This situation was further exacerbated by Freitag's discriminatory policy that largely excluded those who were available from important posts, and assigning them instead to secondary duties.[148]

A similar problem existed with the NCO corps that would be of vital importance for the effectiveness of the formation. As a result, virtually all principle positions of command, and the greater part of the Division's cadre, consisted of German senior and junior officers. In the winter of 1943 and spring of 1944 the departments within its headquarters were staffed almost entirely by Germans. There were only four 'token' Ukrainians attached to it in secondary roles. The staff appointments were:

Divisional Commander: *SS-Oberführer* Fritz Freitag
Adjutant: *SS-Sturmbannführer* Johannes Georgi[149]
Section Ia (Operations Officer): *Major* Wolf Dietrich Heike (from Jan. 1944)
Adjutant: *SS-Obersturmführer* Rudolph Michel,[150] *SS-Obersturmführer* Herbert Schaaf[151]
Section Ic (Intelligence/political matters): *SS-Obersturmführer* Günter Mussbach, *Waffen-Hauptsturmführer* Dmytro Ferkuniak
Section IIa (Divisional records): *SS-Hauptsturmführer* Erich Finder,[152] *Waffen-Hauptsturmführer* Dmytro Paliiv
Ord.Offz. 1: *SS-Untersturmführer* Friedrich Lehnhardt
Ord.Offz. 2: *SS-Obersturmführer* Herbert Oskar Hanel[153]
Kdt.St.Qu: *SS-Obersturmführer* Ernst Gebhardt
Section III (Military justice): *SS-Sturmbannführer* Hans Ziegler,[154] *SS- Hauptsturmführer* Gerhard Hermann, *Waffen-Obersturmführer* Dr Stadnyk
Section IVa (Quartermaster General, supply food and uniforms):
SS-Sturmbannführer Otto Sulzbach[155]
Section IVb (Medical): *SS-Obersturmbannführer* Dr Max Specht[156]
Section IVb (Pharmaceutical): *SS-Hauptsturmführer* Werner Beneke[157]
Section IVb (Veterinary): *SS-Sturmbannführer* Dr Oskar Kopp[158]
Section IV (Dental): *SS-Obersturmführer* Meyer
Section V (Automotive and Mechanical): *SS-Sturmbannführer* Heinz Behrendt[159]
Section VI (Spiritual care, Education, Entertainment and information, Recreation): *SS-Hauptsturmführer* Karl-Robert Zoglauer,[160] *Waffen-Hauptsturmführer* Uhryn-Bezhrishny
(The Divisional chaplain was Reverend Dr V. Steciuk)

Understandably, Freitag was also opposed to the appointment of officers without recent experience. Inevitably it was a policy that always favoured the German officers.[161] During the initial organisational stage, all of the regimental commanders had been Ukrainian. But Freitag, as soon as he was able, unceremoniously replaced the regimental commanders with exclusively German officers. His pretext was that Hitler had ordered "only Germans were to be used as staff officers".[162]

The first to arrive was *SS-Sturmbannführer* Hans-Boto Forstreuter.[163] He was a former battalion commander from a *Kampfgruppe* (battlegroup) of the 4th SS *Polizei Panzergrenadier* Div, who was appointed to command the 2nd Regiment (30th) with effect from 15 November 1943.[164] Three months later, on 20 February 1944, *SS-Obersturmbannführer* Friedrich Dern[165] transferred from 6th SS *Gebirgsdivision* 'Nord' and Paul Herms[166] arrived to take up command of 1st Regiment (29th) and 3rd Regiment (31st) respectively. In the interim, with effect from 1 January 1944, *SS-Obersturmbannführer* Beyersdorff[167] assumed command of the 14th Artillery Regiment.[168]

In the following months, Freitag managed to effect the removal of the majority of the senior ranking Ukrainians. He had little confidence in those who remained, and expanded the number of German postings to cover all except one of the infantry battalions and all the Divisional sub-units. The first of the German infantry battalion commanders to assume their positions was *SS-Hauptsturmführer* Siegfried Klocker[169]. He became commander of the I/2nd Regiment (30th) on 6 November 1943.

Of the sub-unit commanders, among the first to take up their postings was *SS-Sturmbannführer* Remberger[170] who arrived on 8 November 1943. He became the commander of the 14th Pioneer Battalion. Then came *SS Hauptsturmführer* Wolfgang Wuttig[171] who was already in place as commander of the Signals *Abteilung* by 8 December 1943. *SS-Hauptsturmführer* Karl Bristot[172] joined on 15 December 1943, to command the 14th Fusilier Battalion. *SS-Hauptsturmführer* Hermann Kaschner[173] was appointed to the Anti-tank *Abteilung* as of 5 January 1944. *SS-Obersturmbannführer* Franz Magill[174] was posted to head the Supply section on 2 March 1944.[175]

Thereafter, only three Ukrainians held positions of command at the battalion level, or above, in combat units. There was *Waffen-Hauptsturmführer* Michael Brygidyr[176], a former *Hauptsturmführer* with *Schutzmannschaft* 201, who commanded the 1st battalion of the 29th Regiment. Another was *Waffen-Hauptsturmführer* Mykola Palijenko[177] who commanded a battalion of heavy artillery. The third was *Waffen-Sturmbannführer* Pobihushtschyi, who temporally commanded a battalion of the 29th Regiment. He too was replaced, by *SS-Hauptsturmführer* Wilhelm Allerkamp who had joined the Division on 27 March 1944.[178] Other Ukrainian officers took up positions as company, battery or platoon commanders.[179] The majority of company commanders were Ukrainian. Those who were not considered suitable for use in combatant roles were utilised in the supply and support services.

Despite the decision to raise the Galician Division as a regular frontline Waffen-SS combat formation, the consolidation of the German *Polizei* establishment, under the umbrella of Himmler's SS empire, meant that links inevitably existed between the two in one form or another. That was reflected in the fact that the majority of the German officers came mainly from the 4th *SS-Polizei Panzergrenadier* Division (formed in 1939 from members of the *Ordnungspolizei,* i.e. uniformed civilian *Polizei* and *Allgemeine-SS* reservists) or other *Polizei* formations. Ultimately, at least three of its regimental commanders, Beyersdorff (artillery), Forstreuter (WGR 30), and later *SS-Standartenführer* Rudolph Pannier (WGR 31) transferred from the 4th *Polizei* Division. They had joined the Division the following year as replacements, together with a minimum of eight battalion and two battery commanders[180]. Those included the commanders of the Signals, (Wuttig and later his successor Heinz), Fusilier, (Bristot) Anti-tank (Kaschner) and Pioneer (Remberger) battalions.[181]

Like Freitag, the commander of the 29th Regiment, *SS-Obersturmbannführer* Friedrich Dern, had previously served in *Polizei* units,[182] most notably as commander of the 1/14th SS-Inf.Rgt. (*Sonder-Battalion zur Verfügung Kommandostab Reichsführer-SS*). That formation comprised three companies that were subsequently split up and assigned to the infamous *Einsatzgruppen* A, B and C. His activities during his tour of duty with this unit were sufficient to ensure that he faced allegations of war crimes. For those he was subsequently tried and sentenced in the early 1960s.[183] That Dern was the calibre of officer with whom Freitag sought to surround himself is evidenced from Freitag's appraisal written some four months into Dern's tenure as regimental commander. It read:

> Evaluation, Dern.
> Dern, Regiment Commander – SS Freiw.Gren. Rgt.29
> D. has been the Regiment Commander of SS Freiw.Gren. Rgt. 29 since 20.2.44. D. exhibits his straight and open personality and has a firm and decisive appearance. His physique is robust and fully combat ready.
> D. has a solid military knowledge and experience and is leading the regiment to my full satisfaction. Despite all the difficulties appearing in connection with a unit composed of foreign nationals.
> D. is trying with untiring effort, to bring his regiment to a high level of training and conduct.
> D. is an old National Socialist and is always concerned with the well being of his subordinates. Because of his conduct and seasoned experience he always sets a good example for all, and he can easily convey his thoughts to his subordinates. Towards his superiors D. is restrained and tactful. D. is loved amongst his equals.
> D. is performing his assigned duties well.[184]

SS-Obersturmbannführer Franz Magill, who headed the Supply Section, had equally notorious antecedents, prior to his posting to the Galician Division. Magill graduated, from the post of riding instructor at the SS Academy at Braunschweig, to command a squadron of cavalry in the *SS-Totenkopfverbände*. In September 1939 he was assigned to SS *Kavallerie* Regiment 1. Later he was commander of SS *Kavallerie* Regiment 2 that undertook anti-partisan operations in the remote swamps of the Prypiat marshes. One punitive sweep conducted in these swamps between 27 July and 11 August 1941, ultimately accounted for the deaths of 6,526 'bandits' and 'plunderers', i.e. assumed partisans or those who assisted them. In his report on this action Magill noted that:

> 'Driving women and children into swamps was not as successful as it should have been, since the swamps were not deep enough for them to sink. At a depth of one metre, most cases reached solid ground (probably sand) so that drowning was not possible.'[185]

On 15 November 1941, Magill who had developed "an enjoyment of alcohol"[186] was re-assigned to the staff of the HSSPf. in White Russia with the rank of *SS-Sturmbannführer*. He went on to command the most disreputable of all the units in the German armed forces, the *SS-Sonderbataillon 'Dirlewanger'*.[187] It was a unit with an unsurpassed reputation for much wanton cruelty. On 2 March 1944, he was 'put out to grass' and appointed as chief supply officer to the Galician Division. [188]

Other officers, such as *SS-Hauptsturmführer* Karl Bristot,[189] who commanded the Fusilier Battalion, possessed qualities and key attributes as well as the type of combat experience that Freitag felt to be vital in his officer corps. At the time of his appointment, Bristot already held several impressive combat awards. They included the Iron Cross, both 1st and 2nd class, the Infantry Assault Badge, the so-called *Ostmedaille*, and the Wound Badge in both black and silver for having been wounded three times in combat. In addition, he had received the highly prestigious *Deutsches Kreuz in Gold* (German Cross in Gold) whilst participating in the fighting on the Leningrad Front. Possessing in Freitag's words, "a straight and open personality" he was described by him as having a "calm and even tempered, demeanour", who "through his conduct as a National Socialist gives a good example to his men", leaving Freitag to conclude "I am intending to propose him for promotion at the nearest future opportunity".[190]

Of the remainder, several had been sent to the Division by the *SS-Führungshauptamt* (SS Inspectorate of Headquarters[191]) having first been rejected by other formations. Thus, in marked contrast to the attempts by the Military Board to attract the best possible Ukrainian recruits, the Division, as was the case with many other European Waffen-SS Divisions, effectively became a dumping ground for a great many second-rate German officers and NCOs.[192] Without consideration of their suitability, German cadre personnel were transferred to it from various *Polizei*, SS and Waffen-SS formations, including the 1st *'Leibstandarte'*, 3rd *'Totenkopf'*, 4th *'Polizei'* and 5th *'Wiking'* divisions. Indeed, the service records of the personnel who served with the Division reveal that this extended to former concentration camp personnel such as *SS-Untersturmführer* Herbert Hanel[193]. He had served at Majdanek. There was even an eastern Ukrainian named Grigorij Osowoy[194] who transferred from the camp at Trawniki.

In several cases they received promotions to non-commissioned or even commissioned officers' ranks simply because they were fluent in both German and Ukrainian.[195] While some could provide good specialised instruction, few were well enough disposed towards the Ukrainians to establish cordial relations with them. Most remained distant and aloof, firmly convinced of their superiority. More importantly there existed a hardcore element of Nazi party members who formed the 'political backbone' of the Division. Those men, such as *Alt Parteikämpfer SS-Sturmbannführer* Otto Sulzbach and *SS-Hauptsturmführer* Johannes Kleinow, shared Freitag's attitude towards the Ukrainians. They harboured prejudices against them and the Division.[196] Their presence created a lasting atmosphere of tension.

A few individual German officers were more favourably inclined toward the Ukrainians. The most prominent was a Wehrmacht *Major*, Wolf-Dietrich Heike[197] who arrived at Heidelager on 10 January 1944. A decorated and seasoned veteran, familiar with the rigours of the Eastern Front,[198] he was officially 'on assignment' with the Galician Division and took up the post of Ia (General Staff/Operations officer[199]). In that position, Heike's influence on all matters pertaining to the Division was considerable.

Unlike his British or American counterpart, his duties as General Staff/Operations Officer entailed assisting directly with organisation, training and tactical command. His pragmatic and sympathetic approach to the Ukrainians, and the political aspirations that they associated with the formation, could perhaps be attributed to his Wehrmacht background, as opposed to the Polizei background of a large proportion of the other officers. By virtue of his position, Heike was able to serve as a moderating influence on Freitag, who was evidently satisfied with his performance describing him in his personal evaluation as having an "Honest and serious character and strong minded personality", and a "healthy ambition". "Slim with an athletic figure", he was a "good horse rider, who was capable of full achievement". "Above average intellectually" Freitag acknowledged "his organisational talent is outstanding" and that he "fulfilled all responsibilities with industry and diligence, especially in building a foreign division with its occurring difficulties."[200] Despite this appraisal, it is interesting to note that Freitag never recommended Heike for the promotion that he clearly deserved.

SS-Hauptsturmführer Friedrich Wittenmeyer[201] who joined the Division on 28 March 1944, as a battalion commander with WGR 30, later served as a temporary regimental commander with WGR 31. He adopted a similar approach to the Ukrainians. As a result, he was generally held in high esteem by those who served under him. The ethnic German officers, especially the Slovak *Volksdeutsche*, usually had less difficulty in establishing a good rapport with the Ukrainian recruits. That was partly because their native languages were very similar which necessarily facilitated better communications.

From the cadre of *Reichsdeutsch* and *Volksdeutsche* officers, Freitag demanded honesty and dignity, by his own standards, in order that they might set a suitable example to their Ukrainian comrades.[202] On occasion, amongst his own Germanic colleagues, he did not hesitate to punish those whose conduct he did not consider to be appropriate. Equally, as a staunch Nazi, those who shared his political views were often favoured or protected.[203]

The strongest opposition to Freitag's policy of utilising Germans in positions of command, wherever possible, came from *Waffen-Hauptsturmführer* Dmytro Paliiv. Aged 47 years in 1943, with a distinctly skeletal appearance, Paliiv had been an officer in the Ukrainian *Sich* Riflemen during WWI. He was a former journalist, and a member of the Polish parliament.[204] A major proponent of the Division from its inception, he was appointed to Freitag's staff, as political adviser, on the recommendation of Professor Kubijovych. He also acted as unofficial liaison between the Division, the Ukrainian Central Committee and the Military Board. In this position, as the principle spokesman for the Ukrainians, he made tremendous efforts to maintain Ukrainian interests within the Division which frequently brought him into conflict with Freitag.

Paliiv recognised that failure to create a Ukrainian officer/NCO corps, with recent training in a modern army, would critically handicap the Division in what the nationalist element saw as its projected role as the nucleus of a future Ukrainian army. Under the prevailing circumstances, Paliiv chose to pursue a long-term solution to the problem. He ensured that as many Ukrainians as possible attended specialised training programmes for officers and NCOs. Thanks to his efforts, in addition to the 600 Ukrainian officer candidates who eventually completed their courses and became full officers in the Division, by the time the war had ended, a further 2,000 men had successfully finished various specialised programmes for NCOs.[205]

The Struggle for an Identity

There was an almost total absence of Ukrainians from senior positions of command. There was an insistence on using 'Galician' for the Division's title, and on the adoption of the Galician lion as its symbol. There was the mandatory use of the German language, the requirement that the recruits swear an oath to Hitler as commander in chief of the German Armed Forces, and also the 'political' education. All those were measures designed to impose German perceptions on the Ukrainians. Those initiatives certainly allowed the Germans to maintain symbolic supremacy. Nevertheless, even if it was denied an outwardly perceptible Ukrainian character, a combination of three factors assured that the Galician Division remained intrinsically Ukrainian.

The first, and most important factor, in that respect, was the role of the UPA in relation to the Division. Wächter had originally anticipated that the formation of the Division would help to cripple the UPA by diverting potential sympathisers into a controlled army unit. However, in practice it offered the insurgents the potential to strengthen their position. Through its many supporters within the Division's ranks, not only was the UPA able to obtain limited amounts of weapons and equipment for use against the Germans, if need be, but also first class training, at all levels, for its own personnel. In some instances, when soldiers of the Division were granted home leave, they were used by the UPA cadres as instructors for their partisans.[206] The location of Heidelager close to Galicia further facilitated such activities that the Germans were never able to successfully suppress.

Thus, with a ratio in the Division of approximately nine Ukrainians to every one German, at best the Germans only exercised limited control over the unit. They knew it to be infiltrated with UPA members and sympathisers. Even the most committed Nazis and racists among its German cadre realised that to prevent a mutiny, a modus vivendi had to be established which made some allowances for the aspirations and sympathies of their Ukrainian charges.

The second factor was the presence of the Ukrainian Catholic clergy. The appointment of chaplains was one of only two major concessions that the Germans made and kept. The SS-authorities had developed a deep-rooted distrust of the Ukrainian Catholic Church. That came after Reverend Dr Laba's sermon of 28 April 1943 had shown it to be openly supportive of Ukrainian nationalist ideals. For that reason, and because the Waffen-SS was predominantly atheist, the chaplains were regarded by the Divisional command as being politically suspect. They were then forced to operate within the bounds of strict German censorship. Despite the restrictions imposed upon them, they provided vital moral and spiritual support. As a result they quickly became both a focal point for the devoutly religious Ukrainians and a centre for their national identity.

Each regiment and independent battalion was assigned a field chaplain who was responsible to Dr V. Steciuk, the senior religious officer and member of the Divisional staff (section VI). Their role and functions were set out by Father Myhailo Levenets. He issued basic guidelines, directing the chaplains to make every effort "towards gaining the trust of the men and getting to know their character and soul in the finest detail, so that the chaplain can, at the decisive moment, have the desired influence on the troops".

Other specified duties included assisting with applications for family support, made by relatives of the volunteers. They had to ensure that the daily *Wehrmachtbericht* (Wehrmacht report) be made available to the men in Ukrainian, at least every other day. They educated the men regarding conduct towards the civilian population, defending against sabotage, etc, and encouraging cultural work, i.e. press, choir. (see Appendix VI).

Mass was celebrated in Ukrainian every Sunday, and on every major religious holiday, in the form of a field service with a sermon. It was always well attended. It also presented the priests with a perfect opportunity to thwart the German attempts at political propaganda, and to propagate Ukrainian ideals.

The third contributory element was the existence of the Military Board and its affiliation with the Galician Division.[207] Although Wächter had already taken steps to restrict its influence, this civilian organisation was still able to care for the interests and welfare of its soldiers, as well as helping to maintain contact between the soldiers and the population of Galicia.

The Military Board was also responsible for the production and publication of a weekly tabloid-sized Ukrainian language newspaper *Do Peremohy* ('To Victory'). Published in L'viv under the capable editorship of the well-known writer and poet Myhailo Ostroverkha, the first issue appeared on 21 December 1943. It contained military news, together with articles about Ukrainian military history, and reports about life in the Division, written by the German and Ukrainian *Kriegsberichters* who contributed to the journal.[208] All reports submitted for publication were subjected to stringent censorship by the Germans. According to a former Ukrainian *Kriegsberichter,* they "eliminated anything which smelt of Ukrainian nationalism".[209] The journal also published essays, artwork, and literature contributed by the Ukrainian recruits. Since the sale of the paper was restricted to members of the Division it soon became very popular on the black market. Despite constant German opposition to its editorial policy, publication continued until 7 January 1945.[210]

As Christmas 1943 approached, the Military Board focused its attention on conducting fund-raising activities[211] and the collection of Christmas gifts for the soldiers of the Division. A sum exceeding 1,000,000 Zloty was raised from money given by the population of Galicia. 20,000 Christmas parcels were packed from the articles donated, each weighing two kilos.[212] Distribution of the parcels, containing 'Christmas comforts', to all Galician volunteers who were undergoing training throughout various camps in Europe, was the arranged by Section VI of the Divisional staff, headed by *SS-Hauptsturmführer* Zoglauer. The parcels were distributed in the week before Christmas by trucks that called at training establishments and specialist schools at Mielefeld, Osnabrück, Hamm, Verdun, Lübeck, Rallstedt, Hilversum, Oldenburg, Karlstadt, Radolfzell, and Moerchingen, among others.[213]

Of equal import, the Military Board presented a gift of 100,000 Reichmarks to the Division, via its commander *SS-Oberführer* Freitag, plus 25,000 Reichmarks for each of the Galician Volunteer regiments.[214] The poorer families of the soldiers also received parcels containing everyday articles.[215]

Such efforts contributed appreciably to the success of the Division's first Christmas, a great ceremonial event. The culmination of the traditional German *Wiehnachtsfeier* (Christmas festivities) was an evening meal for the senior staff. *SS-Oberführer* Freitag spoke on behalf of the Germans, as did *Waffen-Hauptsturmführer* Dmytro Paliiv on behalf of the Ukrainians. It was followed by a performance by the Divisional orchestra. Every Divisional member at Heidelager, irrespective of their nationality, received a Christmas package, and two bottles of alcohol. The Ukrainians attended their Christmas church services and entertainment was provided. It was a performance arranged by the Military Board, and staged by the 'Merry L'viv' theatre troop and a Bandura[216] ensemble. On

Christmas Eve, traditional Ukrainian dishes were served to those in attendance and in the festive spirit. All that was in spite of total numbers of desertions that by mid-December had risen to 184.[217] The Divisional commander agreed to a request to allow leave, and on 3 January 1944, some 800 men left to join their families for their Ukrainian Christmas. [218]

Governor Wächter had already proudly informed Himmler of the Military Board's endeavours in two letters dated 18 and 19 December 1943. In them he pointed out the considerable capacity for sacrifice that the donations showed in the Galician people who continued to support the Division. At the same time Wächter kept Himmler abreast of the developments within the Galician Division and the Galician SS Volunteer regiments. Wächter had recently visited them in their respective training camps, together with his adjutant, *Oberst* Alfred Bisanz, Dr Makarushka and an entertainment troupe of twelve artists.[219]

Himmler was evidently impressed, and replied in a letter dated 31 December 1943. He congratulated Wächter on his work in Galicia and on the very successful fund raising activities of the Military Board. He also expressed his pleasure with regard to the report on the Galician SS Volunteer regiments. He had promised to provide them with some urgently needed footwear. At the same time, Himmler signalled his intention to address a more pressing concern. That was the progress with the formation of the Division, which at this juncture lacked both manpower and several senior officers for key regimental and battalion command positions. Acknowledging the need for action, he concluded by stating that he would "discuss the problem of the accelerated formation of the division in the next few days and arrive at a suitable solution".[220]

The First Moves Towards Consolidation

The first steps had already been taken towards expediting the formation of the Division. On 11 December 1943, the *Reichsführer* consented to the disbanding of the Galician Polizei Regiments 6 and 7.[221] Subsequently, Himmler issued an order, dated 23 December 1943, that directed that 2000 volunteers be surrendered to the 14th *Galizian SS-Freiw.* Division at the training ground at Heidelager.[222] Of this number, 1200 men were to be drawn from *Gal. SS-Freiw.* Rgt.6, 745 from *Gal. SS-Freiw.* Rgt.7, and a further 55 men from the *Gal. SS-Freiw.Ers.Btl*[223] based at Heidenheim. Thereafter *Galizischen SS-Freiwilligen Regimenter* 6 and 7, whose personnel had completed their basic training, were dissolved[224] and on 29 December the first transport left for Heidelager.[225] The German officer cadres of both regiments, who were not deemed suitable for combat units, were returned to other *Polizei* formations. The majority of the German NCOs of the 7th were sent to *Polizei* units in Bozan (Bosnia).[226]

From the remnants of the two regiments one reserve battalion known as *Galizisches SS-Freiwilligen-Ersatz-Battailon* was formed on 9 March 1944.[227] Commanded by *Major der Sicherheitspolizei* Jordan, it consisted of four companies and had a total strength of around 900 men. The unit remained in south Western France at Tarbes, where its companies performed different duties in rotation, (*Jagdkommando, Wachkomando, Einsatzkommando and Bereitschaftskomando*), until it too was transferred to the Division in mid-May 1944. The inclusion of the 2,000 men meant that by 31 December 1943, the Galician *SS-Freiwilligen* Division's total strength stood at 12,634, including 256 officers, 449 NCOs and 11,929 enlisted men.[228]

Another order by the *Reichsführer*, dated 22 January 1944, was intended to provide further trained manpower via the incorporation of *Schützmannschafts-Batl.* 204, (which as *Wachbataillon* was responsible for security at Heidelager) into the Galician Division[229]. However it was not implemented. Although Himmler's original intention had been to expand this battalion into the 1st *SS-Freiwilligen-Grenadier-Regiment*,[230] it had remained directly subordinate to the *Polizei* authorities. Moreover HSSPf. Koppe, under whose jurisdiction it operated, made no move to comply with the new directive.[231] Instead, according to a former member of *Schützmannschafts-Batl.* 204, a general announcement was made in late January 1944, to its personnel, that "they could ask for a transfer to the [Galician] Division"[232]. As a result "about twenty men volunteered" whereupon they were assigned to the Division's *Nachrichten* (Signals) *Abteilung*[233], once again leaving the battalion independent and virtually intact until it was finally dissolved five months later.

The first batch of Ukrainian recruits were sent to Brno, where SS-Pz.Gren.Ausb.u.E.Btl. *10 (SS-Panzergrenadier Training and Replacement Battalion 10) was based. Consequently, the Ukrainian recruits were temporarily attached to this unit, whose designation was subsequently inscribed on their* Erkennungsmarken *(identity discs). The obverse of the* Erkennungsmarken *showing the unit description.*

The reverse of the Erkennungsmarken *shows the recruit's number and blood group type ('B').*

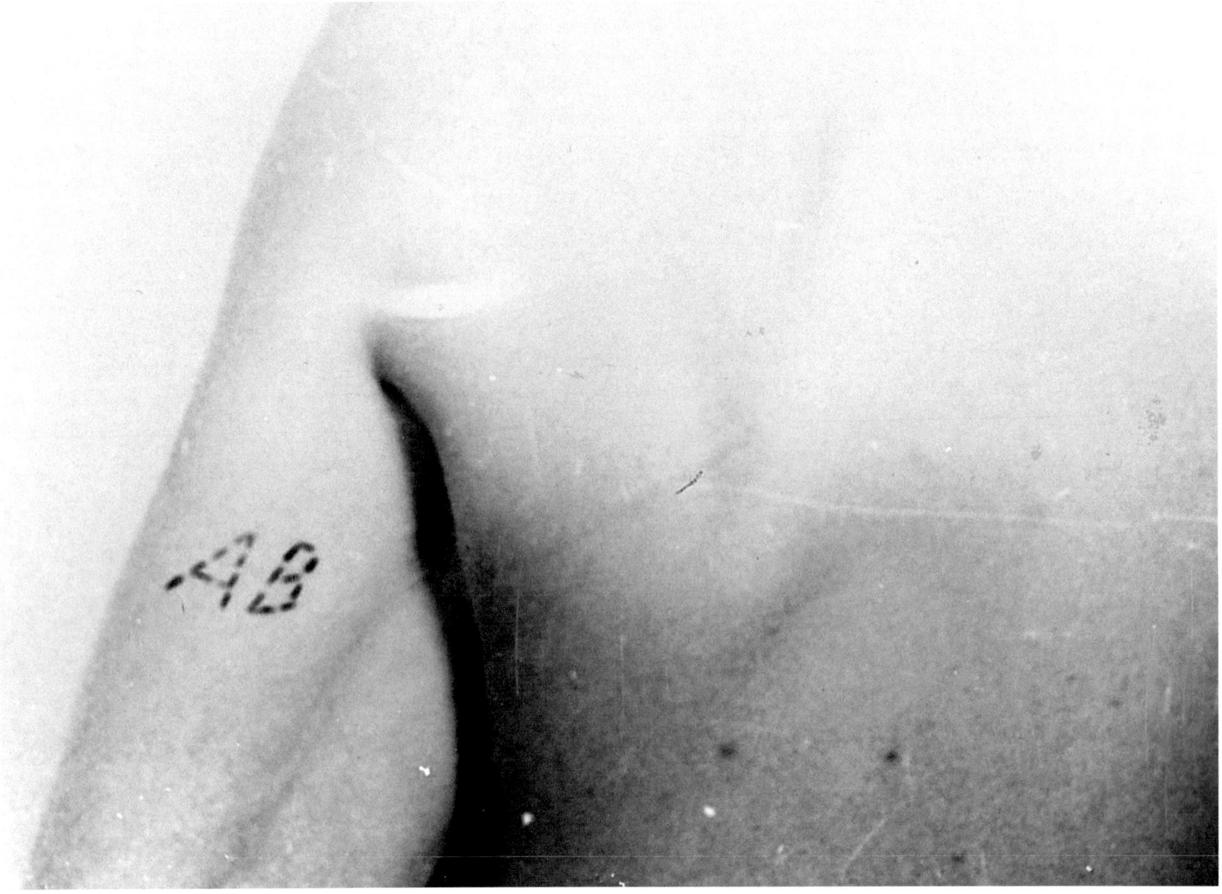

In August 1943, in accordance with a unique practice developed by the SS, the first Ukrainian recruits at Heidelager were tattooed under their left armpit with their blood groups to assist with blood transfusions in the event of a wound being received in combat.

Preparation of meals for members of SS-Ausb.Btl. z.b.V. *(note variation of collar patches).*

Waffenreinigung *(weapons cleaning) for members of the 3rd Company* SS-Ausb.Btl. z.b.V. *at Heidelager.*

Waffenreinigung *(weapons cleaning),* SS-Ausb.Btl. z.b.V. *Summer 1943, Heidelager.*

Heidelager, summer 1943. Ukrainian recruits from SS-Ausb.Btl z.b.V. *dressed in summer denim drill fatigues march to their training exercises behind their German company commander, who leads the column on horseback.*

Members of the SS-Ausb.Btl z.b.V. *await their turn at the rifle range, Heidelager, August 1943.*

In training at Heidelager, live ammunition is distributed for target practice at the rifle range.

An Ukrainian machine-gun team training at Heidelager, August 1943.

Group of older Ukrainian officers and NCOs. On the far right is Wolodymyr Kosak, who became the highest decorated Ukrainian to serve with the Division.

One of the German company commanders of the SS-Ausb.Btl z.b.V. *with his guest at Heidelager, August 1943. Unusually, instead of the slanted SS runes on the right collar patch commonly worn by German personnel attached to the Division, this* SS-Obersturmführer *wears the lion device on both his collar patch and armshield, in conjunction with the 1933 model of the SS service dagger worn by all ranks in the* Allgemeine-SS *who had served for three years as a candidate. The diamond-shaped badge worn on the lower left arm appears to denote that this individual was a Technical Officer.*

On Sunday, 29 August 1943, the members of the SS Ausbildungs-Battailon z.b.V. *were sworn in at Heidelager. Members of the Military Board and the UCC were present and are shown here being greeted by members of the Battalion's training staff. The commander of* SS-Ausb.Btl. z.b.V. SS-Sturmbannführer *Bartelt is at right foreground (wearing cuff title).*

The soldiers of SS-Ausb.Btl. z.b.V. *paraded in a three-sided hollow square for the ceremony, which began with a field service (Feldgottes-dienst) presided over by Rev. Dr Laba (in white in the centre). In the foreground is the choir.*

Governor Wächter (right), the camp commander SS-Brigadeführer *Bernhard Voss (centre) and the Battalion commander* SS-Sturmbannführer *Bartelt (left) inspect the Battalion.*

As part of the programme of entertainment which followed the official ceremony, entertainers from Merry L'viv *performed for the soldiers. Here male and female members of the dance troupe are seen wearing Ukrainian national costume.*

A group of Ukrainian soldiers from SS-Ausbildungs-Battalion z.b.V. *during their basic training at Heidelager, with their NCO instructor in the centre. Back row, second from left, is Mychailo Prymak.*

Members of 4th Group 10th Company SS-Ausb.Btl. z.b.V. *during basic training, Heidelager summer 1943.*

Hot food is dispensed from a mobile food kitchen known as a Gulaschkanone *to soldiers undergoing their basic training in the field.*

Both the Divisional lion device and the trident were a popular adornment in front of barracks at Heidelager.

Members of 3rd Company, Heidelager, 7 September, 1943. Almost the entire group are wearing SS runes on their collar patches.

1. Jurij Holub.
2. Ilariy Kushnirenko
3. Skybinskyj
4. Stefan Hawrysch
5. Karpynec
6. Evhen Schypailo
7. Anatol Skorobohatyj
8. Myroslav Scharko
9. Wasyl Ruzylo
10. Jaroslav Kinash
11. Mychailo Wowk
12. Victor Belej
13. Jaroslav Pankiw
14. Myron Golembyovskyj
15. Bohdan Klymenko
16. Jarosalv Kurdydyk
17. Bohdan Jasinskyj
18. Pavlo Kruschelnyckyj
19. Jaroslav Mryhlod
20. Roman Kohutiak
21. Roman Wysockyj
22. Not known
23. Vsewolod Tiutko
24. Rymec
25. Jurij Holobrockyj
26. Roman Hawrylak
27. Not known
28. Not known
29. Ihor Hawryliw
30. Roman Bontschuk
31. Evhen Romanovytsch
32. Roman Pantschuk
33. Bohdan Mykytyn
34. Jurij Melenkovytsch
35. Bohdan Rudytschiv
36. Dmytro Maslij
37. Mychailo Medvid
38. Roman Lentschyckyj
39. Not known
40. Not known
41. Ihor Kryschtalovytsch
42. Not known
43. Halkevytsch
44. Ivan Lasch
45. Vasyl Marusyn
46. Not known
47. Not known
48. Roman Lechickyj
49. Mykola Ohluk
50. Bohdan Kandiuk
51. Senyk
52. Myron Zbudovskyj
53. Roman Holovka
54. Stefan Stadnyk
55. Vasyl Beniuk
56. Mychailo Zacharkiw
57. Oleh Ratytsch

Ukrainian recruits during a break in the training at Heidelager, summer 1943. Seated on the left is Jaroslav Hawrych.

Heidelager, 27-29 September 1943. 3rd Company, SS-Ausb. Btl. z.b.V. *at the end of a three-day exercise.*

Heidelager, 27-29 September 1943, during a meal break at the conclusion of a three-day exercise.

штемплювати.

Jaroslav Kunytskyj

(Eigenhändige Unterschrift des Inhabers — Ruf- u. Familienname)

(Власноручний підпис власника — Ім'я і назвисько)

The first page of the Soldbuch *of volunteer Jaroslav Kunytskyj.*

Friends and relatives with members of the SS-Ausb.Btl. z.b.V., *October 1943, at Heidelager. The camp football pitch can be seen in the background.*

Several prominent members of the Organisation of Ukrainian Nationalists with previous military experience received personal orders from General Shukhevych to join the Division in order to exercise some 'political muscle'. Some of these men can be identified in this group of former officers pictured during their officer retraining course at Leshany, 31 August-1 November, 1943. Left to right: Bohdan Pidhayny (OUN), German instructor, Myroslav Malecky (OUN), Dmytro Ferkuniak, Mychailo Kachmar (OUN), and Ihor Pospilovskyj.

This picture was taken in October 1943 at the end of the retraining course of officers from SS Volunteer Division Galizien *at the training camp at Leschan. Taken by* Kriegsberichter *Weyer, and originally featured in the Divisional newspaper* Do Peremohy, *the caption reads "Light and heavy infantry weapons in action as seen from the artillery observation post".*

Graduating class of officers from Sitchovi Strilci, Pikovitz, Czechoslovakia, 30 October 1943. The class included former members of the UHA, Polish, Soviet and Romanian armies.

NCO training for infantry artillery at Breslau-Lissa. A group of Ukrainians on the first day of a three-day exercise.

February 1944. SS-Untersturmführer *Dormann accompanies a marching group of Ukrainian soldiers led by their instructors, two German* Unterscharführers, *to fetch their midday meal at the non-commissioned officers school for infantry artillery at Breslau-Lissa. In the second row are three Ukrainian non-commissioned officers who were also instructors; left to right; Mohylnyckyj, Choma and Yarema.*

Swearing-in of new recruit at Heidelager, autumn 1943. In November the Galician Division received a new commander, SS-Oberführer *Fritz Freitag (left), seen here with* Waffen-Hauptsturmführer *Dmytro Paliiv (centre facing the camera), who oversaw the oath-taking at Heidelager of the new recruits who continued to be inducted into the Division throughout 1943.*

Autumn 1943, Heidelager. Swearing-in of new recruits. On this occasion Rev. Mykhailo Levenetz presided over Holy Mass.

Ukrainian recruits taking the oath, Autumn 1943.

Freitag delivers a speech to the men of his new division whilst Waffen-Hauptsturmführer *Dmytro Paliiv translates. Winter 1943/44.*

Winter 1943/44 at Heidelager. An unidentified German officer addresses soldiers of the Division while Waffen-Hauptsturmführer *Dmytro Paliiv translates.*

Galician soldiers training with a medium PAK (anti-tank) gun in the winter of 1943/44. A similar picture appeared in an edition of Do Peremohy *('To Victory') published in L'viv.*

Heidelager, winter 1943. Two Ukrainian soldiers on guard duty. On the left is Jaroslav Liszczynskyj.

Non-commissioned officer training at the Pioneer School at Pikovitz. Young Ukrainian officer candidates learning to build a permanent wooden bridge.

NCO candidates addressed by an instructor on the parade ground during their training at the Infantry NCO School at Radolfzell an Bodensee, which took place 15 November 1943-12 March 1944.

NCO candidates in distinctive camouflage smocks before field exercises at the Infantry NCO School at Radolfzell an Bodensee, 15 November 1943-12 March 1944.

Group of Fusiliers during training at the Army training ground at Eschweiler, November 1943-March 1944, wearing Wehrmacht uniforms. Recruits were only permitted to wear Wehrmacht uniforms, whilst Divisional SS uniforms could only be worn on Sundays and holidays.

Governor Wächter together with members of the Military Board inspect the 3rd Company of Galizischen SS-Freiwilligen *Regiment 4 at Zabern, south of France, November 1943.*

Members of Galizischen SS-Freiwilligen *Regiment 4 assembled at Zabern, south of France, for Mass in the town square before the oath-taking ceremony. November 1943.*

Members of Galizischen SS-Freiwilligen *Regiment 4 assembled at Zabern, south of France, for Mass, prior to swearing the oath. November 1943.*

Members of Galizischen SS-Freiwilligen *Regiment 6 undergoing training in western France, Autumn 1943.*

Originally published in the Divisional Newspaper Do Peremohy, *this picture shows members of* Galizischen SS-Freiwilligen *Regiment 7 at the oath-taking ceremony in November 1943, during Governor Wächter's visit to the Regiment at its home base at Salies de Bearn, near Bayonne, in the south of France. Speaking at the podium is the Regimental commander Heinrich Huber, here wearing the uniform of a SS-*Sturmbannführer. *Immediately behind him, wearing a greatcoat, is the regimental chaplain,* Feldgeistlicher *Danylo Kowaluk.*

Heidelager, December 1943. Waffen-Hauptsturmführer *Dmytro Paliiv (left) in discussion with an unidentified German officer at a* Kameradschaftsabend. *Paliiv served on the Divisional staff as political adviser and also as unofficial liaison between the Division, the Ukrainian Central Committee and the Military Board.*

Stanyslaviv, 2 January 1944. Three Ukrainians during a short Christmas leave from the Non-commissioned Officers School in Dachau. From left: Burtniak, Stadnyk, Cholkan.

Personnel for SS-Flak Abteilung *14 were selected primarily from the 2nd Company of* SS-Ausb. Btl. z.b.V., *most of whom were students. On completion of their basic training, the bulk of those chosen were sent to München in December 1943 for three months' anti-aircraft training. Personnel from this unit could be easily distinguished by their distinctive black overalls, as worn by all but one of this group. Left to right: (kneeling) not known, Yarema; (standing) not known, Dawydko, not known, Pryshliak, Pasij, not known. The picture like many others in the author's possession, also provides further evidence that against official regulations an Ukrainian (in this case Yarema) wore the SS lightning runes on his right collar patch, as was often the case.*

A group of Ukrainian personnel during their anti-aircraft training, gathered around a medium calibre 3.7cm gun, spring 1944.

5

First Combat Assignments

Whatever the actual or potential political significance that Governor Wächter and the Ukrainians bestowed upon the Galician Division, and also the four additional regiments raised from Ukrainian recruits, there were certain individuals and agencies within the SS establishment for whom such considerations were of little, if any consequence. For them the Division and the four Regiments were, first and foremost, desperately needed military units. They would be deployed whenever necessary, to help shore up and defend what remained of German held territory.

One individual who subscribed to this view was *SS-Obergruppenführer* Wilhelm Koppe,[1] the Higher-SS and *Polizei* Leader in the *Generalgouvernement*. Early in 1944 as the Eastern Front edged ever closer, the stability of the territory under his jurisdiction was seriously threatened by a marauding band of Soviet partisans. Koppe sought to restore order by employing whatever forces he could muster, irrespective of any other consideration. By exploiting his authority, and his direct contact with the *Reichsführer-SS*, he successfully secured the use of the 4th and 5th *Galizischen SS-Freiwilligen* Regiments. That task was made easier because of their temporary secondment to the *Orpo*. For that purpose he also mustered a *Kampfgruppe,* i.e. a battle group, from the Galician Division. In neither case was Governor Wächter or the Division's command consulted. Thus, it was under such inauspicious circumstances that the first Ukrainian recruits were to receive their baptism of fire.

The Operations of *Kampfgruppe* Beyersdorff

At the beginning of February 1944 while the Divisional sub-units continued with general training activities, *SS-Oberführer* Freitag took leave from his duties. He attended the 9th Divisional Commanders' Course held in Hirschberg, in the Sudeten Mountains of Silesia. The course lasted from 3 February until 1 March 1944.[2] In the interim, command of the Division reverted to the senior regimental commander, and commander of the 14th Artillery Regiment, *SS-Obersturmbannführer* Friedrich Beyersdorff.[3]

On 9 February,[4] during Freitag's absence, HSSPf. Koppe contacted the commander of the Heidelager camp *SS-Brigadeführer* Voss by telephone. He in turn passed on an order to the Galician Division that it was to immediately form a *Kampfgruppe fur Antipartisaneneinsatz,* i.e. anti-partisan duties. Specifically, it was intended to be used to combat Soviet partisans of the 1st *Sydir Kovpak*[5] Ukrainian Partisan Division, who were under the command of Petro Vershigora. They had penetrated the territory of the *Generalgouvernement*, where they operated with impunity, and spread fear amongst the civilian population.[6] The strength of the battle group was to be one infantry regiment and one detachment of light artillery, supported by detachments of pioneers and anti-tank grenadiers. The order was ostensibly based on Himmler's personal instruction. It further stipulated that the *Kampfgruppe* was to be placed under the jurisdiction of the SS and *Polizei* leader of the *Generalgouvernement*, and ready to march within 24 hours.[7]

In a radio communication to the SS Operations HQ *SS-Brigadeführer* Voss later recounted receipt of the directive for the formation of the unit. The HQ confirmed that no written order to this effect had ever existed. His message read:

> 'The order given for the operation by a *Kampfgruppe* was given over the telephone by HSSuPf. Ostland, *SS-Obergruf.* Koppe, who in that matter was completely with the opinion of Chief of SS. Ops. HQ.
>
> 'I have forwarded this order to HQ of 14th Division. All further matters will be [arranged] direct between the HSSuPf and 14th Division.
>
> 'At the request of *SS-Obergruf.* Koppe, I promised over the telephone to strengthen the *Kampfgruppe* with four assault guns.
>
> '*There is no written record of either of those matters.*'[8] [Author's emphasis].

The Division's command was understandably reluctant to comply with the order. It involved placing some of its soldiers under the control of the *Polizei* authorities for security duties. It would also have meant the use of personnel who had not yet completed their training, causing considerable disruption to the training schedule. However, efforts by its representatives to have the order rescinded on those grounds were to no avail.

After reviewing all available resources and conferring with his officers, *SS-Obersturmbannführer* Beyersdorff, who had been with the Division less than six weeks, contacted Koppe in Cracow. He notified Koppe that the Division was not in a position to comply with the order at such short notice. He could however provide a smaller battle group that because of organisational and supply difficulties would consist of only one infantry battalion. It would be strengthened with one battery of light field artillery, and various support elements. He also stated clearly that as the officer corps would have to be organised from scratch, forty-eight hours' grace would be required to oversee its formation. As the Division had not yet completed its training, the proposed battle group could not be classified as combat ready.

Koppe responded by agreeing to a temporary postponement to allow the Division more time to make the necessary preparations. In the meantime the modified unit was formed by its staff from the most promising trainees and officers, and put on call in anticipation of its requirement in the near future. A few days later, on 15 February[9] 1944, Koppe called again and repeated the order. On that occasion he demanded the battle group arrive in the district north west of L'viv, within twenty-four hours, and engage the Soviet partisans active in that area. In its final form, the *Kampfgruppe* consisted of approximately 2,000 men. They were drawn from the total of 12,794 men of all ranks who constituted the Division's strength return, as of 13 February 1943.[10] The *Kampfgruppe* consisted of: 1 infantry battalion, 1 light artillery battery of 6 artillery pieces, 1 platoon of pioneers, 1 anti-tank platoon, a signals section, a supply section and a cavalry reconnaissance unit.[11]

The staff of the battle group were as follows:

Commander:	*SS-Obersturmbannführer* Friedrich Beyersdorff
Operations Officer:	*SS-Hauptsturmführer* Johannes Kleinow
Liaison:	*Waffen-Hauptsturmführer* Dmytro Paliiv
Commander (Inf Bat):	*SS-Hauptsturmführer* Karl Bristot
Adjutant:	*Waffen-Obersturmführer* Michael Kaczmar
Commander (Arty battery)[12]:	*Waffen-Hauptsturmführer* Mykola Palienko
Logistics and supplies:	*Waffen-Obersturmführer* Josef Polakiv
Cavalry reconnaissance unit:	*Waffen-Hauptsturmführer* Roman Dolynskyj
Veterinary:	*Waffen-Untersturmführer* Dr Volodymyr Kiszko
Chaplain:	*Waffen-Untersturmführer* Fr. Ivan Durbak
Signals section:	*Waffen-Untersturmführer* Adrian Demchuk

Prior to the battle group's departure, the assassinations took place of two prominent members of the German administration in Galicia, Dr Otto Bauer[13] and Dr Heinrich Schneider,[14] on 9 February 1944.[15] As a result, the Division's command despatched 45 men from the 12th *MG-Lehrkompanie* who were all over 160cm in height and whose drill and posture were excellent. Together with the Divisional band[16] they were to act as an *Ehrenkompanie*, i.e. an Honour Company, at the funeral ceremonies scheduled to take place in L'viv, on Saturday 12 February 1944. After practising a parade march, changing formation, and giving a salute, the entire detachment left Heidelager on 11 February. The convoy was of around twenty *Schwimmwagen*, i.e. open-top amphibious jeeps, two ambulances and four trucks. They arrived in L'viv on the evening of the same day.

The following day, after the funeral ceremonies had taken place, the detachment marched through the city's snow-covered streets in parade uniforms, accompanied by the Divisional band. This was only the second public appearance of soldiers of the Division in uniform.[17] They were well received by the inhabitants of the city who turned out in large numbers to lend their support. In the late afternoon Governor Wächter and his entourage visited the company at their quarters. They congratulated *Obersturmführer* Herbert Schneller, who commanded the unit, on the military bearing and discipline of the *Ehrenkompanie*.[18] The detachment remained in the city overnight before returning to Heidelager. There it was ordered to join *Kampfgruppe* Beyersdorff.

Having assembled the requisite men, horses and equipment overnight, at 11.00am on 16 February 1944, the forces assigned to the *Kampfgruppe* left Heidelager. They proceeded to the Kochanivka railway station where they were to entrain.[19] As the loading process began, the *ad hoc* nature of the battle group immediately became apparent from the obvious inexperience of most of its personnel. The resulting improvisation was described by a participant as "a horrible sight".[20] In particular, problems arose with the horses' tack because it came in several parts which none of the soldiers had experience in assembling. Eventually, after several hours, the unit boarded three troop trains and left for the Cholmshchyna region situated to the north west of L'viv. It was a highly volatile region where the underground forces of the Polish and Ukrainian populations were locked in bitter conflict.

Unlike the artillery, which was moved by rail to Lubachiv, the infantry transports were diverted through L'viv, because of the destruction of a rail bridge on the direct route.[21] While they were waiting on board their trains in the Galician capital, the soldiers were visited by members of the Military Board. They received packages of food, cigarettes, reading materials and other items distributed by the Women's Auxiliary Board, a subsidiary branch of the Military Board.[22] The unit also marched along the main street of the city in full dress uniforms in order to boost the morale of the inhabitants.[23]

A few days later, after frequent stops at various stations, the infantry units joined the artillery in Lubachiv.[24] In that area the battle group was to combine with other Wehrmacht and local *Polizei* detachments, including elements of *Gal. SS-Freiw.Rgt.* 5. Their objective was to eradicate the partisan units that had been active in the Lublin district of the *Generalgouvernement*. To achieve that, the Germans planned a three-phase encirclement operation. It was to be co-ordinated by spotter aircraft that would pass on orders directly to the units involved. *Kampfgruppe* Beyersdorff, the largest of the detachments taking part, was deployed in the southern sector in the areas of Krasnik, Lubachiv, Cieszanów, Zamosc, Tarnogrod, Bilgoraj and Tomaszow.

Such heavily forested areas favoured the activities of the Soviet-led partisans who also received strong support from the Polish population. They frequently provided guides and intelligence information. According to contemporary German *Polizei* reports, the insurgents often wore a variety of attire, including German Wehrmacht and *Polizei* uniforms. Those who wore civilian clothing and spoke Polish were indistinguishable from the local civilians, making the task of combating them a formidable proposition. Operating on horseback, often in small groups, and using sledges for their light cannons and equipment, they exploited their mobility and always held the initiative. Avoiding direct confrontation, they resorted to devious methods, adopting hit and run tactics. After cutting communications lines, they would attack administrative centres, storage and depot facilities. They raided towns and villages, blew up railway lines and mined roads. Pursuit was further hampered by the destruction of bridges on the main routes. In turn, that often necessitated lengthy and tiring detours of up to 20 kilometres on poor field roads.

For their part, the Ukrainian soldiers had received little by way of training in anti-partisan warfare and were obliged to learn the appropriate tactics in the field. Some units of the *Kampfgruppe* had not been issued with any warm winter clothing at the outset, and only received felt boots and winter coats a few days after their arrival in the field.[25] In the initial stages, units primarily conducted reconnaissance missions and patrols. Led by its cavalry unit, which soon proved to be amongst its most effective units, the reconnaissance patrols were often confined to marches in freezing weather, on icy roads, through snow and mud in remote areas, with contact limited to occasional skirmishes.[26] From time to time they discovered evidence of the presence of the evasive insurgents. There were abandoned positions, deserted towns and villages with burnt houses, and heavily barricaded local government buildings.

When civilians were present, they were almost always old people and children. Sporadic engagements did take place towards the end of the operation, but were often unproductive. According to the account of *Waffen-Untersturmführer* Dlaboha, that was because the German commanders were inexperienced in partisan warfare. Beyersdorff preferred the advice of his *Volksdeutsche* officers of Polish origin to that of his Ukrainian officers, such as *Waffen-Hauptsturmführer* Ivan Rembalowych. He had participated in two anti-partisan winter campaigns in 1919–1920.[27] In turn, that resulted in several heated exchanges and arguments.[28]

Details of the *Kampfgruppe's* activities during the period of March 1944 can be found in the daily *Polizei* situation reports sent by the Operations Officer of the *Kommandeur* in the district of Lublin, to the *Ortskommandantur* of the

Wehrmacht in Lublin. According to those reports, on 28 February 1944, *Kampfgruppe* Beyersdorff joined I/SS-Grenadier Batl. (mot.), III./ SS-Pol. Rgt. 17, II./*Gal.SS-Freiw.* Rgt. 5 and II/SS-Pol. Rgt. 25. They had begun an action on 24 February, against 'a large band' of partisans who had gathered in the southern part of the counties of Krasnik, Bilgoraj and Zamosc and who planned to attack Janów.[29] With the arrival of those security forces in the area, the partisan group withdrew to the south eastern part of the forest of Bilgoraj, leaving behind strategically placed mines. It remained there, under pressure from the pursuing units, until it was forced to retreat to the area of Chmielek, Lukowa and Osuchy. In the vicinity of the village of Chmielek, situated between Bilgoraj and Tarnogrod, at 3.00pm on 4 March 1944, elements of *Kampfgruppe* Beyersdorff and II/*Gal. SS-Freiw.* Regiment 5 came into contact with the enemy and fought what was to be its largest pitched battle. They had a combined strength of 300 men, and were equipped with heavy weapons, mortars and cannons, and were supported by *Gendarmerie Zug (mot.)* 72, a motorised platoon.

Approaching from a westerly direction, the assault began in mid afternoon. By 5.45pm, the attacking forces were further strengthened by I/SS-Gend. Batl. and one platoon of self-propelled guns. They attacked from Babice, outflanking the insurgent group, reported to be between 400–1,000 men, and who had left in their rear numerous supplies and horses. The fighting near Chmielek with the strong rear guard broke off at 8.00pm. There had been excessive use of ammunition by both sides. At Osuchy the enemy then retreated eastwards, under cover of darkness.[30] During the fighting, near Chmielek, *Kampfgruppe* Beyersdorff lost 2 dead and 6 wounded, including *Waffen-Obersturmführer* Jurij Cherkashyn. The II/*Gal. SS-Freiw.* Regiment 5 lost 1 seriously wounded by a mine, and 3 lightly wounded. Enemy losses amounted to 17 counted dead, although the report states that "many of the killed were taken away by the partisans on carts." Several *Panjewagons*, together with a saddle and many submachine-gun magazines, were captured along with 13 horses, while a further 5 horses were killed.[31]

On 5 and 6 March, *Kampfgruppe* Beyersdorff, together with elements of the I/SS-Pol. Rgt. 4, II/*Gal. SS-Freiw.* Regiment 5, I/SS-Gend. Btl. (mot.), and supported by two self-propelled guns, continued to pursue the group. They attempted to encircle it, which resulted in a further heavy exchange of fire around midday on 6 March, near the village of Kosobudy.[32] Once again, a large group of partisans managed to escape, and despite significant casualties, continued to undertake further operations in the following weeks.[33] A few days later, the entire *Kampfgruppe* was withdrawn from duty. On 17 March 1944,[34] after a week's rest, the first elements entrained at the railway station in the village of Zwierzyniec for the return trip to the Division.[35]

In the meantime, the Division had relocated to a new training ground at Neuhammer in Silesia. Travelling via Lublin and Kielce, on arrival at their new camp the soldiers were first quarantined for one week in the wooden barracks of the former POW camp Zeisau before being re-integrated.[36] During the entire campaign the casualties suffered by the *Kampfgruppe* were minimal.[37] Among the seriously wounded was an Ukrainian grenadier who lost a leg when he stood on a land mine while crossing a bridge.[38] The dead were buried locally. In recognition of its participation in the operation, the battle group was paraded one last time, for the presentation of decorations by the Divisional commander before being disbanded.[39]

Predictably, the German *Polizei* authorities in the *Generalgouvernement* were critical of the *Kampfgruppe*'s performance. Furthermore, shortly after its return, that negative view gained currency when accusations of misconduct by Ukrainian members of the unit were filed with the Divisional command.

The criticisms were largely unfounded. They made no allowance for the prevailing circumstances under which the unit was forced to operate, and over which it had no control. According to the Division's Ia, *Major* Heike, throughout the campaign the detachment had been subordinated to a *Polizei* general in Peremyshl. He was "completely ignorant of military tactics and command," and had not only been responsible for its inept utilisation, but also for failing to keep the unit adequately supplied.[40] The unfavourable climatic conditions also hampered the performance of the *Kampfgruppe.* They had faced experienced and highly mobile partisans. In addition the suggestion had also been made that the Germans showed a marked reluctance to engage the partisans, often declaring an area *Partisanen Gebiet*, i.e. partisan territory, and simply moving round it.[41]

Even so, the undertaking was not entirely without merit. It provided the officers and men who took part in the campaign with important combat experience. They brought the first decorations for valour to Ukrainians serving with the Division.

As for the allegations of misconduct, Heike maintains in his memoirs that it became apparent to the Divisional command that German units, operating in the same area, often "blamed many of their own misdeeds on the non-German unit from the Division", i.e. the *Kampfgruppe*.[42] Cases of proven breaches of discipline by the Division's soldiers, however minor, were dealt with in draconian severity by *SS-Oberführer* Freitag, but in line with the strict disciplinary code.

The Ill-omened Deployment of the 4th and 5th *Galizischen SS-Freiwilligen* Regiments

In January 1944, as HSSPf. Koppe secured Himmler's approval to form a battle group from the Galician Division, he also obtained permission for the Ukrainians serving with the 4th and 5th Galician *SS-Freiwilligen* Regiments, to be assigned to him for similar tasks.

The controlling *Ordnungspolizei* authority for the 4th Regiment,[43] responded to the plan to utilise it in the east, with a secret telex dated 4 February. It warned that it was "not ready for deployment." By way of explanation, the message incorporated a detailed list of the Regiment's deficiencies. Worst affected appears to have been the signals company. It had not yet been provided with any radios or communications equipment. Neither had it the necessary light motorised vehicles, nor the drivers, horses' tack and 12 recruits with weapons for the battalion's signals platoons. Personnel requirements were given as 15 further recruits to replace "losses sustained", cause unspecified, and a replacement for the Regimental doctor who was classified as "totally unfit for active duty." Attention was also drawn to the fact that 120 of the newly arrived recruits had only limited basic training.

Among the less serious matériel shortages identified were 4 additional riding and 10 draught horses and miscellaneous equipment such as wagons, medical packs, and equipment for 2 field kitchens. The document concluded, by stating that when the above forces and inventory had been obtained, and the difficulties overcome, the Regiment would be ready for deployment. However, a specific date for its readiness could not be given.[44] (see Appendix VII)

In much the same way, a similar report of poor preparation of the 5th Regiment, dated 3 February 1944, was sent by its controlling authority, the BdO. Danzig. It stated that because of matériel and key personnel shortages, it would not be combat ready until 15 March 1944. The reasons for this were cited thus:

> Essential specialist personnel were still needed including 2 veterinarians, 3 German doctors (one for each battalion), 1 foreign doctor's assistant, 1 officer for the signals company, 1 dental technician, and 20 recruits for unspecified positions.
>
> The 16-week basic training for recruits was not scheduled to be completed until 5 March 1944, and earlier deployment would not guarantee success.
>
> 90 of the Regiment's assignment of horses were sick and were not expected to have recovered sufficiently for utilisation until the end of March.
>
> The required complement of arms and equipment was still lacking especially with regard to transportation, i.e. wagons and associated gear, 2 urgently needed motor vehicles, signals equipment, clothing, and various weapons parts.[45]

On 9 February 1944, disregarding their protests and excuses, the office of the *Chef der Ordnungspolizei* in Berlin sent a circular to all relevant authorities. It stated that on the orders of the *Reichsführer-SS*, the 4th and 5th Regiments were to be transferred at once, by train, in full strength, to the BdO. in Cracow (HSSPf. Koppe) who would control their deployment.[46]

Once again, Wächter felt that using the Ukrainian volunteers in this way would defeat their intended political purpose.[47] He was not consulted on the matter by either Himmler or Koppe. Despite his misgivings, he was unable to intervene and prevent their utilisation. Faced with a *fait accompli* he contrived to salvage what he could from the situation.

As the public appearance of Ukrainian troops, in the Galician capital, acting as the honour guard at Dr Bauer's funeral[48] proved to be a great success, Wächter contacted Berger and asked him to prevail upon Himmler for a further authorisation. He wanted to interrupt the journey of a battalion, from one of the Regiments on its way to its area of operations, so that it could be used for propaganda purposes.[49]

Berger passed on Wächter's request to Himmler in an urgent secret telex dated 14 February 1944:

> *Brigadeführer* Wächter requests that one of the *Polizeibataillons* of the 4th *Gal. SS-Freiwilligen-Regiment* passing through Lemberg spends 1 to 2 days in Lemberg in order to take part in a large display. This would not only be of great psychological help in the current situation, but would also be the starting point for the registration of countless new volunteers. The *Hauptamt* of the *Ordnungspolizei* could arrange the interruption of the journey of the 2nd battalion of the 4th Regiment in Lemberg, without any great difficulty, if the RF-SS [*Reichsführer-SS*] authorises this. I request a decision."
>
> Signed *SS-Obergruppenführer* Berger.[50]

Two days later, Himmler notified Koppe via a secret telex that he was "in agreement with any employment of both Galician SS *Freiwilligen* Regiments", noting, "You have full authority. Consider temporary use in fight against the partisans essential and correct." The telex also stated that the decision regarding Wächter's request to use the Galicians for propaganda purposes would be left to Koppe.[51]

Accordingly, in February 1944, on Himmler's authority, Koppe issued instructions for both regiments to leave their respective training areas. The 4th Regiment went to the Zbarazh region in Galicia,[52] and the 5th to the vicinity of Lublin, Hrubeshiv and Cholm, the area to which *Kampfgruppe* Beyersdorff had already been sent.

Koppe raised no objection to Wächter's request, and on 25 February, the 1st battalion of the 4th Regiment, not the 2nd, as had been originally planned, arrived at L'viv station *en route* to its designated sector. The soldiers received an enthusiastic reception from a large crowd of Ukrainian civilians including the women's help service.[53] The battalion then marched to a gathering at the Statthalterpalais. Present on the occasion were several senior members of the German administration in Galicia. There were also local dignitaries, including the *SS-Polizeiführer* in Galicia, *SS-Brigadeführer* Thier, the *Amtschef*, i.e. chief of administration Dr Brandl, the commander of the 4th Regiment *SS-Obersturmbannführer, Major* of the *Schutzpolizei* Siegfried Binz, and representatives of the Military Board, and the Ukrainian Central Committee.

The battalion was assembled beneath the balcony in the Statthalterpalais. There they were addressed, in the name of the Military Board, by Evhen Pyndus. He made the following speech to the young men in uniform:

> 'You have become soldiers with the aim of defending the borders and honour of your country. Your homeland and her people are proud of you. You are representatives of your people and you help to create a new and just Europe. Keep high our honour! You marched here at a time when the enemy of our homeland is coming closer. Do not forget that the Ukrainian soldier in 1914–1918 had shown unsurpassed toughness, courage and valour. Our people do not fight for the first time against the destructive forces of the east. You will show that the spirit of heroism has not vanished and that the spirit of glory has not died. You will prove that you are worthy successors of your fathers. The Military Board, that cared for you so far, will continue to care for you in future. The Ukrainian people expect from you vengeance for the harm that the enemy has done and an appropriate answer to the Jewish Bolshevik murderers. The Military Board wishes you soldiers luck and hopes that you may accomplish this with honour so that your writer Franko[54] can say openly "not far is the hour when for you, oh! Home-land, we will win honour glory and freedom.'[55]

Governor Wächter then addressed the members of the battalion. He pointed out that they were being deployed in Galicia, along with their parent regiment. There the volunteers would have the opportunity to protect and defend their own immediate homeland from Bolshevism. Wächter then went on to rail against the forces within the Ukrainian community that had opposed support for the Division:

> 'Do you remember the lies, claiming that only as cannon-fodder have the Germans enlisted you, and that after only a few weeks they will toss you to the front untrained? Now, after months of hard training, you stand here, well trained and longer drilled than any German soldiers.

'What was it the liars said? 'The Germans will put you into action far away from home, in the south or in the Balkans and will leave you to bleed to death far from home'. Now you are marching proudly through your immediate homeland.

'What was it the slanderers shouted? 'You will be dragged off to slavery, badly fed and badly dressed'. Yet here you are standing before us, healthy and stronger than ever before, dressed in clean clothes and well equipped as befits proper proud soldiers.

'In defiance of these slanderers, you are, therefore, going to prove your worth by refuting the words of these incited and misled countrymen of yours, by your manner.'

Wächter feared what he viewed as the deleterious influence of the UPA on the Ukrainian soldiers. He therefore ended the speech with a call to reject, once and for all, the unscrupulous methods employed by the partisans who brought the name of the Ukrainian people into disgrace. Instead, he urged them to "fight openly and in a disciplined and soldierly manner" thereby restoring the good name of the Ukrainian people in what was to be a new, great and happy future.[56]

Although Wächter's anxieties in that respect were well founded, his rhetoric calling for a rejection of the nationalist partisans (UPA) was completely ineffectual. As later events would prove, rather than reject them, and to help further the nationalist cause, the Ukrainian soldiers of both regiments sought out UPA units at the first opportunity. Whenever possible they would clandestinely handed over weapons, ammunition and supplies.[57]

At the conclusion of the speech, the battalion formed into a column and marched to the station, singing.[58] With their propaganda activities in L'viv over, the battalion rejoined its parent 4th Regiment. They then concentrated their activities in the Zolochiv area, where the Regimental command post was based, in Brody, and the Ternopil-Zbarazh districts. Those regions were designated as staging points for actions designed to secure the rear areas of the German army fighting on the Eastern Front. They were constantly being disrupted and menaced by Polish and Soviet partisans.

While the 4th Regiment was active in Galicia, the 5th Regiment arrived in the Cholm district. There it took over the task of supervising local conscripted labourerers who were constructing bunkers and defensive fortifications along the Buh river, and of guarding the positions from attacks by partisans. Almost as soon as they arrived in their respective zones, the Germans encountered problems with both regiments. The deficiencies from which both suffered then began to manifest themselves.

The component battalions of the 4th Regiment, under *SS-Obersturmbannführer und Major der Schutzpolizei* Binz, were sent to different localities. There they conducted reconnaissance missions, repaired roads, cleared mines and carried out routine security operations against partisans. In the Cracow area some elements were assigned to *Kampfgruppe* Rheingold to fight against the partisan brigade Naumow, in the forests of Bilgoraj, 100km south of Lublin.

In late February, parts of the 2nd battalion were involved in an attack on the large Polish village of Huta Peniatska. That village, with approximately 488 inhabitants, was openly acknowledged to have become a well fortified outpost for both Polish and Soviet led partisan groups[59] whose numbers along with civilians from neighbouring villages increased the population to nearly 1,000. The partisans, in addition to attacking German supply columns, and disrupting the rear areas of the German Army, were also known to have fought against the UPA. They also terrorised the local Ukrainian population by raiding the surrounding villages.

The first attack was made on 23 February 1944. It failed, and resulted in the deaths of two Ukrainian soldiers. Their bodies, reported to have been found naked and mutilated, were recovered for burial, after a second successful assault made five days later. During it 8 to 12 Ukrainians were wounded, one of them fatally.[60]

The subsequent 'pacification action' included the destruction of the village, and the liquidation of many of the civilian population. That 'action' was known to have taken place shortly after the attack, and has remained the subject of a great deal of controversy to this day.

One of three members of the Military Board, Myhailo Khronoviat, who visited the Regiment at the time,[61] witnessed the entire event. In the account that he gave, he described how after the village had finally fallen and the

Ukrainians had moved on, a German (*Schutzpolizei*) unit (unspecified) arrived. They destroyed the village, setting fire to the houses, which began exploding because of the ammunition stored in them, and killed many of its inhabitants.[62]

In contrast several Polish and Soviet sources allege that Ukrainian soldiers from the battalion were present and took part in the pacification. However, only inconclusive evidence was produced in support.[63]

By mid March the main force of the Regiment, consisting of the 1st and 2nd battalions was engaged in fighting partisans on a sector that stretched for 170 kilometres in the district of L'viv.[64] The 3rd battalion, also identified as *Kampfgruppe* Mitscherling[65] after its commander, was deployed in the area east of Zbarazh. There it was under the overall command of XLVII *Panzerkorps*/4th *Panzer* Army. On 6 March, it was subordinated to the battle commandant of Ternopil, General Major Schrepffer.[66] On the previous day, 5 March, it was in position east of Lubianky when it unexpectedly found itself in action against the rapidly advancing Red Army. It was attacked by strong tank forces. Without any anti-tank weaponry the battalion inevitably sustained substantial losses[67] and was forced to retreat to the south.

On 7 March, it withdrew further to Stupky and the main road Proskuriv-Pidvoloczys'ka-Ternopil and even further during the following night to Smykivtsi (7km east of Ternopil). Finally, under heavy pressure from the attacking elements of the 336th Soviet Rifle Division, it fell back to Ternopil.[68] By 11 March, its strength had been reduced to 120 men.[69] They were included in the defence of *Festerplatz Ternopil* ('Fortified Place Ternopil') in the northern sector,[70] together with *Kampfgruppe* Krauss (parts of the II/*SS-Inst. Abtl.* 1st *'Leibstandarte Adolf Hitler'*).[71] Along with a mixed group of approximately 4,500 Wehrmacht troops, the survivors were encircled by Red Army units and virtually wiped out. Less than half a dozen broke out during the night of 16 April[72] and eventually returned to the Division.

From 30 April to 10 May, the remnants of the Regiment were deployed under the command of 340th Infantry Division/4th *Panzer* Army (Army Group South) with some success. In April 1944 Governor Wächter, accompanied by a reporter and photographer from the Divisional newspaper *Do Peremohy,* visited one company of the 4th Regiment based in the Kaminka Strumilova district. He witnessed the bestowal of the Iron Cross 2nd Class on 24 men, 20 German and 4 Ukrainian, for their bravery in combat with Red Army troops in the area.[73]

Further to the north, *Gal. SS-Freiw.* Regiment 5 took part in several actions against partisan units, partly in conjunction with *Kampfgruppe* Beyersdorff. For example, at the end of March, and beginning of April 1944, it fought against a very strong insurgent band in the area near Malkow.[74] In addition, some elements were given the assignment of guarding and supervising the preparation of static defensive positions along the river Buh. That entailed working for prolonged periods in the immediate proximity of civilians, among whom were a number of UPA members who quickly made contact with the Ukrainian soldiers.[75]

The influence of the UPA, and dissatisfaction with their assignment, culminated in continual desertion throughout the period of its security operations. In fact desertion threatened to become endemic. There were 119[76] instances documented in the daily *Polizei* situation reports by the Operations Officer of the *Kommandeur der Ordnungspolizei,* in the district of Lublin, to the *Ortskommandantur* of the Wehrmacht in Lublin. The majority were soldiers, in groups of up to 43 men, identified as either members of the *Gal. SS-Freiw.* Rgt 5, Galician Ukrainian *SS-Schützen*, or simply 'Ukrainian SS men'. They took their weapons with them, some having first killed their officers and NCOs. For example:

> Cholm District. 9 March 1944, During the night of 7.3.44, in the Cholm region, 13 privates from II/*Gal. SS-Freiw.* Regiment 5 (Bug) deserted presumably to the partisans, taking with them rifles, overcoats, 2 machine pistols and two revolvers (0.8)[77]
>
> 16 March 1944. Cholm, on the early morning of 13.3.44, in the Cholm region, 23 Galician Ukrainian *SS-Schützen* in field-grey uniforms with overcoats, national badges, i.e. Nazi eagle emblem on left arm, SS runes on collar patches, left their *Stützpunkt* (fortified station, or strongpoint) Stulno, 0 516 (Bug line), with 21 machine-guns, 2 machine pistols, 1 light pistol, 19 rifles, 6 pistols and the appropriate ammunition, after having killed 2 German NCOs, presumably to go over to the partisans.[78]

> Security sector Bug, 20 April 1944. On the night of 19.4.44 all Ukrainian SS men belonging to *Gal.-SS-Freiw.* Regiment 5, fled from (*Stützpunkt*) 12 Hniszo, after killing 3 German NCOs and wounding an officer. Details not known.[79]

Other units, of squad and even company strength, also made plans to desert. However, at the last moment, they were discovered by the Germans. A crisis was averted by temporarily disarming the units concerned, until they regained control of the troops and restored the situation.[80]

Incidents of that nature only served to undermine even further the already strained relations between the German and Ukrainian personnel in the Regiment. It also created an atmosphere of mutual distrust that lasted until its disbandment.

The area, in which both *Kampfgruppe* Beyersdorff and the 5th Regiment were deployed in an active mobile role, was also one in which the age old Polish/Ukrainian antagonism was strong amongst the mixed but predominantly Polish population. They were largely hostile to the presence of the Ukrainian soldiers. The nature and ferocity of the fighting, in which some of its elements were involved, is evident from a surviving telex report from the representative of the SSPf in Lublin to the HSSPf. *Ost* in Cracow, 1944. Although fragmentary, it gives a revealing insight into the actions that took place in its operational sector between 6 and 13 May 1944. The fragments read:

> Re: roem. one [a]– partisan – report.-
> Ref: telegram dated 10.5.44. 1780/44 (g)
>
> Secret
>
> To 1(b) *gal.SS-freiw.* regt. 5 13.5.44 reconnaissance detachment ahead. Zabuce [map reference] 0 516 and soltysy 0 516, (eastwards of the Bug), 23km south of wlodawa). 6 partisans captured. 35 partisans and partisan helpers shot while fleeing or offering violent resistance. In 16 houses hand-grenades exploded when incendiary ammunition was used. Villages 80% razed [by fire]. 2 attacks by small partisan groups, from the woodland eastwards and south of the aforementioned villages, successfully repelled.
>
> To 7: (c) base naleczow 0 104 15.5.44 overrun by partisans. Cossacks disarmed and stripped. No further information available at this time.
>
> (d) On the 15.5.44 at about 06:30 hours, 4 mines were laid by partisans on the janow to krasnik road. Near the sawmill modliborzyce 0 182. When an armoured vehicle drove over, one mine exploded.
>
> Result: vehicle destroyed, 1 Pole killed, 1 Pole seriously injured, and 1 Polish policeman based in Janow lightly injured. The other mines were de-activated.
>
> (e) On the 14.5.44 a small railway bridge, between belzec and mazila 0 657 at km 114, was blown up by partisans. No further information available.
>
> (f) On the 15.5.44 at 0:02 hours, on the Warsaw to Lublin road between wolka-profecka and pulawy 0 89, the gz train 90341 hit a mine. Locomotive derailed on left front axle. 80cm of rail torn away. No personnel losses.
>
> (g) Addition to roem. One a report of 15.5.44 section 7g). Expert findings have shown that the 20 x 20cm hole in the boiler-wagon was not caused by an anti-tank gun, but by an adhesion mine, i.e. magnetic mine.
>
> (h) 14 May 1944 19–22 hours the base at ryki 0 63 was attacked by partisans. Base received reinforcement from the Luftwaffe at Deblin. According to Luftwaffe report about 30 partisans were killed. No friendly losses. Several houses went up in flames during the fighting.
>
> (i) 15 May 1944 22:44 hours. Lukow to Deblin road between kryzwda 039 and okrezeja 0 39 at km 30.1 passenger train 1119 hit a mine. 30cm of right hand track blown away. About 30m track damage. Locomotive derailed on all axles. One passenger carriage derailed on front axle. No personnel losses. Route clear again since 10:00 hours on 16.5.
>
> Signed Ia. (representative of) *Wehrheim* [81]

During its utilisation, 40 *Kriegsverdienstkreuzes* 2nd Class – 24 with and 16 without swords) were issued to German members of the 5th Regiment. Recipients also included *SS-Oberscharführer* Richard Andersohn, *SS-*

Oberscharführer Rudolf Baronyay, *SS-Untersturmführer* Emil Weis. They were all members of 3./*Gal.SS-Freiw.* Regt. 5, and were awarded the *Kriegsverdienstkreuze* (2nd Class with Swords) for bravery during the partisan attack which took place on 13 May 1944, described in the above telex.[82]

The problems that continued to afflict both regiments throughout this period arose mainly because neither was utilised in an appropriate manner, nor sufficiently equipped for its designated task.

Such considerations were ignored by HSSPf. Koppe. Having been informed of the difficulties, at a time when both regiments were still active and under his control, he broached the subject in a speech about security questions in the *Generalgouvernement*, in Cracow on 15 April 1944. In his view, the performance of the Ukrainian regiments had fallen short of expectations. Conveniently overlooking the fact that he had been responsible for their utilisation in the first place, and was the obvious causes of their problems, Koppe announced that, "In this area one had, until now no good experience of the regiments of this Division." At the same time he expressed the opinion that a great risk was being taken by the arming of the Polish and Ukrainian *Polizei*,[83] no doubt alluding to the killing of several German officers and NCOs by Ukrainian members of *Gal. SS-Freiw.* Rgt. 5 before they deserted.

Notwithstanding his apparent dissatisfaction with them, Himmler issued an order seven days later, dated 22 April 1944. It was for the disbandment of *Galizischen SS-Freiwilligen* Regiments 4 and 5 and their transfer to Neuhammer.[84] Koppe ignored that order.

Koppe's disparaging comments cast damaging aspersions over the Ukrainian formations. They threatened to jeopardise much of the progress that Wächter had made in convincing the higher German authorities of the wisdom of permitting the formation of Ukrainian military units. In the course of the next few weeks, Wächter was repeatedly forced to refute his statements, in order to rehabilitate the Ukrainians in the eyes of his superiors. Many of them continued to view the rehabilitation with considerable suspicion.[85] Wächter himself was seen as being too much of a 'trouble-maker.'

March–June 1944

While both *Kampfgruppe* Beyersdorff and *Galizischen SS-Freiwilligen* Regiments 4 and 5 were still engaged in their respective security tasks, in response to the continual requests by its command the Galician Division was finally transferred to another training ground. This was Neuhammer, on the river Queis near Sagan in Lower Silesia, which had just been vacated by the 13 *SS-Freiwilligen b.h. Division (Kroatien)*. The relocation required thirty train-loads of men and matériel. It began with the despatch of advanced detachments in mid-February 1944,[86] and took three weeks to effect.[87]

Unlike Heidelager,[88] which had single-storey primitive wooden barracks, and lacked a number of permanent facilities and fixtures such as vehicle parks, supply and storage depots, Neuhammer was a very large brick camp with purpose-built modern facilities. The move to a new training ground, situated further away from Galicia, brought with it several practical benefits for the Division. Notably they had a camp commander who was less inclined to acquiesce to every demand he received for help from senior ranking officials. He was more supportive towards its needs and worked closely with it in assisting with the procurement of much-needed weapons, horses, vehicles and other essential matériel. There was a dramatic fall in the number of desertions, which had been a constant concern for its command at Heidelager. The accelerated improvement in all areas of training was no longer subject to the distraction caused by visiting friends and relatives.

Right up to February 1944, when the Division left Heidelager, it continued to take delivery of regular shipments of new equipment, weapons and supplies. The shipments included a large consignment of 4,420 rifles, the standard carbines 98k model, from army supply depots in Spandau and Breslau. All was as reported by the Division's quartermaster *SS-Obersturmführer* Schaaf on 19 January 1943.[89] It also received senior officer personnel for its command staff and field units. March 1944 saw the arrival of two more men who assumed positions as battalion commanders in infantry units, *SS-Hauptsturmführer* Allerkamp (CO II/WGR 29) and Wittenmeyer (CO II/WGR 30). Another German officer, *SS-Sturmbannführer* Sepp Syr,[90] was appointed to the Division with effect from 10 March 1944.[91] A decorated veteran, with extensive experience in reconnaissance units, Fusilier Syr had previously served with the 1st SS Division *'Leibstandarte'*, the 8th SS *'Kavallerie'* Division *'Florian Geyer'*, and the

15th Latvian *SS-Freiw.* Division. He was assigned to the Galician Division as a battalion commander for the three-month period ending 16 June 1944.[92] His role during that period was ambiguous. He may have assisted with the forming of the Fusilier Battalion, but there is no evidence to suggest that he ever took formal command of it.

Soldiers who had undergone specialist training also continued to return from their respective schools, such as the 61 NCOs and men who had undergone a course with SS Signals Training Abtl. 4, at Moerchingen. They returned on 12 March 1944.[93]

Also in March, at long last, there was completed the formation of the motorised anti-aircraft battalion (*SS*-Flak *Abteilung 14*) with a strength of 860 personnel[94] commanded by *SS-Hauptsturmführer* Serge von Kuester.[95] In its final form [96] it consisted of one light battery of 2cm guns,[97] a medium battery of 3.7 cm guns,[98] and a third heavy battery of four, highly-prized, high velocity 8.8 cm semi-automatic guns.[99] The latter became something of a showpiece during inspections and tours by visitors.

At the same time the previously established reserve battalion, 14th *Feld-Ersatz* Battalion, was reorganised under the command of *SS-Hauptsturmführer* Johannes Kleinow and expanded to a strength of 800 men.[100] The purpose of that unit, consisting of four companies, was in the first instance, to serve as a source of reserve officers, NCOs and soldiers for all the Division's units. It was also responsible for the retraining and the classification of the ranks of former officers.

Freitag's own estimation of the Division's evolution was summarised briefly in a routine progress report dated 15 March 1944, in which he revealed both his concerns about, and his continuing bias against, the Ukrainian officers. It read:

> [...] 4. Short Evaluation by the Commander.
>
> Training situation: The training of the Artillery, Flak *Abteilung*, *Panzerjäger* Company, *Pionier* and signals groups is making good progress.
>
> The co-ordinated training of the Grenadier regiments and Fusilier Battalion can only begin after the arrival of the NCOs and volunteers from the Waffen SS schools, from the reserve army detachments, and those previously assigned to the *Kampfgruppe*. Their return is under way. The contingents assigned to the *Kampfgruppe* were continuing their training while doing their duty. The *Kampfgruppe's* return to the division is in progress. The lack of suitable German instructors is continuously being felt adversely. Morale of troops: good. The positive attitudes of the new NCOs arriving from the Waffen SS schools should be especially stressed.
>
> Special Difficulties: The laziness and unreliability of the mass of Galician officers is impairing the future formation of the Division. The discipline of the Galician officers is improving since the arrival of individual German commanders.
>
> Combat readiness: At this time not given, because Division is in the process of formation.[101]
>
> Signed Freitag

With regard to the remaining matériel deficiencies, one of the most serious was the number of horses assigned to the Division. It had only 2,996 horses of the required complement of 4,925, leaving a shortfall of 1,929.[102]

In spite of that, in late March 1944, the Division was finally able to begin full-scale battle training. It was due for completion in June. In the following weeks intensified and combined exercises of company, battalion and regimental sized units began, as well as manoeuvres on a divisional scale. They were conducted from dawn until late at night. There was special emphasis on effective interaction between various weapons and services, the co-ordination of light and heavy weapons fire, using live ammunition, and forced marches.

In late March, amid all that activity, at the request of *SS-Oberführer* Freitag, a former SD (*Sicherheitsdienst*) officer who harboured a particular antipathy toward the Galician Ukrainians,[103] was transferred to a newly created and unique sub-section of Section 1c (Military intelligence) of the Division's staff.

Ukrainian born *SS-Hauptsturmführer* Heinrich Wiens[104] had had a sinister career prior to joining the Division. He had previously served with *Einsatzgruppen* D[105] a formation that spent its time hunting down and liquidating Ukrainian patriots, partisans, Jews, and others proscribed by Nazi racial and political policies.[106] The remit of

Section Ic/a (counter-intelligence), of which he was in charge, covered desertion, censorship of mail and most importantly the elimination of the OUN activists within the Division. Wiens, who was fluent in Ukrainian, Russian, Polish and German, was ideally placed and eminently qualified. He helped Freitag to identify the ardent Ukrainian nationalists, and to counteract the dominant sentiment that they exemplified.[107] Whatever the motive for his appointment, Freitag evidently thought very highly of him and was pleased with his work.[108] That continued until his disappearance, just before the end of the war.[109]

In an immediate effort to frustrate his work, the only Ukrainian member of Section IC, *Waffen-Hauptsturmführer* Ferkuniak, advised the principal OUN adherents. They included *Waffen-Obersturmführers* Kaczmar, Maleckyj and Pidhayny. Ferkuniak said that they should let it be known amongst the soldiers that, to avoid serious consequences, the Ukrainians should refrain from expressing their political views in their private letters. It was a measure that met with some success.[110]

In mid-April 1944, a Training and Reserve Regiment (*Ausbildung und Ersatz* Regiment 14) was established commanded by *SS-Sturmbannführer* Mathias Huber. Thereafter all new recruits would first be sent to that unit. The Regiment consisted of a command staff, three battalions, (each of which was made up of four companies[111]) 13th–15th training companies, *Kraftfahr* (driver and mechanic) training company, a reserve battalion with staff company (responsible for receiving and accepting new recruits), and a *Genesenden* (convalescent) company.[112] Stationed at Heidelager (from 15 April to 15 July 1944), it was directly subordinated to, but independent of the Division.[113] Within two months of its establishment, it had a complement of over 5,000 recruits and was expanding. Its sheer size was in itself a problem for the Divisional command, as at that time only 40 to 50 qualified German and Ukrainian instructors were available for training. A high proportion of instructors was unable to take part in practical training because of their wounds.[114] Initially co-operation between the Regiment and the Division was poor but improved steadily.

A strength return for the Galician Division, dated 17 April 1944, revealed it had 13,999 men, i.e. 291 officers, 666 non-commissioned officers and 13,042 men, serving in its ranks.[115]

In accordance with tradition in the German armed forces, on 20 April, the Führer's birthday, promotions in military rank were given, as appropriate, to deserving German and Ukrainian personnel. On that day Fritz Freitag was raised to the rank of *SS-Brigadeführer und Generalmajor der Waffen-SS und Polizei*.[116] There were promotions too for the younger Ukrainian graduates from the non-commissioned officers' schools. They had recently returned to the Division to assist with the training of new recruits.[117]

As the training schedule entered its final stages, regular reports were submitted to the higher German authorities regarding the state of the Division's battle readiness. Governor Wächter, and those who sympathised with his views, ensured that those also stressed the political nature of the formation and the relevance of its involvement in military action with regard to Ukrainian interests.[118] Based on those criteria, a number of suggestions were incorporated within them. Firstly, because of its inexperience, it was considered advisable to send the Division to a quiet sector of the front to allow it to acclimatise to the rigours of combat. Secondly, notwithstanding previous experiences, the venue of its first action would be on Ukrainian soil, preferably in Galicia, as neither the northern nor the southern salients of the Eastern Front were considered appropriate to Ukrainian interests. Its staff further proposed an open field engagement, as opposed to one in a forested or urban area for which it was felt the Ukrainians would not be suited.

Continuing with his incessant manoeuvrings of a diplomatic nature, Wächter saw to it that one copy of a report, based on those recommendations, was sent to the Commander in Chief of Army Group North Ukraine (AGNU) *Generalfeldmarschall* Walther Model whose headquarters were in Galicia.[119] Model, who concurred with Wächter's view with regard to the potential significance of a proper deployment for the Galician Division, showed an enthusiastic interest in the report. He promised actively to support its recommendations. To facilitate that he included the Division in the preparations for his planned operations in that area. Moreover, and as a preparatory measure, albeit a somewhat premature one, he took the practical step of despatching 10 experienced Wehrmacht officers and NCOs to the Division, to acquaint all regiments with the terrain in the proposed area of operations.[120]

The end of April 1944 marked the first anniversary of the promulgation of the formation of the Galician Division. It was then rapidly nearing readiness for deployment. Having made a recent trip to Neuhammer to evaluate the Division's development for himself, Governor Wächter regarded that as an opportune moment to send a full report to Himmler on its progress and on the overall situation in Galicia.

In his eight-page letter, dated 3 May 1944, Wächter sought to convince Himmler that from the German perspective, in spite of the initial doubts, the creation of the Galician Division had been a worthwhile venture. It was the "barricade that kept the entire youth of Galicia from slipping into a nationalistic hostility to the Reich and at the same time, the point of departure for a European-conscious youth, receptive for the Reich concept."

He then gave a brief résumé of some of the difficulties facing the administration authorities in Galicia, following successive German setbacks. He listed the negative effect they were having on the population, especially in relation to the growth of both the Ukrainian nationalist and Soviet partisan movements. In Wächter's view the successful reversal of these adverse developments was inextricably linked with the introduction of a positive political agenda for the Ukrainians:

> 'The question of a national slogan is of decisive importance. It is understandable that young volunteers are more likely to go for a clear and positive political programme than for vague hopes. Many difficulties in the Division and in the [*Polizei*] regiments can be explained by this fact.'

To temper such obvious criticism, Wächter aligned his own view with Himmler's. He reaffirmed his belief in the long-term success of the maxim that Himmler had already expounded on this issue, that "Nothing can be extorted from Adolf Hitler and his German nation, but everything can be gained by proving yourselves to be decent and loyal." That slogan, Wächter noted, would be understood by and appeal to intelligent young people, especially the young officer candidates in the Galician Division who were fully cognisant of its implications and who would serve as an example to the other troops:

> 'I am convinced that this good section will then constitute the nucleus of a growing youth movement in partnership with the Reich. These young men, who in many cases used to be Bandera supporters themselves, i.e. UPA supporters, now find themselves in conflict with the Bandera supporters operating in the woods of their country. When they have experienced the pride of having proved themselves at the front, their contempt for the shirkers and murderous arsonists in the woods will increase.'

Mindful of the detrimental impact of Koppe's recent public criticisms of the performance of the Ukrainians, during their assignments in the *Generalgouvernement,* he continued:

> 'If the various negative events in Galician Regiments 4 and 5 are held up to refute my optimism, they cannot convince me. By keeping in steady contact with the leaders and troops of the Galician SS regiments and with the Division, I am well acquainted with the situation and have come to the following assessment. The deployment of the Regiments was ill-fated from the start. I list the following:
>
> 'Inadequate armament, this was bound to have serious consequences in the various encounters with Soviet tanks.
>
> 'The distribution of the troops, where split up into tiny bases, was easily influenced by nationalist envoys. Acting against this was virtually impossible just because they were so split up and the communications were so inadequate.
>
> 'Their deployment (especially in the case of the 5th Regiment) in areas which were totally undermined by the radical Polish-Ukrainian national struggle.
>
> 'Their deployment at a time of retrogressive frontline development led to manifestations of disintegration even among the German troops.
>
> 'A corps of leaders, some of whom had no personal experience of the front and only limited military experience.

> 'Last but not least, the lack of a link between troops and leaders who could have motivated the men in their own language with easily understood arguments. The existence of a Galician-Ukrainian corps of non-commissioned officers would have had a very positive effect here.
>
> 'In spite of these considerable disadvantages, some troops of the regiments put up a good performance, especially where the leadership was flawless, and where they had some heavy weapons to back them up at the Front. I was told this repeatedly by Wehrmacht officers who were acquainted with the facts.'[121]

Fearing disastrous consequences, if the Galician Division was deployed without regard to Ukrainian interests, and with his preparatory measures in this respect underway, Wächter beseeched Himmler to ensure a "politically favourable active deployment" whatever happened, preferably against the Soviets in Galicia. He went on to add that *Generalfeldmarschall* Model, who had previously successfully used Hungarian troops for tactical political purposes, had already expressed an interest in using the Division in conjunction with his Army Group currently located there. Wächter acknowledged the risks involved in such an undertaking. But he then stressed that the utilisation of the Division in such a way would not only amount to a demonstration of confidence in the Ukrainians, on the part of the Germans, but would also have the additional advantage of helping to undermine their nationalist partisan movement.

Wächter alluded to the "flawless military impression" that the Division had made on him during his recent trip to Neuhammer. He then concluded his letter by requesting that he be allowed to report to Himmler, in person, since over fourteen months had passed since their last meeting.[122] No doubt Wächter hoped such a meeting would afford him the opportunity to extract concessions from Himmler, as he had after they last met, early in March 1943.

Wächter's report appears to have elicited the required response. A few days later, he received confirmation that his request for a personal audience with Himmler would finally be granted and that the Reichsführer would be conducting an official inspection of the 14th Galician Division at Neuhammer in the near future.

The *Reichsführer's* Review

On 16 May 1944, an aircraft carrying the *Reichsführer-SS* landed at Neuhammer. Himmler's diary of official appointments indicates that the scheduled time of arrival was 7.00pm.[123] Governor Wächter was also present. Both men were greeted by *SS-Brigadeführer* Freitag. They were then taken to the officers' mess where formal introductions were made to the assembled regimental and independent battalion commanders and other high-ranking members of staff. The visit then began with a speech by Himmler to the predominantly German, senior officer corps. A surviving audio recording made at the time reveals that, as a conciliatory gesture towards the presence of the Ukrainian contingent, the speech was translated into Ukrainian, sentence by sentence, by *Waffen-Hauptsturmführer* Dmytro Paliiv.[124]

On that occasion the gist of the prepared address that Himmler gave, reflected an attempt to assuage the many criticisms levelled at the Division, by the Ukrainians themselves. Himmler had been made aware of those through his correspondence with Wächter. He therefore began his address by acknowledging what he knew to be their dissatisfaction with the its 'Galician' title. He stated unequivocally that the Division was actually composed of Ukrainians.[125] He then suggested the designation 'Galician' did not reflect an attempt to denationalise the Ukrainians, but was merely a means of regional identification, in the same way that inhabitants of Bavaria were called Bavarians.[126]

His speech continued with some references to the historic link between Galicia and the Reich through its former 150-year association with the Austro-Hungarian Empire. He used that to justify the partitioning of Galicia from the remainder of Ukraine in 1941. Then he mentioned the oppression and persecution of the Ukrainians in the territory under the Poles, and later under the Russian Bolsheviks. Deliverance from those sufferings, he pointed out, together with the removal of the Jews, "who often sullied the name of Galicia", had only come about "through German intervention and with the blood of the German soldiers."

In reply to the ardent Ukrainian nationalists, to whom he referred as "eternally dissatisfied," and who accused the Germans of enlisting the Ukrainians as cannon-fodder, he emphasised that the Division had been given a whole year of thorough training and practice, in discipline, drill, and weapon-craft, before being committed to combat.

Another important criticism from the same quarter, i.e. the lack of Ukrainian officers within the Division, presented a more awkward problem especially in light of the official German policy of reserving senior positions of command exclusively for Germans whenever possible. Himmler attempted to gloss over the issue with the following explanation:

> 'A further assertion made by our 'friends' is: you know of course that the Germans will not let any single one of you rise to any kind of high position. Not one of you will become a proper officer. I believe you are witnesses to the contrary. Every position is filled by a man who is capable. *I did not ask, nor did the Division's commander ask: Is he German or is he Ukrainian?* [Author's emphasis] On the contrary, the only question we asked ourselves was "Does he lead his battalion in such a way that there is no unnecessary loss of blood? Is he a man that can teach his subordinates military virtues and can train them to do their job well? Is he a man who leads his battalion to victory or defeat? Is he a man who buys victory at the expense of far too many lives, or is he such a leader that the dead, the fallen are fewer?
>
> '250 men from the ranks of the Division have been sent to the *Junker* schools, [officer academies] and it is my firm intention to pick out regularly the best and most talented from the youth of Galicia and to further each one according to his capabilities. Every man from your ranks, who becomes an officer or a Führer in the community of the European divisions of the Waffen-SS, is a source of great joy and pride to me.'

"The performance of such men in this war," he said, "would ultimately determine the status, worth and importance of each individual people in the Europe of the future." Himmler reiterated his confidence that the Ukrainians, like the Estonians, Latvians, Bosnians and Albanians who had also been formed into divisions by the Waffen-SS and were under his command, would uphold the 'unprecedented military glory' that the divisions of the SS had fought for and attained.

In an effort to suppress the strong nationalist sentiments amongst the Ukrainians, Himmler then proceeded to forbid the discussing of politics within the Division. He then demanded that his audience must uphold a number of cardinal virtues, including loyalty and obedience, which for Himmler were axiomatic. In the case of the former, Himmler was simply recapitulating a standard theme from one of his many speeches,[127] while as regards the latter he elucidated thus:

> 'There is something I want to tell you: obedience starts the moment you receive an order to do something you find unpleasant. I know if I ordered the Division to exterminate the Poles in this area or that area, I would be a very popular man. But if I tell you, or give you the order, that the Division is to follow this or that route to the front, in full battle order, and fight against the Russians, then that is what will be done. The Führer will manage to handle the Poles alright! For they have ill-treated you in the same way as they have ill-treated our fellow Germans in Poland. You do nothing before the order is given. I expect you, the *Führerkorps*, whether German or Ukrainian, to set a good example to your men by your exemplary obedience in every, I repeat every, respect.'

He then called for comradeship between the Germans and the Ukrainians "in this division of Europe." He demanded that the German SS, officers and men, must treat their Ukrainian comrades "just as if you had been born along with them, and carry the wounded Ukrainian Galician comrade from the battle as if he were your brother."

In closing Himmler stated: "I dismiss you, my leaders, from this summons, from this officers' conference. Tomorrow I will take a look at this battalion and that battalion to see what you can do and what you have learnt as soldiers and leaders. And shortly afterwards you will give a sample of your talent, your worth, your bravery, your obedience, your loyalty and the sanctity of the oath you took to the Lord God to fight against the enemy, Russia and Bolshevism, at the front. I know you will not disappoint the SS and you will not disappoint me who called upon you, and at the end of this war the Führer will be able to say: the division set up by the brave people of Galicia has always done its duty. This people deserves to take its place in Europe."[128] (For the full text of the speech see Appendix VIII).

From his anti-Polish comments, it is evident that Himmler had misjudged Ukrainian motives for supporting the formation of the Division. According to the testimony of *Waffen-Obersturmführer* Julian Temnyk, who was present, in response to Himmler's attempt to incite the Ukrainians against the Poles, *Waffen-Hauptsturmführer* Dmytro Paliiv, the spokesman for the Ukrainian officers, took the floor and said:

> 'Let it be permissible in your presence, *Herr Reichsführer*, for me to state that we Ukrainians are not preparing to slaughter the Poles, and that is not why we voluntarily enlisted into the Division Galicia. But after observing German policies in eastern Europe, we cannot fail to see how you Germans continue to incite us against the Poles and the Poles against us. I feel that it is necessary to inform you that your policies in eastern Europe are not correct and lead to nothing good. Forgive me for such an unpleasant rebuttal, but that is the way it is.'[129]

In the absence of any record of Himmler's reaction to Paliiv's comment, it may be assumed that he bore the embarrassment stoically enough at the time.[130] However, such impudence from an Ukrainian, whom Himmler considered to be his racial inferior, was hardly likely to have gone unnoticed. It may also explain why, a few days after his visit, Himmler issued the following order to the Chief of the security *Polizei* and SD (Security and intelligence Service) designed to disassociate the Ukrainians from the elite SS establishment once and for all:

> 'In the criminal report of the *Reichssicherheitshauptamt* of 26.5.44, reference is made to an Ukrainian SS man under item 2. This should be correctly defined as an Ukrainian serving in the combat units of the SS. I ask you to ensure that the term 'SS Man', which is so precious and high standing to us, is avoided in all reports, as well as in all official and non-official announcements concerning the people of foreign race which we today organise under the order of the SS.'[131]

Early on the morning of 17 May, Himmler, Wächter, Freitag and the camp commandant set out to conduct a thorough inspection of the Division. With its constituent units spread out over such a large site, the Divisional commander placed his car at Himmler's disposal. Waffen-SS war correspondents were at hand to record and photograph every stage of the visit for propaganda purposes.[132] Equipped with binoculars, the party was conveyed in Freitag's 4 x 4 Steyr-Daimler staff car to various sites within the training complex. They observed artillery batteries in action, anti-aircraft batteries, firing both at air and ground targets, infantry support gun crews, mortar teams, and machine-gunners who gave demonstrations of weapons proficiency for his benefit. The inspection encompassed sections from almost every sub-unit, communications staff, supply and provisioning services, veterinary, medical, signal, automotive and pioneer units, as well as combat exercises involving all combined forces conducted under battle conditions.

The inspection was followed by a review of select units chosen from all sections of the Division beginning with its band and followed by the infantry, ending with the motorised units and the heavy artillery. The parade lasted almost an hour and a half. The visit concluded with a closed meeting with Freitag, Wächter and Bisanz to discuss various issues connected with the formation including its imminent deployment.

During the course of his visit, Himmler solicited the comments of men of all ranks and had ample opportunity to acquaint himself with the various concerns of the 'Galician Division' at first hand. Evidently he was pleased with Governor Wächter and satisfied with the Divisions progress and the level of its training, "repeatedly voicing his complete approval".[133]

As a sign of his approval, Himmler promoted Wächter to the rank of *SS-Gruppenführer und Generalleutnant der Polizei* in recognition of his work,[134] and consented to the proposals concerning the critical issue of the venue for the Division's first engagement. Himmler also ordered ten other promotions, as of 17 May 1944, two German and eight Ukrainian. The most senior was Hans-Boto Forstreuter (CO *SS-Freiw.*Gren.Rgt.30) promoted to the rank of *SS-Obersturmbannführer*. The other German, Serge von Kuester (CO *SS-Freiw.*Flak.*Abtl.* 14) was promoted to the rank of *SS-Sturmbannführer*. The most senior of the Ukrainians was Mykola Palienko (12.9.1896) *Abteilungsführer* in *SS-Freiw.*Art.Rgt. 14 who was advanced in rank to *Waffen-Sturmbannführer*, followed by six medical doctors: Jaroslav Karpewitsch (8.7.07) *Regimentsartz SS-Freiw.*Gren.Rgt. 30: Wolodymyr Lubinetzkyj (28.10.13) *Regimentsartz SS-*

*Freiw.*Gren.Rgt. 29: Dionis Dakura (31.12.04) *Regimentsartz SS-Freiw.*Gren.Rgt. 31: Michael Hryhortschuk (1.6.06) *Regimentsartz SS-Freiw.*Art.Rgt. 14: Jaromyr Olesnyckyj (27.12.14) 2./*SS-Freiw.San.Abtl.* 14: Stefan Symko (5.6.13) 2./*SS-Freiw.San.Abtl.* 14, all of whom became *Waffen-Untersturmführer.*[135]

On the early evening of 17 May,[136] Himmler left Neuhammer with Governor Wächter. He boarded his plane and flew to L'viv to visit Model's headquarters and confer with the *Feldmarschall* on the Division's future military engagements. In this respect, part of Model's planned Operation '*Schild und Schwert*', ('Shield and Sword') as outlined in his order dated 17 May 1944,[137] involved an attack by 1st *Panzer* Army to the south of the Dnestr river, and north of Kolomyia. For that purpose, one option within the order allowed for 1 Hungarian reserve division, and the Galician Division, to be deployed behind the front of 1st *Panzer* Army.[138]

With regard to the forthcoming deployment, the last significant potential difficulty was averted a few days later. The order of 15 May 1944 came into force on 22 May by virtue of which the Galician Division's 1st General Staff Officer, *Major* Heike was to have been re-assigned to the 3rd *Totenkopf* Division. That order was finally rescinded thereby preserving the Division's command structure.[139]

An opportunity to assess the development of the Division was also extended to a delegation led by Professor Kubijovych and Alfred Bisanz. They visited Neuhammer along with a group of fathers of some of the soldiers, for two days, on 2 June.[140] The guests watched the Ukrainian soldiers during exercises, inspected their living quarters, and spent some time with their sons, which greatly raised morale. Kubijovych, Bisanz, and Dr M. Roslak, as a representative of the parents, all gave short speeches to the troops. Before they left, a parade by selected units took place from what had become a modern and well-equipped infantry division.

Consolidation

June 1944 saw the final stages of the implementation of the Division's organisation, and the consolidation of all the remaining affiliated Galician *Polizei* units. It was eleven months after the first call up was issued.

On 1 June, the SS-FHA issued an order for the Training and Replacement Regiment (*SS-Gren.Ausb.u.Ers* Rgt 14/*Galiz.* Nr.1) at Wandern to provide the necessary personnel for the formation of the missing 3rd battalions of each of the infantry regiments.[141] Nine days previously on 23 May, the Ukrainian soldiers of the *Galizisches SS-Freiwilligen-Ersatz-Bataillon* Tarbes had already arrived at Neuhammer from their base in the south of France, following the disbandment of their unit.[142] They were then transferred to the 14th *Feld Ersatz Bataillon*. While some remained with that unit, a few days later the remainder were assigned to the Division's various combat units and to the Training and Replacement Regiment as training assistants.[143]

The formation process of the third battalion was also aided by an influx of the Ukrainian soldiers of the 4th and 5th *Galizischen SS-Freiwilligen* regiments (less the majority of the German officers and NCOs). Repeated petitioning of the *Polizei* authorities in Berlin by Governor Wächter, the Military Board, the UCC and the soldiers themselves, led to two orders from Himmler for their disbandment. The first dated 22 April 1944,[144] was not carried out, causing a second to be issued dated 9 June 1944.[145] It directed that both regiments be released from the *Ordnungspolizei* and made an integral part of Waffen-SS. Following that, came the long overdue liquidation. The transfer to the Galician Division, for which they had originally enlisted, then took place. Eight days later, on 17 June, a report was sent by telex to the *Chef der Ordnungspolizei* detailing the disbandment arrangements for the German personnel, vehicles and equipment.[146] As the Ukrainian soldiers in both units, those especially of the 4th Regiment, had had recent combat experience, several were immediately incorporated into the 29th, 30th and 31st regiments and the 14th *Feld Ersatz Bataillon*. [147]The rest were given over to the charge of *Waffen-Sturmbannführer* Pobihushtschyi for retraining.[148]

Ironically, the last unit to be absorbed was *Schützmannschafts-Bataillon* 204 following the arrival at Heidelager of Guard Battalion 5 that was sent to relieve it. A subsequent order dated 20 June 1944, was issued to this effect and read:

> As of 20.6.44 *Schutz* Batl. 204 is dissolved. Those men still required by the commander of the troop training area Heidelager, will, until the final transfer to the 14th Gal. Div. be attached to the 5th *Wach* Btl.[149]

Consequently, approximately 250 German-speaking enlisted men joined the Division[150] while the officers and NCOs were transferred to *Schützmannschafts-Bataillon* 207[151] based at Miechow.

In mid-June, as deployment drew ever closer, at Wächter's behest *Generalfeldmarschall* Model sent a telegram inviting *SS-Brigadeführer* Freitag, his Operations Officer *Major* Heike and adjutants, to the HQ of Army Group North Ukraine for talks on the Galician Division's future utilisation. Freitag and his entourage left at once for L'viv, where they met firstly with Governor Wächter. In recent discussions with some of his closest, like-minded German associates, he had already given vent to his grave misgivings about the suitability of the former *Polizei* general as Divisional commander and expressed his anxieties at the shortage of properly motivated German NCOs within its ranks.[152]

Wächter took the opportunity to raise and elucidate on, various organisational and political problems concerning the Division. At some length, he took the opportunity to convey to Freitag the possible political ramifications for the Ukrainians of its successful combat deployment. *SS-Standartenführer* Günter d'Alquen[153] who was also present, then gave details of operation *Skorpion* (Scorpion). It was a propaganda campaign, to be launched under d'Alquen's direction on the Galician front, aimed at encouraging the desertion to the Germans of Ukrainians serving in the Red Army. To support this initiative, Freitag was informed that the Division was to provide a contingent of educated Ukrainians who would actively participate in the operation. A number of groups were subsequently formed and utilised in this way, apparently to good effect.[154]

From Wächter's office, Freitag and his accompanying officers moved on to Model's HQ, based in Dubliany, a suburb of the city situated directly to the north east. They had come for a conference on the Division's tactical deployment. *Generalfeldmarschall* Model, having listened to Freitag's assessment of the Division's capabilities, including its strengths and weaknesses, confirmed its allocation to the 1st *Panzer* Army under the command of *General der Panzertruppen* Erhard Raus, which was located in the Stanyslaviv region. This proved to be a most appropriate choice. By now Model's initial plans for 'operation *Schild und Schwert*' had undergone some modification[155] as had the proposed role of the Division.

By 9 June 1944, the Division was ear-marked for possible deployment, again in a reserve capacity, as part of LIX Corps, in the sector of 371st Infantry Division.[156] In accordance with that, after further consultations at his regional Corps HQ, General Raus assigned the Division to secondary positions in LIX Corps sector, near the village of Monastyrys'ka, east of Stanyslaviv. It was an arrangement that was agreeable to all parties.[157] There it would be able to gradually acclimatise to the rigours of frontline combat. Freitag notified Model of the satisfactory outcome of the meeting with General Raus before starting the return journey to Neuhammer. From there he began the preparations for the transfer, the first echelons of which were due to leave for the front fourteen days later.

In the remaining two weeks before it departed, the Division's equipment was given a final service and its vehicles painted with camouflage colours.[158] As it was now a fully operational frontline formation, it continued with large-scale manoeuvres lasting two to three days,[159] night exercises and last minute weapon training. However, some difficulties were still being experienced with communication in the vital signals section commanded by *SS-Hauptsturmführer* Wolfgang Wuttig. Few trained German radio and telephone operators were available, while many Ukrainians found it difficult to translate military communications from German into Ukrainian.[160] Later that was to hinder effective operations and place it at a distinct disadvantage when it was engaged in combat.

On 21 June, the final preparations for departure began. All three infantry regiments were given orders to leave their barracks and set up camp in a nearby forest, so that the soldiers could get accustomed to frontline conditions.[161] In the next seven days additional items of uniform, weapons and equipment, in some cases the newest and most modern examples, were issued.[162] Ammunition was distributed and *Verladung* (loading) officers appointed to supervise and direct the movement of men and matériel to the front.

Morale amongst the Ukrainian soldiers, who had heard the rumour that the Division was to be deployed on Ukrainian soil in Galicia,[163] was generally high. Many however, were anxious to return home, to defend their families from the Soviets who had already overrun most of Ukraine and parts of eastern Galicia.

Change of Plans at the Eleventh Hour

On 25 June 1944, an advance party, consisting of a group of officers from the Division's general staff, left Neuhammer for the proposed operational area in the Stanyslaviv district, to make the necessary arrangements for its arrival.

The following day, without any warning, its command received notification from the German Army High Command (OKH) that the deployment orders had been changed. Instead, it was to be assigned to the 4th *Panzer* Army which held the front east of L'viv, in the centre of the battle lines of Army Group North Ukraine, in anticipation of a major Soviet offensive in that area.[164]

A few days earlier, on 22 June 1944, symbolically the third anniversary of the German invasion of the Soviet Union, and to complement the Allied landings in Normandy,[165] the first phase of the Soviet summer offensive, known as Operation Bagration[166] had begun on the Eastern Front. The offensive had begun in Belorussia with the total destruction of the German Army Group Centre (*Heeresgruppe Mitte*).[167] The awesome size of the forces that the Soviets unleashed in that area were so great, that in a period of just twelve days, twenty-five German divisions simply disappeared, in the worst defeat ever suffered in German military history.[168]

Even before they had completed the destruction of Army Group Centre, the Soviet High Command (STAVKA) had begun massing forces in the Brody region, in preparation for the second phase. It was the L'viv – Peremyshl' Operation, later known as the L'viv – Sandomierz Operation, after the Soviets had achieved more than they originally planned. The objective was to occupy L'viv in western Ukraine, and the city of Sandomierz in Poland, thereby overrunning Galicia and the southern part of the *Generalgouvernement* (Poland).

According to a recently declassified, Soviet secret report on the operation, the First Ukrainian Front, under Marshal I.S Konev, was to undertake that offensive. Subordinated to it, including Front operational reserves, were 74 rifle divisions numbering 843,000 troops, who were grouped together as seven infantry armies, (1st, 3rd and 5th Guards, 13th, 18th, 38th and 60th armies).[169] (See Appendix IX).

Armoured and mechanised support, for what was the most powerful single Front entity in the Red Army, was provided by a total of 2,041 tanks and self-propelled guns. They were grouped together as three tank armies, 1st Guards Tank, 3rd Guard tank and 4th Tank, and two independent Cavalry Mechanised Groups named after their commanders Baranov and Sokolov. Amongst them they comprised 7 tank corps, 3 mechanised brigades, 4 separate tank brigades, 18 tank regiments, and 24 self-propelled artillery regiments.[170]

Operational support for the Front consisted of 9,797 guns and mortars (4,887 guns and 4,910 mortars – not including anti-aircraft guns[171]) grouped in 4 artillery divisions, 8 gun artillery brigades, 1 howitzer artillery brigade, 4 howitzer artillery regiments, 6 anti-tank [destroyer] brigades, 36 anti-tank artillery regiments, 19 mortar regiments, 1 mortar brigade, 4 Guards mortar brigades and 14 Guards mortar regiments.[172]

The ground forces were complemented by 2nd Air Army, which comprised 9 aviation corps, 3 aviation divisions, 4 aviation regiments and 4 separate aviation squadrons. Altogether they comprised 3246 aircraft (679 bombers, 1419 fighters, 1046 assault [ground attack] aircraft and 102 reconnaissance and spotter planes).[173]

Konev's own figures for the forces involved reveal only one significant discrepancy, and that was the number of men under his command. He cited them as numbering 1,200,000, i.e. 357,000 more than is stated in the Soviet General Staff Report.[174]

Defending the sector directly opposite the First Ukrainian Front, stretching from the Prypiat marshes to the Carpathian Mountains, was Army Group North Ukraine now under the command of *Generaloberst* Joseph Harpe.[175] It consisted of the 4th[176] and 1st *Panzer* armies[177] and the 1st Hungarian Army. Together they amounted to a total of 31 German divisions, including 4 *Panzer* and 12 Hungarian divisions or brigades.[178] Almost all were under strength, some quite significantly, the average size being between 7 and 9,000 men.

The Army Group had 181 tanks,[179] 43 within 4th *Panzer* Army, additional self-propelled guns,[180] and limited Luftwaffe support. (See Map 1 for disposition of forces as of 12 July, 1944).

There was some discrepancy over the actual fighting strengths of the German forces involved, as quoted in the previously cited Soviet General Staff report, especially with regard to armour and aircraft.[181] Notwithstanding that, according to their own calculations the Red Army in that sector enjoyed an overall superiority, outnumbering the

Germans 1.5/2 to 1, in artillery, tanks and quantity of divisions and by a ratio of 4.5/1 in aircraft, although they should be regarded as extremely conservative estimates.

Moreover, the German forces also had to contend with the considerable impact of the increasing activities of partisan units operating behind their lines, which disrupted communications and supplies to the frontline units.[182]

The position of the already depleted Army Group had deteriorated significantly since the collapse of Army Group Centre. To partially compensate for the recent loss of most of its reserves,[183] the decision was taken to divert the Galician Division to reinforce the front in the sector against which the full weight of the Soviet offensive was expected to fall.

Before returning to the HQ of Army Group North Ukraine to obtain fresh deployment orders, the Galician Division's Operations Officer, *Major* Heike, informed Governor Wächter of the peremptory decision by the OKH to redeploy it, at short notice, in a different sector. Wächter was alarmed at the possible consequences of the new orders, which at a single stroke negated most of the concessions that he had won for the Division, in relation to ensuring it a cautious introduction to combat. Wächter agreed with *Major* Heike that he would make urgent representations to get the orders revoked.[184]

Proceeding to the Army Group headquarters, *Major* Heike was informed that the Galician Division had now been assigned to the XIII Corps of the 4th *Panzer* Army. It was established, in position, in the Brody district 96kms east of L'viv. On arrival, it was to occupy a secondary defensive line and as far as possible continue with its battle training.[185]

The requests to rescind the standing orders met with some sympathy from the Army Group's staff. However, after recent developments on the eastern front, they were not prepared to grant the Galician Division any special dispensation. Its utilisation, in the dire military situation, took precedence over its propaganda value, in terms of potential long-term political developments. Under those circumstances all attempts by Governor Wächter and the Division's representatives to alter the decision inevitably resulted in failure.

In the meantime, on 28 June, orders were given for the bulk of the newly redesignated 14th *Waffen-Grenadier-Division der SS (galizische* Nr. 1*)*[186] to entrain for the Eastern Front. As it relied heavily on draught-horses for its transportation and supply vehicles,[187] the first unit to leave was the veterinary company, under the command of *SS-Sturmbannführer* Dr Kopp, along with its equipment and a large quantity of hay.[188] It was followed by other priority units, including the Flak *Abteilung* commanded by SS-Sturmbannführer von Kuester. *SS-Obersturmbannführer* Beyersdorff's Artillery Regiment proceeded to the Belys military railway station at Neuhammer and, oblivious of the witches' cauldron into which they were about to be thrown, boarded trains and headed east. Thereafter a further four railway transports left each day.[189]

In the wake of the Division's departure, on 15 July 1944, the Training and Reserve Regiment which consisted of about 7,000 men, was transferred temporarily to the training facility at Wandern near Frankfurt-an-der-Oder.[190] It stayed there one month, until 15 August, before finally moving to Neuhammer.[191] There it joined the personnel allocated to form the 3rd battalions of the three infantry regiments which had remained behind at the camp and the bulk of the personnel from the *Galizischen SS-Freiwilligen* Regiments 4 and 5.

To their great disappointment, another group of over 200 Ukrainian soldiers, mostly drawn from those who held administrative positions, also stayed behind having been selected to attend a five-month *Unteroffizier* (NCO) course at a Wehrmacht-run school in Laibach (Slovenia). Among this group the desire to join their companions, who had left for the front in Galicia, was so strong that they had to be kept under guard until the train arrived to transport them to the school.[192]

A New Assignment

On 30 June, after a two-day rail journey, the first echelons arrived in the new district and detrained at the station in the town of Ozhydiv, where XIII Corps had its headquarters.[193] The remaining transports followed over the course of the next few days. From Ozhydiv all arriving units proceeded generally to defined assembly areas.

The unloading of the Division's matériel took place day and night. It was interrupted several times by the sudden appearance of Soviet aircraft in the vicinity of the station, seeking a vulnerable target. As a countermeasure, along with two 3.7 cm guns from XIII Corp's Flak Rgt. 33 deployed at the station on the wagon platform, the Division's battery of 8.8 cm anti-aircraft guns and several of its 2cm cannon were installed in, or close to the rail depot. Unloading was then resumed under the protection of the guns that were able to successfully contain most of the attacks, prevent any casualties and keep the level of damage to a minimum.[194]

With the movement orders well under way, Governor Wächter summoned *SS-Brigadeführer* Freitag to attend a final meeting in L'viv. By then the Division's deployment was completely beyond his influence. Wächter could only reiterate to Freitag the significance of the forthcoming engagement, and remind him that the ultimate responsibility for its performance was in his hands.[195]

As they discussed the ramifications of the new battle orders in L'viv, *Major* Heike and his adjutant reported to the commander of XIII Corps General Artur Hauffe[196] at his HQ in Ozhydiv for a briefing on the overall situation and the new instructions for the Division's tactical deployment. In his memoirs *Major* Heike states that neither the Corps commander nor his Chief of Staff *Oberst* Kurt von Hammerstein knew anything about the as yet unblooded 14th *Waffen-Grenadier-Division der SS* (*galizische* Nr. 1). Both were dubious of its combat capabilities.[197] To make matters worse, in contrast to General Raus, they also proved to be somewhat less inclined to make any allowances for its special needs and idiosyncrasies, as a unit made up of foreign nationals.

The prospect of additional reinforcements in their sector, was however welcomed, especially since all of XIII Corp's Wehrmacht infantry divisions were at medium or minimum strength. Added to that, the Galician Division was better armed and equipped than the Corps' other regular army formations, which was a further source of encouragement.[198]

In his assessment of the situation, General Hauffe envisaged a Soviet advance on L'viv, in the event of which XIII Corps would bar the way especially in the area of Zolochiv.[199] Therefore, rather than a direct frontal attack against prepared German positions, the Soviets were expected to employ a pincer movement from the north and south of the Corps area. In that eventuality the Galician Division would be given the task of preventing any attempt at outflanking the Corps. If the German front was penetrated, it would be committed to a counter-attack to close the resultant gap, contrary to the standard German practice, when confronted with possible encirclement, of breaking up divisions into individual units and deploying them as semi-autonomous groups.

A special request was tendered that as a non-German formation, it should always be deployed as a whole unit and remain under its Divisional command.[200] Evidently, the import of this request was not fully realised by the commanding General and his staff, as later events would prove with alarming clarity.

As part of the 4th *Panzer* Army, XIII Corps held a sector of the front that included the town of Brody and the outlying areas immediately to the north, south and east. Following a previous encirclement, lasting from the end of March until mid April 1944, the Corps had successfully held out until it was relieved by a German counter-attack.[201] From mid-April until late June 1944, the Brody sector had remained quiet. This afforded the Germans the opportunity to recuperate and strengthen their positions. The frontline known as the HKL (*Hauptkampflinie,* i.e. main line of resistance) had been well developed in an engineering sense, with defences to a depth of 6–8 kms. It consisted of three to four trench lines, the first being continuous and full profile. They were connected by a dense network of communications trenches, several rows of barbed wire entanglements, anti-tank and anti-personnel minefields and the same obstructions along the probable tank axis. Mined obstacles were constructed in forest sectors, and key bridges, roads and buildings were also prepared with explosive charges for demolition.[202] More importantly, work began on building a static defensive line in its rear area, known as the Prinz Eugen *Stellung* (Prince Eugen defence position). Within it the Galician Division was ordered to occupy the so-called 'Rudolf Position' and having done so, continued with the construction of the defensive installations and emplacements.[203]

In July 1944, XIII Corps consisted of:

A headquarters unit, based in Ozhydiv with a commanding general and his staff, support, rear echelon and supply services,[204] together with attached Corps artillery group, anti-tank, and pioneer units,[205] [total strength 555[206/207]] and the following infantry units:

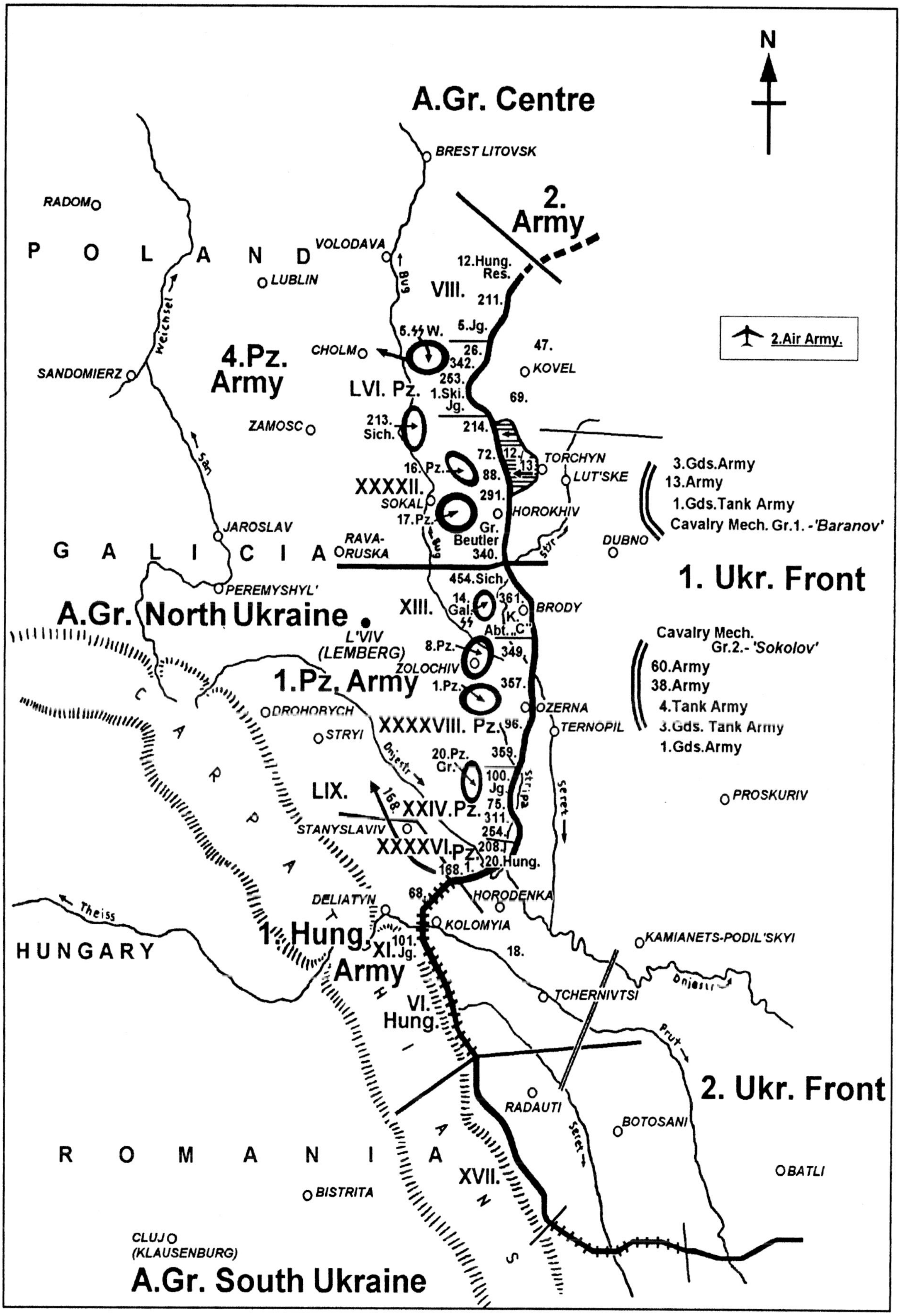

Map 1 Disposition of Army Group North Ukraine on 12 July 1944

454th Security Division: total strength 5,929[208] commanded by *Generalmajor* Johannes Nettwig that was in position on the Corps' left flank north of Stanyslavchyk.

361st Infantry Division: total strength 10,131[209] under Knights Cross holder *Generalmajor* Gerhard Lindemann which was in the centre of the Corps' lines, west of Brody.

Korpsabteilung C:[210] total strength 11,312[211] under the command of *Generalmajor* Wolfgang Lange composed of the 183rd, 217th, and 339th divisional groups, (each at approximately regimental strength) which held the front around Boratyn and Hai Starobridski.

Later, the 349th Infantry Division, total strength 10,588[212], commanded by Knights Cross holder *Generalleutnant* Otto Lasch, was attached to the Corps and covered its right flank near Shyshkivtsi.

These units were augmented by the assault guns of *Sturmgeschutz*-Brigade 249, and II./Flak Rgt. 33 for anti-aircraft support which was added to the Corps strength at the beginning of July.[213]

Lastly, there were the remaining garrison forces within the city of Brody itself which comprised the remnants of three infantry battalions with a combined strength of 743 men,[214] *Sicherheit* Battalion Bauer[215] and elements of the 361st Infantry Division including a *Panzerjäger* platoon[216] that altogether amounted to a further 1,352 men.

With the addition of the 15,299 men of the 14th *Waffen-Grenadier-Division der SS* (*galizische* Nr.1) which was designated as the Corps tactical reserve, XIII Corp's total theoretical paper strength stood at approximately 55,100 men of which about 43,175 (including 11,000 from the Galician Division) were actually deployed in the field.[217] On XIII Corp's left was LVI *Panzerkorps* (4th *Panzer* Army) while on the right was LVIII *Panzerkorps* (1st *Panzer* Army) both of which had infantry divisions manning their fronts.

Based on information obtained from reconnaissance reports and the interrogation of Red Army prisoners, XIII Corps command anticipated an attack in its sector beginning in mid-July.

No further reinforcements were available to the Corps. Any attack would have to be repulsed with minimal armoured support, as the whole of the 4th *Panzer* Army had fewer than 50 operational tanks within its entire sector. Their effectiveness was limited as they suffered from a crippling shortage of fuel.[218] Likewise, critical air support would also be largely absent, as much of the Luftwaffe had been diverted from the Eastern Front. They had to cope with the Allied landings in Normandy and increasingly heavy British and American bombing raids on German cities and industrial targets.

So as to leave no doubt about the realities of the situation, in his command briefing, General Hauffe revealed that the latest intelligence reports indicated massively unequal odds in terms of the known ratio of enemy to friendly forces in the vicinity of his weakened corps. That would in all probability render it inadequate for the task that it had been assigned.[219]

By the end of the first week in July the last rail transports had arrived, along with *SS-Brigadeführer* Freitag, who came to the district by car. Altogether, of the 15,299 men serving with the *14. Waffen-Grenadier-Division der SS* (*galizische* Nr. 1) (consisting of 346 officers: 1,131 NCOs, and 13,822 enlisted men),[220] approximately 11,000 deployed at Brody.[221] Of the officers, about 150 were Ukrainian.[222] Freitag reported the arrival of all the Division's operational and administrative forces to the necessary authorities. After that its general staff allocated positions to individual sections which took up their places and began digging in (see map for location of units).

The terrain in the sector that XIII Corps was defending, was mostly flat, with the exception of the hills of Iaseniv and Pidhirtsi which were cut by the Seret and Buh river valleys. The soil was mainly rich loam that quickly became soaked during rainy periods. The area was heavily forested, with small, populated points, many situated in hollows, and punctuated with occasional swampy meadows. The abundance of forests and wooded groves provided ample natural cover, especially from the air. Moreover the region had the additional benefit of further natural obstacles formed by three rivers, the Seret, the Styr and the lower reaches of the Buh. The road network was well developed. However, the predominantly dirt roads became difficult to traverse after rain, especially for wheeled transport.

The Galician Division held a line between 10–12 kms from the HKL, approximately 36 kms in length, running from SW of Stanyslavchyk in the north, to a point SE of Iaseniv close to the Seret river in the south (see Map 2). Its three infantry regiments were placed in a linear disposition. *Waffen-Grenadier-Regiment* 31[223] (hereafter WGR 31)

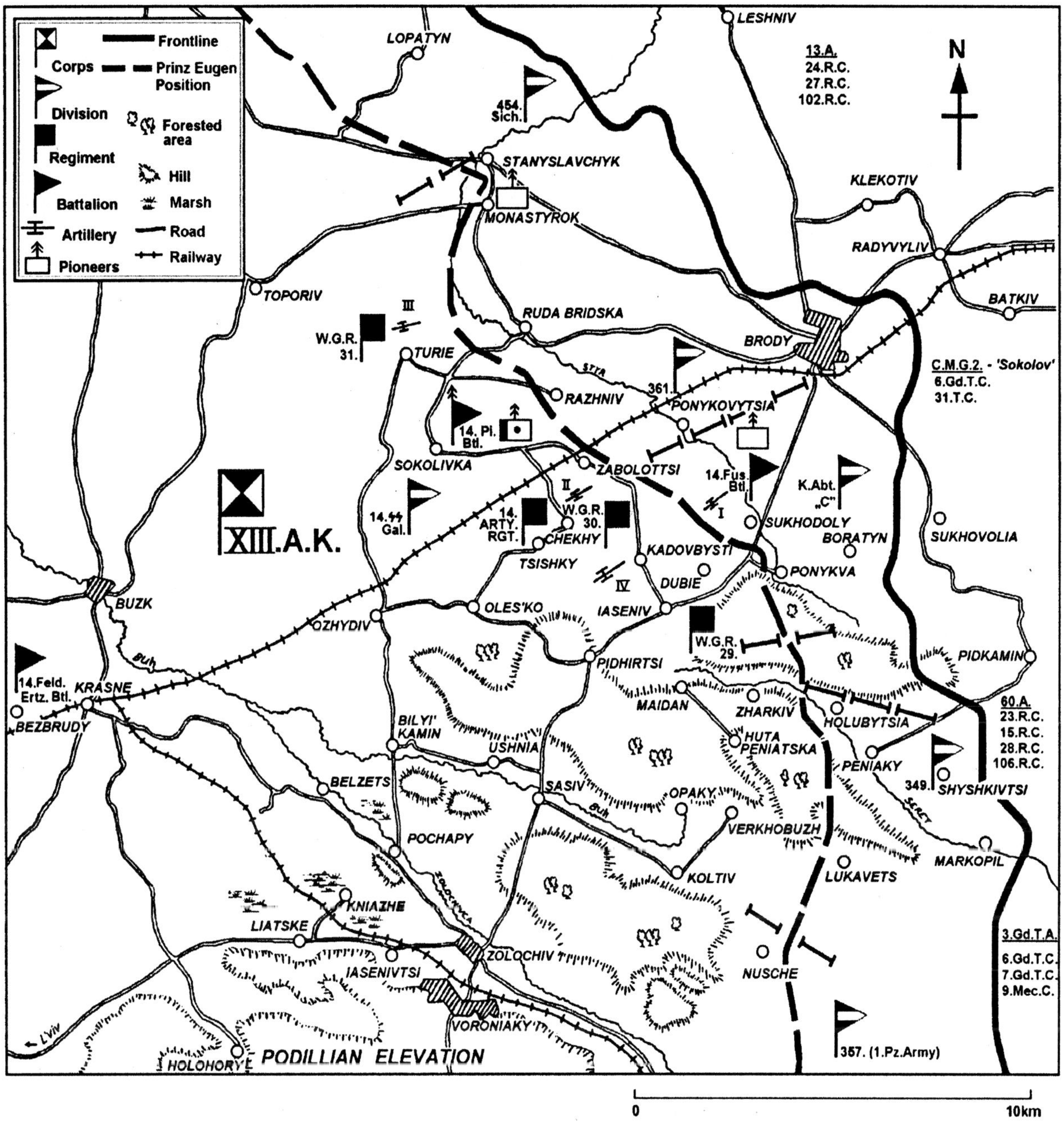

Map 2 Disposition of 14th W.-SS Div. Gal. with XIII Corps, 12 July 1944

supported by the 3rd Artillery Battalion was based in the area of Turie and assigned the northern flank. In position, covering the centre, near the village of Chekhy was WGR 30[224] supported by the 2nd Artillery Battalion. WGR 29,[225] together with elements of the *Panzerjäger* company,[226] took up position on the southern flank beside the village of Iaseniv.

The Division's headquarters were situated in the rear of the three infantry regiments, between Sokolivka and Ozhydiv, as were its supply and support units. The command post of the artillery battalion was established nearby in the vicinity of the village of Tsishky, a short distance from the 4th (Heavy) Artillery Battalion. Meanwhile, the flak batteries were deployed in defence of strategic positions according to the capabilities of their weapons.

The most forward unit was the Fusilier Battalion[227] that occupied a position in front of the Division's main line near Sukhodoly, east of the Styr River. This served as an intelligence unit, establishing observation points to monitor Soviet activities.[228] Situated just behind the battalion, to provide it with covering support was the 1st Artillery Battalion.

Bivouacked in the forest just outside Sokolivka, the Pioneer Battalion was assigned the task of felling trees and preparing materials for the other sections that had been ordered to build bunkers, trenches, gun positions and fortifications.[229]

The 14th *Feld Ersatz Bataillon* commanded by *SS-Hauptsturmführer* Kleinow was one of the last units to arrive on 7 July. It was stationed furthest to the rear, some 20kms behind the Division's positions. Its four companies were located in the proximity of Krasne, in the villages of Kutkir, where there were two companies, and in Kuduriawci and Bezbrody where they continued with their training.[230]

As the Division occupied its sector, its German command staff was confronted by the acknowledged risks associated with using it on home territory. Because of previous experiences with Ukrainian troops, the possibility of desertion to the ubiquitous UPA units, which were known to be active in the area, was considered to be a very real threat. That was more so because of the recent reoccupation of parts of eastern Galicia by the Soviets.[231] There were also concerns about its employment in an area populated by both Ukrainians and Poles.

Those anxieties were initially partly obviated by the fact that, by order of the Corps command, billeting in villages of operational units was strictly forbidden, because of attacks from Soviet aircraft. It required all units to set up quarters in wooded areas nearby. For the first two or three days contact with the population was also forbidden. Later that was relaxed and the soldiers quickly mingled with the local Ukrainian civilian population who referred to them as 'our boys'.[232]

Cordial relations with the civilians engendered a number of benefits and enabled many to supplement their rations with food willingly provided by the villagers. Others, not wishing to place any further burden on the local population, chose instead to augment their dietary requirements by 'fishing' with hand-grenades in the nearby rivers.[233]

In contrast, to meet their own supply needs, XIII Corp's German units in the area formed 'requisitioning detachments' that forcibly procured cattle, pigs, sheep, grain and horses from the peasants, in exchange for worthless government bonds. That left them with very little. Understandably that gave rise to frictions with the Ukrainian soldiers who, upon learning of the seizures, often intervened with their weapons on behalf of the peasants.[234] Thereafter, to avoid difficulties, further necessary requisitioning was undertaken with the assistance of the Galician Division.[235]

While contact with the local population did not result in the large-scale desertions that the Germans had feared,[236] it did facilitate the opening of communications between the local UPA units[237] and almost all the Division's sub-units. It led to unofficial co-operation between the two forces. For its part the UPA was able to furnish the Division with intelligence information regarding the strengths, dispositions and activities of the Red Army forces in the regions they had already occupied. In return, the Division undertook the unauthorised provision of quantities of weapons, ammunition, supplies and uniforms to the UPA. They even managed to undertake limited weapons training sessions with the insurgent personnel.[238] The Division also recruited limited numbers of young men in the area who had no military training but whom the UPA had instructed to join. It was an attempt to thwart the Soviet policy of conscripting all able-bodied men in areas which they had re-occupied and sending them into battle with little, if any, training.[239] A *Waffen-Unterscharführer* serving with WGR 29 recalled:

> 'On 2 July 1944 at 11.30am we, i.e. staff company WGR 29, entered the village of Iaseniv situated about 15kms south west of Brody which had become an important transport and communications centre for the German armies fighting in Ukraine. As a former member of *Prosvita* ('Enlightenment') I had already visited the region in 1942–43 and had made many friends in the village. The population greeted us warmly and made us feel at home. In almost every house in the village you could find an UPA member. They were simple village boys, mostly farmers sons, poorly trained and without ammunition, equipped mostly with revolvers.
>
> 'The front was quiet for the first couple of weeks after our arrival, during which our two *Unteroffiziere* (NCOs) Krasij and Smyk used every spare minute to train the UPA recruits. At that time an [unofficial] agreement was reached between the Division and the local population whereby all the young men in the area with any sort of military training would join the UPA, while those without training were to join the division.

On a single day 120 volunteers were registered at the HQ of the 29th Regiment and transported to the Reserve Battalion at Krasne for training."[240]

Throughout the first week in July the Division continued to establish itself within the so-called Rudolf Position that together with the *Lange-Riegel* (Long Bolt) position, formed part of the Prinz Eugen *Stellung*. All units were kept busy with a variety of tasks associated with its envisaged role of defending a static defensive line. Anti-tank obstacles were erected and concealed. Firing positions for guns of all sizes and calibres were selected and cleared and infantry support weapons sited. The signals units laid telephone lines to regimental HQs. The pioneers placed barbed-wire barricades and laid minefields in front of the prepared positions. To avoid detection, at every opportunity supply work was carried out at night.

From 6 July the Army Group had expected the Soviet attack to begin and consequently on that day all units of the XIII Corps were put on a state of alert[241] giving fresh impetus to the work.

Regular reconnaissance missions were undertaken by small groups from all three infantry regiments. They served the dual purpose of assisting the Divisional command with establishing the location, strength and intentions of the enemy forces opposite, while at the same time enabling the Ukrainian soldiers to obtain battle training under frontline conditions.

As soon as it was practical the heavy artillery battery, under the command of *Waffen-Sturmbannführer* Palienko, was brought into action in support of the Corps units which were holding the frontline. In doing so they gained valuable experience.

To improve their own occupied positions and determine the composition and strength of the German forces, the 1st Ukrainian Front's headquarters planned its own *Razviedka boem* (reconnaissance-in-force). By the second week in July, that had translated into a noticeable increase in terms of Soviet air reconnaissance and long range artillery fire. Such activities augured an imminent offensive. Advance patrols and attack groups infiltrated the German lines, sometimes to a depth of several kilometres, resulting in the outbreak of skirmishes, some of which involved the forward units of the Division.

Significantly, within XIII Corp's sector, based on available intelligence information in the days proceeding the Soviet offensive, its Divisions repeatedly reported to the Corps' HQ that they did not expect to find themselves facing the main thrust of the assault. Instead, they held up a large scale holding attack on their section of the front.[242]

L'viv, February 1944. Whilst waiting at the railway station in L'viv en route to the front, part of Kampfgruppe *Beyersdorff was asked to parade though the streets of L'viv to boost the morale of the inhabitants. Here an officer on horseback leads the column from the* Kampfgruppe, *while a second mounted officer follows at the rear.*

The column proceeds through the snow-covered streets of L'viv. Pictures taken on the same occasion have appeared in other publications incorrectly captioned as showing members of the Ehrenkompanie *(honour company) returning from, or going to, the funeral of Dr Otto Bauer. Unlike the soldiers in the photograph who are wearing combat uniforms identifiable by the presence of items such as gas mask canisters, entrenching tools and* Zeltbahns *(reversible tent quarters that could be worn poncho-style), members of the* Ehrenkompanie *wore parade uniforms from which these items were absent.*

The incorrect positioning of the Divisional arm shield on the lower right arm of the soldiers of the Kampfgruppe occurred by default rather than design since they were hastily issued and affixed immediately prior to departure.

March 1944, Sverkha, on the Buh river. Action against partisans. A machine-gun group from Kampfgruppe *Beyersdorff at the ready. Widely-circulated contemporary photographs demonstrate that some elements of the group were issued with reversible winter clothing seen being worn here, only after their arrival in the field in February 1944.*

March 1944, Sverkha, on the Buh river. Action against partisans. A machine-gun group from Kampfgruppe *Beyersdorff patrol in front of the wire emplacements.*

Unidentified Ukrainian officer in winter clothing at the entrance to one of the static underground bunker positions, Sverkha, on the Buh river, March 1944, Kampfgruppe *Beyersdorff*.

March 1944, Kadlubyska, in the province of Polissia. Unidentified German officer and four NCOs officiate at the funeral of an Ukrainian member of Kampfgruppe *Beyersdorff, who originated from the town of Drohobych.*

Grave of Waffen-Untersturmführer *Bohdan Sobolewsky, from* Kampfgruppe *Beyersdorff, who shot himself just before the group's departure upon learning members of his company had illegally appropriated food from the local inhabitants.*

March 1944, Ukrainians soldiers dressed in winter greatcoats on active duty in the Bilgorajschyna district.

Anti-partisan action in the region of Hrubeshivshchyna-Cholmshchyna. Elements of the 4th Regiment in action, winter 1943/44.

In April 1944, Governor Wächter visited one company of Galizischen SS-Freiwilligen *Regiment 4 based in the Kaminka Strumilova district to witness the bestowal of the Iron Cross 2nd Class to 24 men, for their bravery in combat with the Red Army. This picture of Governor Wächter with Wasyl Wykluk and Wasyl Bilecky – two of four of the Ukrainian* Waffen-Grenadiers *who received the Iron Cross 2nd Class, featured in the Divisional newspaper* Do Peremohy.

Eight of the group with their awards; the four NCOs on the left are German and the four Waffen-Grenadiers *on the right are Ukrainian.*

Governor Wächter (white lapels on great coat) and other dignitaries follow behind the coffins of Roman Andriichuk and Oleksa Bobak, both members of Galizischen SS-Freiwilligen *Regiment 4, killed on 23 February 1944 at Huta Peniatska.*

The burial at the Heldenfriedhof, *Brody, on 2 March, 1944, was accompanied by priests administering the appropriate religious rites.*

Governor Wächter and Alfred Bisanz (bending over in the back of the car wearing a black greatcoat), arrive at Neuhammer for an inspection April 1944.

Training with an 88mm gun in an anti-aircraft role at Neuhammer. The crews for these highly-prized guns were often selected from university graduates.

A group of Ukrainians celebrate Easter at Neuhammer 1944. The Divisional armshield is just visible having been incorporated into the tapestry in the centre of the decorations.

Neuhammer, April 1944, discussion of exercises. From left: Waffen-Unterscharführer *Parfeniuk,* Waffen-Unterscharführer *Kuchar,* Waffen-Unterscharführer *Biletchko,* Waffen-Hauptsturmführer *Evhen Nikitin,* Waffen-Untersturmführer *Lubomyr Ortynskyj, not known.*

Sharpshooting and camouflage techniques were both featured in the training programme. In the upper picture an older volunteer practices both.

Lunch in the field for Waffen-Untersturmführer *Anton Dyhdalewysch (left) (CO, 3rd Coy., Pioneer Btl.) and* Waffen-Unterscharführer *Klufas (right), Neuhammer, April 1944.*

The Pioneer Battalion was equipped with Schwimmwagens, *bicycles and horses for speed of movement. Three Ukrainian NCOs with SS-*Sturmbannführer *Remberger's* Swimmwagen *(note rare curved perspex windscreen). Neuhammer, April 1944.*

The 3rd Platoon of the 3rd Company of the Pioneer Battalion was equipped with bicycles and horses to facilitate rapid movement. Neuhammer, April 1944.

Two NCOs from the 3rd Company of the Pioneer Battalion on horseback. Neuhammer, April 1944.

Neuhammer, 14 April 1944, Waffen-Untersturmführer *Dyhdalewysch with his NCOs from the 3rd Company, Pioneer Battalion. From third from left: Bentzal, Kaczmarchuk, Dyhdalewysch. Wilshynsky (partly hidden); on Dyhdalewysch's left, at the front, Bohdan Kutny. Dyhdalewysch later perished during the Battle of Brody when the Swimmwagen in which he was travelling took a direct hit from a Soviet tank in the vicinity of Pidhirtsi.*

Ukrainian candidates at the Non-commissioned Officers School at Lauenburg, Spring 1944.

At the rifle range, the Non-commissioned Officers School, Lauenburg, Spring 1944.

Group of Ukrainians with their instructor, Lauenburg, Spring 1944.

Freitag, by now a full SS-Brigadeführer und Generalmajor der Waffen-SS, *inspects the Division at Neuhammer prior to the bestowal of awards.*

Waffen-Obersturmführer *Roman Levycky receives a decoration from the Divisional commander at Neuhammer.*

Heidelager, April/May 1944. Group from Schützmannschafts-Btl. *204, outside barrack 'Sorgenkind'. Sitting: first two from left not known, third from left* Hauptmann *Wasyl Tatarskyj,* Hauptmann *Jaroslav Poterejko, fifth and sixth not known,* Feldwebel *Laba, Pylyp,* Unterscharführer *Repola; first row: (first three not known), Hrynevych, Hnatkiw, Chura, Nestor, Kopcha, Pryshlak, Kucan, Kvichko; second row:* Unterscharführer *Shashkevych,* Unterscharführer *Kotylo,* Feldwebel *O. Horodyskyj,* Feldwebel *A Hawirko,* Unterscharführer *Bachurskyj,* Unterscharführer *Lach, German* Feldwebel *Held,* Unterscharführer *Hubach.*

Major *Hennesen, battalion commander, gives the last salute; immediately behind him and to his right is* Hauptmann *W.Tatarskyj, and Hauptmann Y. Poterejko (peaked cap). April/May 1944, at Heidelager.*

Service commemorating President Symon Petlura and Colonel Evhen Konovalets. Rev. Hauptmann *J. Markevych; conducting the singers is Orest Horodyskyj. April/May 1944, at Heidelager.*

May 1944, en route *from Neuhammer to the Officers School at Kienschlag, two Ukrainians entertain their comrades by playing* banduras. *Left to right: Volodymyr Jurkewytsch, Jaroslav Babuniak, (looking on) Roman Yanchyshyn.*

The Galician Division's Fieseler Storch *light reconnaissance aeroplane, later used to good effect in mountainous terrain during anti-partisan operations.*

June 1944, Neuhammer, evening concert for Wächter and the Military Board in the officers' mess. Left to right: not known, Paliiv, Wächter, Freitag, Bisanz, Heike.

June 1944. Wächter speaks to the Division's officers during a visit to the Division. Left to right: Governor Wächter (speaking at the podium), Waffen-Hauptsturmführer *Dmytro Paliiv,* SS-Brigadeführer *Freitag, Oberst Bisanz, not known,* Major *Heike.*

Preparation for weapons inspection at Neuhammer, April 1944; Waffen-Unterscharführers *Kutny (left) and Bardal.*

General von Loeper, Freitag and the commander of the Neuhammer camp.

Commander of WGR 29, SS-Obersturmbannführer *Freidrich Dern and two unidentified German* SS-Sturmbannführers *at the horses stalls, Neuhammer.*

Flamethrower demonstration during exercises at the 12th Kriegs-Reserve-Junker-Lehrgang an der SS-Pz.Gren.Schule *Kienschlag, 15 May-9 September 1944. A total of 101 Ukrainians successfully graduated from this course.*

Unidentified Ukrainian Waffen-Untersturmführer *sitting in a* Swimmwagen *at Neuhammer. The Divisional lion device can be seen just below the windscreen.*

Waffen-Obersturmführer *Petro Markevych, commander of 8/II/WGR 30, with members of his company. Markevych was subsequently wounded and captured by the Soviets at Brody.*

At 19.00hrs in the evening of 16 May 1944, the Reichsführer-SS arrived at Neuhammer to inspect the Galician Division. Himmler greets senior members of the Division's staff beneath a portrait of Field-Marshal von Hindenberg. Left to right: Paliiv (standing beside the microphone) unknown, Himmler, Freitag.

Shortly after his arrival, Himmler addressed the Division's officers. Paliiv translated for the benefit of the Ukrainians who were present, sentence by sentence.

The following day, on 17 May, Himmler watched field exercises. In Freitag's car – Himmler in the front, Freitag in the back, wearing light overcoat.

From left to right: Major *Heike (here wearing the uniform of a* SS-Sturmbannführer*), Governor Wächter,* Reichsführer-SS *Himmler,* SS-Brigadeführer *Freitag.*

Pointing, CO WGR 31, SS-Obersturmbannführer *Paul Herms, explains the exercise to Himmler. To the left of Herms, at the back, wearing an army belt, is the commander of the Pioneer Battalion,* SS-Sturmbannführer *Josef Remberger.*

Himmler reviewing exercises. Left to right: (adjusting binoculars) Himmler, Freitag, Herms.

During the visit, Himmler spoke with members of the Division of all ranks and openly solicited their comments.

Himmler and Freitag inspect the troops. 17 May 1944.

The 'Triumvirate' – Freitag, Himmler, Wächter.

Himmler and a proud-looking Wächter reviewing a parade of the Division's units.

Himmler and Wächter reviewing a parade of the Division's units. 17 May 1944.

During 3-5 June 1944, a delegation comprising members of the Military Board, the Ukrainian Central Committee and parents of the Division's soldiers visited Neuhammer. Here Waffen-Hauptsturmführer *Paliiv instructs the Ukrainian officers with reference to the exercises.*

The same visit. The Divisional commander, SS-Brigadeführer *Freitag, is in the centre. The Divisional vehicle emblem of a golden rampant lion and three crowns is clearly visible on the car. 3-5 June 1944, Neuhammer.*

SS-Feldgendarmerie Truppen *14 was responsible for internal policing duties within the Division. When on duty, members of this sub-unit wore distinctive insignia including a* Ringkragen *(gorget), on which the eagle, buttons and insignia were coated with fluorescent yellow paint and a cuff title worn of the left sleeve bearing the inscription* Feldgendarmerie *in gothic lettering. Both these items of insignia can be clearly seen on this NCO pictured with the Galician Division's band.*

Three grenadiers with their NCO from the Division's Signals Abteilung *in the field. The specialist insignia of the signals unit (a lightning bolt design) is visible on the lower left sleeve of all four men.* Waffen-Grenadier *Roman Kulynycz is on the far right of picture.*

6

Brody, Phase I: *Kessel von Brody* (Encirclement at Brody)

On 13 July the expected Soviet attack began, a day earlier than originally planned, with a minor action. XLII Corps of 4th *Panzer* Army was given permission to withdraw. Covered by strong rearguards, they withdrew from a 'bulge' toward Torchyn, in order to shorten the German line. Marshal Konev promptly followed up this move by ordering Gordov's 3rd Guards Army to pursue the retiring units. They were assisted by air formations from the 1st Guards and 5th Assault Aviation Corps who, on that day, flew 664 sorties against the withdrawing units and various strong points. The forward battalions from units of 3rd Guards Army and 13th Army, with armoured and artillery support, successfully overcame the foremost German defensive line and gained several kilometres of ground.[1]

The next day the First Ukrainian Front launched its main offensive with two blows falling in decisive sectors adjacent to XIII Corps. There the Soviets had concentrated the bulk of their infantry, cavalry and mechanised forces, to the north near Horokhiv, and to the south in the vicinity of Nusche.

In the northern sector, following the earlier successes of the forward elements, the assault began with a twofold objective. Firstly they delivered an attack along the Stoinaiv/Kaminka Strumilova axis that would envelop the German forces west of Brody, from behind. Secondly they developed the offensive towards the ultimate objective of Rava Russka.

Having successfully pierced the German frontline near Horokhiv, a part of 13th Army's infantry forces, accompanied by hundreds of tanks and aircraft, quickly began to push south west towards the northern perimeter of XIII Corps in the general direction of Radekhiv.[2]

On 14 July, sub-units of the 291st and 340th infantry divisions fell back and hastily occupied part of the Prinz Eugen *Stellung*. Simultaneously, in an attempt to restore the front, 4th *Panzer* Army counterattacked with two *Panzer* divisions hitherto held in reserve, 16th and 17th (which between them could deploy only 43 serviceable tanks) against the enemy penetration in the Horokhiv and Druzhkopil region.[3] Even with the limited support of German bombers, and before they could make any significant headway, the counter-attack was halted by vastly superior Soviet forces. The 3rd Guards Army and Putkov's 13th Army inflicted heavy personnel and equipment losses on the *Panzer* units and on the 291st and 340th infantry divisions. That left the Soviets free to continue their advance and expand on the breakthrough.[4]

Over the next three days Marshal Konev further consolidated the initial gains on the northern flank of XIII Corps. He added further infantry, mechanised and tank divisions, including Lieutenant-General Baranov's Cavalry Mechanised Group and then Colonel-General Katukov's 1st Guards Tank Army. All then poured through the gap that had been created.[5] Baranov's Cavalry Mechanised Group moved into the penetration sector under the protection of an umbrella of aircraft from 2nd Air Army. They then immediately advanced to the south-west to fulfil their assignment of capturing Kaminka Strumilova and seizing and holding a bridgehead on the western bank of the Buh river. The execution of this manoeuvre was intended to block the retreat path of XIII Corps and other German forces west of Brody, while concurrently preventing them from receiving any further reinforcement.

The Soviet Offensive in the South and Breakthrough in the Area of Sasiv–Zolochiv

Events on XIII Corps' southern flank followed a similar course. As it was there that the Galician Division was sent into action, what ensued in that sector will be related in greater detail.

On the 14 July, in conjunction with the Soviet strike on the northern flank, a second offensive thrust began at the juncture of the 1st and 4th *Panzer* armies. That had threatened to split them apart and encircle XIII Corps.

The frontal attacks, on 14 July, against the positions of *Korpsabteilung* C were successfully repulsed.[6] Further to the south the Soviet 38th and 60th armies under generals Moskalenko and Kurochkin respectively, attacked at the weakest point of the front where the 349th and the 357th infantry divisions met.[7] In preparation, an extraordinarily heavy, concentrated and continuous artillery barrage took place during the afternoon. It continued with a powerful air strike, delivered by 618 bombers and ground attack aircraft of 2nd Air Army, aimed against the main centres of defence. For 50 minutes, between 3.40pm and 4.30pm, there were more than 1,000 aircraft continually above the battlefield in 38th and 60th armies' penetration sectors.[8]

The assault that followed in 60th Army's offensive sector, led by the infantry divisions of the 15th and 23rd Rifle Corps, fell on the 349th Infantry Division. Its southernmost unit, the 913th Regiment took the brunt. Their forward positions were quickly fragmented and overrun. In the next few hours the 913th Regiment sustained what its subsequent battle report described as 'heavy losses in both men and weapons' and was reduced to a mere fraction of its original strength.[9] The 349th Infantry Division's Fusilier Battalion, initially deployed in front of the 913th Regiment, according to the same report, was 'totally destroyed'. Several of the Division's artillery batteries, sited in the vicinity, were either destroyed, or had to be abandoned, and later, still intact, fell into enemy hands. The remnants of those battered units, formed into ad hoc battlegroups, were forced to retreat to the west in violent fighting. They were under constant harassment by enemy aircraft that were active until sunset.[10]

The explanation offered for the 349th Infantry Division's failure to hold the front, as cited in its subsequent battle report, was given as follows:

Reasons for the breach:

1. Intense bombardments, constant heavy air attacks. No action from our own Luftwaffe and meagre quantity of ammunition, much too insufficient for a major counterattack.
2. Far too wide defence front (4–6 km per Btl.). Consequently total engagement of all infantry and weapons in the frontline, with scant reserves.
3. At the outset, immediate severe initial losses in men and heavy weapons.
4. Destruction of communications network.
5. The right flank was surrounded for hours, so that the positions of the right wing, despite its weak force, had to be re-shaped and lengthened.[11]

Once they had broken through the prepared German positions, the 60th and 38th armies continued their advance towards Zolochiv and Sasiv. By doing so they drove a wedge between XIII Corps and its right-hand neighbour XLVIII *Panzerkorps*.

First Counter-attack by 14th Waffen-Gren.-Div. der SS (*galizische* Nr. 1) and 1st and 8th *Panzer* Divisions Fails

The German command responded to this development by immediately committing its tactical reserves, comprising the 14th *Waffen-Grenadier-Division der SS* (*galizische* Nr. 1), and the 1st and 8th *Panzer* divisions.

In accordance with rigid German military doctrine, XIII Corps command ordered part of its reserve to reinforce the positions of the 349th Infantry Division. The Galician Division's *Waffen-Grenadier-Regiment* 30 (hereafter WGR 30) with artillery support[12] was removed from its own command. It was subordinated directly to the Corps' command. Ordered to move out of its reserve position[13] it had to assist the 349th Infantry Division in halting the penetration to the east of the village of Koltiv.[14] The rest of the Galician Division was placed on full alert but remained in place.

Because of the urgency of the order, WGR 30 had no alternative but to begin its advance. Neither the Divisional staff nor the regimental commander, *SS-Obersturmbannführer* Forstreuter, had time to familiarise themselves with the terrain in the projected area of engagement.[15] As the Regiment set out, it received its baptism of fire from enemy aircraft that strafed the marching columns, inflicting casualties, destroying vehicles and halting its advance.[16] Then came the first encounters with the disorderly groups of retreating veteran German infantry that

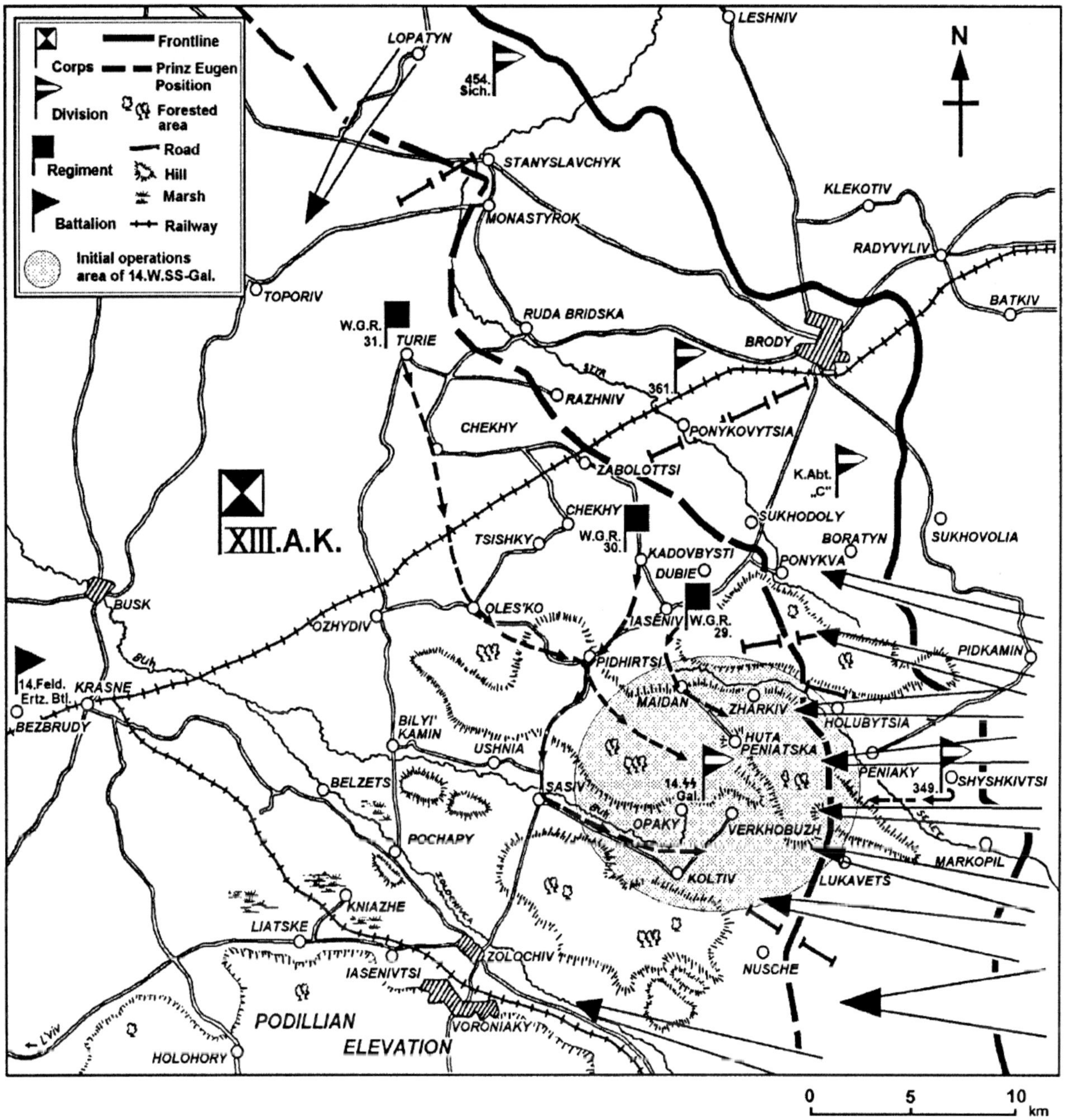

Map 3 Counter-attack by the Galician Division.

came from the shattered units of the 349th Infantry Division that had been holding the frontline. A Ukrainian platoon commander from 3/I/WGR 30, wrote:

> 'On 14 July the 30th Regiment according to orders, had to march and occupy the frontlines in the Koltiv region because of the break in the German lines by the Soviets. It was a hot day and marching was very difficult. Reaching Pidhirtsi shortly after noon, the regiment encountered heavy bombardment and aircraft attacks that continued for more than three hours prohibiting it from moving. By evening and in heavy rain the regiment started to move again. Towards morning it passed Sasiv [turned east towards Koltiv] and had to plough through German soldiers running away from the front. Some were without weapons, many shouting that the Russians were not far behind and that we should turn back, some were sitting and staring, some were even crying. This was a very demoralising example especially for our soldiers from the 'Galician Division' who had never seen real fighting and its cruelties.'[17]

Nevertheless, another Ukrainian grenadier, from the same regiment, who was present, recalled the self-belief that still pervaded as they moved into attack:

> 'It was still early in the morning when we marched through Koltiv. There were smouldering houses and corpses of civilians here and there. Worried villagers, especially women, brought us delicious curdled milk which we drank with great pleasure while marching. Right after the village the road went into wild forest. There, we were confronted by soldiers. Some were on horse wagons, others running fast on foot towards and then past us, always looking back. Some were tending their wounds while they were running. It was not a pleasant experience for us freshly arrived from our peaceful base at Neuhammer but (although I am sure not many will admit it) this was the Wehrmacht fleeing (we called them *brotboitli*[18]) not us Waffen-SS. We'll show them how to behave in the frontlines! How naive we were.'[19]

They reached the line of deployment, on the morning of 15 July at around 8.00am. In a wooded area in the vicinity of the villages of Koltiv and Lukavets, its two infantry battalions and support units came into contact with Red Army units.[20] Before the Ukrainians had even properly deployed, Soviet infantry attacked. They were supported by numerous T–34 tanks and Ilyushin ground attack planes that inflicted heavy casualties. Thereafter, WGR 30 set about a desperate attempt to close the breach.

No sooner had the battle begun than the Regiment was beset by almost exactly the same problems that the 349th Infantry Division had experienced the previous day. The extended length of the position occupied by the Regiment meant its individual companies were thinly spread. In turn that undermined their effectiveness. The essential communications links between the Regimental headquarters and battalion commanders, were virtually non-existent. Those that were available were only usable for a short period. In addition, throughout the day the front in that sector remained fluid, preventing its artillery battalion from providing effective support for the infantry. Although the insertion of the WGR 30 relieved the pressure on the weakened 349th Infantry Division, they were outnumbered three to one.[21] Armed with only light infantry support weapons and without any air cover, they were, predictably, unable to accomplish their mission. Despite that, it was to the credit of the regimental commander, *SS-Obersturmbannführer* Forstreuter and his surviving officers, that some companies although heavily depleted, did at least manage to narrow the gap. However, by doing so they suffered further significant losses in manpower and matériel.

The veteran 349th Infantry Division had itself been routed almost at once. Perhaps to mitigate its own failings, the later report from the Chief Operations Officer gave a highly critical evaluation of the Galician Division's early contribution to the fighting:

> '15 July the [349] Division was reinforced by part of the *SS-Freiwilligen Division 'Galizien'* [sic.] whose weaponry was first-class but whose fighting value was zero. In the following days, the best equipment fell into Russian [Soviet] hands because the Galicians, with only a few exceptions were unable to withstand any Russian [Soviet] attacks and represented a burden for our infantry. It must however be taken into account that this was a newly established non-German unit, not battle hardened, which was first deployed during a retreat and was therefore particularly vulnerable to the material superiority of the Russians, i.e. Soviets, in this area.'[22]

The same day, in conjunction with the attack by WGR 30, 1st *Panzer* Army (as 4th *Panzer* Army had previously done) ordered its mobile tactical reserve consisting of the 1st and 8th *Panzer* divisions to strike at the Soviet spearhead. The German command was very confident that those two powerful veteran formations would repair the broken front, and re-establish contact with XIII Corps.

The counterattack by 1st *Panzer* Division was executed with perfect smoothness and caught the 38th Army by surprise. The attack penetrated the left flank in the vicinity of Oliiv, and temporarily threw back its combat formations by 2–4 kms in several sectors. [23]

In marked contrast, a little further to the west, only a small part of the 8th *Panzer* Division actually managed to engage the enemy in the region of Kruhiv, before being forced into XIII Corp's area.[24] The Soviet General Staff report on the battle, states that air reconnaissance revealed the concentration area of the approaching tanks. To prevent any further incursions into 38th Army's flank, Konev, who recognised the threat that the German armoured formations posed, immediately ordered the 2nd Air Army commander Colonel-General S. A. Krasovskyji "to destroy the enemy tank grouping by large scale attacks from bombers and assault aircraft."[25]

In compliance with that order, 2nd Air Army delivered bombing and assault strikes against the *Panzer* divisions located north and north east of Zborov. A total of 1,848 sorties were completed during the afternoon of 15 July. 17,200 bombs of different types were dropped and 1,700 rocket missiles and 83,000 conventional missiles were launched. A total of 716 tons landed on the German armour, in an area of only 7 square kilometres.[26] As a result, 1st *Panzer* Division sustained considerable losses in both tanks and personnel, and was forced to disengage from the fighting, to withdraw and reorganise.

The brunt was borne by the 8th *Panzer* Division who fared worst. The commander of the Division had disregarded his explicit instructions, to advance on a carefully reconnoitred route through a wooded area. Instead, to save time, he moved his forces along the main Zolochiv/Zborov road, which he had been expressly forbidden to do. Caught in transit on an open road, they suffered what were described as 'devastating losses'.[27] As long columns of tanks and lorries went up in flames, all hopes evaporated of closing the gap in the front at the first attempt.[28]

In the aftermath of the combat on 14 and 15 July, in the southern sector the Soviets had achieved a small but decisive breakthrough that the Front commander Marshall Konev was determined to exploit. The armoured vanguards, followed by the infantry, pushed through the villages of Harbuziv, Perepelnyky, Iwaczow, Nusche and Trostianets' Malyi[29] until they reached the main paved road at Pluhiv. Along it the strong armoured and mechanised units advanced towards Zolochiv.[30] In so doing they formed a narrow corridor approximately 16 kms long and 6 kms wide between XIII Corps' southern flank and the hastily restored defensive positions on the northern flank of XLVIII Corps.

At the end of the day XIII Corps, together with sizeable parts of the 340th Infantry Division and the 349th Infantry Division, had become separated from their respective parent Corps.[31] They were isolated from their neighbouring Corps to both the north and south. Moreover, the failure of the counterattacks meant that German offensive capabilities had been sharply reduced.

Creation and Expansion of the 'Koltiv Corridor'/Further Attempts to Close the Gap/ Remainder of the Galician Division Committed/Withdrawal to the Prinz Eugen *Stellung*

By the morning of the 16 July, the Soviet Front command had shifted the main weight of the attack to the southern sector. There the progress of their offensive had been slower, especially in the area of 38th Army where German resistance had "succeeded in upsetting 38th Army's offensive and complicating its operations on subsequent days."[32] To accelerate the penetration of the German defensive positions, Konev had already begun moving substantial, fresh veteran armoured, and infantry reinforcements, into what became known as the Koltiv corridor. It was constantly being expanded in a west and north-westerly direction.[33] The main forces of General Pavlo Rybalko's elite 3rd Guards[34]Tank Army, (6th and 7th Guards Tank Corps and 9th Mechanised Corps) were committed into the corridor between Koltiv and Trostianets' Malyi. Ultimately over 1,000 Soviet tanks and self-propelled guns were to pass through it. The narrow sector, and lack of roads, forced the army's formations to move westwards along a single route, in a continuous compact column, in the general direction of Krasne. That placed them in an extremely vulnerable position, although it was largely offset by the presence of fighter support. It came in the form of large fighter formations that supported the push of the mobile forces into the existing penetration area.

Hoping to take advantage of the difficult Soviet situation, and fearing the arrival of large tank and mechanised forces in its rear areas, the German command continued to counterattack throughout the day. It was an attempt to liquidate the spearhead.

XIII Corps, threatened with the prospect of complete encirclement, began by strengthening the precarious position on its right flank. To achieve that, the Galician Division's two remaining regiments (WGRs 29 and 31), together with their artillery support units and other combat elements, constituting the last of its tactical reserve, were belatedly brought up (see Map 3). Under the direct command of XIII Corps staff, they received orders to abandon the defensive positions they had built and join up with the battered remains of WGR 30 in the field.[35] In the first stage, they were to move to their assembly area, south of Pidhirtsi, after which they were to advance towards the front in a south-easterly direction.[36]

On the morning of 16 July, as an added contingency measure, and because of the rapidly worsening situation in that sector, XIII Corps also ordered the creation of a blocking force composed of elements of *Korpsabteilung* C. That force, commanded by *Major* Lawatsch, was given the task of securing the line Pobocz-Maidan Peniatska-Zharkiv.[37]

Even before either of the tactical manoeuvres had been effected, by midday on 16 July it had already become apparent that, by virtue of the enemy's immense superiority, and the rapidity of the advance, the preventative measures taken to contain the Soviet thrust in the south, were in vain. Following the fall of Zolochiv, it was clear that a large-scale retreat would be necessary if XIII Corps was to have any hope of avoiding complete encirclement. Thus the units on the Corps' left flank (454th Security Division, 361st Infantry Division, and *Korpsabteilung* C) received orders to withdraw to the unmanned Prinz Eugen *Stellung*. The orders specified, unequivocally, that the withdrawal was not to begin until mid-night on 16 July by which time *Major* Lawatsch's blocking force and the Galician Division would be in position. The heavy weapons and rear echelon units were to relocate to the woods south of Ozhydiv. They were to be followed by combat elements and a rearguard that would conduct a fighting withdrawal, but only when they were under severe enemy pressure.[38]

The 349th Infantry Division, having been unable to hold the Prinz Eugen *Stellung* in its sector, was also instructed to disengage from the enemy and withdraw to the general line Koltiv-Opaky-Huta Verkouzhs'ka.[39] Retirement to new positions offered XIII Corps' command distinct advantages. The primary strategic intention behind the move was to narrow the front, thereby freeing up part of its forces. Those could then be re-grouped, and utilised in accordance with the demands of the developing situation.

The withdrawal to the section of the Prinz Eugen *Stellung,* stretching from Stanislawcyk to Wolochy, by the 361st Infantry Division, the 454th Security Division and *Korpsabteilung C.*, proceeded according to plan.[40] XIII Corps then ordered the 361st Infantry Division to form a *Kampfgruppe* from its reserve battalion (*Kampfgruppe* Haid[41]). They were to be despatched by truck to the area east of Sasiv, and then to Koltiv, to assist the 349th Infantry Division in an attack scheduled for the following morning.[42]

Further to the south, the Koltiv sector was comparatively quiet in comparison with the ferocity of the fighting of the previous two days. To a degree the sector had begun to stabilise, partly because of the reorganisation of the Soviet forces in the area.[43] During a temporary lull in the fighting, the two surviving regiments (911th and 912th) of the 349th Infantry Division, along with the remnants of its other sub-units and their heavy weapons, were able to pull back to its new line without significant difficulty.[44]

On 16 July behind the front, the progress of the Galician Division's WGRs 29 and 31, and other combat support units, was severely retarded. They were proceeding separately, by forced marches, towards Pidhirtsi. There were constant attacks from the ever-present dive-bombers and ground-attack planes. Upon reaching their staging area, without any appreciable rest or respite, both regiments were moved on, to the Front. In the evening they moved out separately for an attack.[45]

WGR 29 proceeded towards Maidan and Huta Peniatska, while WGR 31 moved further south and deployed in the vicinity of Verkouzhs'ka, Opaky and Koltiv. There the Ukrainian infantry found little evidence of the 349th Infantry Division and *Korpsabteilung* C. They were supposed to be holding the front. In several cases, individual elements of the Wehrmacht units, contrary to their explicit orders, and rather expeditiously a few hours before, had already started to leave their emplacements and retire westwards.[46] As a result, several of the Galician Division's combat units became embroiled in sporadic battles in the wooded areas around, Peniaky, Opaky and Verkouzhs'ka on the night of the 16 July, with elements of the Soviet 15th and 23rd rifle corps.

WGR 30 had lost almost half its total strength[47] in its first engagement, including all of its Ukrainian company commanders killed, wounded or missing.[48] By then it was no longer effective as a cohesive fighting unit. Consequently, it was withdrawn from the front and pulled back for reorganisation to Ruda Koltowska, behind the northern bank of the Buh river. There, as well as being used as the Divisional reserve, it was assigned the task of clearing the surrounding woods of the enemy infiltrations, and securing the main Koltiv-Sasiv road.

17/18 July: *Korpsabteilung* C Split up for Emergency Assignments/Final Attempt to Close the Gap, All Units Engaged at the Front

By dawn on 17 July, XIII Corps had moved into its new position and re-grouped its forces. *Korpsabteilung C* now occupied the centre of XIII Corps' lines, facing north east. To its left was the 361st Infantry Division (less *Kampfgruppe* Haid) at the railway line 1.5km north east of Zabolottsi. To its right the Galician Division at the forest tip, 1.5km south-west of Wolochy. While two of *Korpsabteilung* C's divisional groups held the front, Div.Gr. 339, with artillery support,[49] was withdrawn and received the order to reconnoitre in a southward direction over Bilyi Kamin' for an attack on Pochapy and Zhulychi. For that the Lawatsch blocking force was dissolved.[50]

Around midday on the 17 July, *Korpsabteilung* C was also ordered to move its Fusilier Battalion into the vicinity of Iaseniv. It had to secure the main road in that area, and counter a renewed Soviet strike towards Maidan. To the north of the sector, where the 1st and 2nd battalions of the Galician Division's WGR 29 were deployed, the brunt of the attacks was principally borne by the reinforced 68th Guards Rifle Division (of 23rd Rifle Corps) led by expendable penal battalions suitably primed with extra vodka rations. A *Waffen-Unterscharführer* recalled the attack:

'On Monday 17 July, our unit [staff company 29th Regiment] under the command of *SS-Obersturmführer* Weiss along with the 8th Heavy Weapons Company under the command of *Waffen-Obersturmführer* Yaskevych was ordered to counter-attack against the Soviet units which had virtually wiped out our 1st Battalion. For this we were armed with MG 42s, rifles, hand-grenades and *Panzerfäuste*.

'We marched through Hayi Dubecki in an easterly direction. On the way we came across wagons loaded with dead and wounded. Leaving the company under the command of *Waffen-Unterscharführer* Levko, *SS-Obersturmführer* Weiss took a group of 22 men and heading south east towards Zharkiv reached the edge of a wood where a small unit of the 1st battalion was holding out under attack and heavily outnumbered by two companies of Soviets.

'From our concealed position we watched the Soviets attack, against all military training in tight formation stumbling and shouting obscenities. With cries of U-r-r-a! the drunken ranks of the Soviets were advancing one after the other not even bothering to fall to the ground and take cover. We waited in silence until they got to within 100 metres of us and then opened fire from the flank with seven MG 42s. They were taken completely by surprise and within minutes the remaining Soviets were fleeing in panic into the wood leaving some fifty corpses on the battlefield. We advanced another 200 metres or so and tried to make contact with the unit that had been holding out. By now the sun had set and the evening air was heavy with the smell of alcohol from the dead Soviets. Our fighting unit had secured the defensive positions of the first battalion. This was the first, and last, successful engagement of the staff company unit.'[51]

Similarly, WGR 31 was locked in combat, throughout the day and the following night, with the 99th Rifle Division (23rd Rifle Corps) and elements of the 336th Rifle Division (15th Rifle Corps). They were in the vicinity of Opaky, Verkouzhs'ka and Koltiv. In both cases, the Division's Pioneer Battalion, *Panzerjäger Abteilung* and Fusilier Battalion were used to reinforce weak points, and localities in which the fierce Soviet assaults were particularly heavy. At some points the local Polish population, as had been anticipated, was sometimes hostile to the Ukrainian soldiers, as evidenced in this account:

'I was a *Waffen-Oberschütze*[52] serving with the independent *Panzerjäger* company under the command of *SS-Obersturmführer* Rader[53] which was occupying a position about 2kms east of Iaseniv. At 3 or 4pm our platoon received orders to pack up and move to a position about twenty kms to the east. We travelled on the roads and across country in our *Raupenschlepper Ost*[54] towing our anti-tank guns to the village of Huta Peniatska. Here our platoon was deployed in a cemetery as infantry support for two companies of Ukrainian fusiliers.

'At first light we came under heavy mortar fire from the Soviets. Then, with cries of OORAHH! two Red Army battalions mounted a frontal bayonet charge. When they were five hundred metres in front of us we opened fire using anti-personnel shells as very effective direct fire artillery. We continuously shortened our range, until finally we were firing over open sights. Eventually we could not fire for fear of hitting our two Ukrainian companies that counter-attacked. The Soviets stopped, started to return automatic fire and began to withdraw in disorder to a village. We opened fire again, but a few minutes later our platoon was ordered to retreat to our Company HQ in Iaseniv leaving the infantry behind. The battle had lasted about two hours.

'In the afternoon, somewhere between Huta Peniatska and Iaseniv we stopped in a clearing in the forest. While our platoon commander tried to get further instructions by radio we came under mortar fire which stopped after we shot the observer whom we located in a tree. We received instructions to proceed to the village of Maidan. We arrived there in the late afternoon and stayed there overnight. At three or four o'clock in the morning we were attacked by Soviet infantry. Our platoon was ordered to retreat while the Ukrainian infantry in the village covered our withdrawal. In the excitement the driver of my tractor caught the wheel of the gun against a tree. I ordered him to back up which he did with such force that he 'jack-knifed' and the bracket attaching the gun to the truck, which was already cracked, broke.

'I ran to the first house and asked a man in Ukrainian to give me some chains so I could attach the gun to the truck. He answered in Polish 'I don't have chains'. The same thing happened at the next two houses and I realised that it was a Polish village. When I returned empty handed to my men who had come under fire, one of them had already been killed. I was confused. My men who were farmers' sons themselves told me that there is no such thing as a farmer who doesn't have a chain, so I ran back to the first house and put a pistol to the farmer's head and said 'either I have the chains in five seconds or you are dead.' He gave me the chains and we attached the gun to the tractor with them. Unfortunately by that time (5.00am) Maidan was in Soviet hands and when we started to move through the village we received machine-gun fire from houses and windows on all sides. I ordered the men to fire *Panzerfäuste* at the houses which burst into flame and in the confusion we managed to slip through the village and back to Iaseniv where the *Panzerjäger* Company reassembled and received some food and supplies.'[55]

To the rear of the frontline, the Division's artillery batteries struggled to manoeuvre into new firing positions in support of the infantry. The earth roads, already badly damaged by bombardments, were transformed into mud, by heavy rain that began on the night of 16 July. The support and medical units experienced the same difficulties as they persevered to maintain ammunition supplies, and to evacuate the constant stream of wounded to casualty clearing stations. They too were on roads where motor vehicles and horsedrawn supply carts sank up to their axles and the horses were exhausted.[56] From its headquarters in a small wood a few kms south of Oles'ko, in the centre of its lines, the Division's staff maintained contact with all its individual sub-units and co-ordinated their movements and actions. They endeavoured to comply with the directives that it had been given in what was later described as "the most difficult and most unclear frontal sector of the Corps."[57]

Elsewhere in the south, on the 17 July, the 349th Infantry Division, reinforced with *Kampfgruppe* Haid, had been ordered to attack to retake the Prinz Eugen *Stellung* in the vicinity of Kruhiv-Peniaky. The attack began as planned, but quickly ran into strong Soviet defensive positions that were supported by heavy IS–2 heavy tanks. Although some progress was made, with only local reinforcement and minimal armoured backing from a handful of self-propelled guns and tanks,[58] the infantry units found themselves in an identical situation to the Ukrainians. They were quickly pinned down and unable to move. A strong Soviet counter-thrust captured Huta Verkouzhs'ka. The 349th Infantry Division was unable to retake it. When darkness fell on 17 July, the attack ground to a halt.[59]

Once again, XIII Corps' command had overestimated the capabilities of its forces. None had been able to achieve their objectives, in that difficult sector, where the course of the frontline was in a constant state of flux.

Following the failure of the attempt to retake control of the south-eastern most part of the Corps' area, on the night of 17 July *Korpsabteilung* C's Div. Gr. 339 was reinforced with artillery and six self-propelled guns. They were given fresh instructions. They had to make a renewed effort to seal off the area of enemy penetration in the south. Div. *Gruppe* 339 was ordered to march south until it reached Ruda Koltowska. There it was to attach itself to the 349th Infantry Division. Both units were then to attack southward to take the village of Obertasiv. They had to join with the 8th *Panzer* Division, which had reorganised and was still assumed to be striking northward, to re-establish a solid front.

Divisional *Gruppe* 339 and elements of the 349th Infantry Division managed to achieve their objective and reached their destination, the high ground north of Obertasiv, on the morning of 18 July.[60] However, the attack by the 8th *Panzer* Division, which had been placed under the command of *Generalmajor* von Mellenthin, had to be aborted when, for the second time, direct orders were disobeyed, this time by the commander of the *Panzer* regiment, thereby preventing it from reaching the target area.[61]

Simultaneously, *Korpsabteilung* C's Fusilier Battalion had received fresh orders from XIII Corps to advance from its assembly area south of Maidan, and with the support of 2 self-propelled guns, retake the village of Huta Verkouzhs'ka.[62] On its right flank were elements of the Galician Division. Their combat units were still heavily involved in trying to gain control of the forested area, and in local counterattacks, to try to eliminate the many infiltrations.

In the extremely dense woodland south of Maidan, contact between the Fusilier Battalion of *Korpsabteilung* C and elements of the Galician Division on its immediate right was soon lost.[63] The battered units of the Galician Division, which had re-committed WGR 30, were confronted by an enemy equipped with liberal quantities of ubiquitous aircraft, tanks, heavy artillery and mortars. They made little impact on the attacking Soviet forces in its area of operations. Unable to overcome far stronger opposition and following bitter close combat with heavy losses, its units were forced to break off their engagement and retreat.[64] It then received fresh orders to set up a blockade of the Iaseniv and Sasiv valleys and not to allow the enemy passage into the surrounding woodlands and XIII Corps' rear.[65] With its right flank exposed, the Fusilier Battalion of *Korpsabteilung* C found itself in an untenable position. It too fell back to Maidan under cover of darkness.[66]

Against manifestly unequal odds, XIII Corps made a last attempt to seal the gap created by the Soviet advance in the south and link up with the relief forces. It had failed. As a result the Prinz Eugen *Stellung* had to be abandoned and XIII Corps' left wing had to be bent back to form a front facing north.

General Hauffe still did not appreciate the full danger or the radically worsening operational situation. As prisoners subsequently revealed, "Many officers reported to General Hauffe (XIII Corps Commander) about his forces' situation and expressed the opinion that he should withdraw, but the general demanded that they hold out in the hope that help would arrive."[67]

The Meeting of the Soviet Pincers at Busk/Escape of Supply Units/Encirclement is Completed

At that time, alarming news arrived at the Galician Division's HQ that its supply and reserve units, stationed about 15 kms to the rear, had come under attack from the leading elements of the Soviet assault forces near Krasne. They were therefore retreating westwards. The 14th *Feld Ersatz Bataillon* managed to disengage, with minimal casualties, and hurriedly escaped ahead of the approaching tanks. They had abandoned their few heavy weapons and most of their equipment. Several of XIII Corps' other supply and support units did the same in their situation further to the rear.[68] Their comrades further to the east were not however so fortunate.

By the end of 17 July Lieutenant-General Baranov's Cavalry Mechanised Group of the northern pincer had captured Kaminka-Strumilova, deep in the rear of XIII Corps. Having dispersed an attack by two German divisions, 20th *Panzergrenadier* Division and 100th *Jäger* Division, in the area, they threw a detachment forward to the Derevliany region. There, on the 18 July, the 2nd Guards Cavalry Division (from Baranov's Group) linked up with the 71st Mechanised Brigade[69] of the 3rd Tank Army in the south, whose forces had occupied the important road junction at Busk at noon on the same day. Before maintaining its westward advance, the latter left part of its forces, i.e. 71st Mechanised Brigade, 50th Motorcycle Regiment and the 91st Independent Tank Brigade, in a strong screen along the northern bank of the Buh, from Sasiv to Derevliany, facing north and north-east. Small sub-units from those formations then occupied all of the river crossings, the important villages and towns and cut all the roads. Six days after the main Soviet offensive had begun, the encirclement of XIII Corps, for the second

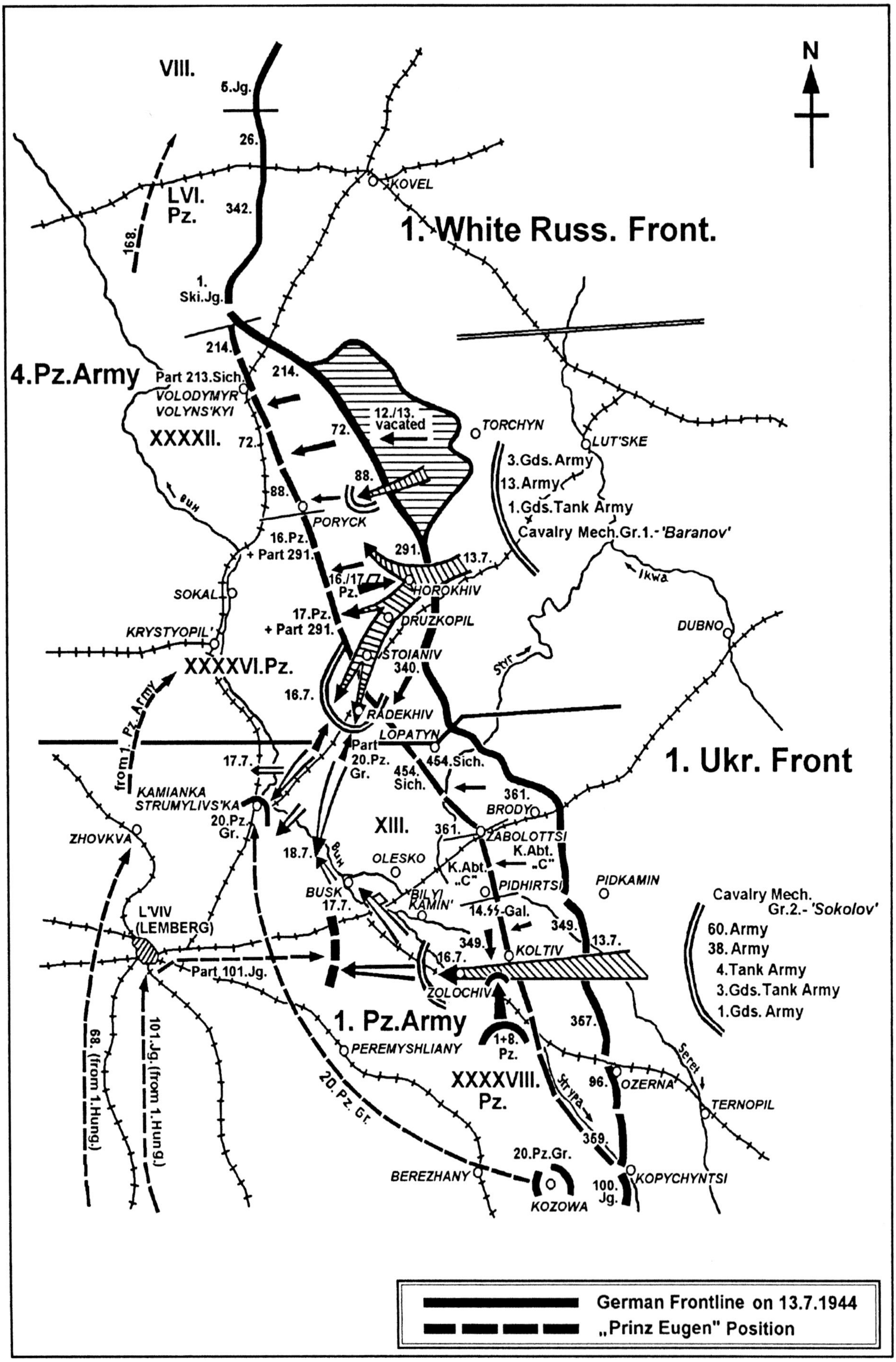

Map 4 Encirclement of XIII Corps, 13–18 July 1944

time in four months, along with a variety of smaller units[70] collectively referred to in the Soviet battle reports as the *Brody* grouping, was thus complete (see Map 4).

Deprived of their withdrawal routes, the greater part of six divisions, 454th Security Division, 361st Infantry Division, 349th Infantry Division, 340th Infantry Division, *Korpsabteilung* C, and the 14. *Waffen-Grenadier-Division der SS* (*galizische* Nr. 1) had been confirmed as having been entrapped in the *Kessel von Brody*.[71] Its external boundary ran along the general line Toporiv, Busk, Sasiv, Koltiv, Opaky and Kadovbysti.[72]

When the news of the encirclement arrived in Moscow the following day, Stalin ordered twenty shots to be fired from 224 guns in celebration.[73]

7

Brody, Phase II: The Destruction of the Entrapped Forces: 18–24 July

The Breakout Plan is Formulated/*Korpsabteilung* C Withdrawn from the Front/Breakout is Delayed

The operational encirclement and isolation of the Brody grouping from the other German forces west of the Buh, was successfully completed. As a result, Marshall Konev gave orders for his mobile forces to push on towards their strategic objectives. These were Rava Russka on the northern axis, and L'viv on the southern axis.[1] Simultaneously, to facilitate the maintenance of the offensive on the Galician capital, the 1st Ukrainian Front undertook the immediate start of the swift liquidation of the entrapped German forces. The main factor which dictated that mission was the presence of the group, which was surrounded over a large area to the south west of Brody. This required large forces to contain the group, the presence of which partly immobilised the manoeuvre capabilities of the Front's combat formations along the L'viv axis.[2] Moreover, the possibility could not be excluded that the Brody grouping could still link up with the remaining tank forces south of Zolochiv. That would have severed the base of the Soviet spearhead in the south.

The task of dismembering and eliminating the Brody group was allocated to 60th Army's forces, reinforced by the 4th Guards Tank Corps from the Front reserve, and in co-operation with a portion of the 4th Tank and 13th armies' forces. [3]

XIII Corps was surrounded in an oval-shaped pocket covering a distance of approximately 40 kms on its north-west/south-east axis, by 24 kms on its east/west axis. They were subjected to a barrage of artillery fire and air strikes by close support aircraft, from all directions. The intensive shellfire wrecked the field telephone installations and shredded telephone wires. Internal communication facilities were severely disrupted on both the Corps and divisional level, making it appreciably harder to maintain centralised command and preserve order.[4]

With all its overland supply routes severed and its retreat path to the west blocked,[5] XIII Corps only hope of avoiding complete destruction was to break out of the encirclement. General Hauffe finally agreed. Following advice, from a westward reconnaissance, against an attempt in that direction,[6] on the afternoon of 18 July, the XIII Corps command elected to try to join with the XLVIII *Panzerkorps* via a thrust to the south roughly level with the main L'viv/Zolochiv road.

To accomplish that, preliminary orders were issued for XIII Corps strongest unit, *Korpsabteilung* C, initially to take up positions on the Zahirtsi-Tsishky-Chekhy ridge north east of Khvativ, on the night of 18 July. Its two remaining divisional groups (183rd and 311th) were to hold that line until being relieved from the front by the 361st Infantry Division and the Galician Division respectively. The component units of the *Korpsabteilung* C were then to gather in the woodland on either side of the road to Bilyi Kamin' and in the Havarechyna/Horishnia area on the 19 July, in preparation for the breakout attempt which it was to lead.[7]

Meanwhile the Soviets, having been alerted to the presence of the Galician Division by virtue of the unique Waffen-SS camouflage clothing and Galician insignia worn by its personnel,[8] set about attempting to annihilate it. Having reverted to the command of its own staff,[9] on 18 July the Galician Division's area of operations extended from Iaseniv in the north to Koltiv in the south. There, on the east and south-eastern edge of the pocket all three of its depleted infantry regiments and other weakened combat units were involved in a gruelling series of defensive engagements. They faced periodic massed attacks, from three sides, consisting of heavy concentrations of well-equipped Red Army infantry backed by armour.

WGR 29, which had the highest ratio of Ukrainian combat officers,[10] was deployed in the vicinity of Iaseniv. There it came under severe pressure from a strong Soviet thrust from elements of the 102nd Rifle Corps (13th Army) with armoured support coming from the direction of Brody.[11] After penetrations in the fronts of both its I and II battalions, the Regiment was ordered to retreat to the Zahirtsi/Pidhirtsi line. The fighting was especially

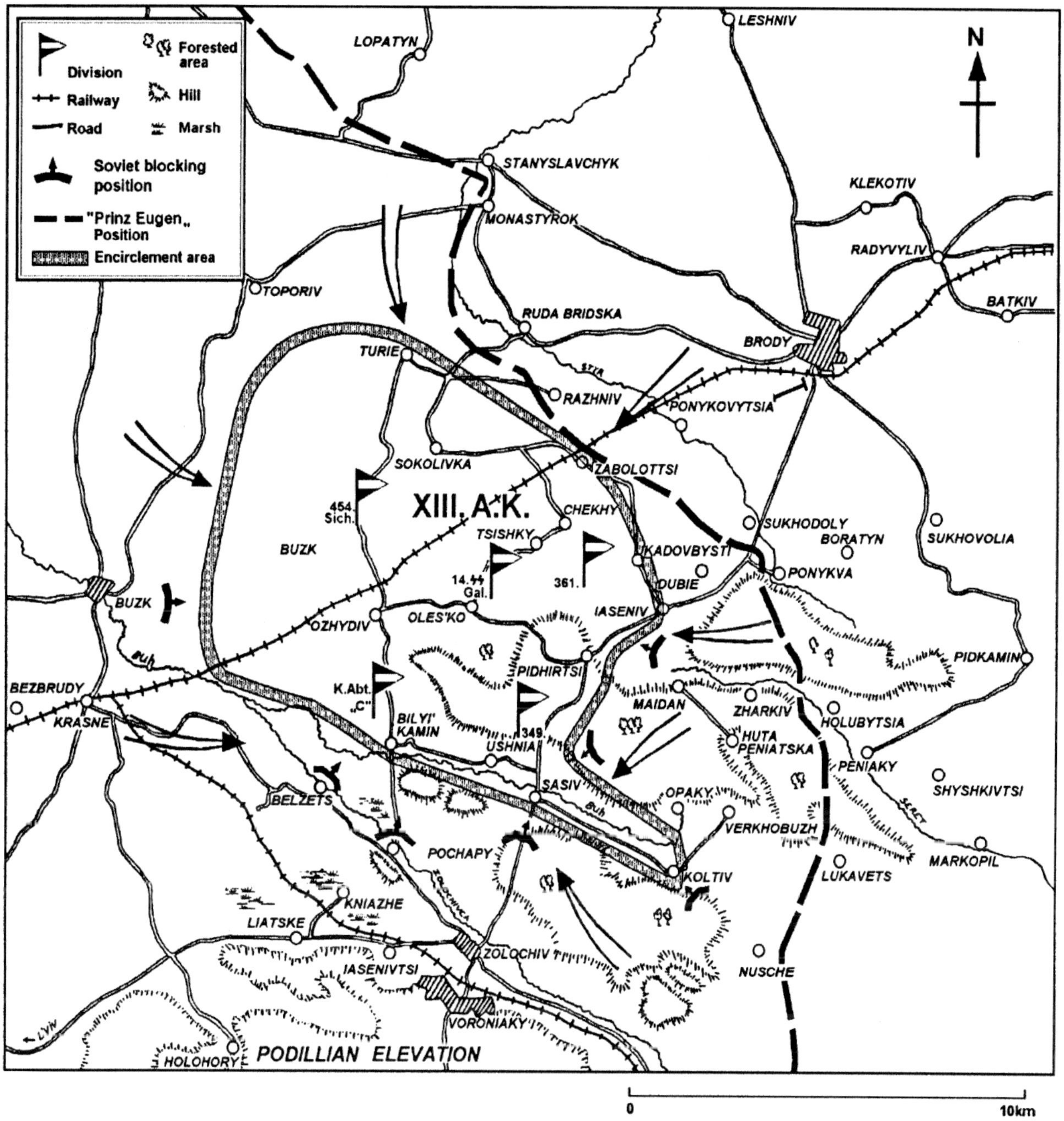

Map 5 Encirclement area of XIII Corps, 18 July 1944

heavy in the vicinity of the villages of Pidhirtsi with its commanding heights and Khvativ. Both changed hands several times.[12]

Facing south, parts of the WGRs 31 and 30 were defending the area around Ushnia and sections of the main road running from Sasiv to Koltiv, which formed the southern perimeter of the pocket.[13] Their opponents were 60th Army's 23rd Rifle Corps, 359th and 99th Rifle, and 68th Guards Rifle divisions reinforced by elements of the 336 Rifle Division (15th Rifle Corps) and 91st and 93rd independent tank brigades (from 3rd Guards Tank Army and 4th Tank Army respectively). There the fighting was equally severe. Some measure of the intensity of the combat in the area can be gauged from the fact that in the period 17–19 July the German forces defending the village of Koltiv came under attack twelve times. Soviet infantry, in regimental strength, was supported by heavy artillery and numerous tanks, in one case by thirty-five. Similarly, Sasiv where groups of Ukrainian troops were also deployed, was repeatedly assaulted, by infantry in battalion and regimental strength, on eight separate occasions.[14]

The Division's Artillery Regiment gave its full support throughout, and reinforced all local counterattacks and provided cover during retreats. Its batteries were so busily engaged that the frequent changes of position were accomplished without the assistance of horses, so that the crews had to manhandle the guns themselves.

Albeit unwittingly, in the course of the fighting the Galician Division's soldiers found themselves responsible for a number of prisoners. Tragically, some of the older captives (aged 40–45 years) were found to have been fighting against their own sons.[15] The prisoners were found to be equipped with a few automatic weapons, but apart from ammunition, most carried little or nothing else and seldom had any food except corn seeds.[16] Whenever possible those who had been forcibly conscripted into the Red Army from the local population (known as 'booty Ukrainians'[17]), were disarmed, released and allowed to return home, or simply left behind untouched.[18] The rest were taken to regimental or battalion command posts where they were passed on to the custody of the Division's military police unit for interrogation.[19] Some implored their Ukrainian captors to allow them to remain under their protection. Prisoners feared their fate, often with good reason, if they were handed over to the Germans, as illustrated in this account by a *Waffen-Unterscharführer* serving with 9/II/WGR 30:

> 'I was standing at the edge of a truck full of soldiers near the forest. To the left was a glade to which the Germans escorted between 10–20 Soviet prisoners. They were about fifty feet from us. Suddenly a shrieking begging broke out from the group of prisoners 'Kamerad, Kamerad, nicht schiessen!' But 'Kamerad', a German who stood with an automatic gun before the group paid no attention to the desperate pleadings of the prisoners. A series of shots sprayed the prisoners who collapsed, screaming and moaning. The 'Kamerad' then walked to each prisoner and shot each one to make sure they were dead. This killing of prisoners that could only be observed by those standing at the edge of the truck, angered the soldiers, especially the Ukrainians. I said aloud in German, "That's the reason why the Germans have to leave Galicia instead of being on the other side of the Urals. That's why you're losing the war'.[20]

On the night of 18 July, the first stage of the preparations for the breakout began. They involved the replacement of the elements of *Korpsabteilung* C that were to act as the spearhead, so that they could withdraw to their assembly areas. This operation coincided with renewed efforts by the designated elements of the 1st Ukrainian Front to reduce the already compressed and constantly shrinking area, via a series of concentric attacks.

In his secret after-action battle report written four months later, the commander of *Korpsabteilung* C General Lange, gave his account of the hand-over. He seemed reluctant to concede that the Ukrainians had some fighting spirit:

> '19 July 1944. The relieving of the Div.Gr. 183 [by the 361st Infantry Division] proceeded according to plan. The Div. *Gruppe*, with its attached units, had by midday [on 19] reached the woods south of Ozhydiv. At that time, the Gren.Rgt.Gr. 311 first handed over [the positions] to the 14. *SS.Freiwi.Div-Galizien* [sic.] so that the covering of the withdrawal could be carried out under pressure from the enemy which in the interim had also moved in tanks on the main Lemberg [L'viv] – Brody road.
>
> 'The increased enemy activity at that point was made more critical for the XIII Corps when the enemy met with only minimal resistance. The 14th *SS-Freiwi-Div.-Galizien* had during its first deployments shown an unusually low ability for holding position.
>
> '*As was anticipated, the Galicians in no way showed themselves to be the fanatical defenders of their homeland against Bolshevism, therefore their superior armament and equipment, could barely be brought to effect and consequently this armament found itself in the hands of a totally undisciplined, disordered mob over whom the minimal German leadership, despite their utmost efforts, could have little effect.* [Author's emphasis].
>
> 'In the afternoon the [Galician] Division also lost Pidhirtsi and Khvativ. To counter the danger within the encirclement the 311th Grenadier Regiment and *Korpsabteilung* C's Fusilier Battalion were sent to consolidate the position under orders of XIII Army Corps. In the event they did not encounter any action. The *SS-Freiwi.Div.Galizien* [sic.] retook Pidhirtsi and Khvativ with support from self-propelled guns.'[21]

In the meantime, on the morning of 19 July, at XIII Corps HQ, in the presence of General Hauffe, his Chief of Staff *Oberst* von Hammerstein issued the detailed orders for the breakout plan to the divisional Ia's of all the Corps units.[22]

According to the plan it was expected to take three days. At dawn, 3.30am, on 20 July, *Korpsabteilung* C would spearhead an attack from its position at Bilyi Kamin' in a south-westerly direction over the Buh river towards the Podillian Elevation.[23] For that purpose, *Sturmgeschütz* Brigade 249 and a battalion of the 361st Infantry Division, would be attached to it. The route involved the crossing of two rivers, as well as 15 kms of marshy ground before negotiating a heavily wooded area situated on an incline. It was thought to be the area in which an attack would be least expected and therefore offer the best chances of success.[24]

The 349th Infantry Division was to provide flank protection as the attack force moved southwards. The Galician Division, along with the 361st and 454th divisions had to form the rearguard. Those divisions located furthest to the north were ordered to remain in place and await orders to fall back. Their task was to defend their positions as long as possible and prevent any serious breach of the perimeter. Any breach would not only effectively terminate any chance of a breakout, but lead to the destruction of the entire Corps.[25]

To assist with the breakout, elements of the LVIII *Panzerkorps,* which were erroneously assumed to be holding a solid front five kilometres south of the main L'viv-Zolochiv road[26] would simultaneously strike north towards the beleaguered Corps. Only when the breakthrough was successful, and a suitable corridor was established, would the wounded, supply services and heavy weapons be evacuated, followed by the three divisions that formed the rearguard.

On 19 July, as the preparations progressed, events continued cruelly to conspire against the Ukrainian soldiers. They were entrenched to face the unabated fury of strong infantry attacks by fresh Red Army formations, some of which included women.[27] With the weakening of the perimeter area, the already hard-pressed rearguard units had to absorb additional pressure. It came primarily from 102nd Rifle Corps (162nd, 172nd rifle and 117th Guards Rifle divisions), along the northern and north eastern perimeter. Pressure also came from 23rd Rifle Corps (68th Guards, 99th and 359th rifle divisions) on the pocket's eastern and south-eastern perimeter.

Because of the high attrition rate among its forward units, the Galician Division was increasingly forced to rely upon the placement of minefields in front of its forward positions. Any such additional fortification work was, however, rendered virtually impossible during daylight because of the proximity of the enemy lines. A limited amount of such work could be undertaken at night, but that did little to deflect the full force of the attacks. Individual breaches when they occurred, could only be contained by the desperate expedient of transferring soldiers from the Division's supply and support units, which were still functioning, to emergency battle groups of mixed German/Ukrainian composition.[28]

As part of the rearguard, the Galician Division held a section of the northern perimeter running along the line of Adamy Stolpin, Perevolochna, Sokolivka, over the Brody/Krasne rail line to Tsishky.[29] North of Oles'ko, between Sokolivka and Tsishky, units of 162nd and 172nd rifle divisions of 102nd Rifle Corps were supported by large formations of Soviet T–34 tanks that joined up with other units coming from the west near Busk. Attacking from north to south the armour crossed the rail line. It made a concentrated attack towards Oles'ko, in the centre of the Galician Division's lines, and several kilometres behind its most easterly positions. To counter this outflanking manoeuvre, the Division's command hurriedly despatched the remnants of the *Panzerjäger* and hastily reorganised scratch infantry companies. The latter comprised soldiers from all branches of services armed only with *Panzerfäuste,* and together they were sent to the vicinity with orders were to hold on at all costs. The *Panzerjäger*, together with the infantry, destroyed several of the tanks at close range and drove off the rest, thus preventing a major breakthrough and temporarily averting a potential disaster.[30]

Further fierce battles were fought around the villages of Kadovbysti and Chekhy by the exhausted remains of WGRs 29 and 30. The Division was also required to shift battalions that still had less than five days' battle experience to cover weak spots in other sectors, such as Opaky. Here veteran German units were constantly struggling to contain elements of 99th and 359th rifle divisions and having to retreat.[31] With its units thus dispersed over a wide area, its dependence on field radios to transmit and receive orders and reports was all the more acute. All were in short supply and those that were available began to malfunction with overuse, or could not be used at all because of the nature of the terrain.

The difficulties in that respect were exacerbated by the fact that many of the Ukrainian communications personnel had an insufficient command of the German language to interpret, or pass on orders, and instructions, to other units. In the absence of fresh orders, individual units that had lost contact with regimental, battalion and company commands were forced to work independently, causing the Division to lose its cohesion. In several instances, soldiers sent to command posts in the rear to receive new orders, arrived only to discover that the posts had been abandoned, and then overrun by marauding groups of Soviet tanks and infantry which had infiltrated the Division's lines.[32]

WGR 31 started to disintegrate following the death of its commander *SS-Obersturmbannführer* Paul Herms, and most of his staff, north of Sasiv.[33] WGR 29 whose commander, *SS-Standartenführer* Friedrich Dern, was injured on the morning of 19 July and evacuated to Pidlyssia for treatment,[34] was in a similar predicament.

Denied the use of their aircraft because of the heavy rain and mist on that day, the Soviets constantly bombarded the Division's positions. Artillery, heavy mortars and the lethal *Katyusha* rockets[35] wrought terrible destruction, devastating entire villages within minutes and shattering the morale of the soldiers in the target area.[36] The particularly heavy casualties amongst the Ukrainian officers had an exceptionally damaging effect. Without an Ukrainian officer in command, some units which had fought bravely up to that point, lost their discipline and abandoned their positions as self preservation took over.[37] Urgent requests to regimental staffs for additional replacement German officers brought no response.[38]

The Divisional headquarters began receiving reports from some surviving unit commanders that their positions had become untenable.[39] After more than seventy-eight hours of combat with no respite, and against vastly unequal odds, the Division was weakening. They were plagued by communications problems, had lost many officers, and had few remaining rations. Ammunition was in short supply because of the excessive expenditure caused by the constant defensive actions. The 14th *Waffen-Grenadier-Division der SS* (*galizische* Nr. 1) began to show signs of collapse.

An offer of assistance, by a delegation from the UPA which arrived at the Division's HQ at that time, was declined in the interests of both parties.[40] Even had it been accepted, it is unlikely to have made any appreciable difference to its overall condition, which was deteriorating rapidly.

By the evening of 19 July, shortly before the breakout was due to commence, the situation in the Galician Division's sector had become critical as units of the Soviet's 172nd Rifle and 117th Guards Rifle divisions made a number of serious penetrations around Oles'ko, Khvativ, and Zahirtsi. Unable to stabilise the front with its own internal resources, the Division had to call upon the help of remnants of other units, principally from the 361st Infantry Division. With enormous difficulty the attacks were successfully contained and local counter-attacks organised to regain lost or strategically important ground.

The Division's commander, *SS-Brigadeführer* Freitag, received the news of those developments with growing consternation. Having already lost several key regimental, section and battalion commanders, either killed, wounded or missing, Freitag then lost his nerve. When the Corps commander General Hauffe requested a situation report, Freitag replied that he was not in a position to give one since the Division was no longer under his control. At that critical juncture, irrespective of any other consideration, he promptly resigned his command.[41] By so doing Freitag not only disassociated himself from the Galician Division, and hence part responsibility for the rearguard, but as later events would prove, he almost certainly increased his own personal chances of survival.

General Hauffe accepted Freitag's abdication. He placed the remains of the Galician Division under the commander of the 361st Infantry Division, *Generalmajor* Gerhard Lindemann, who immediately took over command of all units designated for the defensive of the Corps rearguard. Freitag was assigned to the staff of XIII Corps.

From that point on, although some larger groups were still functional, the Galician Division could no longer be considered as a unified whole. From the remnants of the individual and identifiable combat and support units that no longer existed, special battle groups were established, as they had been by all the Corps divisions. By subordinating those groups to neighbouring units, and utilising his own local reserves, with considerable skill General Lindemann managed to restore the front. That was an essential prerequisite for the successful organisation of the breakout that followed.

20 July 1944

In the early hours of 20 July 1944, the breakout finally got underway. Originally scheduled to begin at 3.30am, the time assigned for preparation was extended, mainly because of road congestion caused by the horse drawn vehicles of the Galician Division, and because the smaller tracks had become flooded due to the rain.[42]

An hour and a half later than originally planned, at 5.00am, the three assault groups formed from *Korpsabteilung* C switched to the offensive. Initially they made good progress, penetrating the first inner Soviet ring and fighting their way through Bilyi Kamin' and over the Buh river. Continuing in a southerly direction, by early afternoon elements of *Korpsabteilung* C had crossed the bridge over the Zolochivka river. They reached and secured their initial objectives, the villages of Belzets, Pochapy, and Zhulychi,[43] pushing back units of the 336th Rifle Division (of 15th Rifle Corps) in the process.[44]

Behind the leading elements, the long columns of the Corps motorised and horse-drawn train and supply vehicles together with the heavy weapons and other war matériel that the orders stipulated were to be saved, set out along the same route. Many, sometimes fatal, accidents occurred amongst the Ukrainian drivers who having received only four weeks' instruction. That was sufficient for driving light personnel cars. Subsequently they had been given three and five ton trucks, fully loaded with men and equipment, to drive.[45] Confined to the few paved roads, for fear of becoming bogged down and stuck in the marshy terrain,[46] their movement betrayed German intentions to 2nd Air Army's reconnaissance aircraft. In his after action report, General Lange once again sought to place the blame squarely on the Ukrainians. They were now under the command of General Lindemann and for the most part were operating without orders.[47] He wrote:

> 'In an inexcusable way, the numerous horse-drawn vehicles belonging to the 14. *SS.Freiwi.Div-Galizien* [sic.] moved in the direction of Bilyi Kamin' in broad daylight. Thus they revealed to the Soviets – as confirmed by s.Qu [Staff Headquarters] – the direction of the breakout and blocked all roads and paths so that all decisive troop movements were significantly hindered'.[48]

Once the direction of the planned breakout had been established, on that clear summer's day, 2nd Air Army promptly sent large assault aviation and bomber forces against the personnel and transport massing in the Bilyi Kamin/Sasiv regions. The air assault was designed to contain the breakout, prevent them from concentrating their forces and weapons at critical points, and destroy the remaining encircled group.[49]

The most recently released post-war Soviet account later estimated that between 19 and 22 July, the 2nd Air Army's formations conducted a total of 2,340 sorties, of which bombers accounted for 402, assault aircraft 1,136, and 802 by fighters, against the German positions at Brody.[50] At regular intervals the main roads, access roads, battery positions, intersections and bridges came under constant bombardment and strafing from Soviet aircraft. There was little opposition from the Luftwaffe.[51] In the vicinity of Bilyi Kamin' and Pochapy, the few operational flak batteries did their best to defend the retreating columns. One battery, of the Galician Division's flak unit, hit an estimated 27 planes on that day, until it too was put out of action.[52] Several bomber and fighter aircraft, flying at altitudes as low as 100 metres, were also brought down by rifle fire.[53] Some planes crashed amongst the troops, injuring some and killing others.[54] After each attack the wreckage of burning vehicles, dead horses and destroyed equipment rendered whole sections of roads impassable, paralysing all movement. Further casualties were caused by ammunition exploding on the trucks.

General Lange later acknowledged that, at an early stage, if all vehicles and equipment had been pushed clear of the tracks and abandoned, the chances of survival would have been considerably improved.[55] The blocked roads created chaos among the disengaging rearward portions of XIII Corps as they fell back, still fighting, from Sasiv and Oles'ko towards Ushnia and Bilyi Kamin'. The chaos put an end to their last hope of conducting an orderly retreat. In the ensuing turmoil, a number of the larger units splintered into groups of varying sizes.[56] In the absence of any definite orders or directions they sought to save themselves by breaking out on their own.

Hit equally hard by air strikes, the leading groups from *Korpsabteilung* C that had already experienced difficulties with the broken terrain along the breakout route, also encountered stronger resistance from Soviet ground

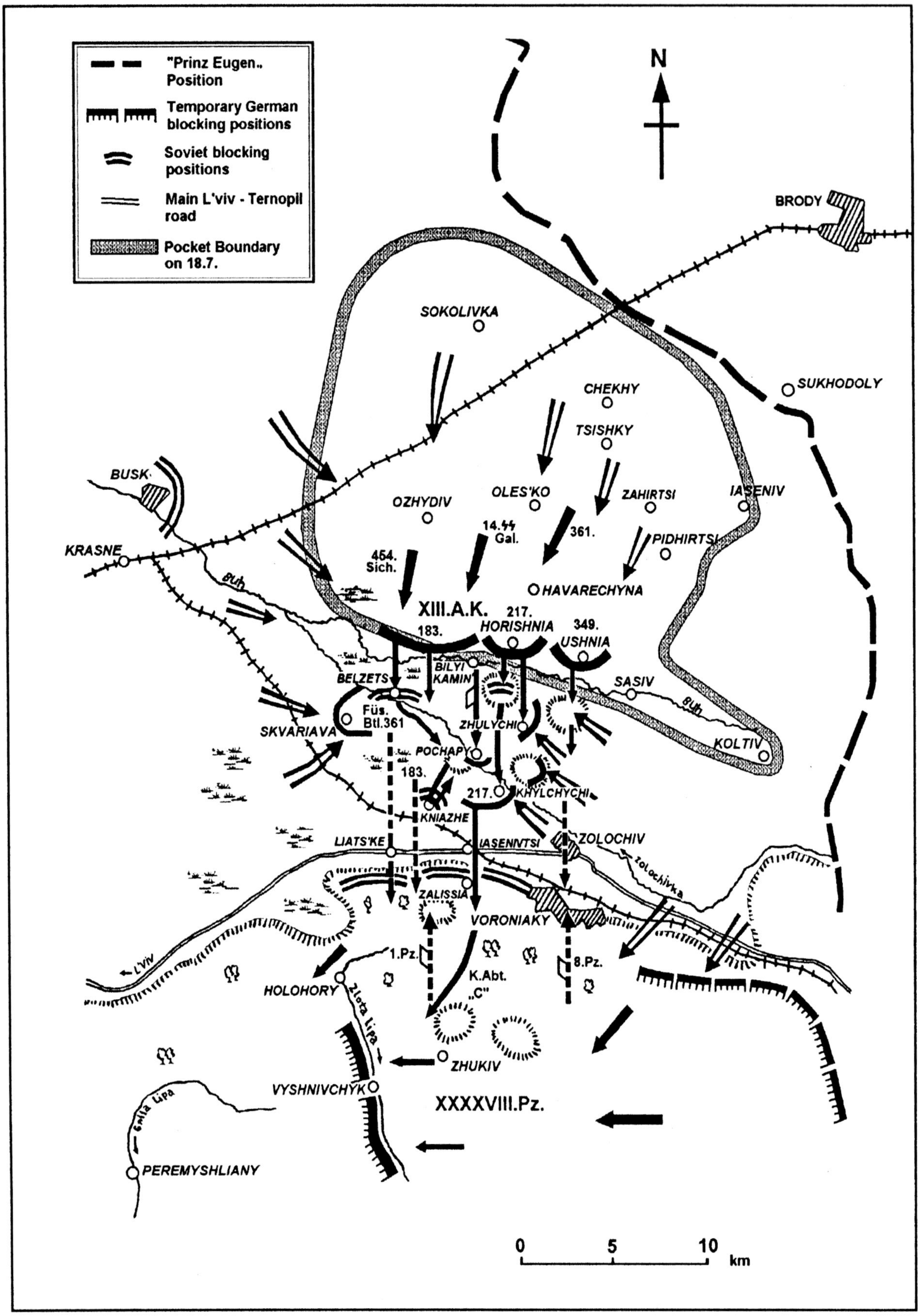

Map 6 Breakout from the pocket, 20–22 July 1944

forces. They were primarily the 8th Anti-tank Artillery Brigade, 107th Rifle Division and a number of other rifle and artillery units. Under the commander of 60th Army and Colonel-General Kurochkin, they had been moved forward to the Belzets/Bilyi Kamin region, together with Lieutenant-General Pluboiarov's 4th Tank Corps (1st Guards Army). They were directed to the area around Kniazhe and Pochapy, to spoil the escape attempt.[57]

By the late afternoon of 20 July, around 4.00pm, although one group had reached the village of Khylchytsi, the advance had lost its momentum and came to a temporary halt.[58] The same day, the news arrived of the attempted assassination [*Attentat*] of Hitler. A German soldier serving with the Galician Division's Pioneer Battalion later described the impact of the announcement as made to his unit:

> 'The toughest battle was fought by the grenadiers, riflemen and pioneers, on 20 July 1944. Then they received the news of the assassination attempt on the Commander in Chief of the German troops [Adolf Hitler]. The news struck us like a bomb. The company commander informed his men and the interpreters translated the news. Because they thought they had misheard, there were several questions regarding the actual facts. [The news] made a deep impression on everyone. Their faces made gaunt by the severe hardships, appeared even more sunken, but they did not say a word. There wasn't even time to talk about it. The Soviet attacks kept us in suspense and defence was our primary concern. The headquarters must have received the news with horror as well. Despite the reported accumulation of enemy troops at our frontline, we received no orders to attack, nor any orders for any other deployment. We were also lacking reliable information regarding the status of our neighbours. My unit was separated from the Pioneer Battalion. In an army unit I tried to get a clear picture of the situation, but even here nobody knew the course of the HKL [main line of resistance] and the extent of the encirclement.'[59]

In such a confused situation, and with only a few communications channels still functioning, it was unlikely that the news was disseminated on a large scale.[60] Nevertheless, not all the Germans who learned of the event retained the same equanimity, and their conduct and fighting morale suffered:[61]

> 'After the attempt was made known some German personnel became despondent, threw away their weapons and simply waited to be taken prisoner. This, in turn, had a bad affect on the morale of the Ukrainian soldiers.'[62]

On the evening of 20 July, XIII Corps staff re-assessed the situation and, despite the setbacks, decided to continue with the original plan. Orders were given to resume the breakout in the direction of Liats'ke and Zolochiv at 1.00 am on 21 July, whatever the cost.[63]

However, the reality of the situation then meant that the chances of the Corps breaking out as a unit were, at best, negligible. At that stage, the Corps command had to resort mainly to the use of couriers equipped with cars and motorcycles, or horses, in order to transmit orders.[64] Contact with the commanders of the leading, flanking and rearguard units could only be maintained in the same unreliable and time consuming way. All that further reduced the possibility of a concentrated attack that under the circumstances was vital. Moreover, there was no sign of the link up with the relief forces which should have been advancing towards the surrounded Corps, but had in fact been brought to a standstill by strong Soviet infantry and anti-tank positions.[65]

Under such adverse conditions, on 21 July the battle groups of *Korpsabteilung* C made a renewed but unsuccessful effort to break out of the encirclement. During the course of the day some small groups succeeded in slipping through the Soviet ring via a few short-lived breaches.[66] They included around 3,000 men from XIII Corps Wehrmacht units. Approximately 400 men from the Galician Division escaped via an opening created by a battlegroup from the 1st *Panzer* Division near Liats'ke, west of Zalissia. They then headed in a general south-westerly direction. There they joined the members of the supply and support units who had managed to avoid entrapment and other elements that had already broken out. On that day the commander of the 14th *Feld Ersatz* Battalion, *SS-Hauptsturmführer* Kleinow reported the presence of the largest contingent from the Galician Division that had gathered outside the pocket, by radio to the SS-FHA in Berlin as follows:

> To SS *Führungshauptamt* Berlin,
>
> The troops from various units from the 14 Gal. SS Div. are dispersed. Vet. comp. 4/18/113, butcher comp. 35 PLOZ, mechanics (repair) comp. combat strength unknown. Connection to the Div. not possible. According to directive of the battle commander the assembly point SAMBOR [sic] was arranged. Further present is the *Felders*. Batl. 14, 11/56/954, but without any orders. Recruits are in the first and second week of training. Equipment 5%.
>
> From CO *Felders*. Batl.14.[67]

However, the bulk of the leading groups of *Korpsabteilung* C were unable to make a decisive break-through on 21 July. They were rolled back, dislocated by the enemy armour and artillery and repulsed by the stubborn opposition from the infantry, sustaining heavy losses in the process. Ferocious fighting broke out for the villages of Pochapy, Khylchytsi, Kniazhe and Zhulychi as 60th Army's formations quickly sealed the gaps that had been made. To the north, elements of 13th Army continued to press in on the bulk of the assault forces and rear echelon units that were still trapped in the encirclement. The radius no longer exceeded four kilometres,[68] and by the day's end, units of the 172nd Rifle Division of 13th Army's 102nd Rifle Corps had captured Sobolivka and burst into the northern outskirts of Bilyi Kamin.[69]

Following the failure of the previous day's attempt, on the night of 21 July, the Corps command who were becoming increasingly pessimistic, gave orders for the remaining troops to breakout on a broad front. Thereafter, there was no more co-ordination or contact between the disintegrating units. Then it was 'every man for himself.'

Last Chance for Freedom/Temporary Breaches Made in the Soviet Ring

In the early hours of the 22 July, three mixed groups made up of the remnants of the units that spearheaded the breakout forces, assembled at the railway embankment south of Boniszyn. Led by Generals Lasch and Lange,[70] at 3.00am, under cover of darkness, they began their last desperate effort. They had to fight their way over the 3–4 metre high railway embankment (or through it, via conduits[71]) and across the open ground to the main Zolochiv – L'viv road. There they had to storm the last Soviet positions at the edge of the forest between Liats'ke and Voroniaky. In his previously cited battle report General Lange recounted those events, sparing no epithet when describing his own heroism and that of the German soldiers who took part:

> 'The enemy, which had remained entirely still up to this point, immediately opened up with maximum fire from well-prepared positions. Tanks, anti-tank guns, anti-aircraft guns, mortars and flanking machine guns attempted to hold down our attacking troops. A battle began that has only a few precedents in the history of war, and which can be compared with the storming of the Spicheren Heights and of Langemarck by our fathers, grandfathers and brothers. Without artillery support (the battery of Art. Rgt. 219 which had taken up position at the south exit of Deniszyn, made an insignificant contribution), led by both their generals, *Generalleutnant* Lasch and *Generalleutnant* Lange, officers and grenadiers with unprecedented bravado, the keenest disregard for death and an effervescent 'Hurra' stormed toward the enemy positions like a mighty wave. They broke through the positions disregarding the heavy losses like an unleashed elemental force and thrust forward to the main road. Several blocking tanks were eliminated in close combat and even the ever-increasing artillery bombardment which began at dawn and came from both east and west and later from the north, into the flanks and the rear of the attacking troops could not dam the mighty *Sturm*. Wave after wave crashed forward. At about 05.00 hrs the heights south and southwest of Iasenivtsi had been taken. The village itself and also Zalissia were in our hands. With an effervescent *Sieg Heil*! the officers and men cheered both their Generals at the edge of the forest south of Zalissia". [...][72]

Numerous other *ad-hoc*, uncoordinated, assault groups that had been formed followed the same path. They all suffered appalling losses or were completely wiped out in their attempt to cross the Valley of Death.[73] Elements of the 14th *Waffen-Grenadier-Division der SS* (*galizische* Nr. 1) escaped, after violent combat, through a breach made west of

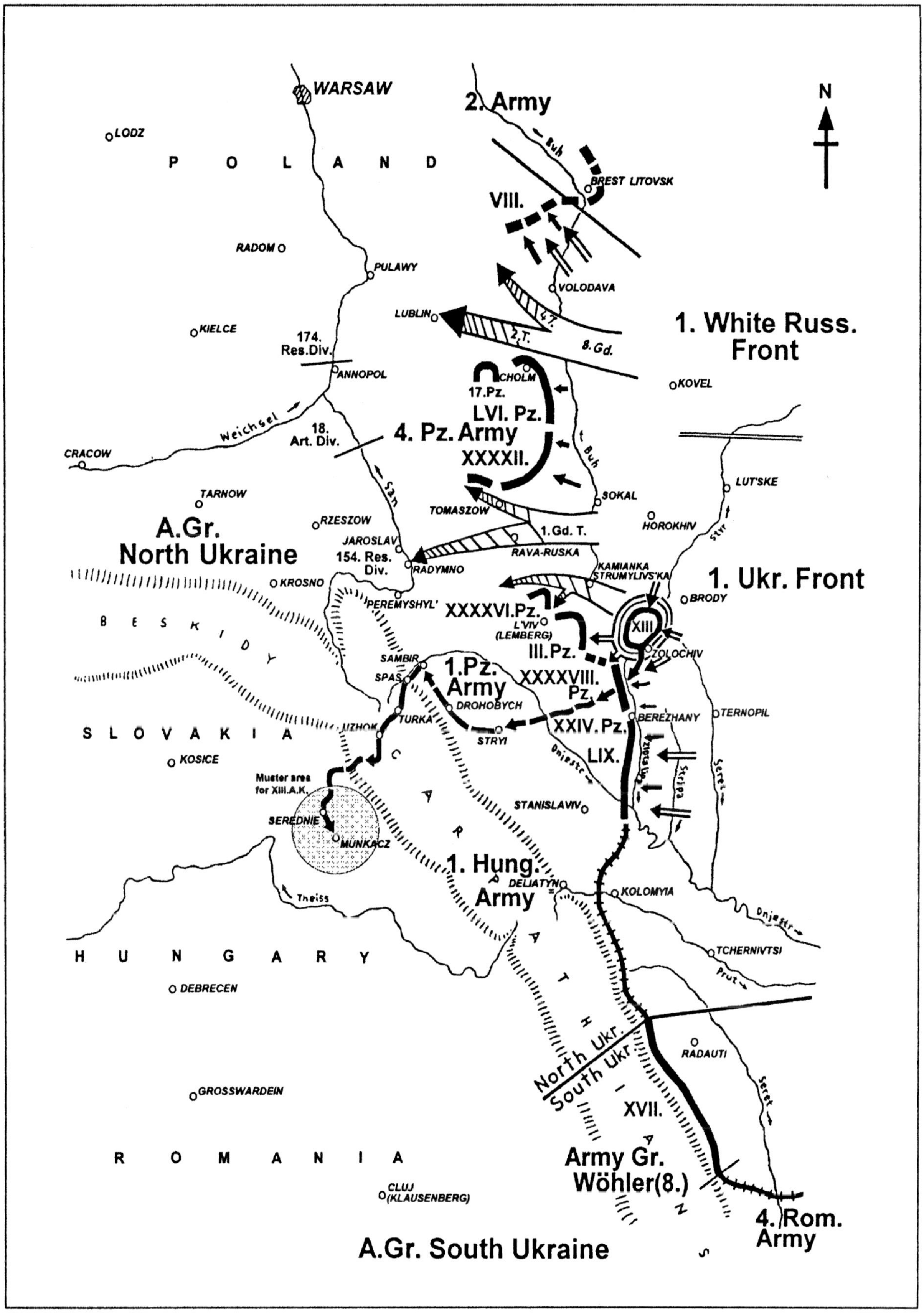

Map 7 Position of Army Group North Ukraine, 22 July 1944, and the retreat of XIII Corps

Zolochiv at a point south of the village of Kniazhe between the villages of Liats'ke and Iasenivtsi. The breach was initially less than three kilometres wide. They were under well-directed, continuous fire from tanks, artillery, mortars, anti-tank guns, and machine guns. In the late afternoon, *SS-Brigadeführer* Freitag by virtue of being attached to XIII Corps staff which was located at an outpost in the escape breach,[74] also escaped in a mixed group of Wehrmacht and Waffen-SS personal which included many German staff members of the Galician Division.

Yurij Kopystansky, a driver serving with the Galician Division's *Kriegsberichter* unit was with one of those groups. He recalled:

> 'We were told that the gathering place for the breakout was south-west of the village of Pochapy, and they added that the first attempt to breakout had failed. Farther down we met one of our divisional officers who gave us packages of biscuits for which we were glad, not having eaten food for three days. We reached the outskirts of Kniazhe, and from a field towards us came a Lieutenant-colonel, covered in medals. We asked him where the gathering place was. His answer was short: 'Shit, we won't come out of this'. A few minutes later he was dead, having shot himself.
>
> 'There were remnants of various Ukrainian and German units lying on the ground. From 14.00–16.00 hours Soviet artillery was shelling continuously. Experts were telling us that it was a minimum of 25 batteries firing. We noted several officers, not far away, lying down talking. We approached them and my friend Misko Furman asked why they were not trying to breakout. Misko said it was better to die trying, than dying doing nothing. One of the Wehrmacht majors asked if there were many like Misko who wanted to try and breakout. We replied there were. The major gave the order to prepare to breakout. He looked at his map and said we would breakout between Kniazhe and Iasenivtsi and that 500 metres from here were three light tanks. Someone had to go and order them here. A lieutenant volunteered to do so. He said that another three Tiger tanks were 8kms away on the hill of Voroniaky but they could not be of any use as the hill was too steep for them to negotiate and below was marshland in which they would sink because they were too heavy.
>
> 'We formed a battle line of about 1,500 men. No one wanted to surrender. As I knew, all Ukrainians kept a bullet aside for themselves just in case. We had three light tanks, a few submachine-guns, rifles, pistols, and grenades. That was all. The tanks moved forward and we followed. Below the hill in the valley stood four T–34s. Our tanks moved up the hill stopped and engaged in a fight with the Soviet tanks. One of our tanks destroyed a Soviet tank with a direct hit. After an additional three shots another Soviet tank was destroyed. The Soviets managed to destroy two of our tanks. We thrust forward, with a loud 'Hurrah!' shooting at will and creating panic among the Soviet troops. They started to retreat. Our last remaining tank moved forward and shot the third Soviet T–34 tank. The last one started to retreat when it too was hit by our tank and blew up. This gave us more confidence in ourselves and with vigour we pushed as hard as we could. Soviet machine guns and mortars were thinning our line fast.
>
> 'To get out of this carnage we had to reach the hill at Voroniaky where our tanks were supposed to be. I was close by the major who was commanding the breakout. I liked his tactics. The Soviets were retreating and we were in pursuit shooting at them and shouting 'Hurrah!' at the top of our voices. We had the Soviets on the run. The hill of Voroniaky was approx. 2 kms away and our line was getting thinner by the minute. The Soviets were hitting us with everything they had. We reached the railroad but getting over was not easy as the embankment was 2–3 metres in height. The Soviets machine-guns were shooting along the railway line continuously. We were desperate and those who tried to cross over died. We saw a dead solider lying over an MG 42 machine-gun. We promptly took that gun which saved some lives. I started to shoot in the direction of a Soviet machine-gun and silenced it for a while. At that time a lot of men leapt over the railroad line. I had my chance. Those of us who made it pushed forward to the Zolochiv/L'viv highway. Past the highway lay a meadow covered with lots of bushes. Only another 600–700 metres to the hill at Voroniaky. It would be easy if it wasn't for the carnage.
>
> ' "What now?" I asked the major. Calmly, he said to wait. Abruptly the Soviets stopped firing. The major remarked that it would be bad now and that the Soviets would be attacking us. He ordered us to move

> forward and we started to run. The Soviets began a heavy bombardment with their mortars and machine-guns. A T–34 came from the village of Iasenivtsi, shooting at us from its turret. Men were falling dead and wounded, crying out in agony and pleading for help. No one paid attention to their pleas. The hill was getting closer and the bombardment was dreadful. I saw the major fall dead. I felt a sharp pain in my right foot. My shoe was full of blood. I crawled towards the hill without stopping and kept on crawling until I reached the top of the hill where there were two Tiger tanks. Two crewmen ran to me with water and helped me closer to the tanks. I did not see anyone come after me to the top of the hill. Out of 1,500 men that had tried to breakout only 46 reached their goal alive.'[75]

Having broken through the third and final Soviet ring, the survivors were confronted with the Podillian Elevation situated directly opposite the breakout point. The whole area was covered in thick brush and woodland, and was constantly under concentrated fire from Soviet troops and *Komsomol* (fanatical Communist youth troops) who had dug in with machine guns, heavy mortars and light artillery.[76] Negotiating the steep incline accounted for further heavy casualties as well as the loss of the handful of remaining vehicles, horses and heavy weapons that had miraculously reached the break out point. The badly wounded had to be left, where they fell, to the mercy of the Red Army. Many preferred suicide rather than burden their comrades.[77]

Later that day, the 60th Army's formations including parts of the 359th, 336th and 107th rifle divisions among others, created blocking positions to close the breaches and re-establish their encircling ring once and for all. The German soldiers were demoralised and disheartened by continuous air strikes, artillery fire, tank and infantry attacks. They were exhausted, not only by uninterrupted combat, but also by the absence of hot food and a shortage of rations during the previous four days. By the evening of 22 July the first individual German soldiers, small groups, then entire units, began to throw away their weapons,[78] destroy their *Soldbuchs*, i.e. pay-books and identity papers, and surrender in numbers:[79]

> 'Some of the Germans, whose spirit was broken, surrendered to the Soviets. Some units fought on but most did not give a damn. Our fellows, i.e. Ukrainians, knew that if we fell into the hands of the Red Army that would be the end because we had recovered some bodies of our officers near Huta Peniatska that the Soviets had captured. Their eyes had been gouged out and they had been stripped of everything – watches, personal belongings, boots, so we knew if we fell in their hands the same would happen to us.'[80]

The remaining troops were now crowded together, amidst burning villages, and under ceaseless bombardment. They were then in an even smaller area from which there was little hope of escape. Amongst those trapped was a former member of the independent *Panzerjäger* company who, during the course of the battle, had received a field promotion to the rank of *Waffen-Unterscharführer*. He recalled his own experiences:

> 'In another village south-west of Oles'ko I found an Ukrainian *Waffen-Untersturmführer* who tried to organise what was left of the *Panzerjäger* Company. So far all he had found besides myself and two other men was one 7.5cm gun which he asked me to take command of. I agreed but said I needed more men and he replied that he would try to find some. We were exhausted and tried to get some rest for the next couple of hours while we waited for him to return. Without any warning the Soviets opened fire on the village with *Katyushas*. The village was completely destroyed and I never saw the officer again. One of the men who was with me was badly wounded. I saw a German officer talking to another soldier nearby and I called to him to help me with my friend. He just got in his car and drove off. We left the gun and the two of us that were left buried our comrade and began to walk towards the south-west.
>
> 'On the way I met a group of Ukrainians who had found a box of hand-grenades which they were busily putting detonators in. They invited me to take some, which I did. I recognised one of them as my friend from high school, Nestor Zhoubrit. He told me that in the next village there was a German Army major who was trying to organise a breakout group. This German major started to organise groups into platoons of about 50 men and for the first time he didn't bother separating Germans and Ukrainians, he simply counted them off in groups. When he found an officer whether he was German or Ukrainian he placed

the officer in command. Then he divided the groups into ten, and I was given command of one of those groups of ten men.

'We moved the same night again in a south-westerly direction and in the morning we reached a village where we encountered very strong Soviet fire. Behind the village was a hill covered with a forest which we had to reach because we knew our group was not strong enough for a face to face fight. We ran towards the village yelling 'Slava'. Even the Germans were yelling 'Slava' and I thought the Germans must think the Soviets were more afraid of us than they were of them. Finally we reached the village. The Soviets fought stubbornly and we had to fight for every house and every yard of ground. The Soviets had two tanks and they moved behind us placing one tank on the road leading to the forest. We couldn't move our wounded because the tank was in the way so I was ordered to destroy it.

'In all the excitement I didn't realise that I had been given the old type of *Panzerfaust* which had a range of 35 metres and when I fired the charge fell short. I realised that in a few seconds the tank would turn its turret and cut me to pieces so I had to do something. I took a magnetic anti-tank grenade, and ran towards the tank but I tripped and fell. Just as I did the tank's machine-guns fired and the bursts went over my head. I started rolling as fast as I could to get within six metres of the tank that was its dead angle.

'Finally I reached what I thought was a safe distance but the tank moved again. I had to act quickly so I grabbed the magnetic anti-tank grenade, jumped up and threw it with all my force at the tank. The magnets were very strong and stuck to it. Three and a half seconds later it exploded but I still did not know whether I had destroyed the tank. I jumped on to it with a hand-grenade in my hand and opened the hatch, which someone had unlocked from the inside. I pulled it open and was ready to throw my hand-grenade in when I noticed that the whole crew, including the tank commander who was a woman, were all dead. This had an extremely bad effect on me and I started to be physically sick. Finally I located the German major and told him what happened. He found a German doctor who gave some something to calm me down and stop the vomiting.

'Eventually we reached the forest and the major decided that our casualties were so heavy that it was impossible even to try and break through as a group and that our only hope was to split into small groups of a few people and try to sneak through. He explained to us that we were to go south-west to Zolochiv and that if we reached Zolochiv we would be safe.

'My group of ten men, started to go through a forest, walking at night, while during the day we would go as deep in the forest as we could and try to rest. We lay in a circle with a sentry on each side but we were so exhausted everybody fell asleep. None of us had any food. For a couple of days all I had to eat were raw oats from the field. I had some cigarette papers, and I ate them too as I figured at least there would be something in my stomach.

'On 28 July, while it was still dark, we left one forest and attempted to cross to the next one that was about two or three kilometres away. Between the two forests was a village that we had to pass. As soon as we reached the road a column of Soviet trucks appeared which were heading for the village. We jumped in a ditch which was full of water and bulrush, but they didn't see us because they had black out lights which only illuminated the road immediately in front. Once the trucks reached the village there was movement and we heard singing and screaming. I realised that this was still close to the front, and that they would have sentries making it very difficult for us to get passed. As it was almost dawn we decided we had better go back across a field of wheat to the forest we had come from. Almost as soon as we began to make our way back it grew light. As the men were farmers' sons I asked them whether they felt we could stay hidden lying down in the field. They said we would be noticed for sure if we were walking so we lay down and fell asleep.

'We awoke to the sound of the Soviets firing machine-guns over our heads. They had a loudhailer and thinking we were Germans spoke to us in German and asked us to surrender. Then they realised that we were Ukrainians and started to speak to us in Ukrainian – 'Surrender and Stalin will forgive you all your crimes, just come over to us.' I said to the men, 'Look if you want to surrender go ahead but I am not going to. The way I understand it is that if you surrender you will die a slow death. I would rather die here, if you want get up and go, go ahead'. As a reply they just started fixing bayonets. A few minutes later when the

> Soviets stopped talking to us, we jumped up, yelled 'Slava' and ran forward. I was hit over the head and collapsed unconscious. I don't know what happened to the others.
>
> 'When I came to I found myself in a barn with about forty or fifty Germans. There were no other Ukrainians. I was interviewed by a Red Army colonel who asked me some questions that I answered, as I expected to be executed anyway. The next day these troops moved out of the village and were replaced. Since I was still wearing my camouflage jacket which was only issued to our division and made me easily identifiable, a Wehrmacht soldier who had two tunics, (one winter and a second regular Wehrmacht canvass one) gave me one so I could pretend to be a German.
>
> 'The next day I was interviewed and when they asked me questions in Russian I replied in German (I did not speak good German but they did not speak any at all). Then after three days we were moved to a camp at Brody where I met my friend from high school in Jaroslav who I had last seen taking the tops off grenades. He spoke to me in Polish and told me that most of the prisoners were from the 361st Division, which was from Silesia, and that most of the Germans in this Division spoke Polish and were pretending to be Poles who had been conscripted. He said that we should also pretend to be Poles because we knew that there was a Polish division in the Soviet army and there were rumours that all the Poles would be drafted to this division and it would be easier to escape from the army than from a prison camp. It sounded logical to me so from that time on I started to pretend to be a Pole.'[81]

Over the next few days a slow trickle of determined groups and individuals continued to filter through the Soviet lines, but the bulk of XIII Corps remained trapped. The declassified Soviet General Staff report on the battle, states that the Corps commander General Hauffe was captured.[82] He was taken prisoner, along with his staff and a large proportion of the rearguard units, including their commanders Generals Lindemann of the 361st Infantry Division, and Nettwig of the 454th Security Division. They were sacrificed to allow their comrades to escape.[83]

Once outside the encirclement, the two largest groups of German staff officers and Ukrainian soldiers from the Galician Division, were reunited and gathered around *SS-Brigadeführer* Freitag and *Major* Heike respectively. The entire group had an approximate strength of 800 men, some of whom were from other XIII Corps units.[84] With the worst of the fighting behind them and in the absence of the captured General Lindemann, under whose command the Galician Division had been placed, *SS-Brigadeführer* Freitag assumed overall command.

Travelling on foot, the group continued to head in a south-westerly direction. On the way they encountered small contingents of enemy troops and tanks that had established numerous defensive emplacements. They were in blocking positions of varying sizes in villages and at road junctions along the main retreat route. The ensuing short, but often violent, skirmishes resulted in still further losses.[85]

After about 10 kms, close to Holohory, the group met some tanks and armoured personnel carriers of the 8th *Panzer* Division[86] that formed the retiring rearguards of the XLVIII *Panzerkorps*, from whom *SS-Brigadeführer* Freitag was able to obtain some transport. The group then resumed its retreat, led by Freitag in a borrowed motor vehicle. They went in the direction of Chemeryntsi under the protection of the German tanks. Their withdrawal was covered by the tanks, against attacks from the pursuing Soviets who were still in close proximity.

They marched in the direction of the German lines, away from the main roads whenever possible, to avoid being spotted by marauding aircraft. The column passed Pidkamin', crossed the Dnestr river and reached the town of Stryj. After a brief rest, Freitag issued orders for the remnants of the Galician Division to push on to a muster area about 48 kms away, at Staryi Sambir, the village of Spas situated on the northern slopes of the Carpathian Mountains.[87] The column moved off again to the west towards the town of Drohobych. There, Freitag met the head of the Military Board, *Oberst* Bisanz to whom he gave a biased summary of the Division's failure in battle, denigrating the moral and soldierly fortitude of the Ukrainian soldiers in the harshest terms. Freitag and his Ia then left the group to report the departure of the remainder of the Division to the commander of the 1st *Panzer* Army, General Raus, at his HQ.[88] They left Bisanz to inform Dr Wächter about the disaster that had befallen it at Brody.

For a few days after the main column had left Drohobych, mixed groups, of varying sizes made up of XIII Corps stragglers, continued to arrive in the vicinity. Following their comrades in the direction of Spas, some Ukrainian soldiers attached themselves to other units from the 1st *Panzer* Army and a *Kampfgruppe* from the 18th *SS-Freiwilligen Panzergrenadier* Division *Horst Wessel*. They were also passing through the same area while falling back to the west.[89]

Others came into contact with elements of the UPA that controlled the mountain passes in the area.[90] The insurgent bands frequently relieved the German soldiers of their weapons, but spared their own countrymen. Instead they attempted to persuade them to defect to the insurgent ranks. An Ukrainian *Waffen-Unterscharführer* serving with 3 Platoon, 3/I/WGR 30 wrote:

> 'My group of about 60 men broke out of the encirclement on 22 July. We were one of the last groups to break out. Our route that took us through Pochapy, Kniazhe, Stryj, and Drohobych, followed in wake of remnants of the Division. Around the 25 July the group which I was leading were resting on the outskirts of the vicinity of the town of Sambir.
>
> 'I was wakened by sentries who told me that UPA people had arrived. These were two young men who insisted that we hand over our weapons to them. I refused and told them that if we did and were later caught by the Germans with no weapons, we would be shot as deserters. I told them if they wanted weapons they should go and look fifty kilometres away at Brody, where they could find artillery, machine guns and all the weapons they wanted. I asked them to take me to their commander. They agreed and together with two other men from my group we were taken to meet him. I asked him why we should give them our weapons and in reply he suggested that our group join forces with his. I returned to my group and asked them whether they wanted to join or go back to the Division. The response was a unanimous decision in favour of joining.
>
> 'For six days we stayed with the UPA unit during which time we were treated more like prisoners. The UPA group were local men who knew the area, but we did not so I repeatedly asked for a map so that I could get my bearings – but this was never provided. On the sixth day a girl came to our group, which was resting at the edge of a wood, and told us that German and Hungarian soldiers were in the village nearby. The UPA men wanted to avoid a confrontation. I asked for a map so that we could split into three groups but they still refused to give me one. We started to receive heavy artillery fire from the German and Hungarian troops in the village. During the attack the UPA men fled leaving our group alone to fend for itself without any idea of where we were. We decided to surrender to the German units in the village. We made white flags and approached the village shouting 'don't shoot'. The Germans recognised our uniforms and held their fire. I asked to be taken to a German officer. Our group was disarmed and debriefed. We said that we had been marching in the woods since we broke out and had not had any contact with anyone from the Division or any Ukrainian or Polish partisans since. After some time we were taken away on lorries to rejoin our Division.'[91]

Around 500 Ukrainian grenadiers, and the majority of the German officers from the Divisional and regimental staffs, congregated in the designated muster area, the village of Spas.[92] While the full extent of its losses were still unknown, from the small group which had thus far assembled, with the exception of the predominantly German officer staff,[93] it was obvious that only small fragments remained of most of the combat echelons and support services. A German platoon commander, who joined the Division at this time, described the general mood as extremely negative, with the "German officers rivalling each other in cursing the Galician volunteers – probably for not doing what they themselves should have done".[94]

Having received the news from Alfred Bisanz that Freitag and most of his staff were gathering in Spas, Governor Wächter set out to join them there to assess the state of the Division's remnants, at first hand. On the afternoon of 25 July, he arrived in the village. Despite being deeply perturbed by the success of the continuing Soviet offensive, he greeted 17 surviving Ukrainian officers individually. He offered a few words of encouragement, thus acknowledging their courage in combat, and promising them that ultimately their political dreams would be fulfilled as a reward for their sacrifices.[95]

Governor Wächter then held a meeting with Freitag who went on to give his wholly negative account of the Division's participation in the battle. He berated the Ukrainian soldiers, whom he accused of cowardice, while at the same time blaming them for the Division's near annihilation. According to Heike, in acrimonious tones Freitag went on to "express the belief that he had lost all face before his superiors, and that his career was finished, all because of the Ukrainians".[96]

Governor Wächter retorted that in Berlin, the office of the German High Command was fully cognisant of the adverse conditions under which the battle had been fought, and of the part that the Galician Division had played. The Soviet military superiority had been so great that virtually the whole of Galicia had been wrested from the Germans.[97] He continued by stating that, in contrast to Freitag's account, the Division's performance during the battle had been viewed positively, especially in light of the fact that it was its first engagement. The general opinion was that the Ukrainians had fought well.[98]

After the meeting, undeterred by Freitag's vehement defamation of the Ukrainian soldiers, Wächter promptly left for Cracow and as a pre-emptive measure against Freitag's accusations, contacted Himmler's office to convince the *Reichsführer* of the viability, and political importance, of rebuilding the Division from the manpower still available to it.

With regard to his own, by then redundant, position of Governor of Galicia, Wächter complained to Himmler that *General-governor* Frank had denied his appeal to be released from his administrative obligations in the *Generalgouvernement*. He wanted to request an appointment in the Waffen-SS.[99] In a secret telex, dated 1 August, Himmler replied that he had ordered *SS-Obergruppenführers* Kaltenbrunner and Stuckart to request Wächter's release so that he could assume a new commission as head of Military Administration in Italy, under *SS-Obergruppenführer* Karl Wolff. Himmler commented, "You would be of immense use in this equally interesting and difficult field."[100]

Following his departure, Freitag, whose mood was probably somewhat tempered by Wächter's comments, assembled his fellow officers both German and Ukrainian, and sought to vindicate his own behaviour. According to *Waffen-Hauptsturmführer* Ferkuniak who was present, Freitag gave a short address. He admitted initially that all three infantry regiments had fought well. Then, with extraordinary logic, Freitag gave all the credit for the successful breakout to the German officers, 90% of whom were present in Seredne. Freitag stated that the German officers had stayed and fought courageously. He simultaneously claimed that the Ukrainian officers had run away from the battle, despite the fact that over 70% of them lay dead on the battlefield. Freitag used that as the basis for an attempt to justify why he had relinquished his command during the battle. The Division's only surviving Ukrainian battalion commander, *Waffen-Hauptsturmführer* Brygidyr was singled out by Freitag, and criticised for his tactical deployment of his battalion (I/WGR 29). Freitag claimed the deployment had led directly to its collapse.[101] "That occurrence and the events that followed," he continued, "showed that the Ukrainians did not have the will to fight and started to disperse. This is what caused my resignation as commander of the Division. Only German soldiers, NCOs and officers rallied around their commander and by their own force got out of the encirclement."[102]

Understandably, those remarks gave rise to feelings of resentment amongst the Ukrainians. They believed, and not without some justification, that they were being made scapegoats to preserve their commander's reputation.[103] They were further aggravated by Freitag's failure even to acknowledge the fact that he had only escaped due to the bravery and fighting spirit of his Ukrainian escort. Two of them had had to literally drag their exhausted commander up hills, with an *ad-hoc* harness fashioned from two belts, because he was physically unfit.[104] As a result of Freitag's allegations, some of the senior German officers developed a hostile attitude towards the Ukrainians, so much so that according to the testimony of one Ukrainian officer, "During this period the Ukrainians were isolated, and treated as [if they were] prisoners of war."[105]

Leaving Spas, the remnants of the unit, together with additional survivors who had found their way there, began the last stage of their journey across the Carpathians towards the Hunyadi *Stellung*, a German defensive line protecting the mountain passes into Hungary, and into the Mukachiv district in Hungary.[106] It was the officially allocated collecting point for all XIII Corps units.[107] A marching column of 864 men[108] was formed, and placed under the command of *SS-Sturmbannführer* Remberger. He was the commander of the Pioneer Battalion, and travelled at its head in a car with two German NCOs. Following behind on foot, were mostly Ukrainian officers, NCOs and soldiers, while bringing up the rear were three German officers on horseback. Under such an 'escort' the column proceeded down the ravine road through Turka to the village of Uzhok where they slept the night. The next day the troops boarded a freight train that arrived on 29 July at the village of Seredne situated between Uzhorod and Mukachiv in the foothills of the Carpathians. During the next two weeks the group was joined by a slow trickle of survivors, known as *Rückkämpfer*, i.e. 'retreat fighters', many of whom had successfully fought their way back to the German lines, either in groups or singly.

In Seredne the group finally began to assume a recognisable appearance as a fighting formation. All units were billeted in private houses in Seredne itself or villages close by. For the first time since the breakout the soldiers had access to limited facilities and services, and the opportunity to recuperate from the recent traumatic events. Some replacement items of uniform were provided for those who were in urgent needed of them, and hot food was available from field kitchens. Almost all food was heavily spiced with paprika. The soldiers who had received back-pay in Hungarian currency, i.e. pengos, were also able to purchase a few other essential items.[109]

Shortly after their arrival, the Divisional command began the process of preparing detailed reports about its actions, the current status and strength of its remnants. The surviving staff officers of the other XIII Corps units did the same. When the registration process had been completed in Seredne, it was clear that after one year of training, for all practical purposes the Galician Division had effectively been destroyed, after just ten days in battle.

Of the original strength of about 11,000 men of the Division who deployed at Brody, a total of 2,807 men together with their portable weaponry were accounted for by a two-man team which had been charged with the task of registering the survivors.[110] The majority, approximately 1,190 men, were reported earlier by *SS-Hauptsturmführer* Kleinow. They came from the supply and support units such as the veterinary and technical supply companies as well as from the 14th *Feld Ersatz Bataillon*. They had been only marginally involved in the fighting and had therefore escaped largely intact with minimal losses.[111] In addition to that number, possibly as many as 800 personnel were expected to rejoin the Division. They had either been wounded and evacuated prior to the encirclement, or had reached the west and had been assimilated back into other German units.[112] Thus the total number of returnees increased to as many as 3,600 men.[113]

The inventory of lost war matériel listed virtually the entire complement of the Division's heavy weaponry, equipment and supplies. It included such as artillery pieces, anti-aircraft guns, vehicles, horses, and wagons. All had been left behind on the battlefield at Brody, or had been abandoned during the breakout.

The remaining 7,400 men were classified as 'missing in action'.[114] For the few with families resident outside of Galicia, official notification to this effect was sent to the next of kin by the information office of war casualties (*Auskunftstelle fur Kriegerverluste der Waffen – SS*) (see Appendix X).

Among the known fatalities were four of the highest ranking Ukrainians who deployed at Brody. They were *Waffen-Sturmbannführer* Mykola Palienko, CO Heavy Artillery Battalion, and three *Waffen-Hauptsturmführers*, Dmytro Paliiv, Peter Roschanetz and Ivan Rembalowych. The absence of those men, especially Paliiv, who had rendered innumerable services to the Division from its inception, would be acutely felt in the following months.

One contributory factor that helped to reduce the Galician Division's losses was the fact that an element of its personnel had been recruited from the Brody area. Those soldiers in turn were able to assist their comrades, both German and Ukrainian to escape. Their assistance was acknowledged by a former German member of the Pioneer Battalion:

> 'What saved us was the fact that our Ukrainian comrades knew the area. This enabled us to avoid the purely Polish villages where assaults from the population would have been likely.'[115]

The Ukrainian soldiers also took advantage of the friendly population who hid their own countrymen, some for many months.[116] It should however be noted that to this day its casualty figures have never been appraised with any degree of certainty.[117]

Of those who could not be accounted for, some, possibly as many as 1,500 elected to join the UPA either through choice or force of circumstances. That was instead of returning to the Division during the battle or in its immediate aftermath, having broken through the encirclement.[118] There is no doubt that the influx of soldiers from the Galician Division, during July 1944, added immeasurably to the UPA's structure. Those who defected later became the backbone of many of its elite units.[119]

The other battle-hardened German units that had formed XIII Corps produced similar reports. In the region of 5,000 men of *Korpsabteilung* C who formed the spearhead of the breakout forces escaped the encirclement with only side-arms and without vehicles, horses, other weapons, supplies or equipment.[120] A total of 73 officers, and 4,059 NCOs and men were listed as killed or missing.[121]

By comparison, the 361st Infantry Division that deployed fewer troops at the beginning of the battle than the Galician Division, and together with it formed the rearguard, suffered losses that equated directly with it. In the period between 16 and 22 July, it sustained almost as many casualties, with total losses amounting to 6,310 officers and men, dead, missing or wounded.[122] The necessary manpower required to rebuild this, and the other German formations, was not available and they were subsequently disbanded and the survivors incorporated into other divisions.

As for XIII Corps, the final report of the Corps liquidation commission, applicable to its regular army units only, recorded 21,766 killed or missing in action.[123] Together with the 7,000 killed or missing men from the Galician Division, that brought the total lost to approximately 29,000. That figure corresponded with General Lange's own estimate of a total of 25–30,000 killed in the encirclement.[124] On the other hand, the recently declassified, secret, Soviet General Staff report stated that, during the course of the battle, their forces destroyed more than 30,000 soldiers and officers, 85 tanks and self-propelled guns, over 500 guns of various calibres, 476 mortars, 705 machine-guns, 12,000 rifles and submachine-guns, 5,843 vehicles, 183 tractors and trailers and 2,430 motorcycles and bicycles. It also claimed that over 17,000 soldiers and officers were taken prisoner,[125] 28 tanks and self-propelled guns were captured, as were over 500 guns of various calibres, more than 600 mortars, 483 machine-guns, 11,000 rifles, and submachine-guns, over 1500 vehicles, 98 tractors and trailers, 376 motorcycles and bicycles, in excess of 3,000 horses and 28 warehouses full of military goods.[126]

An estimated total number of survivors of all XIII Corps units had been given by the adjutant of the 349th Infantry Division as 15,000 officers and men,[127] while a slightly lower figure of 12,000 was subsequently given by *Oberst* Wilck.[128]

In any event, it too ceased to exist, and its remaining staff were called in for reassignment to other army units.

When the Galician Division's staff had prepared the necessary reports, they were forwarded for evaluation to the appropriate military and political authorities.[129] *SS-Brigadeführer* Freitag and his Ia were then summoned to the SS Main Office for debriefing.

On 2 August, the day before their departure, at a meeting of the Division's surviving officers, an account was read out, prepared by *SS-Sturmbannführer* Zoglauer for the authorities in Berlin. It told of the Division's recent fighting and activity. According to *Waffen-Hauptsturmführer* Dmytro Ferkuniak who was present, everything positive was omitted, even Freitag's earlier comments made at the village of Spas that initially the Ukrainians had fought bravely. It went on to say that the Division had not yet matured nor proved itself in battle. That, it said, was proof that the Ukrainians were not ready for independence. The reasons for Freitag's resignation were repeated and underscored in the report, which recommended the Division's disbandment.[130] On 3 August, both men flew to Berlin, leaving the senior regimental commander *SS-Obersturmbannführer* Beyersdorff in charge of the remnants in Seredne.[131]

In Berlin, Freitag reported directly to Himmler who, prior to the meeting, had already received from other sources detailed factual information concerning all the tactical developments during the battle of Brody. Although concerned over the loss of most of its vehicles, equipment and heavy weaponry, the *Reichsführer* expressed his relief that at least part of the Division had been extricated from the encirclement, as that could serve as the basis for its immediate reformation.[132] He dismissed Freitag's criticisms of the Ukrainians, by stressing that the veteran German units had also been unable to prevent the Soviet advance, and had suffered similar losses.

Then he ordered Freitag to begin the reorganisation of a new version of the Division at Neuhammer, where its Training and Reserve Regiment was by then stationed.

In reply, Freitag advised against Himmler's decision. Instead, he suggested that either the Division should be disbanded, and the remaining personnel distributed among other German formations or, alternatively, another commander be appointed in his place and that he be given command of the 4th *SS-Polizei* Division.[133]

Himmler was in desperate need of new manpower[134] and could ill-afford to discard his investment or allow the complete dissolution of the Division. The Warsaw rising[135] had broken out as recently as 1 August 1944. Since then the Germans had been actively involved in suppressing it. Such recent events had helped serve to convince him that as an alternative to its envisaged utilisation as a frontline combat formation, the Galician Division could still play an important role on a secondary front or in security operations against partisans.[136] Waving aside Freitag's protestations, he therefore insisted that it be reformed from the cadre that had broken out of the encirclement. Also included would be its Training and Reserve Regiment and the previously established third battalions of its infantry regiments. Moreover he stated that Freitag should remain as its commander because of his previous experience with the Ukrainians.[137]

To mitigate Freitag's obvious reluctance to comply with his order, Himmler agreed to the introduction of a number of measures designed substantially to increase the 'reliability' of the Division. Foremost would be the assignment of a further 1,000 German officers and NCOs to it.[138]

Thus without any consultation with the Military Board, which had played an active part in the Division's original formation, the decision was taken to rebuild it. The first official notification to that effect was actually given by Himmler to *SS-Brigadeführer* Hans Juttner on 7 August 1944.[139] In a document Himmler stated that [during the encirclement, the] "Division commander and the German commanders behaved and fought outstandingly". It also identified Juttner, in his capacity as the *Chef SS-Führungshauptamt,* as being one of those responsible for the proposal to rearm and equip the Division.[140]

The Military Board was not informed until three days later when it received the news under the cover of a letter from Governor Wächter dated 10 August.[141]

From Berlin, *SS-Brigadeführer* Freitag and his Ia travelled directly to Neuhammer to arrange accommodation for the remnants of the Division. Having done so Freitag took the opportunity to visit the *SS Panzergrenadier Schule,* at Kienschlag in Bohemia. There the course for Ukrainian *SS-Untersturmführers* was coming to an end. On the day of his arrival, all Ukrainians who were in attendance were gathered in the lecture hall of the main building and presented to Freitag, whereupon he delivered an address. In a speech seemingly calculated to humiliate the Ukrainians and vilify their fighting reputation, Freitag emphasised the most deleterious aspect of their conduct at Brody. He sought to apportion to them the full responsibility for the crushing defeat of XIII Corps

Whatever the intended effect was to have been, his tirade ultimately achieved little save unnecessarily antagonising his audience. They were soon to be serving as officers in the Division that he commanded. The school's German course commander, *SS-Sturmbannführer* Rudolf Klotz, was fully cognisant of the circumstances under which the battle had been fought, and he also took exception to Freitag's unprofessional conduct. Offended by this apparent display of acute xenophobia, he later made a point of speaking out in their defence.[142]

On 13 August, *Major* Heike flew to rejoin the remnants of the Division in Transcarpathia. He took the news with him that the Division could not be liquidated because of political considerations.[143] A few days later open-topped freight wagons arrived, and the transfer of the first groups to Neuhammer began, via Budapest and Vienna.

Untermenschen with Iron Crosses

By the end of August the last survivors of Brody had been transferred from northern Hungary to Neuhammer. The bulk consisted of the 1,600 members of the Division's three infantry regiments and 1,200 men from the 14th *Feld Ersatz Bataillon* and the veterinary and technical companies.[144]

As Neuhammer was occupied by other formations, the Galician Division, including the members of the Training and Reserve Regiment, and those who had returned from Brody, were temporarily quartered in the primitive wooden barracks of a nearby former prisoner of war camp. After several days and repeated petitioning by the

Division's command, all its soldiers were able to move into the better accommodation within the main camp compound. The exceptions were members of the 14th *Feld Ersatz Bataillon* who remained in place until the end of September. The unfriendly attitude cultivated by some of the Germans, especially the NCOs, towards the Ukrainians continued to permeate and sour the atmosphere. Calling Ukrainians 'traitors' became an everyday occurrence. The singing of Ukrainian national songs was forbidden and, for some, food and cigarette rations were reduced.[145]

After Mass, on the 1 September 1944, a parade was held for the bestowal of decorations and the announcement of promotions for those who had won them at Brody. For the presentation the Germans received appropriate ration cards for replacement uniforms. However, the Ukrainian officers wore the same uniforms in which they had returned from the battle.[146] Along with a variety of lesser decorations and awards,[147] a total of 101 Iron Crosses 2nd Class were conferred on soldiers serving with the 14th *Waffen-Grenadier-Division der SS (galizische* Nr. 1*)* of which 79 were awarded to Germans[148] (see Appendix XI). The remaining 22 were awarded to Ukrainians. The highest proportion were awarded to members of both WGR 29 (5) and SS Art. Rgt. 14, (5). *Waffen-Obersturmführer* Wolodymyr Kosak[149] and *Waffen-Untersturmführer* Father Michael Levenets, who served as chaplain on the regimental staff, were among the Ukrainian recipients. Several Germans, including the chief Liaison Officer *SS-Obersturmführer* Rudolph Michel, received the Iron Cross 1st Class. Many were undoubtedly deserved. Significantly, no conclusive evidence has yet come to light of authorisation from *SS-Brigadeführer* Freitag for the awarding of the Iron Cross 1st Class to any Ukrainian, for their participation in the battle of Brody.

Several German officers were recommended by Freitag to be advanced in rank, for their valour, with effect from 1 September 1944. Unit commanders Karl Bristot (Fusilier Battalion), Hermann Kaschner (*Panzerjäger Abteilung*), and Johannes Kleinow (*Feld Ersatz Batl.*) were promoted to the rank of *SS-Sturmbannführer*. The commander of the Artillery Regiment Friedrich Beyersdorff became a *SS-Standartenführer*.[150] *Major* Heike was the Division's Ia and only Wehrmacht officer. Several witnesses later testified that he had remained with the Division throughout the battle, directing actions[151] and being injured in the arm in the process.[152] He received neither decoration nor promotion.[153]

A strength return for the Galician Division as of 4 September 1944, listed 134 officers, 522 NCOs, and 4,419 men totalling 5,075.[154] At the same time the Division's independent Training and Reserve Regiment (A.u.E.Rgt.14.) recorded a total of an additional 8,835 men of all ranks.[155]

On 5 September 1944, a secret circular order was finally issued by Hans Juttner, chief of the SS-FHA, setting down the framework on which the new 14th *Waffen-Gren. Div. der SS* (*galizische* Nr.1) was to be rebuilt. The order named the unpopular *SS-Brigadeführer* Freitag as being responsible for its immediate re-formation. It gave instructions that all weapons, equipment, vehicles and horses necessary for that purpose were to be sent directly to its home base of Neuhammer.

It further directed that the basis of the reconstituted Division was to be the 3,000 survivors of Brody. Additional manpower was to be drawn chiefly from three sources. Firstly were the approximately 8,800 men of its Training and Reserve Regiment (*SS-Gren.Ausb.u.Ers.Rgt.* 14). Secondly were the units ordered for use in the formation of the third battalions of the 29th, 30th and 31st regiments. Lastly, there were the remaining soldiers of the 4th and 5th *Galizischen SS-Freiwilligen* regiments who had not deployed at Brody.

Training of specialists was to be completed by 15 November 1944. The Division was to be ready for deployment in the field by 31 December 1944. It was an unrealistic deadline for battle readiness, in view of the influx of new untrained recruits, and the chronic shortages of ordnance prevailing at that time.

Most importantly, the order also specifically stated that Ukrainians were to be debarred from the Divisional staff, regimental staff, communications section and other administrative positions. Those posts were to be reserved exclusively for Germans. The same applied to all battalion and department staff, commanders, adjutants, and security officers, as well as the appropriate communications personnel. The only exceptions were to be drivers and horse grooms etc. Ultimately, Freitag was able to extend the order to the vast majority of technical posts, such as harness makers and craftsmen, which were also given to Germans. The Ukrainians became apprentices.

A further detail contained within the document was designed to address some of the difficulties encountered with communications during the Battle of Brody. It said that 60% of all personnel assigned to the Signals *Abteilung* (*SS-Nachr. Abtl.* 14), irrespective of rank, were to be Germans.

Lastly, all units were to submit status reports by the 15 September 1944, the same day that refitting, reinforcement and retraining was to commence.[156]

During September, at Freitag's request, the SS-FHA helped facilitate the Division's reconstitution as promised. They sent a further 1,000 German officers and NCOs to the Division to make up for losses at Brody and to form the skeleton cadre.[157] The most senior was the replacement commander for WGR 31, holder of the Knights Cross, *SS-Standartenführer* Rudolph Pannier.[158] Like Freitag he transferred from the 4th *SS-Polizei* Division. Similarly, *SS-Hauptsturmführer* Werner Heinz[159] took over as commander of the Signals *Abteilung* from *SS-Hauptsturmführer* Wolfgang Wuttig who was captured on 22 July.[160] The only other significant change, with regard to principle positions of command, was the appointment of an experienced combat veteran *SS-Obersturmbannführer* Carl Marks.[161] He was to be the new commander of the Training and Reserve Regiment from 15 August 1944.

As before, of that group, the ethnic German officers and NCOs, especially the Slovak *Volksdeutsch*, were best suited to the Division. Four were subsequently made battalion commanders. The most senior was *SS-Obersturmbannführer* Karl Wildner,[162] whose appointment was effective from 21 August 1944, as was that of another experienced veteran, *SS-Hauptsturmführer* Ludwig Kuchta.[163] Both were assigned to WGR 29. *SS-Sturmbannführer* Albert Czermin[164] was posted to WGR 30, whilst *SS-Sturmbannführer* Elemer Scholtz[165] and *SS-Sturmbannführer* Wilhelm Podlesch[166] became battalion commanders in WGR 31. Along with some of the Romanian *Volksdeutsch*, and with their Slavic background in common, they soon developed good relations with the Ukrainians.

Conversely, as had been the case in the original formation, a significant number of German NCOs who came directly from various *Polizei* formations did not adapt easily. They often lacked the necessary combat experience. Further, their service prior to joining was either inappropriate or not conducive to conducting a successful training programme in a combat formation.[167] The personnel of two rifle battalions, mainly of Romanian *Volksdeutsche*, were incorporated into the Division at that time but proved to be unsuited.[168]

Despite their often inferior calibre, the sheer number of Germans posted to the Division fulfilled all Freitag's expectations. Indeed they eventually became so numerous that all command positions, at battalion and company level, could have been filled by them, leaving one or two NCOs available for each company. With so many Germans at his disposal, Freitag therefore planned to create a reserve of German officers and NCOs. That caused considerable dissatisfaction amongst the trained Ukrainians, especially the Brody veterans. They frequently had to give up their commands, in favour of inexperienced Germans, and be reassigned as instructors to the Training and Reserve Regiment, and the *Feld Ersatz Bataillon*. Some were relegated to postings within the supply and support services.[169]

Prior to Brody, Ukrainian personnel had accounted for a handful of staff positions. There were two battalion commanders in combat units, *Waffen-Hauptsturmführer* Brygidyr (CO I/WGR 29), and *Waffen-Sturmbannführer* Palienko (CO IV Abt. SS Art.Rgt. 14). Almost all company and battery commanders were Ukrainian. After Brody a large number of those positions were given to Germans.[170] There were a few notable exceptions who retained higher position, including *Waffen-Obersturmführer* Lubomyr Makarushka.[171] As Paliiv's successor he served on the staff as liaison officer between the Division and the Military Board. *Waffen-Hauptsturmführer* Dmytro Ferkuniak continued to serve in Section Ic on Intelligence and political matters. *Waffen-Untersturmführer* Father Levenets served as Divisional chaplain, and *Waffen-Sturmbannführer* Pobihushtschyi served with the Training and Reserve Regiment.

Of the only independent unit that had had Ukrainians commanding all four of its companies before Brody, three retained an Ukrainian company commander after Brody. The fourth commander was *SS-Sturmbannführer* Bristot of the Fusilier Battalion. Even more interesting, it was considered an elite unit within the Division that uniquely accepted volunteers only. The first company was commanded by *Waffen-Untersturmführer* Ivan Zaryckyj, the second by *SS-Untersturmführer* Krause, a *Volksdeutsch*, the third by *Waffen-Obersturmführer* Stefan Hulak, and the fourth by *Waffen-Obersturmführer* Roman Bojcun.

While a limited number of Ukrainian officers were permitted to keep their company commands, the rest were given subordinate positions as platoon commanders. That also applied to the 200 Ukrainian officers and NCOs, in September 1944, on completion of their respective training courses. They successfully graduated from German academies, having met exacting standards, and returned to the Division (see Appendix XII). While the best graduates stayed on for a further four weeks to complete the *Kompanieführerlehrgang* (company commanders course) at

Kienschlag, the rest took up posts as platoons commanders. None were appointed to or ever held any position higher than that of company commander and no Ukrainian officer over 40 years of age was allowed to command a front unit.[172] This discriminatory policy also manifested itself within the ranks of the non-commissioned officers, the higher positions again often going to Germans or *Volksdeutsch* personnel.[173]

By 10 September 1944, with the influx of new personnel, the Division's depleted ranks had expanded to 148 officers, 572 NCOs and 5,796 men totalling 6,516.[174] As of that date the Division's Training and Reserve Regiment listed a total of 7,534 men of all ranks.[175]

Ten days later, quantitatively all the necessary manpower was available to the Division to begin the reformation process. It had a strength return as of 20 September 1944, listed 261 officers, 673 NCOs, and 11,967 men, a total of 12,901, although that was still short of its authorised strength of 14,689 all ranks.[176] The bulk of the additional personnel absorbed by the Division were drawn directly from the Training and Reserve Regiment and had undergone very little if any training. For example 1/I/WGR 30 was reformed from former personnel of the 9th Company of the Reserve Regiment, most of whom were fresh recruits.[177]

To comply with the deadline set by the SS-FHA requiring the Division to be ready for deployment by the end of the year, a planned, intensive retraining programme began immediately. Progress was impeded by several factors. Firstly, there was a dearth of qualified training instructors among the recent intake of German officers and NCOs. That meant that the burden of basic training rested mainly with the Training and Reserve Regiment (which was officially incorporated into the Division[178]) and the instructors assigned to it.

Secondly, while unlike other Waffen-SS formations, the Galician Division did not suffer from a shortage of recruits, there was a noticeable difference between those from the first formation, the nucleus of whom had been volunteers, and the new intake. It should be noted that these replacements were no longer exclusively west Ukrainians from Galicia. They included refugees, from both east and west Ukraine, who had enlisted to escape Soviet occupation and conscription into the advancing Red Army.[179] That influx of east Ukrainians brought with it political schisms hitherto unknown within the Division. Eventually they became a considerable cause of concern for the west Ukrainian nationalist contingent.[180]

There were also those who had been taken by force by the Germans, and pressed into military service. During the German retreat from western Ukraine in the spring and summer of 1944, to meet their manpower needs, German and Hungarian soldiers cordoned off villages and rounded up all the able bodied males, and in some cases females, between the ages of 15 and 50.[181] In that way thousands of young Ukrainians were drafted into the depleted ranks of the Galician Division, or other Waffen-SS and Army formations.[182] Those drafted into the Galician Division under such circumstances were sent directly to its Training and Reserve Regiment straight from civilian life. Some were later found to be unfit for service. But they could not be discharged, nor allowed to return home, as the whole of Ukraine was by then under Soviet occupation. They were therefore kept on, but assigned light duties.[183]

Additional draftees were persons who had been forced to work in Germany, i.e. former members of *Polizei* and *Schutzmannschaft* detachments previously used to guard industrial installations, and Ukrainians who had served with the Red Army and become prisoners of war. Unlike those who had been recruited into the first formation, they were not tattooed with their blood group under the left armpit.

To a certain extent the use of conscripts proved to be counter-productive as they often lacked the enthusiasm and the positive attitude of their predecessors. The ardent Ukrainian nationalist survivors of the original formation could, at least, draw a little inspiration from the possibility that the Galician Division could be a decisive factor in the creation of an independent Ukrainian state. Such a creation was anticipated in the wake of the chaos that would occur after the expected German defeat. Moreover the non-discriminatory policy meant that from then on, the composition and fighting value of its component units varied greatly from regiment to regiment, and even company to company.

A third problem was the negative atmosphere in the camp[184] caused by the deterioration of German/Ukrainian relations. That development was noted by the Military Board.[185] As before, the main cause was the anti-Ukrainian disposition of *SS-Brigadeführer* Freitag and some members of his staff. Freitag's uncompromisingly critical attitude, as expounded to the Ukrainian officer candidates at Kienschlag, ostensibly underwent something of a radical change after 30th September 1944. He was unexpectedly awarded the highly coveted and much esteemed *Ritterkreuz,* or Knight's Cross, for the Division's part in the Battle of Brody.[186] The award was made on the basis of a report submitted for consideration to the appropriate authorities by the commander of the 3rd *Panzer* Army *Generaloberst* Raus. It was accompanied by a short introductory note. Raus sought to exonerate himself for having had any part in it, stating that "In view of the short period during which 14th Galician Division was part of the 1st *Panzer* Army, it is not possible for me to make *a definite and exhaustive assessment.*' [Author's emphasis][187]

The report itself described how Freitag "distinguished himself while breaking through the surrounding forces at Zolochiv, by virtue of his leading, dynamic approach and tough action against (Ukrainian) weaklings" who were "innately weak and apt to waver, lacking any of the manly or fighting virtues of the Germans". It went on to say that:

> 'When the reinforced Gren. Rgt. 30 looked as though it was going to get dragged into this retreat, it was the Division commander who with the regiment commander immediately re-secured the situation in that area and prevented the threatened breakthrough of enemy forces.
>
> 'When later in the battle numerous 'volunteers' of the Division deserted due to innate cowardice and in some cases even turned their weapons on their own officers and NCOs, it was in the main the Division commander who there and then restored order with unhesitating personal action, and took the appropriate brutal measures against the miserable wretches.'

No mention was made of the fact that Freitag resigned his command. Neither was any indication given of the sources upon which the report was based, nor names provided of witnesses to his alleged heroism (for the full text see Appendix XIII). Indeed, Freitag had already expeditiously taken the precaution of relieving his most embarrassing and outspoken critic, *Waffen-Hauptsturmführer* Brygidyr from his command of I/WGR 29, and obtaining his dismissal. His discharge from the Waffen-SS on the request of the command of the 14th *Waffen-Gren.Div. der SS* and transferral to *Reichssicherheitshauptamt* B (Central Security Department – RSHA) was confirmed in the last document in his military service record.[188] In his memoirs *Waffen-Hauptsturmführer* Dmytro Ferkuniak describes the reason for his expulsion thus:

> 'On September 20, Bisanz, Schulze (*SS-Hauptsturmführer* Dr Schulze who headed the *Ergänzungsamt der Waffen-SS, Ergänzungsstelle Warthe* (XXI), Nebenstelle Lemberg) and a Ukrainian member of the Military Board visited the Ukrainian Division. In the hall of the Division's staff, Bisanz asked me about the behaviour of the Germans [at Brody]. I told him to go and ask the Germans themselves, they would tell him the truth. But Brygidyr told him everything, adding that it would be to the common good if Freitag were replaced. I went to Berlin on 22 September and when I returned two days later I was told that Freitag had ordered Brygidyr's arrest and his transportation to Berlin to the Gestapo.'[189]

Within four weeks of the bestowal of the award, Freitag issued a Divisional order of the day addressed to 'Men of my Division' which read:

> 14. *Waffen-Gren. Div. der SS* (*galiz.* Nr.1) Div.St.Qu. 19.10.44
> Commander
>
> The Führer has decorated me with the Knight's Cross of the Iron Cross. I bear this high award for all of the brave and exemplary German and Ukrainian officers, NCOs, and men of my division, who in those difficult days at Brody demonstrated in action, composure and character, what a soldier should be, and created a tradition for the 1st Ukrainian Division.
>
> For the Germans in my division, my decoration represents the highest praise and the recognition of their work in creating this Division, and their bravery in the battle for the eternal future of our people. For the Ukrainians it represents similar recognition and the certainty that the Führer fully appreciates all the brave deeds of the Ukrainians, and also the certainty that he has full appreciation for the actions of the Ukrainians for their people and their homeland, in their fight for freedom.
>
> We all wish to renew our vow to the Führer, that we will pursue unto victory, our joint battle against the Bolshevic hordes and their Jewish-plutocratic helpers.[190]

Freitag
SS-Brigadeführer und Generalmajor der Waffen-SS
Division commander

In the order, in which Freitag took the hitherto unprecedented step of singling out the contributions of the "brave and exemplary German and *Ukrainian* [Author's emphasis] officers, NCOs and men",[191] as a conciliatory act, for the first time, in its text, he referred to the Division as the "1st Ukrainian Division".

In reality there was no genuine conviction behind that remarkable change in his attitude towards the Ukrainians.[192] Nine days later he issued an official directive dated 28 October, concerning problems with political education and other matters in the Division. As a solution to the re-occurring difficulties, Freitag ordered that every unit leader, up to and including the rank of company commander, was to appoint an Ukrainian *Verbindungsmann* (Liaison Officer). They were to have the task of making the officers aware of any difficulties that they may not have been able to identify for themselves, as a result of barriers of rank or language. They would also be given direct access and ability to make direct representations to their leader. The order ended by stipulating:

> 'Finally, I now wish to create a relationship of mutual trust between the German and Ukrainian men, as is required by the fighting community of our Division. *I forbid any second class treatment of Ukrainians*.' [Author's emphasis][193] (See Appendix XIV).

Notwithstanding those and other minor problems such as inadequate food rations, in some respects training proceeded more smoothly than it had with the first formation. It was partly due to the continuity gained by the preservation of the majority of the Division's general staff, and the experienced unit commanders who were able to organise, and carry out training, independently within their sections. For a short period of approximately five weeks, training was conducted in the field, with special emphasis on active defence.[194] Hand to hand combat, night exercises, weapons training and route marches all featured prominently in the training schedule. In light of the experiences at Brody, members of supply and support units also received weapons training, as well as the relevant specialist instruction. While some NCO courses and a limited amount of officer training was available within the Division, the majority of candidates were sent to various specialist Waffen-SS and Wehrmacht academies. Approximately 1,000 of its soldiers were also sent for training with Wehrmacht reserve units.[195]

A few of the best Ukrainian soldiers, who had battle experience, were sent to the youth camp in the Austrian village of Malta. For a short period they had to pass on the benefit of their combat experience to the young Ukrainians, aged 15–18, whom the Germans had been recruiting in Galicia since April 1944.[196] It was one camp of several in which the Germans placed young men, and some women, recruited from both east and west Ukraine.[197] Some received pre-military training prior to their wholesale conscription into the Luftwaffe as auxiliaries or *Flakhelfer*. In that capacity they served as anti-aircraft gunners, searchlight operators, or with signals and transport sections often in the most threatened cities, such as Berlin, Dresden, and Hamburg.[198]

Theoretically, on reaching the age of eighteen the young men could request transfer to the Galician Division where they would automatically qualify as officer and NCO candidates. In practice the Luftwaffe jealously guarded this source of manpower and did not encourage contact with the Galician Division. Ultimately it was only from one such camp in the Austrian village of Malta, that approximately 280 youths later transferred, after completion of their training.[199]

Organisationally, the Division took on the same form as it had prior to the battle of Brody, that of a Type 44 Infantry Division and consisted of the same combat and support units with minor deviations. The three infantry regiments 29th, 30th and 31st were reformed with three, instead of two, battalions each. The Flak *Abteilung* formerly consisted of mixed heavy and light batteries. It was re-built as a combined *Flak/Pak Abteilung*[200] with only one battery of 3.7cm guns and approximately 200 personnel.[201] The heavy battery of four high velocity 88mm guns was never replaced.

In the reorganised Division, the *SS-Feldgendarmerie Truppen* 14 was expanded from platoon to company strength. With approximately 100 men they would presumably facilitate the enforcement of rigorous discipline amongst the 'innately weak Ukrainians who were apt to waver'. *SS-Untersturmführer* Wilhelm Drapatz,[202] promoted *SS-Obersturmführer* on 9 November 1944, was appointed commander, as from 15 September 1944. The whole unit was directly under Divisional command. All Drapatz's officers and around half of the NCOs and men were German *Volksdeutsche* who spoke and understood Ukrainian. Equipped mostly with bicycles and a few motorcycles, according to an Ukrainian who served with the *SS-Feldgendarmerie Truppen* 14, the whole unit was never together in one place and the soldiers were always on duty in pairs, one German and one Ukrainian, so that a German was always present.[203]

A new sub-unit was also established, commanded by a German, after the Division obtained approximately fifty Alsatian dogs trained in security and tracking. Training for their handlers was undertaken at the Research Station for Homing-pigeons and Dogs.[204] Later when engaged in anti-partisan operations in difficult or inaccessible terrain, the existence of this unit proved to be invaluable. However, the dogs did tire easily! As a result, they were later transported between locations by truck.

All types of equipment, weaponry and ammunition were in much shorter supply than they had been when the Division had first been formed. It was a problem felt most acutely in the Reserve Regiment that did not even have sufficient uniforms and shoes for its soldiers.[205] It was even harder to obtain the necessary motorised vehicles of all types, and the gasoline on which to run them. To make up for the shortfall a variety of makes and models were pressed into service, even some French Renault vehicles. A number of two/three-ton trucks were converted to run on gas, in particular the Imbert wood-burning pattern. Those were utilised for transport and supply purposes,[206] as were horses in large numbers.

Since a significant percentage of the Division's quota of horses were in very poor condition or suffering from diseases, several horse-requisitioning parties were formed. They were sent to various localities throughout the *Generalgouvernement,* with the task of procuring the requisite number of animals for its various units. Taking advantage of the situation, some of the more disillusioned soldiers seized the opportunity to desert. Others found themselves engaged in pitched battles with partisans, or even the leading units of the advancing Red Army.[207]

As a unit composed primarily of foreign nationals, permission was sought and given for it to establish a field hospital of its own. Thereafter its soldiers could be treated without having to be sent to Army reserve hospitals. The medical staff was predominantly German including the complement of 32 nursing staff who worked under the overall direction of a German head nurse.[208]

The Division was also given the use of a rest home in the *Generalgouvernement*. An elegant two story building known as Montana, it was situated a kilometre outside the well-known spa town of Zakopane, in the Tatry Mountains. The home received its funding from the *Generalgouvernement* and Ukrainian institutions such as the Military Board and the Ukrainian Central Committee. It was run by a German *SS-Oberscharführer* with a resident civilian staff of Ukrainians from both east and west Ukraine. It had sleeping accommodation for a maximum of thirty people, privates and NCOs. There its most deserving soldiers, both German and Ukrainian, and those who were recuperating from their wounds, could convalesce amidst beautiful mountain scenery. Throughout the duration of their stay all normal duties were excused, except in emergencies, and the soldiers had ample opportunity to relax and visit the cinema, or even the local dentist in the city.[209]

Cultural and recreational activities for the Division centred on cinema screenings and performances by its orchestra. *Ad-hoc* choirs assembled in individual units for special occasions. Other entertainment, such as recitals by Ukrainian artists, was arranged by the Military Board.[210] Together with the Ukrainian Central Committee and a special commission established by the Division, they helped the Ukrainian soldiers locate and contact their relatives within the refugee community.

To complement this initiative, *SS-Brigadeführer* Freitag allowed the wives of German and Ukrainian soldiers to visit their husbands and stay in special quarters in the camp for a maximum of a fourteen-day period. This privilege was well received and appreciated by those who were able to take advantage of it. However, almost without exception, they were the senior German officers.

The German authorities still made little effort to honour Wächter's assurance that maintenance arrangements would be made for members of the soldiers' families. Provision of monetary aid for the soldiers' dependants was especially important, in view of the fact that many had been forced to flee westwards as refugees.[211]

Waffen-Obersturmführer *Mychailo Lischynsky with soldiers from his company shortly after their arrival in the Brody area.*

Many of the roads in the Brody area, like the one shown, were not paved and after heavy rain quickly became impassable for wheeled vehicles.

A group of soldiers deploys in the Brody area, July 1944

The route of retreat was soon marked by burning villages, such as the one pictured here.

Machine-gun team in action in the Brody pocket, July 1944.

Eventually the decision was made to break out towards the south. Machine-gun team during the fighting in the Brody pocket, July 1944.

The Soviets enjoyed vast superiority in every respect at Brody, none more so than in armour. Here an older pattern Soviet tank destroyed during the heavy fighting in the Brody pocket, July 1944.

Soviet fighter and bomber aircraft attacks dominated the battlefield and destroyed exposed vehicles moving along the roads, hindering troop movements and blocking the routes for retreat. Brody pocket, July 1944.

German tanks move from the south to support the breakout attempt. Brody, July 1944.

Although massively outnumbered, the prospect of relief by German armour attacking from outside the pocket was an enormous psychological boost to the soldiers of XIII Corps trapped in the pocket. Here a Panzer *from the relief forces moves toward the pocket at Brody, July 1944.*

Before, during and after the Battle of Brody, soldiers from the Galician Division came into contact with UPA personnel operating in the area. In the aftermath of the battle some Ukrainians, such as Evhen Smyk (pseudonym 'Viy', standing first from left), who had joined the Division on instruction from the OUN, deserted to the UPA. As a commander of a group, Smyk continued to fight with the UPA for several years until the remainder of his group killed themselves with hand grenades after being encircled in a bunker on 7 April 1948.

The UPA units with which the retreating soldiers came into contact varied hugely in size and effectiveness. At least half of this well-equipped group carry prized automatic weapons.

The Galician Division was given the use of a rest home in the Generalgouvernement, *known as 'Montana', near Zakopane, in the Tatry Mountains, where its most deserving soldiers and those who were recuperating from their wounds could convalesce. Two Ukrainian* Waffen-Grenadiers *at 'Montana' in the winter of 1944.*

Drawing by an Ukrainian who was captured at Brody, depicting the treatment of prisoners by their Soviet captors.

In the aftermath of Brody, the rebuilding process was greatly assisted by an influx of over 250 soldiers who were at that time undergoing officer and non-commissioned officer training at various schools. Pictured here are Ukrainian officer candidates with the rank of Waffen-Junker *attending the Infantry Officers' School at Braunschweig, in Posen Treskau, 15 July- 15 December 1944. From over 200 hundred who started the course, 86 graduated. From left: (standing) Stefan Kukurudza, Jaroslav Kunyskyj, Walter Kataman, Jaroslav Owad, Mychailo Palij, Ostap Andruszczakewycz Wolodymyr Lutciw. Autumn 1944.*

Officer training included extensive theoretical and practical instruction. Here Ukrainian officer candidates take part in map reading exercises at Posen Treskau, with their German instructor for military tactics SS-Hauptsturmführer *Schneider. Autumn 1944. Left to right: not known, not known, Remeniuk, not known, Kataman, Duda, Jakubiak, Owad,* SS-Hauptsturmführer *Schneider, Kunyckyj, not known, Hladij, Laluk, not known, Krenta, Luciw, Lahodynskyj, not known, not known, not known, Iwanoczko (facing camera with hands clasped), Andruszczakewycz, not known, Kurkurudza, Charambura, Pasika.*

A Germany company crosses the river Warta whilst another company waits its turn. Posen Treskau, Autumn 1944.

Group of Ukrainian officer candidates at Posen Treskau: (from left) not known, Ostap Andruszczakewycz, Bohdan Laliuk, Wolodymyr Luciw, Jaroslav Owad, (seated) Jaroslav Kunyskyj. Autumn 1944.

Young Ukrainian officer candidates undergoing pioneer training at the officer school at Hradishko. During NCO training at Pikovice, instruction was given by Ukrainian officers, whereas at Hradishko it was carried out exclusively by Germans, many of whom had been wounded and were classified as unfit for active combat duty. Here SS-Untersturmführer *Schweiger, a decorated* Totenkopf *veteran, passes on the benefit of his experience at the front. Left to right: Germa* Junker, SS-Untersturmführer *Herbert Schweiger, Bohdan Kutny, Bohdan Onyszkewycz, Bohdan Romanowskyj.*

Waffen-Standartenjunkers *returning to the Galician Division after graduation from the Pioneer Officers' School at Hradishko, 1 September, 1944. Left to right: Bohdan Romanowsky, Myroslav Kotys, Taras Kaczmarchuk, Bohdan Kutny, Bohdan Onyschkewycz, Jaroslav Bencal, Jaroslav Chomyn, Jaroslav Fenyk, Oleh Harmatij. These young Ukrainians who had graduated from the German academies equalled and often surpassed their equivalent German counterparts as officers.*

8

Revolt in Slovakia

The reformation of the Galician Division at Neuhammer was hardly underway when it was unexpectedly disrupted. An order came to organise a *Kampfgruppe* for immediate use against the Soviet-backed uprising that had broken out in Slovakia against the pro-German government of President Monsignor Joseph Tiso.[1]

The strategic aim of the planned rebellion, which had begun on 29 August 1944, was to assist the rapid penetration of Soviet troops across the Carpathians and into the rear of the German armies in Romania and Hungary. Thereby it was hoped to undermine the whole southern sector of the Eastern Front. It was put into effect by members of the cabinet, under defence minister General Catlos, and backed by a large part of the Slovak army under General Golian. After the mobilisation, carried out during September, it had grown to a formidable strength of approximately 44,700 men. They were equipped with tanks, artillery, 2 armoured trains and over 250 aircraft.[2] The 1st Czechoslovak Army in Slovakia formed the backbone of the insurgent forces. It was reinforced and co-ordinated by 2,200 soldiers of the 2nd Czech Airborne Brigade,[3] and 7,000 partisans, including a number of Soviet commanders and specialists.[4] The Soviets also supplied additional air support (as of 17 September) in the form of the 1st Czechoslovak Air Fighter Regiment together with 250 tons of arms and supplies.

With the embers of the Warsaw rising still smouldering, the Germans were keen to quell the insurrection in Slovakia. They needed to restore the main communication and transportation lines to military traffic as quickly as possible. By 2 September 1944, they had assembled an *ad-hoc* force of emergency mobile *Kampfgruppen* from their forces in eastern Slovakia and northern Hungary, to suppress the revolt. The actual area was swiftly restricted by a combination of ill-preparedness, treachery and hesitation on the part of the Slovaks. Under the direction of *SS-Obergruppenführer* Gottlob Berger, *Kampfgruppe* Schill,[5] *Kampfgruppe* Schafer[6] and the Tatra *Panzer* Division[7] initially made good progress as they moved towards the principal tactical centres of the rebellion, namely Banska Bystrica (Neusohl), Brezno (Briesen) and Zvolen (Altsohl) in the mountainous Tatra region in central Slovakia.

However, by mid September, the advance had lost its impetus. The insurgents withdrew further into their mountain strongholds where the Germans could not exploit their heavy weaponry. On 14 September Berger,[8] who had promised Himmler that "he would a settle the matter, i.e. the rebellion, in four days," was replaced, as overall commander in Slovakia, by *SS-Obergruppenführer und General der Waffen-SS und Polizei* Hermann Höfle.[9] The offensive resumed but it was clear that the German authorities had underestimated not only the scale of the revolt but the resources that would be needed to subjugate it. Thus, on 19 September the Galician Division's command received urgent notification that it was to organise a *Kampfgruppe* with the strength of a reinforced battalion. It was to be sent to join the forces in Slovakia already engaged in suppressing the uprising.[10]

The Division's staff issued the proper instructions and began preparations. In an effort to carry out the order, which originated from the SS-FHA, at short notice, and to minimise disruption to its reformation plan, the III/WGR 29 was chosen as the basis for the improvised unit. The battalion had not been deployed at Brody and was composed partly of soldiers from the disbanded *Galizischen SS Freiwilligen* Regiment 5 that had earlier been active in the Cholm, Lublin and Hrubeshiv regions. The soldiers of the III/WGR 29 were complemented by some of the best and most experienced Ukrainian officers, NCOs and specialists from WGRs 30 and 31 and the Division's various sub-units. The majority of them were veterans of Brody. Several volunteered, after being told that Ukrainian families and refugees in Slovakia were in danger from the Communists.[11]

The *Kampfgruppe* had a battle strength of approximately 1,500 men.[12] It consisted of three infantry companies (9th, 10th, 11th) and one heavy weapons company (12th) each of which had approximately 200 men, together with the following support units:

Kampfgruppe HQ (III/W.Gren. Rgt. d. SS 29)
III/Waffen-Gren.Rgt.29 (Gal.Nr.1)
1 battery light artillery
2 anti-tank platoons
2 pioneer platoons
1 signals unit
1 *Jagd* platoon
1 supply unit[13]
Also attached to the unit were chaplain *Waffen-Obersturmführer* Reverend Bohdan Levytsky and 2 medical doctors, with 10 men acting as orderlies.[14]

The man appointed to command the formation was an experienced soldier, aged 47 years. *SS-Obersturmbannführer* Karl Wildner had joined the Division less than four weeks previously. It was to be his first combat assignment. The various company and unit commands were divided between German and Ukrainian officers.[15]

Reflecting the numerous shortages that the Galician Division suffered, supplies of weapons and ammunition were limited and the standard of equipment and condition of the horses allocated to the *Kampfgruppe* was poor.[16] For mobility, it had at its disposal only 5 motor vehicles, 2 passenger cars and 3 motor cycles. There were draught horses for the transportation of the light artillery guns and the supply and ammunition wagons.

The first of three echelons entrained for Slovakia at Neuhammer on the 22 September.[17] They were to be followed by a second and third within 24 hours. On arrival, *Kampfgruppe* Wildner[18] was to move to its staging point on the south-western perimeter of the remaining insurgent-held territory. Immediately adjacent was *Kampfgruppe* Schill, to whose command it was subordinated when they joined the attack. Shortly after detraining at the station at Oslany on 28 September, even before it had reached its assembly position, enemy aircraft attacked the marching units of the *Kampfgruppe*. The commander of the 9th company, *SS-Untersturmführer* Lilinger, became the first casualty.[19] Thereafter, as a precautionary measure, detraining took place between stations in the same area.[20]

In the vicinity of the mountain village of Pila, Wildner organised his force. He began preparations for an attack on the town of Nova Bania situated approximately 10kms to the south. A reconnaissance group had previously established that the town could be reached from the west via mountain trails. In the early hours of 2 October the unit started its approach. The mountainous terrain made access difficult to negotiate and was especially unsuitable for the horse driven wooden ammunition carts. Within hours, the carts began to break on the rough trails and had to be abandoned, after their cargoes had been loaded on to the horses. Notwithstanding that problem, the first Ukrainian soldiers reached Nova Bania by late afternoon. By the evening the town had been captured from the partisans. They had been taken completely by surprise, so much so that their meals were still on the tables.[21]

Having occupied Nova Bania, and secured the area nearby, the *Kampfgruppe* proceeded north-east towards the town of Zarnovica. Some elements took part in light defensive fighting around Dolny Hamre and Svaty Kriz, and an assault on Stare Kremnica. On 9 October it received orders to continue north along the main Nitra-Ziar road, take the town of Bzenica and advance towards Vyhne and Banska Stiavnica. It was there that the first serious encounter took place with the partisan units. They had withdrawn to positions in the locality.[22]

As soon as Banska Stiavnica and the main access routes leading to the town had been secured, the unit moved southeast about 10kms in the direction of Kolpachy. In that area, around 17 October, the *Kampfgruppe* was reinforced by a platoon of *Flammenwerfern,* i.e. flamethrowers, from the *Kettgen Bataillon*. They fought what was to be the largest single engagement of the campaign. On the outskirts of the village of Babina, entrenched in heavily fortified positions were approximately two infantry battalions of insurgents. They were supported by 4 light bombers, 2 tanks and a battery of heavy artillery. After heavy fighting, against unequal odds, the *Kampfgruppe* successfully dislodged the enemy forces. Before they abandoned their positions, the enemy set fire to part of the village and the railway station, then retreated into the Low Tatras without being given a chance to regroup.[23]

To co-ordinate its forces for that action, and other smaller engagements that followed, the *Kampfgruppe* was mainly reliant upon despatch riders. The portable radio equipment, issued for the purpose, seldom worked because of weak signals caused by the mountains and dense forests.[24]

At the end of September 1944, just as *Kampfgruppe* Wildner had begun combat operations in Slovakia, the *Reichsführer*[25] responsible for anti-partisan warfare in the rear areas was confronted by a new potential danger. It threatened the whole strategic situation in the region. As a result of the gains made during the Soviet 'Carpathian-Dukla' operation, which began on 9 September, Red Army troops were threatening to break through the positions of 1st *Panzer* Army and cross the Dukla pass. The pass gave access to Slovakia via its eastern frontier. The Red Army had the objective of linking up with the insurgent army in central Slovakia.[26] If that aim was achieved the Soviets would have had at their disposal a force capable of extending their initial victory by a rapid thrust. Its most probable direction was expected to be southwesterly towards the rear of the German front in Hungary.

Thus the prompt subjugation of the Slovakian interior had become even more imperative. Authorisation was duly given in the following days, for further reinforcements to be despatched to that area. Foremost were three additional Waffen-SS units. They were the 18th *SS-Freiwilligen-Panzergrenadier* Division *'Horst Wessel'* and the 14th *Waffen-Grenadier Division der SS* (*galiz.* Nr.1), both of which already had a *Kampfgruppe* deployed in Slovakia, and the infamous *SS-Sonderregiment 'Dirlewanger'*.[27] They were augmented by a variety of smaller reserve and security units that were mostly designated for use as occupation forces. The largest were two *Volksgrenadier* Divisions, the 271st and 708th which between them deployed 6,981 and 6,018 officers, NCOs, and men respectively.[28]

The Galician Division received its movement orders from the SS-FHA in a document dated 28 September 1944. They directed that together with its Training and Reserve Regiment (SS-Gren.Ausb.u.Ers.Rgt.14),[29] it was to be transferred immediately from Neuhammer to the *Schutzzone,* i.e. defence zone, in Slovakia, where it would continue with its reformation. There, for supply and territorial purposes, it would be subordinated to the overall German commander for Slovakia, *SS-Obergruppenführer* Höfle in Bratislava (Pressburg). For normal military duties it was to remain under the direct command of the SS-FHA. In view of the recent start of its re-formation, the Division, excluding *Kampfgruppe* Wildner, was initially to be available only for local security deployment in its own vicinity. The formation of any additional combat groups, and their deployment against partisans, was to take place only with the authorisation of the head of the SS-FHA.[30] The Division's commander and his first assistant were to report to the German commander for Slovakia, for further instructions.

SS-Brigadeführer Freitag and *Major* Heike left at once. They travelled by rail to Bratislava for a conference with Höfle and his Chief of Staff von Uechtritz, concerning the details of the transfer and the assignment in Slovakia. At Höfle's HQ, Freitag reported that as the Division was still in the process of re-forming, and as most of its available weapons, ammunition and supplies had been allocated to *Kampfgruppe* Wildner, it could not be considered as deployable. Höfle, recognising the potential the formation afforded him, responded by promising energetic support in supplying it with weapons and provisions to assist with its reformation programme. He then proceeded to provide a summary of the political developments in Slovakia that had led to the uprising and the military actions that had come about as a result.

In accordance with his plan, the Galician Division was to replace the Tatra *Panzer* Division. It was needed for the final attack on the centre of the uprising, scheduled to begin in mid-October. It was to be assigned to the city of Zilina (Sillien) and its predominantly mountainous environs where it would essentially form an occupation force along the upper Vah valley. It would be responsible for defending the main communications lines and centres of military production, along with their workforce. It would maintain order and assist with the suppression of general partisan activity in the region. The technical details of the change over were to be arranged by the respective divisional commanders.

The following day, Freitag and *Major* Heike drove to Zilina to discuss the details of the exchange of control with the commander of the *Tatra* Division, General Friedrich-Wilhelm von Loeper. At the meeting the area of

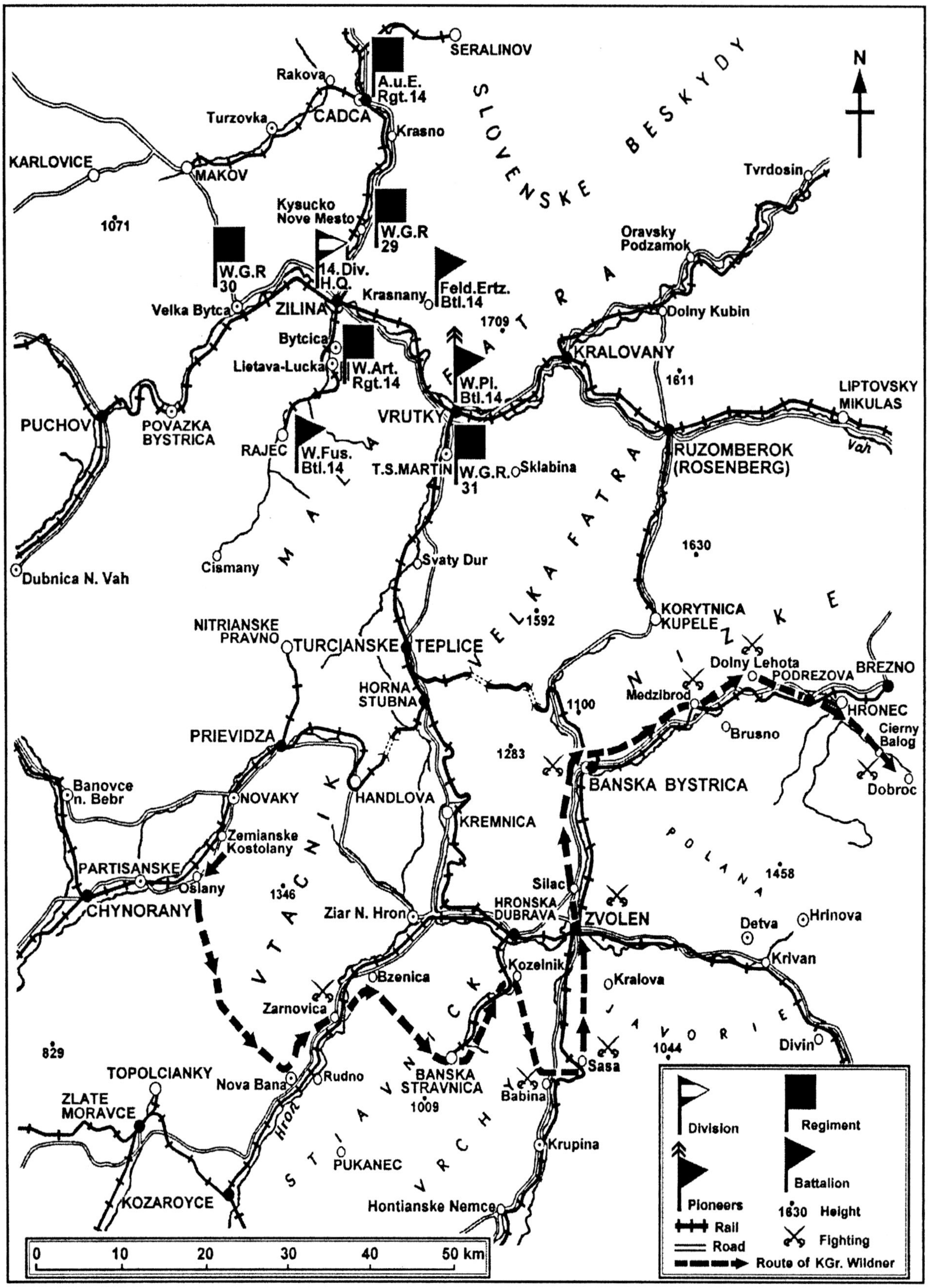

Map 8 Disposition of the Galician Division in Slovakia, September 1944, and the route of Kampfgruppe Wildner

operations within which the Division was to maintain security was defined. It had to cover the area of Ruzomberok, Dolny Kubin, Cadca-Rakova (3km WNW Cadca), Turzovka-Kolarovice (15 km NW Zilina), Povazska Bystrica-Svaty Dur (18km SW Vrutky), Sklabina-Podzamok (10km SE Vrutky).[31] The primary task was to protect the main railway line that ran from Zilina to the industrial town of Ruzomberok. It was of considerable strategic importance for moving troops and military supplies to the front. On the return journey, the line was used for ferrying the wounded to hospitals, and damaged vehicles to repair shops in Germany. It was also used for transporting completed guns from the artillery works at Ruzomberok. It was busy day and night.

As the largest and most substantial unit, all other formations involved in anti-partisan operations within its operational area would be subordinated to the Division, both operationally and for supply purposes.[32] Their duties clarified, both men returned to Neuhammer to oversee the transfer.

On 4 October, WGR 30, which was to form its advance party, entrained at Neuhammer for Slovakia. After a twenty-four hour journey it arrived on 6 October and began to prepare the defences and make suitable arrangements to accommodate the whole of the Galician Division.[33] The remaining echelons followed WGR 30 by train on 15 October.[34] By 17 October all combat and support units including the Training and Reserve Regiment[35] had detrained in Slovakia. The Division's strength at that time had almost reached its full, authorised strength and was recorded as 14,285 (285 officers and 13, 999 NCOs and men).[36] Upon arrival, basic deployment (subject to changes) was as follows:

1. Divisional Staff, Supply troops, Signals unit, Administration section, field hospital – in the city of Zilina.
2. Waffen-Grenadier-Regiment 29 – to the north of Zilina: Regimental HQ in Kysucke Nove Mestro.
3. Waffen-Grenadier-Regiment 30 – West of Zilina: Regimental HQ at Velka Bytca.
4. Waffen-Grenadier-Regiment 31 – South east of Zilina: Regimental HQ at Turcansky Svaty Martin.
5. Waffen-Fusilier Battalion – South west of Zilina: HQ at Rajec.
6. Waffen-Artillery Regiment – South of Zilina: HQ at Bytcica[37] Lietava Lucka.
7. *Panzerjäger Abteilung*: HQ at Turcansky Svaty Martin.
8. *Waffen-Pionier* Battalion: HQ in Vrutky.[38]
9. *Feld Ersatz Bataillon* 14- South east of Zilina: HQ at Krasniany.[39]
10. Training and Reserve Regiment, temporarily in Zilina area and then north east of the city: HQ at Cadca.[40] (see Map 8)

Some units were billeted in the recently vacated barracks of the former Slovakian Army, some were quartered in public buildings such as schools, cinemas or village halls. Others in outlying areas were billeted in private dwellings.

The Division's operational district was divided into defensive security zones, i.e. *Sicherungsbereiche*. To maximise its potential, its various sub-units occupied dispersed centres within the zones, sometimes in company or platoon strength. As soon as it arrived on Slovakian soil, the Division took over the static point defences and the guarding of local munitions factories, mines, bridges and tunnels and other strategically important sites. They safeguarded the main arterial transportation and communication routes. At the same time all sub-units were required to conduct security operations and anti-partisan sweeps within their respective areas.[41]

The extremely poor overall condition of the Division which, like the 708th *Volksgrenadier* and 271st *Volksgrenadier* divisions, was not yet fully armed,[42] meant that it was barely equal to its tasks. Virtually every company was significantly under strength and consisted mostly of fresh recruits with little or no basic training. The necessary numbers of officers and NCOs needed for administrative and training purposes were simply not available. It meant that often these duties had to be devolved to the most intelligent enlisted men or those with the most experience. The frequent transfer of personnel from company to company, at short notice, was another contributory factor that impacted negatively on their effectiveness. The provision of weapons and equipment at that time could only be described as lamentable. To cite a typical example, during its first week of deployment in Slovakia, the 1/I/WGR 30 had only two-thirds of its required weapons, i.e. 3 machine-guns, 3 submachine-guns, 2 pistols and 80 rifles. They suffered from severe shortages of ammunition and equipment. Within the company footwear was in a deplorable condition, as was clothing. There were only 20 helmets and 60 belts for 120 soldiers, who also lacked many other important accessories.[43]

A lesser burden was also caused by the recent influx of the newly promoted Ukrainian officers as company and platoon commanders. They lacked both administrative and, more importantly, practical frontline experience. Battalion commanders were compelled to hold regular instruction talks on the contemporary situation, and current tactical problems.

In spite of those considerable afflictions, continuing efforts by all units to clear the local terrain had, according to the official situation report on events in Slovakia, produced 'good results'. Within two weeks, prisoners and booty had been taken, and the surviving, strong, groups of partisans driven out of its whole sector and into the remote mountains and forests.[44]

At the same time, once the presence of the 14th *Waffen-Grenadier Division der SS* (*galiz.* Nr.1), became known, the Soviet partisan leader Colonel Popoff immediately sought, by a variety of propaganda methods, to unsettle the Ukrainians, especially in the area of Zilina, and induce them to defect. In the same two-week period 50 desertions were recorded.[45]

The Operations of *Kampfgruppe* Wildner and *Kampfgruppe* Wittenmeyer

During the first half of October *SS-Obergruppenführer* Höfle continued to assemble his forces for a final concentrated strike against the insurgent forces. The Galician Division was ordered to form a second task force to take part in the action.[46] It was an *ad-hoc* unit with limited offensive capability, and was formed on 15 October from WGR 30, the first to arrive in Slovakia. They were placed under the command of *SS-Hauptsturmführer* Friedrich Wittenmeyer. It consisted of the III/WGR 30, reinforced with 13/WGR 31, a section of artillery, pioneers, anti-tank grenadiers, signals unit and a supply unit.[47] Once mobilised and supplied it was to proceed to the north-east perimeter of the insurgent pocket. There it had to free the main railway line and road, from Ruzomberok to the east. It had to break the partisans' control and advance towards Brezno.

Both *Kampfgruppe* Wildner and *Kampfgruppe* Wittenmeyer took part in the final offensive that began on the morning of 19 October 1944. German forces closed in from all sides, along eleven routes, towards the centre of the rising. Despite brave efforts on the part of the defenders, and temporary delays in localities where the terrain prevented the Germans from deploying their heavy artillery and tanks, the insurgents, although well armed, could not withstand the intensity of the assault. Organised resistance soon collapsed.

From its assembly area of Poradi and Spisska Nord Ves, about 36 kms east of Ruzomberok, *Kampfgruppe* Wittenmeyer was deployed in conjunction with a unit of local Hlinka Guard militia, together with a unit of ex-Luftwaffe personnel, both of approximately company strength.[48] They set out with the primary objective of opening and safeguarding the main road and rail lines east of Ruzomberok. On the very first day it became obvious that because of the wet and muddy ground, the operation would be difficult. The light artillery guns quickly became bogged down and stuck in the mud. They could only be freed by using oxen from a nearby village. The following day, to overcome the problem, Wittenmeyer requested and received *Panzerspähwagen*. They enabled the artillery guns to be moved. They were then able to provide the necessary support for the infantry units.[49]

Within a short time, thus equipped, the battle group was able to achieve its objective. They drove the partisans who were in the proximity, into the impenetrable High Tatry Mountains. Thereafter, it joined the attack on the insurgent pocket in a secondary role, advancing from the north-east towards Brezno/Banska Bystrica. Between the 19 and 23 October, elements were involved in fighting in the area of Vernar and Kralova Lehota. On 24 October, having broken through the enemy positions and occupied Kralova Lehota, the battle group was reported to be "fighting slowly on the village of Maluzina" 21 kms north of Brezno, which it captured the next day. It freed the railway line for rail traffic, after track repairs, in the process.[50] The next report on its progress, dated 27 October, read "K.Gr. Wittenmeyer took Nisch (10km south of Krl. Lehota). Main road Rosenberg-Poprad is free of enemy." "The Ukrainian volunteers of the *Freiwilligen 14.Waffen-Gren.Div.SS* deployed here fought *exceptionally*." [Author's emphasis][51] On 28 October the unit was reported to have "cleared villages situated just south and north of the road Rosenberg-Poprad of the stronger partisan groups and secured many munitions dumps, provisions, and valuable light and heavy weapons."[52] Persevering through deep snow, in very difficult terrain, it continued its activities in the vicinity. It provided security for the recaptured area and pursuing the remaining part of the insurgent army into the High and Low Tatras. Then on 15 November it was withdrawn and returned to its parent formation.

Although it played a limited part in the final offensive, during its operations *Kampfgruppe* Wittenmeyer uncovered a significant amount of weapons and other war materiel,[53] and earned its commander promotion to the rank of *SS-Sturmbannführer* on 9 November.[54]

Kampfgruppe Wildner

Simultaneously, in the south-western sector, operating alongside *Kampfgruppe* Schill, *Kampfgruppe* Wildner fought a series of engagements of varying severity, with the insurgent units around the towns of Banska Stiavnica and Zvolen. The regular Slovak soldiers, in the absence of reserves to facilitate relief, were often on the verge of exhaustion and showed little inclination to fight. Towards the end of October they abandoned their heavily fortified defensive emplacements and withdrew towards Banska Bystrica. As they retreated they blew up all the bridges on the river Hron. Tired and demoralised, whole formations surrendered, frequently to the Ukrainians in preference to the Germans.[55] As far as he was able Wildner, who was himself a Slovak national, saw to it that groups of regular Slovak soldiers, especially the older men, were disarmed. Their weapons, mainly rifles, were distributed throughout the *Kampfgruppe*, before they were released.[56] Other prisoners, mostly the younger Slovak nationals, Red Army officers and men, and in at least one instance, two American airmen,[57] were sent to the rear for interrogation, once they too had been disarmed. In that way the *Kampfgruppe* was able to overcome many of the weapon deficiencies that had plagued it from the outset[58] although the acquisition of this weaponry was somewhat mitigated by a shortage of appropriate ammunition.[59] The captured medical supplies, mainly quantities of poor quality Soviet-made bandages, and various provisions, such as coffee, sugar, bread and fat were equally beneficial.[60]

On 28 October 1944, converging from several points, the German forces entered the recently evacuated town of Banska Bystrica. The town was the headquarters of the rebellion. The last insurgents retreated northwards to the area between Liptov Osada and Brezno in the Low Tatras. On 30 October 1944, a victory parade was held in Banska Bystrica. It was attended by Höfle, the Slovakian State President, Tiso, and delegations from the 18th *SS-Freiwilligen-Panzergrenadier* Division *'Horst Wessel'* and *Kampfgruppe* Schafer.[61] On that occasion, in a statement made on 31 October, President Tiso, publicly expressed his gratitude to the Waffen-SS and Army units, including the Galician Division, involved in freeing the Slovakia Republic from Bolsheviks and Communist partisans.[62] The official OKW report, announcing the collapse and destruction of the organised rebellion movement in Slovakia, followed a few days later.[63]

Kampfgruppe Wildner had in the meantime moved up to occupy Kralova and Radvan in the suburbs of Banska Bystrica. After a few days it received orders to secure the larger villages, in the region to the north east of the city, and in the surrounding mountains. There it was to attack the small pockets of well-armed Soviet and Czech partisans who were still active, and force them to disperse. An Ukrainian platoon commander who took part in the action later wrote:

> 'Passing the village of Medzibrod my platoon from 10th Company searched three freight cars at the railway station. We discovered families of Ukrainian refugees, about 30–40 people in total including children, hiding in them. A few days earlier they had been in the hands of the Communist partisans. As the area had been secured by the *Kampfgruppe*, I told them to head towards Banska Bystrica which was about 20kms away. In the next villages, Brusno and Predajna we met a few groups of former Slovakian soldiers returning to their homes. Lots of weapons were lying around which were a welcome 'gift' for us. They were mainly light infantry weapons such as Czech-made rifles, pistols and automatic weapons of mixed Czech, Soviet, and German origin, only some of which had ammunition, most having none. The company spent the night in Podbrezova. Early in the morning the *Kampfgruppe* under the command of *SS-Obersturmbannführer* Wildner started the assault on pockets of armed partisans and remnants of the 2nd Czech Airborne Brigade. The 10th

> Company encountered partisans in the mountains most of whom (50 or so) surrendered. But there was still some fighting during which two of our soldiers were wounded, before the last groups gave themselves up. Four Soviet officers and one female soldier were transferred to Battalion headquarters. After we returned to Podbrezova the company received orders to proceed to Hronec and then Cierny Balog. By 16 November the *Kampfgruppe* was back in Banska Bystrica/Kralova for a few days rest before it received transportation to rejoin the Division in Zilina.'[64]

On its return journey, parts of the *Kampfgruppe* engaged in short but heavy fighting, in the Povazska Bystrica and Turcansky Teplice regions, to the south west and south east of Zilina respectively.[65]

After ten weeks of fighting, it finally arrived in Zilina on 30 November 1944. They were greeted by the commander of WGR 29, *SS-Standartenführer* Dern with his staff and the Divisional band.[66] The unit was then disbanded and returned to WGR 29. The soldiers were given two days' rest before being assigned to security duties in Zilina.[67] The wounded were transferred for treatment to the Division's hospital in the city. There, according to a report about the rationing situation for the patients, submitted by *SS-Obersturmbannführer* Dr Max Specht, the Head of Section IVb (Medical) of the Division's staff, the allotment of meat, fat and sugar was minimal. It was totally inadequate for recuperating patients.[68]

In view of the duration of the campaign, and the nature of the fighting, the total number of casualties sustained by *Kampfgruppe* Wildner, seventeen killed and sixty-seven wounded,[69] was comparatively low. Several of the Ukrainian soldiers who had distinguished themselves were recommended for and subsequently received decorations. To supplement a variety of lesser combat awards that were made,[70] an estimated total of 32 soldiers were decorated with the Iron Cross 2nd Class.[71] German personnel received the award in both the 1st and 2nd Class.[72]

According to Heike, the Galician Division sent a third group to the area of Ruzomberok. The strength and disposition of that group was and is unknown. It encountered no partisans. They had all dispersed by that time.[73]

With the successful conclusion of the uprising, Höfle honoured his pledge, and assigned a significant portion of the predominantly Czech-made armaments, with appropriate ammunition, and other war matériel from the captured stocks of the Slovak Army to the Galician Division. Small arms, rifles, light and heavy machine-guns, infantry support artillery and other artillery pieces of all calibre, including three of the excellent 7.5cm Pak 40 anti-tank guns,[74] were obtained in quantity over the next few weeks. It further supplemented the weaponry acquired by its two *Kampfgruppen* during their operations. From the 309 artillery pieces captured by the Germans, the Division's Artillery Regiment was able to obtain 90% of the German-made field howitzers that it came to use.[75] Almost all of the light guns originated from the large caches of weapons found by *Kampfgruppe* Wittenmeyer.[76] As a rule, the best equipment was retained by its combat elements while the remainder was passed to the support and supply units.

Equally important was the allocation of a number of horses and motor vehicles. Mostly they consisted of Skoda private passenger cars, Slovak military trucks and motorcycles.[77] In total, over 800 trucks were captured, the bulk of which went to the 18th *SS-Freiwilligen-Panzergrenadier* Division *'Horst Wessel'*.[78] Of those allotted to the Galician Division, not all were in working order although the workshop company was able to salvage and repair several which had been damaged. The acquisition of extra motor vehicles proved to be a major asset. They facilitated the formation of a motorised echelon that could be sent quickly to any sector where it was needed.

The remaining equipment and stores of provisions it received, such as ammunition trucks, field kitchens, horse-blankets, spades and much needed footwear, were distributed by the Ib (Quartermaster) *SS-Hauptsturmführer* Herbert Schaaf to all sections. The abundance was such that the Division could be considered fully armed and equipped and partly mobile.

Anabasis in Slovakia

German dominion had been re-established and the frontline in the east temporarily stabilised in the Carpathians. In the next few weeks the so-called *Schutzzone* of western Slovakia underwent a period of relative tranquillity. The surviving elements of the Slovak army, and Communist partisan groups, had dispersed. Having managed to escape the final encirclement, they fled. They reorganised and established bases high in remote mountain regions. There, after making preparations for the rapid onset of winter, they continued to conduct guerrilla warfare. They launched raids on signal and administrative installations, bridges, storage and supply depots and other similarly susceptible targets.[79]

To accelerate combat training and gain vital practical experience for its soldiers, at every opportunity the Galician Division's command elected to undertake extensive assignments. They involved search and destroy missions against the partisans, in preference to the defence of strategic points and sentry duty. That was entrusted to reserve German units.

The operations extended as far as the Lower Tatry and Fatra Mountains. Although they seldom resulted in any significant engagements, they were extremely arduous for soldiers and horses alike. They often took place in snow and freezing cold winter weather, in mountainous and heavily forested country. The strenuous physical effort was however beneficial in as much as it helped to build up the soldiers' endurance threshold.

Small detachments, and specially formed assault groups known as *Jagdzüge* or *Jagdkompanie,* were formed by almost all the sub-units.[80] They hoped to exploit the key element of surprise. To aid their activities, the Division received a limited supply of specialist equipment such as skis, and small sledges to tow machine-guns and mortars. A large shipment of warm, winter, reversible, camouflage uniforms and winter boots,[81] caused a certain degree of resentment among the less well equipped regular Wehrmacht units stationed in the same area.[82] The small detachments enjoyed a distinct advantage over larger groups whose movements were easily detectable. Acting independently, or guided by indigenous units formed from friendly Slovak elements,[83] they were sent deep into the snow-covered mountains on reconnaissance missions and regular patrols. They had orders to concentrate on the discovery of partisan routes and camps. In that way, continual harassment compelled the partisans to move to other areas and prevented them from consolidating their positions.

From time to time, that difficult and unique type of warfare, with all its inherent peculiar tactics, demanded extraordinary countermeasures. They required equal ingenuity from the Division's soldiers. A *Waffen-Untersturmführer* commanding 5/II/ WGR 30, described one such event and a most resourceful solution to a difficult problem:

> 'The entire company was in a large village, the houses of which were mostly situated along the entire length of a road which ran through it. We were wearing reversible winter camouflage uniforms. While we were in the village, somebody noticed that the company *Waffenwart* [weapons keeper] was missing and it became clear that the partisans had seized him. I ordered a retreat to the far end of the village where we were hidden from view and sent a member of the company back with an ultimatum to the partisans: either they release him in two hours or I burn down the village. Two hours passed in great tension and when there was no sight of him I had two smoke grenades activated which from a distance made it look as though part of village was burning. Apparently it made an impression on the partisans because about ten minutes later they released our *Waffenwart* unharmed'.[84]

Occasional large-scale anti-partisan actions were undertaken. Whenever those took place the commanders of the Division's individual units liased directly with Höfle and his staff. They planned and supervised all major operations from the head quarters in Bratislava. As with the smaller actions, those too met with varying degrees of success,[85] the principal hindrance being the co-ordination of troop movements in the field. Use of the Division's Fieseler Storch light reconnaissance aeroplane partly offset the problem. But maintaining communication via radio contact remained highly problematical, because of the lack of portable radio sets, and the variability of elevation that caused the sets to malfunction. Even when the sets did work, the Ukrainian operators sometimes had problems understanding German commands.[86] The partisans had to be extremely mobile, and also enjoyed the advantage of operating on home territory. Furthermore, according to *Major* Heike, they benefited from the fact that the Ukrainians, "when left to their own devices in impenetrable terrain, frequently failed to follow orders, neglected basic military principles and failed to pay attention to detail".[87] Fortunately the Division's casualties during those operations were minimal. Provision was made for the burial of fatalities to take place in local villages, accompanied by appropriate religious rites.

In Slovakia, all engagements were waged in a proper and controlled manner. The execution of prisoners, the taking of hostages and the destruction of buildings, unless occupied by the enemy and therefore a legitimate target, were expressly prohibited under all circumstances. On their own initiative, many of the Ukrainian soldiers had adopted a lenient attitude towards their prisoners. Those who were not released straight away or not known about by the Germans, were allowed to escape.[88] They were well treated, some of the wounded receiving treatment by the Division's medical personnel.[89] Moreover, in some instances transgressions by the civilian population were deliberately overlooked.[90]

However, not for the first time, other German units stationed in the same district ascribed some of their own misdeeds to the Ukrainians, the main culprits being *SS-Sonderregiment* Dirlewanger and the *Ostturkischer Waffenverband*.[91] Both units committed a number of outrages against the local inhabitants and later attempted to pass them off on the Galician Division.[92]

Isolated instances of mistreatment of Slovaks, or serious breeches of discipline, by the Division's Ukrainian soldiers that did occur were referred to *SS-Sturmbannführer* Hans Ziegler who headed Section III (Legal) of the Divisional staff. Likewise, a few individuals were also found guilty of lesser infractions such as petty theft of personal effects and small items of value taken during house searches. Proven cases were referred to Freitag, who inevitably recommended capital punishment or transfer to a penal company. That in itself was an active deterrent.[93] Later, as will be seen, Freitag requested a special authority that would give him far reaching powers to punish those guilty of transgressions.

As well as their other duties, all units continued with vigorous training that was progressing well. There were two main factors that facilitated development in that respect. One was the gradual replacement of *Reichsdeutsch* and *Volksdeutsche* NCOs, who proliferated within most companies, when the formation had first arrived in Slovakia with Ukrainians. That in turn made communication far easier as, at that time, the majority of Ukrainians had only the most rudimentary command of German.[94] Familiarity grew as personnel had time to settle into new units and get to know their comrades.

Emphasis was placed on sharp-shooting, weapons instruction and night exercises. Specialist training was given, and complementary courses held, as available resources permitted. Correct and thorough training remained a high priority, despite the rapidly deteriorating war situation. Some of their fellow countrymen had been conscripted by the occupying Red Army, and were thrown into the frontline with little or no training. However, the opportunity for further development, via NCO and officer courses for the soldiers of the Division, continued to be available until the last weeks of the war.[95]

Assault exercises were conducted with live ammunition in areas where partisan units were known or suspected to be present. It was regarded as training for anti-partisan warfare. To a certain extent that combat experience compensated for the fact that given the physical characteristics of the district in which the Division was deployed, large-scale manoeuvres, similar to those performed at Neuhammer prior to its departure to the front at Brody, were not a practical proposition. The deep, narrow valleys and irregular terrain were not conducive to the battle deployment that involved regimental or battalion sized groups.

As the partisan activity subsided and encounters became less and less frequent, the Division settled down to garrison duty in a country that, disturbed only by frequent air-raid alarms, had almost completely escaped the ravages of war. Sunday concerts were given by the Divisional orchestra which regularly toured the regiments in Slovakia. When free from duty the Ukrainian soldiers were permitted to visit bars or cinemas. There they mingled with the Slovak community with whom, on the whole, they quickly established excellent relations. This was partly due to a similarity in the Slovak and the Ukrainian languages. Strong religious ties were common, as recalled by a Waffen-grenadier serving with WGR 29:

> 'Slovaks liked the Ukrainians and we liked them. They regularly invited us to their homes. We attended their church on Sundays. We met their young people and became very friendly.'[96]

This rapport with the population, and the general decrease in partisan actions, had other less desirable side effects. Discipline was becoming lax, and there was an increasing danger of complacency amongst units that were inactive for prolonged periods.

Food was plentiful, as rationing was not in force. Forays into the mountains, chasing partisans, produced the occasional deer to supplement military rations. Other foodstuffs could be bought from the shops that offered a bewildering array of meat, cakes, wines, spirits, real coffee, and sweets. Other luxury consumer goods, such as watches, were unknown in most occupied countries in late 1944. The only restriction, on the acquisition of many valued commodities, came about as the result of Freitag's order to issue military pay half in Slovak Kronen and half in German Marks.[97] Despite the considerable risk involved, some Ukrainian soldiers sold military equipment and items of uniform to the civilian population, to try to generate the required local currency. Occasionally they resorted to bartering.[98]

Seeking to take advantage of the ease with which the Ukrainian soldiers integrated with the native population, Soviet agents posed as Slovak nationals. They attempted to befriend them in the hopes of procuring useful intelligence about troop movements, unit strengths and other classified information. On the whole, their efforts were ineffectual. Civilians suspected of being enemy agents were arrested and handed over to section Ic, military intelligence, for interrogation.[99] The effectively waged and sustained propaganda campaign was more efficacious. Both the Soviet and Slovak partisans encouraged desertion. To that end, safe conduct passes and leaflets were produced and distributed. They promised among other things that those who surrendered voluntarily would not be punished, and would be allowed to return to their homes.

Section VI of the Divisional staff, religion, entertainment, education and information, was headed by *SS-Sturmbannführer*[100] Karl Robert Zoglauer. He was responsible for counteracting the Soviet propaganda. A circular letter dated 6 November 1944, issued by that section emphasised the inconsistencies in the Bolshevik propaganda. In the leaflets the essence and content of which rigidly followed the same formula, neither Communism and the USSR, nor Bolshevism and the Bolshevik army were mentioned. Instead only Russia, i.e. the Soviet Union, and the Russian Army, were, in the hopes of appealing to the local Slovak population. It went on to remind the soldiers of the "hunger, chaos and destruction" offered by the "liberators of the European people". It concluded by stating that if the soldiers gave themselves up, they would not be allowed to return home. Instead, they would be drafted into the Red Army, along with all the men aged between 18–50 years in the Bolshevik occupied territories, as had recently been the case in Slovakia. They would be given three days' training before being sent to the front.[101]

To reduce susceptibility and as a further disincentive, all units were constantly rotated between different localities. Even so, many of the Division's soldiers remained billeted away from proper military barracks, but were in small villages. In conjunction with that, contact between the soldiers, and members of the population, was restricted by confining it strictly to business matters. It was a policy that proved to be unenforceable.

Nonetheless, in spite of such measures, desertions of both officers and enlisted men were recorded by virtually every unit during the Division's stay in Slovakia. The total number reached approximately 200,[102] a figure that exceeded the number of fatalities. They were estimated at 126[103] in the same period. It seems the majority sought to cross the Carpathian Mountains to join the UPA, while others deserted to avoid disciplinary measures, or found themselves a *sleczna* (girlfriend) whose families often offered to provide a suitable hiding place. Conscripts, Communist agents who had infiltrated, opportunists, and those with divided loyalties[104] all took the opportunity to leave the Division. It is worth noting that the total number of deserters includes a small percentage of soldiers who were taken prisoner during active operations.

Approximately 39 deserters were caught and publicly executed by firing squad, in front of their assembled comrades.[105]

In mid-November, the Division absorbed a group of Ukrainians who arrived in Slovakia having been temporarily seconded to the 5th *SS-Panzer* Division *'Wiking'*. They were part of a group of 'around one thousand'[106] Ukrainians from the Galician Division's Training and Reserve Regiment.[107] They had been assembled on 8 July, at Heidelager, prior to being seconded to the 5th *SS-Panzer* Division *'Wiking'* for training.[108] Their basic infantry training began in Heidelager, and was eventually completed on or about 5 September at another Waffen-SS training establishment at Strasece near Prague in Bohemia.[109] From there, they boarded a train for Modlin, north of Warsaw, in Poland. There, on 10 September 1944 the 1,000 grenadiers were divided up between *'Wiking's'* two infantry regiments, *'Westland'* and *'Germania'*, and its artillery regiments.[110]

To serve the spiritual needs, and improve the morale, of the Ukrainian soldiers, the Military Board recommended that a chaplain, *Waffen-Obersturmführer* Julian Habrusevych, be assigned to the *'Wiking'* Division.[111] The arrangements were made but a series of delays prevented the chaplain from arriving in Modlin until after the surviving Ukrainian contingent had rejoined their parent formation.[112]

As members of the *'Wiking'* Division were at that time engaged in the third defensive battle for Warsaw, the Ukrainian soldiers were split up, no more than 5 per unit.[113] They were sent to frontline defensive positions to the north west of the city, close to the confluence of the Vistula and Buh rivers. Dressed in German uniform, and distinguishable only by the Ukrainian insignia worn on their collar patches and armshields,[114] the Ukrainians, most of whom spoke little or no German,[115] were thrown into heavy fighting. It lasted one month. They faced attacks by powerful Soviet assault forces whose targets were the Vistula crossings and the town of Modlin. Despite their significant numerical weakness, the Soviet attacks were successfully repulsed and the front held, the defenders having sustained extremely heavy losses in the process.[116] By 30 October when the survivors were withdrawn from the frontline, only approximately 800 men were left from the original contingent.[117] The others were dead or wounded.[118]

There were numerous requests from the Military Board and many submissions of petitions to the *'Wiking'* Division command from the Ukrainian soldiers.[119] Himmler finally ordered their detachment and transfer back to the Galician Division. On the occasion of their formal departure on 3 November 1944, and in recognition of their contribution, the *'Wiking'* Division commander *SS-Standartenführer* Ulrich issued a special order. He praised their efforts in helping to hold the enemy, although heavily outnumbered. He thanked them for their "proven commitment to the battle against Bolshevism".[120] The survivors returned to Zilina on 17 November 1944, and were integrated into the various sub-units. Their combat experience proved to be a major asset. According to their instructors they went on to become some of the Division's best soldiers.[121]

The First Concessions

While the reformation process continued in Slovakia, the Ukrainians came a step closer to realising the political agenda for the Division that they so eagerly sought. It came about, as the result of a belated attempt of some elements within the Nazi state. They wanted to mobilise the support, en masse, of the hitherto subjugated eastern peoples, in the defence of the collapsing Reich.[122]

General Reinhard Gehlen, head of Foreign Armies East (*Fremde Heere Ost*), *Generalfeldmarschall* Günter von Kluge, and General Ernst Kostring were among a growing number of notable personalities who advocated the formation of a 'Committee for the Liberation of the Peoples of Russia' (*Komitet Osvobozhdeniia Narodov Rossii*) [KONR]. It would be under the leadership of the anti-Bolshevik Russian General Andrei Andreyevich Vlasov.[123] The Committee was to have its own Russian Army of Liberation known as the *Russkaya Osvoboditelnaya Armiy* [ROA] that would fight as Germany's ally against the Soviets. To appeal to the Russians in the Red Army, political concessions were to be granted in the event of a German victory. Foremost was the formation of a Russian state over which the Russians would continue to exercise political control.[124] According to the federalist concept to which Vlasov and his German sponsors[125] adhered, the ROA would encompass all the other former Soviet nationalities that would be subordinated to Vlasov's overall command, thus unifying the forces struggling against Bolshevism.

Other proponents of co-operation with former Soviet nationals were opposed to the federalist concept. They included Alfred Rosenberg and several prominent members of his *Ostministerium*[126] and Dr Fritz Rudolph Arlt[127] chief of the *Freiwilligen Leitstelle Ost in Amtsgruppe D*, or Eastern Volunteers Desk. It was a special advisory agency within the SS-FHA.[128] They supported the idea of national separatism and autonomy for the non-Russian nations of the USSR and the formation, under German auspices, of several distinct National Committees as representatives of the larger ethnic minorities, along with Vlasov, Primus Inter Pares.[129]

In each case, the Germans were fully cognisant of the fact that it was imperative to secure the support of the Ukrainians, if they were to succeed in that endeavour. They formed the largest, and most important, of the minority populations of the Soviet Union.

At first, attempts were made to establish closer co-operation with the Ukrainian nationalists via the *Ukrainska Holovna Vyzvolna Rada* (Ukrainian Supreme Liberation Council) which formed the political superstructure of the OUN-UPA.[130] In doing so, the Germans hoped to exploit the significant anti-Soviet potential of the UPA. After the German withdrawal it was directing its activities principally against the occupying Soviets,[131] in order to maintain a small second front behind Soviet lines. The German overtures met with limited success amongst local UPA leaders resulting in occasional airdrops of arms and equipment being made.[132] However, the UPA leadership declined to enter into any formal agreement of co-operation.

Persisting in their efforts to realise their plans, and as a further inducement to gain Ukrainian support, the Germans released several prominent Ukrainian nationalist political leaders. Until that time they had been proscribed pariahs, together with many of their followers from various concentration camps.[133] Taras Borovets' (aka Bulba) was freed in August 1944.[134] He was followed by the leaders of the two main branches of the OUN, Stephan Bandera and his deputy Jaroslav Stetsko (OUN-B) who were released on 27 September 1944, from Sachsenhausen where they had been imprisoned since 1941. The OUN-M leader Andrij Melnyk followed them on 17 October 1944.

The Germans were represented by Berger (*SS-FHA*), Dr Arlt (*Freiwilligen Leitstelle Ost im RSHA*), and *SS-Obersturmbannführer* Ludwig Wolff (*Einzel-Leitstelle Ukraine*) among others. They initiated a series of discussions with the various representatives of the organised Ukrainian political and community centres, including Bandera, Melnyk, Skoropadskyj, Kubijovych and others. That was with a view to forming an Ukrainian Committee for incorporation into the KONR. In the negotiations which followed they discovered that although there were differences of opinion among the Ukrainian leaders, they were united, both in their desire for the establishment of an independent Ukrainian state, as well as in their total opposition to any Russian directed enterprise.[135] In that respect the Ukrainians had the unqualified support of other National Committees in particular those of the Georgians (Kediya), Belorussians (Astrausky), and Don Cossacks (Krasnov). All were equally hostile to the KONR project and the Russian claim to political hegemony.[136]

Notwithstanding the failure of their negotiations, as a token gesture a Pro Vlasovitie Ukrainian was found outside the recognised political centres, named Dr Fedir Bohatyrchuk. He was appointed to head a rival Ukrainian committee under Vlasov. Realising that it was imperative to gain the endorsement of the OUN who would have nothing to do with the Russianised Committee, the Germans were obliged to continue their discussions.

The Germans were unable to create a working union with either the Bandera or Melnyk factions of the OUN. Concerned that none of the remaining leaders possessed sufficient stature or support to make him acceptable as the head of the Ukrainian Committee,[137] the Germans made contact with Andrij Levytskyj president of the UNR.[138] As a government in exile the UNR was a non-partisan body that had no direct contact with the underground Ukrainian organisations. In late November Levytskyj nominated General Pavlo Feofanovich Shandruk[139] as leader of the UNC.[140] A pragmatic career soldier who was politically remote, Shandruk was found to be acceptable to all nationalistic factions,[141] and after further talks with Levytskyj, and other Ukrainian representatives, was persuaded to accept the nomination.

Shandruk was summoned to Berlin for a meeting with Dr Arlt, and the head of his Ukrainian section, *SS-Obersturmbannführer* Wolff. They had lengthy discussions concerning the proposed organisation, composition and functions of the committee and its relationship with Vlasov's KONR.[142] During the conference it quickly became apparent to Dr Arlt that Shandruk too demanded what amounted to no less than formal German recognition of an Ukrainian sovereign state. Shandruk set out certain conditions which would ensure that the Ukrainians would be regarded as German allies and not merely as mercenaries.[143]

The conditions were that Germany should renounce all territorial claims in Ukraine. Secondly that the formation of an Ukrainian provisional government be permitted, and that there would be native command for the

Galician Division. There would be the transfer of all soldiers of Ukrainian origin, who were dispersed throughout all formations of the Wehrmacht, to purely Ukrainian units. The organisation of a national army under Ukrainian command would march under the Ukrainian national banner, wear traditional Ukrainian uniforms, swear allegiance to Ukraine and serve only Ukrainian interests. The liberation of the remaining Ukrainian political prisoners from German concentration camps would be guaranteed. Civil rights for freedom of assembly, organisations, freedom of speech and freedom of the press would follow.

Dr Arlt, who was not in a position to make any binding promises, told Shandruk that he would give his full support to obtaining consent to those conditions. However, he advised Shandruk not to make them a sine qua non, but rather 'get in on a developing situation'.[144] In line with Himmler's own recently declared position, that the new Vlasov committee should enjoy an overall authority,[145] Arlt was however obliged to insist that the Ukrainian National Committee be subordinated to Vlasov's KONR. In response, Shandruk was equally adamant. He emphatically refused to recognise even the symbolic supremacy of the KONR, headed by Vlasov, stating that no Ukrainian would support him, because such recognition would be considered treason.[146]

In due course Dr Arlt referred the matter to Berger who had been appointed as Himmler's plenipotentiary in all Russian affairs.[147] But Berger remained insistent upon the condition.[148] In an attempt to resolve that contentious issue a meeting was arranged between Shandruk and Vlasov.[149] After much heated discussion Vlasov proffered an acceptable compromise. Shandruk would retain an Ukrainian Committee that would be formally installed as representatives solely of Galicia and would command an Ukrainian (Galician) Army. At the same time another Division of east Ukrainians who wished to place themselves under Vlasov's banners would be formed under the KONR.[150] Himmler sanctioned the idea, in principle, at his second meeting with Vlasov in February 1945, but then it was Hitler who vetoed the plan.[151]

Thus the formal legalised recognition of the émigré Ukrainian Committee that would have transformed it into a government in exile was withheld for several weeks. That was until the former Governor of Galicia, Dr Wächter, having been appointed as the intermediary between Vlasov and Shandruk, was able to persuade his superiors to acquiesce to Shandruk's demand for an Ukrainian Committee independent of the KONR.[152]

Official German recognition of Shandruk's Ukrainian National Committee was withheld, because of his refusal to subordinate it to Vlasov. In the interim, as a by-product of Arlt's efforts on behalf of the Ukrainians, the SS authorities relented with regard to the question of Ukrainian national identity within the Galician Division.[153] In November 1944, four minor but prestigious gestures became effective that, for the first time, allowed it to convey a perceptible Ukrainian national character. Firstly, the Divisional orchestra was granted permission to play the Ukrainian national anthem as well as the two German anthems.[154] Secondly, approval was granted to fly the Ukrainian flag in the national colours of blue and gold, alongside the German flag.[155] In addition, the increasing usage, of the Ukrainian national symbol, the Trident, was to be permitted especially on Ukrainian celebratory and ceremonial occasions even though it officially remained prohibited.[156] Thirdly, a new oath was authorised with a modified text that read:

> 'I swear before God this holy oath, that in the battle against Bolshevism, and for the liberation of my Ukrainian people and Ukrainian homeland, I will give absolute obedience to the Commander in Chief of the German armed forces and all fighters of the young European nations against Bolshevism, Adolf Hitler, and as a brave soldier I will always be prepared to lay down my life for this oath.'[157]

Finally, and perhaps most significantly from a political point of view, it was formally recognised by the Germans as being a 'Ukrainian' as opposed to a 'Galician' formation and was renamed accordingly. By order of the *Reichsführer*, dated 12 November 1944, the suffix (*galizische* Nr.1)[158] was replaced by (*ukrainische* Nr.1) in the Division's title. It became redesignated *14. Waffen-Grenadier-Division der SS* (*ukrainische* Nr.1), a measure which the Ukrainians themselves and the Division's German sponsors, most notably Dr Wächter, had repeatedly petitioned for. Although its commander *SS-Brigadeführer* Freitag was already referring to the Division by its new name by 15 November 1944,[159] the change in nomenclature was not adopted universally, even within the Division itself.[160]

An explanation as to the reason for the change, purportedly to have been at Freitag's behest, was to be made to the Division's soldiers during *Weltanschaulichen* (political doctrine) lectures,[161] in compliance with the set guidelines contained in a circular produced by Section VI of the Divisional staff which explained:

> The *Reichsführer-SS* has, following the suggestion of the Division-commander, (sic.) ordered the renaming of our Division to 14th *Waffen-Gren.Division der SS* (*ukrainische* Nr.1). The meaning of this order is to be explained to the men during *Weltanschaulichen* studies, according to the following guide-lines:
>
> 1. The Division, while in the *Generalgouvernement* was mainly made up of men from the Galician region, hence the designation 'Galician Nr.1' (*galizische* Nr.1).
> 2. Increasingly as time went by the Division became a melting pot for Ukrainian men from all regions of Ukraine. It is also intended as the future military home for all Ukrainians. Thus the term 'Galician' has become too narrow, and the term 'Ukrainian' has been ordered in accordance with the requirements of the Reichsführer-SS.
> 3. The renaming is closely related to the stepping up of the battle against Bolshevism by the entire Ukrainian people.
>
> The renaming has fulfilled a long-standing wish for all of us. However, this also brings with it a holy duty: "To preserve the unity of Ukraine! For this it is required that: Everyone, try to help everyone else, wherever necessary. We must build a large community of comrades and thus become, for our people and homeland, the necessary fighting community which will enable us to survive all hard battles against our arch-enemy bolshevism.
>
> To emphasise the unity that the new title was intended to convey, the document ended by stating that, "All brotherly differences between east and west Ukrainians must be put aside during this most fateful hour."[162]

Moreover, accompanying the changes, and alongside tired and meaningless German propaganda themes such as 'The New Europe' that were still being expounded in their lectures,[163] the Ukrainian soldiers were openly urged to continue their military training. After the defeat of the Bolsheviks the Division would be the elite of the Ukrainian Army, safeguarding Ukrainian statehood.[164]

It should be noted that by introducing these cosmetic reforms the Germans sought to alleviate some of the tensions which had built up between the Division's German and Ukrainian contingent, now predominantly conscripted. .

Similar considerations almost certainly accounted for Freitag's order dated 10 November 1944, announcing the death of his Excellency the Greek Catholic Archbishop and Metropolitan Andreas Graf von Sheptyskyj in L'viv on 1 November 1944. In the dedication, Freitag who had once been granted an audience with Sheptyskyj, wrote "Our Division has lost in his Excellency one of our most noted friends and oldest benefactors." In memory of the late Metropolitan he ordered a special requiem to be held on Sunday 19 November 1944. All units were to devote one hour to the personality of the late Metropolitan as part of the *Weltanschaulichen* lecture in the week 12–19 November 1944.[165] This conciliatory initiative, despite being well received by the Ukrainians, was manifestly insufficient to improve his reputation, which remained irrevocably damaged.

Indeed, far from representing a genuine commitment to address the clear lines of cleavage which had developed between the two sides, the internal policies that Freitag continued to pursue, offset any progress and ensured that the growing rift became even more pronounced. For example, to circumvent the influence of *Major* Heike, who enjoyed a close and very good relationship with the Ukrainians, the Ukrainian Liaison Officer *Waffen-Obersturmführer* Dr Makarushka was given explicit instructions that matters in his jurisdiction were to be discussed only with the commander of the Division.[166] The effect of this edict was to limit Heike's involvement to purely tactical matters and "exclude him from dealing with questions of Ukrainian interest."[167] In the most blatant illustration, Freitag permitted the commander of WGR 30, *SS-Obersturmbannführer* Forstreuter, not only to remove an Ukrainian officer, Waffen-Untersturmführer Alexander Podolynsky, from his command of the regimental staff company, but then to replace him with a German NCO, *SS-Sturmscharführer* Bessel. To make matters worse, for a few months Podolynsky and *Waffen-Untersturmführer* Rostislav Chomyn were obliged to serve under Bessel as platoon commanders in the company.[168]

Likewise, to suppress disquieting developments amongst the Ukrainians in the Division, in a letter dated 7 December 1944, Freitag sought Himmler's endorsement of the implementation of court martial proceedings. As often as not these proceedings resulted in the death penalty. Freitag considered it "unnecessary bureaucracy" in the current regulations that enforced order, and kept the Ukrainians in line. It read:

14. Waffen-Gren. Div. der SS (ukr.Nr.1)
O.U., 7 December 1944
Commander
To the *Reichsführer-SS's* judge.

For information for referral to the *Reichsführer-SS*.

1. Court of the German *Kdo. Stelle Reichsführer-SS* Senior commander in Slovakia Pressburg.
2. *Hauptamt* SS Legal Department Prien/Chiemsee.

The exceptional situation and the circumstances within the Division, force me to use the harshest measures and most severe penalties in dealing with all breaches of military discipline, political unreliability, and in particular cases of desertion.

A section of the Ukrainian members of the Division have a general tendency to put themselves above the demands of military discipline and to disregard the authority of their superiors. This has repeatedly led to incidents that are unthinkable in a German division. Not only have incidents of disobedience reached an above average level, but also things have often gone as far as confrontation and attacks against superiors, including German superiors. Besides these, there have also been countless incidents where pro-Bolshevik, pro-Polish and anti-German propaganda have been promoted. As a result the number of deserters has, at times, reached an unbearable level. This development has been to a large extent assisted by the fact that the Division is in a region were deserters can easily go underground via partisans, and a hostile anti-German civilian population.

For that reason I saw myself compelled to instruct my court to mete out the severest punishments. Above all I committed them to the speediest sentencing and implementation of the verdict, because only the immediate resolution and punishment of these cases will be a deterrent. It will also contribute to thwarting similar transgressions.

Unfortunately I have had to observe that the efforts of my court have often been hindered by formal difficulties that prevent an immediate resolution of procedure. For example, delays arise because a legal opinion must first be obtained from the court of the senior commander in Slovakia, before a sentence can be confirmed and executed. In addition there exists a regulation, according to which in cases involving political offences or undermining of military strength (*Wehrkraft*), paragraph 5. Section 1 numbers 1 and 2 *KsstVO*, states that the main hearing should only take place following receipt of instructions from the *Hauptamt SS-Gericht* (SS Main Legal Department[169]) Directive sheet of the *Hauptamt's* SS Legal Department Year 1, Number 216. Consequently, according to existing regulations sentences passed against Ukrainian officers must be passed to the *Reichsführer-SS* for confirmation.

In order to avoid these delays, which at this time can simply no longer be tolerated in the interests of maintaining disciplined conduct, I have ordered my court to disregard the questionable regulations, for the time being. In this respect I have allowed the legal opinion to be given, by my own court, as a matter of principle in the trial of Ukrainians. Further to this I have also allowed the trial of Ukrainians for undermining of military strength (*Wehrkraft*) to proceed without authorisation from the *Hauptamt* SS Legal Department, and in some cases I have myself confirmed sentences against Ukrainian officers and arranged for the sentences to be carried out.

I now request a special authorisation according to which:

1. The legal opinion for the trial of Ukrainians can be given by the Divisional court as a matter of principle.

2. The trial of Ukrainians for sabotage and political offences does not require authorisation by the *Hauptamt* SS Legal Department.

3. Sentences against Ukrainian officers can be confirmed by myself, and that even so, I be allowed to sign penal ordinances and injunctions without presenting them to the *Reichsführer-SS* or the *Hauptamt* SS legal Department.

Freitag
SS-Brigadeführer und Generalmajor der Waffen-SS[170]

The authorisation was duly approved. By the time the Division left Slovakia a few weeks later, Freitag had granted all commanders of regiments and independent battalions the right to form their own *Kriegsgericht,* i.e. a court under the War-measures Act. They were empowered to pass sentence on any soldier guilty of a breach of discipline and to carry out executions when necessary. As a direct result, a significant number of Ukrainians were condemned to death, usually by firing squad, in the remaining six months of the war. It is noteworthy that despite several instances of Germans being found guilty of serious infractions, including the accidental shooting dead of an Ukrainian sentry by a drunken German, their sentences were remitted to transfer to a penal company. None faced capital punishment.

As a further safeguard to protect his own position and avoid any unpleasant surprises, Freitag instigated further mechanisms such as the nomination of an individual in each company who was required to produce regular monthly reports. The subject was 'the main topics of conversation amongst the troops'. On completion, the reports were passed on to battalion and then regimental headquarters. There they were collated before finally being presented to sub-section Ic (a) (counter-intelligence) of the Division's staff. Headed by *SS-Hauptsturmführer* Wiens, it was responsible for the collection and analysis of this data. Partly because there was little time available to complete these reports, the contents were either fabricated or deliberately misrepresented. Typically they mentioned either a belief in Germany's invincibility and the new V weapons which would guarantee ultimate victory, or alternatively trivialities such as food, cigarettes and *Marketenderwaren,* i.e. commodities such as alcoholic beverages, soap, tooth paste, shaving supplies etc supplied regularly to the soldiers. Thus the enterprise was effectively sabotaged and the reports were of no real benefit.[171]

Operations in December 1944

In the aftermath of the most recent Soviet offensives on the Eastern Front, the German position in Slovakia, in late 1944, was threatened from two directions. In the east the Red Army had already entered Slovak territory and was involved in an exhausting struggle with the German 1st *Panzer* Army in the Carpathian Mountains. In the south, a westward drive through Hungary had brought the Red Army close to the southern Slovak border that was defended by the 6th Army (reconstituted after its almost total annihilation at Stalingrad).

With the gradual retrograde movement of the German frontline, the 1st *Panzer* Army transferred its rear echelon and supply units to Zilina, in the 14th *Waffen-Grenadier-Division der SS* (*ukrainische* Nr.1) district. The sudden influx of such a large military force resulted in the almost complete cessation of local partisan activity. Consequently the Division's operational area was expanded to encompass the Nitra valley effectively increasing its size two-fold. At the same time it was ordered to assist with the establishment of fortifications in anticipation of the next Soviet onslaught. The Wehrmacht command in the Army rear defence zone started with the building of static defensive positions along the valleys of the Kisuca and Vah rivers, running from the town of Cadca in the north via Zilina to Bratislava in the south. The lines were constructed with the objective of blocking the Vah valley in the east and the Nitra valley in the south. They hoped to eliminate the threat of outflanking the German front in Poland. To expedite the work all units, both frontal and reserve, irrespective of their other duties, were ordered to co-operate.

The Division's sub-units played an active part in the preparations. Within its own sector, especially in the valley of the Turca river, HSSPf. Höfle, on his own volition, had ordered the building of a second line. The new line, built 10 kms to the east of the first position, ran from Martin to Vrutky and northward on the northern extension of the Nitra line. There, to its credit, WGR 31, stationed at Turcansky Svaty Martin, entrenched facing east with great speed.

Equally important was the contribution of the Pioneer Battalion commanded by *SS-Sturmbannführer* Remberger. It carried out technical work and received special commendation for its efforts. It built concealed emplacements at strategic points in the mountains and valleys in the district, and prepared the defence of critical points along natural avenues of approach. It erected a number of anti-tank obstacles, set up minefields, blocked rivers and viaducts, and rigged numerous tunnels and bridges with explosives for subsequent demolition. Finally, the battalion rebuilt an important road bridge in Vrutky that had been destroyed before the arrival of the Division.[172]

To the extent that its other tasks allowed, the Division continued with its training and reformation, making minor refinements to its organisational structure in the process.[173] Regular progress reports were filed with the appropriate German political and military institutions. Because of the close proximity of the frontline, reports went to both 1st *Panzer* Army and 6th Army. In the event of it being given a combat role, its command had adopted a strategy that made allowances for the deployment of the Division as a whole unit. Alternatively it could become three self-contained battle groups based around its three Infantry regiments with additional support from artillery, pioneer, communications and supply units. In the latter case, the first battlegroup was to be ready for marching at short notice, i.e. within 24 hours, and in case of need, a motorised column was formed to facilitate its rapid movement.[174]

In mid-December 1944 the Division received orders to despatch one such group to the Slovakian/Hungarian border. There, part of Plijews 6th Guards Tank Army had penetrated the German front and was advancing up the Sikenica valley along the main road from Levice towards Banska Stiavnica.

The battlegroup formed around *SS-Obersturmbannführer* Friedrich Dern's WGR 29 including Wildner's experienced battalion. It was selected to carry out the mission although, in the event, it appears that only the 3rd Battalion, which had formed the basis for *Kampfgruppe* Wildner, actually saw action. The remainder of Dern's group was held in reserve. In the early hours of the morning of 17 December 1944, the 3rd Battalion was rushed to Banska Stiavnica in a convoy of military trucks and a conglomeration of requisitioned civilian motor cars. They arrived late in the evening of the same day to join elements of the 18th *SS-Freiw. Panzergrenadier* Div. *'Horst Wessel'*, together with parts of the 24th *Panzer* Division and the Dirlewanger Brigade who were holding the German lines in the area. *Kampfgruppe* Schafer, from 18th *SS-Freiw. Panzergrenadier* Division *'Horst Wessel'*, was reinforced by a pioneer battalion from an Army unit, and part of the 24th *Panzer* Division. They moved to the vicinity of Batovce to try and close the local breach. The 3rd Battalion was given orders to take up a reserve position directly south west of Banska Stiavnica. An Ukrainian platoon commander assigned to the 10th Company later wrote:

> 'The following morning we moved a few kilometres to the village of Piarg to secure the main road and defend access to Banska Stiavnica. After a few days the 10th Company was ordered to move by truck to the village of Pocuvadlo and then on foot to the village of Badan. There we were supposed to link up with some German infantry units and tanks that were to support an attack on the village of Jablonovce (Dolny Almas). We spent the night on a ridge of frozen snow waiting for the tanks, but to our disappointment after a long wait they had still not arrived. In the morning we could see the Soviet soldiers down in the valley were burning straw, to prepare their breakfast. As the promised tank support had not appeared, we began to prepare to attack without them, hoping additional infantry units would arrive soon. We started to approach Jablonovce, which we took early in the morning of 24 December. While we were in the village, a German infantry company finally arrived. We arranged with the officer in charge of the German Company to change with them, so that the Germans could spend their Christmas (25 December) in reserve.
>
> 'Meanwhile we held the frontline on the understanding that they would replace us so that we could spend our Christmas (7 January) in reserve. On 25 December the 10th Company received the order to secure the mountain which overlooked the village of Batovce, 7kms to the south. Batovce was occupied by the Soviets and from our position we had an excellent view and could observe their movements. On 26 December we observed a large concentration of Soviet tanks and infantry which were obviously preparing for an attack. In

turn we started to prepare our defence. Around 2.00am on 27 December the offensive began. We watched as the Soviet tanks passed through the valley towards the village of Pukanec. Around 3.00am the Soviets started their assault on our positions.

'After a few hours of intense fighting at 8.00am the 10th company received the order to retreat back to the village of Jablonovce, while the 11th Company on our left covered the retreat. Under heavy fire, my platoon, which was the rearguard, had two killed and 4 wounded (including myself). I later learned that our entire unit had heavy casualties and was forced to withdraw.'[175]

The Soviet attack was held in check in fierce defensive fighting which continued for the next two days in the vicinity of the village of Pukanec.[176]

On 29 December, *Kampfgruppe* Schafer and other German forces in the area, including the Dirlewanger Brigade, launched a series of counter-attacks. They successfully drove the Soviets back and restored the front.[177] On 3 January 1945,[178] 3rd Battalion Wildner was recalled from the line to rejoin its parent regiment, as Dern's battlegroup stood down. It arrived back in Zilina just in time to celebrate Ukrainian Christmas, 7 January. According to Heike, the battlegroup had fought well and received commendations from all those who dealt with it, the artillery units being deserving of special praise. Among the notable casualties lost during the fighting was *Waffen-Untersturmführer* Grocholsky who died during the Soviet attack on 26 December.[179] Both Germans and Ukrainians were subsequently decorated for their valour during offensive and defensive engagements.

Epiphany – New Year Celebrations

In a subdued atmosphere and with the uncertainty that surrounded the desperate German military situation, the Division commemorated the Christmas and New Year 1944/45 in Slovakia in comparative tranquillity. In an address at this time, broadcast by radio, *SS-Brigadeführer* Freitag expressed the wish that 7 January 1945, might be the last Christmas celebrated by the Division outside Galicia.[180] That sentiment could not however hide the realities of the situation, which everyone knew to be worsening rapidly. As if to emphasise this, on 7 January the Divisional newspaper appeared under the name *Do Peremohy,* To Victory, for the last time before changing its name to *Do Boyu* (To Battle).[181]

For most combat units, the extent of the festivities was limited to the observance of a holy evening supper, on Christmas Eve. It consisted of traditional Ukrainian dishes of borsch, fish, and kutia. Special Christmas parcels containing a gift of cake, a bottle of wine or spirit as appropriate, cigarettes, real chocolate or comparable luxury commodities, were also distributed to each soldier.

Professional entertainment was provided by Ukrainian artists, who stayed with the Division until mid-January 1945. They gave performances for several of the sub-units.[182] Among many reserve units improvised festivities were arranged enlivened by the singing of Ukrainian Christmas carols, music, dances, and plays organised by the soldiers themselves.[183]

On 7 January, Ukrainian Christmas day, Reverend Dr Laba presided over a special field service at the Division's headquarters. He shared *Prosfora* (blessed bread) with its commander *SS-Brigadeführer* Freitag. The modest celebrations took place in the presence of the leaders of the Military Board, the Ukrainian Central Committee, *Oberst* Bisanz, and Professor Kubijovych who arrived in Zilina, together with a party of 25–30 members of the organisations they represented.[184] In small delegations they visited several of the reserve units, making speeches to boost morale and bringing with them news of the developments concerning the formation of the Ukrainian National Committee.[185]

In Zilina, *Oberst* Bisanz held a series of private talks with the senior general staff officers including Major Heike, with whom he discussed German attitudes towards the Ukrainians, the recent political developments, and their repercussions with regard to the Division. Confidentially, Heike was also told that the Wächter-Arlt cabal had instigated steps to have Freitag removed and a more suitable commander appointed in his place.[186]

The same topics formed the basis of a subsequent conference with Freitag. During it he was informed of the imminent public proclamation of the establishment of the Ukrainian National Committee headed by General Shandruk, and its formal recognition by the German government. Bisanz unsuccessfully endeavoured to persuade Freitag that in light of General Shandruk's envisaged appointment as 'supreme commander of all Ukrainian Armed forces' the formation of which had already begun, that he was no longer suitable as the commander as his attitude towards the Division was in any case wholly inappropriate.

Freitag was fortified by the knowledge that Bisanz lacked the authority to effect a change of command. Knowing that the 'official' German line at the time was still disposed toward Vlasovs 'federalist' concept and did not support an independent Ukrainian Committee, Freitag refused to debate the issue. He could not be induced into relinquishing his command. Similarly, a subsequent attempt to get Ukrainians assigned to positions of responsibility also met with failure since, as long as he was not compelled to do so, Freitag would not revise his fundamental attitude. He continued to exclude Ukrainians from crucial positions on the Division's staff.

The visitors left on the 8 January 1945, having accomplished very little in practical terms. From the moment of their arrival until their departure, Bisanz and Kubijovych were kept under surveillance by the German security services in Slovakia. A three-page secret report on their activities also emphasised among other topics their respective attitudes towards the German military situation in the east. It was prepared by the former chief of Police, and SD in Galicia *SS-Obersturmbannführer* Dr Josef Witiska,[187] for *Gestapo* Müller, the head of the *Sicherheitsdienst* (SS security and intelligence service).[188]

On 19 January, according to traditional Ukrainian customs, the seasonal religious festival concluded with the observance of *Yordan* (water blessing).[189] A former *Waffen-Untersturmführer* from 13/WGR 30 described the occasion within his unit:

> 'I vividly remember the day when we celebrated *Yordan* (Epiphany) in Velka Bytca on 19 January, 1945, in an old Ukrainian tradition. In the centre of the town square a huge cross (measuring about 10ft) was erected, made out of ice blocks. In front of the cross a platform was built adorned with pine trees on the left and on the right and in the centre of the platform was a small podium to serve as an altar. A large cask filled with water was placed next to the podium. At precisely 10.30am the troops stationed in the town – about 300 men – arrived at the square and formed a U-shape facing the altar. They were dressed in parade uniforms. It was a nice clear day with the temperature just below freezing. The Division's priest celebrated a Mass, blessed the water and the troops. A platoon fired three salvos. After Mass the troops returned to their quarters marching and singing Ukrainian military songs. A large number of local people gathered in the town-square and observed the Mass and proceedings. They liked what they saw. No German personnel participated in the celebration.'[190]

Even more lavish festivities were held, within the Training and Reserve Regiment in Cadca, on the same day. At least one of the regiment's German battalion commanders, *SS-Hauptsturmführer* Wilhelm Schramm (CO III Btl.) was present. He witnessed a Mass, conducted by Chaplain Danylo Kowaluk, and accompanied by the regimental choir.

For the duration of the Ukrainian Christmas and New Year period the Division continued to perform its security tasks and all units were kept in a constant state of alert, ready for deployment in the field.

In response to an alarm received on 16 and 17 January, *Kampfgruppe* Wildner was sent for the third and final time to the Slovakian/Hungarian front.[191] The unit was to have been transported by truck but because of heavy snowfall of almost one metre, the battle group was forced to make the second part of its journey to the village of Babina on foot. The *Kampfgruppe* had barely taken up positions before its mission was aborted. It received the order to withdraw to Zilina and to rejoin the Division, which, in the interim, had already left for a new operational theatre.[192]

Transfer to Slovenia

As the deadline set by the SS-FHA for the 14th *Waffen-Grenadier-Division der SS* (*ukrainische* Nr.1) to become fully operational had already expired, its command awaited the imminent arrival of new deployment orders.[193] In the meantime, plans were made to accommodate the possibility of it being sent to the nearby front. The likelihood of this happening in the immediate future, in anything other than an emergency, was somewhat mitigated by political considerations in respect of the ongoing developments with the Ukrainian National Committee. Influential individuals like Wächter and Arlt, both of whom had a vested interest in the Division's fate, were also anxious to exploit its political potential and to avoid another debacle like that at Brody the previous summer.

An equally significant factor in the argument against prematurely committing the Division to battle and without due consideration, was the overall state of its battle readiness which led its commander to believe it was not yet ready to be sent to the front. Despite having overcome the initial dearth of vital weapons and equipment from supplies obtained in Slovakia, the influx of a large number of untrained replacements into its ranks, in the course of the previous months, had had a negative impact on progress with its reformation and retraining. Added to that, paradoxically, its activities in Slovakia while undoubtedly of benefit, had denied it the sustained and uninterrupted period of intensive training that it needed to become a fully effective fighting unit "by the end of 1944", as originally specified.

Therefore, as a contingency measure, provision was made for transfer to a secondary front in a new sector, on foot if necessary, where it could be used for anti-partisan and security duties.[194] In that eventuality, its general staff officers felt that the most likely destination would be the German front in Poland. That was in view of the fact that Freitag had already met with the command of the army group in Cracow for official discussions concerning the details. The Army Group had expressed an interest in using the 14th Division to fight partisans and maintain security in its rear.[195]

In spite of everything, following an earlier established pattern, it was ultimately an urgent demand for assistance, this time from the HSSPf. for *Alpenland* (Yugoslavia) in early January 1945, that decided the issue. Circumstances determined its destination that came as a surprise to its command.[196] Plans to clear the partisan units from that region during the winter offensive of 1944, with their available forces, were not successful. The German special operative HQ in Ljubljana for the destruction of *Banditen* demanded fresh reserves to accomplish the task. Consequently, on 21 January 1945, notification was received at the Division's headquarters, that it was to transfer to Styria (South Steiermark) along with its Training and Reserve Regiment. There it was to be deployed against partisans in the district and complete its reformation.

On arrival it was to be subordinated to the command of the HSSPf. *SS-Obergruppenführer Generalleutnant der Polizei und Waffen-SS* Erwin Rösener[197] in Ljubljana. Commander of the rear areas of Army Group E, he would determine its exact area of deployment. As the requisite rail transportation was not available transfer was to be effected by *Fußmarsch,* i.e. a foot march.[198] A supplementary order from *SS-Obergruppenführer* Höfle stated that the use of the main Zilina – Bratislava – Vienna road was prohibited, as it was restricted to priority traffic carrying supplies for the frontline units.[199]

To comply with the order, it was estimated that an additional 400 horses and 100 wagons would be required to move the vast amount of matériel, uniforms, food and ammunition that the Division had accumulated. As Slovakia was predominantly agricultural draught horses and wagons were relatively plentiful. Permission was subsequently granted by Höfle to procure the deficit from local sources. That was to be on the basis of a voluntary transaction with cash reimbursements to the farmers as compensation to cover their losses. Detailed requisition orders were then issued to unit commanders. Regardless of the strict limits imposed on quotas, in their eagerness to obtain transportation the Division's combined units requisitioned horses and wagons from civilians and other German formations stationed in the area. Approximately 800 hundred horses and 150 wagons was the number in excess of that deemed necessary. Following complaints, over 200 horses and 100 wagons were returned by the Division's command. The commanders of units found to be culpable of taking more than their allocation were severely reprimanded and penalties meted out for contravening orders.[200]

To effect the transfer, a detailed marching plan was devised that divided the Division's sub-units into two marching columns, *Marschgruppe* A and B. They were to travel along two parallel routes, pass through Slovakia, and cross the main bridges over the Danube, at Bratislava and Kloster Neuburg. Then, they would go on through Austria to their eventual destination in Slovenia. It was to be a long and difficult march covering a total distance of around five hundred kilometres.

Marschgruppe A, led by *SS-Brigadeführer* Freitag, was by far the larger of the two and had furthest to travel. It consisted of the headquarters unit together with WGRs 29 and 30, the Training and Reserve Regiment, the signals *Abteilung*, parts of the anti-tank unit, the Artillery Regiment, and the supply services. Its projected route was Cadca-Zilina, then along the Vah valley to Povazska Bystrica, Trencin, Nove Mestro near Vahom, Neustadt. It went across the lower Carpathians to Maleckyj, then passing north of Vienna, to Kloster Neuburg, across the Wiener Wald to Wiener Neustadt, Semmering, Bruck, Graz and Marburg on der Drau.

Somewhat smaller was *Marschgruppe* B led by the commander of WGR 31, *SS-Standartenführer* Rudolph Pannier. It comprised WGR 31, the Fusilier Battalion, the Pioneer Battalion, and the 14th *Feld Ersatz* Battalion. That group was to follow the route Vrutky, St Martin, then along the Turiec and Nitra valleys to Piestany, across the lower Carpathians to Bratislava, passing south of Vienna to Wiener Neustadt, Hartberg, Gleisdorf, Graz and finally onto Marburg on der Drau.

As fuel for the motorised equipment was unobtainable in any appreciable quantity, apart from a few vehicles, mainly light cars and motorcycles, which were to accompany the marching groups for liaison and communications purposes, the remainder were to be transported by rail. The motorised echelon, together with some of the heavy weapons including anti-aircraft weaponry and provisions, which were not easily moved by road, and with the Division's medical personnel, formed *Marschgruppe* C. It was supervised by the commander of the *Panzerjäger Abteilung*, *SS-Sturmbannführer* Hermann Kaschner.

With the finalisation of the plans, preparations for the commencement of the march began in earnest. All soldiers were issued with appropriate winter clothing,[201] a *Nachkommando* (rear group) was formed under the direction of the 1st *Ordonnanz Offizier SS-Obersturmführer* Michel that, in the wake of departure, was required to oversee the clean up. Prior to its departure, Freitag ordered the Division to strip itself of all extraneous baggage and threatened that if he found any officer with a personal suitcase he would "personally throw it in the Drava".[202]

The Division's Headquarters in Zilina received a written directive from Himmler in the form of a telex from Himmler dated 26 January 1945, concerning the transfer:

> Re: Relocation of the 14.*Waffen-Gren. Div. d. SS* (*ukrainische* Nr.1)
>
> Following order RF-SS to be acknowledged and executed:
>
> 1. The 14th *Waffen-Gren.Div.d.SS* (*ukrainische* Nr.1) is to relocate to quarters in the Untersteiermark region. It will immediately commence its march on foot along the Pressburg/Wien (Vienna) route.
> 2. The *Höh.SS-u.Pol.Führ. Alpenland* will ensure accommodation in buildings in garrisons, in villages and towns.
> 3. Transport of non-mobile parts, i.e. heavy repair equipment etc by train, other than this transport, on foot where possible
> 4. The march is to be utilised as a combined marching exercise with integrated combat exercises. The Division's foremost sections will commence the march at the latest by the 26 January, and will arrive at its new location by 28 February at the latest.
> 5. I am to receive daily reports from the Divisional Commander via the nearest telegraph station or by radio.
> 6. Naturally motorised vehicles are to be embarked.
>
> Signed H. Himmler
> Addition *SS–Hauptamt SS-Gren. Ausb.u.Ers.Rgt.* 14 (*ukrainische Ausb.Rgt.* Nr.1) is also to be transferred to the new location concurrently.[203]

By that time the first groups in battalion and company strength were already on their way, while the remaining units set out at regular intervals to avoid congestion during the course of the following days. For security purposes the marching routes, and the final destination, were known only to the commander and his most senior staff officers.

The march itself presented numerous logistical problems for the supply units. Supply points were set up along the route, to be followed by officers of sections 1b (Quartermaster Supply – weapons and ammunition) headed by *SS-Hauptsturmführer* Herbert Schaaf and Section IVa (Quartermaster General, supply food and uniforms), under *SS-Sturmbannführer* Otto Sulzbach, in conjunction with the commanders of 17th (Vienna) and 18th (Salzburg) Military Districts.

In addition, for each battalion or sub-unit, a *Vorkommando* (quartermaster's advance group) was sent one day ahead to arrange accommodation. The units that followed were given a daily route, with a detailed road map, and assigned overnight rest areas. To maintain sufficient progress, three days were spent marching an average of 30–50 kms, often along snow-covered roads, followed by one day of rest. The columns stretched out over a distance of 60–70 kms with all equipment, weapons and artillery transported by horse-drawn wagons, while the soldiers marched on foot in winter conditions. As one *Waffen-grenadier* recalled "uniforms and shoes were wet all the time".[204]

Several heavy snowdrifts and poor road conditions in the lower Carpathian Mountains made it extremely difficult for the draught horses pulling guns and other heavy equipment. Höfle relented and gave permission for the heavy artillery and part of the Pioneer Battalion to detour on to a section of the main road from Piestany to Bratislava. Despite that, the horses belonging to the units persevering on the snow-bound secondary roads still found it very hard to pull their heavy carts. Frequently their cargoes had to be unloaded to enable them to negotiate the climbing of steep hills and only when the empty carts had been pulled to the top of the hills were they reloaded.

Passing through Bratislava, Freitag and *Major* Heike stopped at Höfle's HQ where in his absence, his Chief of Staff Ia von Uechtritz, commended the Division for performing its tasks in Slovakia. Afterwards Freitag, together with the senior regimental commander *SS-Standartenführer* Beyersdorff and his adjutant *SS-Hauptsturmführer* Muller, took the opportunity to review a march past by the Artillery Regiment.[205]

In several important respects the tour of duty had been beneficial. It had the opportunity to re-equip with weapons and other war matériel which it lacked, obtained from the partisans and from the captured stocks of the Slovak Army. Its soldiers had reached a high level of fitness during the anti-partisan missions in the mountains which demanded considerable endurance, and elements of it had gained valuable combat experience fighting against the Red Army.

As intended, the route for both columns passed close to Vienna where west Ukrainian refugees, some of whom were related to the soldiers, who had fled from the advancing Soviets, were held in several transit camps. In the interests of discipline, and to discourage desertion, no leaves were permitted. Local military police and authorities were given instructions to prevent the soldiers from entering the city. Nonetheless, some enterprising individuals who had reason for doing so, or out of sheer curiosity, succeeded.[206]

In early February 1945 in the vicinity of Bruck, shortly after passing Vienna, the Division stopped for a much-needed 8-day rest. That afforded an ideal opportunity to repair equipment and put things in good working order. There was also a chance to satisfy some basic personal hygiene requirements before continuing on the last non-stop stage of the journey. At that juncture, the provision of food to meet the needs of the entire formation proved to be problematical. The city did not have sufficient supplies due to a transportation breakdown and a general food shortage in the Reich, where severe rationing had long been in force.

During its transfer, the Division was classified as a Reserve Unit, unlike units actively engaged in combat, therefore it was eligible to receive only the lowest rations. It was felt all the more acutely as it had just left Slovak territory where almost every kind of foodstuff was available in abundance. The provisions that the Division had brought along with it, together with the gifts of food many soldiers had received from the civilian population in Slovakia[207] were largely sufficient. They compensated for the drastic reduction in rations that then occurred. In one recorded instance some soldiers from II/WGR 29, resorted to the 'appropriation' of 300 kgs of butter, in twelve 25 kg barrels, from a local warehouse to supplement their rations. That prompted an official complaint to the Division's command.[208]

The final and most hazardous stretch of the journey between Bruck/Graz – Marburg got underway in mid-February, under the direction of *Major* Heike. He had taken over from *SS-Brigadeführer* Freitag who had been taken ill and was unable to return to duty for ten days.[209] As the columns got closer to their destination, they came within the range of Allied aircraft, operating out of airstrips in Italy, which strafed the main roads during daylight hours causing casualties in men, horses and matériel. To lessen its vulnerability to air attack, orders were given for marching to continue by night only, bringing its own unique difficulties.

Marschgruppe C included the Division's *Feldlazarett* (Field hospital) together with its complement of staff (48 nurses and 12 doctors) and patients. It was the first echelon to arrive at its new destination. A *Waffen-Unterscharführer* who had been wounded during combat in Slovakia recalled:

> 'On 26 January the patients from the Division's hospital relocated from Zilina by rail. The train that we boarded was bound for Vienna. We had not gone far when the train stopped at a station and I got out to see if I could find some hot food, which was often available at stations for military personnel. As I was recuperating from my wound, I could only move slowly and had to walk with a stick for support. I suddenly saw the train on which I had been travelling leaving the station. I called to a German officer and explained to him what had happened and that my train had just left without me. I showed him my ticket which stated that I was wounded and he advised me not to worry because another train bound for Vienna was due through the station in about four hours time.
>
> 'As luck would have it just at that moment, another train pulled into the station and I recognised our Divisional insignia on the artillery guns and vehicles. I told the German officer that this was my division and he shouted to the driver that he was not to leave until I had boarded the train. I was fortunate because the train was carrying the staff and equipment of our Divisional *Feldlazarett* who looked after me during the journey. On one occasion the train was attacked by British aircraft. On 28 or 29 January 1945 the train arrived in Marburg, Slovenia. Here the Division's *Feldlazarett* was relocated in a bombed-out barrack. I was fortunate to receive a reasonably quiet corner with three walls. The fourth wall had been bombed and I had a beautiful view of the nearby hill. I was also lucky to be able to move on crutches, which I did everyday before 10.00am, because at that time American bombers started attacks for approximately two hours. For some reason the hill was not bombed and soldiers from the hospital were able to find sanctuary there. In addition to the bombing, Tito's Communist partisans were everywhere. On 10 February I left the hospital in Marburg and received a 14-day leave before reporting to the convalescent company in Marburg. But unfortunately the whole of that time was spent in Marburg under heavy bombardment.'[210]

Following the arrival of *Marschgruppe* C in Marburg, along with the *Feldlazarett,* the Divisional flak company which consisted of nine 3.7cm flak guns, was amongst the first of its units which became operational. It had immediately established itself within the city, and was actively engaged in anti-aircraft defence. [211]

By the end of February *Marschgruppe* A had reached the new district. On 28 February, at 10.00am, the march was officially ended by special order.[212] It was not until the end of the first week in March that the remaining elements had arrived.[213] The Division's command reported by radio to the RFSS-*Feldkommandostelle* and the HSSPf. in Ljubljana that "the march had proceeded according to plan" and "without any special problems".[214] Rough terrain and winter conditions had been particularly difficult for the horses whose numbers had been severely depleted. In the course of departure approximately one hundred men deserted from the Division. The total strength, less the Training and Reserve Regiment, was given in an official chart dated 1 March 1945, as being 14,000.[215]

No sooner had they arrived in Slovakia, than all the Division's sub-units began anti-partisan sweeps to provide security for Zilina and its environs. An unidentified unit from the 14th Galician Division armed with a machine gun conducting anti-partisan operations in Slovakia, Autumn 1944. Private photographs taken on active duty were officially forbidden, which explains the poor quality.

Anti-partisan action in Slovakia, conducted by personnel from the light artillery. Second row, third from left: Stephan Sadiwsky, who was from the village of Koropec, was a former member of the Red Army who had fought in defence of Moscow and later at Stalingrad, before being captured by the Germans. After escaping from a German POW camp near Minsk, he made his way across the frontline, back to his home village, whereupon he joined a local UPA unit, before eventually enlisting into the Galician Division in June 1944. Wounded twice during his service with the Division, he survived the war and settled in England.

Two Ukrainian platoon commanders from 13/WGR 30, Waffen-Untersturmführer *Shypailo (right) and* Waffen-Untersturmführer *Korczak in Slovakia. Korczak wears the ribbons of the Iron Cross Second Class in his button hole, won for his bravery whilst attached to* Kampfgruppe *Wildner.*

Medzibrod, Slovakia, 3 November 1944, Waffen-Hauptsturmführer *Tatarsky at the head of his company 10/III/WGR 29, during the Wildner campaign.*

Two Slovak regular soldiers captured by Divisional units in winter 1944.

Ukrainian soldiers of the Galician Division playing chess and draughts whilst relaxing in their billets on active service in Slovakia, winter 1944. The SS runes can been seen on the helmet of the man standing third from right.

Ukrainian soldiers with their NCO going to fetch the food and supplies by horse-drawn cart. Slovakia, Winter 1944.

Ukrainian Waffen-Grenadiers *and a NCO, relaxing in a small town in Slovakia, autumn 1944.*

A group of Ukrainians from the Galician Division at an unknown location in Slovakia, autumn 1944. Third from left is the author's father Waffen-Kanonier Petro Melnyk, who served with the Division's heavy artillery battalion.

Waffen-Unterscharführer *Michael Prymak, 12/WGR 29, with a civilian whom he later arrested and handed over to the Battalion HQ in Banska Bystrica after it had transpired that he was in fact an armed Soviet agent who attempted to procure classified information. Slovakia, Winter 1944.*

A full-length portrait of a typical Waffen-Grenadier *in Slovakia, autumn 1944.*

A similar portrait, this time of an unidentified mounted Ukrainian officer taken at the same location in Slovakia, Autumn 1944.

Throughout the Division's stay in Slovakia, training continued. Here Ukrainian recruits practice firing a rifle on a bed of fir tree branches, for insulation against the cold. Slovakia, Winter 1944

Waffen-Untersturmführer *Roman Herasaymowych, commander 1/I/WGR 30 (left) and* SS-Oberscharführer *Wittman, Precin, Slovakia, November 1944, leading the company back after exercises, the plans for which have been tucked in to the tunic cuff. Amongst Wittman's combat decorations visible on his tunic is the rare* Bandenkampfabzeichen *(Anti-partisan badge).*

Waffen-Untersturmführer *Herasaymowych, commander, 1/I/WGR 30, with four of his NCOs, three German and one Ukrainian. During this transitionary phase German NCOs and platoon commanders were gradually replaced by Ukrainians. Left to right:* SS-Oberscharführer *Yost,* Waffen-Oberscharführer *Bezchlibnyk,* Untersturmführer *Herasaymowych* SS-Hauptscharführer *(also company* Spiess*) Meister, not known.*

Regimental and battalion commanders of WGR 30 at a briefing during a training exercise, Marshova, Slovakia, November 1944. Left to right: Waffen-Untersturmführer *Komorowsky,* Waffen-Untersturmführer *Skira, not known, not known, regimental commander* SS-Obersturmbannführer *Forstreuter, not known,* SS-Sturmbannführer *Wittenmeyer (facing camera with binoculars, CO 3rd Battalion), SS-Sturmbannführer Czermin (CO 2nd Battalion, carrying binoculars), not known.*

Marshova, Slovakia, Winter 1944. The commander of 6/II/WGR 30 Waffen-Obersturmführer *Pidhayny explains an exercise to members of his company.*

Mass at the funeral of two Ukrainian soldiers killed in action by partisans Turzovka, Slovakia, Winter 1944.

Zilina, January 1945, three young Ukrainian Waffen-Untersturmführers *from WGR 30 report for a meeting at Headquarters. All three wear the warm reversible camouflage suits issued to the Division's soldiers in the winter of 1944/45.*

Waffen-Obersturmführer *Roman Lazurko (centre, wearing white snow suit), with soldiers from his platoon from 13/WGR 30 in Velika Bica, 14 January 1945.*

Feld Ersatz *Regiment, 19 January 1945, Cadca, Slovakia. The Regimental choir on their way to a lavish ceremony to celebrate Epiphany* (Yordan).

Commander of 3rd Btl., SS-Sturmbannführer *Ewald Eduard Schramm, arrives for the festivities in his battalion staff car.*

Feld Ersatz *Regiment, 19 January 1945, Cadca, Slovakia. Chaplain* Waffen-Hauptsturmführer *Danylo Kowaluk conducts the service. The Ukrainian national symbol, the trident, is clearly evident.*

Epiphany, 19 January 1945. The Pioneer Battalion built an impressive cross and alter out of ice blocks to celebrate Yordan.

January 1945, Slovakia, members of Kampfgruppe *Wildner from WGR 29 during a rest period. Left to right: M. Skremeta, P. Kiszchuk and M. Prymak. In contravention of regulations, all three are wearing scarves, which were presents from local* slecznas *(girlfriends).*

Portrait of Waffen-Unterscharführer *Mychailo Prymak, late January 1945, Slovakia, around the time that he was awarded the Iron Cross 2nd Class for destroying a Soviet anti-tank gun with a direct hit whilst fighting with* Kampfgruppe *Dern, Slovakia.*

The original caption for this picture, dated 19 January 1945, reads 'Ukrainian Waffen-Grenadiers *guard a rail transport. A machine gun is ready against attacks by low flying aircraft'.*

During February 1945, aside from a small section which utilised rail transportation, the bulk of the Galician Division undertook a forced march across the White Carpathian Mountains, when the formation was transferred from Slovakia to Slovenia. Warm reversible winter clothing was issued in Slovakia and was worn during the march.

Horse-drawn wagons laden with equipment passing through a town February 1945. The horses found the steep hills and snow-bound roads difficult to negotiate.

11 February 1945, four Ukrainians from WGR 31 during the march from Slovakia to Slovenia. Left to right: Cholkan, Waffen-Untersturmführer *Stachiw, Wawryk, unknown.*

9

Against Tito in Slovenia

Immediately upon arrival the Division's sub-units encamped on both sides of the Austrian/Slovenian border, mainly on the side inhabited by the Slovenes. They were lodged in public buildings secured by the *Vorkommando*. As that was not always possible, on occasion companies were accommodated in private dwellings in mountain villages. In doing so, every attempt was made to minimise the burden on the civilian inhabitants. Occasionally, however, to overcome problems that later arose, in moving heavy equipment such as field kitchens, some units were forced to resort to 'borrowing' oxen from them.[1] Initially a few difficulties and heated disputes arose with the German civilian administration.[2] They were on Austrian territory in the Deutschlandsberg area, where to compensate for the diminished *Heimat* (Home) rations that were issued, several companies had arbitrarily requisitioned food from the local population. Otherwise relations with the civilian administration were correct and in some cases cordial.

The Slovenes themselves soon proved to be less amiable than the Slovaks and with few exceptions were generally reserved or even hostile towards the Division's soldiers.

The provinces of Styria (Stajerska) and Carinthia (Gorenjska) were divided into security zones, one of which was assigned to the Division. The neighbouring zones to the south and south-west contained a *Polizei* and a Wehrmacht formation respectively. The German occupation forces in these provinces held the principal cities and towns and patrolled the connecting main road and rail links. They abandoned the villages and countryside, with its craggy mountains, deep river valleys, and numerous dense impenetrable forests, to the control of the partisans. HSSPf. Rösener considered combating these partisans to be a major priority as the security forces at his disposal (which were largely confined to heavily fortified outposts)[3] were so inadequate that the establishment of any normal administration in the region was impossible. Moreover, the protection of the main transportation routes in the territory could no longer be assured even during daylight hours.

The centre of the Division's deployment was therefore to be the partisan infested mountainous forests of the Pohorje, south of the river Drava. A further influencing factor on determining the tactical disposition of its units was the proximity of the Eastern Front. Therefore, after some discussion, the Division's command decided to place two infantry regiments, reinforced by detachments of artillery, west of Marburg (Maribor) in a line north to south. All heavy weaponry and anti-tank detachments were stationed in the vicinity of the city to ensure mobility in all directions. A temporary deployment was arranged as follows:

Headquarters: (Administration section) in Selnica ob Dravi (Zellnitz am Drau)
WGR 29 south and SW Marburg: Regimental HQ Slovenske Konjice (Gonobitz)
WGR 30 SE Slovenj Gradec (Windisch-Graz): HQ Velenje (Wöllan)
WGR 31 in the Drava valley at Ruse (Reiffing), Fala (Fall) Radlje ob Drava (Radl): HQ Lovrenc na Pohorju (St Lorenzen)
Fusilier Battalion in Slovenska Bistrica: HQ Ob Pulsgau
Artillery Regiment: HQ 1 and 4 *Abtl.* at Slovenska Bistrica: 2 *Abtl.* with WGR 30: 3 *Abtl.* with WGR 31
Panzerjäger Abteilung: HQ Slovenska Bistrica/Ptujska Gora
Pioneer Battalion at Marenberg (Hohenmauthen)
Signals *Abteilung* – Ruse
Supply Detachment: HQ Leibnitz/Spielfeld
Transport Detachment: HQ Slivnica
14th *Feld Ersatz Bataillon*: HQ Spielfeld[4]
Training and Reserve Regiment: HQ Deutschlandsberg
Division Field Hospital: Marburg (temporarily) then Celje (Cilli)[5]

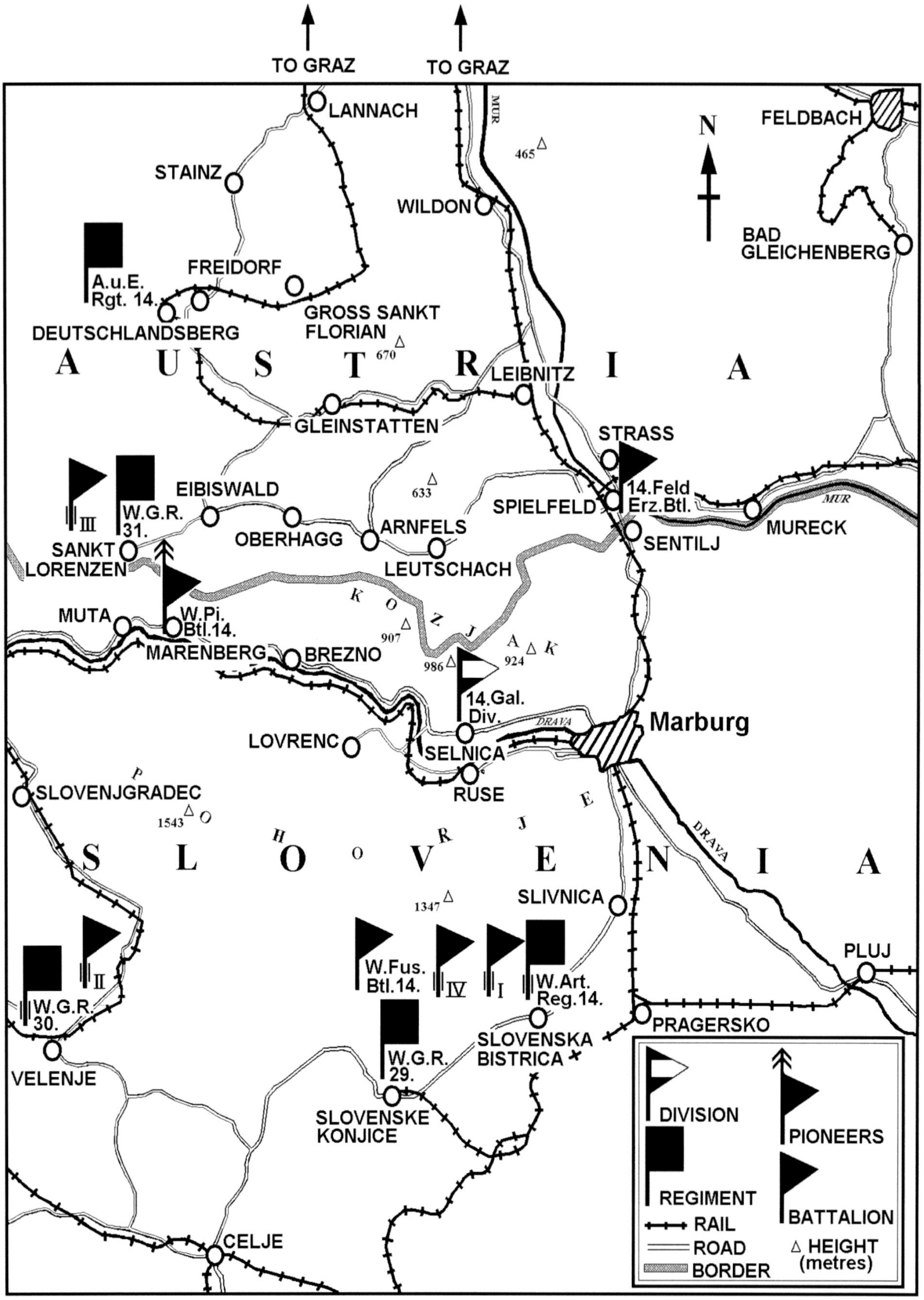

Map 9 Disposition of the Galician Division in Slovenia, February 1945

The headquarters of all sub-units were located close to the railway to facilitate re-supply from the Division's main rail supply point at Pragersko (Prager Hof). Throughout its stay in Slovenia the location of units changed a number of times in accordance with the prevailing circumstances. Each time a unit relocated a *Nachkommando* remained behind, to ensure the vacated area was left in good order.

Within the Division's operational area, two types of partisan were active. The first smaller group was known as *Chetniks.* Under the leadership of Colonel Dragoljub 'Draza' Mikhailovich they were royalist, pro-Allied and anti-Communist. Recognised by King Peter II as the Yugoslav Army of the Homeland, they operated in small organised, disciplined, uniformed and well-armed squads east of Marburg. They posed no immediate threat to the Division having established a temporary *modus vivendi* with the Germans against their common enemy. The second far larger and more formidable group, were Tito's communist partisans.

Under the command of Marshal Josip Broz-Tito, a Croatian Communist, whose forces from November 1942 were known as the "National Liberation Army of Yugoslavia" (NOVJ, *Narodnoosvobodilna vojska Jugoslavije*), this insurgent army had from June 1941, waged a bitter and protracted war against the Germans. Tito's partisan formations, some of which grew to strengths of 30,000 plus, included men of all ages, women (in both combatant and non-combatant roles[6]) and even children. They operated exceptionally well from their heavily fortified camps located in remote forests, caves and wooded mountains. There they assembled to receive air-dropped supplies from the British, Americans and the Soviets. Dressed in a diverse mixture of civilian attire, uniforms of their own country and German uniforms, they conducted frequent surprise raids. Their targets were such as individual drivers, resting places, troop and supply trains, headquarters units, and ammunition and supply dumps. Highly motivated, their local numerical superiority, which was further supplemented by support from the indigenous population, was nonetheless partly offset by their poor level of training and armament.

Tito's principal forces were active in the district that was known by them as the '4th Partisan Operative Zone'. It consisted of the '14th Partisan Division', composed of a HQ and the Šercer, Bracic and Tomsic brigades, and two independent brigades, 6th *Slander* and 11th *Zidanšek*. In early March 1945, those units were still engaged in attempting to cross into the Dolenjska region situated on the left bank of the Sava river south of Ljubljana. It was an area that encompassed the towns of Grosuplje, Trebnje and Novo mesto. They had previously failed to cross. In preparation for a renewed effort, to be made in two or more parts at timed intervals, the formations were dispersed over a wide area. They were ordered to employ mainly defensive tactics and to avoid large frontal battles with enemy units.[7]

The same tried and tested strategy, in place in Slovakia, was again adopted in Slovenia. Each of the Division's sub-units was assigned to a locality in which they were responsible for combating partisans and maintaining security.

From the moment of their arrival all the Division's units were engaged in either defensive or offensive activities during which every soldier was to become acquainted with the unmistakable nature of the war in the Balkans. Small-scale partisan attacks began at once. Amongst the first casualties were two soldiers, one of them having had his ear cut off. They were from the *Vorkommando* of WGR 30 that had arrived in Marburg ahead of the main body of the Division.[8] In the first few days it was not uncommon for individual soldiers, or small groups, who ventured into the woods not to return. Sometimes their dead bodies would be found, mutilated, days later.[9]

Defensive measures therefore concentrated on clearing the main transport and communication arteries around the towns where the various units were stationed. They had to provide security for vital industrial installations, power plants and other strategic objectives. Simultaneously, offensive actions were undertaken by assault groups and mobile patrols that began combing through the woods in the Bachern mountain range (Pohorje plateau) south of the river Drava. Day and night they searched for the bases of the *Bachern Brigad,* i.e. the colloquial German name for Tito's partisans in that region. Their actions met with varying degrees of success, but also highlighted some of the intractable internal problems within the Division as illustrated in the following account of a platoon commander from WGR 31:

> 'My assault platoon was assigned to St Lorenzen, a small village south of the river Drava at the foot of the Pohorje mountain range, where according to the intelligence obtained from the previous German garrison,

Tito's partisans had a stronghold. Before we had a chance to find appropriate billeting, the regimental commander *SS-Standartenführer* Pannier sent us on an armed reconnaissance mission deep into the Pohorje. We were to report our findings and receive our further orders by radio. We took along enough ammunition, hand grenades and rations for a few days, and passwords, which were changed daily. Previous German garrisons did not venture into the mountains so the terrain and situation were completely unknown to us.

'After an exhausting day-long march we arrived almost at our assigned location in the centre of the Pohorje, without having encountered the enemy. I ordered a short break and tried to make radio contact with our regimental headquarters but was unable to do so because of the distance and mountainous terrain. I therefore had to act on my own initiative. We continued to advance for about 400 metres when I noticed an empty stand behind the bushes. Fresh tracks indicated the recent presence of an enemy sentry. A little further ahead a mountain farmstead became visible. I ordered my troops to take up attack formation as we approached the buildings. The houses were empty but in the hearth the fire was still burning and in two large cauldrons some soup was boiling. Judging by their size the meal was for 200 people or more. We searched all the farm buildings but found nothing except evidence that a large number of people had been living there for some time. While we had been resting nearby the partisans must have been alerted and had left, taking everything with them.

'After several unsuccessful attempts to make radio contact with regimental headquarters, I decided to occupy the partisan camp and await further developments. Despite its delicious smell I ordered the soup to be thrown away as it could have been poisoned. Having worked out comprehensive defence plans, I placed sentries at strategic locations including the empty sentry post. After an evening meal from our rations, we rested, weapons in hands. The night passed without incident.

'In the morning I ordered my troops outside to rehearse our defence plans. Suddenly I saw some troops in mixed German uniforms together with some civilians coming towards us following the same path that we had used. I immediately realised that they were partisans, raised my submachine-gun and shouted: 'Hands up! Drop your weapons!' My soldiers followed my example and within seconds they had been disarmed without a shot. There were about 15 men in German uniforms of various services, who were returning to their stronghold, unaware of our presence. They had mistaken our sentry for their own as their previous sentry had also worn a German uniform. Our sentry, who did not speak German, seeing German uniforms and as they spoke to him in a foreign language which he did not understand, let them pass. By way of this mutual misunderstanding the partisans had come straight into our hands. Later I tried to interrogate them, but without success, since I didn't understand Slovenian, and they didn't understand German. That afternoon *Waffen-Untersturmführer* Zenko Kozak arrived with some reinforcements having been sent by Pannier to assist us. Kozak agreed to escort all captives back to regimental headquarters with his group, while I remained behind with my platoon to continue our mission. We resumed our positions and posted reinforced sentries.

'During the night we heard some shots coming from the direction of our sentry. We ran outside and in the dark I saw visible flashes of discharges coming from the nearby woods. I took up position with one squad opposite the area where enemy fire was coming from and sent the other two squads to the flanks. There was an intense exchange of fire and we threw some hand grenades in their direction, after which we heard branches being broken as they fled. We gave chase for a short distance firing in the dark and then retreated to our compound suspecting a diversionary manoeuvre. In the fighting one of our men had been wounded.

'On our way back we found one enemy dead in the woods whom we left, intending to inspect him and the battlefield in the morning. We prepared for renewed enemy attacks but none came. In the morning we found the dead man in German uniform, like the other captured partisans but on closer inspection I recognised him as an NCO from the signals platoon of the regimental HQ. It looked as if one of our detachments had inadvertently stumbled in our way in the dark and both groups had taken the other for the enemy. After this, I decided to end the mission and return to our regiment to make a report.

'We made a stretcher for the dead German and began a slow and exhaustive trip back to regimental headquarters. Late at night we arrived and found *SS-Untersturmführer* Hubert Krimbacher, who had reported that his platoon had encountered overwhelming enemy forces that tried to encircle them. They had managed to escape but had to leave the dead or gravely wounded man behind. He was astonished when he learned that we had been his 'enemies'.

'It transpired that Pannier, together with his adjutant Weiss had started to interrogate the captured partisans with the help of an interpreter. One of them appeared to be very co-operative and indicated that he knew the location of the partisan headquarters and was willing to take Pannier's troops there. Without any previous notice, at night and without any radio communication, Pannier immediately sent the signals platoon that consisted exclusively of Germans on this mission, believing that German troops were more likely to succeed. The plan was to attack the partisan stronghold in the middle of night in order to surprise them and capture them easily. Two partisans had led *Untersturmführer* Krimbacher's platoon directly towards us, and then ran away as soon as the battle started leaving us to fight it out.

'In the investigation that followed everything was properly recorded but no charges were ever made. The German NCO paid with his life for Pannier's mistake. As a result of this incident one could hear the enlisted men comparing the respective fighting spirits of the Ukrainians and the Germans. Until then the Germans had boasted of their superiority in battle, often belittling the Ukrainians.'[10]

It is indicative of Freitag's discriminatory attitude that, at that time, the smallest transgression on the part of an Ukrainian, resulted almost inevitably in the death penalty. It was intended as an example, and as a means of maintaining discipline. However, Pannier's conduct went unpunished.

After a number of such actions within a ten-day period, the Division's district remained quiet and Marshall Tito's forces kept at a safe distance. More importantly, the main road from Marburg to Celje on which military columns, convoys and transportation facilities had previously been under constant threat from attack, had been cleared for all traffic, day and night.[11]

The original deadline set by the SS-FHA for the Division to be 'battle ready' by 31 December 1944 had long since elapsed.[12] At the beginning of March a letter arrived at Divisional headquarters enquiring as to its current operational status. Freitag duly replied that he did not yet consider it to be fully combat effective.[13] In response the Division was notified that its armaments should be given to units that were, and that the Division itself should be moved to the region of Salzburg for further training.[14] No immediate action appears to have been taken. However, it prompted Freitag to take remedial measures. He issued a secret internal directive to his unit commanders. In it he instructed them to discharge *Unbrauchbare Elementen,* i.e. useless and unwanted elements.[15]

Having been told that they were to be released, from military duty into civilian life, a significant number of these sub-standard soldiers were later redirected to *Arbeitsbataillons,* i.e. construction battalions. Amongst the approximately 400 men[16] selected from WGR 31 who were assembled for an inspection by *SS-Standartenführer* Pannier, at the regimental HQ in Lorenzen, was Jaroslav Senchyna, a clerk serving with the 11/III/WGR 31. By his account, having handed back rifles, belts, bayonets, pay books and insignia, but not their uniforms, the entire group marched to Marburg. From there they travelled by train to Feldbach in Austria. There they were included in a larger labour force supervised by the Organisation *Todt.* Many were Jewish women and children from Hungary. All were put to work building defensive positions.[17]

The Ukrainian National Army

It was a conscious decision by the German authorities to move the Division to a remote theatre of operations. Ukraine was once again being subjected to the brutalities of Soviet occupation. The move inevitably produced a marked decline in the morale of the Ukrainian soldiers. The only remaining source from which any immediate encouragement could be derived was the continuing developments with the 'Ukrainian National Committee' that in late February to early March had entered into a decisive stage.

At a time when the Western Allied armies had already crossed the German frontier and were poised to cross the Rhine, the Red Army was a mere 64kms from Berlin. But, after months of negotiations, an 'Ukrainian National Committee', independent of Vlasov's authority, came into being.[18] On 23 February 1945, Alfred Rosenberg, as the representative of the German Government, formally empowered Shandruk to head the 'Ukrainian National

Committee'. It was to be the sole representative of the Ukrainian people.[19] The official act of recognition was promulgated seventeen days later, in writing, by Rosenberg on 12 March 1945.[20] (See Appendix XVI).

Rosenberg's declaration was made in his, by then, impotent capacity as *Reichsminister* for the Occupied (sic.) Eastern Territories, and without the consent of the other German agencies. Ratification, by way of a written order from either Hitler or Himmler, was noticeably absent. The practical consequences were necessarily limited.[21] Nevertheless, following receipt of this authorisation, Shandruk was able to proceed with his plans that he had already initiated for the organisation of the committee and the establishment of an Ukrainian National Army. The nucleus was to be the 14th *Waffen Grenadier Division der SS* (*ukrainische* Nr. 1). Having filled the committee's executive positions, and appointed Professor Volodymyr Kubijovych and Oleksander Semenenko as his first and second deputies,[22] priority was given to the unification of all Ukrainian military formations into the Ukrainian National Army. General Shandruk himself became Commander in Chief.[23]

Towards that end, a projected 2nd Ukrainian Division had already begun to take shape. At the Nimek (Niemegk) training camp near Berlin, approximately 500 Ukrainian men formed the 1st company of the *Vil'na Ukraina* Anti-tank Brigade,[24] to boost their strength. Those units, and the 14th *Waffen Grenadier Division der SS ukrainische* Nr. 1 were to become the 1st Division of the Ukrainian National Army. Without consulting Shandruk, the Military Board, or any other Ukrainian body, the Germans began a recruiting drive. Former members of various *Schützmannschaft* battalions had fled with the retreating Germans. There were numbers of disillusioned forced labourers and former prisoners of war held in camps in Germany. Many had unknown or criminal service histories. All sought to join the 14th *Waffen Grenadier Division der SS* (*ukrainische* Nr. 1), as individuals, or in groups.[25] Not all succeeded in doing so. As far as possible, given its already overstretched resources, the Division undertook limited screening. They rejected those who were either unfit or unsuitable for enlistment. Others preferred to return from whence they came.[26]

At the end of February 1945, concurrent plans were made to incorporate into the Division the Volhynian Self-Defence Legion made up of battle-trained and experienced men. The Volhynian Legion was originally a partisan unit belonging to the Melnyk faction of the OUN[27] that specialised in anti-partisan warfare. From October 1943, it had been under the direct control of the *Sicherheitsdienst* (SD) as the *Schützmannschaft Bataillon der SD* Nr. 31 or the Ukrainian Legion of Self-Defence.[28] From July 1944,[29] it was commanded by *SS-Sturmbannführer* Biegelmeyer.[30] At its peak it reached a strength of approximately 600 officers and men, including a few German SD officers and NCOs.[31] The Legion had undertaken several independent anti-partisan actions at various locations in the Volhynia and Cholm regions of the *Generalgouvernement*, from February 1944 to the end of October 1944.[32] During that time at least one reinforced company, under the command of Oberst Petro Diachenko, was utilised for several weeks along with the German forces, in the suppression of the Warsaw rising in August 1944.[33] The Legion was then deployed, in its entirety, at the railway station at Klaj, between Cracow and Bochnia, before being moved again to the Austrian side of the Yugoslav/Austrian border by train in late February 1945.[34] There, in the first week of March, *SS-Brigadeführer* Freitag met *SS-Sturmbannführer* Biegelmeyer in the village of Unterschwarz where the Legion had its HQ, for discussions on the merger of the two units. No Ukrainians were consulted, nor did any take part in those talks. Pending full integration the unit remained in the region as a separate entity.

Unaware of the plans to unify all Ukrainian units, the majority of the Volhynians opposed the merger, especially those who had previously served as officers in the Division and had subsequently been dismissed as unsuitable.[35] They were concerned that they would lose their separate Ukrainian identity and independence. Hence, on 5 March 1945, the day that the official incorporation was to have taken place under the Ukrainian flag, the Division's designated representatives *Major* Heike and *SS-Standartenführer* Beyersdorff, together with its band, arrived at the Legion's camp in a village on the river Mur. They found that, during the night, over 200 of the Volhynians had deserted, taking their portable weapons and equipment. Led by Lieutenant Roman Kyveluk, ('Voron'), the group had established contact with the Chetniks, who agreed to help them cross the river Mur by ferry.

They then set out to return to the Carpathian Mountains with the intention of joining with the existing Ukrainian resistance movements active in that area.[36] Having crossed the Mur without the promised help, the Ukrainians were met by Chetnik liaison officers. They were supposed to act as guides, in the St Leonard district east of

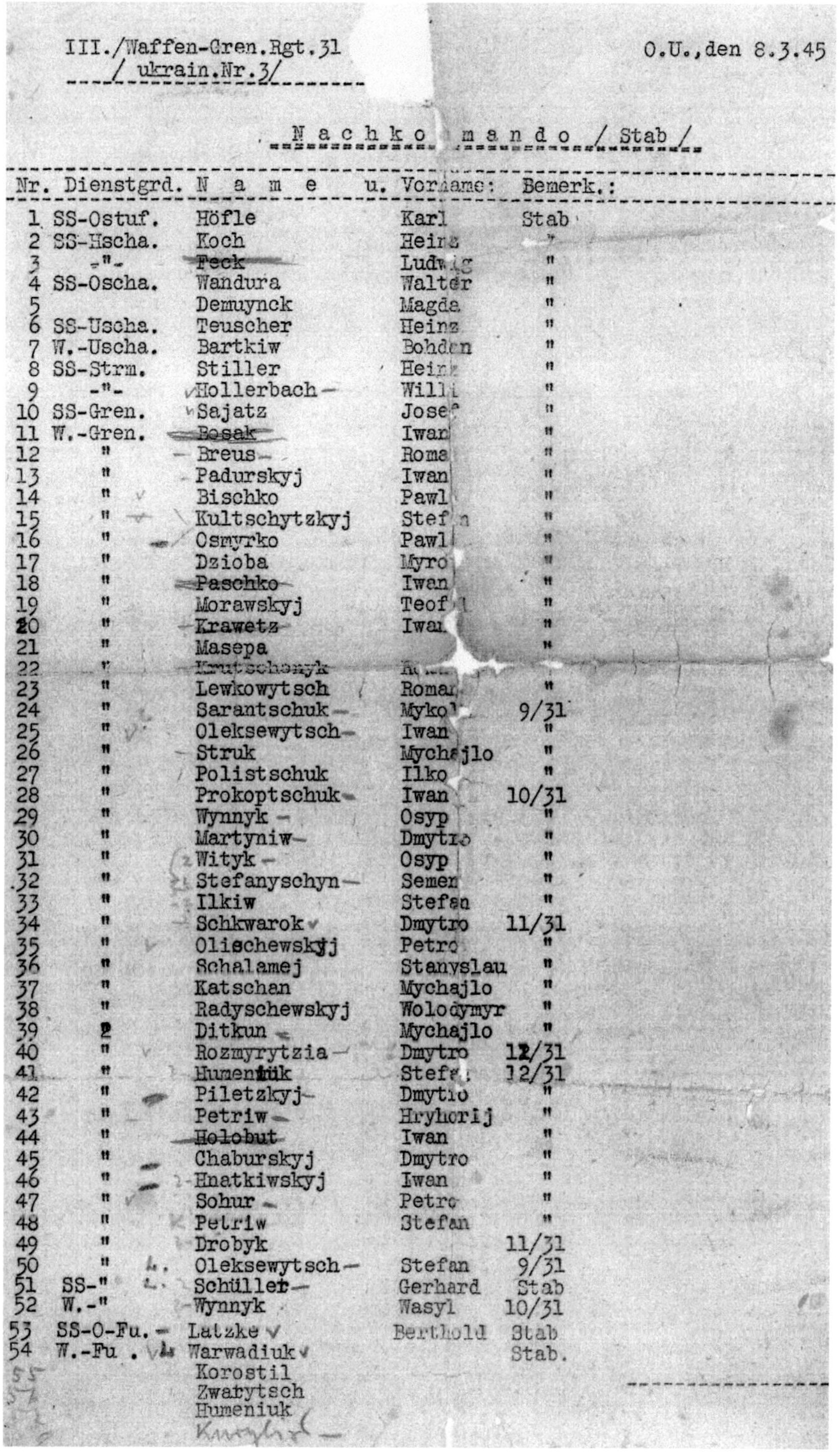

III./Waffen-Gren.Rgt.31
/ ukrain.Nr.3/

O.U., den 8.3.45

Nachko mando / Stab /

Nr.	Dienstgrd.	Name	u. Vorname:	Bemerk.:
1	SS-Ostuf.	Höfle	Karl	Stab
2	SS-Hscha.	Koch	Heinz	"
3	-"-	Feck	Ludwig	"
4	SS-Oscha.	Wandura	Walter	"
5		Demuynck	Magda	"
6	SS-Uscha.	Teuscher	Heinz	"
7	W.-Uscha.	Bartkiw	Bohdan	"
8	SS-Strm.	Stiller	Hein	"
9	-"-	Hollerbach	Willi	"
10	SS-Gren.	Sajatz	Jose	"
11	W.-Gren.	Bosak	Iwan	"
12	"	Breus	Roma	"
13	"	Padurskyj	Iwan	"
14	"	Bischko	Pawl	"
15	"	Kultschytzkyj	Stef n	"
16	"	Osmyrko	Pawl	"
17	"	Dzioba	Myro	"
18	"	Paschko	Iwan	"
19	"	Morawskyj	Teof	"
20	"	Krawetz	Iwa	"
21	"	Masepa		"
22	"	[illegible]	[illegible]	
23	"	Lewkowytsch	Roman	"
24	"	Sarantschuk	Mykol	9/31
25	"	Oleksewytsch	Iwan	"
26	"	Struk	Mychajlo	"
27	"	Polistschuk	Ilko	"
28	"	Prokoptschuk	Iwan	10/31
29	"	Wynnyk	Osyp	"
30	"	Martyniw	Dmytro	"
31	"	Wityk	Osyp	"
32	"	Stefanyschyn	Semen	"
33	"	Ilkiw	Stefan	"
34	"	Schkwarok	Dmytro	11/31
35	"	Olischewskyj	Petro	"
36	"	Schalamej	Stanyslau	"
37	"	Katschan	Mychajlo	"
38	"	Radyschewskyj	Wolodymyr	"
39	"	Ditkun	Mychajlo	"
40	"	Rozmyrytzia	Dmytro	12/31
41	"	Humeniuk	Stefan	12/31
42	"	Piletzkyj	Dmytro	"
43	"	Petriw	Hryhorij	"
44	"	Holobut	Iwan	"
45	"	Chaburskyj	Dmytro	"
46	"	Hnatkiwskyj	Iwan	"
47	"	Sohur	Petro	"
48	"	Petriw	Stefan	"
49	"	Drobyk		11/31
50	"	Oleksewytsch	Stefan	9/31
51	SS-"	Schüller	Gerhard	Stab
52	W.-"	Wynnyk	Wasyl	10/31
53	SS-O-Fu.	Latzke	Berthold	Stab
54	W.-Fu.	Warwadiuk		Stab.
55		Korostil		
56		Zwarytsch		
57		Humeniuk		
		[illegible]		

List of 58 soldiers assigned to the Nachkommando of III/WGR 31 dated 8 March 1945

Marburg.[37] The Chetniks promptly betrayed the location of the Ukrainian soldiers to the German security *Polizei* in Marburg. The *Polizei* gave instructions to deliver the group to a previously determined location. There they would be met by a detachment from the Division that was to oversee the enforced merger.

The merger took place on 9 March. The members of the legion were surrounded by a detachment from the Division in company strength, under the command of *Major* Heike. Representing the Ukrainian contingent were *Waffen-Untersturmführer* Father Levenets, *Waffen-Obersturmführer* Pidhayny and the Liaison Officer *Waffen-Hauptsturmführer* Makarushka who acted as interpreter.[38] To mollify their apprehensions, the Volhynians were offered surrender terms on Freitag's behalf, and assured that there would be a full amnesty for all those involved.

After careful deliberation, the offer was accepted by their leader, Roman Kyveluk. Shortly after, the merger went ahead in the village of Frauheim.

In that way, around 600 Volhynians including two doctors and two priests[39] were absorbed into the 14th *Waffen Grenadier Division der SS* (*ukrainische* Nr. 1), in early March 1945. The officers and NCOs, numbering approximately 80 men, were permitted to retain their ranks and were subsequently put through a training course during which they were given instruction in tactics and in the handling of weapons, such as the *Panzerfaust*. Later, together with the enlisted men they were divided up between the Division's sub-units.[40] Because of their expertise they were often used as search platoons in subsequent actions against partisans. For example around 50 of them were sent to the Fusilier Battalion from which a *Jagdzug* was formed. Commanded by *Waffen-Untersturmführer* Iliasewych, it was under the direct orders of the battalion commander.[41]

Kyveluk, who had led the renegades, was summoned to Divisional Headquarters on Freitag's orders. In reply to fellow legion members, who warned him not to go, Kyveluk who was known to be a sincere and honourable man, stated that he could not do otherwise because of his 'officer's honour'. En route he was shot, purportedly for theft.[42]

While the fate of the Volhynians was being decided, the Division began one of several larger scale anti-partisan operations that it undertook during March 1945. Some were in conjunction with other German Wehrmacht and *Polizei* units and local garrison forces. Operation *Donnerwetter* ('Thunderstorm') was reported to have begun on 8 March 1945, and concluded ten days later on 18th.[43] During that period, the 14th Division was at first engaged in battle with both the Šercer and Bracic brigades. They had been ordered to go to the Mozirje mountains and the Pohorje, to deceive the Germans into believing that they had abandoned the idea of going to the Dolenjska region.[44] At the same time, while in that region, the insurgents were to collect weapons, munitions and supplies dropped by Allied aircraft.

As the biggest and most effective of the participating units, the 14th Division was entrusted with the most demanding part of the operation. The objective was to gradually constrict the operational area of the partisans by pushing them back into their last defensive positions. There they were to be eliminated.

The Division's sub-units advanced across difficult terrain to their assembly positions in the upper Savinja and Saleška Valleys in the Mozirje mountains before beginning their operations, after only a brief rest. The mountainous approach routes were extremely difficult for the soldiers to traverse. The use of trucks and horses for the transportation of heavy weapons, field kitchens and supplies of food and ammunition was ruled out. For that purpose mules were available but in such limited quantity that they could only be used to transport a small fraction of the total of the Division's requirements. The remainder had to be manhandled. To ensure the availability of sufficient provisions, the heavy radio equipment had to be left behind. That meant the Division was forced to adhere rigidly to a prearranged plan which, once commenced, could not be altered. They were placed at a distinct disadvantage for the duration of the operation.

The Division's infantry units were split up into platoon-sized groups. They ventured into the remote mountains having received the following days' instructions and route from their company commanders. Often with no appropriate maps[45] for orientation, without hot food or shelter, and with inadequate footwear for mountain climbing, the heavily laden soldiers moved into the steep, snow-covered mountains. They went in single file, through snow that was sometimes waist deep. The fighting that followed took place in biting cold and occasional snow blizzards.

The day after the offensive had started both the Šercer and Bracic brigades had been surrounded by elements of the 14th Division on the south side of the Mozirje Plateau. There, between 9 and 11 March, the Division's units advancing from the towns of Mozirje and Šmihel came into contact with the Šercer brigade near the villages of Gostencnik and Radegunda. There, for the next three days, they defended its positions from constant attacks. They used women as nurses, cooks and other auxiliary personnel.

On 11 March 1945 the Division's units were also reported to be fighting against the Bracic brigade on the Medvedjak Mountain. Due to heavy pressure, bad connections between the Bracic brigades' battalions, and under the protection of its 3rd Battalion, all its units and the HQ of the 14th Partisan Division were forced to retreat to the south, in the direction of the village of Poljane. Pursued by the Division's units that launched attacks with heavy artillery and mortar support from the direction of Mozirje and Šoštanj, the fighting continued in the region

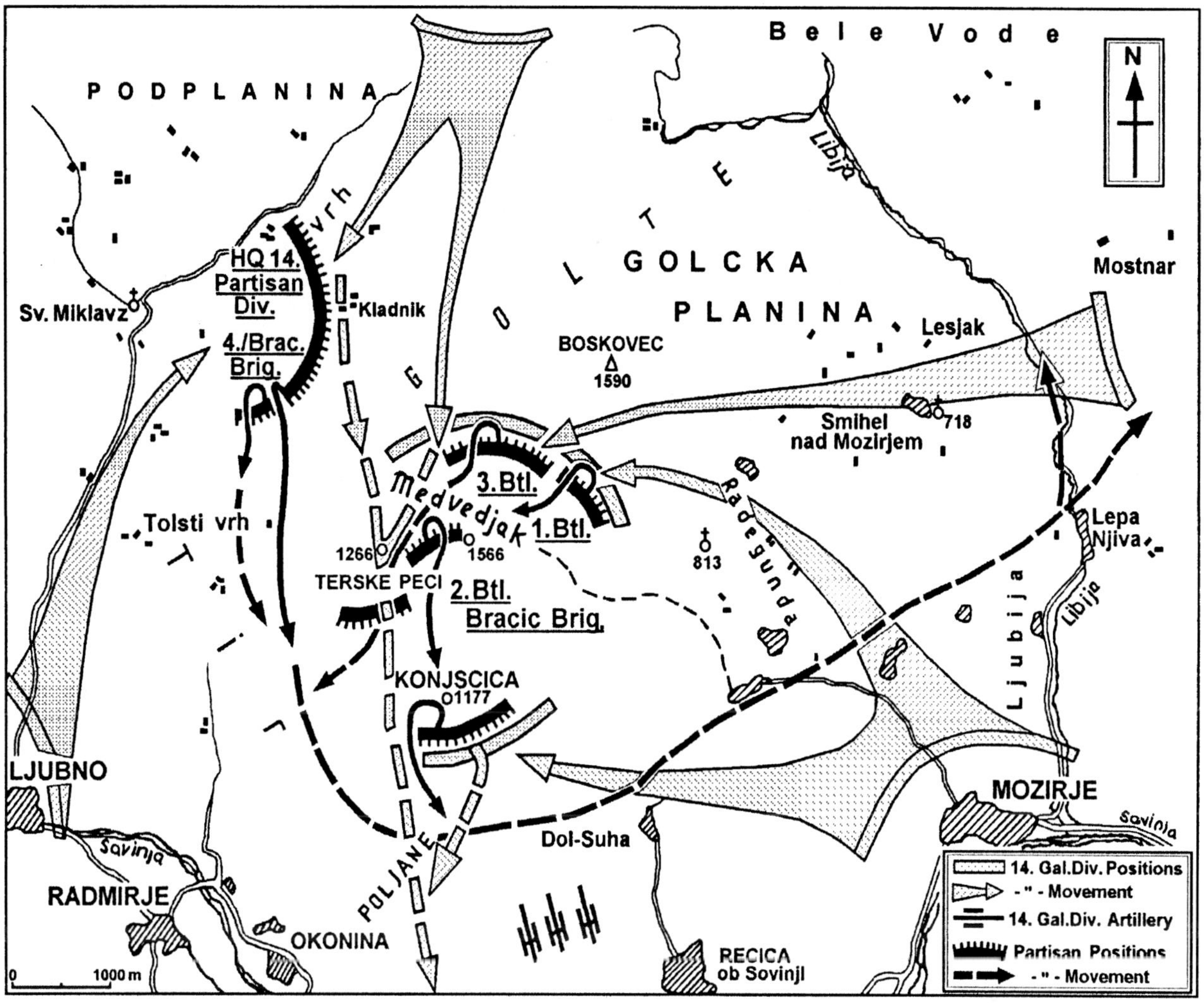

Map 10 Operations of the 14th Waffen-Grenadier-Division der SS *(*ukrainische Nr. *1) against the 2nd SNOUB* 'Mirko Bracic' *at Medvedjak, Slovenia, 11 March 1945*

of Bela Pec. At last, on the night of the third day, the partisan units were finally able to retreat from the Mozirje plateau in difficult circumstances. Most of the men of 3rd Battalion of the Bracic brigade that formed the rear-guard, were able to extricate themselves but only with the utmost difficulty. They were lucky to escape near Terske peci. The battalion commander reported:

> 'Due to the critical position on the Medvedjak the commander gave orders to the political commissar of the 2nd Company that the company must hold its position, against heavy attacks by units of the 14th Waffen SS Division *Galizien*. The scenes above the ridge, defended by the partisans, were amazing. The enemy was coming from the other side of the rock ridge and throwing grenades from a distance of around 15–20 metres that the partisans picked up and threw back. The attack of the Ukrainians was covered by their MGs. It went on for several hours during which time two partisan MG gunners and their assistant were killed. The Ukrainians suddenly appeared on the left side and were seriously threatening the right flank too. The battalion retreated to the edge of the wood and defended itself.
>
> 'Near Terske Peci its men were faced with a decision of how to proceed, because they were confronted with a deep rock precipice. However, a large group of the 3rd Battalion with their wounded managed to save themselves by using ropes, which were hastily prepared and then by dropping themselves over the deep precipice into the valley below, taking the ropes with them. The enemy soon reached the precipice but wasn't prepared to risk following. The 3rd Battalion was then safely guided towards the valley by its

commander and two locals. During the retreat, there were further clashes with the Ukrainians. 3rd Battalion later made contact with the Brigade HQ, whose commander Captain Milenko Knezevic, believed it had been destroyed in the fierce battles."[46]

Despite its escape, the strength of the Bracic brigade was reduced from 472 on 9 March, to 393 on 15 March. It was a loss of 79 men, including those killed, captured, missing, deserters and transfers to other partisan units, all in less than a week.[47]

Like its sister formation the Šercer Brigade also escaped from encirclement by doubling back and slipping undetected through the Division's lines under cover of darkness.[48] Its losses for that period were reported as 17 dead, 21 wounded and 55 missing, some later returned, together with the loss of 25 rifles, 4 machine-guns and 3 submachine-guns.[49]

The Division's own losses appear to have been minimal.[50] The wounded who required medical attention were immediately despatched to its field hospital in Marburg. There, German soldiers from other units, and even some Slovenian civilians were also treated.[51]

A rumoured incident involved the burning of a partisan field hospital, along with all the patients who could not walk, including a British airman. It was discovered, at the time, by soldiers of the Galician Division. Subsequently, it was investigated by the RAF and discounted, because the statement given by the principle witness, Flight Sergeant Parker, contained no evidence to that effect.[52]

After three days of fighting in the area of the Mozirje mountains, the Division continued with offensive actions in the area between the Zgornja Savinja Valley and the Tuhinje Valley, at the Menina plateau.[53] There it battled against the Zidanšek and Šlander brigades which together with their operative HQ and 4th Battalion of the 3rd Brigade NO, i.e. *Narodna Obramba* or National Defence, were successfully surrounded on the Menina plateau from 13–15 March. The subsequent partisan accounts of that action describe, in dramatic detail, how elements of the 14th Division came close to capturing the Šlander brigade's secret camp, and how the insurgent forces evaded their pursuers. They avoided the numerous ambushes and blocking positions established along the mountain ridges, and skilfully managed to break through the encirclement near Cirkuše, close to the Division's artillery positions.[54]

All large-scale operations, undertaken by part or the whole of the 14th Division in Slovenia were, according to its Ia, *Major* Heike, fraught with difficulties which combined constantly to undermine its effectiveness. The major part of the operation was led, personally, by *SS-Obergruppenführer* Rösener and was no exception. He responded to German intelligence reports that a significant concentration of partisans had assembled in the Menina planina mountains, i.e. the Steinen Alps, south of Ljubljana, intending to pick up weapons, munitions and supplies dropped by Allied aircraft.

Typically, remote areas were chosen for the designated drop zones. Together with the times and dates of the flights, they were arranged and co-ordinated by individual partisan brigade HQs, and partisan liaison officers from the Allied Military Mission who were attached to them.[55] Consequently, the partisans had a clear advantage. However, it was sometimes possible for the German forces to establish the location of these zones from the presence of large, low-flying Allied bomber, or transport aircraft, as they circled over the target area. To avoid detection, planes would from time to time drop their supply containers from a high altitude, causing the falling parachutes to get caught in the wind and their precious cargoes of weapons, ammunition, food, clothes and medicines, to fall into German hands.

The preferred secluded sites ensured that, during the drop, actual engagements were rare. In some localities sporadic contact did occur. Then there were skirmishes with the partisan patrols, messengers and other activists who would frequently disappear and pretend that they were "peace loving inhabitants" of small mountain villages who knew nothing about 'partisans'. As a result house searches followed which seldom produced any incriminating evidence, except for the silken parachutes. Of course, those originated from the airdrops, the weapons and munitions having been hidden by the partisans in the forests. When questioned the local women would allege that they had only found the parachutes in the mountains and wanted to use the material to make clothing. The parachutes were duly confiscated and used by the soldiers to make scarves and socks.[56] Several bunkers and wooden emplacements were also discovered. In them were stored the weapons, munitions, tools, provisions and clothing obtained from the airdrops. Everything usable was taken, the bunkers and hide-outs blown up and the items of clothing burned. After considerable effort, this operation was called off without a decisive engagement having taken place.

The large-scale action designed to secure and clear the towns of Solcava, Mozirje and Ljubno and the Boskovec massif, elevation 1,590 metres, situated in the south western corner of the Division's district,[57] was also fated ultimately to fail for reasons beyond its control. Communication problems, caused by the inadequate provision of field radios, were exacerbated by the fact that its Fieseler Storch reconnaissance plane, usually a most effective aid to orientation, could not be used with any appreciable effect. Therefore all efforts to engage and destroy the partisans were frustrated.[58] Further, as with all major actions, once the bulk of its forces were in the field, other partisans acting on information from local informants became very active. They conducted raids on the weak garrison forces left behind, cut telephone wires and generally caused havoc. The Command was compelled to terminate the undertaking prematurely. Thereafter, only the Artillery Regiment and Fusilier Battalion remained in the southern sector where they successfully engaged the insurgents in the Sava river district.

On account of the failure of those large-scale actions, the Division's command preferred to employ smaller detachments and *Jagdzüge* in local security sweeps. They had proved their worth in Slovakia. The actions were carried out by almost all of its sub-units, some in conjunction with other German units. Typically lasting only a few days, they were generally far more effective. Many of the most notable successes were attributable to the Volyhnians who showed a particular aptitude for anti-partisan warfare.[59] In that way limited amounts of enemy matériel, consisting mainly of small arms, rifles, machine-guns, ammunition and items of clothing were captured.[60] A variety of masterfully camouflaged partisan hide-outs and installations were also discovered and destroyed.[61]

Small groups of soldiers operating in remote areas were, however, prone to ambush, a tactic frequently successfully employed by the partisans.[62] The funerals of those killed on active service were presided over by the Division's chaplains.

As a rule, in compliance with their orders, the partisans sought to evade frontal battles at all costs. Their virulent hatred of the Germans and their ruthless tactics demanded the utmost vigilance from the pursuit groups. They had to contend with hazards including booby-traps,[63] and a multitude of other difficulties, as related by a *Waffen-Untersturmführer* who served as a platoon commander:

> 'The mountainous terrain was the biggest problem. My company (13/WGR 30) with infantry IGs [*Infanterie Geschütze* – infantry guns] had to use the roads which were often icy or slippery, too steep or non existent. We were forced to stay at lower elevations. Any troop movements had to be done at night. During the day only patrols in a *Gansereihe* [single file], utilising terrain cover to the fullest extent, were able to move from place to place. There was also a constant danger from low flying planes. Because of the hilly terrain one could not see nor hear them from a distance, and only became aware of them when they were already on top of you. In Slovakia we were able to march openly every day to a drill area, singing and often children would gather and accompany us. In Slovenia, we had to build MG nests and rifle pits around the perimeter of our quarters, march at night and be on guard at all times. The population was less friendly and it was not permitted to walk alone, only in pairs'.[64]

Although sentry duty was always conducted in earnest, it could not prevent the Division sustaining losses. The more ruthless partisans showed no mercy even for medical personnel.[65] Accordingly, losses were appreciably higher than they had been in Slovakia. They were an estimated 156 killed on Yugoslav territory.[66] The numbers would have been even higher had not some unit commanders, on both sides, entered into unofficial local truces and deliberately avoided contact.[67] Such unusual circumstances may account for the fact that, in exceptional situations, partisans were released after interrogation, as were some Ukrainian troops who fell into enemy hands.[68]

The nature of the Division's assignment in Slovenia meant that, apart from the experience and physical conditioning gained during combat with the partisans, little time remained for other training activities. Any weapons instruction, exercises, drill and NCO training which did take place, amidst often picturesque surroundings, had to take into account the dispersal of its units over a wide area, and the posting of sentries. Although to a certain extent tracking-dogs proved to be useful. However, there were continuous assignments at short notice.

Free time for rest and recreation was scarce. When available it was generally limited to visiting cinemas in the larger towns or trying to befriend local girls, which was not without its own hazards.[69] As the territory had been incorporated into the Reich, military pay was issued in German Marks with which the soldiers could purchase the Divisional newspaper *Do Boyu*. It was published by its own staff and printed in Marburg.[70] As circumstances permitted, members of some non-combatant units also attended services held at local Slovenian churches, where they were able to participate in the Mass.[71]

Surprisingly, with the war drawing to an obvious conclusion, the Division's camaraderie remained good. During its tour of duty in Slovenia, a further 150 desertions of both Ukrainian and German personnel occurred.[72] That brought the total number from autumn 1943, until the end of March 1945, to around 600 men, excluding those who deserted at Brody. It was a desertion rate of less than 3%.[73] At the same time, at least two Ukrainian officers, from WGR 31, *Waffen-Untersturmführers* M. Javorskyj and T. Chmola,[74] and one from WGR 30, *Waffen-Untersturmführer* M.Bihus, were decorated with the Iron Cross 2nd Class for their courage during actions in Slovenia. [75]

The Division's command received all news of the most recent developments on the Eastern Front through the offices of Dr Steindl, the head of the Styrian *Heimatsbund*. The proximity of the Front was getting closer by the day. The foremost units of the Red Army had advanced to within 40 kilometres of Marburg, directly in front of the Division's position. Thus, from early March all its sub-units were put on full alert and plans drawn up for committing it to battle.

An ill-affordable Luxury

By mid-March 1945 the general war situation had worsened considerably. Indeed, on the southern sector of the Eastern Front where the 14th Division was deployed, it had deteriorated to such an extent that the security actions in which it was compelled to participate were considered by its command to be of comparatively little relevance.

Following the failure of the last German offensive of the war in Hungary,[76] the Soviet 2nd and 3rd Ukrainian fronts had pushed Army Group South back towards Austria's eastern provinces. It held the right wing of the German forces on the Eastern Front. In that area it was imperative that the line held, as Army Group South protected the withdrawal of Army Group E[77] (Balkans). They were retreating through Yugoslavia, towards Austria, pursued by Soviet and Bulgarian Armies, as well as Marshall Tito's partisans.

As part of the massive Soviet offensive against Austria, code named 'Operation Vienna', the corps and divisions of Marshall Tolbhukin's 3rd Ukrainian Front launched a powerful assault on Army Group South's defensive line. On 21 March, a Soviet spearhead attacked and successfully penetrated the left flank of the German 6th Army that stood in its path, at the boundary between 6th Army and 6th SS *Panzer* Army. On 6th's right flank was the German 2nd *Panzer* Army. In anticipation of attacks in the area of 2nd *Panzer* Army, on 24 March, Army Group South issued a general directive, stating that the '14. *SS Waffen-Gren. Div.* (*Ukrainer*) [sic.] and the 297th Infantry Division had to occupy secondary positions in its sector.[78] As of that date the Division is identified on a German operations chart as being within 2nd *Panzer* Army.

The same chart provided a rating of each unit's estimated combat value. It showed the 14th Division to be classified unreliable,[79] in accordance with Freitag's estimation given at the beginning of the month.

Despite its secondment to 2nd *Panzer* Army on paper, with the Division's sub-units scattered over a large area, the actual transfer of command was delayed. It was therefore unable to draw supplies from any Army Group, at that time, as would ordinarily have been the case. As it was still considered to be in the process of reformation, for operational and supply purposes it remained under the control of HSSPf. Rösener. They were engaged in combating partisans in the Pohorje region south of the river Drava.[80]

At that point the Division, and its Training and Reserve Regiment, resumed its attempts to clear its district and the rear of the nearby front.[81] While doing so its very existence was jeopardised by the arrival of a sudden and unexpected order. The origins of the order can be traced to the night of the 23 March 1945, when Hitler referred to the Ukrainian SS-Division, i.e. 14th, during a briefing at his headquarters in Berlin. At that meeting he claimed to know nothing about the 14th.

'... I just heard for the first time, to my amazement, that an Ukrainian SS Division has suddenly appeared. I didn't know a thing about this *Ukrainian SS Division*." [Author's emphasis]

It is evident, from the official transcript of the conference, that in the following discussion no one present, including the adjutant of the Liaison Officer of the Waffen-SS (*Adjutant des Verbindungsführers der Waffen-SS*) *SS-Sturmbannführer* Göhler, was able to differentiate between the 14th *Waffen Grenadier Division der SS* and the Ukrainian Division. However, as Hitler suspected, they were in fact one and the same.[82] As a result, the Galician Division was incorrectly identified by *SS-Sturmbannführer* Göhler as the 30th SS Division and the Ukrainian Division as the 14th.[83] Nonetheless, Hitler was furious when he was informed that having been committed to combat in the Brody/Tarnow sector, where it was encircled, the Division had recuperated to the point where it had reached full strength of 14,000 men.[84] But, erroneously, it was resting and "had not been committed since".[85] Once the subject had been broached, Hitler went on to refer to the "self-delusion" of maintaining and arming formations made up of foreigners whose loyalty to the German cause and fighting value, was highly suspect. It could not therefore be considered as "trustworthy". It would be better, he asserted, to take away their weapons immediately and raise new Reich German divisions. Upon learning that the Ukrainian, i.e. Galician Division had what he considered to be "nearly enough weapons to equip two divisions"[86] Hitler retorted:

'I must know what this division is worth. I want to speak to the *Reichsführer* right away tomorrow. He's in Berlin anyhow. We have to investigate exactly what we can expect from a unit like that. If one cannot expect anything there is no sense to it. We can't afford the luxury of keeping units like that.'[87]

Within hours, the *Reichsführer-SS* Himmler, whose standing with Hitler was at an all time low,[88] had dutifully issued an order to the Division. He directed it to temporarily disarm and surrender its weapons and equipment, to facilitate the establishment of new Reich German formations. Replacement weapons were to be shipped in due course.[89] That order arrived at its HQ in Selnica via Army Group South. They had been charged with the task of ensuring that all the weapons and supplies were gathered, taken to a rail depot and loaded on to transport trains bound for Nurnberg, approximately 600kms away.[90] From there, ultimately the weapons and matériel were to be made available to the Commander in Chief of the German forces on the Western Front.

Having previously encountered spurious *Führer* or *Reichsführer* orders, the Division's headquarters was inherently suspicious of this potentially disastrous directive. Consequently, *SS-Brigadeführer* Freitag left for Himmler's *Feldkommando-Stelle,* i.e. Field Command Post, in Salzburg, the next day to seek clarification. There, in the face of his objections, it was confirmed. While, in the absence of the *Reichsführer* himself, there was no immediate latitude for negotiation, Himmler's Chief of Staff promised that he would take up the matter of revoking the order with Himmler personally. Freitag then returned to Selnica to await further developments. In anticipation of the worst scenario, the Division's command temporally suspended its anti-partisan activities. The Artillery Regiment, plus the 2nd and 3rd companies of the Fusilier Battalion which were still south of the Sava river were instructed to return to Marburg.[91] Only WGR 31 was in the field with the 2nd company of the Pioneer Battalion, and they continued with their security operations south of the Sava.[92]

Due to the gravity of the disarmament order, which showed no regard for either the Division or the precarious military situation on the south Austrian front, its command deliberately tried to procrastinate in the hope that, after due consideration, it would be countermanded. Notwithstanding that, in spite of the repeated demands of the Chief Quartermaster of Army Group South that followed, practical considerations prevented its implementation. The requisite 38 freight cars needed to transport all the matériel were not available, and could not be provided by the local transport officials. With Allied forces already in the vicinity of Nurnberg it was also unlikely that the shipment would reach its destination. When notified of such insurmountable difficulties, the Chief Quartermaster promised to review the matter with the OKH.[93]

In the interim, the Division's command sent out a sharply worded teletype message to the higher authorities including Himmler, outlining its concerns. The response was a spate of new and often contradictory orders and directives from various military bodies. Those followed in quick succession. (For an example of one of the disarmament orders see Appendix XVII). A few days later Army Group South sent a commission or acceptance detachment, under the command of a senior ordnance officer from the quartermaster section. Under its pressure, part of the small arms arsenal was collected from the soldiers both Ukrainian and German.[94] The requirement for some units to surrender their weapons[95] spread rumours and great consternation among the ranks.[96] Transportation of the weapons was, however, still impossible. Heavy bombardment of Marburg railway station by Allied planes, halted all traffic for several days. Because of the proximity of the front, and the realistic prospect of mutiny,[97] after a short period the weapons were returned.[98]

Somewhat fortuitously, according to Heike's testimony, late at night on 26 March 1945, the original architect of the Division, Dr Wächter arrived. He was accompanied by the head of the Military Board, *Oberst* Bisanz.[99] Freitag was unwilling to accommodate them at the staff HQ and relented only on Heike's insistence. Both Dr Wächter and *Oberst* Bisanz were well acquainted with the situation at the front, but knew nothing about the disarmament order. Dr Wächter who had a vested interest in preserving the Division, wasted no time in contacting Himmler, the local *Gauleiter* of Steiermark, and the Defence Commissar Dr Siegfried Uiberreither.

Uiberreither had been granted emergency powers, by Hitler, to defend his province to the last. He and other influential individuals attempted to persuade them that compliance with the order was neither in German nor in Ukrainian interests. There is no evidence to suggest that Dr Wächter consulted or even informed General Shandruk, or the recently recognised 'Ukrainian National Committee', at that critical time. In any case they were powerless to prevent such a move. The following day, unable to obtain the assurance that he sought, Dr Wächter approached the local military authorities seeking to circumvent the order.[100] As Freitag had refused requests to allow his Operations Officer, *Major* Heike to accompany Wächter, he took along the first Liaison Officer *Waffen-Hauptsturmführer* Makarushka. Together they hastened by car to the HQ of Army Group South, where Wächter hoped to convince its commander *Generaloberst* Alexander Löhr, that the 14th Division was in fact ready to be given an immediate combat role.[101]

With the Division still under orders to hand over its weapons, WGRs 29 and 30 remained entrenched within a twenty-four hour march of Marburg. In the event of a Soviet attack on such a vital communications and supply centre, the Division's command, on its own initiative, drew up plans for the defence of the city, which it reported to 2nd and 6th armies. WGR 31 and the 2nd Company of the Pioneer Battalion were still in the district, south of Ljubljana, were they had been sent by HSSPf. Rösener to combat partisans.[102] The Training and Reserve Regiment was located across the Austrian border at Deutschlandsberg, where it too was heavily engaged in battling insurgent forces.

Dr Wächter came back from the Army Group HQ, to report that its commander had recognised the merit in his arguments. He had also agreed that he would arrange for the Division to be sent to fight at the front against the Red Army. Wächter's tireless efforts seemed finally to have brought a reprieve, if only a temporary one. On the evening of 28 March 1945, the Division received notification, via Himmler's Field Command Post in Salzburg, that "no arms were to be given up. Further orders would follow."[103]

In the meantime, the situation at the front was becoming critical. As had been anticipated, Soviet reconnaissance forces had detected a weakness in the German frontline on 6th Army's southern flank at its juncture with 2nd *Panzer* Army.[104] There, at the end of March, the 57th Army, 1st Bulgarian Army and elements of 27th Army, broke through the German and Hungarian formations manning the *Reichsschutzstellung*. A hastily dug line of field fortifications, it was the last barrier before the Reich frontier and threatened to drive deep into Styria, south-eastern Austria.[105]

On Wächter's return, *Major* Heike as Operations Officer travelled to the HQ of 2nd *Panzer* Army to report to its Chief of Staff the condition and battle readiness of the Division. He requested immediate deployment orders be issued.[106] The proposal met with approval of the 2nd *Panzer* Army's Chief of Staff who indicated that pending its formal acceptance, it was to be assigned to closing the breach between 2nd and 6th armies, i.e. a line running from Feldbach to Gleichenberg.

On 31 March, Army Group South issued an order subordinating the Division to the 2nd *Panzer* Army commanded by *General der Artillerie* Maximilian de Angelis. In turn, 2nd *Panzer* Army assigned it to the command of *General der Kavallerie* Gustav Harteneck's I *Kavallerie* Corps.[107] It had the lowest combat effectiveness in the whole of 2nd *Panzer* Army and joint lowest of the whole of Army Group South.[108] In accordance with the general directive, the advance by I

Kavallerie Corps on the Soviet breakpoint, between Feldbach and Radkersburg, was scheduled to begin the following day at 6.30am.[109] At the same time Rösener sent a message to the *SS-Gauleiter* Dr Siegfried Uiberreither, which read "I am going to release immediately to *Brigadeführer* Freitag part of the 14th SS Ukraine Nr.1."[110]

Notwithstanding these developments, Wächter, who knew that the preservation of the Division ultimately depended on a definitive revocation from the very highest authority, felt it prudent to visit the head quarters of Army Group Southeast on 1 April, as there was "Still no decision by OKW".[111]

Until there was such a decision the Division's fate was not assured. Somewhat expediently, even before the deployment orders had been secured, the Division's command, on its own volition, had made provision to that end which it had already begun to implement. Some elements were moved to Spielfeld to protect the Mur narrows and a vital road bridge.[112] Furthermore, the commanders of WGRs 29 and 30 and the 14th *Feld Ersatz* Battalion, that had been selected to participate in the initial advance, had been given orders to begin reconnaissance missions and to survey the approach roads to the threatened sector.

Since the Division could not be deployed *en masse*, because of the geographical dispersal of its units and the non-availability of sufficient motorised or rail transportation, its integration into the frontline took place in stages. Spearheading the attack on the breakpoint was WGR 29, that included Wildner's experienced battalion. Beginning on 1 April, all three of its battalions, supported by a detachment of artillery, marched to the Mur which formed the Slovenian /Austrian border.[113] Movement was restricted to the hours of darkness to minimise the threat of attack from American aircraft. Having reached it, the 1st and 3rd battalions commanded by *SS-Obersturmführer* Karl Wildner and *SS-Hauptsturmführer* Hans Salzinger crossed the river by bridge at Mureck. To avoid congestion, part of *SS-Sturmbannführer* Otto Blankenhorn's 2nd Battalion crossed, at night, further to the east. The infantry were ferried across in pontoons and barges.[114]

The three battalions then moved separately northwards over the hills. They moved parallel with, and a few kilometres behind, the frontline. The Regiment was assigned the task of re-capturing and securing the height of Gleichenberg Kogel and its environs including, the castle and village of Gleichenberg and Bad Gleichenberg. The task was made considerably harder at that time by virtue of the fact that its command had very little intelligence information at its disposal. They knew little of the strength, intents, location and dispositions of the opposing forces.

The 2nd Battalion passed Kronnersdorf and headed northwards in the direction of Krusdorf and Ebersdorf. There its marching columns unexpectedly clashed with forward Red Army elements. A short skirmish ensued and the Soviets were forced to retreat. The battalion continued northwards through Poppendorf towards Gleichenberg. They passed small villages where buildings were still burning as a result of artillery fire. Exploiting the element of surprise, the Ukrainian troops quickly overran the advanced enemy positions and captured intact some of their abandoned heavy weapons. A Waffen-grenadier who took part in that action wrote:

> 'We, the 8/II/WGR 29 went into battle at around 6.00am, just at daybreak and occupied the village of Gleichenberg. The Red Army retreated in a hurry leaving a few six heavy artillery pieces. When I entered a building there was food and Red Army caps lying on the table. We suffered some losses. At about 10.00 am on the first day we captured two Red Army prisoners, both of whom were Ukrainian from western Ukraine – they were sent to the Division's HQ.'[115]

Once past Straden, the 1st and 3rd battalions veered to the right at Krusdorf to Waldsberg, then on to the town of Trautmannsdorf.[116] From there they began their approach towards Bad Gleichenberg from the south. Reconnaissance forces led by the 1st Company of 1st Battalion, commanded by *Waffen-Obersturmführer* Wolodymyr Kosak, captured Trautmannsdorf railway station without loss. Then they took an important height named 'Sulz' that overlooked the Sulzbach valley.[117] In the villages close to the front, cut off from their supplies, the Ukrainian soldiers searched the houses for food:

> 'In these first days we did not meet any civilians in Gleichenberg and since our supplies had not been functioning, we went into the basements of houses looking for food. It was usually apples that we found in the basement stores as well as 'Most' (fermented apple juice with low alcohol content produced by the local farmers) which was stored in large barrels.'[118]

There were occasional encounters with the local inhabitants, whose reaction was not always positive to the appearance of foreigners in German uniforms, whom they called *Kriegsverlänge* or 'war prolongers.'[119] However, the majority of those who had not fled ahead of the Red Army were friendly and proffered their assistance. That was especially true of those who had already come into contact with Red Army soldiers and experienced the consequences at first hand.[120]

At the same time that WGR 29 moved towards the front in the vicinity of Gleichenberg, the bulk of WGR 30 joined the artillery, anti-tank unit and Pioneer Battalion, quartered in Marburg. On 2 April the Regiment was in position within the city and on its south-eastern outskirts.[121] There, all three of its battalions took part in the erection of defensive emplacements and fortifications. They were assisted by the bulk of the Pioneer Battalion that carried out most of the specialist work. The commander of WGR 30, *SS-Obersturmbannführer* Forstreuter, who was stationed at the bridgehead on the outskirts, was appointed the local commander. He was given the task of defending Marburg. On the morning of 2 April it was declared a 'closed city' to be defended to the last man.[122] On the same day, in readiness for its move to the front sector, the Regiment despatched its advance party including its 13th Company, to Mureck.[123]

The third infantry regiment, WGR 31 which had been recalled from the Konice district on 1 April,[124] was proceeding by continuous forced march with short breaks, i.e. "we slept walking"[125] along the main route of Ljubljana-Trava-Celje-Marburg. As it was not expected to arrive for several days[126] it was intended that it be kept in reserve.[127]

Of its remaining combat units, part of the Pioneer Battalion stayed in position, north of Marburg, making preparations for blowing up the bridges.[128] More importantly, the 1st and 4th companies and the *Jagdzug* of the Fusilier Battalion, together with the commander and his staff, who were considered to be the most powerful and effective element of the Division, were temporarily subordinated. They were then under the command of *Generalmajor* Josef von Radowitz's 23rd *Panzer* Division, in the area of Radkersburg.[129] Neither of those independent battalions was therefore available to take part in the first wave of the counterattack in their entirety. That in turn undermined the Division's overall effectiveness.

During the fortification work around Marburg, and along the Mur river, the Division had absorbed a considerable part of its reserves of fuel and supplies. There was no immediate prospect of replacement. It was therefore authorised to stop the retreating German and Hungarian units that filled the main routes, and requisition their fuel, weapons, ammunition and supplies. That, however, proved to be a problematical undertaking. Many of those formations were poorly disciplined and, especially in the case of the German units, hostile to the Division. It soon became necessary to barter or buy the necessary matériel from them.[130]

Unlike the Germans, the Hungarians who were frequently accompanied by their families,[131] were often glad to be rid of their small arms. They willingly gave them up along with some supplies[132] and accoutrements such as binoculars and compasses.[133] It was also possible to form another artillery detachment from the Hungarian units, albeit with a very limited ammunition supply. Later they fought courageously alongside the Ukrainian soldiers in their sector, until taken away by higher authorities in mid-April 1945.

Further Orders: The Crisis Continues

The Division's deployment orders for its new combat assignment were already well underway, when OKW issued the promised "further orders" via the SS-FHA. Those once again threatened to bring about its premature liquidation. On 3 April 1945, it received a new instruction to surrender its best hand weapons to the 10th *Fallschirmjäger* Division. It was forming within I *Kavallerie* Corps/2nd *Panzer* Army in the Graz area, some 60kms distant. It read:

> To KDrd. 14 *Waffen Gren. Div. d.SS Ukrain.* Nr. 1, Marburg/Drau
> From SSFHA, Amt. II Org.Abtl.I.B, 3 April 1945
>
> On the order of the OKW, the following weapons are to be handed over from the arsenal of the 14th Div: 6,600 MPi [submachine-guns], 80 Zielfernrohrgewehre, [rifles with telescopic sights] 54 k. Karabiner 43. [semi-automatic rifles].[134] The aforementioned weapons are to be surrendered to the 10th *Fallschirmjäger* Div. and rapidly transported to Graz. Army Group E has been notified and is responsible for overseeing this order.
>
> Signed *SS-Obersturmbannführer* Pruss.[135]

The result was the further temporary disarmament of the Division's units that were still in and around Marburg.[136] A *Waffen-Unterscharführer* recorded in his diary:

> 'On 3 April all weapons of 9/II/WGR 30 were taken away, except for two MG 42s and the officers and NCOs pistols [which were] retained for defence purposes.'[137]

However, even the movement of a limited amount of the Division's best light personal weaponry to a destination ten times closer than had been originally intended, could not be carried out.

In his narrative, Heike states that the Luftwaffe general whose unit was to receive the weaponry, arrived at that time after his light reconnaissance plane had been shot down near the Division's supply depot. He claimed that he had been authorised to take over the arms.[138] Evidently, on the night of the 3 April Hitler had further deliberated over the Division's fate. He decided that it would be more expedient to separate and arm its minority German contingent at the expense of the Ukrainian Division, and then incorporate the Germans into a division undiluted by foreigners. Hence, the Luftwaffe general's authorisation further allowed him to appropriate German Waffen-SS cadre personnel from the Division. In that case it would not have to hand over any weapons, as the one thousand or so men under his command had no infantry training. All that was confirmed in an order transmitted on the following day that read:

> Secret Command matter
> 4 April 1945
>
> Op Abtl/Ia, Nr.4178 g. Kdos.,
> Notice after talk by the Führer, night 3/4.4.45
> H.Gr. Sud
> Führer has decided that the 14.*Waffen-Gren.Div. der SS* (*ukrainische*.Nr.1) is to provide cadre for the 10. *Fallsch.Jg.* Div. Hereby transfer the German personnel from Waffen-SS to Luftwaffe.[139]

Under the prevailing circumstances, the new directives for the Division, to relinquish its weapons or transfer its German Waffen-SS personnel to a Luftwaffe paratroop unit, were considered to be no less impractical and absurd as any of the previous orders.[140] In view of that, taking advantage of its recent incorporation into 2nd *Panzer* Army and its battle orders, Dr Wächter and the Divisions staff ignored that and following instructions. They passed them on to higher authorities to deal with.[141] The Divisional command then returned all the weapons that had been collected from its soldiers.[142] Rösener's Operational HQ in Ljubljana promptly responded to that decision with an abortive radio message to the GOC of uniformed *Polizei* in Salzburg, *Oberst* Wolter and the commander of rural *Polizei* in Graz instructing them to "Stop immediate issue of arms to 14. *Waffen Gren. Div. der SS* (*Ukrain.* Nr. 1)."[143] Fortunately neither was remotely capable of doing so.

Oblivious to that directive, and in defiance of its standing orders from OKW and the SS-FHA, the Division's command then went ahead with the directive from 2nd *Panzer* Army. They gave orders for its remaining units to join the counter-attack to close the breach made by the forces of the 3rd Ukrainian Front.[144] The Luftwaffe general departed after having been given some supplies.[145] Another potential disaster was averted, but the issue was still as yet unresolved. A Waffen-SS officer was despatched from Himmler's command post. He spent the next ten days at the Division's staff operations department, observing its general staff.[146] It was a development that augured the final twist in the tale that came a week later.

Defensive Battles in Oststeiermark, April 1945

Following the decision not to comply with the order received from the SS-FHA, on 3 April the Division immediately began its main attack. It had to close the Soviet breach north of Straden in the Gleichenberg sector.[147] Simultaneously, the remnants of the 5th SS *'Wiking'* Division, part of 6th Army, advanced on the Division's left flank against the Soviet forces that were attacking along the Raab valley towards Feldbach.[148] Meanwhile, the 3rd *Kavallerie* Division of I *Kavallerie* Corps, moved on its right.

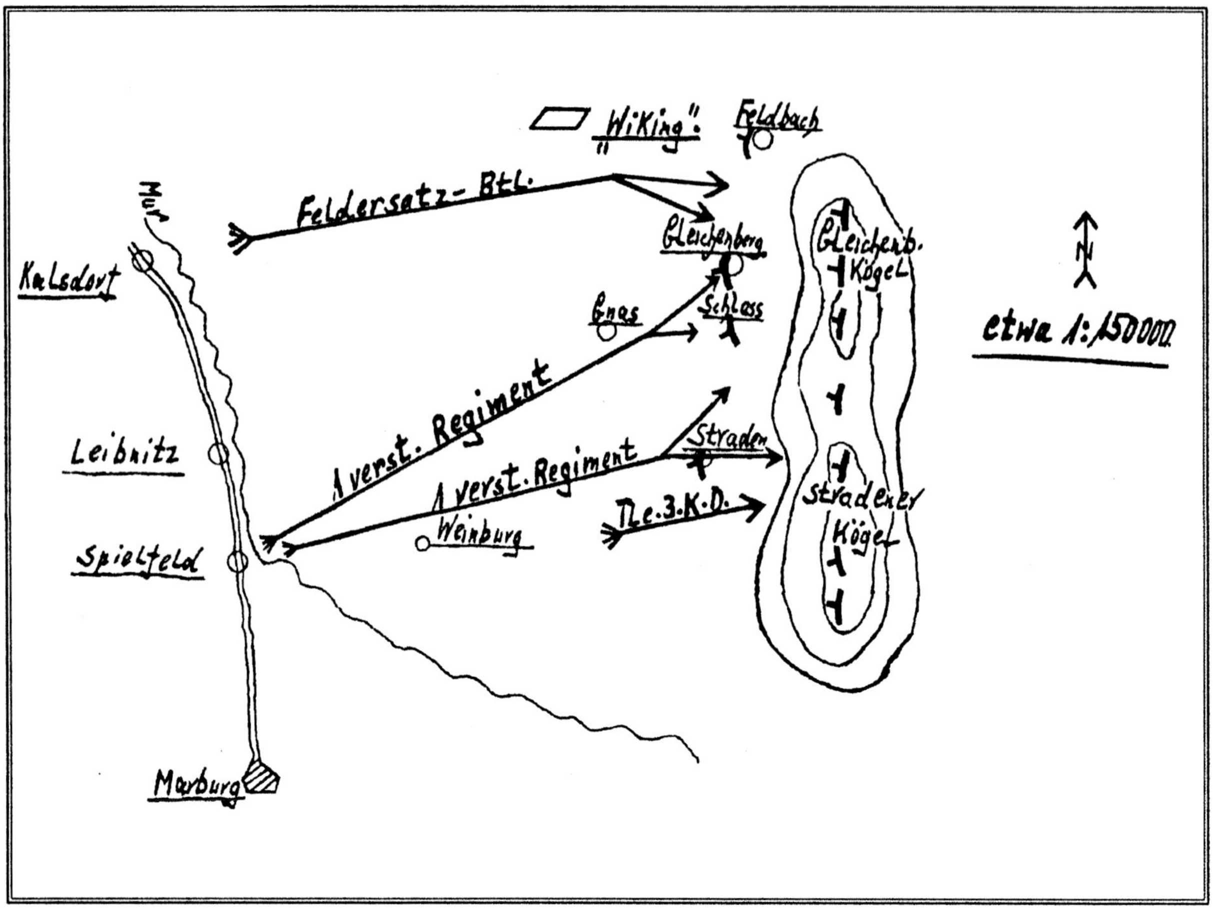

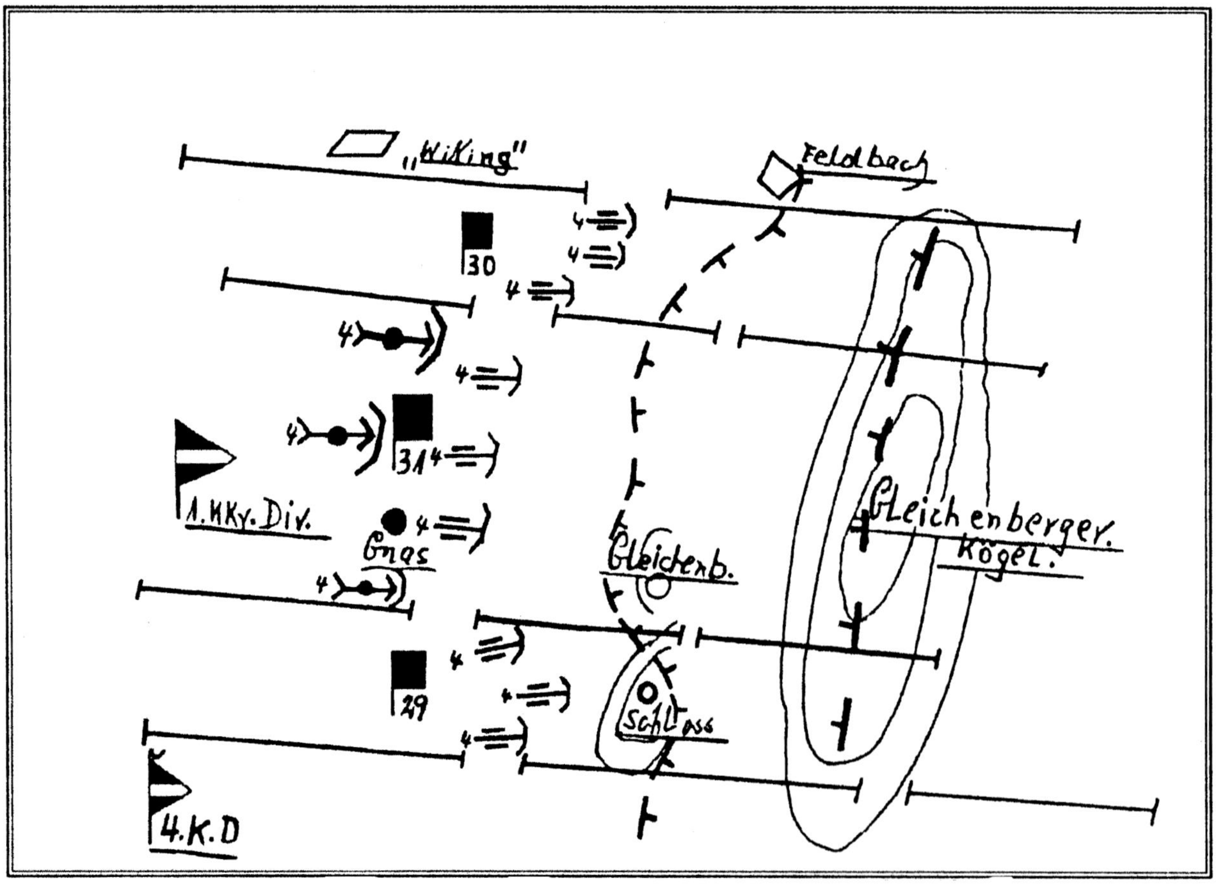

Map 11 (above) *The Galician Division's initial attack by WGRs 29 and 30, and* Felders. Btl. *1, 6 April 1945*
Map 12 (below) *The Galician Division's positions in the Feldbach sector, 18 April 1945*

The Division's headquarters were relocated from St Peter to Gnas for a short period, before finally moving south-east to the village of Straden, where Freitag was with his Operations Officer *Major* Heike. Later the HQ of the Artillery Regiment was also located in that village. It was an excellent tactical observation point, from which the Division's command could oversee the deployment of most of its fighting echelons in the field. Behind the front, the Pioneer Battalion assembled east of Trautmannsdorf in the vicinity of Gnas where it was temporally held as the Divisional reserve.[149]

In the vanguard of the advance, the initial attacks of all three battalions of WGR 29 had made good progress. Having met with only weak enemy forces that were quickly overcome, the Regiment seized its main objective, i.e. the high ground in the vicinity of Gleichenberg Kogel (elevation 598m), which included Gleichenberg Castle and another elevation named Sulz. On the eastern side of the Sulzbach valley, elements came under concentrated fire from fortified Soviet positions at Gleichenberg, and the Austrian resort town of Bad Gleichenberg. Heavy fighting followed for Gleichenberg. The personal bravery and exemplary leadership of *Waffen-Obersturmführer* Ostap Czuczkewycz[150] later won him the Iron Cross 1st Class. However, the Ukrainian soldiers were unable to capture and hold the whole of the village. Similarly, other elements of the Regiment had been forced to retreat from Bad Gleichenberg. They regrouped under cover of darkness in a wood just outside the town. Next morning with artillery support, they attacked the position in strength, but were unable to dislodge the Red Army units entrenched there.[151]

While WGR 29 halted the breakthrough and closed the gap in the Gleichenberg sector, on the night of the 4 April 1945, the bulk of WGR 30 was alerted for an immediate move in the direction of Straden.[152] Its assignment was to capture Stradner Kogel (elevation 609m) and occupy the frontline directly to the south of WGR 29. Starting at dawn, in extreme heat, the Regiment's forced march, from Marburg via Mureck, to its assigned positions lasted until 11.00pm on 5 April. The 3rd Battalion commanded by *SS-Sturmbannführer* Wittenmeyer, was the first to be sent into action and took up the foremost part of the line around Kolldorf. Overextended, it quickly sustained heavy losses and had to withdraw and reorganise.[153] The 1st and 2nd battalions also moved into combat positions in the vicinity of Wilhelmsdorf/Hochstradener Kogel.

During the night their officers had first been given a short briefing on the situation.[154] In doing so, WGR 30 had occupied, without the customary preparations and planning, what ultimately proved to be a tactically very poor defensive line. It immediately undermined its effectiveness. Having arrived in the line, the Regiment was unable to make any real progress with its positions. Initially constructed at night, the company and platoon commanders could not select the most suitable places to dig their emplacements. Several units had no maps of the locality and the line was under constant Soviet observation. Even in daylight the Regimental HQ, which was situated in an empty farmhouse, came under artillery and heavy mortar fire.

Further, the forward defensive posts were spread out along the extended length of a hilly and heavily wooded section of the front. There had not even been enough time to lay telephone lines between the battalions and their regimental headquarters ½ km away. As a result, messages had to be delivered by hand. Communications between units were made almost impossible. Consequently the likelihood of the Regiment being able to co-ordinate its forces, in the event of an attack, was slim at best.[155]

The third combat element to deploy with the first wave, the 14th *Feld Ersatz Bataillon*, had made its way north, independently, from Spielfeld to the district south west of Feldbach. As the extreme left flank of the Division, it formed part of an emergency force assembled from various *Kampfgruppen* by 6th Army (General Balck) and *Wehrkreis* XVIII (General Ringel), for a counterattack in the Raab valley. For that purpose, it was subordinated to the overall command of *Panzer* officer *Oberstleutnant* Wolf of 6th Army.[156] On 5 April the 1,200 men of the 14th *Feld Ersatz Bataillon* advanced en masse from its staging area at Unterwiessenbach. They went in an easterly direction through Oedt[157] towards Burgfried, a suburb of Feldbach. Its insertion in this area relieved the pressure on the *Fallschirmjäger* troops who were thrusting eastwards along both sides of the Feldbach/Leiterdorf road.

Notwithstanding the precarious positions recently occupied by WGR 30, the Division's general line of advance had shown good progress in all areas which raised morale and boosted the confidence of the Ukrainian soldiers. By 6 April, WGRs 29 and 30 held positions that stretched from Gleichenberg Castle to Hochstraden just north of

Frutten. That sector, as later events would prove, was too ambitious for its limited resources. It included the Gleichenberg and Stradner Kogel, situated in a north/south line approximately 6kms apart, as well as Gleichenberg Castle. By so doing, it had achieved its general objective of capturing and securing the two elevations, thereby sealing the important breach between the German 2nd and 6th armies. It enabled I *Kavallerie* Corps to move the 3rd *Kavallerie* Division off the frontline and into a reserve position. The achievement was summarised in the secret daily report of the OKH for 6 April 1945, as follows:

> '2. Pz. Army: An attack in a north-easterly direction by the 14.SS.Div. on the left flank of the army reached the region 3 kms south of Gleichenberg.'[158]

Somewhat fortuitously, the success of the Division's initial mission coincided with the arrival of 82 young Ukrainian officers with the rank of *Waffen-Untersturmführer.*[159] One group of officers, often referred to by their comrades by the colloquial term *Pistolets*, reported for service at the Division's HQ near Straden in the second week in April. There they were met by Dr Wächter[160] and Freitag, who addressed them concerning the need for officers at the front. They assigned individuals to the regiments to which they had originally belonged. Immediately integrated into its various sub-units as platoon or company commanders, many were sent straight into combat and participated in the battles in the days to come.[161] Most had no battle experience. Amongst Germans battle experience was a mandatory requirement for all officers.

Dr Wächter left shortly after, to visit his contacts in Italy. He wanted to continue with his plans to transfer the Division, the Cossack Corps and the eastern Turkic formations to northern Italy, via the small town of Tolmezzo in the Carnian Alps. With the help of *Generalfeldmarschall* Kesselring's successor, the Commander in Chief of the German forces in Italy, who was General Heinrich Freiherr von Vietinghoff, Wächter proposed to hand over those formations to the Western Allies.[162] To that end he instructed the Division's command to obtain the necessary food supplies, especially livestock, that would be needed for it to cross the Alps. Before he left, Wächter also gave notice of the impending arrival of General Shandruk.[163]

The Soviet Counterattack

The Soviet attempt to regain the ground that they had lost was not long in coming. Facing I *Kavallerie* Corps in the second week in April was the Soviet 6th Guards Rifle Corps[164] and elements of 64th Rifle Corps.[165] The main attacks, in the Division's sector, were spearheaded by the 20th Guards Division, 61st Guards Rifle Division, (6th Guards Rifle Corps) and 10th Guards Div (64th Rifle Corps).[166] The estimated ratio at that time was four or five to one in favour of the Soviets.[167] The relative strength of the heavy weaponry and artillery was considerably worse. The huge disparity in that respect was compounded by the fact that, on the German side, there was an acute shortage of ammunition for the artillery and heavy weapons that were available.[168] Although the I *Kavallerie* Corps had neither tanks nor planes at its disposal, comparatively few Soviet tanks were in evidence in an area that did not easily lend itself to the deployment of armour.[169] Moreover, the nature of the mountainous terrain with its thick forests was not conducive to the utilisation of aircraft, thus preventing the Soviets from capitalising on their total air superiority.

In WGR 29's locality, the main thrust by 20th Guards Rifle Division struck in the direction of Trautmannsdorf. The attack forced elements of WGR 29 to retire from their exposed positions in the Sulzbach valley, on the outskirts of Bad Gleichenberg, and from Gleichenberg, which was recaptured by the Red Army. Gleichenberg Klogel also had to be abandoned, after changing hands several times. As the fighting took place day and night, the sequential relief of the first echelon infantry units was instituted. The purpose was to involve the forces more fully in combat acclimatisation. It would also allow the troops a few hours in the rear to rest, to eat, and attend to basic hygiene, before being re-committed at the front.[170]

Wildner's battalion (I/29) retired to Sulz, with orders to hold the hill at all costs. However, the commander of the 4th (heavy weapons) Company, *SS-Obersturmführer* Schneller, ignored the instruction and ordered his company to retreat.[171] The Soviets then pressed forward and by 10 April, after heavy fighting, had retaken Trautmannsdorf village and station.[172] In the process they by-passed the elevation on which two companies, reinforced with a *Jagdzug*, were still entrenched.[173] A newly arrived *Waffen-Untersturmführer*, who had been assigned to command the 1st Platoon of the 1st Company that was part of the trapped force, later wrote:

> 'The first company (1/Btl) held a frontline position at the outskirts of the Austrian town of Bad Gleichenberg, located in the valley east of Graz. I reported to the company commander, a young Ukrainian *Waffen-Untersturmführer*. He in turn made me his deputy and put me in charge of the 1st Platoon that consisted of 4 NCOs and about 40 grenadiers. The Soviets attacked mercilessly, without let up. Because our position in the valley was very vulnerable, we found it more advantageous to pull back a few hundred yards to the hill, called Sulz, from where we had a better view of the enemy and a better defence. We held this hill with another company for about four days. In the meantime I received reinforcement to my platoon of one squad (11 men) from the Ukrainian Volhynian Legion.
>
> 'For a while all seemed to be fairly normal and under control until, suddenly on the fifth day, the Soviets started bombarding our hill with heavy artillery and Katyushas which made a tremendous noise and inflicted a lot of damage and quite a few casualties. The wounded were taken to the field hospital … .
>
> 'We defended our position well but our own artillery was not very effective in helping us so that by the evening our hill was practically cut off. We also lost telephone and radio contact with our battalion command. Our ammunition supply was now running low and we were beginning to get hungry. There were 4 Ukrainian officers (the most senior of which was *Waffen-Obersturmführer* Wolodymyr Kosak), about a dozen NCOs and approximately 200 men. The situation was grave. After a short discussion among the officers and an evaluation of our situation, we concluded that our best chance would be to try and break through. This could not be accomplished during the day so we had to wait for nightfall.
>
> 'In the meantime we suffered more casualties, so *Waffen-Obersturmführer* Kosak ordered me and another *Waffen-Untersturmführer* to cover the break through with our platoons. Most of our troops broke out during the night. By morning about forty of us were still on the hill Sulz. Our supplies of ammunition were practically gone leaving us no choice but to run down the hill no matter what and to cross the railway tracks on which the enemy was concentrating his mortar fire.
>
> 'Ignoring the exploding mortar rounds, we all jumped across the tracks and made it out of the encirclement without any losses. We then ran fast to the next hill where our troops, who had abandoned Sulz during the previous night, were protecting our retreat. While we were resting hidden behind the hill the enemy managed to change position and one of his mortar shells exploded amongst us, killing one and wounding three others from my platoon. Because we had no contact with our battalion command, in the evening under the cover of darkness, *Waffen-Obersturmführer* Kosak as the senior officer ordered me to take a group of men and try and re-establish contact with other units of our battalion. Walking in no-man's land throughout the night we finally stumbled on our anti-tank artillery unit and were received very warmly by 3 Ukrainian officers who gave us something to eat. Here I used their radio to report to our battalion commander what happened to us and of the current whereabouts of the remainder of the two companies.'[174]

By 13 April 1945, the 20th Guards Rifle Division had made a deep penetration in the Division's lines in that locality which temporarily threatened the entire sector. To prevent a major breakthrough, on that day I *Kavallerie* Corps brought in the 3rd *Kavallerie* Division (*Reiterregiment* 41, *Kavallerie* Regiment 5 and parts of *Reiterregiments* 31 and 32), and later *Panzeraufklärungsabteilung* 16, which together with elements of the Division, successfully contained the attack.[175]

However, the Soviet pressure continued unabated around Gleichenberg Castle. It was situated on a steep hill, surrounded by woods, with a commanding view that dominated the entire area. It was also the scene of fierce fighting. It came under attack from three sides and was so heavily bombarded by artillery and mortar fire that even though its walls were two metres thick in places, it sustained considerable damage.[176] The Ukrainian units of WGR 29 within the castle fought bravely despite being surrounded. They held out until 15 April, when *Waffen-Obersturmführer* Wolodymyr Kosak, led a local counterattack. They cleared a path in hand-to-hand fighting that freed the surrounded troops in the castle, and at the same time re-established the frontline.[177]

Elsewhere, directly to the south, the heaviest fighting occurred around Stradner Klogel, and the plateau, 1,000 metres south of the elevation. A series of attacks and counter-attacks, in quick succession, resulted in a fluid frontline. Over the course of the next ten days there was unavoidable close-quarter combat.[178]

The 20th Guards Rifle Division committed two of its regiments (60th Guards Rifle Regiment and 57th Guards Rifle Regiment) whose first probing attacks forced a retreat of the Division's most advanced positions near Kolldorf and Hochstraden. It was the prelude to a full scale Soviet assault on Stradner Klogel. In that sector, WGR 31 having just completed its forced march from Slovenia, was to have been kept in reserve,[179] but had to be committed to the fighting.[180] Following extensive pressure twice, on 8 and 10 April, the Ukrainian infantry, many of whom were experiencing their baptism of fire, were dislodged from their positions after strong attacks by the 61st Guards Rifle Division. On both occasions the 3rd *Kavallerie* Division came to their assistance and successfully counter-attacked, forcing the Red Army off the mountain and back to the village of Plesch.

During one critical situation, Freitag became so alarmed by the developments at the front, that in the presence of the commander of the I *Kavallerie* Corps, *General der Kavallerie* Harteneck, he reacted instinctively. Just as he had done at Brody, he announced his resignation as Divisional commander and also his responsibility for its performance in action. General Harteneck refused Freitag's resignation and ordered him to remain at his post.[181] In due course, with additional support, primarily from the veteran 3rd *Kavallerie* Division, the crisis passed and the front held.

The commander of the 2nd *Abteilung/Reiterregiment* 32, (3rd *Kavallerie* Division) *Rittmeister* Franz Rudolph Zilm described the participation of his unit in the early battles on 6 and 7th April. After acknowledging that heavy fighting was in progress in Gleichenberg where "the Ukrainians fought courageously and took heavy losses", Zilm goes on to say that the Ukrainians "were however unsuited for woodland combat and quickly lost Stradner Kogel." Zilm's own unit then attacked and seized the villages of Wilhelmsdorf and Frutten. With the support of additional squadrons which were then moved in, they stormed Stradner Kogel with a broad assault from the south. On the mountain, they encountered both Red Army units and the Ukrainians, who had secured themselves in company strength. Whereupon, according to Zilm's account, "In the darkness everyone started fighting everyone else, Germans fought against Russians and by mistake against Ukrainians. Ukrainians fought against Germans and Russians, Russians against Germans and Ukrainians. In the resulting confusion there were inevitable casualties. According to Zilm, on that occasion the Ukrainians "panic-stricken and inexperienced, took until the morning to calm down and recover their composure", and some then "broke into tears when they realised that they had injured at least five of our own soldiers".[182]

The 3rd *Kavallerie* Division had lost its self-propelled anti-aircraft guns, which had been hit and disabled. They then came under heavy fire from enemy mortars that caused significant casualties in dead and wounded. On 8 April they were moved into the reserve in the village of Haag for re-supply. The Ukrainians then retook responsibility for the whole height whereupon the Soviets launched a furious counterattack to regain the territory that had been recently wrested from them. A *Waffen-Untersturmführer* commanding a platoon from 14/WGR 30 recalled his experiences of the attack:

> 'In the early morning hours of 8 April 1945, on the left flank of II/WGR 30, the enemy opened up with artillery fire. A barrage of relentless bombardment that lasted for about 5 minutes breached a wide enough gap in our frontline positions for their assault group of about 30 men to break through. They were advancing rapidly and shooting haphazardly. Once they had encountered our resistance and suffered their first casualties they started a retreat that turned into a panicky flight. I grabbed their heavy machine-gun, which they had abandoned, and fired rounds of their own ammunition in pursuit. Their breakthrough was to have been followed by a massive attack. They did not know that this had been thwarted from the beginning by *Sperrfeuer* (blocking fire) laid down by our heavy artillery.
>
> 'One battery of the Division's artillery regiment (10th) was attached to II/WGR 30, as reinforcement. The commanding officer of that battery was *Waffen-Untersturmführer* Roman Krawchuk who deserves recognition for a job well done. In that counterattack *Waffen-Untersturmführers* Eugene Shypailo and Roman Lazurko were active participants.

'On the same day I was wounded by an enemy sharpshooter, with a gunshot wound which penetrated my left upper thigh right through. I was sent to the Division's field hospital from where I was transferred to the military hospital at Klagenfurt. For the action described above I received the Iron Cross Second Class.'[183]

Stubborn resistance by individual companies could not however hold off the Soviets for long. Within hours they had taken control of the mountain forcing the 3rd *Kavallerie* Division to repeat its attack.[184]

On 9 April, the Ukrainian infantry moved back into the line, surprising the Red Army units and pushing them back 1.5km east on a segment of 3km.[185] They had not had time to dig in, and establish their positions on and around Stradner Kogel, before there was a heavy barrage from artillery and the dreaded *Katyusha* rockets that lasted two hours. Then the Red Army attacked again. Several gaps were opened in the Ukrainian lines through which Soviet assault troops moved forward. In an effort to seal the numerous penetrations within its own forces, all three companies of the Pioneer Battalion were committed to the fighting at the foot of Stradner Kogel. As regular infantry[186] they fought alongside the 2nd and 3rd companies of the Fusilier Battalion. They suffered severe casualties that day, among them the commander of WGR 31 *SS-Standartenführer*, Rudolph Pannier, who was wounded.[187] However, the Division was unable to stop the Soviets from temporarily regaining control of the elevation.

The 3rd *Kavallerie* Division was again brought in from the reserves to counter-attack, this time approaching from Rosenberg (4kms south of Straden). By the evening a mixed force of riders from the 31st, 32nd, 41st and 5th *Kavallerie* regiments and Ukrainian infantry had secured the mountain which was once again in German hands.[188] The secret daily report of the OKH for 9 April 1945, recorded the fighting for this day:

'2nd *Pz.* Army. The enemy succeeded in penetrating the frontline in the sector of the 14th SS-Gren. Div. and occupying the mountainous terrain 5 kms wide to the south east of Gleichenberg. Part of the 3rd *Kavallerie* Division was engaged in a counterattack.'[189]

The next day the Soviets attacked in such overwhelming strength that they forced a general retreat of all units, approximately 2km west to the Sulzbach valley on the line Waldsberg Dirnbach-Stainz. The Ukrainian units regrouped around the village of Straden. The daily report of the OKH for 10 April 1945, noted:

'2. *Pz.* Army: In the sector of the I *Kavallerie* Corps north of Radkersburg, the enemy could only achieve small penetrations. However, at the right flank and in the middle of the 14th SS Div. the enemy broke through. The creation of a new frontline by 3rd and 4th *Kavallerie* divisions is in progress.'[190]

Stradner Kogel was finally lost on 11 April.[191] The intensity of the fighting showed no sign of abating, although that time it was the 3rd *Kavallerie* Division that bore the brunt. Close to the village of Stallhans east of Frutten, *Reiterregiment* 32 was unable to contain a breakthrough of the German line by elements of the 61st Guards Rifle Division. On that occasion they were saved by the timely intervention of Ukrainian infantry units. In the previously cited account, the commander of the 2nd *Abteilung*, *Rittmeister* Zilm stated that when on 12 April, the 6th and 8th squadrons came under heavy pressure, an assault group led by *Leutnant* Jurgen was only partly able to control the enemy penetration when, "without having to be asked the Ukrainians came to help us. *They wanted to show that they were not inferior to us*.' [Author's emphasis][192]

All three *Waffen-Grenadier* Regiments engaged the Soviets in the area of Bad Gleichenberg and Straden. To the south two companies of the Division's Fusilier Battalion, together with its staff and its *Jagdzug*, were subordinated to the 23rd *Panzer* Division, in the German bridgehead at Radkersburg. The 4th Company was deployed on the eastern side of Radkersburg, while the 1st Company and *Jagdzug* were in position north of the 4th Company, in the vicinity of the village of Zelting.

On 6 April the detachment was holding a line about 2kms in length. Together with other German and Cossack units in the area they became embroiled in bitter defensive fighting, against elements of the Soviet 73rd Guards Rifle Division and the 113th Rifle Division,[193] around Murauen by Radkersburg. A former member of the 1st Company of the Fusilier Battalion recounted:

> 'April 7. Everybody in that area (Radkersburg) was mobilised. Wehrmacht, some units of the 44th [*Reichs-Gren.* Div. *Hoch-und Deutschmeister*], also Hungarian troops. The Soviet attack was very intense and strong. Wehrmacht and Hungarian troops were retreating, us too. There was also a unit of Cossack Cavalry who stormed the Soviets galloping on horses. We were retreating towards Straden and didn't know much about what was going on.'[194]

On that day, the *Jagdzug* and one platoon of the 1st Company of the Fusilier Battalion began an attack at 7.00pm near Zelting. After heavy fighting these platoons had almost taken the Soviet positions when they received an abrupt order to retreat beyond their initial starting positions.[195] The fusiliers were then forced back several times. Shortly after, having lost several men killed and wounded, the detachment pulled back to the west to a position south of Purkla. Eventually it reached Mureck where it was used to fill the gap in the line left by the Wehrmacht crossing the river Mur. There the fusiliers continued to engage Red Army units for almost a full week.

On one occasion during the heavy fighting that ensued, *Waffen-Untersturmführer* Volodymyr Malynovych noticed an enemy force advancing through a ditch towards the ferry on the river Mur. On his own initiative he began shooting the approaching Soviets with a machine-gun. Together with the support of the heavy mortar platoon of the 4th Company and a few machine-guns, the enemy units were turned back. As a result of his action Malynovych was recommended for and received the Iron Cross Second Class.[196] A few days later the two companies of fusiliers were sent for one week's rest near Gleichenberg. There they were rejoined by the 2nd and 3rd companies. The commander of the 23rd *Panzer* Division later reported that while under his command, the performance of the Ukrainian fusiliers had been commendable[197] and several others received decorations for their bravery.

As part of 6 Army, on the Division's extreme northern flank, in Feldbach and in the nearby villages of Kalvarienberg and Steinberg, the 14th *Feld Ersatz Bataillon* counter-attacked. They moved from Oesterreichberg through Burgfried to Petersdorf (south of Mühldorf) against an enemy force of around 1,300 men who had the advantage of superior fire-power and heavy weapons support.

On 5 April at midnight, one company commanded by an Ukrainian officer and supported by four 7.62cm self propelled guns received an order to commence attack at 5.00am as cover for *Kampfgruppe* Heymann [10th *Fallschirmjäger* Division] They were to advance through Burgfried in the direction of Height 470 (Steinberg). In his diary, the company commander recorded how, "after overcoming tough enemy resistance and taking about ten Red Army soldiers prisoner in the waterworks, the company advanced until it reached a railway dam. There it took up positions between a *Fallschirmjäger* mortar unit on the right and elements of the 1st *Panzer* Division on the right, and in the process made a significant contribution to the successful recapture of the town."[198]

The Soviet counterattack had finally been contained and the front stabilised along the western side of the Sulzbach valley. The cost of that accomplishment was considerable. The Division's casualty rate had been estimated at 1,600 killed and wounded,[199] (most from WGR 30) which equated to over 11% of its fighting strength of 14,000.[200] That was ample testimony to the ferocity of the combat. The constant changes in the situation at the front necessitated some regrouping. WGRs 29 and 30 had to be pulled out of action to rest and for refitting and refurbishing in secondary positions. Both regiments received replacements from the 14th *Feld Ersatz Bataillon*. However, because of excessive casualties, including two key battalion commanders, *SS-Sturmbannführer* Wilhelm Podlesch (III/WGR 31) and *SS-Hauptsturmführer* Ludwig Kuchta[201] (III/WGR 29) and several trained officers killed in action or wounded, the replacements had to be reduced from three to two battalions.[202] The wounded were evacuated to the Division's field hospital in Völkermarkt.[203] Some of the more serious cases were later transferred for treatment to military hospitals in Austria. Most of those were overcrowded, under-staffed and suffered from acute shortages of all types of medication.

As neither the Gleichenberg nor Stradner Kogels had any particular strategic significance, control of both elevations was finally relinquished to the Soviets. No further attempts were made to recapture them.

The Division's new right hand neighbour was the 4th *Kavallerie* Division (I *Kavallerie* Corps), while to the left was the 5th SS *'Wiking'* Division (6th Army).

The Final Reprieve

On 10 April, as the fighting around Gleichenberg and Stradner Kogels was reaching its climax, the highest German authorities finally arrived at a compromise solution. It put an end to the uncertainty surrounding the fate of the Division and its association with the 10th *Fallschirmjäger* Division, once and for all.[204] The SS-FHA sent a new secret order that read:

> To 14. *Waffen Gren. Div. d.SS* (*Ukr.* Nr. 1)
> Secret!
> 1. Contrary to all previous orders the disarmament of the 14th *Waffengrenadier div.d.SS* (*Ukr.* Nr. 1), is not to be carried out.
> 2. The German staff personnel of the 14th *Waffengrenadier div.d.SS* (*Ukr.* Nr. 1) of 2,000 officers, NCOs and men is to be supplemented by the inclusion of 3–4,000 Luftwaffe ground crew.
> 3. 14th *Waffengrenadier div.d.SS* (*Ukr.* Nr. 1) is to remain a unit of the Waffen-SS.
>
> Signed Blume[205]

Significantly, no mention was made of the 'Ukrainian National Army'. It was in the process of being formed, under the auspices of the recently officially recognised 'Ukrainian National Committee', headed by General Shandruk. Instead, it is implicit, from point 3, the Division's continued direct affiliation to the Waffen-SS was regarded, at least by Himmler and the SS-FHA, as a *sine qua non*.

Following receipt of the order, approximately 2,500 surplus German Luftwaffe personnel, who were originally destined for the 10th *Fallschirmjäger* Division, reported for service.[206] That was a figure somewhat less than the originally proposed number of 3 to 4,000 men

The influx of such a large number of German soldiers, only days after the routing of the Ukrainians on the Stradner Kogel provided Freitag with the inspiration for a radical solution to stiffen the resilience of his Division. To do this, he intended to assimilate the 'trustworthy' German personnel at once, in one of two ways. The Luftwaffe men were predominantly NCOs, holding ranks from corporal to sergeant-major. Their number also included around 70 officers whose ranks ranged from officer candidate to captain.[207] In his first option Freitag envisaged immediately incorporating them as platoon or squad commanders in fighting units. According to that plan, they would replace the equivalent number of Ukrainian soldiers who were currently holding those positions. Once disarmed, the Ukrainians would then be sent to 'military labour battalions'. A second alternative was to regroup the Division so that each regiment contained an entirely German battalion,[208] thus creating an exclusively German element within each of its major combat units.

Under different circumstances Freitag may well have implemented either plan. But the insurmountable organisational difficulties involved with the Division at the front, prevented him from doing so.[209] Furthermore, the Luftwaffe men who were mostly former ground crew, and a few pilots, had not been re-trained as infantry and lacked vital combat experience. To compound matters they had no weapons. Many were distrustful of the Ukrainians whose loyalty they suspected.[210]

After protracted deliberations, it was decided that they should undergo a period of intensive, basic, infantry training before being included in the combat elements. That forced Freitag, temporarily and with considerable reluctance, to abandon his plans. The maximum number of 1,200 men was subsequently assigned to the 14th *Feld Ersatz Bataillon*. Ironically they received their instruction from Ukrainians whose limited command of the German language necessitated the extensive use of interpreters.

The remainder were sent to its other sub-units to replenish the losses. That brought the total number of Germans serving with the Division to an estimated 3,600.[211] The commander of WGR 29 opposed the inclusion of the Luftwaffe men in his regiment. However, unlike the commander of WGR 30, *SS-Obersturmbannführer* Forstreuter wanted the largest possible contingent assigned to him. According to his former *Ordonnanz Offizier*, that was because he simply "didn't trust the Ukrainians".[212] As an experiment, Forstreuter was allocated enough of the new German personnel to reconstitute a third battalion within WGR 30. The other two regiments had already received replacements from reserve units and were also able to form a third battalion.[213] Because of the continual dearth of signals specialists, i.e. radio and telephone operators, and other technicians, those with the requisite skills were quickly absorbed into the relevant sections. The rest were sent to different companies where they were given administrative or non-combatant roles and generally seem to have done their best to avoid combat postings.[214]

By 18 April the frontline in Oststeiermark had stabilised to the west of the Sulzbach valley. I *Kavallerie* Corps then held a line that ran from north to south from Feldbach to Gleichenberg and to the west of the following, Trautmannsdorf-Waldsberg-Dirnbach-Stainz-Straden-Karla-Radochen.[215]

The Division, having re-committed WGRs 29 and 30, was now assigned to the defence of its own sector of the front. It stretched from the outskirts of Feldbach on the extreme left flank, to the village of Gleichenberg on the right flank, a distance of approximately 8kms. It also continued to occupy Gleichenberg Castle, which cut through the enemy lines and formed a pivotal point of resistance in its line of defence. The three infantry regiments were deployed in a linear disposition. WGR 30 was to the north (HQ near Brundlegg), WGR 31 was in the centre (HQ near Hof), and WGR 29 (HQ near Katzendorf) covered the southern sector bordering with 4th *Kavallerie* Division.[216]

It should be noted that the strength of the new defensive line varied. In some cases it was undermined by the acute shortages of weapons and equipment that were experienced amongst some of the infantry, especially the scratch units organised as the result of the heavy losses. A *Waffen-Oberscharführer* serving with WGR 29 recalled:

> 'I was assigned about a platoon of soldiers. I did not know them or where they came from. As it turned out, they were loyal to each other and we spent the last days of the war together. We came to the company command post and were told where to take our positions. We dug in and for a few weeks held our flank position. We had about enough ammunition to defend ourselves for about ten minutes, no hand-grenades, no compass, no binoculars and no ammunition depot close by. During that time no officer inspected our position and the company command post was about 100 metres away. It was our good luck that the Red Army did not attack.'[217]

With the resulting movement of its infantry, the Division's HQ and that of the Artillery Regiment were relocated west to the village of Obergnas.

The individual batteries of the Artillery Regiment were evenly distributed and deployed so as to provide cover for the entire sector. A detailed fire plan was produced that took the capabilities of the heavy artillery into account. The 2nd and 3rd companies of the Fusilier Battalion held the line north of Gleichenberg Castle, while 1st and 4th were kept in reserve.[218] Also situated to the rear was the Divisional reserve which comprised the 14th *Feld Ersatz Bataillon*, and the Pioneer Battalion. The latter, in accordance with orders, was withdrawn from the front and utilised only for technical pioneer work.[219] Its most important task was the construction of two temporary bridges to assist with the Division's anticipated withdrawal. They were situated about five miles apart, on either side of the existing permanent concrete bridge spanning the river Mur in the vicinity of Kalsdorf. The first bridge was under construction by the 1st Company and the second by the 2nd Company,[220] whose commander *SS-Obersturmführer* Dzillum later wrote:

> 'After a day of rest for my company in Kalsdorf, I received an order from the battalion commander, *SS-Sturmbannführer* Remberger, to set up a temporary bridge across the Mur and to construct a big ferry. Both objects were to be camouflaged against air-reconnaissance. The locality was very favourable for this project because the terrain on both sides of the Mur was wooded. Furthermore the existing road-bridge across the river was prepared for demolition. The building of the bridge and ferry was a very difficult project because we only had light pioneer equipment like cross-cut saws, axes, spades, shovels, sledge hammers and ropes at our disposal. Floating supports and pontoons were not available. The pioneer equipment was pitiful. We used punts that we managed to find in the area to ram beams into the river. All the men involved, officers, NCOs and grenadiers received the highest praise for their accomplishment of this project with the most primitive tools.'[221]

The Pioneer Battalion also carried out special tasks. For example, at the request of two mayors in the area of Kalsdorf, a bomb disposal unit of the 2nd Company successfully defused three unexploded bombs without any difficulty. One of the bombs had to be dug up from between two houses where it had landed before being taken into open terrain and exploded.[222]

As the frontline had settled into static defence positions, the troops were able to consolidate their emplacements, constructing trenches and bunkers and laying minefields to establish a defence in depth. Reserve units were reorganised and employed in building secondary and tertiary lines of defence in case of encirclement. In that way the Division slowly gained control of its sector. Although it was outnumbered by a ratio of three to one[223] it effectively defended the sector until the end of the war. The Soviet attacks became progressively weaker and all minor advances were successfully repelled.

Internal supply units functioned effectively, moving the matériels required by the troops from dumps in the rear to the forward units. There were however shortages of munitions. To supplement rations, foodstuffs were sometimes obtained from the local population.[224] Occasionally livestock was taken from Austrian farmsteads in no-man's-land, before it fell into enemy hands.[225] With few sanitary facilities available, 'lice-chasing' was a popular pastime amongst the troops.

The Training and Reserve Regiment had a strength of approximately 3,000.[226] In early April 1945 it had relocated to Völkermarkt. Its battalions and companies, spread out over a wide area encompassing several villages, were billeted in schools and other public buildings. There, they continued to pit their wits against Tito's insurgent forces who no longer confined their operations to the remote hills. The suppression of their ever more daring exploits in the rear areas, kept all the regiments' units fully occupied.[227]

Although no large-scale actions were conducted by either side, minor skirmishes occurred as the result of regular armed reconnaissance missions and patrols. The Division's command sought to capture enemy soldiers in order to discover Soviet intentions and unexpected troop movements. Several perilous raids, requiring considerable skill on behalf of the participants, ended in failure.[228] With their own homeland far behind enemy lines, the Ukrainian soldiers were not always eager to participate in such actions. It is evident from the following account of a *Waffen-Untersturmführer* whose platoon was given one such assignment:

> 'Following an order received by our regiment (31st) my assault platoon was chosen to launch a surprise attack at night on a section of the enemy trenches and capture one or more Soviet prisoners. Our plan was to attack at a segment of the front opposite the sector held by a company commanded by another Ukrainian. The *Waffen-Untersturmführer* had submitted some beautiful sketches of the location of enemy trenches in front of his company. There was no time to acquaint myself with the terrain and enemy position. However, I was reassured by everyone that the information contained in his sketches was correct. It had been compiled as the result of scouting missions conducted by his company. I was also promised that our artillery would concentrate its fire on the chosen location, prior to the attack, to soften up the enemy positions. This was to commence following a signal given by radio, or at an appointed time. We prepared for our mission, checking our weapons and covering our faces with soot. After midnight we left our lines. Following a route that I had memorised from the maps and sketches we advanced in attack formation.
>
> 'The night was quiet except for occasional single rifles shots. We passed some of our dead and Soviet dead lying in the woods. The terrain was covered with sparse trees and hedges. We moved forward taking special care not to stand on any dry branches until we reached our staging positions for our attack. So as not to alert the enemy to our presence, I forbade the radio operator to use his set. At the agreed time we heard the artillery shells exploding a short way in front of us. After five minutes the artillery stopped shelling and we moved forward. When we arrived at the target area we found no sign of enemy positions, only a few holes made by our artillery which had alerted the enemy. We continued to advance for some considerable distance from our staging area and still found no enemy trenches.
>
> 'We entered some denser woods and began to climb a slight incline when suddenly we heard the alarm and the enemy started to fire tracer bullets and flares which lit up the battle field as through it were daylight. At the same time we began to receive heavy machine-gun fire. We dropped to the ground and started to run back the way we had come. Rolling down the incline under enemy fire I joined my troops at the bottom of

> the hill. After a hasty check I established that no one had been killed, but two injured, although they could both walk by themselves. We managed to return hastily to our lines without any further incident. The *Waffen-Untersturmführer* was waiting for me and I gave him a piece of my mind. As a company commander he had not gone on these scouting missions himself but sent his subordinates, who not wanting to expose themselves to excessive danger had not ventured too far and reported something that looked plausible. He in turn had dressed up their reports in beautiful form and sent them to the regimental command.'[229]

The 'dependable' Germans too, proved to be equally unwilling to risk their lives in such missions, with the war so close to its inevitable conclusion. The commander of WGR 29, from the regimental *Jagdzug*, assembled a commando unit consisting entirely of Germans, to attempt a similar raid into enemy territory. It too ended in fiasco.[230] Other attempts were more successful as evidenced by an article in the penultimate edition of the Divisional newspaper *Do Boyu* entitled "Before Our First Lines", which summarised the Division's achievements thus:

> 'The Styrian sector has been quiet for sometime. Our own raids and reconnaissances were successful. Many attacks from the enemy were repulsed by our defenders. In the sector south of Straden, our troops broke through two fortified enemy positions. Our troops destroyed three houses in which the enemy was stationed. The enemy retreated before our fighting group who crossed the river Mur near Radkersburg and reached Neidorfl via Prentlhoff. In our whole sector our raiding and reconnaissance groups captured 5 anti-tank guns, 1 infantry gun, 3 mortars, 23 heavy machine-guns, 9 light machine-guns, 5 submachine-guns and many rifles. They took 15 Bolsheviks prisoner of war. The Bolsheviks suffered 68 killed before our lines.'[231]

Psychological Warfare

Across from the Division was the 20th Guards Rifle Division (6th Guards Rifle Corps, 3rd Ukrainian Front). From their static defensive positions both sides attempted to encourage the other to desert. In that respect, the Soviets had the upper hand, and soon showed themselves to be far more adept and resourceful, utilising a variety of methods. North of Gleichenberg Castle, where the Fusilier Battalion was deployed, to emphasise Germany's calamitous war situation, the Red Army units drew a large map showing the positions of the frontlines on both the eastern and western fronts.[232] The Ukrainians were also bombarded with propaganda leaflets.[233] With the two frontlines sometimes as little as 500 metres apart, verbal exchanges often took place. Periodically, Red Army intelligence units called to the Ukrainian soldiers through loud-hailers, promising amnesty if they were to surrender, and urging them to desert so that they could return to their families.[234] To give the broadcasts a personal slant individuals were named, together with their relatives and friends living under Soviet occupation. They were an easy target for reprisals by the NKVD. A *Waffen-Untersturmführer* recalled his experiences in this respect:

> 'The Communists did not limit themselves merely to playing Ukrainian national folk songs and melodies, they [also] encouraged our soldiers to desert. Here and there individual soldiers or groups went over to the enemy. To add insult to injury some of the turncoats voluntarily or under duress helped the Communists with their propaganda. They would call from the enemy side over loudspeakers, identify themselves stating their names and units and tell their former comrades that no harm had come to them and they were "proud to have become soldiers of the victorious Red Army". They suggested their former comrades kill their officers and desert. They would name the Ukrainian officers. I heard that my name was mentioned on several occasions.'[235]

Susceptibility varied from unit to unit.[236] While some proved to be completely impervious to the promises, Soviet agents and sympathisers within the Division, and those with no stomach to fight on, availed themselves of the first opportunity to abscond. In doing so they took with them their light arms and also important information about the tactical disposition of individual units and other details. One group from the 9/II/WGR 29,[237] led by a former Red Army officer, was enticed by the propaganda, as was a squad of 30 men from 1/I/WGR 31.[238] From the beginning of the defensive fighting, until the end of the war, 98 instances of desertion were recorded[239] They were from all ranks of the Division, officers, NCOs and enlisted men. However, viewed in perspective, that number was negligible considering the large number of soldiers in its ranks. It was at the critical time of general disintegration and incidences of desertion in the core German divisions.

Nonetheless, a series of countermeasures were instigated designed to eradicate the tendency with all the ramifications that it entailed. Units were rotated from frontline to reserve positions, or had their deployment sector changed at short notice. In characteristic fashion, to discourage desertion and to maintain 'exemplary discipline', Freitag issued an internal directive to all regimental and battalion commanders. He encouraged them to impose the death sentence frequently for proven cases of dereliction of duty.[240] In the case of desertion, those who were caught were given a brief mock trial. Usually they were then executed by firing squads.[241] A *Waffen-Untersturmführer* serving as a platoon commander with *Jagdkompanie* WGR 29 was chosen to attend on one occasion:

> 'I was present at an execution of a young soldier who was sentenced by a military court to death by firing squad for desertion. I was ordered to take the whole platoon [to watch]. The intention was to depress and scare everybody. The firing squad was commanded by a German officer.'[242]

Hanging was also commonplace. The bodies of those executed in that way were often left publicly displayed for several days, on a railway bridge or beside a road, as a warning for those with similar intentions.[243]

The Division's own attempts to persuade the Soviets to change sides were largely ineffectual. Several prominent individuals, including *Waffen-Untersturmführer* Father Michael Levenets, took part. Some isolated instances of line-crossing, from the Red Army to the Division, were recorded, although the total number of defectors is unlikely to have reached double figures.[244]

After the hard fighting that had taken place during the previous three weeks in Austria, on 20 April 1945, Hitler's last birthday, awards and promotions were given to the Division's most deserving personnel. *Waffen-Obersturmführers* Wolodymyr Kosak and Ostap Czuczkewycz (both of WGR 29) were awarded the Iron Cross 1st Class.[245] A further 28 awards of the Iron Cross 2nd Class, to Ukrainian soldiers, were cited in the last edition of the Divisional paper *Do Boyu* dated 6 May 1945.[246] (15 were awarded to *W-Grenadiers* and *Oberschütze,* 2 were awarded to *W-Sturmanns*, 12 were awarded to *W-Untersturmführers*. The same source states that 11 War Merit Crosses 1st Class, and 189 War Merit Crosses 2nd Class, were given.[247]

On that date the Division was still listed as being under the command of the 2nd *Panzer* Army, I *Kavallerie* Corps.[248] With the reorganisation of the I *Kavallerie* Corps, the Division was subordinated to the 6th Army, commanded by *General der Panzertruppen* Balck, who in turn assigned it to IV SS *Panzerkorps* under *SS-Obergruppenführer* Herbert Gille.[249] Its operational sector then extended to Feldbach, and included the east/west railway line.

In March 1945, Schützmannschaft Bataillon der SD Nr. *31 or the 'Volhynian Self-Defence Legion' was incorporated into the Galician Division. Part of their number made an abortive attempt to join up with the local Chetnik forces. This renegade group was eventually forced to surrender and merge with the Galician Division, on 9 March 1945, in the village of Frauheim, Slovenia. Here Heike (centre) and (to his left) the Division's liaison officer* Waffen-Haupsturmführer *Makarushka are accompanied by an unidentified officer.*

Major *Heike and* Waffen-Haupsturmführer *Makarushka, 9 March 1945, in the village of Frauheim, Slovenia.*

Five officers of the Legion in the village of Oberschwarze, Austria, on the Mur river. Feldwebel *Domarackyj,* Leutnant *Lytwyn, (dismissed from the 14th Division),* Hauptmann *Oksentijiw,* Leutnant *Roman Kyveluk (leader of the group of legionnaires, who was later shot on Freitag's orders), and* Leutnant *Charvickyj.*

The Legion had its own priests and medical section. A group of nurses from the Volhynian Legion, March 1945, Frauheim, Slovenia. Left to right: N. Boruczyk, T. Potapenko, H. Pisotska, A Hrycenko, O. Wazhna.

9 March 1945, Frauheim, Slovenia. Part of the group of NCOs from the Legion which refused to join the Division. In the sheepskin, first row, fifth from right, Orest Horodysky.

Well-armed group from an infantry unit in a village in Slovenia, March 1945, during an anti-partisan action.

March 1945, Slovenia. An Ukrainian soldier dressed in white snow camouflage overall in typical terrain.

Group of cavalry from the Division in Slovenia, March 1945. Second from right is Waffen-Hauptsturmführer *Dolynsky.*

A post-war picture of Gleichenberg Castle, which was in ruins after heavy fighting by WGR 29 in April 1945. When elements of WGR 29 first arrived, the castle was still inhabited and most of its contents were present and intact.

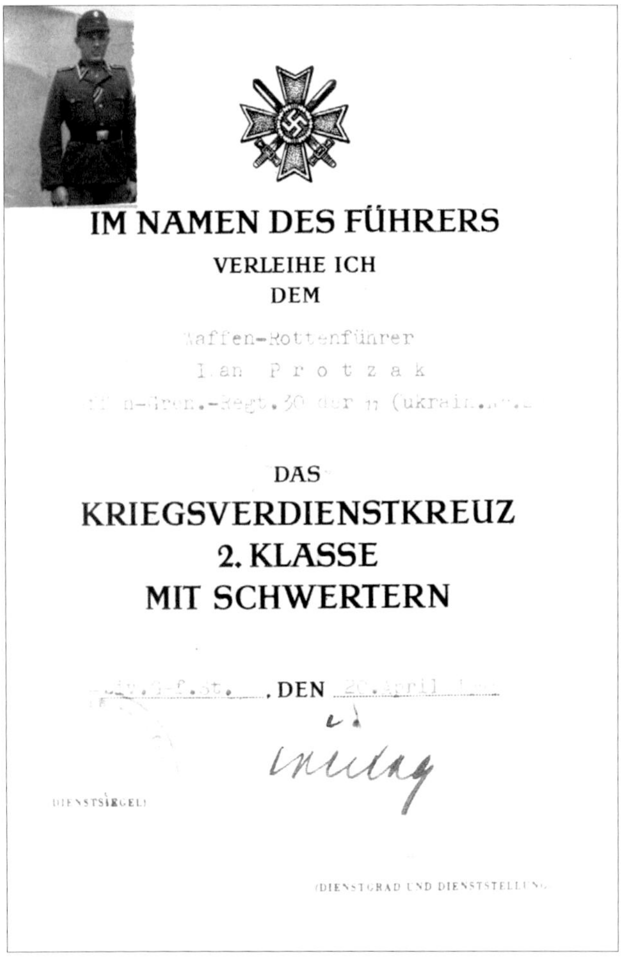

IM NAMEN DES FÜHRERS

VERLEIHE ICH

DEM

Waffen-Rottenführer

I.an Protzak

n-Gren.-Regt.30 der (ukrain.

DAS

KRIEGSVERDIENSTKREUZ

2. KLASSE

MIT SCHWERTERN

, DEN 20.April

(DIENSTSIEGEL)

(DIENSTGRAD UND DIENSTSTELLUNG)

The citation, dated 20 April 1945, for the Kriegsverdienstkreuz 2.Klasse mit Schwerten *(War Service Cross 2nd Class with Swords) awarded to* Waffen-Rottenführer *Iwan Protzak, WGR 30 (*Ukrain. Nr. *2).*

10

Reality or a Symbolic Gesture?

On 17 April 1945, after a ten-day journey via Prague and Linz, General Shandruk and his entourage arrived at the headquarters of the Division's Training and Reserve Regiment in Völkermarkt. Accompanied by Dr Arlt, *Oberst* Bisanz, and Dr Wächter, who joined them en route near Spittal,[1] the purpose of the visit was to oversee the incorporation of the 14th *Waffen-Grenadier-Division der SS* (*ukrainische* Nr.1) into the Ukrainian National Army

In Völkermarkt, the first senior German officer whom Shandruk encountered was the commander of the reserve regiment *SS-Obersturmbannführer* Carl Marks. Much to Shandruk's annoyance, having been informed of the arrival of an Ukrainian general, Marks proceeded to ignore him completely. An act of such gross insubordination would have automatically brought about court-martial proceedings against an Ukrainian in similar circumstances. Thus slighted, Shandruk returned to the hotel in which he was quartered, intent on removing Marks from his command. Actually effecting his dismissal proved to be a far more formidable proposition than he had anticipated. Upon learning of Marks' conduct, both Dr Wächter and Dr Arlt intervened on his behalf and placated Shandruk with profuse apologies. It was a clear indication that for reasons of expediency they were determined to preserve the Division's internal command structure, at least temporarily.[2]

In contrast to his earlier nonchalant reception by a German officer, Shandruk received a warm welcome from the older Ukrainian officers in the Reserve Company who had gathered to meet him. After brief talks, his dignity restored, he gave orders for them to change their German ranks and insignia for the Ukrainian equivalent, i.e. those of the Army of the Ukrainian People's Republic 1919–1921. By the next day it had been done.[3]

His tour of inspection continued on 19 April, when he left for the Division's field HQ at Obergnas. Dr Wächter, Dr Arlt, *Oberst* Bisanz, and *Waffen-Hauptsturmführer* Makarushka were present on that occasion. Also present was Colonel Myhailo Krat,[4] a former Ukrainian officer who had not seen active service since 1920. Shandruk intended to appoint Krat as the new Divisional commander in place of Freitag.

On the previous evening, Freitag was forewarned of the coming visit by Wächter and Arlt. Freitag's general demeanour towards Shandruk was uncharacteristically approachable. He gave a written and oral report on the Division, its position, contact with its neighbours, and an estimate of the opposing enemy forces. All that was supplemented by a full description from *Major* Heike, of frontal fortifications and deployment of its units and reserves. The reports and various tactical details were then discussed with Freitag, after which Shandruk insisted that henceforth the formation be known as the 1st Ukrainian Division of the Ukrainian National Army.[5] Simultaneously, the 29th, 30th and 31st regiments were renamed nos 1, 2 and 3. So as to leave no doubt, he later issued a written instruction to Freitag to announce the renaming, as well as several other points in the next Divisional orders which were to appear a few days later.[6]

To acquaint himself with organisational and internal matters from an Ukrainian perspective, Shandruk invited *Waffen-Hauptsturmführer* Lubomyr Makarushka to join him for a private talk that lasted for several hours. On the spot he promoted Makarushka to the rank of Major of the UNA. Makarushka expounded on a long list of grievances. The first was that the Division was firmly in the hands of the Germans, who held the vast majority of command posts and amongst whom there was a marked propensity to treat the Ukrainians with contempt. The second was that all supplies were in German hands. The third grievance was Freitag's predilection for court-martial proceedings when dealing with transgressions by Ukrainians. Fourth was the Division's almost total dependency on horse-drawn transportation that impeded logistics and movement. The single most important issue to be broached throughout the extended consultation was the proposed change in command.

Following an evaluation of the pros and cons, it was decided that in the current situation, and in view of the expected early end of the war, appointing an Ukrainian as a new Divisional commander would not serve the best interests of the Division. Similarly, Shandruk later rejected the idea of replacing with Ukrainians all the German commanders in the Division and in its Reserve Regiment. His justification for those decisions was that any hostile activity towards the Germans would deprive it of provisions. The Division was surrounded by large units of German troops. The possibility existed, that the orders and directives, issued by Ukrainian officers, could have been sabotaged by Germans at all levels.[7] Thus, fearing adverse consequences if Freitag was removed, Shandruk left him in command. Consequently Krat returned to the Army staff in Völkermarkt.[8]

As a nominal acknowledgement for retaining his command, Freitag requested two German NCOs should stand guard, in place of Ukrainian soldiers, outside the farmhouse which served as his new quarters and above which flew the Ukrainian national flag.

Over the next six days, Shandruk's presence became known throughout the Division, raising the morale of the Ukrainian soldiers. Together with Makarushka he dutifully visited many units at the front, a practice not engaged in by Freitag. While so doing, Shandruk distributed to every group he could reach, limited quantities of a new cap badge embossed with the Trident emblem. It was a replacement for the traditional SS Death's Head insignia. With the chief chaplain *Waffen-Untersturmführer* Father Levenets, he visited the graves of soldiers killed in fighting and attended the services held for them.

On 25 April 1945, Shandruk ordered the Division to be sworn in as the *Persha Ukrainska Dyvizija Ukrainskoi Nacional'noi Armii,* i.e. 1st Division of the Ukrainian National Army. Thereby he completed the final formality of transferring it to the Ukrainian National Army.[9] That was a further indulgence that his German sponsors were prepared to accept. Like the name change, it had a symbolic meaning only. No practical consequences would affect the overall tactical control of the Division, which remained German until the final surrender.

As most of the Division was holding the frontline, the ceremony was conducted in the presence of WGR 30. The previous day it had been pulled out of action at Unter Giem and temporarily moved into reserve.[10] In an open field, surrounded by hills and woods near the village of Odet, the regiment formed into a hollow square. They were assembled in full complement, together with delegates sent to represent WGRs 29 and 31, and the other sub units. Mass was conducted, after which two young Ukrainian *Waffen-Untersturmführers* dressed in their parade uniforms, laid their hands on a medium calibre mortar and, together with all those present, repeated the oath after *Waffen-Untersturmführer* Father Levenets:[11]

> 'I swear to Almighty God on His Holy Gospel and His Living Cross, sparing neither life nor health, always and everywhere to fight with weapons in my hand under the Ukrainian National Banner for my people and for my homeland, Ukraine. Aware of my great responsibility as a soldier of the Ukrainian National Army, I swear that I will carry out all orders of my superiors obediently and without question, and to keep secret all service orders. So help me God and the Holy Virgin, Amen.'[12]

A review took place immediately afterwards, and the Commander in Chief of the Ukrainian National Army greeted several of the young Ukrainian officers. For them, and the vast majority of their comrades, swearing an oath of allegiance to Ukraine was a moving and profound experience. There had been no mention of Adolf Hitler. They were within a few kilometres of the frontline and it represented the culmination of their aspirations to become soldiers of an Ukrainian National Army.[13]

As a rule, the Division's German contingent, perhaps understandably, were somewhat less inclined to view the matter with the same degree of sentimentality. Except for Dr Wächter, Dr Arlt, and the commander of WGR 30, *SS-Obersturmbannführer* Forstreuter,[14] the Division's senior German commanders and general staff officers were noticeable by their absence. That was some measure of the lack of seriousness they gave the ceremony. Despite appearances, Dr Wächter and Dr Arlt were anxious to stifle any official uncensored announcement of those events until such time as they felt it was safe. That was evidenced by Dr Arlt's cautionary remark to an Ukrainian *Kriegsberichter* who had witnessed the ceremony and who was told by Arlt that "*Sie Kriegsberichter darüber dürfen nicht Schreiben*". ["The Kriegsberichter are not permitted to write in the interim."][15]

A photographic record of the highlights of Shandruk's visit eventually did appear as a one-page insert in the last issue of the Divisional paper *Do Boyu*. It was dated 6 May 1945,[16] six days after Hitler's suicide in Berlin on 30 April 1945, and only two days before Germany's capitulation.

One page insert with photographs of Shandruk's visit from the Divisional newspaper Do Boyu dated 6 May 1945

In real terms, the transfer changed nothing. As the 1st Ukrainian Division of the Ukrainian National Army, the Division remained subject to the authority of the *Reichsführer-SS* and consequently depended on the Waffen-SS establishment for its supplies, equipment and replacements. Further, the SS-FHA continued to exercise complete control over all the German cadre personnel assigned to it. As late as 29 April 1945, the *SS-Personalhauptamt* was ordering the re-assignment of individuals for special duties.[17] Tactically, the Division remained subordinate to 6th Army and under the command of *General der Panzertruppen* Hermann Balck.

Despite his newly found exalted capacity, the limitations of Shandruk's authority and influence as the 'Commander in Chief of the Ukrainian National Army' were becoming all too apparent. While the dismissal of the more odious Germans, of all ranks, was ultimately promised, there was no evidence to suggest that it actually took place. Their continued survival and the failure to implement the eagerly awaited and long overdue major radical reform measures, was most likely due to the machinations and external pressure from Dr Wächter and Dr Arlt.

However, it should be noted that Shandruk signalled his intention to address some secondary concerns in the next Divisional order, i.e. Divisional Order Number 71. It was issued on 27 April 1945, entitled "The Ukrainianisation of the Division" (for the full text, see Appendix XIX).[18] The contents of the order set out the envisaged military and political consequences for the Division according to the agenda of Dr Wächter. He and all the others subscribed to the popular belief of the inevitability of a conflict between the Western Allies and the Soviets, after a defeat by Germany.

The order began as Shandruk had requested. It stressed the change in the Division's nomenclature and stated that General Schandruk was the Commander in Chief of all Ukrainian units including the 1st Ukrainian Division. Everything was to be made common knowledge among the troops. The Division, as the 1st Ukrainian Division, was a purely Ukrainian combat unit, with a small percentage of German leaders. It was to continue to fight Bolshevism on the Eastern Front. Dr Wächter, *Oberst* Bisanz, and Dr Arlt were to act as its political advisers.

It then outlined the main arguments for preserving the status quo within its unsatisfactory current command and personnel structure. Under the heading 'Political consequences', it stated that negotiations regarding the Division's inclusion within the 'anti-Bolshevik Kampfbloc' (literally 'anti-Bolshevik fighting bloc'), are in progress and appear to be progressing favourably". In the event of that happening, the document continued, there were two alternatives. The first preferred option was that the Division would retain all weapons, and the same uniforms, while its entire German cadre would remain complete within it. The Luftwaffe had still to be decided. It was important because:

> 'The maintaining of all units with any combat capacity whatsoever, will be decisive in the final battle against Bolshevism which lies ahead of us with 100% certainty. It is therefore the duty of every member of the Division, whether German or Ukrainian, to do his utmost to maintain the unit in its entirety as a fighting force against Bolshevism. The tighter and more complete the internal cohesion of the unit, the more successful will be the coming march against Bolshevism. It is vital that we maintain and keep together the remaining valuable blood that has been brought together by its hatred of Bolshevism. The Division, in its composition and in particular in the working relationship between the Germans and the Ukrainians, forms a firm blood-bonded basis for the future co-operation of both peoples.'

Without so much as a hint of irony this section concluded by saying that if they were to remain, the Germans would have to "show chivalry towards the Ukrainians".

The second alternative considered the possibility of the departure of the German personnel prior to the transfer, in which case suitable Ukrainian replacements would have to be found. The Germans, once released, would immediately be placed under the command of the nearest German combat unit, preferably an SS unit. For the fanatics, it warned against following the philosophy of the *Werwolf,* "which remains foolish."

The order also revealed that, as a contingency measure, some thought had been given to exploring the possibility of a merger of the 1st Ukrainian Division with General Anders' anti-Bolshevik Polish Corps fighting for the Anglo-Americans in Italy.[19] To facilitate that, the document described its composition as being west Ukrainian, i.e. Galician, with 11% Germans.[20] There would be only a few east Ukrainians, and no Russians. It emphasised that there was therefore "no conflict with the Polish government in London, but a distinct conflict with the (Pro-Soviet) Polish government in Lublin".

All those possibilities, it explained, were to be presented to the officers and NCOs, German and Ukrainian. There was also news that the Americans were to be approached as early as possible via the Training and Reserve Regiment, and it was vital to keep the Division from falling into Soviet hands. The measures it stated had been agreed in principle and ratified at both Army and Corps level "completely and without reservation" although no specific details were mentioned. The officers were also to be informed that negotiations with the Western Allies had begun and that it could be hinted at to the NCO corps to maintain combat morale.

Under Section V, 'Immediate measures', the need to hold the front and maintain order and discipline within the Division was emphasised. The following directions were given:

> 'The quartermasters' stores were to be depleted immediately. The remaining bedding, clothing, and equipment would be issued, food distributed and the soldiers equipped with enough ammunition to be able to engage the enemy at any time. Any officer failing to carry out the instructions would automatically suffer summary justice.
>
> 'To ensure full mobility for the imminent withdrawal, all vehicles were to be loaded and ready, with priority given to making the communication centres mobile, i.e. the radio operators and their sets. Non-essential equipment was to be abandoned to make way for food and ammunition. Files, war diaries and Divisional staff papers were to be destroyed. The Division's supplies were to be taken over by its Training and Reserve Regiment, and concealed in the Unterdrauberg and Mahrenberg region.'

As the duration of the war was unknown, but expected to be short, and as an added incentive it stated that, "in the remaining days the Division will be very charitably disposed to nominations for promotion or decorations". As of 5 May those could be dealt with internally.

Only in the penultimate paragraph were commanders instructed to make lists of those German soldiers who were strongly opposed to the Ukrainians. They would be transferred to the 14th *Feld Ersatz Bataillon* that was to become an exclusively German unit. With reference to extreme cases, it stipulated that "Soldiers who hate or are hated by the Ukrainians cannot be kept".[21] The contents of that paragraph were largely academic and neither measure was implemented.

Subsequent to the issuing of the order, the commanders of all sub-units were gathered together and given a summary of its contents and the possibilities outlined therein. At the end of the meeting *Oberst* Bisanz gave a speech in which he called upon all commanders to fulfil their duties conscientiously, as soldiers, at that difficult time.[22] General Shandruk, Wächter and Arlt returned to Völkermarkt on 29 April. Dr Wächter and Dr Arlt immediately left to contact General Shkuro. They hoped to discuss the prospect of joining the Cossacks under his command, for joint action with the 1st Ukrainian Division.[23] The next day General Shandruk oversaw the swearing in of the Reserve Regiment. On 1 May he undertook an inspection of the Division's hospital.[24]

Except for local actions by enemy patrols, and an intensification of artillery fire, in the first days of May the front around Feldbach and Gleichenberg remained quiet. The commander of 6th Army, *General der Panzertruppen* Balck, took the opportunity to summon to his HQ *SS-Brigadeführer* Freitag and *Major* Heike, along with all the other commanders, higher adjutants and Chiefs of Staff. There, he said he was convinced of a positive outcome of the approaching events. During the conference he stressed that available supplies of munitions and fuel, in the depots near the front, would be adequate to repel the enemy advance. He also gave orders for all units to increase the use of reconnaissance groups. They were to conduct raids deep behind the enemy lines, collect intelligence and destroy military installations. In his memoirs, Heike states that General Balck's optimistic assessment was for some "difficult to believe and received with considerable scepticism".[25] However, it did at least offer some encouragement to the officers as they returned to their respective units.

With few positive distractions available in that period of uncertainty and *Paroles* (Ukrainian slang for 'rumours'), General Shandruk gave orders for the solemn observance of Easter. By the Julian calendar it began on Thursday 3 May.[26] For the next four days the Ukrainian soldiers took advantage of the inactivity, and the unusual calm at the front, to commemorate the event as best they could. Units in reserve prepared Easter meals served with meat, mostly roast pork,[27] eggs, pickle, bread and ubiquitous schnapps.[28] Those in the frontline did not have that luxury.[29] The Ukrainian Greek Catholic chaplains said Mass. When possible they arranged for the soldiers to attend confession, one platoon at a time. The *Paska* was blessed and, according to Ukrainian custom, traditional painted eggs were distributed to several units, together with sausage and meat in baskets. As part of the impromptu celebrations, one Ukrainian Company commander ordered the firing of signals-cartridges and flares, for three minutes, at midnight on Easter Thursday. The Soviets observed from their frontline, only two hundred metres away.[30] Another spontaneous moment provided a poignant reminder of the tragic circumstances that had brought the Division's soldiers face to face with their Ukrainian countrymen with whom they usually shared common religious convictions. On that issue a *Waffen-Untersturmführer* serving with 1/I/I (formerly WGR 29) wrote:

> 'Early at dawn on Easter Sunday the soldiers of our Division in the frontlines sang the traditional song *Khrystos Voskres* ('Christ is Risen') and to our surprise the Soviet line joined our troops in singing because there were many Ukrainian soldiers in the Red Army on the other side.'[31]

The news of Hitler's "heroic death while fighting in the defence of Berlin" and the subsequent appointment of Grand Admiral Dönitz as his successor, reached many units, including the 1st Ukrainian Division, after the announcement on the radio.[32] While it may have come as a profound shock to the die-hard German Nazis, for the Ukrainians it was received with complete indifference or even relief.[33] Either way, it led to the mostly inescapable conclusion that the complete collapse of Germany was imminent.

The main concern then facing its command, and all those associated with the 1st Ukrainian Division, was Germany's impending defeat and the consequences that were likely to follow. The process of clearing out continued with renewed emphasis. All units were subjected to a purge of unnecessary matériel and encumbrances in order to increase mobility. It was especially important since it would be necessary to negotiate a retreat path across steep mountain passes to the Western Allied demarcation line.

On the morning of 6 May, a briefing was held for all Divisional chiefs of staff at the command post of IV SS *Panzerkorps*. Unconditional capitulation of the German Wehrmacht was then expected at any time. *SS-Obergruppenführer* Herbert Gille's instructions were that, from 7 May, the entire German front was to disengage from the Red Army and move to territories occupied by the British and Americans. Other than essential items, all matériel and heavy weapons were to be left behind. The first units to withdraw were to be the foremost elements of IV SS *Panzerkorps* that were to retreat on 7 May. The 1st Ukrainian Division was to follow twenty-four hours later, on 8 May, when all the Corps' units had been aligned.

A second conference took place, on the afternoon of the same day, when all divisional commanders and commanding generals were called to General Balck's headquarters for the last time. The main topic of discussion was the avoidance of capture by the Red Army. At the Division's proposal, Völkermarkt was designated as its mustering point. That was in line with Wächter's plan of moving it to Tolmezzo in northern Italy. Requests were also made by its command that it be given priority, when the withdrawal orders were issued, on the basis of its unique circumstances. As an 'Ukrainian Division' the consequences of capture by the Soviets would in all probability be far worse than for regular German formations. Moreover, unlike its mobile neighbours, as an infantry Division its retreat would necessarily be slower. General Balck listened to these representations but refused to commit himself. He made no definitive decisions, although he had the latitude to do so. He was fully aware that the schedule for capitulation on the Eastern Front gave no instructions for a precisely timed cease-fire, because of the potentially disastrous results.[34]

General Shandruk, Dr Arlt, Dr Wächter and *Oberst* Bisanz returned to the 1st Ukrainian Division on the afternoon of the same day. Dr Wächter, in his capacity as *SS-Gruppenführer und Generalleutnant der Polizei*, immediately left for the army headquarters, hoping that by exerting his influence he could obtain an early withdrawal.

The Western Allies had by now entered Austria from the west and northwest. At Shandruk's bidding, Dr Makarushka who was felt to be the Division's most suitable emissary, was directed to leave for the Völkermarkt/

Klagenfurt district.[35] Accompanied by Dr Arlt, who was to act as an interpreter, he was given the assignment of making contact with the British. He had to inform them of the existence of the 'Ukrainian National Army' and get a written order to move the 1st Ukrainian Division to rear of the British lines. Makarushka subsequently met a British unit whose commander agreed to his request that Völkermarkt would be designated as the Division's assembly area. That plan subsequently had to be abandoned. The city had been occupied by a large garrison of Tito's pro-Soviet partisans. They claimed it belonged to them and not to the British. They were hostile to the presence of Ukrainian soldiers.

Under those circumstances, having lost contact with the Division's command, Dr Makarushka took the precaution of sending guides to divert the columns bound for Völkermarkt, to Radstädter Tauern instead which was under British control.

Similarly, to avoid further harassment, he redirected to the north the Training and Reserve Regiment which had begun its retreat on 3 May.[36] In some cases it was accomplished only with the utmost difficulty, especially for those units which were posted south of the Drava.[37] Tito's partisans who had crossed into Austria proper, surprised and ambushed the retreating soldiers, frequently inflicting heavy casualties and capturing prisoners. Over 80 men were taken from the 2nd Battalion alone.[38] Forced to fight their way through, in the fierce battles that ensued the Regiment was broken into small units which made their way independently towards the Allied lines.[39]

The strong presence of partisans, in the vicinity of Völkermarkt, also meant that Dr Wächter's plan for the Division to cross the Alps was no longer feasible.

Capitulation

Along with the destruction of documents and surplus matériel, as instructed by Divisional Order 71,[40] the thinning out of all non-combatant and support units had already begun on 6 May. All divisional commanders relocated their supply, service and logistics units to the rear, on 7 May, mostly during the hours of darkness, to avoid detection. On the roads leading to the west, which quickly became congested, movement was supervised by officers and military police.

Throughout 7 May, Freitag and Heike petitioned the IV SS *Panzerkorps* headquarters for an exact time of withdrawal. However, their urgent requests and protestations made no impression and the only orders they received were to wait. In the early hours of 8 May, Dr Wächter who had been unable to reach 6th Army HQ because his car had broken down, telephoned and stated that to the best of his knowledge 6th Army had already given the appropriate orders. It was not until 6.00am on 8 May, that the Chief of Staff of IV SS *Panzerkorps* finally telephoned, with orders for retirement, to commence without further delay. The 1st Ukrainian Division was to move westwards. The demarcation line, some 200kms to the rear, would have to be crossed before 9.00am on 9 May. In compliance with the surrender terms, after that hour all military movement was to halt. Troops were to remain where they were, until taken in to captivity by the army against whom they had last fought.

Instructions were then issued to the commanders of all the 1st Ukrainian Division's sub-units who were awaiting them impatiently. After abandoning all the remaining heavy equipment and infantry support weapons such as mortars, which had first to be rendered useless, they had to discard steel helmets, gas mask canisters[41] and other superfluous items of personal kit. They had then to disengage from the front completely, by constant and accelerated marching. Two routes were to be utilised as far as Graz. A few units in the north, amongst them parts of the 14th *Feld Ersatz Bataillon*, were to march along the main route to Feldbach, via the Raab valley to Gleisdorf and then to Graz. Meanwhile, the bulk of the Division moved further south from Gnas, to the first collection point at St. Stephan, where the classified regimental documents were burnt.[42] They went next to Enzelsdorf, to the Mur at Kalsdorf, and then north to Graz. There, both columns were to combine and retreat westwards along the *Pakstrasse*, the main route assigned to the majority of 6th Army's units, in the direction of its mustering point at Völkermarkt. Rest stops were forbidden because of the constant threat of a final Soviet offensive.

As the Division's units began to make an orderly withdrawal its artillery batteries continued to fire on the enemy positions until they had expended all their remaining ammunition.[43] The guns were then abandoned, after the breach blocks had been buried. Their crews joined the mass of soldiers marching west, carrying only light weapons and essential provisions. They left behind 729 of their comrades who died during the fighting on the frontline in Slovenia and Austria.[44]

As soon as the first infantry units began leaving their trenches, enemy activity increased. Fortunately, the Soviets only carried out isolated attacks and did not mount an offensive along the entire front.

The first natural barrier to be encountered was the Mur that ran approximately 50kms, or one day's march, behind the frontline. Some difficulties were anticipated because of the small number of bridges spanning the river. To ease the congestion, especially on the existing main permanent concrete bridge, which had been mined but was still intact, barges were utilised by some infantry units so that the crossing proceeded without any significant delays.[45]

Initially, the Division's staff remained in the vicinity of Gnas to assist with the evacuation and to clear up tactical difficulties caused by the earlier retirement of one of the Division's neighbours. Temporally that meant that its left flank was exposed. After a few hours it transferred its headquarters to the west bank of the Mur, where it remained until the bulk of the Division had crossed. Shandruk states in his narrative that, together with Freitag, he waited for the last of the soldiers to cross at the bridge at Leoben, approximately 40kms north of Graz, before moving west to Judenburg.[46]

To cover the retreat, Freitag's orders stated that one reinforced company per regiment was to remain in place until 2.00pm.[47] In practice, the size of the unit that remained was left to the discretion of the individual battalion commanders and hence it varied considerably.[48]

In the case of II/2nd Rgt, formerly WGR 30, that duty was assigned to the 5th Company reinforced with two adjacent platoons. Throughout 8 May, beginning at dawn, the force that had a total strength of approximately 180 men, came under heavy pressure. It managed to repel the Soviet attacks successfully but with severe losses. Unable to wait for darkness before pulling back because of the possibility of being surrounded, at 2.30pm the survivors withdrew in broad daylight along a road towards Feldbach. They then continued in the direction of St Stephan. By that time only 25 men were left from the original contingent.[49]

Amid outbreaks of sporadic fighting, the remaining rearguard units also began to vacate their positions in the early afternoon, as instructed. They booby-trapped command bunkers and other defensive installations. Following their comrades, they crossed the Mur with the last stragglers and mistakenly believed themselves to be safe. Red Army units soon appeared hard on their heels. A *Waffen-Untersturmführer* commanding the rearguard of the 1st Platoon, 1/I/1st Rgt (formerly WGR 29) gave his account of these events:

> 'Marching all night, by early next morning we had crossed the river south of Graz, and lay down to rest on the western bank. Everyone was exhausted and I fell asleep. Suddenly loud noises woke me up. The Soviet troops had caught up with us and their mortar shells were exploding all around us. This surprise attack created panic among our troops. Although we couldn't see the enemy, we started running for cover towards some woods about half a mile away. The officers wanted to establish a defensive line but it was to no avail. In the panic, no one listened and everyone was running blindly. I started to run too, but my feet were swollen in my high officers' boots from all the marching throughout the day and the previous night, and I soon fell behind.
>
> 'As I approached a nearby farmhouse I noticed three saddled horses tied up to a post. Without hesitation I mounted one and galloped until I caught up with our troops, who by now had reached the woods. A couple of exhausted fellow officers held on to the horse's saddle and were running alongside me. On the other side of the woods we came across a field hospital which was being evacuated. There were several empty trucks that everybody climbed on to. I decided to keep the horse as in the event that the road was bombed or cut off I would have a better chance of riding away cross-country. It wasn't long before I had lost sight of the trucks that I was following.
>
> 'Riding on my own for about 10 kms, I caught up with a detail of about 80 German cavalry, who were evidently well rested and rode leisurely. I rode with them for a short while but could not keep up with them for long. Eventually I caught up with some Ukrainian infantry troops who were marching with their horse drawn wagons. I tied my horse to a wagon and climbed on it to rest.'[50]

To slow down the advancing Red Army the 3rd Company of the Pioneer Battalion, commanded by *SS-Obersturmführer* Dombrowskyi, was one of the last to retreat. They constructed anti-tank obstacles, laid mines, and placed explosive charges on trees that were detonated so that they fell blocking the roads.[51] However, there was not enough time to carry out the standing orders to destroy all the bridges over the Mur in the 1st Ukrainian Division's sector. That would have caused the civilian population significant hardship.[52]

At Graz on the west bank of the Mur, both of the Division's main columns converged. As planned they began to retreat along the *Pakstrasse* with the majority of 6th Army's units, towards Twimberg. The Division's staff moved towards the front of the marching column in an attempt to direct and retain control of it. Initially, *SS-Brigadeführer* Freitag and his staff were still able to issue orders to the motorised and horse-drawn elements. But very soon the troops were spread out over a wide area and became intermingled with a variety of German units. Under such conditions its larger units began to disperse, as marching discipline was lost. The cavalry and motorised formations on the Division's left and right flanks were fortunate in that they were able to retain a certain amount of cohesion, because they had transport and sufficient field radios.

Radio contact had been lost with the Training and Reserve Regiment on 7 May. The chief Liaison Officer *SS-Obersturmführer* Rudolph Michel was despatched ahead to report the arrival of the rest of the Division in its district.[53] He later sent notification that he had not found British formations in the area around Völkermarkt, which was infested with partisans. On his own initiative he therefore intercepted the Division's units, at the cross-roads north of Wolfsberg, and redirected them away from the danger to the north via Twimberg-Judenburg-Marua-Mauterndorf-Radstädter Tauern and Radstädt.

A colossal jam soon developed. There were long delays for the retreating troops as they fled through the mountains towards the assumed safety of the Western Allies. Trucks, cars, both military and civilian, motorcycles, horse-drawn carriages, horses, and bicycles were mixed with the majority who made their way on foot. Everything exacerbated the already difficult conditions and slowed all movement. Anything that was not absolutely essential was soon discarded, to speed up the retreat. En route, the 14th *Feld Ersatz Bataillon* deposited all its medical supplies for local use in the village of Hitzendorf south west of Graz.[54] As they passed through small hamlets along the route, the Austrian civilians offered bread and milk to the 1st Ukrainian Division's exhausted and thirsty soldiers, as recalled by one veteran:[55]

> 'The retreating column went through an Austrian village. Here Austrian women and children stood along both sides of the road and handed the thirsty passing soldiers water to drink. I was moved by that expression of human spirit and goodness.'[56]

More importantly, the locals often gave the soldiers intelligence information relating to the advance of Soviet tanks and which villages they had already occupied. Many were saved from falling into Soviet hands.[57]

The long, slow-moving lines on the crowed roads were a prime target for enemy fighters that began strafing them intermittently, from the afternoon of 8 May, causing further casualties.[58] The attacks lasted until 12 May, when the last units reached the safety of the Allied lines.[59]

Having arrived in Judenburg, ahead of the main column, Shandruk met Lieutenant Fediv, General Krat's Liaison Officer and gave him a note appointing Krat as the Divisional commander.[60] There, Dr Wächter rejoined the Division's staff having been to Graz to obtain up to date information about Soviet movements. He warned that tanks from an armoured unit were advancing rapidly along the main road from Bruck to Judenburg. Indeed, that unit later reached Judenburg where its tanks intercepted the Division's column, cutting off the main retreat path. In so doing, several horse-drawn supply wagons, complete with their contents and many personal effects were abandoned in the rush to escape.[61] Some unfortunate Divisional soldiers were captured in those chaotic conditions described by a former member of 7/II/3rd Regiment:

> 'Our column was cut off by Soviets [at Judenburg]. They came with tanks and told us to lay down our arms. They knew we were Ukrainian by the lion on our collars. They didn't shoot us straight away just told us to get in line and disarmed us. Together with four friends I took the first opportunity to escape through the houses down a side street and into the mountains.'[62]

On hearing rumours that the Soviets had occupied Judenburg, those further to the rear of the retreating column scattered into the surrounding mountains. The remnants later reassembled and started on a route from St Veit to Feldkirchen.

Rumours about the fate that awaited the Waffen-SS personnel who fell into Allied hands at that time, provided sufficient incentive for some. Many had already discarded pay-books and other potentially incriminating evidence. Others took additional steps to disassociate themselves from their former membership of a Waffen-SS Division. They obliterated the tattoos of their blood groups from under their left arms. A former member of the 13th *Waffen-Gebirgsdivision der SS 'Handschar'* who was also in the POW camp in Tamsweg, stated in his memoirs how a physician from the 14th SS Division, i.e. a Galician, provided him and others from his unit with hydrogen tablets to remove blood group tattoos. When moistened and dabbed on to the arm, the resulting skin irritation was sufficient to ensure that the tattoos came off within about 2 or 3 days, whilst the skin itself required two to three weeks to heal.[63]

The End of the Division's Command Staff

On the afternoon of 10 May, the Division's HQ was in Tamsweg. On the evening of the same day they moved 3kms north to the village of St Andrij.[64] Dr Wächter's aide-de-camp delivered news that the Western Allies were interning all foreign and Waffen-SS units in Tamsweg. As a Wehrmacht officer, Major Heike left the group to explore the possibility of by-passing the road block and to reconnoitre an alternative route. General Shandruk, Freitag and Dr Wächter remained behind. After long delays caused by the heavy traffic of the stalled column of troops and vehicles on the overcrowded road, Heike finally returned to Mauterndorf with a new route. There he met a few of the Division's German staff officers, among them the commander of the Pioneer Battalion *SS-Sturmbannführer* Remberger. From them, he was informed that the Division's headquarters group had already dispersed and that *SS-Brigadeführer* Freitag had proposed a plan to escape with them into the mountains. When his suggestion was rejected he fell into a state of depression. He committed suicide in St Andrij by shooting himself. His body along with his identity papers was discovered a few days later by the British field security forces.[65]

Shortly after, by his own account, General Shandruk had left to seek out the higher American military command, hoping to enjoy a more understanding reception from a country with an ethnic Ukrainian population of over one million.[66] With him went Dr Makarushka and Dr Arlt. Shandruk eventually did make contact with the Americans and having done so, surprisingly was not interned but allowed to remain at liberty. Consequently, in the months that followed, his primary concerns were evading capture by the Soviets and agitating on behalf of the interned Ukrainians for their release.[67]

SS-Gruppenführer und Generalleutnant der Polizei Dr Wächter had needed no convincing that his arrest was only a matter of time, because of his rank and high profile within the German administration in the *Generalgouvernement*.[68] In Heike's absence, he had felt it prudent to take his leave and disappeared into the mountains to Italy where he had friends. They hid him in a monastery under the assumed name of Alfredo Reinhardt until his death by natural causes in 1949.[69]

Under the circumstances of the remaining leadership being scattered, Heike established contact with a British brigade and reported a number of the Division's units to them. A large field near Tamsweg was then assigned as the mustering point for the Ukrainian units that continued to arrive in the area. Heike stayed at the headquarters of the I *Kavallerie* Corps but continued to visit the soldiers at Tamsweg until the entire camp was moved to Spittal-an-der-Drau. Eventually *Major* Heike himself was taken to a separate POW camp. There, he too was held by British forces.[70]

With the dissolution of the Division's command, each man was left to his own discretion as to the course of action he should take. That meant that almost every member of the Division experienced the act of surrender differently. A few of the more resourceful and enterprising individuals headed into the remote Austrian mountains. They, together with a handful of others, having discarded their military apparel, made their way to camps in Germany. Claiming to be forced labourers they managed to register themselves as stateless persons and were subsequently reclassified as refugees. Thus, having obtained the appropriate paperwork[71] they were able to maintain the status of civilians, thereby evading the fate of their comrades.

However, the overwhelming majority of the officers and other ranks preferred to stay together, in line with Shandruk's original instructions. They capitulated to units of the British 5th Corps that comprised 6th Armoured

Division, 46th Infantry Division, 78th Infantry Division, and 7th Armoured Brigade, in Carinthia. They were identified, prior to 26 May, as 'German mercenaries' serving variously with the 14th SS Ukrainian Division, or 14th SS *Galizien* amongst other titles.[72]

The bulk of the dispersed Ukrainian units therefore rallied at three different points in close proximity, at the city of Spittal upon the Drava River, at Feldkirchen and at Klagenfurt. Amongst those who gathered there, were a number of Ukrainian civilians. They had been taken by the Germans to work on farms in Austria and had joined the retreating soldiers.

At Spittal, which became the main assembly area for the Ukrainian Division, a camp was established in a large meadow with no borders or fences of any kind and only a token British guard. Based on his diary entry, a former *Waffen-Unterscharführer* serving with 9/III/2nd Rgt recorded his experiences at this time:

> 'I happened to be in the first group that traversed the Alps. Having wandered for three days in the mountains, on 13 May we passed the locality of Radentheim, reached the beautiful Millstadt lake, and since it was already late, we decided to stay there overnight and in the early morning go to Spittal. There we met other people [from our Division] and our group increased in size. The following day, in the morning, the group with two or three horse-drawn carts and with all our weapons, entered what was already occupied by the British.
>
> 'Our leaders reported to the British command in the town and we were told to go farther on, that is to leave the town, which we did. We had hardly reached the outskirts when two British soldiers on motorcycles caught up with us and asked us to lay down our weapons which we obediently did, since it was not our aim to fight with the British. While proceeding along the main road, to our left there was an extensive meadow with one huge empty barn. After we laid down our weapons we were instructed to enter the meadow and await further orders. Our group entered the barn. Soon after, or rather all day long, new groups were arriving, some with their rations and field kitchens and some with their weapons that they had to surrender. By the next day, our numbers had grown to two or three thousand people, including *Oberst* Alfred Bisanz[73].
>
> 'We started to organise ourselves into regiments or battalions and submitted our numbers to the British. I believe it was the next day that the British started to supply us with some food delivered by aeroplanes and dropped on our meadow. Nobody ever asked us what we were carrying in our rucksacks. There was no wire along that meadow and only one British soldier walked on the road that separated us from the next field across the way, directing the traffic. If a group of new arrivals was from the Ukrainian Division they were directed to join us on the meadow. Nobody cared if we stayed there or whether at night or went somewhere else. Next day, on 14 May, the British separated the German personnel who had remained with us (many of them had already left).'[74]

Not all the Division's soldiers who surrendered to the British were disarmed immediately. A former member of II/3rd Rgt was part of a group who were allowed to retain the weapons they were carrying, for several days, as they made their way unescorted to their eventual assembly point at Feldkirchen:

> 'Only about 60% of the Division's soldiers were assembled after the war in Spittal, Austria. Most of the 3rd Regiment (formerly WGR 31) and many others stopped on the road to Judenburg having received information that it was being occupied by the Red Army. They turned south into the mountains. This group took with them all horse-drawn wagons full of army supplies including their field kitchens. All day we struggled along poor, log-covered roads, uphill until in the dark we reached the top of the snow covered mountains. During the climb we had to shoot some of the horses, which broke their legs on the bad road. Overnight we slept wherever we could, mostly in and under the wagons. In the morning we continued our march southward down the mountain until about noon we met the first British soldiers of the advance units. All our rifles, machine-guns and some mortars were surrendered to the British. They allowed all officers and others to keep their side arms (mostly pistols) and directed us to set up our camp in nearby fields of clover. In the evening the British commandant asked all the officers (from the rank of *Obersturmführer* to *Hauptsturmführer*) to meet with him. The Germans did most of the talking. When the meeting had concluded, the Ukrainian

officers asked to speak to the British commander and explained to him, through an interpreter, our situation, and requested that we be separated from the Germans.

'The next morning the British commander asked us to provide the Germans with a few horse-drawn wagons, and ordered them to move out of the camp. They soon departed without any goodbyes. We stayed in the fields, without any British guards, for a few more days before we were told to go further south to the town of Feldkirchen, a main gathering point of the Ukrainian Division. At that time we had enough food supplies to feed our people. The British command indicated the road we were to follow and warned us that we may encounter some of Tito's partisans. They said that they did not have enough soldiers to escort us and gave us back some rifles and *Sturmgewehr* (assault rifles) and told us that we would have to defend ourselves if the partisans attacked.

'The horses were well rested and the next day we proceeded towards Feldkirchen. While passing one village, we encountered some partisans who quickly dispersed when they saw that we were armed. By the evening we had arrived in Feldkirchen, where many soldiers of our Division were assembled on a large meadow near a creek. Our senior Ukrainian officers assigned us an area in which to set up our camp. The 2nd Battalion of the 3rd Regiment had brought with it four field kitchens and were ordered to share them with the other soldiers. We settled there for a few days, during which time the Intendant of the 2nd Battalion was able to pay his soldiers in German Marks and divide among them the remaining food, cigarettes and liquor. Altogether about 4,000 soldiers from our Division assembled in that location under the overall command of some of the older officers (such as Sylenko, Nikitin and others). We did not know then about the existence of the camp at Spittal.

'Within a week or so we were ordered to take a train to a permanent camp. We were unloaded overnight in a mountain location which to the best of my recollection was known as Pantofel, where we stayed overnight in a school. There we met, for the first time, Jewish soldiers in British uniforms. Most of them spoke Polish. They gathered around the entrance and offered to buy some items from us. One offered 60 cigarettes for an officer's pistol, but none of our officers accepted the offer. Later we were all searched by British soldiers, who took our weapons and many other items. Maybe 60 cigarettes was a good price for a pistol after all.'[75]

Further to the north on 13 May, *Waffen-Hauptsturmführer* Ferkuniak joined a much smaller group of the Division's soldiers. There were 76 officers, 30 of whom were Ukrainian, and 1,112 NCOs and men. They had given themselves up to the Americans, near Wagrain, in the vicinity of Radstädt. Most of the surviving senior German staff officers including Beyersdorff, Forstreuter, Kleinow, Bristot, Kopp and Finder had access to motorised transportation. They had made their get away in good time, taking with them their personal effects, and their own food reserves for ten to twelve days.[76] Unlike the British, the Americans initially showed no interest in their charges. For the first two months the Americans made no effort to provide the prisoners with food causing one to later comment – "We practically starved for the first few months."[77]

While in American internment, *SS-Standartenführer* Beyersdorff and *SS-Sturmbannführer* Karl Bristot attempted to assert their authority over this group. Even at that stage they wanted an Ukrainian NCO to be executed for not fulfilling one of Bristot's orders. The NCO had walked off the road when he had been ordered to run. *Waffen-Hauptsturmführer* Ferkuniak, who represented the Ukrainians, refused to co-operate and stated that he could not guarantee the lives of those who would carry out such a decision. Beyersdorff responded to this statement by threatening, "Remember that the Ukrainians are here between two German divisions, *'Wiking'* and *'Hohenstaufen'*, who could cause you such a blood bath that the world has not yet seen, should anything happen to any Germans". Not to be outdone, Beyersdorff went ahead and convened a *Kriegsgericht*, i.e. an emergency court empowered to sentence any soldier guilty of a breach of discipline, and to carry out executions. The court would have carried out the punishment had not Ferkuniak invalidated the court, acting as the sole representative of General Shandruk.[78]

Beyersdorff was also quick to denounce his former Ukrainian comrades in arms to the American authorities, as being thieves and criminals. It came about as the result of the hungry Ukrainian soldiers having taken a quantity of eggs, and cans of meat, from a railroad car of the American escort. Although the theft was uncovered by Ukrainian officers, the rations returned, and the culprits handed over to the *Feldgendarmerie*, Beyersdorff used it as an excuse to portray the Ukrainians as bandits, robbers and mutineers before the American authorities. He publicly disassociated the remaining German contingent from the Ukrainians.[79] On that issue, an Ukrainian officer who himself had previously served with the Artillery Regiment recalled:

> 'Beyersdorff called a muster. On 1 June 1,200 men assembled. Beyersdorff spoke, but his usual introduction '*Meine liebe gute Ukrainer*' ('My dear good Ukrainians') was missing. He said that he was very disappointed with the Ukrainians. He tried very hard to educate them to be real soldiers but to no avail because under them a dominant group are thieves and bandits. Therefore he could not endanger his Germans who would have to part with the Ukrainians. *Waffen-Hauptsturmführer* Wolodymyr Kosak was appointed as our commander.'[80]

Ultimately the Germans were separated from the Ukrainians, who were moved to P.W.E (Prisoner of War Enclave) No.24 at Auerbach in Germany, controlled by the 3rd US Army in Bad Tolz.[81] There in July 1945, according to the Geneva Convention, officers and senior NCOs were segregated from the men and kept in a separate cage. Movement between cages was forbidden.

In three groups a smaller number of Ukrainians was also held captive by the Americans, in Austria. They were held in, or moved between, several locations, at various times. The camps included Flachau, Wagrain, St Johann in Pongau, Bad Ausee, Radstädt, Steyr, Saalfeldon, Hallein and Glasenbach, Salzburg.

The few Ukrainians who found themselves in French hands had two options. They could either be repatriated to the USSR, or join the French Foreign Legion.

With the majority of the Division's soldiers having passed into either American or British captivity, the military role of the 1st Ukrainian Division of the Ukrainian National Army in World War II came to an end. Despite the uncertainty and understandable apprehension that lay ahead, most were simply glad just to have survived. However, for some of its German commanders such as *SS-Obersturmbannführer* Forstreuter, the war had finished before he could win the Knight's Cross that he coveted so much.

For the 10,000 men encamped in the area around Spittal and Feldkirchen there was nothing left to do now except await further developments:

> 'We sat, sunned ourselves in the spring sun, admired the beautiful mountains surrounding us and hunted for lice that we brought from the front. No facilities for personal hygiene were available. In time the British began to show more interest in us and gave us some very meagre food rations. These were canned meat and crackers washed down with some brown liquid which was supposed to be coffee.'[82]

Eventually, by mid-May 1945, several elements of the 1st Ukrainian Division that had been allowed to retain some of their portable weaponry, finally had to relinquish them.[83] A few days later, on 19 May, the British began to move the first contingent of 3,000 soldiers by truck from their temporary compounds in Carinthia to a transit camp near the city of Udine, in north-eastern Italy. They were followed by other transports, including one group of 2,000 as confirmed in the entry in 5th Corps War Diary which read "Evacuation of SS troops and Yugoslav subjects continues, 2,000 troops of 14th SS *Galizien* moved to Udine".[84]

On arrival, the British 'Tommies' began searching the men, some very thoroughly, checking rucksacks and pockets for guns and other weapons. At the same time they availed themselves of the opportunity to 'liberate' from their prisoners anything they found useful. The officers were obliged to give up their military equipment such as pistols, binoculars, compasses, maps, watches, and pocket-knives. All ranks had other personal items of value taken from them. Those who protested were hit with a rifle-butt or kicked. One veteran later recalled his indignity at such treatment to which there was no recourse:

> 'When we arrived there [at Udine] in the evening we were ordered by the British to hold our hands over our heads and run quickly in single file into the camp. Search lights were beaming directly into our eyes, blinding us, while two rows of British soldiers on either side were grabbing our wrists and hands, removing watches and rings, tearing off pockets, and looking for loot. We were disgusted with this uncivilised British

behaviour. Our complaints to the British camp commander the next morning were unsuccessful. He even had the nerve to arrogantly ask if we could point out the guilty British soldiers!'[85]

From Udine, transports left for another camp at Mestre, 5 miles north west of Venice. En route, the prisoners had to brave the, often hostile, population, between stopping at barracks and transit camps, where they were searched again:

> 'As we were riding in open trucks, the Italian population thinking we were Germans (we were still wearing German uniforms) were throwing rocks at us hollering '*Porchi Tedeschi!*' ('German pigs!'). Some rocks landed on our trucks but the Italians got them right back the hard way.'[86]

The length of time that different transports stayed at that location varied, but eventually after a few days all were moved to their final destination, camp 5C, which had been hastily established on 4 June 1945, west of the village of Bellaria. It was approximately 13 kms north of Rimini, on the Adriatic coast. There the bulk of the Division's Ukrainian contingent was finally re-assembled and held in captivity by the British, its personnel having been classified with the status of 'surrendered enemy personnel' (SEP).

Post-Mortem

From the outset of the establishment of the first direct German-Ukrainian relations in the Twentieth Century, in 1918, the nature of the relationship that Germany cultivated toward Ukraine was exclusively utilitarian and was merely a tactical necessity designed to advance its foreign policy goals. Thereafter, in the inter-war period, successive German governments showed no inclination to revise this position, which was further exemplified on 15 March 1939. Then, after the pronouncement of the independence of the Carpatho-Ukrainian republic, the expected German support failed to materialise as Hitler's alliance with Hungary took precedence.

Any lingering doubts were finally dispelled days after the German invasion of the Soviet Union, on 30 June 1941. The German reaction to the proclamation of the renewal of an independent Ukrainian state by Ukrainian nationalists, was to execute the protagonists, or arrest and deport them to concentration camps. Shortly thereafter Hitler categorically rejected all proposals that would have allowed Ukraine any degree of independence. He preferred instead to divide its territory, which he considered to be inhabited by sub-humans fit only for slavery. That policy in turn provoked the emergence of anti-Nazi resistance in the form of the Ukrainian Insurgent Army, or UPA, which undertook an armed struggle against the Germans which continued throughout the period of German occupation.

Only after it had become apparent that Germany could not possibly win the war did elements within the Nazi hierarchy present the Galician-Ukrainians with an opportunity to potentially realise their political aspirations by permitting the raising of a military unit from amongst the Ukrainian population of western Ukraine or Galicia. In the last few weeks of the war, when the Germans had been driven out of all Ukrainian territory and had little to compromise except for the residual racist ideology of the die-hard Nazis, they agreed to broaden the scope of the Ukrainian armed forces by taking steps to organise the 'Ukrainian National Army'.

Given the prevailing circumstances, the Ukrainian position was an unenviable one, especially as the disadvantages in agreeing to co-operate in the formation of a military unit were obvious. The main one being a German defeat and everything which that entailed.

At the same time, co-operation offered some advantages. The ultimate creation of the Ukrainian National Army under an Ukrainian commander, General Shandruk, was the first step. On paper, at least, it went towards uniting all the Ukrainian units fighting on the side of the Germans, with a view to using them exclusively for the Ukrainian cause. At the same time, the existence of a disciplined Ukrainian military force, and the resultant training of officers and NCOs could, under certain circumstances, have helped to 'internationalise' the Ukrainian question. It had done so previously, in 1918, when an independent Ukrainian state had been established with German assistance.

Therefore, in the final analysis, the '14th Galician Division/1st Division of the Ukrainian National Army' was the product of Nazi-German self interest and expediency on one hand, and Galician-Ukrainian self interest, mixed with idealism and a degree of opportunistic thinking, on the other.

Within the context of WWII, the '14th Galician'/'1st Ukrainian Division's' influence on the field of battle proved to be negligible, but paradoxically there is some evidence to suggest that its potential far-reaching political significance, which for the Ukrainians was the very raison d'être for agreeing to its formation, was realised in part. Indeed, Stalin's concern about the continued post-war existence of the formation, in the west, lead to his demand for its forced repatriation.[87] Somewhat controversially, the British, to whom the bulk of the unit had surrendered, steadfastly refused to do so.[88]

The Ukrainian members of the 1st Ukrainian Division were, therefore, fortunate to escape the unenviable fate of hundreds of thousands of other Ukrainians, Russians, Cossacks, Latvians and many others. They had also fought against the Stalinist regime and were handed over by the Western Allies. Thereupon they were murdered, or condemned to lengthy terms of imprisonment in appalling conditions, in Siberian gulags. There, most perished.

In due course, around 8,500 Ukrainians, who had surrendered to the British, were shipped to Great Britain between 29 April and 10 June 1947. After a further period of internment, they were released. They were allowed to remain in Great Britain, or to emigrate and settle as free men, in several countries including Canada, the USA, Australia and Argentina.

Predictably, the history of the Division's wartime activities has, since that time, remained the subject of dis-information campaigns, especially from the Soviets and the Poles. Campaigns have aimed at discrediting the Ukrainian nationalist movement, by linking it with war crimes. Despite the paucity of any unequivocal evidence in support of such allegations, this is an issue best addressed elsewhere.[89]

ПРИСЯГА

вояків 1. УД — УНА, введена в квітні 1945 р.

Присягаю Всемогучому Богові перед Святою Його Євангелією та Животворящим Хрестом, не шкодуючи ні життя ні здоров'я, скрізь та повсякчас під Українським Національним Прапором боротися зі зброєю в руках за свій Народ і свою Батьківщину — Україну. Свідомий великої відповідальности присягаю як вояк Українського Національного Війська виконувати всі накази своїх начальників слухняно й беззастережно, а службові доручення тримати в таємниці. Так нехай мені в цьому допоможе Бог і Пречиста Мати, амінь.

Присягаю на Український Національний Прапор, не шкодуючи ні життя ні здоров'я, скрізь і повсякчас зі зброєю в руках боротися за Український Народ та за свою Батьківщину — Україну. Свідомий великої відповідальности, присягаю як вояк Українського Національного Війська виконувати всі накази своїх начальників слухняно й беззастережно, службові доручення тримати в таємниці.

On 25 April 1945, General Shandruk ordered the Division to be sworn in as the Persha Ukrainska Dyvizija Ukrainskoi Nacional'noi Armii *(1st Division of the Ukrainian National Army). The text of the new oath of allegiance sworn by the Division's soldiers makes no reference to Adolf Hitler.*

Waffen-Untersturmführer *Motyka, commander of the 1st Platoon, 1/I/1st Regiment is presented with a hoe (*Motyka *is translated as 'hoe') as a present before the company bunker, in the vicinity of Gleichenberg, May 1945. The trident cap badge is visible on his cap in place of the SS Death's Head emblem.*

A group of soldiers from the 1st Platoon, 1/I/1st Regiment with Waffen-Untersturmführer *Motyka in front of the company bunker in the vicinity of Gleichenberg, May 1945. The trident cap badge is discernable on the cap of the man standing second from left.*

Soldiers of 1/I/1 (formerly WGR 29) retreating from the frontline. Centre, wearing poncho, Waffen-Untersturmführer *Owad, right* Waffen-Unterscharführer *Holowko.*

A column of soldiers from the '1st Division of the Ukrainian National Army' winds its way through an Austrian village heading for the Western Allied demarcation line. Austria, May 1945.

Soldiers of the '1st Division of the Ukrainian National Army' consult a map during a break in the retreat across the mountains to escape the advancing Red Army. Austria, May 1945.

A group of Ukrainians in the Austrian town of Spittal-an-der-Drau during British captivity. From right, standing: Owad, Holowko, Krainyk, Smuk.

From April 1944, the Germans recruited youths (both male and female) known as Yunaky *from Galicia between fourteen and eighteen years of age to undergo pre-military training as* Flakhelfer *(flak auxiliaries) at several youth camps, including those at Perovorsk, Malta, Dembica and Nepolomytsi near Cracow. Some of the young men, for example from the camp at Malta, were transferred to the Galician Division on reaching the age of eighteen, where they automatically qualified as officer and NCO candidates. In this picture taken in early June 1944,* SS-Gruppenführer *Wächter and* Oberst *Bisanz arrive for the official opening ceremony of the Chernyk camp in Perovorsk, near Jaroslav, in the* Generalgouvernement. Kriegsberichter *S. Konrad (extreme left) took notes.*

The event was filmed for propaganda purposes and incorporated a swearing-in ceremony. Oberst *Bisanz and Wächter look on as representatives of the young Ukrainians prepare to swear the oath.*

Bisanz (second left) and Wächter (third left) in conversation with some of the youngest boys and the camp staff about the training programme. Representatives of the Hitlerjugend *which administered the programme, as well as the Luftwaffe, were also present.*

The event was reported by Kriegsberichter *S. Konrad (extreme left).*

Young Ukrainians await inspection at the Chernyk camp, which held about 300 boys.

Another youth camp was located in the Austrian village of Malta. Secondary school students underwent their basic training here, which lasted from 10 July 1944 until 30 September 1944. These Yunaky*, pictured in front of Naseberg mountain, wore blue Luftwaffe uniforms with SS insignia and arm brassards in the Ukrainian national colours of blue and gold, bearing either the Galician lion emblem (for Galician Ukrainians) or Trident emblem (for those from Greater Ukraine) and diamond-shaped cap badges in these colours.*

The training programme placed a heavy emphasis upon marching, drill and sports activities such as swimming, boxing and football. There was also a secondary school curriculum and formal lessons and tuition in the German language for those who interrupted their studies to join the Yunaky.

Yunaky *at the Malta camp with one of their sports instructors.*

Two Yunaky *members in the grounds of the camp at Malta.*

Approximately 240 youths later transferred to the Division at Neuhammer, after completion of their training, whereupon they were dispersed amongst various units. Here a group assemble before their departure to the Galician Division.

Governor of Galicia Dr Otto Wächter pictured on 18 April 1944, in L'viv, as a SS-Gruppenführer.

Oberst *Alfred Bisanz, head of the Military Board.*

Official portrait of Divisional commander SS-Brigadeführer *Fritz Freitag, after the award of the* Ritterkreuz.

General Pavlo Shandruk, commander of the Ukrainian National Army, pictured in April 1945.

Major *Wolf-Dietrich Heike, Divisional Ia. Heike's* Soldbuch *shows that he was never officially transferred to the Waffen-SS and was only seconded, hence he is pictured here in a Wehrmacht uniform with the rank of* Major.

SS-Obersturmführer *Rudolph Michel,* 1. Ordonnanzoffizier *(picture taken in Slovakia, 12 December 1944).*

SS-Sturmbannführer *Karl Zoglauer, commander* Abt. *VI, Divisional staff (Spiritual care, Education, Entertainment & Information, Recreation). This section became the mouthpiece for Freitag's internal policies (picture taken in Slovakia, 28 November 1944).*

SS-Obersturmbannführer *Dr Oskar Kopp, commander,* Abt. *IVc (Veterinary).*

Waffen-Obersturmführer *Liubomyr Makarushka (right), who was Paliiv's successor and served on the Division's staff as liaison officer between the Division and the Military Board, with* Waffen-Untersturmführer *Hawrylak (left).*

Commander of WGR-29 SS-Obersturmbannführer *Friedrich Dern, in civilian clothing, indicted for war crimes after the war.*

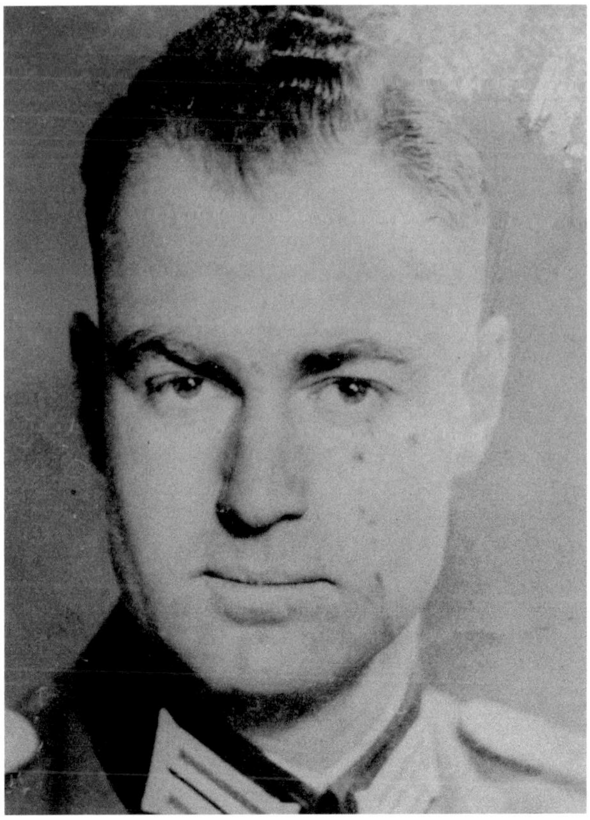

Commander of WGR-30 SS-Obersturmbannführer *Hans-Boto Forstreuter, who "did not trust the Ukrainians", seen here wearing the uniform of the 4th* SS-Polizei Panzergrenadier *Division.*

SS-Obersturmbannführer *Paul Herms, CO WGR-31, killed at Brody.*

Replacement commander of WGR 31 after the death of SS-Obersturmbannführer *Paul Herms, Knight's Cross holder* SS-Standartenführer *Rudolph Pannier, who became a morphine addict after being heavily wounded, and whose mistakes Freitag overlooked. Seen here with the rank of* SS-Obersturmbannführer.

Commander of 14th Artillery Regiment, SS-Standartenführer *Friedrich Beyersdorff, here in the uniform of the 4th* SS-Polizei Panzergrenadier *Division.*

Replacement commander of Ausb. u. Ers. *Rgt. 14., and former member of the* 'Leibstandarte Adolf Hitler', SS-Obersturmbannführer *Carl Marks, seen here as a* SS-Untersturmführer.

SS-Obersturmbannführer *Franz Magill (commander* Div. Nachschubtruppen*), pictured here in an* Allgemeine-SS *uniform with the rank of* SS-Untersturmführer.

SS-Sturmbannführer *Friedrich Wittenmeyer, who variously commanded II/WGR-30, III/WGR-30,* Kampfgruppe *Wittenmeyer and temporarily WGR-31, in the uniform of the 4th* SS-Polizei Panzergrenadier *Division, facing camera in the centre, carrying binoculars.*

Commander of Fusilier Btl. 14, SS-Sturmbannführer *Karl Bristot, here as an* Untersturmführer *in the* Allgemeine-SS.

Commander of Pioneer Battalion SS-Sturmbannführer *Josef Remberger (right) and* Waffen-Untersturmführer *Dyhdalewysch, commander of 3rd Coy., Pioneer Btl. (left wearing a camouflage jacket), Neuhammer, April 1944.*

SS-Obersturmführer *Wilhelm Drapatz, commander,* SS-Feldgendarmerie Truppen *14, Slovakia, November 1944.*

Waffen-Hauptsturmführer *Michael Brygidyr, commander of I/ WGR 29, the only Ukrainian battalion commander of a combat unit. Although officially forbidden to do so, Brygider is seen hear wearing the SS runes instead of the lion device on his right collar patch.*

The Galician Division's highest decorated soldier, Waffen-Obersturmführer *Wolodymyr Kosak (promoted* Waffen-Hauptsturmführer, *1 May 1945), commander 1/I/WGR 29, pictured on 20 April 1945, after receiving the Iron Cross 1st Class for his bravery during the fighting at Gleichenberg. Other awards worn on his tunic include the Iron Cross 2nd Class, the* Infanterie-Sturmabzeichen *in Silber (Infantry Assault Badge in Silver) and the* Verwundetenabzeichen in Silber *(Wound Badge in Silver).*

Waffen-Obersturmführer *Stefan Hulak, commander, 3rd Company, Fusilier Battalion.*

Waffen-Obersturmführer *Roman Bojcun, commander, 4th Company, Fusilier Battalion, pictured here in the uniform of* Schützmannschaft *201.*

Commander, Galizischen SS-Freiwilligen *Regiment 4* Major der Schutzpolizei *Siegfried Binz.*

SS-Hauptsturmführer *Siegfried Assmuss, first commander of* Schützmannschaft Bataillon der SD Nr. *31 or the 'Volhynian Self-Defence Legion' This formation was incorporated into the Galician Division in March 1945.*

There has been, and remains, a great deal of confusion over the insignia worn on the uniforms of members of the Galician Division throughout its existence. This has come about as a direct consequence of German inconsistency, caused in part by shortages, local variations and simple ignorance of official instructions.

Kragenspiegel (Collar Patches)

Officially, uniforms for this division were to be those of the Waffen-SS, initially to be worn without the SS runes on the right collar patch and with SS rank insignia on the left collar patch. Notwithstanding this unequivocal instruction, photographic evidence shows that these criteria were not always stringently applied.

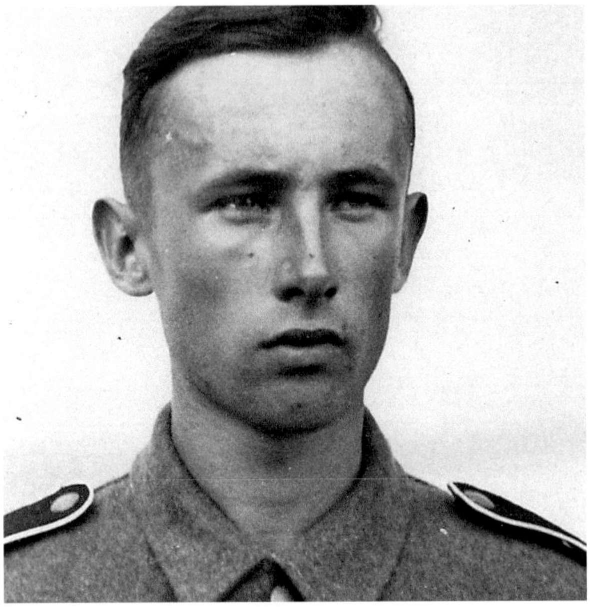

All recruits who joined the Galician Division received standard field grey Waffen-SS uniforms. Some were issued with tunics without any kind of collar patches, such as in this picture of recruit Roman Wysocky, taken at Heidelager on 20 August 1943.

*SS regulations clearly stipulated that members of 'non-Germanic' divisions should not have worn the SS runes on the right collar patch, however some groups of Ukrainians - such as the first contingent who were inducted at Brno - were issued uniforms with the SS lightning runes which they did not remove, and in some cases wore for many months, as shown in this picture of a group of Ukrainians from 3rd Company, SS-*Ausb.Btl.z.b.V., *Heidelager, summer 1943 - all wear SS lightning runes. Top row, left, is Jurij Holobrockyj.*

After a few months, as supplies became available, the blank patches were issued, as shown here in this picture of a recruit at Heidelager taken in the summer of 1943.

Finally, the blank patches, or those bearing the SS runes, were replaced with collar patches depicting the Galician lion. Two variations of the basic collar patches for other ranks are known to have existed. Waffen-Grenadier *Klymchuk, wearing the first pattern lion patch.*

Waffen-Grenadier *Sadiwskyj wearing the second variation.*

The officers' collar patch bearing the lion device was edged with aluminium silver thread, worn here by Waffen-Untersturmführer *Liashevych.*

A portrait shot of Standertenjunker *Marian Ciolko taken in October 1944, showing the lion patch being worn in the correct manner.*

Another Waffen-Untersturmführer *wearing the collar patch worn upside down.*

In some cases recruits received all three patches, as demonstrated by this series of three pictures showing the same individual wearing all three variations. This individual is seen here wearing first the blank collar patches, then the SS lightning runes and finally the second pattern lion device.

Finally, a collar patch bearing the Ukrainian National symbol of the trident was authorised when the Division became the '1st Division of the Ukrainian National Army'. It appears that only the officers' version with the piping of silver thread was actually manufactured in very limited quantities, and is known to have been worn by some officers, including Waffen-Sturmbannführer *Evhen Pobihushtschyi. All four examples of the collar patch from the author's collection. Top left: Second pattern lion device; top right, Trident officer's patch; bottom left, officer's lion device; bottom right, first pattern lion device.*

The Divisional armshield depicting a rampant lion with three crowns existed in several variations. Here Waffenjunker *Lutciw wears the first pattern together with a privately jewelled silver ring bearing the Death's Head emblem, which the author has in his collection.*

A group of five Ukrainian NCOs. Centre, Waffen-Oberscharführer *Zenon Goiiv. The fourth and fifth men from the left wear the second BEVO pattern armshield.*

Waffen-Untersturmführer *Lutciw, wearing the third example, with a black border*

A portrait of Waffen-Standartenjunker *Ciolko in full uniform.*

Three versions of the Divisional armshield from the author's collection.

Trident Cap Badges

The round version was rarer.

Two examples of trident badges issued to personnel serving with the Division. The first, oval, example was more common.

A portrait of Petro Melnyk taken in British captivity at the POW enclave at Rimini shows the original lion collar patch worn in conjunction with the trident cap badge of the 1st Division of the Ukrainian National Army. The belt buckle is of Slovak origin and was obtained during the Division's stay in that country.

Two stamps issued by the Military Board in L'viv in 1943, designed by artist Sviatoslav Hordynsky, and sold to raise funds for the Galician Division.

Affiliated Polizei Units

From its very inception – but especially in the final months of the war – former members of various Schützmannschaft *and* Werkschutz *battalions enlisted in the Division. A young Ukrainian serving with a* Schützmannschaft *unit, who later went on to join the Galician Division.* Schuma *uniforms were often a mixture of surplus pre-war black* Allgemeine-SS *parade uniforms with light blue collar facings and cuffs added. This picture was taken on 20 May 1944.*

Another individual wearing Schuma uniform and insignia, who also enlisted into the Galician Division.

Two young Ukrainians pictured on 5 August 1944, prior to joining the Galician Division, wearing Werkschutz *uniforms. These battalions generally guarded factories and industrial plants.*

Major *Nykolyn, chief of Ukrainian police in Berczany after his release from Schützmannschaft 204. His uniform incorporated a trident cap badge. Nykolyn and Jaroslav Poterejko were the two Ukrainian originators of* Schützmannschaft *Btl. 204.*

A group from Schützmannschaft *204 in Kazimierza Wielka, Poland, shortly before the unit was dissolved in June 1944. From left: Merlin (German), Bezchlibnyj, Swyrydenko, Harkawenko, Mykolayenko, Kowalenko,* Leutnant *Zuk, Woronowskyj, Charchenko, Horodyskyj; kneeling: Washchenko, Demyk.*

April 1944 at Heidelager – Feldwebel *Parolish in the uniform of* Schützmannschafts-Batl. *204.*

Group from Schützmannschafts-Btl. *204. pose with a machine gun. From top left: Dutcha, Yarworskyj, Horodyskyj, Solomka, Klym, Kushyk, Kachmaryk, Tchervinskyj Baran, Struk. April/May 1944, Heidelager.*

Obverse of the Führerschein *and* Soldbuch *issued to Petro Maslij.*

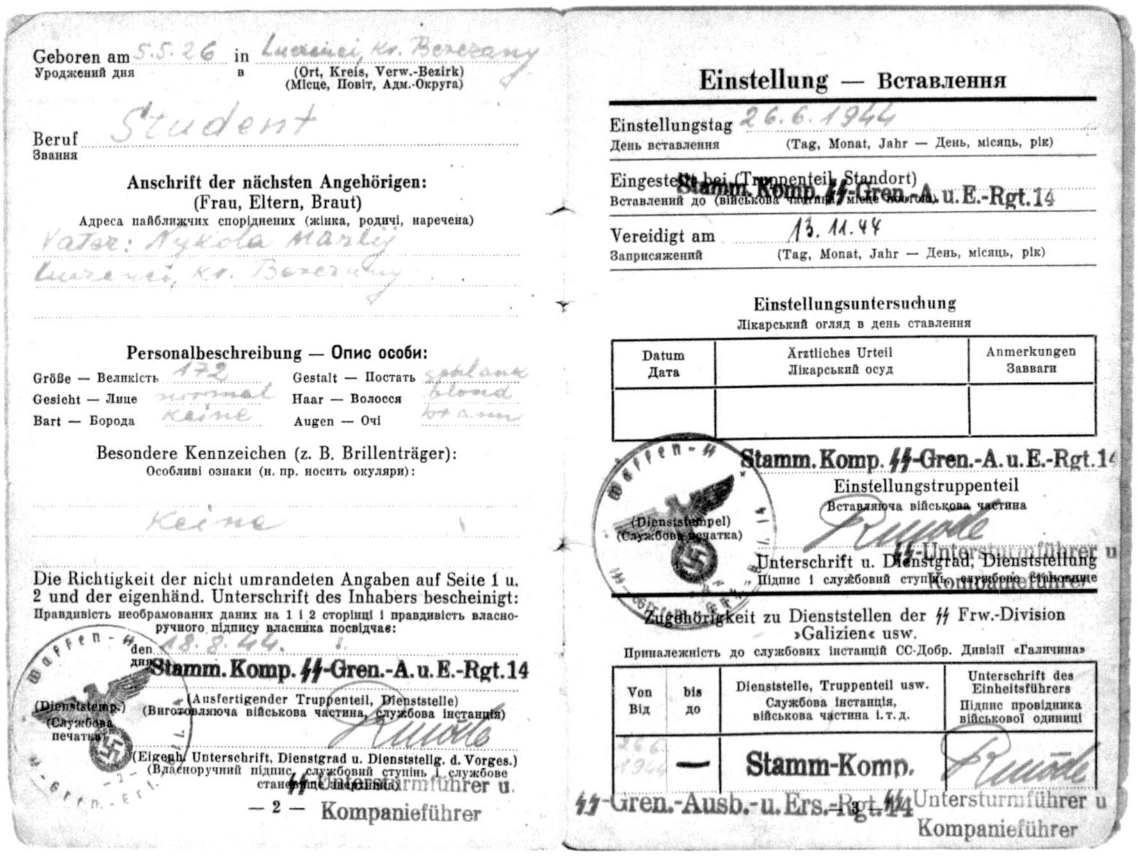

Pages 2-3 of Soldbuch *of Petro Maslij, showing personal and physical details including occupation, place and date of birth, height and hair colour.*

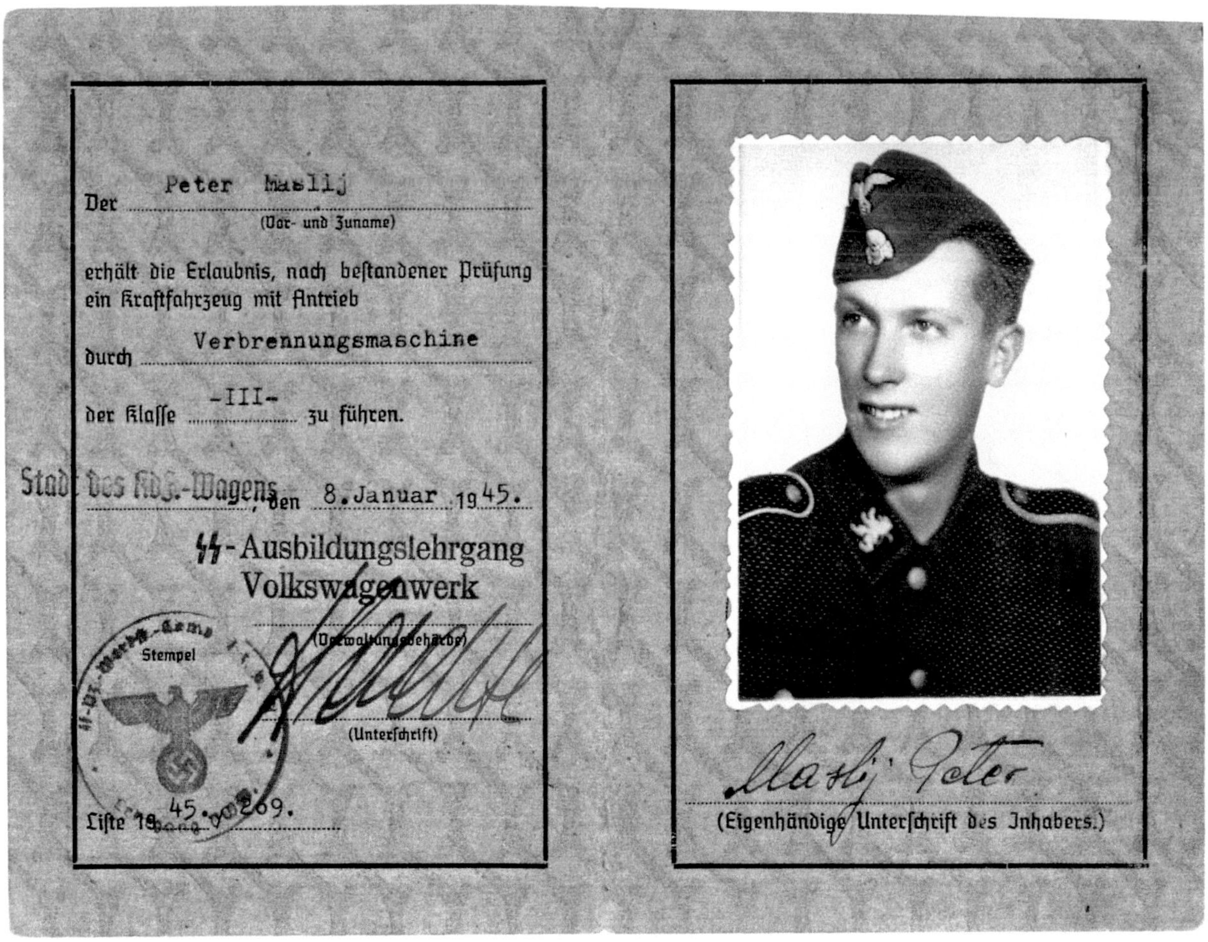

Der Peter Maslij
(Vor- und Zuname)

erhält die Erlaubnis, nach bestandener Prüfung
ein Kraftfahrzeug mit Antrieb

durch Verbrennungsmaschine

der Klasse -III- zu führen.

Stadt des KdF.-Wagens, den 8. Januar 1945.

SS-Ausbildungslehrgang
Volkswagenwerk
(Verwaltungsbehörde)

Stempel

(Unterschrift)

Liste 1945. 269.

Maslij Peter
(Eigenhändige Unterschrift des Inhabers.)

Reverse of Führerschein *issued to Petro Maslij. The photograph has been unofficially attached by the owner and consequently lacks the validation stamps on the top left and bottom right.*

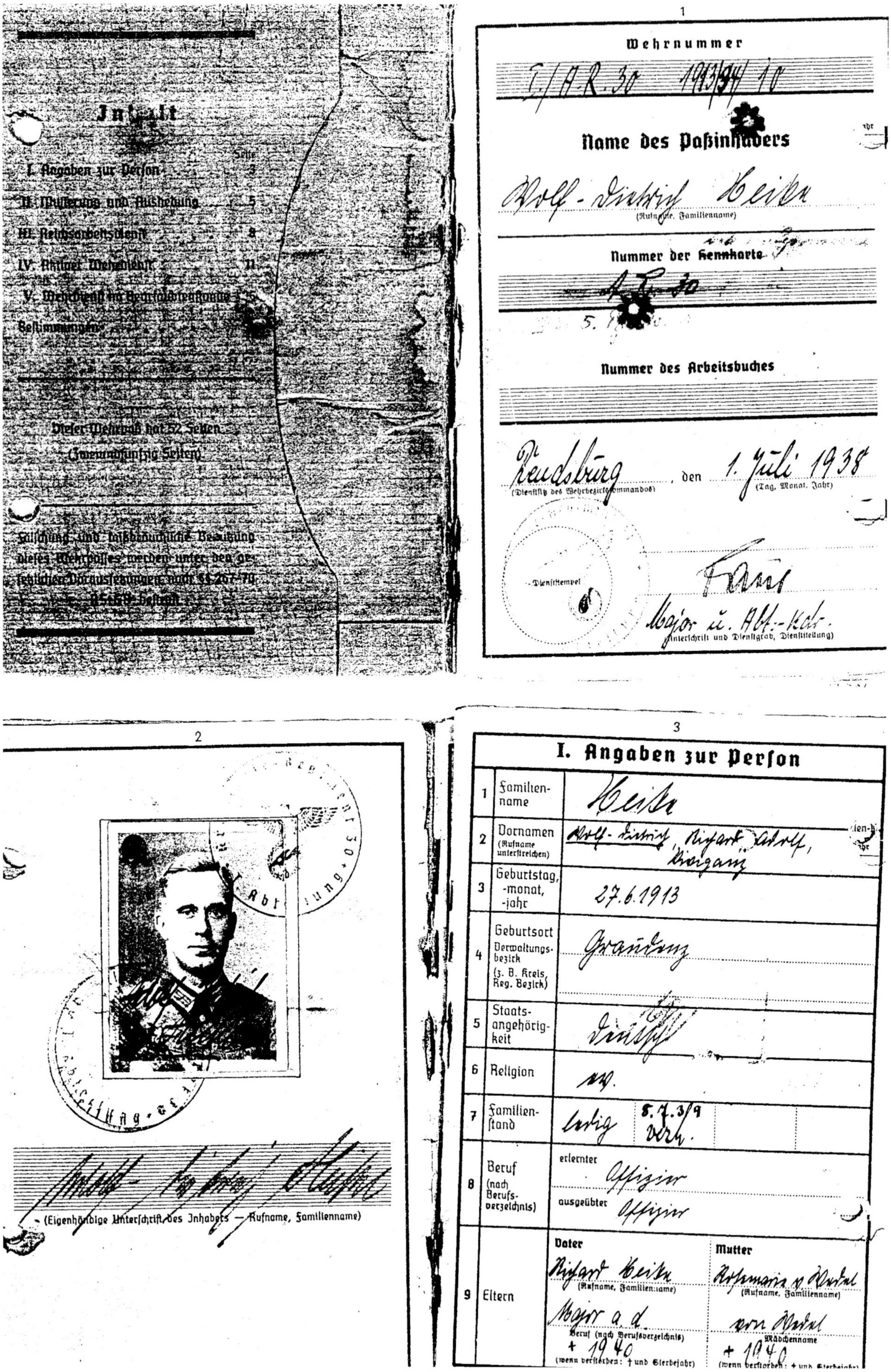

Inhalt

Dieser Wehrpaß hat 52 Seiten (Zweiundfünfzig Seiten)

Fälschung und mißbräuchliche Benutzung dieses Wehrpasses werden unter den gesetzlichen Voraussetzungen nach §§ 267–70 ... bestraft.

1

Wehrnummer

Name des Paßinhabers

Wolf-Dietrich Heike

(Rufname, Familienname)

Nummer der Kennkarte

Nummer des Arbeitsbuches

Rendsburg, den 1. Juli 1938

(Dienstsitz des Wehrbezirkskommandos) (Tag, Monat, Jahr)

Dienststempel

Major u. Abt.-Kdr.

(Unterschrift und Dienstgrad, Dienststellung)

2

(Eigenhändige Unterschrift des Inhabers — Rufname, Familienname)

3

I. Angaben zur Person

1	Familienname	Heike
2	Vornamen (Rufname unterstreichen)	Wolf-Dietrich, Richard, Adolf
3	Geburtstag, -monat, -jahr	27.6.1913
4	Geburtsort, Verwaltungsbezirk (z. B. Kreis, Reg. Bezirk)	Graudenz
5	Staatsangehörigkeit	Deutsch
6	Religion	ev.
7	Familienstand	ledig; 8.7.39 verh.
8	Beruf (nach Berufsverzeichnis)	erlernter: Offizier; ausgeübter: Offizier
9	Eltern	Vater: Richard Heike (Rufname, Familienname); Major a.D. (Beruf (nach Berufsverzeichnis)); + 1940 (wenn verstorben: † und Sterbejahr). Mutter: (Rufname, Familienname); von Wedel (Mädchenname); + 1940 (wenn verstorben: † und Sterbejahr)

Extracts of Soldbuch *of W.D.Heike, the Division's Ia. Pages 1, 2 and 3 give personal details, pages 12, 13, 22 and 23 provide details of active service, and awards and decorations.*

12

noch **IV. Aktiver**

Zugehörigkeit zu Dienststellen des Heeres

von	bis	Dienststelle (Truppenteil usw.)	Stammrollen-Nr. Ranglisten-Nr.
4.4.34	15.1.36	2. (Preuß.) A. R. Schwerin	
16.1.36	5.10.36	A. R. 20, Itzehoe	
6.10.36	9.11.38	I./A. R. 30 Rendsburg	
10.11.38	31.3.39	II./A. R. 66 Lübeck.	
1.4.39.	10.12.40.	2./A. R. 30, Flensburg	10.
19 10.12. 1940	16/8.41	4./A. R. 120	Kr. 3
17/8.41.	31.8.42	Stab/110. Inf. Div.	25
1.9.42	18.10.1942	Stab/5. Pz. Div. (im Rahmen der Gen. Stabsausbildung zur Abt. Ic kdrt.)	
1.9.1942	14.3.1943	Führer-Res. OKH	
15.3.1943	24.6.1943	**Kriegsakademie**	556
25.6.1943	6.XI.43	Stab 122. Inf. Div. (Ib)	80
1.12.43	31.12.43	Führer. Res. OKH (Dienst regelt PA/P3)	

13

Wehrdienst

oder der Luftwaffe (auch im Kriege)

von	bis	Dienststelle (Truppenteil usw.)	Stammrollen-Nr. Ranglisten-Nr.
1.1.44	1.6.44	14. Geb. Div. (Ia)	
1.6.44	1.1.45	z. b. V. OKH, Gen St. d. H.	
1.1.45		Führer-Reserve OKH (Dienst regelt PA/P3)	

22

noch **IV. Aktiver**

Beförderungen und Ernennungen*)

Mit Wirkung vom	Befördert oder ernannt zum
1.10.34	Gefreiten befördert,
1.12.34	Unteroffizier befördert,
1.6.35	Fähnrich befördert,
1.10.35	Oberfähnrich befördert,
1.4.36	Leutnant befördert,
23 6.10.36	Führer des Nachr.-Zuges I./A. R. 30 ernannt
12.10.37	Abt.-Adjutanten ernannt.
1.3.39	Oblt. befördert (113)
1.2.42	Hauptmann (645)
	gem. Verfg. OKH 2529/42 PA/Ag P1/Ref. 11 v. 20.4.42.
	neues R.D.A.: 1.7.41. (44a)
	gem. Verfg. OKH 510/43 PA/Ag Chef-Abt. I Gru II/Ref. 11 neues R.D.A. 1.7.40 (44c)

*) Bestätigung der Beförderungen und Ernennungen nach Abschluß der aktiven Dienstzeit durch den Entlassungstruppenteil usw. mit Dienststelle, Unterschrift, Dienstgrad, Dienststellung und Dienststempel.

23

Wehrdienst

Beförderungen und Ernennungen*)

Mit Wirkung vom	Befördert oder ernannt zum
1.8.43	Major gem. H.PA/P3 Nr. 1937/43 g v. 3.9.43 R.D.A. 1.8.43/25a

noch 23

Orden und Ehrenzeichen*)

D.A. IV. Klasse am 1.4.38

24 E. K. 2. (4.11.39)

Sudetenmedaille 20.2.40

E.K. I. 6.11.40.

[illegible] Fah. S. 38

*) Bestätigung der Beförderungen, Ernennungen und Verleihungen nach Abschluß der aktiven Dienstzeit durch den Entlassungstruppenteil usw. mit Dienststelle, Unterschrift, Dienstgrad, Dienststellung und Dienststempel.

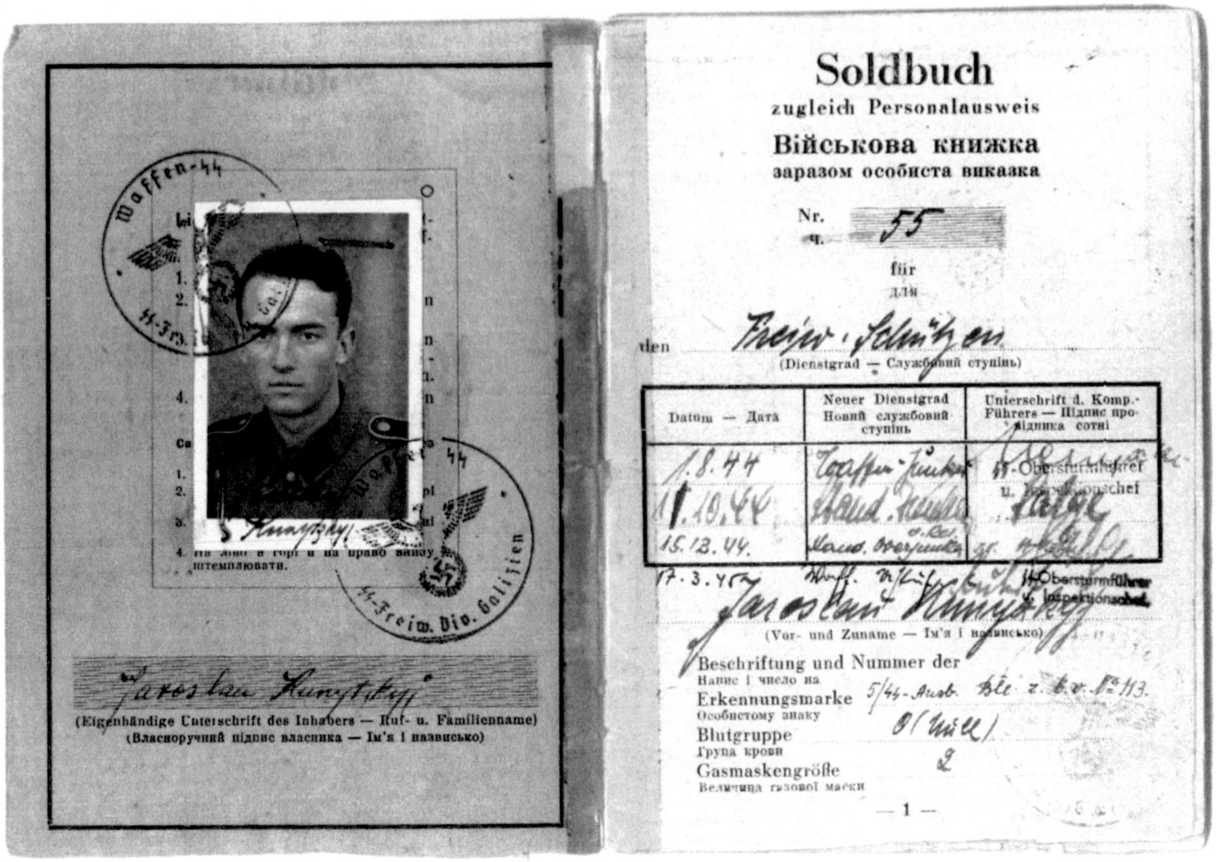

Inside cover and page 1 of Soldbuch *issued to Jaroslav Kunyskyj.*

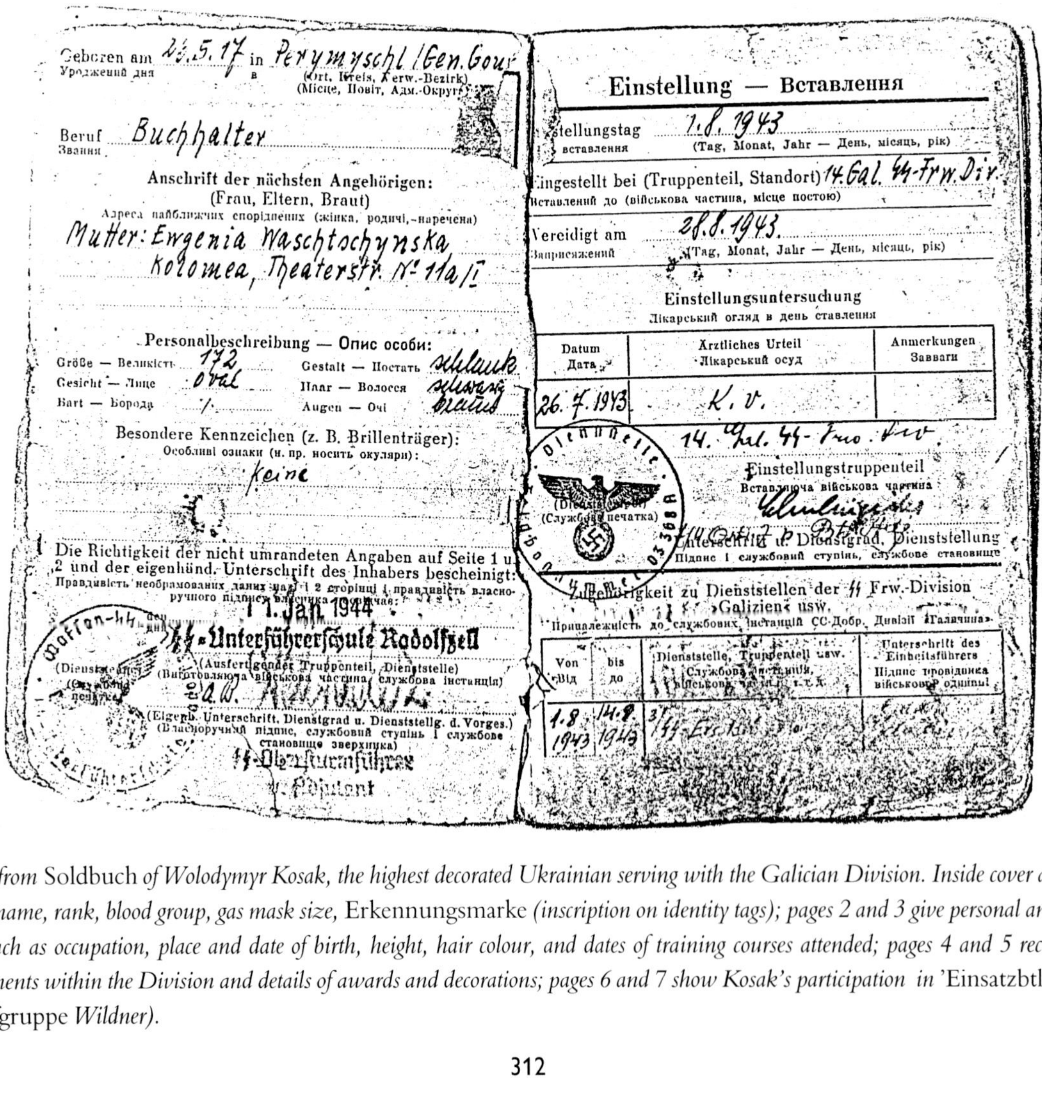

Extracts from Soldbuch *of Wolodymyr Kosak, the highest decorated Ukrainian serving with the Galician Division. Inside cover and page 1 give full name, rank, blood group, gas mask size,* Erkennungsmarke *(inscription on identity tags); pages 2 and 3 give personal and physical details such as occupation, place and date of birth, height, hair colour, and dates of training courses attended; pages 4 and 5 record service appointments within the Division and details of awards and decorations; pages 6 and 7 show Kosak's participation in* 'Einsatzbtl. *Wildner' (*Kampfgruppe *Wildner).*

Soldbuch
zugleich Personalausweis
Військова книжка
заразом особиста виказка

Nr. 1 891

für
для

Freiw.-SS-Obersturmführer
(Dienstgrad — Службовий ступінь)

Datum — Дата	Neuer Dienstgrad Новий службовий ступінь	Unterschrift d. Komp.-Führers — Підпис провідника сотні
1.5.1945	SS-Hauptsturmführer	[illegible] SS-Stubaf

Wolodymyr Kosak
(Vor- und Zuname — Ім'я і назвисько)

Beschriftung und Nummer der Erkennungsmarke — Напис і число на особистому знаку
Blutgruppe — Група крови
Gasmaskengröße 2 — Величина газової маски

Lichtbild 37×52 mm, Brustbild ohne Kopf-[bedeckung]

(Eigenhändige Unterschrift des Inhabers — Ruf- u. Familienname)
(Власноручний підпис власника — Ім'я і назвисько)

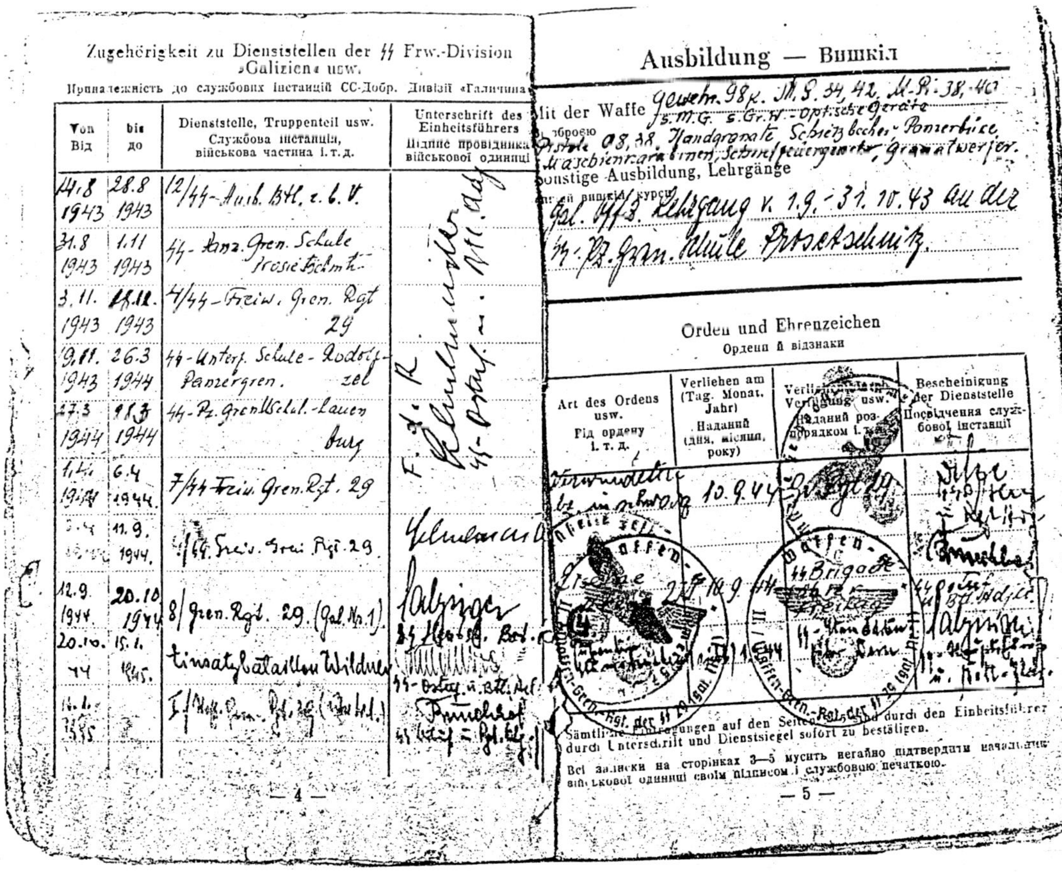

Zugehörigkeit zu Dienststellen der SS Frw.-Division »Galizien« usw.
Приналежність до службових інстанцій СС-Добр. Дивізії «Галичина»

Von Від	bis до	Dienststelle, Truppenteil usw. Службова інстанція, військова частина і. т. д.	Unterschrift des Einheitsführers Підпис провідника військової одиниці
14.8 1943	28.8 1943	12/SS-Ausb. Btl. z. b. V.	
31.8 1943	1.11 1943	SS-Panz. Gren. Schule Kiensche-Böhmen	
3.11. 1943	18.11. 1943	4/SS-Freiw. Gren. Rgt. 29	
19.11. 1943	26.3 1944	SS-Unterf. Schule Radolfzell Panzergren.	
27.3 1944	11.3 1944	SS-Pz. Gren. Schl. Lauenburg	
1.4. 1944	6.4 1944	7/SS-Freiw. Gren. Rgt. 29	
	11.9. 1944	[illegible] Gren. Rgt. 29	
12.9. 1944	20.10 1944	8/ Gren. Rgt. 29 (Gal. Nr. 1)	
20.10. 44	15.1. 1945	Einsatzbataillon Wildner	
16.1. 1945		I/ Waff. Gren. Rgt. 29	

— 4 —

Ausbildung — Вишкіл

Mit der Waffe — зброєю: Gewehr 98k, M.G. 34, 42, M.P. 38, 40, s.M.G., s.Gr.W., optische Geräte, Pistole 08, 38, Handgranate, Schießbecher, Panzerbüchse, Maschinenkarabiner, Schnellfeuergewehr, Granatwerfer.

Sonstige Ausbildung, Lehrgänge — Інший вишкіл, курси: Gal. SS Lehrgang v. 1.9.–31.10.43 an der SS-Pz. Gren. Schule Kienschlag

Orden und Ehrenzeichen
Ордени й відзнаки

Art des Ordens usw. Рід ордену і. т. д.	Verliehen am (Tag, Monat, Jahr) Наданий (дня, місяця, року)	Verliehen durch Verfügung usw. Наданий розпорядком і. т. д.	Bescheinigung der Dienststelle Посвідчення службової інстанції
Verwundeten-abzeichen in schwarz	10.9.44	[illegible]	[illegible]

Sämtliche Eintragungen auf den Seiten 3–5 sind durch den Einheitsführer durch Unterschrift und Dienstsiegel sofort zu bestätigen.
Всі записки на сторінках 3—5 мусить негайно підтвердити начальник військової одиниці своїм підписом і службовою печаткою.

— 5 —

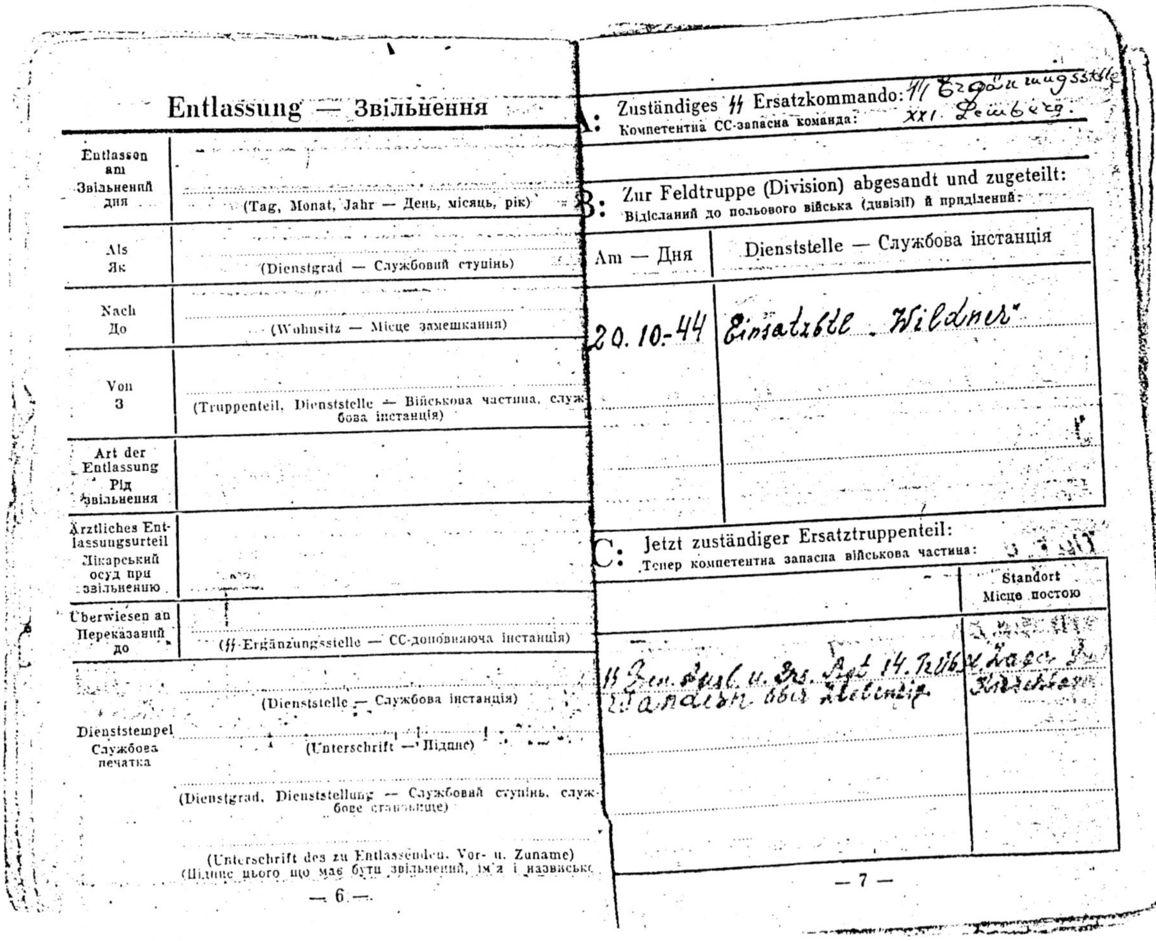

Entlassung — Звільнення

Entlassen am Звільнений дня	(Tag, Monat, Jahr — День, місяць, рік)
Als Як	(Dienstgrad — Службовий ступінь)
Nach До	(Wohnsitz — Місце замешкання)
Von З	(Truppenteil, Dienststelle — Військова частина, службова інстанція)
Art der Entlassung Рід звільнення	
Ärztliches Entlassungsurteil Лікарський осуд при звільненню	
Überwiesen an Переказаний до	(ϟϟ-Ergänzungsstelle — СС-доповнююча інстанція)
	(Dienststelle — Службова інстанція)
Dienststempel Службова печатка	(Unterschrift — Підпис)
	(Dienstgrad, Dienststellung — Службовий ступінь, службове становище)
	(Unterschrift des zu Entlassenden. Vor- u. Zuname) (Підпис цього що має бути звільнений, ім'я і назвисько)

— 6 —

A: Zuständiges ϟϟ Ersatzkommando: ϟϟ Ergänzungsstelle XXI. Lemberg.
Компетентна СС-запасна команда:

B: Zur Feldtruppe (Division) abgesandt und zugeteilt:
Відісланий до польового війська (дивізії) й приділений:

Am — Дня	Dienststelle — Службова інстанція
20.10.44	Einsatzstelle „Wildner"

C: Jetzt zuständiger Ersatztruppenteil:
Тепер компетентна запасна військова частина:

	Standort Місце постою
ϟϟ Gren. Ausb. u. Ers. Rgt. 14. Gal. Div. Ersatzkp. über Lebensly. [illegible]	Lager [illegible]

— 7 —

Dienstausweis *and extract of* Polizei Dienstpass *belonging to* Oberwachtmeister *Willi Bock, formerly a member of 4th Gal. Rgt. (16.11.43-22.5.44) and from 23.5.44 until 9.5.45,* Aus. u Ers. *Reg. 14, giving service details.*

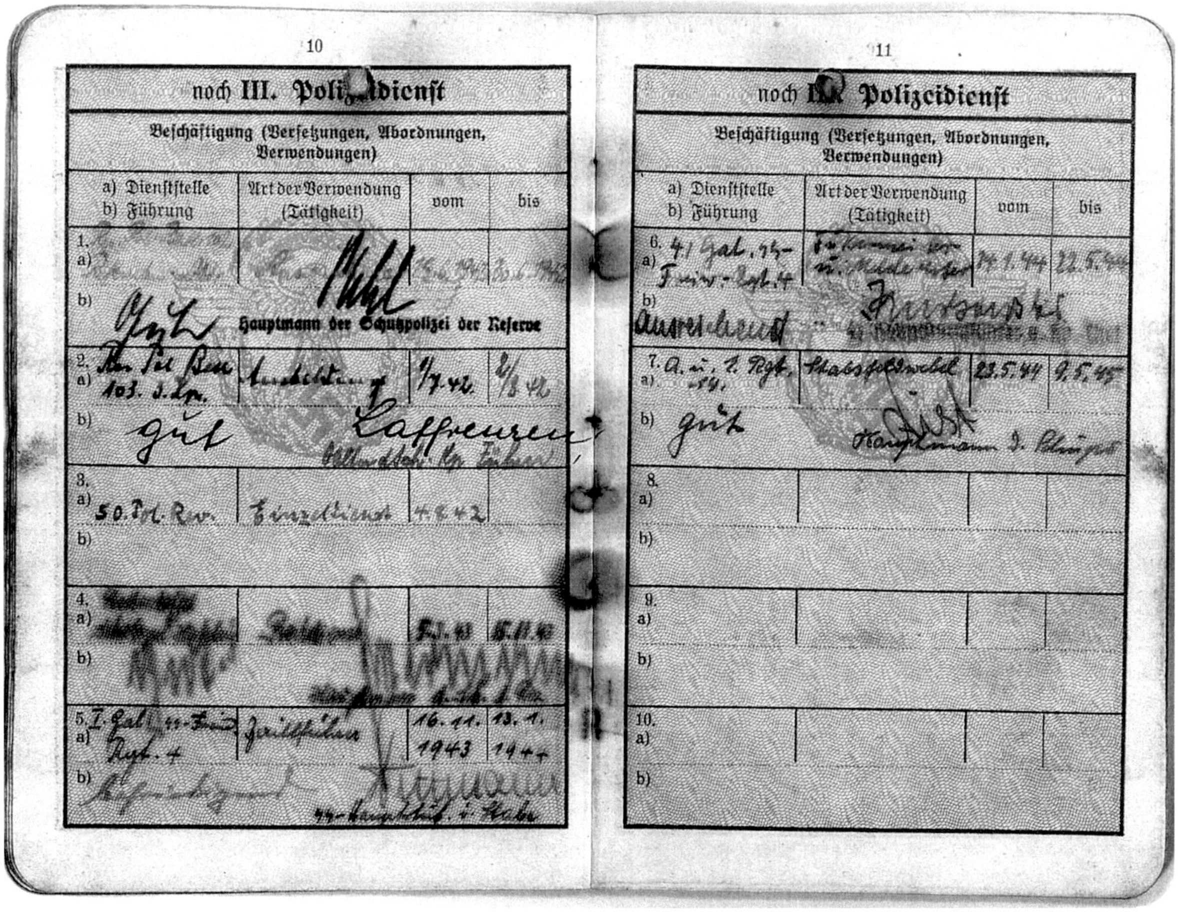

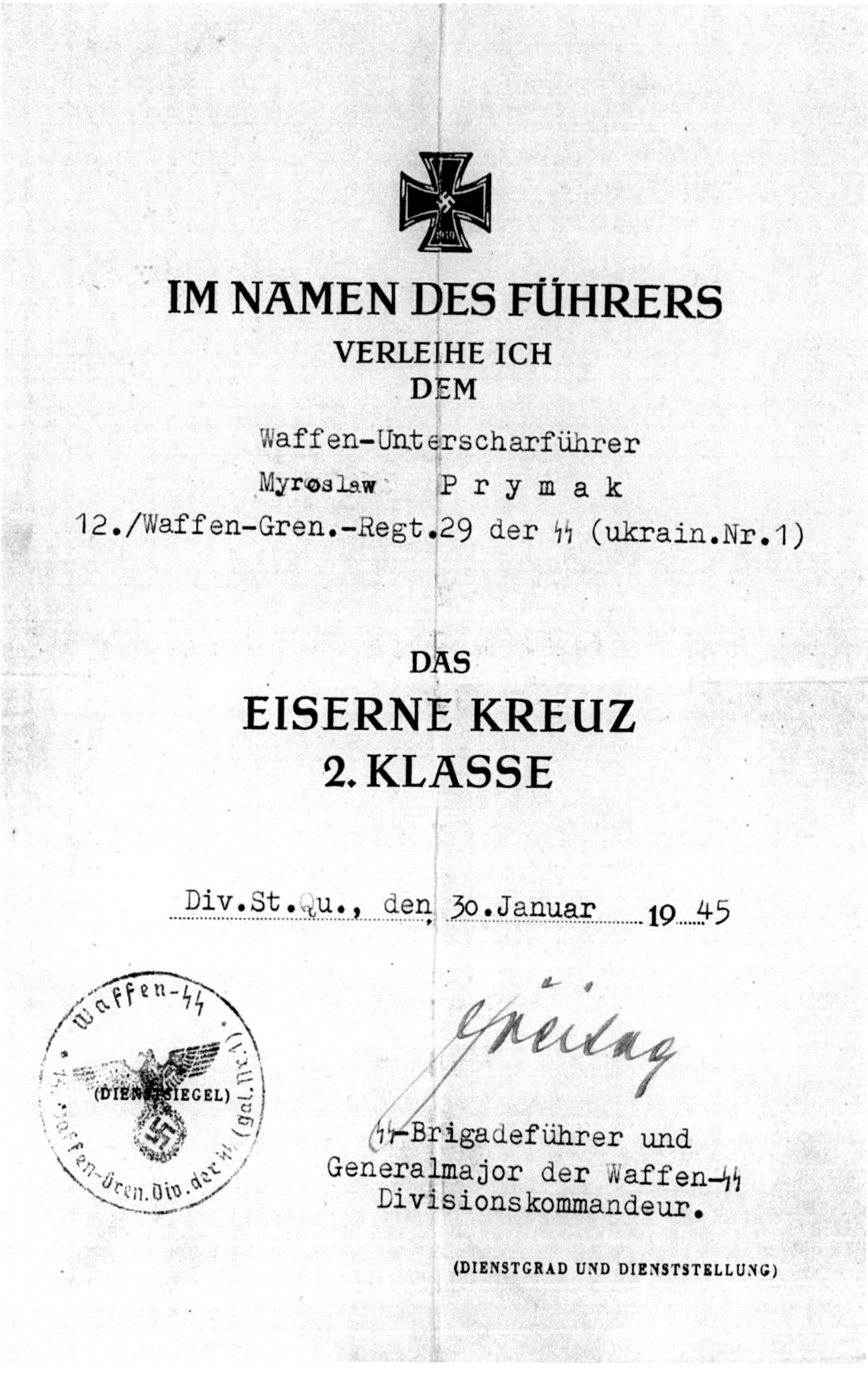

IM NAMEN DES FÜHRERS

VERLEIHE ICH

DEM

Waffen-Unterscharführer

Myroslaw Prymak

12./Waffen-Gren.-Regt.29 der SS (ukrain.Nr.1)

DAS

EISERNE KREUZ

2. KLASSE

Div.St.Qu., den 30.Januar 1945

SS-Brigadeführer und
Generalmajor der Waffen-SS
Divisionskommandeur.

(DIENSTGRAD UND DIENSTSTELLUNG)

*Citation for the Iron Cross 2nd Class awarded to Myroslaw Prymak of 11./Waffen-Gren.-Rgt. 29 der SS (*ukrain. *Nr. 1).*

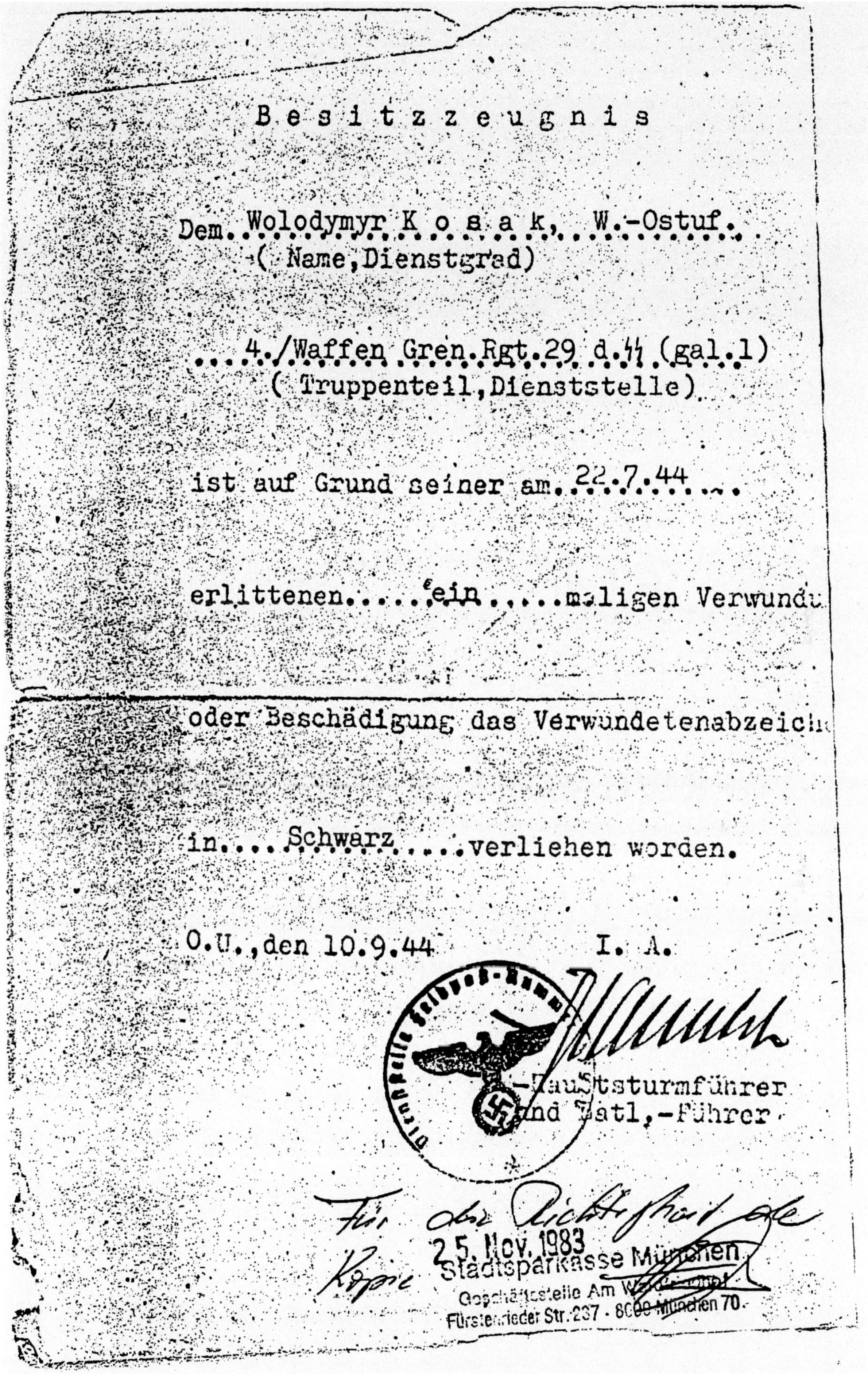

Besitzzeugnis

Dem. Wolodymyr Kosak, W.-Ostuf.
(Name, Dienstgrad)

4./Waffen Gren.Rgt.29 d.SS (gal.1)
(Truppenteil, Dienststelle)

ist auf Grund seiner am 22.7.44

erlittenen ein maligen Verwundu

oder Beschädigung das Verwundetenabzeich

in Schwarz verliehen worden.

O.U., den 10.9.44

I. A.

-Hauptsturmführer
und Batl.-Führer

Für die Richtigkeit der Kopie

25. Nov. 1983
Stadtsparkasse München
Geschäftsstelle Am W...
Fürstenrieder Str. 237 · 8000 München 70

Copies of Wolodymyr Kosak's citations for the Black Wound Badge

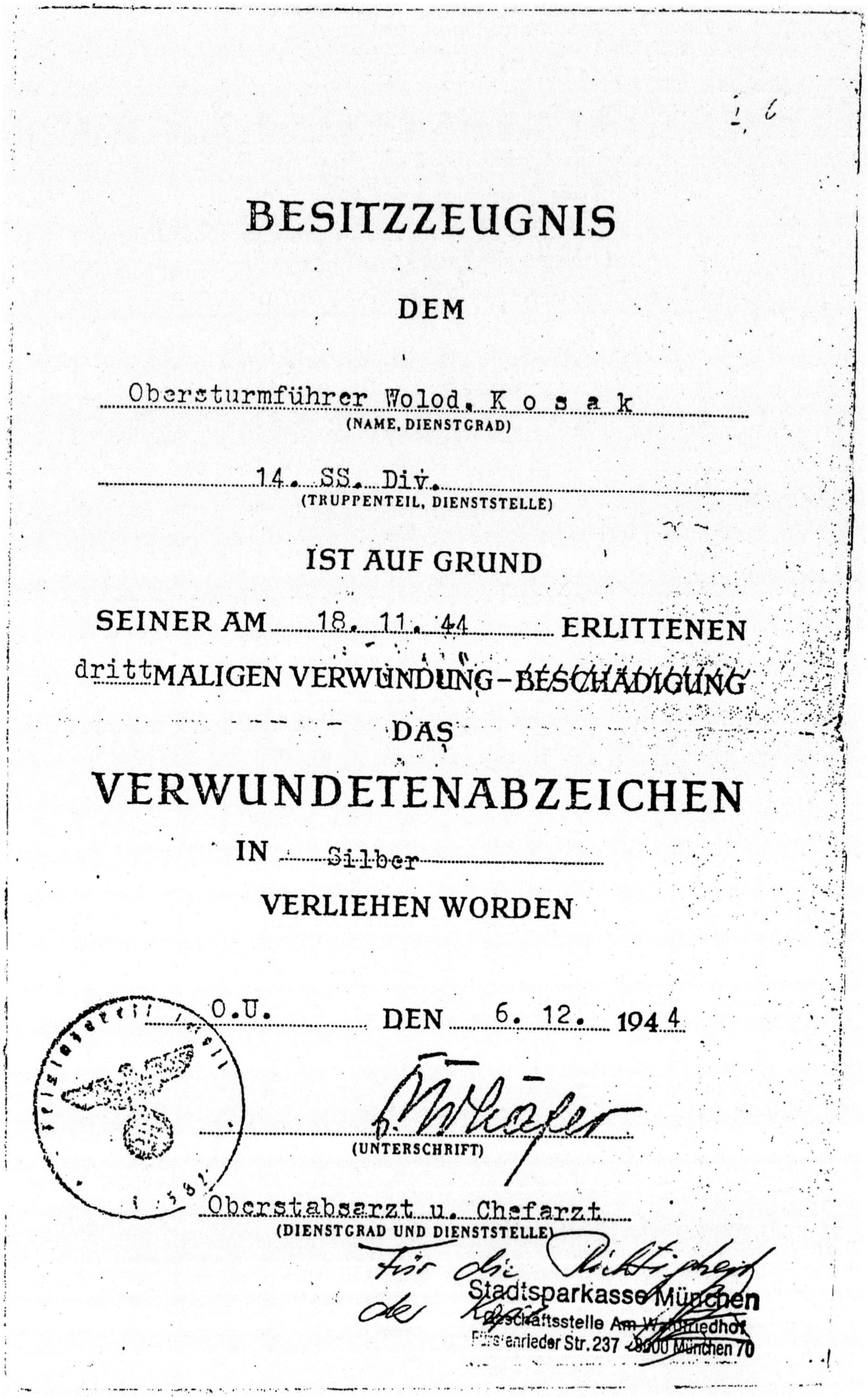

BESITZZEUGNIS

DEM

Obersturmführer Wolod. K o s a k
(NAME, DIENSTGRAD)

14. SS. Div.
(TRUPPENTEIL, DIENSTSTELLE)

IST AUF GRUND

SEINER AM 18. 11. 44 ERLITTENEN

drittMALIGEN VERWUNDUNG – ~~BESCHÄDIGUNG~~

DAS

VERWUNDETENABZEICHEN

IN Silber

VERLIEHEN WORDEN

O.U. DEN 6. 12. 1944

(UNTERSCHRIFT)

Oberstabsarzt u. Chefarzt
(DIENSTGRAD UND DIENSTSTELLE)

Stadtsparkasse München
Geschäftsstelle Am Waldfriedhof
Fürstenrieder Str. 237 8000 München 70

Silver Wound Badge

BESITZZEUGNIS

DEM W-Obersturmführer
(DIENSTGRAD)

Wolodymyr K o s a k
(VOR. UND ZUNAME)

4./Waffen Gren.Rgt.d.ᛋᛋ Nr.29 (gal.1)
(TRUPPENTEIL)

VERLEIHE ICH DAS

INFANTERIE-STURMABZEICHEN

IN SILBER

O.U. den 1.September 1944
(ORT UND DATUM)

(UNTERSCHRIFT)

Waffen-ᛋᛋ
(STEMPEL)
ᛋᛋ-Frw. Gren. Rgt. 29

ᛋᛋ-Standartenführer u.Rgt.-Kdr.
(DIENSTGRAD UND DIENSTSTELLUNG)

Für die Richtigkeit
der Kopie

Stadtsparkasse München
Geschäftsstelle Am Waldfriedhof
Fürstenrieder Str. 237 · 8000 München 70

25. Nov. 1983

Silver Infantry Assault Badge

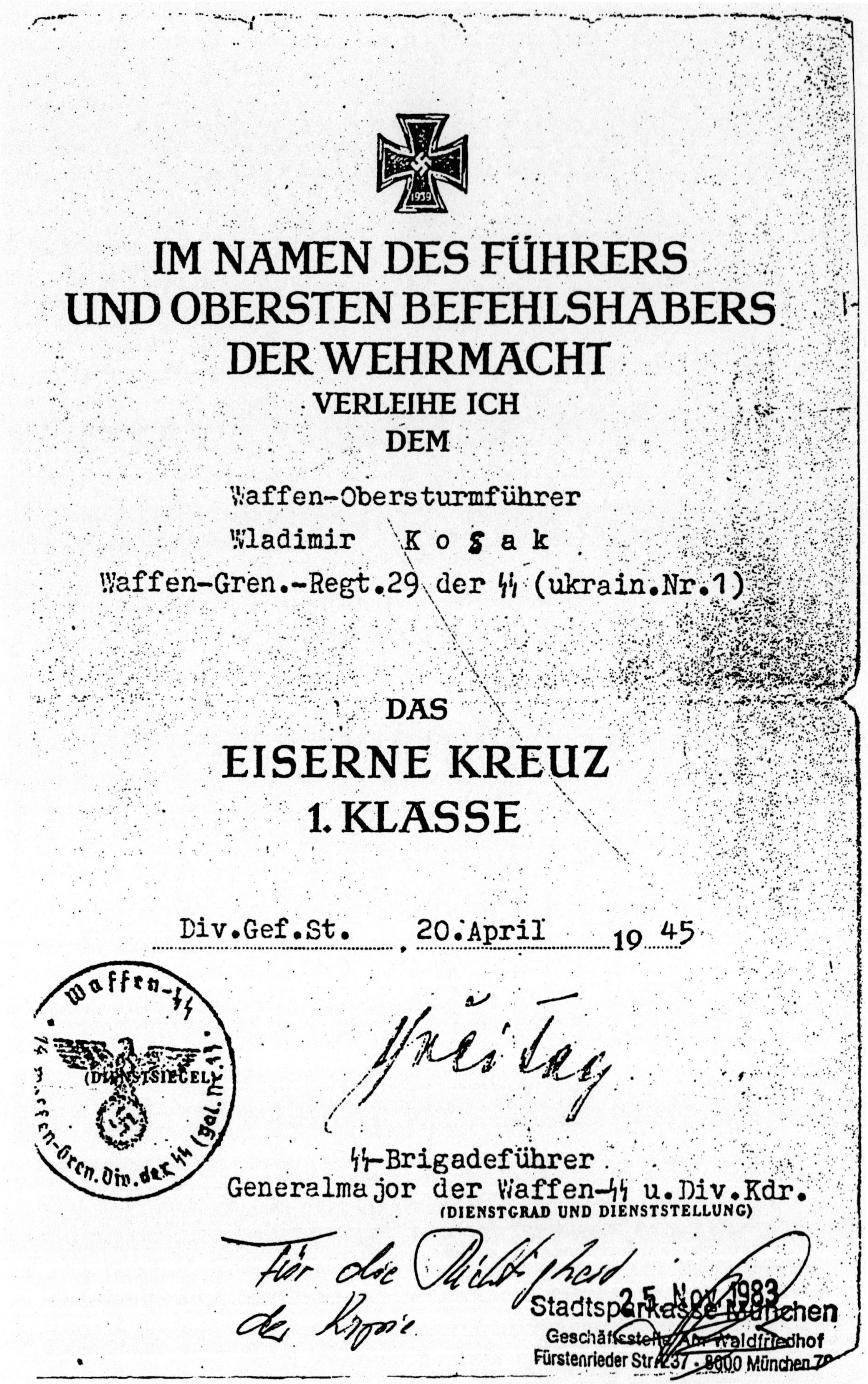

IM NAMEN DES FÜHRERS
UND OBERSTEN BEFEHLSHABERS
DER WEHRMACHT
VERLEIHE ICH
DEM

Waffen-Obersturmführer
Wladimir Kosak
Waffen-Gren.-Regt.29 der SS (ukrain.Nr.1)

DAS
EISERNE KREUZ
1. KLASSE

Div.Gef.St., 20. April 1945

Waffen-SS
(DIENSTSIEGEL)
14 Waffen-Gren.Div.der SS (gal.Nr.1)

Freitag

SS-Brigadeführer
Generalmajor der Waffen-SS u.Div.Kdr.
(DIENSTGRAD UND DIENSTSTELLUNG)

Für die Richtigkeit der Kopie

25 Nov 1983
Stadtsparkasse München
Geschäftsstelle Am Waldfriedhof
Fürstenrieder Str. 237 · 8000 München 70

Iron Cross 1st Class

SS- u. WAFFEN-JUNKERSCHULE
BRAUNSCHWEIG
(POSEN-TRESKAU)

An den

SS-Frw.- Grenadier

L u t z i w , Wolodymyr

geboren: 3. Januar 1923

Ich befördere Sie mit Wirkung vom 1. August 1944

zum

WAFFEN-JUNKER

z. Z. Posen-Treskau, den 15. August 1944

Waffen-SS Junkerschule Braunschweig

DER KOMMANDEUR
DER SS- u. WAFFEN-JUNKERSCHULE
BRAUNSCHWEIG

SS-Brigadeführer u.
Generalmajor der Waffen-SS

Group of three promotion certificates for Wolodymyr Lutziw for: Waffen-Junker

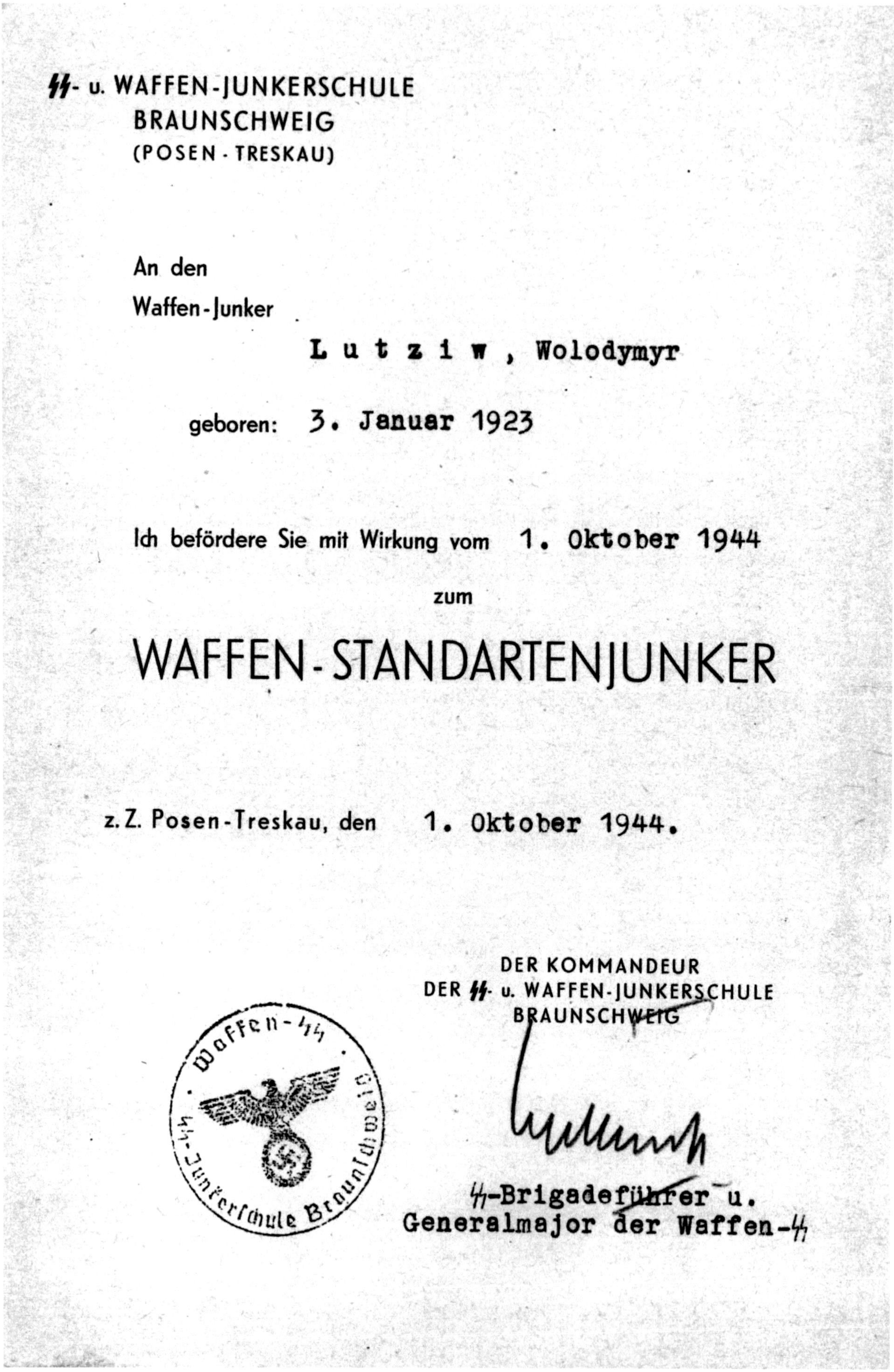

SS- u. WAFFEN-JUNKERSCHULE
BRAUNSCHWEIG
(POSEN - TRESKAU)

An den
Waffen-Junker

L u t z i w , Wolodymyr

geboren: 3. Januar 1923

Ich befördere Sie mit Wirkung vom 1. Oktober 1944

zum

WAFFEN-STANDARTENJUNKER

z. Z. Posen-Treskau, den 1. Oktober 1944.

DER KOMMANDEUR
DER SS- u. WAFFEN-JUNKERSCHULE
BRAUNSCHWEIG

SS-Brigadeführer u.
Generalmajor der Waffen-SS

Waffen-Standartenjunker

SS-Führungshauptamt
Der Chef des Amtes XI

An den

Standartenjunker d. Res. der Waffen-SS
L u t z i w , Wolodymyr

SS-Nr. -.- Geb. 3.1.1923

Ich befördere Sie mit Wirkung vom 15.12.1944
zum

Standartenoberjunker d. Res. der Waffen-SS

Berlin, 10.12.1944

SS-Brigadeführer
und Generalmajor der Waffen-SS

SS-FHA/XI/I/67/Gl.

Standartenoberjunker d. Res. der Waffen-SS

Appendix I

Guidelines for Speakers in the Recruiting Commissions 28 April 1943

From the Archives of the Brotherhood of Former Combatants.
28 April 43
Lemberg
Generalgouvernement
Governor of the District of Galicia, Tgb.104\43g
Secret !

Kreishauptmann or representative 2 copies
Stadthauptmann Lemberg or representative 2 copies
Land- und Stadtkommissare or representative 1 copy
Kommandeur der Sicherheitspolizei und des S.D 30 copies

Re: Guidelines for Speakers in the Recruiting Commissions

You will find enclosed some guidelines for the speakers in the recruiting commissions of the *SS-Schützen-Division Galicia*. They have also been sent to the *Wehrausschuss* and its agents in the districts and regions.

I would ask you to look on these guidelines as a rough idea of what I consider a suitable argument, at present, when canvassing for recruits. It is left to the speakers themselves, of course, to work out their speeches in detail, but the essential points of the guidelines are to be respected.

I wish to make the following points:

- Statements that suggest any kind of brotherhood between Germans and Ukrainians are to be avoided.
- The impression is likewise to be avoided that we are dependant on the help of the Ukrainians.
- The Ukrainians are not to be addressed as allies. All that should be said is that they will be treated in the same way as German soldiers.
- Neither a positive nor a negative response should be given to the wish of the Galician Ukrainians for an independent state, or to aspirations for a Greater Ukrainian state. Should the case arise where this is not possible it must be made clear that the fulfilment of the political aspirations of the Ukrainians in Galicia can only be seen as a consequence of the new formation proving its worth and not as a premise of its existence.
- Naturally we must avoid anything that could be taken to imply that we look on Galicia as our property where we can do as we please. It should be strongly emphasised that we respect Galicia as the home of the Galician Ukrainians. Any mention of settlement questions is therefore to be avoided.
- Drastic insults to Bolshevism, the Soviets and the Russians have also to be refrained from. It must be realised that the local populations have had their own experiences with the Soviets, not all of which have been unfavourable. For this reason, the proven disadvantages and faults of Bolshevism should be pointed out in a clear and factual way.
- A position can be adopted against the Poles in as far as, unlike the Ukrainians, they have not understood their European responsibility in the fight against Bolshevism. This should be accentuated in such a way as to flatter Ukrainian conceit. Under no circumstances must insults be made against the Poles.
- Ukrainian members of the recruiting commissions have not been informed of this letter. It is to be destroyed after the contents have been memorised.

Appendix II

Report on Recruitment, up to and including 2 June 1943

From the Archives of the Brotherhood of Former Combatants.

District	Volunteered	Accepted	Rejected
Berezhany	3,567	2,731	836
Drohobych	2,195	2,085	110
Zolochiv	2,476	2,312	164
Kaminka Strumilova	2,112	2,012	100
Rava Russka	2,579	1,777	802
Kolomyia	11,325	8,537	2,788
Sambir	2,094	1,640	454
Stanyslaviv	8,827	6,276	2,551
Chortkiv	7,343	5,078	2,265
Ternopil	3,118	1,749	1,369
Kalush	850	623	227
Stryj	2,690	1,604	1,086
L'viv (city)	2,915	2,802	113
L'viv (district)	10,909	8,710	2,199
Total strength in Galicia	63,000	47,936	15,064
Peremyshl	1,821	1,429	392
Iaroslav	2,732	1,502	1,230
Sianok	14,446	2,008	12,438
Total strength in Cracow	18,999	4,939	14,060
Grand total strength	81,999	52,875	29,124

Appendix III

Formation of the *SS-Freiw.* Division *'Galizien'*, 30 July 1943

From the Imperial War Museum

30 July 1943
Berlin-Wilmersdorf, Kaiserallee 188
SS-Führungshauptamt
Edc.Amt. d.Waffen-SS
Org.Tgb. Nr.982/43 g. Kdos.

SECRET COMMAND-MATTER
Re: Formation of the *SS-Freiw.* Division *'Galizien'*
Enclosure: 3 sheets (only for departments involved in the processing)
Distributor: Special distribution 70 copies.

1. The Führer has ordered the formation of a *SS-Freiwilligen* Division *'Galizien'* (*SS-Frw.* Div. *'Galizien'*). The *SS-Frw.* Div. *'Galizien'* is to be set up according to the enclosed organisation, at the SS training camp Heidelager.
2. Organisation and equipment: see enclosures 1 and 2. See enclosure 3 for additional plans authorised by SS-FHA.
3. Formation will be achieved via:
   (a) Galician volunteers currently in the SS Training Battalion (*SS-Ausb.* Btl.) at the SS training camp Heidelager. Specialist NCOs from various colleges and training units.
   (b) Additional Galician volunteers.
4. Appointment of officers will be done by SS-FHA, Section 5, Dept. 2a. Medical and administrative leaders will be respectively appointed by the SS-FHA, *Amtsgr.* D, the Personnel Office of the SS-*W.V. Hauptamt*.
5. Regarding the supply of weapons, equipment, vehicles and horses special orders will be issued by SS-FHA, Dept. 1b (*Abtl.* Ib), Section 10 (*Amt.* X) and where appropriate by Section 6 (*Amt.* VI).
6. Field postal numbers will be issued by SS-FHA, Section 2, Dept 1c/Fp.
7. Allocation of the Field post office and of the Feldgend. Tr. will be achieved via SS-FHA, Section 2, Dept. 1c.
8. KSt [*Kreigsstarkenachweisung*] and KAN [*Kreigsausrustungsnachweis*] will be provided, without the need for a request, by SS-FHA, Section 2, Dept. Org./St AN. Provision of regulations will be via special orders.
9. The directions of the *Reichsführer-SS*, Tgb.Nr.309/41 g.Kdos. dated 6.11.41 regarding the formation and deployment of foreign volunteer units, are to be appropriately applied.
10. The Oath is as follows: "I swear by God this holy oath, that in the battle against Bolshevism, I will give absolute obedience to the commander in chief of the German Armed Forces, Adolf Hitler, and as a brave soldier I will always be prepared to lay down my life for this oath."
11. The language to be used for commands: Galician
    The language to be used for orders: German
12. Uniform is that of the Waffen-SS. Initially with no runes on the right collar patch, and with SS rank insignia on the left collar patch. The SS-*WV-Hauptamt* will be asked to provide the necessary clothing and personal equipment.
13. *SS-Brigadeführer und Generalmajor der Waffen-SS* Schimana is responsible for the formation of the *SS-Frw.* Div. *'Galizien'*.
14. Reserve units for the *SS-Frw.* Div. *'Galizien'* will be arranged at a later date.

Signed Juttner
SS-Obergruppenführer und General der Waffen-SS

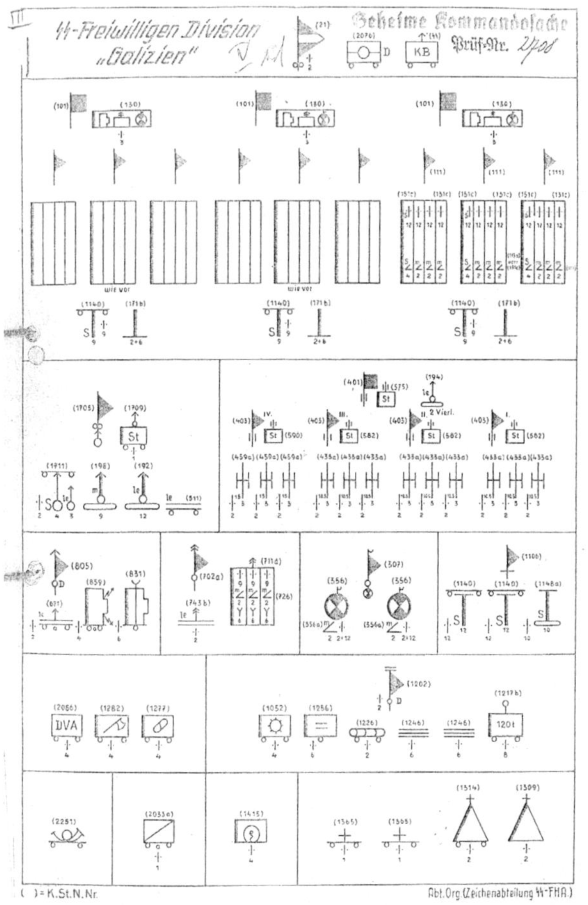

Appendix IV

30 July 1943

HFD, H/10/56

30 July 1943
Lemberg
General-Gouvernement
Governor of the District of Galicia
Dr. WA./ Ra

ZL. 19/43 g Secret, Private!

To the *Reichsführer-SS und Chef der Deutschen Polizei* Heinrich Himmler
Berlin SW11, Prinz Albrecht-Straße Nr. 8.
Re: *SS-Schützen* Division *Galizien*.

Reichsführer!

Following my presentation of 1 March this year, you issued the order for the formation of the Galician *SS-Freiwilligen* Division.

I have, on your behalf and in accordance with your basic guidelines, completed the technical, and particularly the political, preparations. I therefore feel some responsibility for the further development of the division. More so, because the formation of the division is of exceptional importance in relation to the general political situation in the district of Galicia and to the morale of the population. In view of this responsibility, and the fact that I do not have the opportunity to consult with you in person, I now present the following comments in writing:

In the various training camps where Galician SS volunteers are currently in training, an order was announced stating that the volunteers should only be referred to as 'Galicians' and that on no account should any title including the word 'Ukrainian' be used. Concerning this I feel obliged to raise the following points:

1. 'Galicia' is a geographical and state territorial concept, and not a national one. Along with a few Germans, millions of Poles and Ukrainians live in Galicia. The Ukrainians, like the Poles, are unique in both language

and culture. In particular they hold strongly opposing attitudes towards the Reich. It cannot be our task to merge Ukrainians and Poles to become 'Galicians'. Such a development would be contrary to our interests, which involve preventing pan-Slavonic tendencies. The consequences of such a development would be both racially and geographically utterly impossible to predict.

2. The existence of a Ukrainian national culture had already been acknowledged as a fact, during the years 1939 and1940, i.e. prior to the creation of the district of Galicia. Since then we have had the following recognised and officially appointed by the German authorities: 'Ukrainian committees', 'Ukrainian delegations', a 'Ukrainian Police', Ukrainian newspapers etc. Additionally, in the constitution of the *Generalgouvernement*, the cultures are divided into Poles and Ukrainians.

3. I further note that all German literature appearing in the Reich concerning Eastern issues, has referred to the Galician-Ukrainian population as 'Ukrainians'. This includes the book written by Franz Obermeyer *Die Ukraine, Land der Schwarzen Erde* ('Ukraine, Land of the Black Earth'), which was first published in 1942, and is widely circulated here.

4. I, along with my colleagues, refer to the citizens of the Galician district as the 'Galician population', when making an appeal to both Ukrainians and Poles. If however I wish to make an appeal aimed at just the Poles or just the Ukrainians, then I must refer directly to the peoples concerned by the appropriate name. This is reinforced by the existence of provisions here, which, as described in point 2, simply do not allow an alternative mode of address. In view of the guidelines issued by you, since the formation of the volunteer division, which is of course only open to the Ukrainians of Galicia and not to the Poles, I now refer to 'Galician Ukrainians'.

5. The question as to whether the 'Galician Ukrainians' should be referred to as 'Ruthenians', as was sometimes the case under the old monarchy, can at this point in time only receive a negative reply. The title 'Ruthenians' has not been used since the year 1918. 'Ruthenian' means 'Friend of Russia', and was, during the Polish period only applied to the small groups of Galicians friendly towards Russia. This term is passionately rejected by Galician Ukrainians. Its reintroduction especially in this war is not possible.

6. The descriptions of Galician Ukrainians as only 'Galician' is incorrect and, in my view, also politically wrong. This description clearly conveys to these people the intention of removing their national identity, while not actually achieving this. Particularly during this war, where the powerful revolutionary concepts of bolshevism can only be countered with equally potent nationalistic concepts, our anti-Bolshevik activities must override such an emphatic attempt at the neutralisation of this ethnic group.

7. In the district of Galicia it has so far been possible to enlist the genuine and active co-operation of the population. In this respect Galicia stands in stark contrast to the many other occupied eastern regions. Essential to this was the maintaining of decent and just treatment for the population, and the consequent continuation of a political approach securing the trust of the population in German leadership. This approach was made easier by the 150 years of Austrian, and therefore European, history in this region, also by the existence of a clear orientation towards the west among the older generation. It was possible to involve broad sections of the Polish, but especially the Ukrainian population in anti-Bolshevik policies. Among the Ukrainians this succeeded particularly because of a nationalism which rejected the red Muscovite. I have, along with my colleagues, via constant and careful work, attempted to move these nationalistic tendencies onto an anti-Bolshevik track, in order to procure increased achievements for the Reich. Via further gradual educational work, the already evident national awareness should be developed into a special awareness of Galician-Ukrainian origins, and thus create an awareness of belonging to the Reich. Such an awareness still exists in sections of the older generation, but has, as a result of 25 years of Polish and Bolshevik rule, been extensively lost among the young. I am convinced that this national awareness cannot be eliminated by using orders. I seriously fear that such measures will trouble what are essentially good-willed and positive people, and thus achieve a result opposite to the one desired by us. Ethnically the volunteers are essentially 'Ukrainian', with an Ukrainian language and a strong independent culture. It is the person who is prepared to fight against Bolshevism on behalf of his culture, who will therefore respond negatively to such measures.

8. That this approach is necessary here, can be seen from the fact that the leaflet from the *SS- und Polizei Führer* in the District of Galicia, requesting the citizens to take part in the fight against the Kolpak [sic.] partisans, explicitly addresses the 'Ukrainians'. A leaflet in whose conception I, incidentally, had no involvement whatsoever. Any other approach to this awkward problem, will, if applied within the home region of these volunteers or among the troops, have a disruptive effect, since the volunteers are, as I have emphasised, very sensitive regarding nationality. Similarly, it is my conviction that the bad experiences with various other military formations of foreign national origin, can be traced back to the fact that the inhabitants experienced in their home country an approach which was totally alien to that experienced under the nationalistic symbolism of the marching troops.

9. At this particular point in time these questions acquire an extraordinary relevance. The current general political and military position of the Reich depends to an unusual degree on our relationship with people of foreign national groups within the realm of German rule. In Galicia there exists the additional factor, that waves of unrest are increasingly spreading through from Wolhynia and Lublin. The march of the Kolpak partisans through five counties (*Kreishauptmannschaften*), and their current three-week long residence in Galicia has created here a serious crisis regarding confidence in the authority of the Reich. We are making the most intensive efforts to restore this authority, especially in view of the necessity of bringing in the plentiful harvest and of preserving supply routes to the front. Essential to this is the preservation of the population's trust in the justness of German actions, and also the strict upholding of any declarations, as well as the respecting of racial identity.

If you, *Reichsführer*, take a position, regarding issues concerning the SS Division, which demonstrates to these people – who are, as I have repeatedly emphasised, very politically aware – that we intend to remove their national identity, then they will feel their trust betrayed and will most certainly back out. However, if an alternative approach were used, then they would just as certainly become loyal and reliable soldiers. The former approach would in any case be pointless, for as we know, from our struggle as National Socialists, one cannot simply take away the national identity from a strong national culture, and in this case we are indeed dealing with a very healthy and robust farming community.

In the interests of gaining 10,000 reliable SS men and in the interests of preserving the political direction in Galicia, which is of service to the Reich throughout, I request that you, *Reichsführer*, earnestly examine the points presented.

As a result of the still active commitment of large sections of the non-German population to the goals of the Reich, Galicia can be seen as a starting point for the repair of the subversive developments. Here in the East, as I see it, they are increasing on a daily basis. If the situation is turned around here also, then one of the most promising developments will be shattered with the same blow.

Looking at the position of the Reich, I am convinced that the key to victory or failure lies, now as ever, in the East with the Reich's Eastern political activities. I therefore ask you *Reichsführer* for your understanding perusal.

Heil Hitler!
Your obedient servant
Wächter
2 Enclosures

Appendix V

Note concerning Ordinance of 6 August 1943

BA-KO, R19/104

Chef der Ordnungspolizei
Berlin, 12 August 1943
Kdo. IO (3) 1 No. 484/43

QUICK NOTE
Re: I/SS-Pol. 8
Concerning: Ordinance of 6.8.1943 – Kdo.IO(3)1 No.166/13

1. In a change of the above ordinance, the I./SS Pol. 8, that is presently in Mährisch-Ostrau, will not be disbanded for the time being.
2. The *Pol.-Schützen* Rgt. 36 should be reinforced using resources from this Btl. according to numerical regulations. The transfer of NCOs and troops to *Pol.-Schützen* Rgt. 36 is being decided by the commander of the *Ordnungspolizei* in Prague according to his jurisdiction.
   Armament & Equipment
   The NCOs and troops are to receive 1 gas mask each.
   Armament of the force should come from the nominal equipment of *Pol.-Schützen* Rgt. 36.
   The field kitchens should be relinquished to *Pol.-Schützen* Rgt. 36 against the proper receipt.
   Clothing
   Furnishing of service clothing is being regulated by the ordinance from 12.7.1941 (MBliV.S13030) as amended by ordinance 5.8.1942 (MBliV.S1644).
3. The remaining forces of I./SS-Pol.8, numbers of which should be immediately reported to me, should be consolidated into two companies and should remain in Mährisch-Ostrau, together with its battalion staff, and be available for my disposal. These are intended for later incorporation in *Gal. SS-Freiw.* Rgt. 7 and into SS *Freiw.* reserve units.

Distribution:
(a) Commander of the *Ordnungspolizei* in Prague
(b) Pol.-Schützen Rgt. 36 } through BdO. Prague
(c) I./SS-Pol. 8 }
(d) *Polizei Waffenschulen* I – IV
(e) Signals and ordnance office of the *Ordnungspolizei* in Berlin-Adlershof.
(f) *Polizei-San. und Ersatzabteilung* in Berlin SO 36, Wrangelstr. 97/99.

Appendix VI

Basic guidelines for field chaplains of the Division issued by Father Myhailo Levenets (undated)

From the Author's archive.

1. Every Sunday, as a matter of principle, a field service with a sermon is to be held. If the unit finds itself too far away from the location designated for the service, then it should take part in the local Roman Catholic service, provided that the field chaplain has made prior contact with the priest responsible for that area, and got to know him. In addition, it is the duty of the field chaplain, with permission from the unit's leader, to hold a daily service with a sermon for the unit. This service is to be held in the early morning hours, without disturbing normal duties.
2. Care will be taken to ensure that for eligible relatives – of the volunteers of the division – who live in the Reich, an application for family support will made and passed to the appropriate higher department.
3. The field chaplain has a duty to discuss the following military educational material with the regular troops at least twice a week: development of character, soldierly virtues, readiness for self-sacrifice, living together as comrades, fighting spirit etc.
4. A considerable amount of cultural and educational work with the troops is desirable: press, choir, congregational singing, comradeship evenings, and the like. The informing of the unit leader and consideration of combat circumstances are to be respected in all cases!
5. A weekly review of the press is to be prepared. Should the Ukrainian newspapers not be available, then the Wehrmacht report should be made available to the men in Ukrainian, at least every other day.
6. It is the duty of the field chaplain to constantly educate the men regarding conduct towards the civilian population, defending against sabotage, keeping of secrets and silence, sanctity of personal effects etc.
7. All efforts of the field chaplain are to be directed towards gaining the trust of the men and getting to know their character and soul in the finest detail, so that he can at the decisive moment have the desired influence on the troops and help the commander lead the unit to its objective.

Appendix VII

March and combat capability of *Gal. SS-Freiw.* Rgt, 4

From the Archives of the Brotherhood of Former Combatants.

Ia, copies to Jn. Wg. K., N San. 2, Vet., with a request for acknowledgement and further measures.
Telex BdO. Stg Nr 123, 4/2 1730

To the *Chef der Ordnungspolizei* in Berlin,
Re.: March and combat capability of *Gal. SS-Freiw.*Rgt. 4
With reference to: FS-Erl. v.3.2.44 Nr. 552 – Kdo. 1 Org 3 1 Nr.78/44

Secret
Gal. SS-Freiw. Rgt. 4 is not ready for deployment.

1. Still required are:
   (a) All radios and communications equipment for the Signals Company
   (b) All horse harness for the Signals Company
   (c) *Pkw* (light vehicles) for the Signals Company with drivers
   (d) 1 field wagon for the Pioneer Platoon with soft covers
   (e) Entrenching tools for 105 field wagons
   (f) 4 riding and 10 draught horses and replacements for the two riding horses unfit for duty. (Section d not yet arrived)
   (g) 12 recruits, with weapons, for the battalions' Signals platoons 15 further recruits to replace losses sustained
   (h) Replacement for the regimental doctor who is totally unfit for active duty
   (i) 11 medical packs, 3 rucksacks with field collars (*Feldkragen*)
   (k) Equipment for 2 field kitchens
   (l) One tank full of petrol for all vehicles as marching reserve
   The above forces and inventory have been notified to T.
2. Other obstacles:
   (a) 120 newly arrived recruits have only limited basic training.
   (b) 2 lorries, 1 passenger vehicle and 3 motorbikes are under repair. Parts not available up to now.
   (c) Latest shipment of horse tack again fails to fit throughout. Alteration by saddlers will take another two-three weeks.
3. As soon as the aforementioned forces and inventory have arrived and the obstacles are overcome, the Regiment will be ready for deployment. A date for this cannot be given by the Regiment.

BdO. Stuttgart –1a 3/10 Nr. 118/43 Secret.
I.V. gez OPHORST

Appendix VIII

Speech of the *Reichsführer-SS* at the summons of the officer corps of the Galician *SS-Freiw.* Infantry Division, Neuhammer, 16 May 1944S

BA-KO, R 52 III/3c

My Comrades,

About a year ago, on 28 April 1943, an appeal went out calling upon volunteers to enrol for the formation of a division in your home country. The division was given the designation, 14. *SS Freiwilligen-Division*, i.e. *Galizische Freiwilligen-Division*. As I am in the habit of discussing openly all things and questions with my officer corps, I wish to discuss the following questions with you also.

I know that some of you are unhappy about the fact that the division is called Galician and that you are sometimes, or even frequently, addressed with the name Galician. I am well aware, of course, that the inhabitants of Galicia, that is to say those of your ilk, are Ukrainians. Just as in Germany, the Germans who are at home in Pomerania are called Pomeranians and those who are at home in Bavaria are called Bavarians and call themselves Bavarians. In exactly the same way the designation Galician has been chosen according to the name of your beautiful homeland, of which you can be truly proud. Your homeland has become even more beautiful – and I can safely say this – since it lost, through our intervention, those inhabitants who often sullied the name of Galicia, namely the Jews.

I know the sorrowful history of your people. For centuries, your brave people suffered under the Russians and the Poles. The section of your people that lives in Galicia came to Austria in the year 1772 after the break up of Poland. For 150 years this section of your people has experienced the blessings of greater freedom, and of German order and justice as well. Of your people, you are the ones who have a proper understanding of the West and can convey this understanding (to others). The future of your fellow countrymen will depend to a great extent on your discipline and your good sense. After the 1918 war you went through a terrible time under the Polish state. You suffered the same oppression and persecution under the Poles as the Germans did in Poland. Worse still were the years 1939 to 1941 under the Russians, i.e. under the Bolsheviks.

Three years ago, the Führer Adolf Hitler decided to attack Bolshevism, i.e. Russia. With the blood of your German comrades, the blood of the German soldiers your country was freed from Bolshevism. There were some among your people, who out of the purest love for their people, expected more from Germany, greater gifts and rights. In the last few years, the Führer in his wisdom has decided differently. It behoves none of us to be dissatisfied, since we know and have seen how wisely the Führer, whom the Lord God has sent us all, has done everything since he has lead Germany and liberated Europe. On the contrary, I believe it is our best policy to await his decision, about the order of the peoples in Europe, at the end of the war. The Führer decided in 1941 that the part of the Ukrainian people that lives in Galicia, which belonged to the Reich, for 150 years, should take it's place as a government (province) in the *Generalgouvernement*. The other part that had 25 years of Bolshevik education and Bolshevik rule behind it was, according to the decision of the Führer, to be administered in a different way. There were some who were not pleased about this, although today when Bolshevism has temporarily re-occupied this country, they are forced to experience for themselves through their own suffering what a bitter lot they have got in exchange.

And now I come to you, the Division. The appeal went out a year ago. A large number of the Ukrainian people of Galicia have enrolled voluntarily, old and young, fathers and sons. Right away, the propaganda against the Division and against all of you was started by those who are eternally dissatisfied, who are never an asset to their people, by those who never think anything moves fast enough, by those who always want to reap before they have sown. They said that the men who registered here were only taken on by the Germans as cannon-fodder. The registration was a year ago and every man of the Division is witness against this slander. To this I must add that we Germans, as soldiers, have never been in the habit of letting other people do more of the fighting in a war than we do ourselves. When something difficult is to be done somewhere, then we do it ourselves.

So, in the course of a year, we have given you a thorough training. I know that this also did not please some outsiders, for they said that the Germans who were training you were just tormenting you with their drill. One can really say that malevolent people can always find fault with something, no-matter what one does. We soldiers – and these others are not soldiers – must make one thing clear: there is a big difference in going in the woods any old how and going into battle at the front as a division. Anybody can shoot from the bushes and shout insults from the bushes. Whoever does that is not a patriot. But he who practices discipline, drill, weapons-craft, and trains himself and his men, he is really doing something for his people. For when you go to the front with the skills you have now acquired and you are given a position where you are defending or attacking 20, 30, or 40 kilometres you will be a shield for your homeland and people, custodians of order, of command and of obedience. And you know that the prosperity of a people is based on command and obedience.

A further assertion made by our 'friends' is that you know of course the Germans will not let any single one of you rise to any kind of high position. Not one of you will become a proper officer, commander, company chief or commander. I believe you are witnesses to the contrary. Every position has been filled by a man who is capable. I did not ask, nor did the Division's commander ask "Is he German or is he Ukrainian?" On the contrary, the only question we asked ourselves was "Does he lead his battalion in such a way that there is no unnecessary loss of blood? Is he a man that can teach his subordinates military virtues and can train them to do their job well? Is he a man who leads his Battalion to victory or defeat? Is he a man who buys victory at the expense of far too many lives? Is he such a leader that the dead, the fallen, are fewer?"

You, my officers and commanders of this Division, must all keep in mind your first and foremost rule. Regardless of whether you are German or Ukrainian, you are responsible for the life and health of every single one of your men. 250 men from the ranks of the Division have been sent to the *Junker* schools, and it is my firm intention to pick out regularly the best and most talented from the youth of Galicia and to further each one according to his capabilities. Every man from your ranks who becomes and officer or a commander in the community of the European divisions of the Waffen-SS is a source of great joy and pride to me.

I am not the kind of man who makes any promises or tells you something pleasant about the future. It would be pretty cheap if I told you after the war you would get this, would get that, would get these rights and those liberties- the way the British do on the other side. If I promise something I have got to know that I can keep that promise and I do keep it. There is only one thing I can say: the status, worth and importance of every single people in Europe of the future will be determined solely by the performance of each individual people in this war. I place great confidence in you. We are not in the habit of boasting. But we, SS men and SS officers, can claim that the divisions of the SS have fought for and attained unprecedented military glory in this most difficult struggle.

When your governor, Dr Wächter, suggested to me that I should form a division from the Ukrainian sons of Galicia, I was faced with a decision that called for considerable consideration. Don't get me wrong. But when one single division is formed by the Waffen SS and under the command of the *Reichsführer-SS* fails to do its duty, then the military prestige of the SS for which thousands and tens of thousands have laid down their lives is sullied. The unblemished glory of troops who have never failed would be destroyed. I was confronted with exactly the same problem when I set up a division of Estonians, two divisions of Latvians, a division of Bosnians, now the second, and one of Albanians. So I asked your governor "Is this a decent and loyal people?" And thereupon your governor, who is an old SS commander, answered as an SS man "Indeed, *Reichsführer*, you will be able to rely on this decent farming people." I then gave my assent and have now carried through this decision. So you are now the representatives of your people in Europe. In accordance with the rights granted to you, you alone wear on your collar patch the future coat of arms of your country. In the same way, alone of your entire people, you will wear on your arm the colours of your country as a national shield, in accordance with the rights granted to you.

I have gone one step further. I have ruled that every member of this Division, every German included, shall wear the uniform bestowed to this Division as his official uniform. I have placed my confidence in you and I know you will not disappoint me. I demand from you, my commanders, and from my non-commissioned officers and men likewise, a number of virtues.

Firstly, discussing politics will not be tolerated in the Division. We are soldiers. The only politics that concern us is the battle against the enemy, who would kill us all, in fact your people first. The only politics that can have any meaning for the people are those on the main battle line, politics that are not implemented by speeches, newspapers and pamphlets but with gun, grenade, and cannon and in hand to hand combat. Say to anyone who whispers anything different in your ear "Look here, the best policy we Ukrainians can follow is as soldiers in this Division. For we embody the honour, the glory and the achievement of our people."

The second thing I demand from you is order, order in great things and in small things. Order is the basis of the nation and its culture, and order is the foundation of states. The soldier whose uniform is not in order is himself not in order. Sooner or later he will let himself go, stop being obedient and then become like those on the other side with the Bolsheviks. Later, in peacetime, when this war is over and I am travelling through your country, I would still like to be able to recognise every man in this Division in his citizen's or peasant's clothes because he is so neat and clean.

Another point, if you do not keep things neat and tidy and do not look after your weapon and have it looked after, this neglect of order and duty can cost you and your men your lives tomorrow. Your weapon cannot fire, if you do not look after it and clean it. Your young men will not do this of their own accord if you, their leaders, do not tirelessly train them to do it. When a man forgets something and neglects his duty, we are in the habit of punishing, not only the man himself, but also his officer, his non-commissioned officer, and his platoon leader. For the lowest commander, the officer has more prestige, more standing and more rights and for this reason more duties. The higher any one of us is placed, the greater are the duties he has.

The third thing I demand of you is obedience. There is something I want to tell you. Obedience starts the moment you receive an order to do something you find unpleasant. I know if I ordered the Division to exterminate the Poles in this area or that area, I would be a very popular man. But if I tell you or give you the order that the Division is to follow this or that route to the front in full battle order, and fight against the Russians, then that is what will be done. For the Führer will manage to handle the Poles, they who have ill-treated you in the same way as they have ill-treated our fellow Germans in Poland. You do nothing before the order is given. I expect you, the officers, whether German or Ukrainian, to set a good example to your men by your exemplary obedience in every, I repeat every, respect.

The fourth thing I demand is comradeship. It would not be difficult if I asked all you from the same village to stick together. It is a bit more difficult when I tell you that the whole company, no matter from how many villages the men come from, must help each other through life and death. It is a disgrace when one man leaves the other in the lurch. It is a disgrace when one man steals something from another man. It is a disgrace when one man does not help another man. It is more difficult still when I demand that all Ukrainians in this Division must help each other as comrades in life and death. And it is more difficult again when I demand that every man in this Division, whether Ukrainian or German, helps each other. From you, my German SS officers and men, I demand you are comrades to the others just as if you had been born along with them. To the best of your ability you will pass on all the knowledge and skills you acquired in Germany to your comrades and to your subordinates who are just as much your comrades. I expect you, my German SS officers and men, to carry the wounded Ukrainian Galician comrade from the battle as if he were your brother.

And from you, Ukrainian officers and men of the Division, and from you Germans, I expect that you vie with each other to be the best comrades. And from all of you together, I expect that you will never allow any malicious agitator or agent to drive a wedge between you. You see, none of those malicious agitators and propagandists are out there at the front. There, this Division has to fight as a united whole, out there where the Russian bullet and Russian grenade do not ask whether they are now hitting a German or Ukrainian. They are fired to shoot dead and destroy yet another in the grey uniform with the eagle on the sleeve.

Never allow anything to split you up. Be brothers and comrades in this Division of Europe, in this Division which has sworn the holy oath to the man who is the Führer of us all. He is the Führer of us Germans whose race he stems from, but also of all the others who live in Europe.

And the fifth and last thing I expect from you, is loyalty to this man I have just mentioned, who will be Europe's saviour and architect of your future. In a few weeks the Division will have completed its training and will go to the front.

I dismiss you, my leaders, from this summons, from this officers' conference. Tomorrow I will take a look at this battalion and that battalion to see what you can do and what you have learnt as soldiers and leaders. And shortly afterwards you will give a sample of your talent, your worth, your bravery, your obedience, your loyalty and the sanctity of the oath you took to the Lord God to fight against the enemy Russia and Bolshevism at the front. I know you will not disappoint the SS and you will not disappoint me who called upon you. At the end of this war the Führer will be able to say the Division set up by the brave people of Galicia has always done its duty. This people deserves to take its place in Europe.

I herewith close this summons.

Appendix IX

Soviet order of battle, 1st Ukrainian Front, 13 July 1944

1st Ukrainian Front

Commander: Marshal of the Soviet Union I.S. Konev
Chief of Staff: Army: General V.D. Sokolovsky
Commissar: Lieutenant-General K.V. Krainiukov

3rd GUARDS ARMY

Commander: Colonel-General V.N. Gordov
Commissar: General I.S. Kolesnichenko
Chief of Staff: Major-General F.T. Rybal'chenko
120th Rifle Corps
- 197th Rifle Division
- 218th Rifle Division
- 273rd Rifle Division

21st Rifle Corps
- 253rd Rifle Division
- 136th Rifle Division
- 81st Rifle Division

76th Rifle Corps
- 181st Rifle Division
- 106th Rifle Division
- 149th Rifle Division

22nd Rifle Corps
- 389th Rifle Division
- 329th Rifle Division
- 58th Rifle Division

Independent Army Units
- 150th Independent Tank Brigade
- 39th Tank Regiment
- 293rd Guards Self-propelled Artillery Regiment
- 13th Breakthrough Artillery Division
- 47th Howitzer Artillery Brigade
- 88th Heavy Howitzer Artillery Brigade
- 42nd Light Artillery Brigade
- 17th Mortar Brigade
- 101st Super-heavy Howitzer Artillery Brigade
- 40th Guards Gun Artillery Brigade (less 1 btn)
- 1528th Howitzer Artillery Regiment
- 26th Anti-tank Artillery Brigade
- 179th Guards Anti-tank Artillery Regiment
- 316th Guards Anti-tank Artillery Regiment
- 868th Anti-tank Artillery Regiment
- 1643rd Anti-tank Artillery Regiment
- 563rd Anti-tank Artillery Regiment
- 1stGuards Mortar Brigade
- 12th Mortar Brigade
- 526th Mortar Regiment
- 569th Mortar Regiment

497th Mortar Regiment
8th Guards Mortar Regiment
21st Guards Mortar Regiment
69th Anti-aircraft Artillery Division
45th Independent Armoured Train Battalion
49th Independent Armoured Train Battalion
40th Engineer Brigade
16th Assault Engineer Brigade (less 79th and 89th btns)

13th ARMY

Commander: Lieutenant-General N.P. Pukhov
Commissar: Major-General M.A. Kozlov
Chief of Staff: Lieutenant-General G.K. Malandin
24th Rifle Corps
350th Rifle Division
287th Rifle Division
71st Rifle Division
27th Rifle Corps
6th Guards Rifle Division
112th Guards Rifle Division
121st Guards Rifle Division
102nd Rifle Corps
117th Guards Rifle Division
162nd Rifle Division
172nd Rifle Division
Independent Army Units
87th Tank Regiment
327th Self-propelled Artillery Regiment
1st Guards Artillery Division
1st Guards Gun Artillery Brigade
2nd Guards Gun Artillery Brigade
3rd Guards Light Artillery Brigade
39th Gun Artillery Brigade
111th Howitzer Artillery Regiment
493rd Anti-tank Artillery Regiment
1076th Anti-tank Artillery Regiment
1644th Anti-tank Artillery Regiment
1645th Anti tank Artillery Regiment
128th Mortar Regiment
476th Mortar Regiment
323rd Guards Mortar Regiment
10th Anti-aircraft Artillery Division
1287th Anti-aircraft Artillery Regiment
58th Independent Armoured Train Battalion
79th Anti-aircraft Artillery Division
89th Anti-aircraft Artillery Division
20th Independent Pontoon Battalion

60th ARMY

Commander: Colonel-General P.A. Kurochkin
Commissar: Major-General V.P. Olenin
Chief of Staff: Major-General G.A. Ter-Gesparian (from 23.7. Colonel S. M. Protas)
23rd Rifle Corps
359th Rifle Division
99th Rifle Division
68th Rifle Division
15th Rifle Corps
322nd Rifle Division
148th Rifle Division
336th Rifle Division
28th Rifle Corps
107th Guards Rifle Division
246th Rifle Division
106th Rifle Corps
100th Rifle Division
306th Rifle Division
Independent Army Units
59th Tank Regiment
1827th Self-propelled Artillery Regiment
1889th Self-propelled Artillery Regiment
17th Breakthrough Artillery Division
50th Howitzer Artillery Brigade
92nd Heavy Howitzer Artillery Brigade
39th Gun Artillery Brigade
37th Light Artillery Brigade
108th Super-heavy Howitzer Artillery Brigade
24th Guards Gun Artillery Brigade
33rd Gun Artillery Brigade
155th Gun Artillery Brigade
805th Gun Artillery Brigade
7th Guards Anti-tank Artillery Brigade
350th Anti-aircraft Artillery Regiment
640th Anti-aircraft Artillery Regiment
645th Anti-aircraft Artillery Regiment
1178th Anti-tank Artillery Regiment
1593rd Anti-tank Artillery Regiment
408th Anti-tank Artillery Regiment
138th Mortar Regiment
3rd Guards Mortar Division (2 brigades)
83rd Guards Mortar Regiment
98th Guards Mortar Regiment
23rd Anti-aircraft Artillery Division
217th Anti-aircraft Artillery Regiment
21st Independent Armoured Train Battalion
37th Independent Armoured Train Battalion
59th Engineer Brigade
15th Assault Engineer Brigade (2 btns)

38th ARMY

Commander: Colonel-General K. S. Moselenko
Commissar: Major-General A. A. Epishev
Chief of Staff: Major-General V. F. Vorob'ev
52nd Rifle Corps
316th Rifle Division
304th Rifle Division
340th Rifle Division
101st Rifle Corps
211th Rifle Division
305th Rifle Division
70th Guards Rifle Division
67th Rifle Corps
121st Rifle Division
241st Rifle Division
140th Rifle Division
183rd Rifle Division
Independent Army Units
12th Guards Tank Regiment
1228th Self-propelled Artillery Regiment
349th Self-propelled Artillery Regiment
3rd Breakthrough Artillery Division
15th Light Artillery Brigade
1st Howitzer Artillery Brigade
5th Gun Artillery Brigade
7th Mortar Brigade
116th Heavy Howitzer Artillery Brigade
135th Gun Artillery Brigade
25th Super-heavy Howitzer Artillery Brigade
11th Guards Anti-tank Artillery Brigade
296th Guards Anti-tank Artillery Regiment
1663rd Anti-tank Artillery Regiment
491st Mortar Regiment
18th Guards Mortar Brigade (3rd Guards Mortar Division)
65th Guards Mortar Brigade
88th Guards Mortar Regiment
21st Anti-aircraft Artillery Division
296th Guards Anti-aircraft Artillery Regiment
39th Engineer Brigade
15th Assault Engineer Brigade (less 3 btns)

1st GUARDS ARMY

Commander: Colonel-General A.A. Grechko
Commissar: Major-General I.V. Vasil'ev
Chief of Staff: Lieutenant-General A.G. Batiuna
107th Rifle Corps
129th Rifle Division

127th Rifle Division
167th Rifle Division
74th Rifle Corps
147th Rifle Division
276th Rifle Division
155th Rifle Division
30th Rifle Corps
30th Rifle Division
141st Rifle Division
18th Guards Rifle Corps
161st Rifle Division
237th Rifle Division
151st Rifle Division
395th Rifle Division
4th Guards Tank Corps
12th Guards Tank Brigade
13th Guards Tank Brigade
14th Guards Tank Brigade
3rd Guards Motorised Rifle Brigade
Independent Army Units
1st Guards Tank Regiment
130th Anti-tank Artillery Regiment
222nd Anti-tank Artillery Regiment
269th Anti-tank Artillery Regiment
317th Anti-tank Artillery Regiment
1075th Anti-tank Artillery Regiment
1506th Anti-tank Artillery Regiment
1642nd Anti-tank Artillery Regiment
1672nd Anti-tank Artillery Regiment
756th Anti-tank Artillery Regiment
752nd Anti-tank Artillery Regiment
525th Mortar Regiment
264th Mortar Regiment
329th Guards Mortar Regiment
240th Guards Mortar Brigade
25th Anti-aircraft Artillery Division
580th Anti-aircraft Artillery Regiment
120th Anti-aircraft Artillery Regiment
31st Guards Anti-aircraft Artillery Brigade
6th Engineer Brigade
3rd Pontoon Brigade (2 btns)

18th ARMY

Commander: Lieutenant-General E.P. Zhuravlev
Commissar: Major-General S.E. Kolonin
Chief of Staff: Lieutenant-General F.P. Ozerov
11th Rifle Corps
24th Rifle Division
226th Rifle Division
271st Rifle Division
17th Rifle Corps
2nd Guards Airborne Division
8th Rifle Division
317 Rifle Division
95th Rifle Corps
66th Rifle Division
138th Rifle Division
351st Rifle Division
Independent Army Units
1448th Self-propelled Artillery Regiment
146th Guards Gun Artillery Brigade
839th Howitzer Artillery Regiment
196th Guards Anti-tank Artillery Regiment
1646th Anti-tank Artillery Regiment
9th Mountain Mortar Regiment
477th Mountain Mortar Regiment
494th Mountain Mortar Regiment
496th Mountain Mortar Regiment
5th Guards Mortar Regiment
2nd Guards Mountain Mortar Brigade
3rd Guards Mountain Mortar Brigade
544th Anti-aircraft Artillery Brigade
33rd Independent Armoured Train Battalion
9th Engineer Brigade
6th Pontoon Brigade

1st GUARDS TANK ARMY

Commander: Colonel-General of Tank Forces M.E. Katukov
Commissar: Lieutenant-General of Tank Forces N.K. Popol'
Chief of Staff: Lieutenant-General M. .A. Shalin
11th Guards Tank Corps
40th Tank Brigade
44th Tank Brigade
45th Tank Brigade
8th Guards Mechanised Corps
27th Guards Tank Brigade
19th Guards Mechanised Brigade
20th Guards Mechanised Brigade
21st Guards Mechanised Brigade
Independent Army Units
1st Guards Tank Brigade
64th Guards Tank Brigade
11th Guards Tank Regiment
6th Motorcycle Regiment
40th Guards Gun Artillery Brigade (1 btn)
353rd Anti-aircraft Artillery Regiment
362nd Anti-aircraft Artillery Regiment
265th Mortar Regiment
270th Mortar Regiment
79th Guards Mortar Regiment
405th Guards Mortar Brigade
53rd Guards Mortar Brigade
4th Guards Anti-tank Artillery Division
358th Anti-tank Artillery Regiment
1018th Anti-tank Artillery Regiment
399th Self-propelled Artillery Regiment
400th Self-propelled Artillery Regiment
1454th Self-propelled Artillery Regiment
13th Guards Independent Motorised Engineer Battalion
14th Guards Engineer Brigade
6th Pontoon Brigade (2 btns)

4th GUARDS TANK ARMY

Commander: Colonel-General P.S. Rybalko
Commissar: Lieutenant-General of Tank Forces S.I. Mel'nikov
Chief of Staff: Major-General of Tank Forces D.D. Bakhmet'ev
6th Guards Tank Corps
51st Tank Brigade
52nd Tank Brigade
53rd Tank Brigade
22nd Guards Motorised Rifle Brigade
7th Guards Tank Corps
54th Tank Brigade
55th Tank Brigade
56th Tank Brigade
23rd Guards Motorised Rifle Brigade
9th Mechanised Corps
69th Mechanised Brigade
70th Mechanised Brigade
71st Mechanised Brigade
Independent Army Units
91st Tank Brigade
47th Tank Regiment
59th Guards Heavy Tank Regiment
71st Guards Heavy Tank Regiment
29th Guards Heavy Tank Regiment
57th Tank Regiment (IS2 heavy tanks)
33rd Gun Artillery Brigade (one 152mm btn)
10th Guards Anti-tank Artillery Brigade
1660th Anti-tank Artillery Regiment
108th Anti-tank Artillery Regiment
312th Anti-tank Artillery Regiment
272nd Mortar Regiment
467th Mortar Regiment
616th Mortar Regiment

36th Guards Mortar Regiment
91st Guards Mortar Regiment
439th Guards Mortar Brigade
440th Guards Mortar Brigade
441st Guards Mortar Brigade
1719th Anti-aircraft Artillery Regiment
1381st Anti-aircraft Artillery Regiment
1394th Anti-aircraft Artillery Regiment
268th Guards Anti-aircraft Artillery Regiment
287th Guards Anti-aircraft Artillery Regiment
702nd Self-propelled Artillery Regiment
1449th Self-propelled Artillery Regiment
1507th Self-propelled Artillery Regiment
1893rd Self-propelled Artillery Regiment
1894th Self-propelled Artillery Regiment
53rd Engineer Brigade (2 btns)
182nd Engineer Brigade (miners)

4th TANK ARMY
Commander: Colonel-General D.D . Leliushenko
Commissar: Major-General V.G. Guliaev
Chief of Staff: Major-General of Tank Forces K.I . Upman
10th Guards Tank Corps
61st Guards Tank Brigade
62nd Guards Tank Brigade
63rd Guards Tank Brigade
29th Guards Motorised Rifle Brigade
6th Guards Mechanised Corps
16th Guards Mechanised Brigade
17th Guards Mechanised Brigade
49th Guards Mechanised Brigade
Independent Army Units
93rd Tank Brigade
72nd Heavy Tank Regiment
51st Motorcycle Regiment
9th Guards Anti-tank Artillery Regiment
51st Anti-tank Artillery Regiment
357th Anti-tank Artillery Regiment
1689th Anti-tank Artillery Regiment
62nd Anti-tank Artillery Brigade
740th Anti-tank Artillery Brigade
240th Mortar Regiment
29th Mortar Regiment
312th Guards Mortar Regiment
52nd Guards Mortar Brigade
248th Guards Mortar Brigade
68th Anti-aircraft Artillery Division
396th Anti tank Artillery Regiment
359th Anti-tank Artillery Regiment
1st Guards Self-propelled Artillery Regiment
356th Self-propelled Artillery Regiment
374th Heavy Self-propelled Artillery Regiment
88th Engineer Brigade (miners)
3rd Pontoon Brigade (1 btn)
53rd Engineer Brigade (1 btn)

1st CAVALRY MECHANISED GROUP
Commander: Lieutenant-General V.K. Baranov
1st Guards Cavalry Corps
1st Guards Cavalry Division
2nd Guards Cavalry Division
7th Guards Cavalry Division
25th Tank Corps
11th Tank Brigade
162nd Tank Brigade
175th Tank Brigade
20th Motorised Rifle Brigade
Independent Army Units
58th Tank Regiment
61st Tank Regiment
1451st Self-propelled Artillery Regiment
1244th Self-propelled Artillery Regiment
1253rd Self-propelled Artillery Regiment
143rd Anti-tank Artillery Regiment
1497th Anti-tank Artillery Regiment
Anti-tank Artillery Regiment from 3rd Guards Army
2nd Guards Mortar Brigade
319th Anti-aircraft Artillery Regiment
1702nd Anti-aircraft Artillery Regiment

2nd CAVALRY MECHANISED GROUP
Commander: Lieutenant-General S.V. Sokolov
6th Guards Cavalry Corps
8th Guards Cavalry Division
13th Guards Cavalry Division
8th Cavalry Division
31st Tank Corps
100th Tank Brigade
237th Tank Brigade
242nd Tank Brigade
65th Motorised Rifle Brigade
Independent Army Units
136th Tank Regiment
154th Tank Regiment
250th Tank Regiment
1813th Self-propelled Artillery Regiment
1442nd Self-propelled Artillery Regiment
1548th Self-propelled Artillery Regiment
142nd Anti-tank Artillery Regiment
1732nd Anti-aircraft Artillery Regiment
1885th Anti-aircraft Artillery Regiment
1954th Anti-aircraft Artillery Regiment

5th GUARDS ARMY
Commander: Lieutenant-General A.S. Zhadov
Commissar: Major-General A.M. Krivulin
Chief of Staff: Major-General N.M. Liamin
32nd Guards Rifle Corps
13th Guards Rifle Division
95th Guards Rifle Division
97th Guards Rifle Division
33rd Guards Rifle Corps
9th Guards Airborne Division
14th Guards Rifle Division
78th Guards Rifle Division
34th Guards Rifle Corps
15th Guards Rifle Division
58th Guards Rifle Division
118th Guards Rifle Division
Independent Army Units
1073rd Anti-tank Artillery Regiment
469th Mortar Regiment
308th Guards Mortar Regiment
29th Anti-tank Artillery Regiment
55th Engineer Brigade

FRONT RESERVES
47th Rifle Corps
280th Rifle Division
309th Rifle Division
9th Cossack Rifle Division (dsmtd)
Independent Front Units
28th Tank Regiment (IS 122s)
8th Guards Anti-tank Artillery Brigade
1660th Anti-tank Artillery Brigade
23rd Guards Mortar Regiment
37th Anti-aircraft Artillery Division
1288th Anti-aircraft Artillery Division
322nd Guards Anti-aircraft Artillery Brigade
22nd Guards Anti-aircraft Artillery Brigade
42nd Independent Motorised Engineer Brigade
8th Independent Pontoon Battalion
50th Independent Pontoon Battalion
20th Independent Pontoon Battalion

2nd AIR ARMY
Commander: Colonel-General of Aviation S.A. Kasovsky

Commissar: Deputy Commander for Political Units Major-General S.A. Romazanov

Chief of Staff: Major-General of Aviation K.I. Tel'nov

5th Fighter Aviation Corps
- 8th Guards Fighter Aviation Division
- 256th Fighter Aviation Division

7th Fighter Aviation Corps
- 9th Guards Fighter Aviation Division
- 205th Fighter Aviation Division
- 304th Fighter Aviation Division

10th Fighter Aviation Corps
- 10th Guards Fighter Aviation Division
- 235th Fighter Aviation Division
- 6th Guards Fighter Aviation Division

1st Guards Assault Aviation Corps
- 8th Guards Assault Aviation Division
- 9th Guards Assault Aviation Division
- 12th Guards Fighter Aviation Division

1st Guards Mixed Aviation Corps
- 5th Guards Assault Aviation Division
- 6th Guards Assault Aviation Division
- 11th Guards Fighter Aviation Division

5th Assault Aviation Corps
- 4th Guards Assault Aviation Division
- 264th Assault Aviation Division
- 331st Fighter Aviation Division

8th Assault Aviation Corps
- 224th Assault Aviation Division
- 227th Assault Aviation Division
- 236th Fighter Aviation Division
- 10th Guards Assault Aviation Division

2nd Guards Bomber Aviation Corps
- 1st Guards Bomber Aviation Division
- 8th Guards Assault Aviation Division
- 244th Bomber Aviation Division

4th Bomber Aviation Corps
- 202nd Bomber Aviation Division
- 219th Bomber Aviation Division
- 321st Bomber Aviation Division
- 208th Fighter-bomber Aviation Division
- 98th Guards Reconnaissance Aviation Regiment
- 50th Reconnaissance Aviation Regiment
- 2 Independent Aviation Correction Regiments

Appendix X

Notification sent by *Auskunftstelle für Kriegerverluste der Waffen-SS* to Wysockyj Family

From the Author's archive.

Dear Wysockyj family!

Only now, after ascertaining the present address of the relatives of volunteer *Sturmmann* Roman Wysockyj, from the information office of war casualties of the Waffen-SS, am I able to send you news of your son.

It is now more than 7 months since the heavy fighting near Brody in July 1944, and all inquiries regarding the missing men of the regiments have led to nothing, especially as only very few officers, NCOs and men returned. I must, therefore, send you the sad news that your son has not returned either. He fought bravely and loyally at the side of his comrades in the bitter fighting to escape from the encirclement the division had got into. In the heavy skirmishes in the forest, which often continued into the nigh, he was separated from his unit and since then there has been no trace of him. Your son has been registered as missing and it must be assumed, unfortunately, that he has been taken prisoner or fallen in battle. To you this news is a terrible blow, and I can only ask you to bear your sorrow in the proud consciousness that he fought in accordance with his oath for Führer and nation. With him we have lost a good comrade and a loyal comrade-in-arms. But the fighting goes on, and after the victory, the prisoners will return, and you too can still hope that he will return.

In deep sympathy for the terrible fate of your son,
Heil Hitler!

Appendix XI

Award list for Iron Cross Second Class

From the Author's Archive.

See Glossary for details of abbreviations etc.

Waff.-Gren. Div. der SS/gal Nr.1/
Area of operations: Eastern Front, southern sector

Award List Number 1 for the Iron Cross Second Class

Surname	*Forename*	*Birthplace*	*D.o.B.*	*Rank*	*Unit*	*Awarded*
Div. Staff						
Specht	Max	Lemkol	8.11.98	SS-Ostubaf.	IVb.	1.8.44
Kopp	Oskar	Kirschhofen	30.5.10	SS-Stubaf.	IVc.	1.8.44
Sulzbach	Otto	Darmstadt	18.5.09	SS-Stubaf.	IVa.	1.8.44
Behrendt	Heinz	Braunsch.	20.7.09	SS-Stubaf.	V	1.8.44
Zoglauer	Karl	Innsbruck	3.7.07	SS-Hstuf.	VI	1.8.44
Muller	Erich	Hattingen	18.3.15	SS-Oscha.	IIa.	1.8.44
Nödinger	Karl	Ulm	8.7.12	SS-Oscha.	Ia.	1.8.44
Godschan	Walter	Drebkau	12.7.22	SS-Rttf.	Feldg.	1.8.44
Babick	Johann	Neuwise	22.12.06	SS-Strm.	Krftfhr.	1.8.44
Kuhn	Hubert	St.Michel	7.8.26	SS-Gren.	Krftfhr.	1.8.44
Witt	Günter	Schleswig	14.10.26	SS-Gren .	Krftfhr.	1.8.44
Waff-Gren.-Regt.29 der SS/gal.NrI/						
Weiss	Günter	Giessen	28.9.16	SS-Ostuf.	Stb.Kp.	1.8.44
Thessel	Heinz	Dresden	18.7.07	SS-Ustuf.	Rgt.St.	1.8.44
Kosak	Wolodymyr	Peremshyl	26.5.16	W-Ostuf.	4./29	1.8.44
Levenets	Michael	Brody	26.9.11	W-Ustuf.	Rgt.Stb	1.8.44
Konig	Alfred	Hunnora	2.8.13	SS-Oscha.	Rgt.Stb	1.8.44
Duker	Albert	Trier	28.7.09	SS-Oscha.	II./29	1.8.44
Schulz	Herbert	Westenfeld	23.I.23	SS-Oscha.	Rgt.Stb	1.8.44
Erdmann	Paul	Gutstadt	25.2.15	SS-Oscha.	II./29	1.8.44
Grabe	Herbert	Eisleden	14.12.11	SS-Oscha.	Rgt.Stb	1.8.44
Klein	Willi	Schutterzel	23.55.20	SS-Scharf.	Rgt.Stb	1.8.44
Klein	Helmut	Neuenburg	24.9.21	SS-Oscha.	Rgt.Stb	1.8.44
Kinnich	Lutwin	Broos	20.4.07	SS-Uscha.	II./29	1.8.44
Bodnar	Lubomyr	Ungwar	5.11.19	W-Uscha.	14./29	1.8.44
Kinasch	Jaroslav	Stanislau	20.7.23	W-Uscha.	II./29	1.8.44
Daumann	Harry	Tilsit	4.5.22	SS-Rttf.	Rgt.Stb	1.8.44
Pietsch	Herbert	Kattowitz	9.5.20	SS-Rttf.	Stab	1.8.44
Czuczkewycz	Ostap	Romaniv	2.10.07	W-Ustuf.	14./29	1.8.44
Waff-Gren.-Regt.30 der SS/gal.Nr2/						
Trautvetter	Walter	Laucha	9.5.03	SS-Ostuf.	Stab	1.8.44
Royer	Siegfried	Schlatming	15.2.10	SS-Oscha.	Stab	1.8.44
Heis	Helmut	—	4.3.24	SS-Uscha.	14./30	1.8.44
Jung	Heinrich	Berlin	9.10.03	SS-Uscha.	II./30	1.8.44
Bobinskyj	Jaroslav	Galizien	11.2.11	W-Uscha.	I./30	1.8.44
Lechniuk	Jarema	Kamionka	20.10.22	W-Gren.	I3./30	1.8.44
Waff-Gren.-Regt.31 der SS/gal.Nr3/						
Rohda	Gerhard	Memel	18.4.12	SS-Ostuf.	Stab	1.8.44
Funk	Helmut	Schatthausen	27.11.10	SS-Ostuf.	Stab	1.8.44
Amtsfeld	Heinz	Luneburg	17.7.11	SS-Ustuf.	I./31	1.8.44
Wurth	Karl	Koln	22.7.09	SS-Ustuf.	Stab	1.8.44
Dawald	Karl	Zwittan	19.4.20	SS-Uscha.	Stab	1.8.44

Lurssen	Willi	Lindern	26.11.09	SS-Uscha.	I./31	1.8.44
Gardetzkyj	Olesj	Kostiv	25.7.25	W-Uscha.	8./31	1.8.44
Damkowytsch	Josef	Stanislau	5.6.21	W-Rttf.	14./31	1.8.44
Paschytznyj	Myron	Birtscha	20.2.20	W-Strm.	7./31	1.8.44
Kondur	Jurij	Zbarazh	6.5.22	W-Gren.	Stab	1.8.44
Waffen-Fus.-Batl.14 der SS						
Bojcun	Roman	Zloczow	14.8.20	W-Ostuf.	4.Kp.	1.8.44
Gaspar	Lutwin	Besseringen	2.8.23	SS-Uscha.	Stab	1.8.44
Fylypowych	Nikolaus	Kuty	17.4.25	W-Strm.	4.Kp.	1.8.44
Janko	Wasyl	Dobrotiw	19.4.25	W-O.Fus.	2.Kp.	1.8.44
Waffen-Art.-Regt. 14 der SS						
Stolle	Hermann	Wense	21.12.04	SS-Unstuf.	Stab	1.8.44
Braun	Richard	Wetzlar	19.10.21	SS-Unstuf.	III/14	1.8.44
Dlaboha	Michael	Torki	27.1.05	W-Ustuf.	II/14	1.8.44
Weis	Josef	Wien	7.2.09	SS-Stuscha.	Stab.B	1.8.44
Martens	Alexander	Riga	4.10.03	SS-Oscha.	4.Battr.	1.8.44
Krauledat	Willy	Alexkehl	3.04.09	SS-Oscha.	I.Battr.	1.8.44
Schmarze	Heinrich	Pr. Stohen	8.4.13	SS-Oscha.	Stab	1.8.44
Dzundza	Eugen	Kalush	1.6.20	W-Uscha.	I.Battr.	1.8.44
Gurniswytsch	Marian	Tarnopol	24.7.20	W-Strm.	6.Battr.	1.8.44
Butschvnskyj	Roman	Zbarazh	13.3.25	W-Kan.	2.Battr.	1.8.44
Palienko	Wasyl	Podibrady	9.4.26	W-Kan.	1.Battr.	1.8.44
SS-Freiw.-Flak-Abtl. 14						
Wahl	—	—	—	SS-Uscha.	Stab	1.8.44
Piczenki	Joachim	Luggenwalde	13.12.21	SS-Uscha.	—	1.8.44
SS-Pz.Jg.Abtl.14						
Heberling	Kurt	—	10.8.21	SS-Uscha.	Komp.	1.8.44
Schtschudluk	Myron	—	1.5.--	W-Uscha.	Komp.	1.8.44
Lofi	Günter		17.9.14	W-Strm.	Komp.	1.8.44
Waffen-Pi.Batl. 14 der SS						
Haubner	München	—	15.1.95	SS-Hstuf.	Sond.Kp	1.8.44
Krausser	Heinz	Hammersleben	7.11.20	SS-Ustuf.	Stab	1.8.44
Zaberowski	Paul	Berlin	4.11.10	SS-Ustuf.	Stab	1.8.44
Freytag	Paul	Voburg	4.11.14	SS-Uscha.	KIA	1.8.44
Janke	Josef	Neuensee	1.1.12	SS-Uscha.	3.Kp	1.8.44

Waff-San.Abtl. 14 der SS						
Friedrich	Karl	Gera	1.12.12	SS-Oscha.	Stab	1.8.44
Salamon	Karl	Karwen	7.3.24	SS-Uscha.	2.Kp.	1.8.44
Luhring	Helmut	Marburg	2.10.21	SS-Uscha.	1.Kp.	1.8.44
Hersener	Gustav	Helmstadt	3.7.24	SS-Rttf.	2.Kp.	1.8.44
Butzmann	Arthur	Stuttgart	27.7.97	SS-Rttf.	2.Kp.	1.8.44
Sauer	Helmut	Weida	25.3.26	SS-Strm.	2.Kp.	1.8.44
Div.-Nachsch.-Tr. 14						
Zeh	Hans	Dresden	1.12.04	SS-Stuscha.	Stab	1.8.44
Qade	Horst	Parchim	26.12.17	SS-Oscha.	Stab	1.8.44
Kelchard	Eugen	Ulm	22.08.04	SS-Oscha.	Stab	1.8.44
Elmer	Stefan	Batschka	14.05.02	SS-Uscha.	Stab	1.8.44
Battermann	Werner	Hannover	26.04.21	SS-Uscha.	Stab	1.8.44
Waffen-Nachrichten Abtl.14 der SS						
Koppan	Lothar	Havelberg	23.9.19	SS-Ostuf.	2.Kp.	1.8.44
Unterguggenberg	Johan	Mattling	1.2.14	SS-Oscha.	1.Kp.	1.8.44
Martschuk	Wlodymyr	Kolomyia	2.7.15	W-Strm.	1.Kp.	1.8.44
Bulik	Hans	Bremen	13.5.24	SS-Funk.	1.Kp.	1.8.44
Batko	Stefan	Peremshyl	6.7.22	W-Funk.	2.Kp.	1.8.44
Vers.-Tr. Abtl. 14						
Meier	Ernst	Minden	28.2.12	SS-Ostuf.	Adj.	1.8.44
Bollbuck	Walter	Garding	6.11.08	SS-Ostuf.	Verw.Kp.	1.8.44
Holfe	Karl	Wien	18.11.13	SS-Ostuf.	Verw.Kp.	1.8.44
Hullencremer	Erich	Worms	15.10.17	SS-Hscha.	Stab	1.8.44
Helling	Otto	Stendal	5.4.13	SS-Hscha.	Back.Kp.	1.8.44
Siering	Hans	Raschutz	30.10.12	SS-Oscha.	Verw.Kp.	1.8.44
Gladitz	Ewald	Langfeld	12.12.19	SS-Uscha.	Verw.Kp.	1.8.44
Fichtal	Otto	Beilstein	5.2.07	SS-Uscha.	Schl.Kp.	1.8.44
Gkobarla	Paul	Antonienbutte	28.5.05	SS-Uscha.	Back.Kp.	1.8.44
Polzin	Heinz	Berlin	2.10.22	SS-Rttf.	Back.Kp.	1.8.44
Schmidt	Walter	Essen	10.4.23	SS-Strm.	Back.Kp.	1.8.44
Werkst.-Kp.14						
Hornik	Anton	Folmau	19.1.16	SS-Oscha.	Komp.	1.8.44
Vet.-Komp. 14						
Kastner	Karl	Abtsbes	22.5.11	SS-Oscha.	Komp.	1.8.44
Hesse	Josef	Grefenbruck	14.9.16	SS-Uscha.	Komp.	1.8.44
Hoger	Josef	Neu Passau	15.8.21	SS-Rttf.	Komp.	1.8.44
Lemke	Ernst	Linzheim	9.3.24	SS-Rttf.	Komp.	1.8.44

Signed Freitag
SS-Brigadeführer und Generalmajor der Waffen SS

Appendix XII

Secret leaving report on Ukrainian Officer Candidate Olexa Horbatsch, *SS-Artillerie-Schule* II, Beneschau, 24 August 1944

From the Author's archive

H. is a Galician. He comes from a poor, farming family.
Father: Farmer, 75 years old. Siblings: 2 brothers, 1 sister.
Profession: Middle school teacher, single.
Primary school, Grammar school, A-Levels, University (Slavonic and Germanic philology). Drafted into the Red Army in the autumn of 1940, and defected to the Germans in the autumn of 1941.
Rank attained in the Red Army: Sergeant. Enlisted in the Waffen-SS on 17.7.1943. Subsequent retraining at *SS-Artillerie-Schule* II, in Beneschau completed on 10.3.1944. Served in the 9./*SS-Freiw.*A.R.14. Troop type: Artillery.

H. is large and powerful physically, though somewhat clumsy. He is very capable, but does not have enough self-discipline to overcome harder tasks. Appearance and attitude are excellent. He is a reliable, hard working person with an upright and self-confident personality. His manner is controlled and approachable. He has a healthy desire for the esteem of others. He responds well to authority. He is sure of himself, decisive, but somewhat lacking in energy. His manners are good, but require occasional admonishment. H. has an idealistic approach to life. He has a broad sphere of knowledge, and has a good level of general education, especially with regard to historical and philosophical concepts. His capacity for philosophical and moral judgement is well defined and fully mature. Areas of special interest: Linguistic sciences, philosophy.

Mentally he is above average. He picks things up quickly, and is interested and actively involved in lessons. His analytical capacity is well developed, and his capacity for judgement is clear and accurate.

He performs his duties responsibly and with interest. He has a good command of the German language and he is able to teach it to others. His behaviour in command is somewhat soft. His commands are clear and understandable, but are not sufficiently inspirational. Among his comrades he is helpful and comradely. He can assert himself well over those under his command and he is tactful with superiors.

He is suitable to be a Waffen-SS officer.

Deployment as Battery Officer is suggested.

Final Report

Rank	*Name,*	*Forename*	*SS-No.*	*Date of birth*
The Stand. Ju.	Horbatsch,	Olexa		24.9.22

During the *SS-Kriegsjunker* 16th training course at the *Waffen-Junkerschule* 'Braunschweig', from 15 July until 15 December 1944, he demonstrated understanding, as indicated, in the following subjects, and has thus passed the final examination.

1. Applied Philosophy: Fairly good
2. Tactics and Terrain: Fairly good
3. SS and *Polizei*: Fairly good
4. Army: Fairly good
5. Military Duties: Good
6. Physical Education: Fairly good
7. Communication Studies: Fairly good
8. Technical Weapon Training: Good
9. Engineer/Sapper Training: Fairly good
10. Motorised Vehicle Training: -------
11. Riding, Horse-drawn Driving: Fairly good

Appendix XIII

Proposal for award of the Knight's Cross of the Iron Cross to *SS-Brigadeführer* Freitag

Der Reichsführer-SS

Reichsführer-SS Personl. Stab
Verb. Offz. b.OKH/PA/P5

16 September 1944
Tgb.Nr.843/449/1.
(approved by Himmler 16 September)
Number 3692

Proposal for the Awarding of the Knight's Cross of the Iron Cross (Award Date 30.9.44)
Commander of the 3rd *Panzer* Army, Army HQ (Nominated 23.8.1944)
Review concerning *SS-Brigadeführer* Freitag, CO 14th *Waffen-Gren.-Div. der SS* (*galiz.*Nr.1)

In view of the short period during which the [14th Galician Division] was part of the 1st *Panzer* Army, it is not possible for me to make a definite and exhaustive assessment.

Impression: Circumspect, self-assured (sure of one's aim) leader. Great personal bravery, eager for action. He made enthusiastic efforts to get the best out of his Galician SS-Division. He distinguished himself while breaking through the surrounding forces at Zolochiv, by virtue of his leading, dynamic approach and tough action against weaklings.

Raus, *Generaloberst*

SS-Brigadeführer Freitag demonstrated exemplary and total personal preparedness for action, under uniquely difficult combat conditions in the Brody pocket.

His Division in this instance was not made up of German soldiers prepared to fight to the last in combat, but of Ukrainians of the Galician region, innately weak and apt to waver, lacking any of the manly or fighting virtues of the Germans.

Keeping together and leading men, so unfamiliar with war and so averse to hardship, in the carrying out of the most difficult of orders (such as in the Battle in the Brody pocket) requires ultimate and unique involvement on the part of the leader responsible.

Because of the particular circumstances, as of 12 July 1944, the Division was placed at the decisive position in the battle in the pocket, and received as its first impression of combat, the retreat of German units.

When the reinforced Grenadier Regiment 30 looked as though it was going to get dragged into this retreat, it was the Division commander who with the Regiment commander immediately re-secured the situation in that area, and prevented the threatened breakthrough of enemy forces.

Later in the battle numerous 'volunteers' of the Division deserted due to innate cowardice. In some cases they even turned their weapons on their own officers and NCOs. In the main it was the Division commander who, there and then, restored order with unhesitating personal action, and took the appropriate measures against the miserable wretches.

The Division fulfilled its orders, under the most difficult circumstances, up to 19 July 1944. This was achieved with Ukrainians, who, with few exceptions are not inherently disposed as fighters, supported only by a handful of German personnel.

The recognised achievements of the Division, when deployed in the crucial point of the battle must be credited solely to the German leadership and ultimately to the Division commander. The achievements rest mainly on their personal actions during the focal point of the battle. The tragic thing about the deployment of the Division is that despite the exemplary conduct of the Division commander a decisive success in battle was denied.

After the shattering of the Division in the Brody pocket, the Division commander made himself available to the leader of the rear guard troops – *Generalmajor* Lindemann. After Lindemann's heroic death, and despite being wounded himself, Freitag was the last general to leave the pocket. Cautiously and safely he led all remaining troops out of the first encirclement.

In the late afternoon of 22 July 1944 the Division commander gathered about 4,000 men of all divisions of XIII Corps and personally decided to break through the encirclement. It had been renewed by the enemy, to the south-west.

In contrast to other combat units that attempted to breakout towards the west and the south and who, in the main, fell victim to the enemy at Zaskow and Prezemyslany, Freitag led his combat unit out of the encirclement despite the exhaustion of his men.

SS-Brigadeführer Freitag has been deployed at the front since the start of this war, and since the end of 1941 he has been almost continuously deployed in the East. He has fought in the mid-sector of the Eastern Front, as a regimental commander at Wolchow and outside Leningrad, and has proved himself as a troop leader.

Appendix XIV

Political leadership of the troops, 28 October 1944

From the Archives of the Brotherhood of Former Combatants.

14.*Waffen-Gren.Div. der SS* (*galiz.*Nr.1)
Div.St.Qu. 28.10.44

Commander
1357/44

Re: Political Leadership of the Troops

Despite the fact that I have repeatedly emphasised the importance of the political leadership and the doctrinal education and care of the troops, I have discovered that this is still not being understood by all officers and NCOs.

I discovered one training course, of several weeks' duration, where no lectures regarding political doctrine were given.

I further discovered that orders, in this case those concerning political leadership of the troops, have been put aside by desk staff without presenting them to the unit leader. These orders have thus not been passed on to the troops.

I know that the commanders are fully aware of the particular importance for our Division of political leadership. They make every effort to maintain full political control of their units. However as a result of the lack of understanding shown by some officers and NCOs everything that has been created by months of greatest effort, is being destroyed.

I know of one case, for example, where a unit leader who very nearly died as a result of his exemplary care for his men, but was deprived of any success in his training efforts, because of the total failure of his *Stabsscharführer* in the field of leadership.

If an officer now proudly reports to me that he has ordered that German and Ukrainian NCOs take their meals together, then I can only respond that this should have been taken for granted and that such an order should therefore have been given many months ago.

I have also discovered that men returning from training courses etc and awaiting collection from the divisional garrison by their units, have been left waiting for days without rations or other care, simply because their units have failed to collect them.

In addition there are also units in which rations, cigarettes, etc are being withheld from the men.

Such failure in personnel leadership destroys more than we can make good with years of greatest constructive effort.

I Command:

1. With immediate effect every German troop- and unit-leader, up to and including the rank of company leader, is to appoint an Ukrainian *Verbindungsmann* (Liaison Officer), who is given direct access and ability to make direct representations to that leader. These men have the task of making the officers aware of any difficulties the officers may not be able to identify themselves as a result of barriers of rank or language. The names of the Liaison Officers are to be reported to the Div. *Abtl.* VI by 5.11.44.

2. German officers and NCOs, particularly those newly transferred to the Division, must be constantly reminded of the political problem of this Division, and must apprise themselves of the appropriate guidelines for the political leadership of personnel.

Finally, I now wish to create a relationship of mutual trust between the German and Ukrainian men, as is required by the fighting community of our Division. I forbid any second rate treatment of Ukrainians.

I will use appropriate organisations to convince myself that my orders are being carried out and in future I will in cases of 'poor' political leadership of the troops approach that leaders immediate superior regarding inadequate performance of duty.

Freitag *SS-Brigadeführer und Generalmajor der Waffen-SS*
Division Commander
Distribution I & IV

Appendix XV

Strength and casualty lists, *SS-Freiw.* Grenadier Regiment 30, 22 September 1944

	Actual strength			KIA			Missing		
	O	N	M	O	N	M	O	N	M
Rgt. Staff	12(6)	1(1)	22(1)	—	—	1(1)	7(2)	1(1)	16
HQ Company	3(1)	32(16)	224(1)	—	—	1	3(1)	17(5)	204
Staff I/30	4(3)	11(6)	64(2)	—	—	1	2(1)	6(3)	52(1)
1st Company	1	5	136(1)	—	—	—	1	3	126(1)
2nd Company	1	6(1)	142	—	—	1	1	1	121(1)
3rd Company	1	7	133	—	—	2	—	2	111
4th Company	1	4(1)	216	1	—	2	—	2(1)	167
Staff II/30	4(3)	11(5)	52	1	—	1	—	5(1)	46(1)

30 SS *Freiw.* Gren. Rgt.
Liquidation Dept. 22.9.44.
Feldpost Nr. 05–330

Key: O Officers
N NCOs
M Other ranks

Figures given in brackets denote Germans

Appendix XVI

Letter from Alfred Rosenberg, 12 March 1945

From the Author's archive

Reichsminister Alfred Rosenberg
Berlin, 12 March 1945

General Paul Schandruk, Berlin-Charlottenburg, Kant Hotel

In order to maximise the effect of all anti-Bolshevik national forces in this decisive phase of the war, and in the interests of a just order of the nations in Europe, I recognise on behalf of the German government the working staff of Ukrainian national representatives called into existence by you as the Ukrainian National Committee.

I confirm that:

1. The Ukrainian National Committee is recognised by the German government as the sole representative of the Ukrainian people.

2. The National committee has the right to represent its views of the future of the Ukraine and to express this in declarations and manifestos.

When the question is finally settled as to how the Ukrainians fighting in the German army are to be organised, I will intercede in favour of Ukrainian troops in their entirety forming the Ukrainian Liberation Army.

Signed Rosenberg

Appendix XVII

Decrypted Disarmament Order issued to the 14th Galician Division

HW1/3666, Public Records Office, London, England.

HW1/3666
CX/MSS/T508/10
BT 9298

West – Southeast Europe
No. III/011057
From: OKH/General Staff of the Army £H£/QMG. *Abtl.* III
Signed: *Oberst* I.G Moeller-Althaus, 28/3/45

To: Army Group E, Chief QM and to 14 SS (Ukrainian) Div via Army Group E

In accordance with the Führer's order, 14th SS (Ukrainian) Div No.2(+) is to be disarmed in order that its weapons may be made available to the C-in-C West at once as immediate assistance in material. Army Group E will send off at once an acceptance detachment under the command of a senior ordnance officer of the Army Group to 14th SS Div at Marburg an der Drau.

Tasks:

1. To carry out most rapidly the disarming and collecting together of the weapons and equipment at the railway loading stations.
2. Rapid loading in complete trains.
3. To make certain of transport indent and speedy allocation of railway vehicles by director of transport Army Group E.
4. Army Group E is providing transport escort personnel under the command of officers.
5. Destination will be made known later.
6. Report that handing over has taken place to OKH/General Staff of the Army £H£/QMG *Abtl.* III. A numerical, detailed list regarding weapons, equipment etc given up is to follow.

Note: (+) error For No. 1.
The preceding was passed at 1.26pm 3/4/45

Appendix XVIII

Propaganda statement issued by F. Tolbukhin, commander of 3rd Ukrainian Front

To all generals, officers, and soldiers of the German Armed Forces in the southern sector of the eastern front

On 7 May, 1945 in the city of Reims, the act of military capitulation of all German armed forces was signed before the Union of the Socialist Soviet Republics, the United States of America, Great Britain, France and all United Nations – on the Western Front and also on the Eastern Front. As representative of the supreme commander of German Armed Forces, Grand-Admiral Dönitz signed the acts of an unconditional capitulation of the Chief of General staff of the Armed Forces, *Generaloberst* Jodl in the presence of Admiral Friedeburg.

Acts of the unconditional capitulation go in effect on 8 May 1945 at 23:00 hours central European time.

The supreme commander of the German Armed Forces, Grand-Admiral Dönitz has already issued an order of capitulation to all Armed Forces.

I submit (the following):

1. All German units and detachments, led by their generals and officers, have to cease all hostilities and surrender all weapons on 8 May 1945 at 23.00 hours.
2. Generals and officers [are directed] on 9 May from dawn until 9.00 hours central European time to send officers with a white flag to the Russian front line officers in order to receive the instructions about the surrender of weapons and surrender of troops.
3. All weapons, means of transport, communications equipment, war materiel and food stuffs must be turned over to the commanders of the Red Army in good condition.
4. All who surrender their arms and themselves according to the international rules regarding prisoners of war, are guaranteed life, uniform, decorations, personal property, regular nourishment, medical care and shelter in the POW camps until it is time to return home.

Commander of 3rd Ukrainian Front, Marshal of the Soviet Union F. Tolbukhin

Appendix XIX

Divisional Order No. 71

From the Archives of the Brotherhood of Former Combatants.

Divisional Order No. 71
The Ukrainianisation of the Division – Consequences for the Division.

Military consequences

Fact: The Division is part of the Eastern Front and must continue to fight Bolshevism as part of the Eastern Front.

1. The Division is, and remains a purely Ukrainian combat unit only a small percentage of which consists of German leaders, whose positions the Ukrainians are unable to fill because so many of the most intelligent have been liquidated.
2. The success of the Division in combat stands or falls on its unity.

Political consequences

1. The political advisers of the Division, General Schandruk [sic.], *SS-Gruppenfhr.* Dr Wächter, *Oberst* Bisanz, *SS-Ostubaf.* Dr Arlt are either with the Division or will arrive at the required time. They will most definitely be with the division as political advisers at the required time. General Schandruk [sic.] is furthermore the Commander in Chief of all Ukrainian units including the 1st Ukrainian Division. This is of particular importance and is to become common knowledge among the troops.
2. It is vital that we keep the Div. away from grasp of Bolshevism and to maintain its integrity as a single effective anti-Bolshevik combat unit.
3. The deployment and maintenance of the Div. in its current state as an anti-Bolshevik combat unit is being organised in co-operation with the Allied camp. These matters are considered together with the negotiations concerning the future of the Cossack, Caucasian, and Georgian combat units. The negotiations are being done via the political leaders of the Div. with *SS-Obergruppenführer* Wolf, and via Switzerland. The negotiations regarding the Georgians and Caucasians were resolved favourably. These units will retain their weapons and German SS commanders, and remain armed anti-Bolshevik units.
4. When the Americans near their own Eastern Front, it is intended that they should be approached as early and as far back as possible. Herein lies the particular purpose of the *A.u.E.* Rgt. The relocation of the *A.u.E.* Rgt is not envisaged, because of its intended role, in engaging the Americans. Both Army and Corps have been briefed in these measures and have approved them completely and without reservation.
5. The negotiations can however only be carried out on the following basis:
   The Division is to remain, as before, a purely Ukrainian Division, i.e. the 1st Ukrainian Division, which along with the Ukrainian National Army, is to be set up with the authorisation of the Reichs government, and is to have at its head General Schandruk [sic.] as Commander in Chief. The German personnel assigned to the Div. were only essential in the beginning, because Ukrainians suitable for the posts held by

German officers and NCOs, were not available. The leaders and the Ukrainian intelligentsia had been liquidated en masse by Bolshevism. The withdrawal of German personnel following the development of suitable Ukrainian leaders was envisaged from the beginning. In the division there are (11%) Germans. The inclusion of Luftwaffe personnel, which would mean the raising of German personnel to 3,600, is, for the aforementioned political reasons, unviable. A decision regarding future use of the Luftwaffe personnel has been requested. Until a decision has been made, we must tread water. However, the commanders do have the right to immediately enlist any Luftwaffe personnel who are suited to join their troops, and who would not compromise the integrity or morale of the Division. All other Luftwaffe members are to be initially formed into closed training units. It is however stressed that exceptional men should be transferred to the troops of the Division immediately. It is important to remember that the Div. is west Ukrainian i.e. a Galician Division. Only a few individuals are east Ukrainian. There are no Russians in the Division. There is therefore no conflict with the Polish government in London, but there is a distinct conflict with the Polish government in Lublin. This omission of west Ukrainians is necessary to distinguish the division from the Polish Corps fighting for the Anglo-Americans in Italy. This Corps is also anti-Bolshevik. It is very important that the Division is the first combat unit of the Ukrainian National Army, at whose head General Schandruk [sic.] stands as Commander in Chief.

Likely possibilities for the Division

The honour of being part of the coming anti-Bolshevik combat block [*Kampfblock*], while retaining all weapons and the integrity of the Division. Negotiations regarding this are in progress and appear to be progressing favourably. It is in the interests of the matter as a whole that the German personnel (Luftwaffe still to be decided) should stay with the Division. There is also the possibility that without German personnel the unit may join the Anglo-American side. This possibility seems unlikely in view of the circumstances.

1. All German personnel remain complete within the Division.
   When considering how to present this step to the German personnel, or when each German answers to his conscience, the following should be considered:
   (a) The maintaining of all units with any combat capacity whatsoever, will be decisive in the final battle against Bolshevism which lies ahead of us with 100% certainty. It is therefore the duty of every member of the Division, whether German or Ukrainian, to do his utmost to maintain the unit in its entirety as a fighting force against Bolshevism. The tighter and more complete the internal cohesion of the unit, the more successful will be the coming march against Bolshevism.
   (b) It is vital that we maintain and keep together the remaining valuable blood that has been brought together by its hatred of Bolshevism.
   (c) The Division, in its composition and in particular in the working relationship between the Germans and the Ukrainians, forms a firm blood-bonded basis for the future co-operation of both peoples.
   (d) For the Germans to remain in the Ukrainian Division, they must show chivalry towards the Ukrainians who are in the main respectable, and who despite severe setbacks have stood with greatest loyalty by the side of the German Reich right into the very last phase of the battle.
   (e) Following the philosophy of the *Werwolf* remains foolish, as no military or other conditions prevail that would justify this kind of freedom movement. External support for this movement is not present. A *Werwolf* movement under the given assumptions can only result in a cost to the civilian population, that will lead those in question into the fold of the partisans. He who wishes to leave the Division excludes himself from the community. There can however only be a communal fate from which no one is able to exclude themselves.
   (f) It should also be noted that one million Ukrainians currently reside in America and 600,000 in Canada.
   (g) The German personnel would keep, as would the whole Div., the same uniforms until further notice, should the Division be transferred to the anti-Bolshevik battle front.
2. The German personnel leave prior to a transfer of the Division.
   This measure should also be prepared for. Most importantly officers must, as of now, be considered to replace the Germans immediately should they leave. The personnel thus released must immediately be placed under the command of the commander of the nearest German combat unit, if possible an SS unit.
3. In the case of an official capitulation by the German Reich, which can hardly be expected, the Division is to withdraw towards the Anglo-Americans. Thus all units would be ordered to go to assembly areas as far back as possible. Command would then only be conducted by radio and messengers.

Immediate measures

1. Philosophical instruction
   The concepts presented above must immediately be presented to the officer and NCO corps (German and Ukrainian), by the commanders. This is currently the most urgent measure and the highest priority task for the commanders. Nothing is to be kept secret, instead all possibilities and facts are to be clearly presented.
   It should be emphasised as forcefully as possible that the Germans of the Division are in no way deserting the Ukrainians, but intend to continue to stand by them in a joint future. The principle that should be expressed in all theoretical and practical measures, is that the unity of, and the links within the Division, will remain regardless of what the future may bring. The better the relationship between the Germans and the Ukrainians, the better and happier the future. The officers can be clearly informed of the fact that negotiations with the allied camp have commenced. It may be hinted at to the NCOs in order to maintain combat morale. The requirement for the success of all measures that are currently in progress, is that the front be held. The men must also be made aware of the future in a suitable form.
2. How long the Division's current battle is likely to last is impossible to predict; it may be short. All the more important then that we use the remaining days to reward the deserving officers, NCOs, and men. The Div. will therefore be very charitably disposed to nominations for promotion or decorations and will pass these on immediately. They will make an effort to consider all nominations as fully as possible. Particular note is to be made that, as of 8 days from now, every type of nomination can, in view of the prevailing circumstances, be dealt with internally.
3. Special emphasis must be given to keeping order and discipline in the unit. The unit must remain firmly in the hands of its leaders.
4. The unit must quickly receive everything it can transport by itself, by depleting the stores of the quartermasters department. Firstly the Division should immediately be equipped with as much transportable food as possible. Additionally the troops must be equipped with enough ammunition to be able to engage the enemy at any time. Additional supplies of ammunition and food cannot be expected. Emergency rations are to be issued to the troops immediately. If a man eats his rations immediately, then only he will suffer. Replacements cannot be issued. This must be made clear to the troops.
5. Remaining bedding, clothing, and equipment are to be issued to the troops immediately. It is mindless, possibly even sabotage, to continue to hoard valuable clothing and equipment in stores. Any officer who fails to put all his effort into equipping his troops as well as possible by emptying the stores, shall suffer summary justice. The troops must however only receive those things that they can genuinely take with them. Poor clothing is to be replaced immediately with the best available. The administrative officers must work with great flexibility and speed. The troop officers must, as appropriate, put the necessary pressure on their administrative officers. It must be particularly stressed that the transport of stores will no longer be possible. Seizure of goods or plundering by other parts of the Division must be relied upon.
6. Future command will depend mainly on the use of radio for information. Radio communication readiness is to be checked from Divisional level right down to company level. The mobility of the communication centres is of particular importance. In addition communications duties are to be assigned to the best NCOs and men. They are to be mounted to a large extent, to increase mobility. Bulk loads of fuel for loading on to transporters are to be requested from the appropriate departments and stored.
7. All vehicles must be loaded and ready. This also applies to the convoy section of the Division's supply department. The process of clearing out is to continue with renewed emphasis. Any non-essential equipment must be handed over to make room for food and ammunition.

Div. *Abtl.* Ib must put itself in a position where it is able to receive the equipment from all over the unit at short notice.

8. Div. *Abtl.* V must immediately test the remaining bulk supplies of fuel for range (i.e. miles per gallon/fuel value). For all still authorised vehicles, 3 V.S. must be with the unit.

   Files as far as is possible are to be cleared out and destroyed. War diaries are to no longer to be kept and are to be cancelled. [Note: legibility of original document in this section is very poor]. Divisional staff papers are to be destroyed.

9. *A.u.E.* Rgt. must quickly take over the Division's supplies in the Unterdrauberg and Mahrenberg region, and hide them for the Division. Apart from this all stores of the quartermaster's department that lie well in the rear are to be dissolved and transferred to the *A.u.E.* Rgt in the vicinity of the fighting troops. Maximum haste and speed is demanded of all section heads of the quartermaster's department.

10. The commanders are to transfer, via lists, those German soldiers, who for special reasons are strongly opposed to the Ukrainians, to the *Feld Ers.* Btl. Soldiers who hate or are hated by the Ukrainians cannot be kept. The *Feld Ers.* Btl., as a purely German unit, is not envisaged to take part in the actions of the battalion, but will have a different mission. Individual members of the HQ *Feld Ers.* Btl. may yet be included in the Division.

    Emphasis should be placed on the establishment of full mobility for all sections of the Division.

Appendix XX

Declaration of the Ukrainian Committee, 17 March 1945

From the Archives of the Brotherhood of Former Combatants.

Declaration of the Ukrainian Committee

The Ukrainian National Committee has come into being in accordance with the will of the Ukrainian citizens on the territory of Germany and in countries allied with it.

The establishment of the UNC is a new page in the social-political life of the Ukrainian citizens who, filled with a deep love of their country, wish to see their fatherland freed of occupying forces.

The UNC is the representative of these secret wishes of the citizens and it will stride boldly along the road to the creation of a National Sovereign State.

For this reason, the UNC has undertaken to organise an Ukrainian National Army that is to renew the armed struggle for an Ukrainian state.

The Ukrainian National Army, in Ukrainian uniform, under the national battle flags consecrated at the time of the last struggle, with its own Ukrainian command will be under the ideological-political leadership of the UNC. Into its ranks will come, above all, those Ukrainians who are in the German armed forces and other Wehrmacht and police formations.

The future state should be built by Ukrainians who are deeply patriotic, of tough moral fibre and strong in mind and body. For this reason, the UNC will make provision for the legal protection of all Ukrainian citizens in Germany, equal rights of the workers alongside all the citizens of nation states, and above all, for the development of an extremely broad religious, moral, cultural and material care. The UNC will also see to the liberation of all political prisoners.

The foreign borders that for many long years have separated the different Ukrainian regions have created differences in ideas and actions. This must disappear in a common march towards a common aim.

The UNC wishes to accelerate this process of unification of Ukrainian souls not only by setting up a large-scale education programme, but also by stating the collective Ukrainian view on all matters.

In its work the UNC will cooperate with the National Committees of other nations subjugated by the Bolshevism of Moscow which are fighting in exactly the same way as the Ukrainian nation for their independence and freedom.

The UNC is staunchly dedicated to and will not flinch from performing the duties the Ukrainian citizens have entrusted it with. It will certainly perform them, if every Ukrainian individual invests all his energy in the common struggle for the common victory.

Headquarters, 17 March 1945

Signed *Generalmajor* i.G. Pavlo Shandruk (Chairman, Ukrainian National Committee)
Prof. Dr Woldymyr Mychajlowytsch Kubijovych (Deputy Chairman, UNK)
Rechtsanwalt Oleksander Platonowytsch Semenenko (Deputy Chairman, UNK)
Ing. Petro Pawlowytsch Tereshchenko e.d.P.d (General Secretary, UNK)

Appendix XXI

Certificate, *Waffen-Untersturmführer* Volodymyr Lutziw, 31 March 1945

From the Author's archive

Waffen-Untersturmführer Volodymyr Lutziw serving with the *Waffen-Aus. u. Ers.* Rgt. der SS 14, *Führungstab-Befehlshaber Wkr.*- Kdo.XVIII *Gef. St.*, 31 March 1945

Certificate

The person showing this certificate is authorised to conduct searches of supply and baggage wagons, establish emergency units and further to deploy them or hand them over to the nearest front commander for action. Furthermore he has the right to shoot soldiers who disobey his orders or try to leave these emergency units without permission.

This order is valid for all parts of the Wehrmacht including Waffen-SS.

Führungstab Befehlshaber Wkr. Kdo. XVIII in agreement with the CO, Army Group Ia.

Notes

Chapter 1

1. The name Galicia ('Halychyna' in Ukrainian) is derived from the old city of Halych which was the seat of 'Halycko Wolynske Kniaziwstwo'– the Halych princedom, during the 13th Century. The capital of Galicia was L'viv ,also known as Lemberg (in German), L'vov (in Russian) and Lwów (in Polish).
2. Also known as Carpathian Ukraine.
3. Galicia had been added to the Empire in 1772 with the partition of Poland. As a former *Kronland* (Crown-Land) of the Austro-Hungarian Empire, Galicia benefited from the Habsburg's 'divide and rule' nationality policies. In 1914 the Galician Ukrainians won the Austrian government's permission to establish the 'Ukrainian Sich Riflemen' as a distinct unit of the Austrian army. These troops were later to become the backbone of the Ukrainian Galician army. *Ukraine During WWII, History and its Aftermath*, Y. Boshyk, Canadian Institute of Ukrainian Studies, University of Alberta, Edmonton, 1986, p.67.
4. *Rada* means council in Ukrainian. The Russian equivalent is *Soviet*.
5. Dated 22 January this important document was actually produced on the night of 24–25 January.
6. Known as *Brotfrieden* ('peace for bread').
7. See *Encyclopaedia of Ukraine* Vol. 2, G–K. University of Toronto Press, p.183.
8. During the Austro-German occupation of 1918, Ukraine supplied 42000–75000 freight car loads (equivalent to roughly 840000–1.5 million tonnes) of foodstuffs to those countries. Ibid., p.51.
9. Field Marshal von Eichhorn was murdered in Kiev on 30 July 1918, by a twenty-four-year-old Russian Social Revolutionary sailor, Boris M. Donskoij, acting on the orders of the Party's Central Committee in Moscow.
10. Skoropadskyj and his government were evacuated along with the retreating Germans.
11. For more information concerning the Directory of the UNR see *Encyclopaedia Ukraine*, Vol. 1, A–F, pp.675–676.
12. The Trident or Tryzub of Volodymyr the Great (979–1015) was the oldest symbol of national significance and is the national emblem of Ukraine.
13. As part of the so-called 'Third Revolution', enforced collectivisation of agriculture and the creation of *kolkhozes* (collective farms) were required to finance Stalin's vast industrialisation programme.
14. The famine was organised by one of Stalin's principal henchmen, Lazar Kaganovich. For a thorough discussion of the Ukrainian famine see Robert Conquest *The Harvest of Sorrow: Soviet collectivisation and the terror famine*, Hutchinson, London, 1986.
15. During the 1920s there was an influx of some 200,000 Poles into the rural areas of Galicia and 100,000 into the towns and cities, which further aggravated Ukrainian/Polish tensions. See *Encyclopaedia of Ukraine*, Vol. 2, G–K, p.187.
16. The Organisation of Ukrainian Nationalists (Organizatsia Ukrainskych Nacionalistiv – OUN) became the most important Ukrainian force that continued to lead the armed struggle for the independence and sovereignty of a united Ukraine.
17. In 1934 the camp was established by the Polish government. It was for Ukrainian political and cultural activists, members of the Polish opposition, ordinary criminals and communists.
18. During a ten-week period from 16 September to 30 November 1930, in an attempt to suppress and intimidate the Ukrainian populace, Polish police and military units entered approximately 450 villages in eastern Galicia. They terrorised the inhabitants, beat up many of the males and demolished Ukrainian organisational and co-operative buildings.
19. Abwehr = *Amt Auslandsnachrichten und Abwehr*, Intelligence and Counter-Espionage Service of the German Armed Forces and High Command. For contacts between the OUN and the German military intelligence see Lev Rebet *Svitla I tini OUN*, München, Ukrainskyj samostiinyk, 1964.
20. A significant contribution towards the funding of its activities came from Ukrainian emigrants living in the USA and Canada.
21. A comprehensive account of this event is provided by Petro Stercho, *Karpato-ukrainska derzava: do istorii vyzvolnoi borotby karpatskykh ukraintsiv u 1919–1939 rokakh*, Toronto, 1965.
22. *Encyclopaedia Ukraine*, Vol. 5, St–Z, pp.114–115.
23. Trial of Colonel Erwin Stolze in *Trial of the Major War Criminals before the International Military Tribunal*, Vol. II, pp.477–478.
24. Hans W. Neulen, *An deutscher Seite. Internationale Freiwillige von Wehrmacht und Waffen-SS*, p.306, München, 1985.
25. It also made provision for a trade agreement which allowed for the exchange of Soviet raw materials and foodstuffs for German machinery and technical assistance.
26. For example, Ukrainian became the official language in Galicia and great efforts were made to improve the school system and health care.
27. In his essay entitled 'Soviet Occupation of Western Ukraine, 1939–41', Orest Subtelny quotes a letter from The Ukrainian Catholic Metropolitan Andrij Sheptyskyj to the Vatican dated 7 November 1941, in which he estimated that in the L'viv eparchy alone, an estimated 200,000 Ukrainians had been jailed, forcibly evacuated or executed. The figure of 400,000 is given for Galicia as a whole. See Boshyk, op.cit., p.11.
28. See 'Galician Ukrainians in German Military Formations and in the German Administration', essay by M. Yurkevich in Boshyk, op.cit. p.73, and *Kubijovych Ukraintsi v Heneral'nii hubernii, 1939–41*, Istoriia Ukrainskoho tsentralnoho komitetu, Chicago, 1975, p.47.
29. This was partly due to the patronage of a number of highly placed civil servants such as Fritz Arlt, of whom more will be heard later.
30. In addition, both factions of the OUN also formed expeditionary groups, see Lev Shankovskyj, *Pokhidni hrupy OUN: prychynky do istorii pokhidnykh hrup OUN na tsentralnykh i skhidnikh zemliakh Ukrainy v 1941–1943 rr*, München, 1958.
31. *Nachtigall*, which had strength of about 325 men, was formed in Germany in early 1941 and trained at Neuhammer in Silesia. The commanding officer was Dr Albrecht Herzner. *Oberleutnant* Prof. Theodor Oberländer was the Liaison Officer and the Ukrainian senior officer was *Hauptmann* Roman Shukhevych (later Gen. Taras Chuprynka, CO UPA). Members of *Nachtigall* wore regular German army uniforms with blue and yellow ribbons on their epaulets to identify their Ukrainian nationality. Letter to author, M. Kalba, 16 November 1992.
32. *Roland* had the strength of about 280 men and was formed in Austria and trained at Saubersdorf near Vienna Neustadt under the command of *Major* Pobihushtschyi (its *de facto* commander was an Austrian – *Oberst* Riko Jary). *Roland* had a more pronounced Ukrainian character and wore blue and yellow insignia and the Ukrainian Trident on their caps (all that remained of the ex 1918–1920 Ukrainian *Halycka Armija* stock in Vienna). They also wore collar patches, with red cut out insignia, as did the UHA.
33. Myroslav Kalba, *Druzhyny Ukrainskych Nationalistiv u 1941–1942 rocac*, München, 1953, p.23.
34. The Waffen-SS was the fully militarised combat element distinct from the *Allgemeine* SS that formed the general body of the SS and comprised both full- and part-time, inactive and honorary members.
35. See *European Volunteers, 5th SS Panzer Division 'Wiking'*, Peter Strassner, J.J Fedorowicz Publishing, Winnipeg, 1988.
36. The breakdown was given as follows: 64 racially suitable (kv.F. and gv.F.) and 615 racially unsuitable inspected (kv.F. and gv.F.). See Berger to Himmler 28 April 1941: CdSSHA/Be/We. Tgb. Nr 358/41 geh, National Archives, Washington DC, (hereafter abbreviated NA) T-175, roll 110, frame 2634861.
37. Himmler's reply to Berger 31 April 1941: Tgb.Nr.945/41/geh. Be/Schb. Betr. Ukrainer. NA, T-175, roll 110, frame 2634860.
38. "We only have to kick in the door, and the whole rotten structure will come crashing down". *Hitler a Study in Tyranny*, Alan Bullock, Book Club Associates, London, 1973, p.652.
39. First published in 1925, Hitler had written in *Mein Kampf*, "We (National Socialists) stem the Germanic stream towards the south and west of Europe, and turn our eyes eastwards ..." Adolf Hitler: *Mein Kampf*, Zentralverlag der NSDAP, Franz Eher I, München 1942, translated James Murphy, Hurst and Blackett, London 1939, p.258.
40. Nazi racist ideology supported a theory of the *Herrenvolk* (master race) that they were Aryans of Germanic decent. The antithesis was the *Untermensch* (subhuman) (i.e. Slavic peoples) who were fit only for slavery and serfdom. The extreme apostles of the subhuman policy were Erich Koch and ironically the *Reichsführer-SS* Heinrich Himmler, under whose auspices the Galician Division was finally formed.
41. *Nachtigall* was deployed with the 1st Brandenburg Battalion that was attached to the 1st *Gebirgsdivision*. Letter to author, M. Kalba, 16 November 1992.
42. See article in *World War II Investigator*, Vol. 1, No. 2, May 1988, London, England, entitled 'The Mysterious Death of Lieutenant Herzner', p.28.
43. Literally 'Marching Groups'.
44. 8,000 people (including the expeditionary forces of both OUN factions) are estimated to have been involved, see Zynovii Matla, *Pivdenna pokhidna hrupa*, München, 1952, p. 22, and Shankovskyj, op.cit. p.12, n. 63.
45. A veteran of the Galician Division later summarised the reason that the Germans were treated as liberators: "We couldn't believe that these clean, healthy, intelligent people could impose such barbaric rule". Interview, P. Maslij, Scunthorpe, England, 8 February 1992.
46. Among them people accused of being saboteurs for persistently having arrived late at work.
47. For figures see Boshyk, op.cit. pp.12–13.
48. According to a former member of the battalion, *Nachtigall's* entry into L'viv was greeted by the population "...with great ecstasy and tears of joy". Letter to author from M. Kalba 16 November 1992.
49. Interview, M. Dobrianskyj, London, 15 October 1992.
50. German propagandists were quick to exploit the evidence of Soviet occupation. The bodies were photographed and the pictures were published in propaganda publications (the English language edition of *Signal* featured several of them). For the benefit of the local population photographs were also exhibited in shop windows in L'viv.
51. An allegation was made in the final report of the show trial of *Oberleutnant* Prof. Theodor Oberländer (*in absentia*) conducted in East Berlin, that the 2nd Company of the *Nachtigall* battalion was involved in a pogrom carried out against the Jewish population in the city on 30 June 1941. The relevant section reads: 'In summary, it can therefore be determined, with a high degree of probability that an Ukrainian platoon of the 2nd Company of the *Nachtigall Bataillon* was involved in acts of violence against the Jews, who were collected together in the NKVD prison. It is, therefore, guilty of causing the deaths of numerous Jews.' See *Der Fall* Oberländer, Hermann Raschofer, Bonn, 5 August 1960, p. 60. Oberländer was cleared by the West-German investigating authorities. Later he won libel suits against the German newspaper *Die Tat* in Frankfurt, and *Die Volksstimme* in Vienna, as well as against the leaders of the German Writers Union, Bernt Engelmann and Sepp Barant, in München. See Kalba, op.cit., p.121.
52. Individual officers from *Nachtigall*, including Roman Shukhevych and from other Wehrmacht/

German units were present and even participated in the proclamation. Letter to author from M. Kalba 16 November 1992.

53. The son of a wealthy landowner, Archbishop Sheptyskyj's activities during the Russian occupation of Galicia in WW1 led to his arrest and confinement in St Petersburg. In 1940 he sent missionaries into various parts of the Soviet Union. During German occupation Sheptyskyj was the only person with such a high profile to openly defy the Germans by publicly criticising the atrocities against the Jews and other minorities persecuted under the Nazi regime. He wrote letters to Pope Pious XII informing him of the German occupation policies, and a sharp letter of protest to the *Reichsführer-SS* Heinrich Himmler against the mass extermination of Jews in Western Ukraine, and against forcing Ukrainian auxiliary units to assist in those actions. During the war, at considerable risk to himself, he hid 3–400 Jews in St George's Cathedral in L'viv. As regards his letter of support for the newly proclaimed administration, upon learning that the proclamation had been made in the name of the Bandera action of the OUN only, Sheptyskyj expressed his regret at having been misled into giving his support in that way.
54. Interview, M. Dobrianskyj, London, 15 October 1992. According to Dobrianskyj these recordings were given to Ukrainian interpreters serving with the Wehrmacht and their use met with significant success.
55. A copy of this letter was published in *Luxemburger Wort*, 11 December 1986.
56. See Wolodymyr Kosyk *The Third Reich and the Ukrainian Question. Documents 1934–1944*, Ukrainian Central Information Service, London, 1991, p.14.
57. Ibid., Document 21, pp.50–51.
58. Ibid.
59. Ibid., Document 22, p.52.
60. Ibid., Documents 23 and 24, p.53.
61. Letter to author, M. Kalba, 16 November 1992.
62. The commanding officer of *Nachtigall*, *Leutnant* Herzner, noted in his unit's war diary, "The Ukrainians were shocked. Hardly had their fight for freedom commenced and now it's all over". *World War II Investigator* Vol. 1, No. 1, April 1988, London, p.8.
63. In early 1942, after re-training, *Schutzmannschaft* 201, which had a strength of around 650 men, was transported to Belorussia in March 1942, and deployed to guard transports and fight partisans. Letter to author, M. Kalba, 16 November 1992.
64. A summary of events in the Nazi occupied territory of the Soviet Union contains a photocopy of Melnyk's letter. See *Ereignismeldung UdSSR* No.15, 7 July 1941, Bundesarchiv, Koblenz. [Hereafter abbreviated BA-KO]
65. Alfred Bisanz born 1890 in Liubin Veliki near L'viv, was an officer of German origin in the Austrian Army and later Lieutenant Colonel of the 'Ukrainian Galician Army' (1918–1920). For further details see *Encyclopaedia of Ukraine*, Vol. 1, p.237.
66. Taras Hunczak, *On the Horns of a Dilemma, The Story of the Ukrainian Division Halychyna*, University Press of America, Lanham, MD, 2000, pp.5–6.
67. Under the leadership of Kapustianskyj these men had met in Cracow on 29 June 1941. See Myhailo Slaboshpytskyj and Valerie Stetsenko, *Ukrainian Division 'Galicia'*, Association 'Mehociant–Plus', Kiev, Toronto, 1994, pp.24–25.
68. *Svoboda*, Jersey City, NJ, No. 215, 18 September 1941 and Kost Pankivskyj, *Roky nimetskoi* okupatsii, Newark, NJ, 1965, pp. 218–219.
69. Among the propositions, which received no response at that time was that made by Skoropadskyj. According to this proposal, in compensation for the granting of limited autonomy to his homeland, Skoropadskyj, who was living in exile in Berlin and whose political influence in Ukraine was insignificant, stated that he would set up a Ukrainian army of two million men. In the same way the appeal made by Metropolitan Sheptyskyj to Hitler at the beginning of February 1942 was also ignored.
70. Alfred Rosenberg (1893–1946) was a Baltic German who headed the *Ostministerium* (Eastern Ministry) from April 1941 and supporter of autonomous Ukrainian state: "Ukrainian nationalism must be given every encouragement, Ukrainian writers scholars, and political leaders must be given the task of reviving the Ukrainian national consciousness".
71. Stressing that Germany's secret aims must be concealed from the world at large Hitler revealed his future policies – first conquer, second rule, third exploit. For the minutes of the conference see Roman Ilnytsky, *Deutschland und die Ukraine, 1934–45: Tatsachen europaischer Ostpolitik, ein Vorbericht*, Munich, Osteuropa Institut, 1955, p.315.
72. Ibid.
73. In this way a free Ukrainian state was to become a bulwark against the emergence of a future Russian state.
74. Ilnytsky, op.cit. 'Aktenvermerk 16:7:41', p.317.
75. Hitler's opposition to the use of foreign troops was based on ideological and historical reasons. Hitler credited the former national legions that fought in the Austro-Hungarian army, as being a major contributory factor in the fall of the Austro-Hungarian monarchy. His observations of those legions (including the Galician Sich Riflemen) formed the basis of his extreme scepticism of their loyalty and worth. He maintained that view until his death.
76. Ilnytsky, op.cit., 'Aktenvermerk 16:7:41', p.315.
77. The *Generalgouvernement* had previously been divided into four districts – Cracow, Lublin, Radom and Warsaw.
78. This move was also intended to weaken Ukraine as a whole.
79. To show his contempt for the idea of an Ukrainian state, Koch moved the capital of the *Reichskommissariat* from Kiev to the small provincial town of Rivne. Koch's appointment ushered in an era of terror and oppression, and his name became the symbol of German brutality and stupidity in the East. More than anyone else, Koch succeeded in alienating the population of eastern Ukraine from the Germans.
80. Ukraine's fertile soil and incredible grain producing capacity would make it the 'bread basket of Europe'. Hitler demanded Koch extract 3 million tons of wheat per year.
81. These units were used primarily to guard military training camps and other military objects as well as for small-scale anti-partisan activities. The Germans recruited locals for these units in all the occupied eastern territories.
82. *Werkschutz* battalions guarded factories or industrial plants.
83. Anti-Communist sentiments and force of circumstance led many of these men to enlist in these formations although for some recruitment was the result of the offer of material benefits which would otherwise have been exceptionally difficult to obtain.
84. One exception was *Schutzmannschaft* 201.
85. "Within the first few months of German occupation, the signs were visible all over [in Galicia]. When I went to town I noticed many signs, '*Nur fur Deutsche*' ('Only for Germans') on trains, restaurants, hotels, theatres, movie-houses, barbers, stores and even on park benches". Q15 Sokolskyj
86. From approximately 2,800,000 *Ostarbeiter* conscripted for work in Germany, 2,300,000 came from Ukraine. Having promised liberal inducements, which failed to materialise, the German authorities employed press gangs to secure the necessary labour.
87. Koch's policies amounted to outright enslavement and extermination. Among the critics of German policy in the east, typified by Koch's regime, was the *Generalkommissar* in the Crimea, the former Viennese *Gauleiter* Alfred E. Frauenfeld. He described the German occupation Policy as "A masterpiece of ineptitude, the acme of stupidity, proof that those who parade their brutality and give themselves master race airs are at heart uneducated louts", letter from Frauenfeld, dated 10 February 1944, NA T175, roll 125.

    Interestingly, in the post war years Koch was captured by the Poles, who tried him for his treatment of the Polish population of East Prussia, where he was *Gauleiter*. He was never tried by the Soviets or the Nurnberg Tribunal. His death sentence was suspended and commuted to life imprisonment because of his ill health and Koch subsequently lived in Barczewo Prison in comparative comfort until his death on 12 November 1986. As a former committed Communist he is strongly suspected of being Stalin's contact man within the famed 'Rote Kapelle' (Red Orchestra) spy-ring which operated in the Reich throughout the war.
88. *SS-Obergruppenführer und General der Polizei* Friedrich Wilhelm Krüger was nominated as HSSPf. Under him each district had its own *SS- und Polizeiführer* (SSPf).
89. Similar representation was also granted to the Polish and Jewish populations. Although the Ukrainian committee had no political standing and very limited authority, it provided help with food distribution and a number of social amenities, i.e. medical care, educational services, and assistance for refugees during the winter of 1941–42.
90. Among its most noticeable successes, the committee successfully negotiated the return of 85,000 Ukrainian prisoners of war from the German/Polish conflict.
91. Originally known as the Ukrainian National Alliance (UNO), it was renamed the Ukrainian Central Committee in June 1940. *Encyclopaedia Ukraine*, Vol. 5, pp.367–370, *Kubijovych Ukraintsi v Heneral'nii hubernii, 1939–41*, Istoriia Ukrainskoho tsentralnoho komitetu, Chicago, 1975.
92. Prior to this posting Lasch was the governor of Radom.
93. Aptly described as a '*Sammelsurium von Kreaturen*' (assemblage of characters).
94. Such as the public striking of Ukrainian peasants by Germans. Physical abuse is overwhelmingly reported to have been one of the major stimuli to anti-German feeling in the occupied eastern territories.
95. One such example was the request made by Dr Pankivskyj to reopen the Schevchenko Society (established in 1873) to which Lasch responded stating that "There was no need for such an institution". Interview, M. Dobrianskyj, London 15 March 1991.
96. The German security police *Sicherheitspolizei* (SD) ordered the arrest of all members of the OUN-B and gave instructions that "After thorough interrogation (they were) to be secretly liquidated as brigands". See Einsatzkommando C/5 of the security police and the SD–kdo–Tgb No. 12432, 25 November 1941, in *The Third Reich and the Ukrainian Question, Documents 1934–1944*, W. Kosyk, Document No. 59, p.14.
97. Ereignismeldung UdSSR No. 79, 10 September 1941, p. 8, R58/217, BA. Hunczak, op.cit. p.1 and p.5. According to Alfred Bisanz, the UCC was directly supervised by *Abwehrstelle* Cracow and headed by *Major* Hans Dehmel.
98. Pankivskyj, *Roky nimetskoi* okupatsii, New York, Kliuchi, 1965, 2nd ed; *Naukove tovarystvo* in Shevchenka, 1983, p.220.
99. Letters to the author, Kolisnyk 28 September and 8 December 1998.
100. Alfred Kolf, the political officer in the district of Galicia told Pankivskyj that the Germans would campaign for volunteers for the Waffen-SS (with Germanic racial characteristics), especially in the regions of Podilla, Pokuttia, and the Carpathian Mountains.
101. Information conveyed via letters to author, Kolisnyk 28 September and 8 December 1998. The officer file of *W. Unstuf.* Wladymyr Woloschtschuk (born 20 October 1920) records his service in the same unit prior to enlistment in the Galician Division.
102. Within months of occupation young Ukrainians and Poles alike were selected for the infamous *Ostarbeiter* programme. Initially introduced on a voluntary basis, the local German authorities under Lasch were increasingly forced to resort to systematic evacuations when the required numbers of volunteers could no longer be found after news spread of the ill treatment of the workers who were forced to live in appalling conditions.
103. Taras Bulba was the pseudonym of Taras Borovets born 9 March 1908, in Volhynia. Bulba was an excellent guerrilla leader who in 1941 organised the *Polissian Sich*, which was the first unit of the Ukrainian Insurgent Army. This formation originally operated in the Polissian swamps against Soviet military units that had been left behind following

the German advance. Having escaped, they retreated into the treacherous and remote swamps where they mercilessly terrorised the local population, unhindered by German security forces that avoided the area. For further details see *An Army Without a State (Glory and Tragedy of the Ukrainian Insurrection Movement), Memoirs of Otaman T. Bulba-Borovets*, Research Institute of Volyn No. 45, Society of Volyn, Winnipeg, Canada, 1981, pp.319–321.

104. The UPA was sustained above all by OUN-B and fought against Soviet Russia, Nazi Germany, the Poles, and partly against the OUN-M.

105. Lasch was arrested by the *Sicherheitspolizei* and tried for 'misappropriation of public property'. (i.e. Jewish valuables including furs, paintings, carpets etc) for his own use. On 3 June 1942, he was shot without trial on the orders of the *Reichsführer-SS*. See Martin Broszat, *Nationalsozialistische Polenpolitik 1939–45*, Deutsche Verlagsanstalt, Stuttgart 1961, p.82. In a lengthy statement given to the *Chef der Sicherheitspolizei und Sicherheitsdienst* im *Generalgouvernement* during an interview on 26 April 1942, following his arrest, in mitigation of his actions Lasch stated that "nearly all leaders in the *Generalgouvernement* had enriched themselves in this way and even more extensively". For example, on the issue of food, which was rationed throughout the *Generalgouvernement,* and available for purchase only with appropriate coupons, he said that Frank, Buehler [State Secretary in the GG] and Wächter had "probably the best furnished kitchens in the whole Reich, including all subsidiary territories" and that they frequently had big banquets "with many, many courses". See Document 3815-PS, *Chef der Sicherheitspolizei*, No. 89/42. *Geheim*, Cracow, 25 April 1942, reproduced in *The Trials of Major War Criminals before the International Military Tribunal, Nazi Conspiracy and Aggression*, (The 'Red Series'), Vol. VI, pp.745–752. For an interesting insight into Lasch's downfall see Reitlinger's *The Alibi of a Nation*, New York, Viking Press, 1968. p.225.

106. Title equivalent to baron.

107. *SS-Brigadeführer* Otto Wächter: born in Vienna on 8 July 1901 – died 10 September 1949. SS Nr. 235,368/Party Nr 301,093. Married, and by the end of the war the father of six children. Wächter was a keen sportsman and enjoyed swimming, mountaineering and skiing. He served in a Wehrmacht reserve infantry battalion from 17 March 1936, from 11 May 1936 as an ordinary soldier, and from 4 June to 29 July 1936, as an NCO. A long-time member of the Austrian Nazi Party, in the summer of 1934 as political leader he was one of the main participants in the abortive putsch against the Austrian Chancellor Dollfuss, which resulted in the death of the Chancellor and a few days in police custody for Wächter. He held the post of *Polizeipräsident* of Vienna and, after the German occupation of Poland in 1939, he became Governor of Cracow and was involved with the commission for re-settlement of ethnic German nationals. On 9 November 1939, Wächter was promoted to the purely SS rank of *Brigadeführer* and did not hold simultaneous rank in the *Polizei*. On 16 May 1944, he was promoted to *SS-Gruppenführer und Generalleutnant der Polizei*. He never held a rank in the Waffen-SS. See *Personalakt* Dr Otto Wächter NA A3343-SSO-213B.

108. According to state requirements Wächter practised law for seven years between 1924–1931 in the Austrian courts and with local legal firms. He was in private practice in Vienna from 1 January 1931, to 25 July 1934. See Lebenslauf, Ibid.

109. See *Personalakt* Dr Otto Wächter NA A3343-SSO-213B.

110. See *Personal Bericht*, Ibid.

111. See Wächter's speech to the Governor and head of departments, 16.2.44, W. Prag and W. Jacobmeyer, *Das Diensttagebuch des deutschen Generalgouverneurs in Polen 1939–1945*, Deutsche Verlags Anstalt, Stuttgart, 1975, p.800.

112. *Morality and Reality, The Life and Times of Andrei Sheptyskyj*, Paul Robert Magocsi, Canadian Institute of Ukrainian Studies, University of Alberta, Edmonton, 1989, p.132.

113. Frank's comment made during a discussion with members of the *Reichsjugendführung* (National Youth Leadership) on 23 July 1943, that "The Ukrainians should remain subordinates of the Reich, and not become allies", gives a clear indication of his attitude towards the Ukrainians. Prag & Jacobmeyer, op.cit., p.708.

114. Prag & Jacobmeyer, op.cit., p.800.

115. HSSPf. Krüger gives vent to his frustrations with Wächter on this issue and on other maters in a five-page letter to him, see *Abschrift! Der Höhrer SS-und Polizeiführer Ost*, Cracow, 24.11.1942. *Regierungsgebaude*, AZ. Kr/Fi.-P.K. 14/42 *Personalich! Eigenhandig! Einschreiben! An den Gouverneur des Distrikts Galizien, SS-Brigadeführer* Dr Wächter, Lemberg, in Wächter's personal file, NA T175, roll 32.

116. *Der Dienstkalender Heinrich Himmlers 1941/42*, Christians, Hamburg, 1999, p.521, note 73.

117. In doing so Wächter faced something of a dilemma. While he remained a firm believer in the principle of 'Germany first', his administration often went further to accommodate the wishes of the population than it was required to. As often as not, he was frequently obliged to use his influence and connections by first circumventing Frank, and by exploiting the strained relations between Frank and Himmler in order to pursue his policy.

118. Dr Otto Bauer was the Chief of Staff of Wächter's Galician administration and appointed minister of the interior (vice governor) responsible for internal security.

119. Dr Ludwig Losacker was Wächter's deputy (Director of internal affairs in the *Generalgouvernement* and former Vice-Governor of Galicia. In 1943 Losacker was demoted by Himmler because of his critical comments about German occupation policies and sent to a Waffen-SS penal battalion in Italy. He was captured by the Americans in 1945 and subsequently released. See Magocsi, op.cit., p.142.

120. Wächter's itinerary included visits to Kiev and Rivne.

121. Bormann was the head of the party chancery.

122. A large portion of this document is reproduced verbatim in *Echo Der Woche*, 16 October 1950.

123. Without exception, Wächter signed all correspondence '*Ihr stets gehorsamer*' (Your obedient servant).

124. On 1 March 260 men were transferred in this way. See *Fernschreiben*, SSD/HSSPf. OST KRK NR 1007, 25.2.43 1012, *der Hoehere SS-und-Polizeiführer* OST-AZ: KR/FI.-Roem. Zwei A/-*An den Reichsfuehrer und Chef der Deutschen Polizei* Heinrich Himmler. See Wächter's personal file, NA T175, roll 32.

125. GMUND NR.10 25.2.43. 1515 PO, *An Den Hoehren SS-und-Polizeiführer Ost SS-Obergruppenführer und General der Polizei* Krueger, Ibid.

126. According to one estimate, in 1942/43 in the *Reichskommissariat Ukraine,* the strength of the Ukrainian *Schutzmannschaften* was divided amongst 70 battalions. It stood at approximately 35,000 men. In addition, there were a further 15,665 serving in the Ukrainian *Schutzpolizei* and 55,094 Ukrainian gendarmes. The majority of those diverse Ukrainian security forces attached to German army and home guard militia units (UNS) were under the control of the German Army. They were known collectively as the UVV, *Ukrainske Vyzvolne Viysko* (Ukrainian Liberation Army), and may have numbered anything up to 180,000 men.

127. Berger to Himmler, 3 June 1943, Himmler File Document, HFD, H/10/34. Imperial War Museum, London (hereafter cited as HFD followed by index number).

128. In his letter to Himmler dated 4 March 1943, Wächter states "I am sending you further documentation regarding the setting up of the SS formation in Galicia". He must therefore have already broached the proposal with Himmler. See HFD, H/10/2.

129. *SS-Brigadeführer and General der Polizei* Friedrich Katzmann, was born 6 May 1906 in Langendreer. SS Nr. 3,065 from 18 May 1942. Katzmann held the post of SSPf in Lemberg. Ruth Bettina Birn, *Die Höheren SS-und Polizeiführer: Himmler's Vertreter im Reich und in den besetzten Gebieten*, Droste Verlag, Dusseldorf, 1986. p.338.

130. Himmler to Wächter, *Der Reichsführer-SS, Feldkommandostelle*, 18 January 1943, *Personalakt* Dr Otto Wächter NA A3343-SSO-213B.

Chapter 2

1. The first line of a secret letter, from Wächter to Himmler, dated 30 July 1943 (see Appendix IV) suggests that the issue of the raising of a formation from Galician Ukrainians was actually discussed on 1 and not 2 March 1943. However, the Vortragszettel (BA-KO, NS 19/1449, p.38) refer only to a meeting between the two men on 2 March. There is no record of any meeting on 1 March.

2. BA-KO, NS 19/1449, p 38.

3. Letter from *Der Gouveneur des Distrikts Galizien* of 19 March 1943 – 3 BI.Ph. *an den SS-Gruf. Berger, zur Weiterleitung, Betrifft: Neue Distrikteinteilung im Generalgouvernement*. Nürnberg. Doc. NO-3225. Institut Für Zeitgeschichte Archiv, München.

4. Ironically, *Generalgouveneur* Frank had already been forced to abandon a proposal to grant the Ukrainian population complete possession of the land they cultivated after protests from Berger and others that this would interfere with the German re-settlement programme. (See telex from Berger to Himmler 7 August 1942, NR.4510\7.8.42\16.20\SO) HFD, H/1/42.

5. Although Wächter's letter refers to a 'Division', from the available evidence it is likely that the original proposal included the concurrent formation of a separate unit of regimental strength intended for police duties.

6. Friedrich Wilhelm Krüger, born 8 May 1894, SS Nr. 6123: Party Nr. 171191. HSSPf. in the *Generalgouvernement* 1939-43.

7. See letter from Wächter to Himmler 4 March 1943. HFD, H/10/2.

8. Volodymyr Kubijovych, Meni 70, Munich 1970, p 59.

9. From the documentation available to the author at the time of writing, it was not possible to determine the definitive origins of this 'Regiment'. Alexander Dallin accredits its inception to the manoeuvrings of Berger, with the support of two officials from Rosenberg's *Ostministerium*, Mende and Kinkelin, a logical and plausible explanation. Alternatively, it may have formed part of Wächter's original proposal, in which case it was possibly intended to be a separate entity from the 'Division', under the control of the *Ordnungspolizei*. Certainly from February 1943, various *Polizei* battalions were being grouped into German *Polizei* regiments. Under German decrees dated 29 March and 31 April, *Polizei Schützen Regimenter* (Police Rifle Regiments) were to be raised from among the indigenous populations of the occupied eastern territories. These were to consist of three battalions, the first of which would be German, while the second and third would be *Ostvolk*, preferably Ukrainians, but with a cadre of 130 German officers and senior NCOs each. Six regiments were subsequently formed and numbered 31 to 38. See D. Littlejohn, *Foreign Legions of the Third Reich*, Vol. 4, James Bender Publishing 1987, p.43. In his respect no doubt it reflected the growing trend to amalgamate *Polizei* battalions into larger units of regimental strength.

10. The term used in the original document '*vorausgebildete Ukraine*' is somewhat ambiguous. The literal translation is 'pre-trained.' That would be applicable if it referred to the numerous Ukrainian men who had under taken *Baudienst* (construction service). But that was restricted to the *Generalgouvernement*. It had a structure and function analogous to the Organisation Todt, or those who during Soviet occupation had undergone military training which was compulsory in higher educational institutions.

11. See Berger to Brandt, *Der Reichsführer SS Chef des SS-Hauptamtes*, CdSSHA/Be/Vo. VS-Tgb, Nr.1689/43 geh., C.Adj. VS-Tgb. Nr. 923/43 geh. Berlin den 20 Marz 1943. *Betr: Neue Distrikteinteilung im Generalgouvernement*. Nurnberg reference: unpublished series, record group 238, NO – 3172, NA.

12. In the letter dated 8 March 1943, Kubijovych requested the use of a variety of means to form a volunteer Ukrainian military unit on the territory of the *Generalgouvernement*. They would fight side by side with the Germans against the Soviets. On the same day, Kubijovych conferred with Dr Ludwig Losacker in his capacity as Director of

Internal Affairs in the *Generalgouvernement* and as former vice-Governor of Galicia on the same subject.

13. Letter from Wächter to Himmler and Krüger 24 March 1943 with a proposal for a land reform entitled *'Verordnung uber die Beseitigung bolshewistischer Wirtschaftsformen auf dem Gebiete der Landwirtschaft'*. HFD's, H/10/3 and H/10/4. Reference is made to this letter in Wächter's letter to Himmler of 3 April 1943. H/10/11.
14. Secret letter from Himmler to Wächter, *Feldkommandostelle* 28 March 1943. Tgb.Nr. 35/37/ 43g RF/Bn. HFD, H/10/5.
15. Secret letter from Himmler to Wächter, *Feldkommandostelle*, 28 March 1943. Tgb.Nr. 47/82/ 43 RF/Bn. HFD, H/10/6.
16. "...The more generous our manner, the more effective [the reprivatisation] in terms of propaganda value...", Wächter's secret telegram to Himmler dated 3 April 1943, Governor Galicia, Lemberg, NR 76 2.4.43: 1725. HFD, H/10/9.
17. Ibid.
18. Previous experiences with the Germans and the fact that an Allied victory was in sight ensured that both factions opposed the idea of the Division. See Basil Dmytryshyn, *Nationalities papers*, Vol. XXI, No. 2, autumn 1993, p.72.
19. Kubijovych statement AA. In the statement Kubijovych maintains that he was willing to cooperate with the Germans to enable the Ukrainians to receive advanced military training, one of several basic prerequisites to gaining an independent statehood.
20. Ibid.
21. Daluege was the head of the *Ordnungspolizei* (ORPO) Winkelmann was the chief of his office.
22. Berger to Himmler 6 April 1943: cdSSHA/BE/Dr/ VS-Tgb.Nr2239/43g. HFD, H/10/12.
23. In July 1942 Himmler had ordered the SS-FHA to make certain that men serving in the legions were wearing national emblems on their collar patches in place of the SS runes. "I want, purely and simply, for all time, to prevent the admission as the result of exigencies of war, of all men who are not from the strictest point of view qualified to be SS men."
24. Steiner was the commander of the European based 5th *Wiking* Division.
25. Felix Steiner, *Die Armee der Geachteten*, Plesse Verlag, Gottingen 1963, p.179.
26. Himmler remained sensitive to the arguments of those who objected to the formation of the Division on racial grounds. When Kubijovych had approached Paul Dargel, Koch's assistant, with the suggestion of a separate Ukrainian armed unit he had received the reply "There will be no arms for you Ukrainians, neither as *Polizei* or as an army. For you in the future Europe there will be only the broom and the hoe." (Kubijovych statement, AA).
27. Telex from Himmler's secretary *SS-Obersturmbannführer* Dr Rudolph Brandt to Wächter *Feldkommandostelle* 10 April 1943. Bra/V. HFD, H/10/ 13.
28. Those in attendance were: *Gouverneur SS-Brigadeführer* Dr Wächter, *Generalleutnant der Polizei* pfeffer Wildenbruch, *Chef des Amtes* Otto Bauer, *Vertreter des SS und Polizeiführers, SS-Brigadeführer und Generalmajor der Polizei* Stroop, *Oberstleutnant* Wenerer, *Major* Degener, *SS-Sturmbannführer* Sielaff, *Oberst* Bisanz, *Leiter der Unterabteilung Bevölkerungswesen u. Fursorge* Pg Toscher, *Stellvertreter des Leiters der Abteilung Propaganda*, Dr Neuman *Leiter des Präsidialamtes*. No Ukrainians attended. See *'Abschrift'*, (an eight page summary of the conference presided over by Wächter), HFD, H/10/14.
29. Other topics discussed included the establishment of a musical platoon, accommodation, financing, spiritual welfare (the appointment of army chaplains), staff personnel and remuneration. The minutes of the conference provide an illuminating insight into the attitudes of the representatives of the various offices of the Third Reich. Ibid.
30. This is the last reference to the *Polizeiregiment* as a separate entity to be found which suggests that it was superseded by the formation of the Division which consequently absorbed all the personnel originally intended for it.
31. Ibid.
32. Telex from Wächter to Himmler 12 April 1943. HFD, H/10/15.
33. The formation of these *Polizei* Regiments will be discussed later.
34. See telexes to Wächter and Krüger 13 April 1943: Bra/V. HFD, H/10/16.
35. Verbatim *'national-ukrainische Intelligenz-Gruppen'*.
36. Himmler was evidently ignorant of Ukrainian history as, in 1917, Bandera himself was an eight year old boy and therefore necessarily without influence.
37. Daluege to Winkelmann z.Zt.*Feld-kommandostelle*, 14 April 1943. Archives of the 'Brotherhood of Former Combatants'. (Hereafter abbreviated ABFC).
38. Krüger to Himmler, *Der Höhere SS-und Polizeiführer Ost* Kr/Fi.- 560/43, *geheim*, 16.4.1943, HFD, H/10/18.
39. Telex Grothmann to Wächter 16 April 1943, Gro/ V. HFD, H/10/21. See footnote 9, chapter 1 for details concerning assassination of Field Marshal von Eichhorn. The prevalent opinion among the Nazi hierarchy including Hitler, Koch, Himmler and others, was that Eichhorn was murdered by an Ukrainian and this assumption was a major contributory factor which accounted for the anti-Ukrainian sentiment which permeated the upper echelons of the Nazi Party.
40. This date is probably a mistake on Berger's part and should have read 28 April 1943.
41. See telegram from Berger to Himmler 16 April 1943, SSHA 4268. 16.4.43.1055. HFD, H/10/20.
42. In the telex Wächter actually states that "...I therefore intend to make the call to arms on 18.4.1943". As this telex is dated 19 April 1943, it would appear that Wächter quoted the wrong date. Telex no.681 from Wächter to Grothmann, 19.4.43. HFD, H/10/ 22.
43. Ibid.
44. In the memoirs of Myroslav Semchyshyn, a former member of the UCC, he states that Prof. Kubijovych held a meeting at which the pros and contras of the formation of the Division were discussed which lasted four hours (with two hours allocated for each of the viewpoints). The major concern at this stage was that no political guarantees were being offered. See *From the Book of Lev, Ukrainian L'viv, 20th-40th years, Memoirs*, Schevchenko Scientific Society Memoir Library of SSS, No. 4, L'viv, 1998, pp. 132-133.
45. Kubijovych later said that the fact that Metropolitan Sheptyskyj had given his support to the formation of the Division was a major influence in his decision to cooperate.
46. Kubijovych statement, AA.
47. Ibid.
48. There is some argument that in the latter part of the Division's existence, whilst deployed in an anti-partisan role in Slovakia and Slovenia, its soldiers did fight against American and British airmen, who were providing air-dropped supplies for the partisan movements in both countries. However, it is important to note that when deployed in these two respective theatres the presence of the Allied airmen was incidental. At no point during its history did the Galician Division or any of its affiliated units ever engage in combat with organised military forces of British or American origin.
49. Bisanz related this verbally to M. Dobrianskyj. Interview, M. Dobrianskyj, London, 15 March 1991.
50. A standing lion with a raised tail was the coat of arms for Galicia until 1772. In 1884 a crown was added as a symbol of statehood. Under Austrian rule a new coat of arms for the 'Kingdom of Galicia and Volodymyria' was created consisting of a lion with three crowns and a daw. The designer of the Divisional Emblem retained the three crowns to allude to Galicia's Austrian heritage (gold, or yellow, and blue constitute the Ukrainian national colours).
51. The situation with the Latvian Self Administration, who were also negotiating the formation of a Latvian Legion (which later became the '15. *Waffen-Grenadier Division der* Waffen-SS' [*Lettische* Nr.1] with the Germans at approximately the same time, is a case in point. Faced initially with the same uncompromising stance by the German authorities, the Latvians later obtained several significant concessions from the Germans. For example, the Latvians negotiated the appointment of a native Latvian – Rudolf Bangerskis – as 'Inspector General of the Latvian Legion'. That appointment gave a Latvian national simultaneous authority to supervise and inspect the Latvian Legion, a brigade and *Polizei* battalions made up of Latvians. He also had the right to report his observations and suggestions directly to the High Command of the Army and to the *Reichsführer-SS* Heinrich Himmler himself. Other compromises reached with the German authorities included the institution of Latvian as the language of command for the Legion.
52. Verbally to author, R. Drazniowskyj, 27 November 1993.
53. This figure was given as an estimate of the number of men required to begin with.
54. See *'Der Gouverneur des Distrikt Galizien* Tgb.N.104\ 43g, 28/4/1943, *Betr: Aufstellung der SS-Schützen Division Galizien'*: ABFC. The document stated that "... the formation of the Division is to be utilised as much as possible in the sprit of an introduction of the Ukrainian population of Galicia to the concept of being Germanic".
55. Ibid.
56. Directives for Recruitment Commissions for the *SS-Schützen-Division Galizien*. (In confidence! Only for the officials employed by members of the Recruitment Commissions), L'viv, 28 April 1943. AA.
57. Secret letter from *Der Gouverneur des Distrikts Galizien*: zu Tgb.104\43g: Lemberg, 28 April 1943. ABFC.

Chapter 3

1. Detailed coverage of the event was provided by newspapers such as *L'vivski Visti* (L'viv news) No. 93, *Stanislavivske Slovo* [18/83] among others while German cameramen captured the event for posterity and for propaganda reasons. An edited copy of the film is in the author's possession.
2. See *Abschrift, Korrekturen der Reichsführer-SS bereits berücksichtigt* annexed to Himmler's letter to Wächter of 28 March 1943, Tgb.Nr. 35/37/43g. HFD, H/10/5.
3. The literature issued to those who enrolled stated unequivocally that [...] "10. The volunteer receives the same uniform, equipment, food and pay as the German soldier. He receives the most fair and equal treatment. 11. After honorary service, he will be treated similarly in his social welfare, just as German soldiers after their discharge. A similar rule will be applied to those who in any way are wounded or affected by the war. 12. Members of the family that were supported by the volunteer such as: 1. wife, 2. family 3. Children: will receive the same welfare as the families of German soldiers." Instructions for Volunteers for the SS Riflemen Division Galicia. AA.
4. Later, Professor Kubijovych, in his capacity as head of the UCC sent a telegram to the *Generalgouverneur* Frank in Cracow which read: "I wish to express to the Government of the Reich my deepest thanks on behalf of the Ukrainian people of Galicia, for the opportunity for Ukrainians to join the battle against bolshevism with weapon in hand. The entire Ukrainian people nurture feelings of upright gratitude to the Führer of the Greater German Reich, for the authorisation for the formation of the *'SS-Schützen-Division Galizien'*. I request that your Excellency convey this gratitude to the Führer. We are especially grateful for your message to the Ukrainian people of Galicia and your best wishes for today's celebrations." Kubijovych to Frank, 10 May 1943, HFD, H/10/26.
5. *Krakivski Visti*, 1 May 1943, No. 89.
6. *Khronoviat's* function within the Military Board was head of recruitment.
7. For the text of Rev. Laba's speech see HFD, H/10/ 47.
8. Delivery of the recordings was delayed due to them being misdirected. Poscher to Brandt, Lemberg, 9 July 1943, Tgb.Nr. 35/96/43g. H\10\45.
9. 13 July 1943, Himmler's office (Brandt) to Berger See H\10\47.
10. 22 July 1943, Berger to Brandt, CdSSHA/Be/Ra. See H\10\54.
11. Professor Kubijovych had hoped that he would be appointed to this post. General Victor

Kurmanovych was appointed honorary leader of the Military Board.

12. Directives for Recruitment Commissions for the *SS-Schützen-Division Galizien*. L'viv, 28 April 1943. An original of this document is in the author's possession. For details of the statutes see *Minutes of the Meetings of the Military Board Galicia*, edited by Roman Kolisnyk, Shevchenko Scientific Society of Canada, Vol.30, 1990, pp182-183.
13. Ibid. see also *An Den Wehrausschuss Galizien*, Lemberg 28 April 1943. ABFC.
14. The document stated it was not necessary for them to have been born in Galicia but to be resident there for some time, confirmation of which was to be provided by the village head. Directives for Recruitment Commissions for the *SS-Schützen-Division Galizien*. L'viv, 28 April 1943. AA.
15. Directives for Recruitment Commissions for the *SS-Schützen-Division Galizien*. (In confidence! Only for the officials employed by members of the Recruitment Commissions), L'viv, 28 April 1943. AA.
16. For two examples see *L'vivski Visti* ('L'viv News') No. 93, and *Stanislavivske Slovo* 18/83.
17. See *Kracower Zeitung* of 29 April 1943. The report on the formation of the Division appeared under the heading 'Formation of an SS *Schützen* Division *Galizien'* for the Ukrainian Youth'. The article also gave details about the Division's insignia and went on to say that the language of command would be German while the language for orders would be Ukrainian. It also announced that commissions would be given to former Ukrainian officers of the Austro-Hungarian army. A copy of this cutting can also be found in the Himmler papers, HFD, H/10/ 24.
18. Alfred Bisanz and Yuri Krokhmaliuk travelled to Buchach, Stephan Volynets to Sambir and Turka, Myhailo Khronoviat visited Bibrka, etc.
19. The Sich riflemen or *Sichovi Striltsi* was a distinct unit of the Austro-Hungarian army in WWI that later became the nucleus of the Ukrainian Galician Army.
20. Q2: Havrych.
21. It seems likely that the German authorities were aware of, or at least suspected members of the Military Board of propagating nationalist opinions in their recruitment speeches for the Division. However, so as not to hamper recruitment, no preventative action was taken until Dr Bauer issued a memorandum dated 18 August 1943. By that time the first phase of recruitment was nearing its end. It forbade the Military Board from issuing any writings of a political nature without his consent or that of Alfred Bisanz, *chef des Amtes*, Lemberg, den 18 August 1943, ABFC.
22. At the same time a number of women volunteered for the hospital services.
23. There is of course no conclusive evidence of the claim that the majority of those who volunteered in the first three months of the recruitment campaign were politically motivated. However, this statement is supported by numerous personal interviews, questionnaires and letters addressed to the author. The overwhelming majority, in answer to the question 'Why did you volunteer'? gave an answer which corresponded roughly with this statement.
24. Shypailo, letter to author, 2 November 1994.
25. AA.
26. "I was in the last grade at high school (8th). Our teachers and community leaders were for the creation of the Ukrainian army. All people of the 8th grade with some of the teachers registered for the division. It was the duty to serve". Q6 Kolisnyk. There is some evidence that after the initial wave of enthusiasm had passed, in some cases pressure was exerted on school leavers who were told they had to sign these volunteer papers in order to get their last report: Letter to author, M. Klymchuk, 30 August 1990.
27. For example: "On the first day of recruitment, the principal of the trade school in Sanok, Mykhalevych enlisted with all his students". ...."In Sambir, a large group of students from the local college arrived at the draft board led by their principle, Martynetz", etc.
28. The name of the *Plast* organisation is derived from the Ukrainian word *Plastun*, a scout of the Zaporozhian Cossacks. Its main goals were to cultivate skills such as camping and outdoor activities, developing moral character and leadership qualities as well as fostering a sense of Ukrainian patriotism amongst its members.
29. Verbally to author, M. Scharko, 9 March 1999.
30. It is impossible to put a figure on the number who joined purely because of anti-communist sentiments. To give an indication of the strength of the anti-Russian sentiments of the population, Bender & Taylor make the unsupported claim that "...20,000 are said to have volunteered at once as a result of the anti-Russian theme", Bender & Taylor, *Uniforms of the Waffen-SS*, Vol.4, p.22.
31. Rev. Dr Laba's sermon had included the phrase "He who wants to be free must fight for it".
32. Of a random sample of fifty former Division members interviewed by the author, ten had served in other German formations prior to their service with the Division. Three served as auxiliary *Polizei* in various *Shuma* battalions, one served in another Waffen-SS formation, one was in the Brandenburg Division, one was a Luftwaffe auxiliary, three were in regular Wehrmacht formations, in non-combatant roles as *Hilfswilliger* (Hiwis) or helpers, and one as a former member of *Nachtigall*.
33. Interview, I. Nyzchka, Rushden, England, 6 January 1991.
34. *Krakivski Visti*, 16 May 1943, No. 20 reported Kubijovych's enlistment.
35. Q3 Humeniuk.
36. The document also specified that non-commissioned officers of the former Polish army who were in German prisoner of war camps in the Reich were to be placed at the disposal of the Division.
37. Bender & Taylor, op.cit. Vol. 4, p.24, RF-SS, HA B1 Az 9a/Br.Galiz.Div/, v.1.7.1943.
38. At a meeting of the Military Board on 24 November 1943, there was difficulty in listing 50.
39. Two examples are Alexander Yaworskyj and Julian Temnyk. These officers were also members of the Ukrainian Galician Army 1918-1920 and many of them joined Petlura's Army (from central Ukraine as opposed to western Ukraine).
40. Of those who enlisted 30 were dismissed because they were over 50 years of age. Most were aged between 45 and 55 years.
41. Letter to author, Dr W. Krywulak, 4 May 1994.
42. Letter to author, Dr W. Krywulak, 25 May 1994.
43. Letter to author, Dr B. Rozdilskyj, 20 October 1996.
44. In addition nine veterinarians, two dentists, six dental technicians and two apothecaries had volunteered by November 1943.
45. Letter dated 28 June 1943, from Kaltenbrunner to Himmler, IV B3 – 416\43. HFD H/10/38.
46. Brandt to Kaltenbrunner *Feldkommando-stelle*, 16 July 1943, Tgb. Nr. 42/78/43. HFD, H/10/51. That was consistent with Himmler's previously expressed view towards the Church when he had written to Krüger advising him to endeavour to "Make use of the vassalage of the Poles and Ukrainians to the Church and their love for their priests and other village notables, who should be made answerable for their good behaviour with their lives". See Helmut Heiber, *Reichsführer: Breife an und von Himmler*, Deutsch Verlags Anstalt, Stuttgart, 1968, p.132-133.
47. Letter from Berger to Himmler 26 July 1943, HFD, H /10/55. In the letter Berger also gave a brief resumé of Laba's antecedents. Reverend Laba had served as an officer in the Austrian army during WWI on the Italian front in the 3rd *Kaiser Schützen* and the 4th *Bosniakischen Haus Regiment*. During his service he was awarded the second highest Austrian military decoration, and Berger noted had "by all accounts performed very bravely as a soldier".
48. These are named as Dr Vasyl Laba, Dr Ivan Durbak, Dr Osyp Karpynskyj, Dr Josef Kladochny, Dr Volodymyr Stetsiuk, Izydor Sydir Nahayevskyj, Lubomyr Syvenky, Danylo Kovaliuk, Bohdan Levytsky, Emanuel Korduba, Julian Habrusevych, Vasyl Leschyshyn. In addition other chaplains who served with the Division or its affiliated units were Roman Lobodych, Myhailo Levenets, Ivan Holojda, Oleksander Babij, Oleksander Markevych, Ivan Tomashivskyj and Myhailo Ratushynskyj.
49. Ibid.: In the document Berger also mentioned that the priests should undergo basic military training at Sennheim. Berger concluded by saying that the Domherr Dr Laba "was most impressed by the discussion, as he had previously thought that the Reichsführer-SS would resent the deployment of clergymen". Sennheim was a training camp established in Alsace where foreign troops underwent a six-eight week course to learn German.
50. Brandt to Berger *Feld-kommandostelle*, 31 July 1943: Tgb.Nr.36\178\43 g: HFD, H/10/58.
51. Details of Koch's objections can be found in the so-called 'Brandenburg memorandum', 16 September 1943, NA Document NO-3469. For Berger's attempt to refute some of Koch's criticisms of the Division, see his letter to Himmler dated 10 December 1943. NS 19/2191 folder 1, BA-KO.
52. For an example of an anti-Divisional leaflet in both the Ukrainian and Polish languages see V. Veryha *Dorohamy druhoii svitovoi viiny: legendy pro uchast ukraintsiv u zdushuvanni varshavskoho povstannia v 1944 r.ta pro ukrainsku dyviziiu 'Halychyna'*, Toronto, New Pathway, 1980, 2nd rev. ed.; *Bratstvo kolyshnikh voiakiv 1-oi ukrainskoi dyvizii UNA*, Toronto, 1984, pp.216-220.
53. One veteran related an incident to the author in which he returned to his home village of Lubachiv (close to the Polish/Ukrainian border) in uniform to spend a few days leave with his family. Having departed to rejoin the Division, his father was subsequently beaten up by local Polish civilians. Verbally to author, M. Prymak 8 November 1997.
54. For example, see letter from *Oberstleutnant* B. Jewtymowytsch to the head of the historical section of the Military Board, Lemberg 3 July 1943, complaining about the behaviour of Polish civil servants and their disregard for documents issued by the Military Board. ABFC.
55. The OUN-M did not advocate a definite stand.
56. A further cause of their opposition stemmed from the fact that the Division provided competition for manpower, especially with regard to officers. For some of the arguments against the Division see Myroslav Prokop, 'U Sorokrichchia 3-oho Nadzvychainoho Velykoho Zboru OUN' in *Suchasnist*, 1987, No. 3, p.394.
57. Bulletin of the Organisation of Ukrainian Nationalists, Year III, 1943, No. 11, AA.
58. cf. 'Ukrainskyj Narode!' in *Kravivski Visti*, 2 November 1943 nr 245 (983) and Hunczak, op.cit. p.210.
59. The Ukrainian units of the Austro-Hungarian Army that were active during WWI.
60. In his book, Roman Krokhmaliuk describes how, at a time when local UPA leaders who on their own initiative were actively hindering enlistment of volunteers, he met for thirty minutes with the UPA leader Roman Shukhevych, in a private residence in a suburb of L'viv. As untrained recruits to the UPA were becoming an increasing liability, Shukhevych determined to use the Division so that UPA members could get the necessary training that would allow it to become an elite guerrilla force. Thereafter the enlistment rate, especially in the L'viv region, showed a significant increase. See Roman Krokhmaliuk *The Glow in Eastern Europe*, Toronto-New York, *Bratstvo kolyshnikh voiakiv I-oi Ukrainskoi dyvizii UNA*, 1978, pp.40-41,
61. Letter to author, M. Paslij 10 January 1994.
62. For a detailed discussion of the OUN/UPA's relationship with the Division see the article by Lev Shankovskyj in *America*, 12-16 July 1954, Philadelphia. Reprinted in *Ukrainska Dyvisia Halychyna* pp.55-61, Kyiv, 1994.
63. See article by Bohdan Pidhayny entitled 'Two Paths One Aim', taken from the publication *Brody: Zbirnyk stattei i narysiv* ('Brody: A collection of articles and sketches'), pp. 59-64, Oleh Lysiak, *Bratstvo kol. Voiakiv Pershoi UD UNA*, München, 1951. no.1 p.60.
64. Krüger to Berger secret telegram dated 11 May 1943 HFD, H/10/27. The official recruitment figures of the *Wehrausschuss* Galicia quoted 31,034 as having enlisted by 11 May 1943.
65. Enlistment report of the *Wehrausschuss* Galicia, ABFC.
66. In Wächter's secret circular letter dated 28 April 1943, to all local authorities concerning the ambitious recruitment programme which was about to

commence, under section two he wrote: (...) "2) Canvassing. When one considers the large number of fully fit men who have already been drafted, it will not be easy to reach the numbers required for the formation of a division. A total of 20,000 men is needed to start with. Therefore every 100,000 inhabitants will provide, on average, 500 volunteers. I wish you to regard this number as an approximation only. As all use of coercion or even moral pressure is out of the question – these would only destroy the political aim of the undertaking-all our efforts will have to be concentrated on the area of canvassing if our goal is to be achieved." See '*Der Gouverneur des Distrikt Galizien Betr*: TGB. N.104\43G' Secret, Lemberg 28 April 1943, *Betr. Aufstellung der SS-Schützen Division 'Galizien'*: ABFC.

67. Figure quoted in Himmler's reply to Wächter dated 17 May 1943. See telex from Himmler to Wächter 544: HFD, H/10/29.
68. Ibid. In his reply dated 17 May 1943, Himmler said that because of his busy schedule he could not visit Galicia for the time being. But he suggested that, "When next I visit Lemberg I will be very glad to travel with you through these regions incognito and not in an official capacity, to get an impression myself." Ibid.
69. Kubijovych statement, see Heike, Eng. ed. op.cit. p.145. Kubijovych maintains that this came about as the result of repeated petitioning by the MB and UCC. Later recruitment took place in the provinces of Cholm, and Hrubeshiv.
70. Including the towns of Kolomyia, Horodenka, Kosiv and Sniatyn.
71. A German account of the recruitment action in Kolomyia is given in an article entitled 'Ukrainische Freiwillige marschieren' in *Völkischer Beobachter* (München ed.), no. 151, 31 May 1943. AA.
72. The description of the events in Kolomyia was given in a letter to author dated 1 January 1999, by I. Sadoveyj who was present throughout.
73. A copy of the film is in the author's possession. Wächter was so pleased with the success of recruitment in this region that he sent Himmler a photographic record of the formal announcement of the formation of the *SS-Schützen-Division Galizien* in Kolomyia. Brandt noted that the *Reichsführer* "looked through the folder with interest". Secret letter from Brandt to Wächter 29 June 1943. HDF, H\10\39.
74. Enlistment report of the *Wehrausschuss* Galicia, ABFC.
75. Ibid. In Wächter's secret circular letter dated 28 April 1943, he had stated that as a matter of principle, enlistment into the Division was to be limited exclusively to Galician Ukrainians. It was however often virtually impossible to tell whether an individual originated from east or West Ukraine, in practice volunteers were recruited from both.
76. '*Bericht uber die Werbeaktion bis 2.Juni. 1943, einschliesslich*' (see Appendix II). ABFC.
77. The town of Sianok was one such example. Recruitment started on 15 May when the commission began registering all the men in the town fit for combat. By the end of the first day 300 had been registered of which 250 had been accepted and 50 rejected. During the course of the next two weeks, following demonstrations of support that took place in all the villages of the Sianok district, the commission began to register all the males who supported the Division, irrespective of their eligibility. They included a large number of workers employed by the forestry commissions as woodcutters, or in the sawmills, who reported for enlistment *en masse*. These men were later excused from service as their occupations were classified as being essential for the war economy. As a result, a total of 14,446 men had been registered by 31 May 1943, of whom 12,438 were not, and could not be eligible for service in the Division because of their occupation, age, ill health etc and were subsequently rejected or excused service. Nevertheless despite a rejection rate of 86%, the overall figure was still counted toward the total number of registrations.
78. In this the letter Berger referred to the proposed formation as the 'Galician Legion'. This was not however an accurate description as it had already been decided that the formation was to be a division.
79. Berger to Himmler 3 June 1943. HFD, H/10/34. In Bender & Taylor, op.cit., p.22, the date of the order is incorrectly given as being 3 July 1943.
80. Secret interim report from Berger to Himmler dated 21 June 1943 HFD, H/10/36.
81. Ironically, in view of the opening sentence, the figures in the document have erroneously been added together – the correct figure would be 23,518.
82. Berger to Himmler 2 July 1943, kr shas nr.8164 2.7.43 1400 – me – *an den Reichsführer-SS und chef der deutschen Polizei, Feld-kommandostelle*, Urgent! Secret! NA, T175, roll 74, BA-KO, NS 19/1785 folder 1.
83. It is unclear exactly when the *Ergänzungsamt der Waffen-SS, Ergänzungsstelle Warthe (XXI), Nebenstelle Lemberg* came into being. It had 10-12 staff all of whom were German except *Waffen-Obersturmführer* Dr Stephan Molodawec, a general medical practitioner mobilised from Lodz who had served as a military doctor during the German/Polish war in the Polish army.
84. From its inception the German authorities had done their best to limit the potential influence of the Military Board, which Wächter had refused to place under the control of a Ukrainian national. It did however continue to register the volunteers and maintain individual files as well as administer welfare facilities for the Ukrainian volunteers and also published a weekly newspaper (tabloid size with 6-8 pages) for the soldiers of the Division.
85. Of this number the commission also siphoned out those who were known or suspected of being politically unreliable.
86. 'Minutes of the Meetings of the Military Board Galicia' edited by Roman Kolisnyk, *Shevchenko Scientific Society of Canada*, Vol. 30, 1990, pp.57-58. Dr Schulze also mentioned that 70 desertions had already occurred and that the esprit de corps varied between the different training camps in which the Ukrainian volunteers were undergoing their training. Former members of 11 armies had been identified and there are three divisions: trainees, reclaimants and deserters. In some areas of Galicia, as a solution to the problem of the 'draft dodgers' the German authorities resorted to holding the families of the so-called 'deserters' responsible. In practical terms this amounted to German *Polizei* and security units arresting the fathers and brothers of those who had enlisted but failed to report, while in rural areas, to punish the 'deserters' livestock was seized and taken from the farms. Letter to author, M. Klymchuk, 30 August 1990.

Chapter 4

1. *Der Reichsführer SS, Feldkommandostelle* 5 July 1943, Tgb.Nr 35/88/43g RF/Bn. HFD, H/10/43.
2. In his letter to Himmler dated 3 June 1943, Berger had said; "The registered officers and NCOs will, after confirmation with the *SS-Führungshauptamt*, be enlisted as soon as possible in retraining courses, and will form the foundation for the planned division." Cd SSHA/Be/Ra./VS-Tgb. Nr.3561/43g. HFD, H/10/34.
3. Programme of the 'Festive Farewell of the first call up of officers, NCOs and riflemen to the SS-Rifle Division Galicia' issued by the Military Board. An original example is in the author's possession.
4. Professor Kubijovych was to have addressed the volunteers but according to Pankivskyj was forbidden to do so at the last moment by "an order from above."
5. This was a recruit named Yurij Ferencevych.
6. Roman Hawrylak, *Memoirs of Bygone Years* (unpublished manuscript), p 6.
7. The transport consisted of five 2nd and 3rd class passenger wagons for officers, and ten cattle-wagons for recruits.
8. Amongst other things, volunteers were also advised to attend to all his outstanding matters both business and domestic as "after recruitment you will have to wait a long time before you get your first leave to return home". 'Instructions for Volunteers for the SS Rifle Division Galicia'. AA.
9. Identity tags were issued by the depot unit that received the soldier into the army and made out his paybook. Consequently they seldom showed the unit in which a man actually served unless the original was lost and a replacement issued.
10. Uniform was to be that of the Waffen-SS initially without the SS runes on the right lapel and with SS rank insignia on the left lapel. See Juttner's order dated 30 July 1943: *Kdo.Amt der Waffen-SS*: Org.Tgb. Nr.982/43 g. Kdos. v. 30.7.1943 *Aufstellung der SS-Freiw. Division 'Galizien'*. According to official SS regulations, members of 'non-Germanic' divisions should not have worn the SS runes on the right lapel, however the first contingent who were inducted at Brno were issued uniforms with SS runes which they were apparently not required to remove.
11. On the day after arrival at Brno each recruit was issued with their *Erkennungsmarken*, three sets of uniforms, a helmet, a set of eating utensils, shoes, and a knapsack. Details regarding the recruits' stay at Brno were provided in letters to the author by E. Shypailo 18 April 1995, 23 June 1995, and 27 August 1995, Roman Wysockyj, 28 June 1995, and Roman Herasymowycz, 1 and 21 November 1995.
12. The figures are quoted from Ferkuniak, *Spomyny...* p.6.
13. In July 1943 large parts of the camp were still under construction.
14. SS-FHA. Kdo. Amt der Waffen-SS: Org.Tgb. Nr.982/43 g.Kdos.v. 30.7.1943 *Aufstellung der SS-Freiw. Division 'Galizien'*.
15. For example 35 officers chosen to serve in the artillery were sent directly to Beneschau near Prague. See memoirs of M. Dlaboha, *Visti*, nos. 5-6 (43-44), May-June 1954.
16. Among the former officers who accompanied the recruits to Heidelager were Dmytro Ferkuniak, and Wolodymyr Kosak (see Ferkuniak, op.cit., p.6). Kosak's *Soldbuch* (paybook/identity papers) confirm that from 14 August 1943 to 28 August 1943 he was based at Heidelager as a member of the *12/Ausb. Btl. z.b.V.* AA.
17. After the first transport had left L'viv for Brno, the second and subsequent transports were sent directly to Heidelager.
18. As of 27 August 1943, the German staff of the *SS-Ausbildungs-Btl. z.b.V.* included:
    Btl. CO: *SS-Sturmbannführer* Bartelt (4 March 1901)
    Btl. Adjutant: *SS-Untersturmführer* Artur Preuss (30 June 1907)
    Btl. Supplies officer: *SS-Obersturmführer* Alfred Paul (7 December 1914)
    Btl. Medical officer: *SS-Untersturmführer* Erich Schmidt (11 November 1911)
    Führer VI (resp. for ideological instruction): *SS-Untersturmführer* Werner Urlen (23 November 1909)
    For further details of the battalion's German staff, company and platoon (zug) commanders see 84/43 geh. *SS-Ausbildungs Batl. z.b.V.* IIa,Az.:21, Tgb.Nr.84/43 geh.27.8.43 *Betr.: Führerstellenbesetzungsliste an* SS-FHA. RG-48.004m, Reel 6, *SS-Ausbildungs Battailon z.b.V.* Karton 3, File 11, 1943, II, Holdings of the US Holocaust Memorial Museum Archives [Hereafter USHMMA]
19. *SS-Sturmbannführer* Bernhard Bartelt: born 4 March 1901: Party Nr. 711242/SS Nr. 27759: Holder of Iron Cross 1st Class. Information about his career can be found in his *Personal-Akte* Bernhard Bartelt, NA, A3343-SSO-034 and his corresponding RuSHA file A3343-RS-A236.
20. The structure of a rifle company was as follows: one platoon = four squads, three platoons = one company. Selection was made basically by height – the tallest recruits were in the first platoon and the shortest in the fourth. Letter to author, E. Shypailo, 2 November 1994.
21. The heavy weapons companies had around 300 men each while each of the rifle companies had approximately 200.
22. An average daily strength report for the battalion for the month of August 1943 is given as follows: 177 Officers, 422 NCOs, 3,026 men, total 3,625. See 89/43 geh. *SS-Ausbildungs Batl. z.b.V. (SS-Freiw. Div. 'Galizien') SS-Tr.Ub.Pl.* Heidelager, den 1.9.1943, IIb, Az: 9w, Tgb.-Nr.89/43 geh.27.8.43 *Betr.: Monatliche stärkemeldung der Teilnehmer an der Feldpost-bezw. SS-Feldpost*, RG-48.004m, Reel 6, *SS-Ausbildungsbataillon z.b.V.* Karton 3, Filr 11, 1943, II, USHMMA.
23. Leiter Ost Poscher – Berlin 9 July 1943, to the Staatssekretär. ABFC.

24. Letter dated 19 June 1943, from the *Distriktkommissar* of Horochow Harter to the *Generalkommissar* for Volhynia und Podolien. HFD, H/10/35.
25. *Fernschreib* RFSS, RF/Br. NA T-175, roll 70, frame 2586531.
26. Hans Prützmann *SS-Obergruppenführer und General der Polizei*: born 31 August 1901: SS Nr. 3002: Party Nr. 142290.
27. *Der Höheren SS und Polizeiführer Russland Sud*, 8 July 1943. Tgb. Nr. 145\43 (g) HFD, H/10/40.
28. *Der Reichsführer SS Feldkommandostelle* 14 July 1943, Tgb 48\10\43g. HFD, H/10/48.
29. See notes of the conference held on 12 April 1943, HFD, H/10/14.
30. See Wächter's secret letter to Himmler 30 July 1943. Dr WA./Ra ZL. 19/43 g: HFD, H/10/56. The report also contained two enclosures.
31. See letter to Himmler on dated 5 August 1943, '*Betr: SS Schützendivision Galizien*', BA-KO NS 19\1785. This unsigned letter has been commonly and incorrectly attributed to Governor Wächter, however the very first line which begins "I have been informed by the Governor of Galicia..." suggests that the letter was written by someone else, in all probability a high ranking party official who was senior in rank to Wächter (i.e. Rosenberg) ABFC.
32. Himmler to Wächter 11 August 1943, *Feldkommandostelle* Tgb.Nr. 48/10/43g. HFD, H/10/59.
33. Wächter's secret letter to Himmler, 4 September 1943, ZI.19\43. HFD, H/10/63. In this letter Wächter explained to Himmler that his conception of a 'Galician-Ukrainian' was the same as Himmler's and justified his previous position by saying that "these questions should be viewed in the context of a more long term development. The Austrian tradition was interrupted by twenty years of Polish rule and so was to a large extent lost among the younger generation who are providing the volunteers. In my opinion, the desired development requires influence to be applied step by step. This development can, I believe, be set in motion during the war, but cannot be completed until after the final victory".
34. After their meeting in March 1943, Wächter requested a personal audience with Himmler in writing on at least eight separate occasions.
35. The entry in the publication *Verordnungsblatt der Waffen-SS*, by the *Verbindungsoffizier der SS beim* OKH (SS Liaison Officer to the Army High Command) reads: *Die wird unbekannt in 14.Waffen-Gren, Div. der SS (galizsche Nr.1) [VOSS 1848g v. 4.8.44] Unbekannt in 14.Waffen-Gren.Div. der SS (ukrainsche Nr.1)* [VOSS 862g v. 12.11.44]. AA. A copy can be found in Document N 756/170 (Sammlung Vopersal), BA-MA.
36. The majority of the instructors were veterans of the Eastern Front holding combat decorations for bravery, who because of injuries sustained whilst on active duty had been classified as unfit for frontline service.
37. See *Geheim*, August 1943, Nr. 4, *Nachrichtendienst fur die Leiter der Abteilung* VI, I. Führer and *Autoritat* and *II. Schulung oder Erziehung*, pp. 1-6. RG 48.004m, Reel 5, *SS-Ausbildungsbattalion z.b.V.* Karton 3, File II, 1943, II, USHMMA.
38. Ferkunia, op.cit. p.8. Ferkuniak and 8 others were assigned to the 10th Training Company.
39. SS-FHA. *Kdo. Amt der Waffen-SS*: Org.Tgb.Nr.982/43 g.Kdos.v. 30.7.1943 *Aufstellung der SS-Freiw. Division 'Galizien'*.
40. Ibid. The document actually read: 'Language to be used for commands: 'Galician' (sic.): language to be used for orders: German.'
41. Heike, English ed., op.cit., p.9.
42. *Pioniereinheiten der 14 Waffen-Gren Div der SS* (*Ukrain*.Nr 1), U-6, Dr H. Schmitt – unpublished manuscript.
43. Hawrylak, op.cit. p.8.
44. Letter to author, R. Kolisnyk, 30 June 1995.
45. Interview, S. Sadiwskyj, Diss, England, 27 February 1989.
46. Interview, Dmytryk, Rushden, England, 21 October 1990. Injuries included splinters from shells and bullet wounds. Verbally to author, Prymak 3 November 1997.
47. Heike, English ed., op.cit., pp.18-19.
48. *Nachrichtendienst fur die Leiter der Abteilung* VI, II. *Schulung oder Erziehung*, p. 5, RG 48.004m, Reel 5, *SS-Ausbildungsbataillon z.b.V.* Karton 3, File II, 1943, II. USHMMA.
49. All regular SS recruits underwent ideological training, however the influx of non-Germanic personnel into the Waffen-SS forced the *SS-Hauptamt* to give up its uniform ideological indoctrination and prepare a specially tailored program for each national or ethnic group. As the Galician Ukrainians were of Slavic origin the lectures deliberately avoided mentioning the inferiority of the Slav race, which was the very essence of the Nazi ideological doctrine.
50. Letter to author, R. Kolisnyk 6 June 1995. The fact that the recruits received political education at Heidelager was confirmed by several veterans of the Division including W. Sirskyj letter to author, 21 September 1995.
51. Verbally to author, R. Drazniowskyj, 13 March 1997 and Heike, English ed., op.cit., p.70.
52. Verbally to author, M. Prymak, 8 November 1997.
53. According to Ferkuniak the officers had taken the oath the day before on 28 August Ferkuniak, op.cit., pp.8-9.
54. The choir was conducted by Vasyl Ostashevskyj.
55. The text of the officially prescribed oath for foreign troops is given in Juttner's circular dated 30 July 1943, Kdo.Amt d.Waffen-SS: Org.Tgb.Nr 982/43 g Kdos. v. 30.7.1943 *Aufstellung der SS-Freiw. Division 'Galizien'*.
56. *My idemo v biy*, nr. 38 (39). AA. For further information about this special edition see *Do Peremohy – Tyzhnevyk Dyviziyi* ('To Victory – The Weekly of the Division'), *Visti Kombatanta*, nr.2, 1972, p. 41.
57. This visit was arranged by the Military Board that was responsible for administering welfare and recreational facilities for the recruits.
58. *SS-Ausbildungs Batl. z.b.V.* (*SS-Freiw. Div. 'Galizien'*), Heidelager, Post Pustkow.Dist.Krak. II b Az.: 12d Tgb.-Nr.130/43 geh. 19.10.43. *Betr: Stärkemeldung, Bezug: Besprechung RF-SS mit SS-Stubaf.* Bartelt. RG-48.004m, Reel 6, *SS-Ausbildungsbataillon z.b.V.*, Karton 3, File 11, 1943, II, USHMMA.
59. According to Ferkuniak the verification commission was established on 20 August 1943, and consisted of Col. Dobrianskyj, Lt. Col. —, Major Kastel and Capt. Uhryn Bezhrishnyi. It recommended that 16 officers be discharged as unsuitable. See Ferkuniak, op.cit. p.8.
60. Ibid.
61. Inter-company football matches were sometimes played. It should however be noted that no sports equipment or clothing was available for matches and games had to be played in army issue shoes. The only recreational facilities available for the camp were a canteen (where beer could be purchased) and a bordello called '*Haus Waldeslust*' ('House of joy in the woods'). Roman Hawrylak, op.cit., p.9.
62. By 30 October 1943, there were 70 known deserters, see Minutes of the Military Board 30 October 1943, ABFC. The OUN leadership did not encourage these desertions and therefore Roman Shukhevych (aka Gen. Chuprynka) issued instructions that volunteer members of the OUN could only leave the Division as the direct result of an order from the OUN commander. The result was a significant reduction in the desertion rate. See 'UPA and the Division 'Halychyna', Lev Shankovskyj, published in *America*, July 12-16, Philadelphia, 1954.
63. Dmytryshyn, *SS Division Galicia...*, op.cit. p.64. See also Kost Pankivskyj *Roky nimetskoi okupatsii, 1941-1944* (New York, Toronto, 1965) op.cit. pp.244-247.
64. Mykola Fylypowych, *Masheruyut Dobrovoltsi*, unpublished manuscript, p 23. These recruits were sworn in on 17 October 1943.
65. *SS-Haupsturmführer* Johannes Kleinow, born 10 February 1901, Party Nr. 112, 214: SS-Nr. 28,740. Former member of *Schutzmannschaft* 207. See *Personal-Akte* NA A3343-SSO-178A.
66. This staff list includes some platoon commanders, see 105/43 geh. *SS-AusbildungsBatl. z.b.V., IIa, A.:21, Tgb.Nr.105/43 geh v.27.9.43 Betr: Führerstellenbesetzungsliste an SS-FHA.* RG 48.004m, Reel 5, *SS-Ausbildungsbataillon z.b.V.* Karton 3, File 11, 1943, II, USHMMA.
67. Figure given in the 'Minutes of the Military Board', 30 October 1943, ABFC.
68. Of this number 3140 (13 officers and 3127 recruits) were based at Heidelager while the remainder were attending training courses elsewhere. See *SS-Ausbildungs Batl. z.b.V. SS-Freiw. Div. 'Galizien'*, Heidelager, Post Pustkow.Dist.Krak, II b Az: 12 d Tgb. Nr, 130/43 *geh. H Geheim! Betr: Stärkemeldung. Bezug: Besprechung RF-SS mit SS-Stubaf.* Bartelt, RG 48.004m, Reel 5, *SS-Ausbildungsbataillon z.b.V*, Karton 3, File II, 1943, II, USHMMA. For the month of September 1943, the average daily strength for the *SS-Ausbildungs-Batl. z.b.V.* (*SS-Freiw. Div. 'Galizien'*) was 3,842. The specific figures for the three categories were 28 German and 20 Ukrainian officers, 410 German NCOs and 382 German and 3220 Ukrainian men. See Ibid., *SS-Ausbildungs-Batl. z.b.V.* (*SS-Freiw. Div. 'Galizien'*), SS-Tr.Ub.Pl. Heidelager, den 1.10.1943, IIb, Az: 9w, Tgb. Nr. 109/43 geh. H/Kr, *Betr: Monatliche stärkemeldung der Teilnehmer an der Feldpost bezw. SS-Feldpost.* Ibid.
69. See *Der Gouverneur des Distrikts Galizien, An den Reichsführer-SS und Chef der Deutschen Polizei* Heinrich Himmler, Lemberg den, 30 Oktober 1943, Dr WA./Ra, 263, HFD, H/10/67.
70. *SS-Panzer-Grenadier-Schule Galiz. Offz. Lehrgang*, Leschan, den 30.10.1943, *Betr: Galiz. Offz. Lehrgang, Bezug: Schr. Wehrkanzlei* Nr. 4/48/943 v.20.10.43. The original document is in the author's archive.
71. In his memoirs Ferkuniak states that the vast majority of those given the highest rank of *Waffen-Hauptsturmführer* including Barvinskyj, Uhryn-Bezhrishnyi, Dawybida, Kotyl and Wasylew were dismissed within months on one pretext or another following Pobihushtschyi's machinations to remove Dawybida which Freitag used as an excuse commenting "As I see it there is no solidarity among you Ukrainians". Ferkuniak, op.cit., p.12.
72. See Ferkuniak, op.cit. pp.10-11. Some arrived with the rank of *Standartenoberjunker* (officer cadets with substantive rank of warrant officer) and were commissioned shortly after their arrival at Heidelager.
73. There are many recorded instances of complaints by these older officers to the Military Board, about their treatment at the hands of the German NCO instructors. Several of their letters of complaint have been persevered and copies of some are in the author's possession. Three officers, P. Holojda, M. Konkol and V. Poniatyshyn later signed a declaration to this effect dated 31 October 1944, which was verified by Osyp Navrotskyj in his capacity as an executive officer of the Military Board. AA.
74. Ferkuniak, op.cit., p.10.
75. Eugen Pobihushtschyi, born 15 November 1901, in Postoliwka. He saw active service with the Ukrainian Army from 1 November 1918 until May 1920 and then from 15 July 1928 until 19 March 1935 he served in the Polish Army with the 57th Infantry Regiment, rising to the equivalent rank of Captain. With the German invasion of Poland in September 1939, he was captured and held by the Germans as a prisoner of war until his release on May 1940. On 15 May 1941, he joined *Roland*. He attended the *Heeresschule für Btl. Abtl. Führer, Antwerpen* 17 April-13 May 1944, and was described by his course commanders as 'a passionate soldier.' On 15 November 1943, he was confirmed in the rank of *Waffen-Sturmbannführer. Personal-Akte*, NA, A3343-SSO-384A.
76. Hawrylak, op.cit., p.12.
77. Heike, Eng. ed., op.cit. p.14.
78. Ibid., p.14.
79. The 12th *MG-Lehrkompanie* was commanded by *SS-Obersturmführer* Herbert Schneller.
80. 'Anschriften': AA. Additional camps at which Ukrainians underwent training included: Amsterdam, Arolsen, Bielefeld, Brno, Cannstatt, Graz, Hamburg-Rahlst, Hamm, Karlsruhe, Kensberg, Koblenz, Leshany, Lübeck, Maastricht, Mielefeld, Moerchingen, Oldenburg, Orthez, Osnabrück, Radom, Rallstedt, Strassburg, Sennheim and Verdun.
81. *Pioneer Battalion of the Galician Division*, Bohdan Kutny and Taras Kaczmarchuk, unpublished

paper, p 1. Interview, Dmytryk, Rushden, England, 21 October 1990.
82. Hawrylak, op.cit., p.9.
83. Letter to the author, Roman Herasymowycz 21 November 1995.
84. *SS-Führungshauptamt Amt* XI, Abtl.2/I, Az:22b16, Amt V Abtl IIa. 10. Dez.1944, *Betr:* 16 *Kriegs-Junkerlehrgang an der SS-und Waffen-Junkerschule* Braunschweig. AA.
85. By preventing the consolidation of these forces in one location the Germans intentionally or otherwise, mitigated their potential threat in the event of a large-scale mutiny.
86. See message to Gren. *Ers.* Regt. 34 Koblenz, from *Galizien* SS Volunteer Div. SS Troop Training Area Heidelager, signed Bartelt, *SS Stubaf,* 26/11, HW16/101, CX/MSS/ Q.24, 6/12/43, Public Records Office, Kew, London (Hereafter abbreviated PRO).
87. *SS-Brigadeführer* Walter Schimana: born 12 March 1898 in Troppau Czechoslovakia – died 12 September 1948 in Salzburg. SS Nr. 337,753/Party Nr. 49,042. Holder of Iron Cross 1st and 2nd Class awarded for anti-partisan actions). Commander of '*Kampfgruppe* Schimana'. He is shown as being responsible for the formation of the 14th Division in the SS-FHA. Kdo. Ant d. Waffen-SS: Org.Tgb.Nr.982/43 g.Kdos.v. 30.7.1943 *Aufstellung der SS-Freiw. Division 'Galizien'*. For further details of career see *Personal-Akte* Walter Schimana NA, A3343-SSO-078B and his RuSHA file NA, A3343-RS-F0316.
88. During the initial training period because of the shortage of instructors all three infantry regiments and the Fusilier Battalion were joined into one regiment that was commanded by *Waffen-Sturmbannführer* Evhen Pobihushtschyi. Heike, Eng. ed., op.cit. p.17.
89. *SS-Führungshauptamt,* Berlin Wilmersdorf, 22 September 1943, Amt II Org.Abtl.1a/II, *Betr.: Neugliederung der SS-Freiw. Div.'Galizien'*, AA.
90. These units were finally completed in January 1944.
91. J. Hnatkiv, *The Fusilier Battalion of the Ukrainian Division*, unpublished paper, p.1.
92. Prior to this change both individuals and departments within the SS establishment continued to use their own terminology when referring to the Division. Thus at different times it was variously referred to as: '*SS-Freiwilligen-Division Galizien*' (by Himmler in his letter to Wächter dated 28 March 1943 HFD, H/10/5); the '*Ukrainische-SS-Polizei-Schützen Division*' (by Berger in a letter to Himmler dated 6 April 1943, HFD, H/10/12); the '*Galizische Division*' (in a telex from Daluege to Winkelmann of 14 April 1943); '*SS-Schützen Division Galizien*' (both in Wächter's proclamation dated 28 April, – and in Berger's letter to Himmler of 21 August 43); and the '*Legion Galizien*' (In Berger's letter to Himmler dated 3 June 43 HFD, H/10/34). After June 1943 the confusion abated.
93. This order was dated 22 October 1943, see Bender & Taylor, op.cit., pp.28-29. It appears that the actual renumbering of the infantry regiments did not however take place for several weeks.
94. Heike refers to this agreement in his memoirs, Eng. ed., op.cit., p.16.
95. Both Barvinskyj and Kotyl were later dismissed from the Division.
96. *Waffen-Hauptsturmführer* I. Rembalowych.
97. *Waffen-Sturmbannführer* M. Palienko.
98. *Waffen-Hauptsturmführer* P. Sosidko.
99. See Daluege to Winkelmann *z.Zt.Feld-kommandostelle*, 14 April 1943. ABFC.
100. Essentially, Wächter and Berger anticipated that 'undesirable political consequences' would occur in the event of the regiments being formed. For both Wächter and Berger's objections see Berger's letter to Himmler 3 June 1943, CdSSHA/Be/Ra./VS-Tgb. Nr. 3561/43g. HFD, H/10/34.
101. Himmler's circular to all officers: *Der Reichsführer* SS Tgb.Nr. 35\88\43g *Feld-kommandostelle* 24 June 1943. HFD, H/10/37.
102. Born 27 October 1898, SS Nr. 393 251, NS Nr. 8,185 303. On 9 November 1944, Flade was promoted to *Chef Kommando Amt, Hauptamt Ordnungspolizei*.
103. The original circular which bears no heading is dated June 1943 (the day is missing). ABFC.
104. See Berger to Himmler *Feldkommandostelle*, SSHA 4268 16.4.43. 1055. HFD, H/10/20.
105. See Himmler's circular dated 5 July 1943, *Feldkommandostelle* Tgb.Nr. 35/88/43g. HFD, H/10/43.
106. Each company had a strength of about 110 soldiers and was comprised of three infantry platoons, a signals section and various support services such as cooks, tailors, etc.
107. The Ukrainians enlisted into these regiments initially wore blank collar patches. German officers and NCOs of these units wore *Polizei* uniforms that carried appropriate *Polizei* ranks. With the exception of helmets bearing *Polizei* markings, no other *Polizei* uniforms or insignia were worn by the Ukrainian volunteers at any time (although the Ukrainian recruits were issued with some *Polizei* equipment such as rucksacks and blankets).
108. A number of pre-worn uniforms (complete with the SS lightning rune collar patches) were issued to the Ukrainians soldiers, that would account for this anomaly. Letter to author, I. Sadoveyj, 22 August 2000.
109. Figure provided in a recruitment report at a meeting of the Military Board on 30 October 1943.
110. Born 12 March 1898, Party No. 2,639,652, holder of the *Balkenkreuz*, Iron Cross 1st and 2nd class, Wound Badge in Black, and the *Deutsches Kreuz in Gold*. Information taken from his service record See *Personal-Akte* NA A3343-SSO-071.
111. Ibid. These included operations 'Hamburg', 'Altona', 'Franz', 'Erntefest I', 'Erntefest II', 'Hornung' and 'Föhn'. See *Der SS-und Polizeiführer in Weissruthenien*, Minsk, den 30.März 143, 00061, *an den Reichsführer SS und Chef der Deutschen Polizei im Reichsministerium des Innern, Betr.: Vorzugsweise Beförderung des Majors d.Sch.* Siegfried Binz, *geb. am* 12.3.1898 in Ostseebad Binz a/Rügen, *Kommandeur des* I./23, *Heimatstandort*: Recklinghausen. *Bezug*: O-Kdo. II P.I (1a) 37/43 *vom* 13.3.43.
112. By order of the *Chef der Ordnungspolizei* in Berlin dated 25 January 1944, the 4th Regiment's 3rd Battalion was transferred by train from Fernschweiler to Maastricht in the Nederlands where it was temporarily accommodated in the Tapijin barracks. However the same order stated unequivocally that "It [3rd Batl] remains attached (and subordinate) in every respect to the Regiment." *Der Chief der Ordnungspolizei Kdo,* g.I-Ia(I) Nr. 983/43(g), Berlin *den* 25. Januar 1944, *Betr.: Verlegung des III./Galizischen SS-Freiwilligen* Rgt.4. ABFC.
113. *Telegram Der Chef der Ordnungspolizei*, Berlin, den 5. Juli 1943, Kdo, I O (3) 1 Nr. 378/43, ABFC.
114. Recruitment report at a meeting of the Military Board on 30 October 1943.
115. *Telegram Der Chef der Ordnungspolizei*, Berlin, den 5. Juli 1943, Kdo, I O (3) 1 Nr. 378/43. ABFC. *Polizeibataillon* 11, to which *Oberst der Sicherheitspolizei* Franz Lechthaler belonged prior to his posting to the 5th Regiment, operated in the Kauen/Sluzk region where on 27 October 1941, a two day operation was carried out against the entire Jewish population. In the early 1960s, Lechthaler and a *Polizeimajor* named Willy Papenkort, who participated in the action, were brought to trial before the Schwurgericht Kassel, twice. The charges on both occasions were '*Beihilfe zum Totschlag an 550 Menschen im Smolensk and Sluzk*', where according to the report '*Lechthaler war der Kommandeur des Exekutions-Bataillon 1941-1942*.' While Papenkort was freed, Lechthaler was subsequently convicted, and sentenced to a three and a half years, a one to two years, and a two years term of imprisonment. A full description of the action in question (omitting the actual numbers of victims) appears in Nurnberg Documents PS-1104.
116. *Telegram Der Chef der Ordnungspolizei*, Berlin, den 5.Juli 1943, Kdo, I O (3) 1 Nr. 378/43. ABFC.
117. Report given at a general meeting of the Military Board October 1943, at which Dr Schulze incorrectly gave the strength of this unit as being 1,293.
118. See *Der Chef der Ordnungspolizei*, 6 August 1943. Kdo. I 0 (3) 1 Nr. 469/43. ABFC.
119. For further details relating to the formation, organisation and structure of this regiment including the names, ranks and positions to which they were posted of many of the German command personnel see a four page document, *Erlass des Chef der Orpo* (Kdo. I 0 (3) 1 Nr. 526/43 v 7.9.1943 *Betr.: Aufstellung des Gal. SS-Freiw.*Rgts.7. BA-KO, R 19 / 1 106.
120. Born 29 April 1895, Party Nr. 7, 238, 661, SS Nr. 442, 406.
121. Recruitment report of the Military Board on 30 October 1943. See also memoirs of Rev. D. Kowaluk, Visti, Nr. 118, 1965, pp. 36-39. Initially there were problems with training facilities for the 7th Regiment in Salies de Bearn and it appears that some recruits had to be temporarily housed in hotels and boarding houses.
122. Born 13 July 1895, Party No. 4, 663, 977.
123. See *Reichsrangliste der Offiziere der Schutzpolizei und Gendarmerie, 1. Teil, Generale und Stabsoffiziere*, Berlin, Reichsdruckerei, 1941.
124. For a list of the proposed appointments see *Gal. SS-Freiw.* Rgt. 8, Maastricht, den 25.Oktober 1943, *Fernschrift, an den chef des Aufstellungsstabes der Gal. SS-Freiw. Regimenter* 4-8. Berlin, *Betr.: Offizierstellenbesetzung. Bezug: Verfg. vom* 12.10.1943. BA-KO, R 20/66.
125. 1 *Oberstleutnant*, 2 *Hauptmann*, 3 *Oberleutnants*, 2 *Leutnants*, 1 *Leutnant d. Res.*, 3 *Rev.-Leutnants*, 118 *Unterführer* (of which 12 gvH suitable), 1 German doctor, 2 Galician doctors. See *SS-Freiw.* Rgt. 8, Maastricht, den 28.Oktober 1943, *Fernschrift, (Oberstleutnant d.SchP.u.Kommandeur Gal. SS-Freiw.*Rgt.8. Schwertschlager) *an den Befehlshaber der Ordnungspolizei in Nimwegen. Betr.: Vorhandene Offiziere und Unterführer bei der aufgelösten Pol.-Waffenschule* IV, *Aufstellung des gal.SSFreiw.* Rgt.8. *Bezug:* FS. Nr.616 vom 27.10.1943. BA-KO, R 20/66.
126. A document dated 12 August 1943, states that some NCOs and men of the 1st Battalion of the 8th Regiment stationed in Märisch-Ostrau, were transferred to *Pol.Schützen*-Rgt.36, whilst the remaining men were formed into two companies which were to remain with the battalion staff at Märisch-Ostrau until their probable assignment to the 7th Regiment and other Galician reserve units. See *Der Chef der Ordnungspolizei*, Berlin, den 12. August 1943, Kdo. I 0 (3) 1 Nr. 484/43, *Schnellbrief, Betr.*: I./SS-Pol.8, *Bezug: Erlass vom* 6.8.1943 – Kdo I 0 (3) 1 Nr. 466/43, R 19/ 104, BA-KO.
127. For further details including staff appointments etc. see *Schnellbrief Chef der Ordnungspolizei/ kdo.* I 0 (3) Nr. 455 II/43 v 20.8.1943 *Betr.: Aufstellung des Gal. SS-Freiw. Ersatz-Batl.* Heidenheim, R 19/103), BA-KO.
128. Letter to author, I. Sadoveyj, 27 February 1999.
129. Ibid.
130. *Der Reichsführer SS und Chef der Deutschen Polizei*, O-W IV (c) 4614/2/ XII, Berlin NW7, den 21 Dez.1943, *Landesarchiv* Saarbrücken, Bestand Md1, Nr. 81.
131. One *Ordnungspolizei* regiment was dissolved to provide the instructors needed to train the Galician Regiments.
132. Schimana received a telegram from Himmler dated 22 October 1943, notifying him that he was to leave his appointment as the commander of the SS-*Freiwilligen*-Division '*Galizien*' and with effect from 9 November 1943, assume the post of the *Höheren SS-und Polizeiführer* as the replacement for Jürgen Stroop. BA-KO, NS 19/2191 folder 1.
133. Fritz Freitag: Born 28 April 1894, in Allenstein, East Prussia: Party Nr. 3,052,501 \ SS Nr. 393,266. Married with two children, Freitag was the son of a railway official who served in the German armed forces in WWI from 1 April 1914 until 17 December 1918 and the *Freikorps* from 15 January 1919 until 15 April 1919. On 3 February 1920 he joined the *Schutzpolizei* (security police) and rose to the rank of *Oberführer* (Colonel). Freitag transferred to the 4th *SS Polizei Panzergrenadier* Division at the outbreak of WWII. See Personalverfügung der *SS-Oberführer* Fritz Freitag, Personal File NA, A3343 SSO-220.
134. Schimana did not take up his new appointment in Greece until 19 November 1943. According to his service record Freitag's appointment was effective as of 20 October 1943. There must therefore have been an overlap between Schimana's departure and Freitag's arrival. Ibid.
135. See programme for the visit by the CO of the SS *Schützen* Division *Galizien SS-Oberführer* Freitag on 19/20 November 1943. ABFC.

136. Ibid.
137. These units were placed under Himmler's direct command as of 27 June 1941, See *Unsere Ehre Heisst Treue, Kreigstagebuch des Kommandostabes Reichsführer SS. Tätigkeitsberichte der 1 und 2 SS-Inf.Brigade, der 1. SS-Kav.-Brigade und von Sonderkommandos der SS,* Vienna, Frankfurt, Zürich: Europa, 1965, pp.15-23.
138. The two motorised brigades were established by Himmler's order on 1 May 1941.
139. For the purposes of these operations Jews were referred to as 'abettors of partisan activity'.
140. See *'Brigadegefechtsstand, den 29.8.1941, Tätigkeitsbericht fur die Zeit vom* 24.8.1941/12.00 Uhr – 29.8.1941/12.00 Ukr', *Unsere Ehre...*, pp.122-123.
141. From 4 January 1943 to 20 April 1943.
142. For details of Freitag's career, appointment dates, positions see his personal file – N/A, A3343 SSO-220.
143. At time of his appointment as Divisional commander Freitag held both the Iron Cross 1st and 2nd Class, (clasp for Iron Cross 2nd Class awarded 5 February 1942, clasp for Iron Cross 1st Class awarded 6 March 1942) the German Cross in Gold (awarded 30 April 1943), the *Ostmedaille* and the Wound Badge in both silver and gold. For details of his service record prior to joining the Galician Division see *'Personalverfügung der SS-Oberführer Fritz Freitag'*, *SS-Führungshauptamt Amt V/Abtl.* IIa/Ref 2, Az.: 21c 24 Fu.P. PZ, Gren, 29.1.1944. *Personalakte* – NA, A3343 SSO-220. ff 584-695.
144. Freitag does however appear to have had some indirect contact with local Ukrainian militia units whose co-operation he acknowledges in the secret daily activity reports of the 1st SS *Infanterie* Brigade and who are described as having "done a very valuable job as regards clearing the partisans and paratroops from the army rear area". In the same reports he criticises conduct of the local Ukrainian population for being 'two-faced' as it was known to be assisting the Jews hiding in the woods and supplying the partisans with food and information. See 1.SS Brigade IIa /449/41, Abtl,Ic.27/41 geh.E/Schu. Brig.St.Qu. 20.8.194, *Betr.: Tätigkeitsberichter* v.20.8.41/12.00 Uhrs bis 24.8.41/12.00, *Unsere, Ehre Heisst Treue*, p.118. See also 1. SS Brigade IIa/449/41, Abtl,Ic.26/41 geh.E/Schu. Brig.St.Qu. 20.8.1941, *Betr.: Tätigkeitsberichter* v.17.8.41/12.00 Uhrs bis 20.8.41/12.00, Ibid. p.110.
145. Not only the Ukrainians considered Freitag's appointment to be inappropriate. In his memoirs the Division's former Operations Officer wrote "One of the greatest tragedies of the Division was the appointment of such a man as its commander". Heike, Eng. ed., op.cit. p.7.
146. Ibid. For a discussion of Freitag's character and personality see pp. 6-7.
147. Ibid., p 9.
148. Heike states that originally the German political authorities had contemplated filling only the Division staff with Germans but the dearth of Ukrainian officers were not available and of those who did undergo training, many proved to be unsuitable because of out-moded experience in modern warfare and had to be dismissed. Ibid., p 15. In marked contrast in his unpublished memoirs *Waffen-Haupsturmführer* Ferkuniak one of the very few Ukrainians to serve on the Division's general staff, states that this was because "Ukrainian officers were obstacles for the Germans which prevented them from taking complete control over Ukrainian soldiers." Ferkuniak, op.cit., p.12.
149. *SS-Sturmbannführer* Johannes Georgi: born 17 August 1912. See *Personal-Akte* NA A3343-SSO-008A.
150. Rudolph Michel, born 28 December 1920, Osnabrück: SS-Nr.466 716.
151. *SS-Obersturmführer* Herbert Schaaf: born 4 March 1908. SS-Nr. 465057. See *Personal-Akte* NA A3343-SSO-063B.
152. *SS-Hauptsturmführer* Erich Finder SS Nr. 16, 939, was transferred from the 8th SS *Kavallerie* Div. to the 14th Galician Division with effect from 20 April 1944, as IIa. See message to 8th SS *Kav.* Div. from SS. Ops. H.Q. IIA Katz: dated 15 April 1944, Top Secret Copy No.13 CX/MSS, Q.53, 24/4/44, HW 16/101 PRO and *Personal-Akte* NA A3343-SSO-008A.
153. *SS-Obersturmführer* Herbert Oskar Hanel: born 18 July 1912. SS-Nr. 121, 523. See *Personal-Akte* NA A3343-SSO-060A.
154. *SS-Sturmbannführer* Hans-Georg Ziegler: born 31 August 1912, SS-Nr. 254 020. See *Personal-Akte* NA A3343-SSO-021C.
155. *SS-Sturmbannführer* Otto Sulzbach: born 18 May 1909. SS-Nr. 1,364/Party No. 61,317. His appointment with the *SS-Freiwilligen-Division 'Galizien'* was effective as of 16 September 1943. See *Personal-Akte* NA A3343-SSO-170B.
156. *SS-Obersturmbannführer* Dr Max Specht: born 8 November 1898, SS-Nr. 118,403/Party Nr. 2,725,210. See *Personal-Akte* NA A3343-SSO-145B.
157. *SS-Hauptsturmführer* Werner Beneke: born 14 July 1911, SS-Nr. 211 942. See *Personal-Akte* NA A3343-SSO-056.
158. *SS-Sturmbannführer* Dr Oskar Kopp: born 30 May 1910. See *Personal-Akte* NA A3343-SSO-199A.
159. *SS-Sturmbannführer* Heinz Behrendt: born 20 July 1904. SS-Nr. 243,666. See *Personal-Akte* NA A3343-SSO-052.
160. *SS-Sturmbannführer* Karl-Robert Zoglauer: born 3 July 1907, SS-Nr. 46 147. See *Personal-Akte* NA A3343-SSO-025c.
161. In his memoirs Heike states that Freitag's desire to appoint commanders with recent frontline experience (and thus maintain a "margin of certainty") was partly defensible in view of the need to prepare the Division for battle in the shortest possible time.
162. In *My Life's Mosaic*, Pobihushtschyi states "Nobody from the division's staff had informed me that a new commander had arrived to take over command of the 29th regiment, which I was commanding." *My Life's Mosaic*, The Association of Ukrainians in Great Britain, 1982, p.126.
163. *SS-Sturmbannführer* Hans Forstreuter: born 1 November 1912, SS-Nr. 422,180/Party Nr. 3,324,777. Holder of German Cross in Gold, Iron Cross 1st and 2nd class, *Infanterie Sturmabzeichen* and *Nahkampfspange* in bronze. In his *Lebenslauf* dated 20 March 1943, Forstreuter gives his party number as being 3,744,129. See NA, A3342-SSO-215.
164. See *SS-Führungshauptamt, Amt* V/IIa.Iof.1, 16/SSO.Ho. 11.11.1943 *Personalverfügung der SS-Sturmbannführer* Forstreuter, NA, A3342-SSO-215.
165. *SS-Obersturmbannführer* Friedrich Dern: born 5 March 1896, SS-Nr. 38,707/Party Nr. 1,202,729. Holder of Iron Cross 1st and 2nd class. For details see his *Personal-Akte* NA, A3343-SSO-143.
166. *SS-Obersturmbannführer* Paul Herms: born 29 September 1903, SS-Nr. 129,135/Party Nr. 5,274,317. Holder of Iron Cross 1st Class, saw active service with the SS-V.T.-Division (mot.) (with both the *'Germania'* and *'Der Führer'* regiments) and then from February 1942 until April 1943 with the 6th SS *Gebirgsdivision 'Nord'*. For further details of his career see his *Personal-Akte*, A3343-SSO-091a.
167. *SS-Standartenführer* Friedrich Beyersdorff: born 9 August 1892, in Kiel, SS-Nr. 405,820/Party Nr. 4,738,054. Holder of Iron Cross 1st and 2nd class.
168. For the appointment see his service record, *SS-Führungshauptamt* Berlin Wilmersdorf, 1.12.43, IIa/Az 21c 16 Lg-/Ge, *Personalverfung Der SS-Obersturmbannführer* Friedrich Beyersdorff. NA, A3343-550-220.
169. Born 10 November 1911. SS-Nr. 490,441. *Personal-Akte* NA A3343-SSO-181A.
170. *SS-Sturmbannführer* Josef Remberger: born 9 June 1903, in Steinweg nr Regensberg, SS-Nr. 267,977/Party Nr. 1,929,332. Holder of Iron Cross 1st Class. He transferred from the 4th SS *Polizei* Div. *Personal-Akte* NA A3343-SSO-023B.
171. *SS-Hauptsturmführer* Wolfgang Wuttig: born 22 October 1915, SS Nr. 423,123. See *Personal-Akte* NA A3343-SSO-017C.
172. *SS-Hauptsturmführer* Karl Bristot: born 12 September 1915, SS-Nr. 202,908/Party Nr. 4,887,138. Formerly member of the 4th SS *Polizei Panzergrenadier* Division. Holder of *Deutsches Kreuz in Gold*, Iron Cross 1st Class, *Kriegsverdienstkreuz* with Swords, Silver Wound Badge. *Personal-Akte* NA, A3343-SSO-107.
173. *SS-Sturmbannführer* Hermann Kaschner: born 7 November 1914, Party Nr. 5,177,822: SS Nr. 317,675. See *Personal-Akte* NA A3343-SSO-155A.
174. *SS-Obersturmbannführer* Franz Magill: born 22 August 1900, SS Nr. 132,620/Party Nr. 4,137171. Holder of Iron Cross 1st and 2nd class. See *Personal-Akte* Franz Magill, NA, A3343-SSO-288A.
175. For a staff listing as of 22 October 1943, see *Die Waffen-SS und Polizei 1939-45 (Führung und Truppe)*, Kurt Mehner, Militair-Verlag Klaus D. Patzwall, Norderstedt, 1995, p.225.
176. Born 24 September 1902, in Malaschiwzi (Ternopil Oblast). In 1924 Michael Brygidyr completed high school and served in the Polish army in which he graduated from a non-commissioned officers' school. From 15 July 1940 to 19 August 1942 he served in the Wehrmacht and from 20 August 1942 to 5 March 1943, in *Schutzmannschaft* 201 as commander of 2nd Company with the rank of *SS-Hauptsturmführer* before enlisting in the 14th Galician Div. on 17 July 1943. He attended a retraining course at SS *Pz.Gren.Sch.* Prosetschnitz-Galiz. *Offz. Lehrgang* in Leschan. His appointment with the '14th Gal. Div' with the rank of *SS-Hauptsturmführer* was confirmed 1 November 1943. His retraining was completed after attending the 15 Batl. *Führer Lehrgang* at Antwerp from 3-29 January 1944, after which he was appointed as commander of I/WGR 29. For details see his SS-Officer file, NA, A3343-SSO-112.
177. Mykola Palienko: born 12 September 1896, Besidkor, Ukraine. He enlisted in the Galician Div. on 17 May 1943.
178. *SS-Hauptsturmführer* Wilhelm Allerkamp: born 21 September 1913 in Wehsede an der Weser, SS Nr. 357,155, Party Nr. 1429 593. Former member of the 4th *SS-Pol.Pzgren.* Div. See *Personal-Akte*, NA, A3343-SSO-008.
179. Heike states whenever possible Freitag even reserved company and platoon commands for Germans. Heike, Eng. ed., op.cit., p.15.
180. Wittenmeyer, Allerkamp, and Kurzbach, were amongst the most prominent of the German battalion commanders as were Sparsam, and Gläss who were battery commanders all of whom had previously served with the 4th *Polizei Panzergrenadier* Division. Other former members of this division who served on the Galician Division's staff included Schaaf, Kopp, Georgi, and Schmitt.
181. Beyersdorff had commanded a regiment in the *Polizei* Division while Forstreuter had previously commanded a battalion.
182. *Fuhrer* of 98. *SS-Standarte*, Headquarters Marhrisch-Schonberg.
183. See *Das Sonderkommando 4a der Einsatzgruppe C und die mit diesem kommando eingestzten Einheiten wahrend des Russland-Feldzuges in der Zeit vom 22.6.1941 bis zum Sommer 1943*, Zentrale Stelle der Landesjustizverwaltungen, Ludwigsburg, 30.12.1964, pp.43-44. At the time Dern held the rank *SS-Sturmbannführer*.
184. See Beurteilung für *SS-Obersturmbannführer* Friedrich Dern, *Personal-Akte* NA A3343-SSO-181A.
185. For details of this particular action see *Unsere Ehre Heisst Treue*, ('Bericht uber den Verlauf der Pripjet-Aktion', 12 August, 1941) op.cit. pp.227-30, and Ruth-Bettina Birn, 'Zweierlei Wirklichkeit. Fallbeispiele zur Partisanbekampfung im Osten' in Wegner (Ed.), *Zwei Wege*, p.275.
186. Quoted verbatim from an appraisal of Magill by *SS-Standartenführer* Hermann Fegelein dated 8 October 1941. See *Personal-Akte* Franz Magill, NA, A3343-SSO-288A.
187. *SS-Sonderbataillon* 'Dirlewanger' was a Waffen-SS penal detachment under the command of *SS-Oberführer* Oskar Dirlewanger (a protégé of Gottlob Berger) which was comprised of among others, convicted criminals, short term non-political concentration camp inmates, cashiered SS men, disgraced officers from all branches of the Wehrmacht serving without rank insignia.
188. Confirmation of Magill's appointments can be found in his service record (*Personal-Akte* Franz Magill) NA, A3343-SSO-288A. After the war Magill was tried in Braunschweig (20.04.1964) and found guilty of complicity in murder of at least 5,254 cases and at least 100 cases of attempted murder for which he was sentenced to five years' imprisonment. See SKs 1/63 – in JuNSV Lfd Nr. 570 – Vol. 20.

189. *SS-Hauptsturmführer* Karl Bristot: born 12 September 1915, Fohnsdorf (Steiermark), SS-Nr. 202,908/Party Nr. 4,887,138. Formerly member of the 4th *SS-Polizei Panzergrenadier* Division. Holder of *Deutsches Kreuz in Gold*, Iron Cross 1st Class, *KVK mit Schwerten, Verwundetenabzeichen in Schwarz und Silber. Personal-Akte* NA, A3343-SSO-107.
190. See *Beurteilung für SS-Hauptsturmführer* Karl Bristot, den 22. Juni 1944, Ibid.
191. The *SS-Führungshauptamt* was the operations headquarters of the whole SS, responsible for training, organisation and employment with the exception of tactical deployment of the Waffen-SS field divisions.
192. The view that the new non-German SS Divisions were frequently saddled with 'undesirable' officers from other German formations is reinforced by Erich Kern, an Austrian NCO assigned to the 14th Galician Division, see his book *Dance Of Death*, Collins Clear-Type Press, London, 1951, p.194.
193. Papers from his personal file confirm that *SS-Untersturmf.* Hanel (born 18 July 1912, Schlettau/Anaberg), served with *1/SS-Totenkopf-Reiterstandarte* and at Majdanek. AA.
194. Grigorij Ossowoy, born 12 October 1923 in Liman/Kharkiv, Ukraine had previously served with the 44th Inf. Div. at Stalingrad where he was wounded. After recovering from his wounds he was sent to the Trawniki camp in October 1942 before requesting a transfer to the *SS-Freiwilligen* Division *'Galizien'* at Heidelager which was approved on 11 August 1943. Details of Ossowoy's service record and transfer are well chronicled in a series of documents for example, *SS-Standortkommandantur Lublin der Waffen-SS*, Lublin, 11 August, 1943, Az.: 23/43/Vo/Hg, *Betr: Versetzungsgsuch des SS-Wachmann* Georg Ossowoy,[sic] geb. 12.10.1923, *Bezug: Gesuch des* Ossowoy v.1.8.43. AA.
195. There are several such examples of non-Ukrainian individuals who were transferred to the 14th Galician Division because they were bilingual in Russian or Polish, such as Jakob Wiens (born 21 September 1901), a German born in Muntau, Ukraine. Wiens, who spoke both, was a former member of the *Allgemeine* SS who transferred to the Waffen-SS in January 1940. In September 1941, his knowledge of the Russian language was sufficient to earn him a posting to *Der Wirtschafter Russland-Süd* (SS Economic and Administrative Department) in Kiev. In November 1943, Wiens transferred for service with the Galician Division with the commissioned rank of *SS-Obersturmführer* in the Division's *Nachschubtruppen* (supply section), in all probability because of his fluency in both Russian and Polish. Personal statement, Jakob Wiens, München 8 February 1962. AA.
196. In extreme cases individuals were openly arrogant and contemptuous toward the Ukrainians "boasting of their German superiority". The commander of the 30th Regiment, *SS-Obersturmbannführer* Hans Boto Forstreuter and his adjutant *SS-Hauptsturmführer* Kurkowskyj were among the worst culprits for displaying this kind of behaviour (letter to author, Shypailo 20 September, 1994). The assertion that some of the senior German officers displayed something akin to Ukrainophobia is confirmed by the Division's Operations Officer W.D Heike whose memoir gives a balanced view of the German officer personnel assigned to the unit. Heike, Eng. ed., op.cit. pp.12-15.
197. For further details see *Personal-Akte* Wolf Dietrich Heike, NA, A3343-SSO-76A. Heike's claim that he remained a member of, and was paid by the General Staff up until the end of the war (hence retaining his Wehrmacht rank) is substantiated by his Soldbuch, a copy of which is in the author's possession. His rank was therefore converted to that of *SS-Sturmbannführer*. Heike was appointed to the post from 1 January 1944, although he actually arrived at Heidelager on 10 January 1944.
198. On 1 April 1934, Heike enlisted as an officer cadet in the 2nd Artillery Regiment at Schwerin, before going on to attend the Kriegsschule in München. He served as a battery officer in the Artillery Regiment at Rendsburg and on 1 April 1936, was commissioned as a 2nd Lieutenant. At the outbreak of WWII, Heike was serving as battery CO with 2nd Artillery Regiment in the 30th Infantry Division and took part in both the Polish and Western campaigns, receiving the Iron Cross 2nd Class on 4 November 1939. The Iron Cross 1st Class followed soon after on 6 November 1940. On 1 December 1940, he was posted with his battery to the newly formed 110th Infantry Division with which he later fought against the Soviet Union becoming on 1 October 1941, 01 (first orderly officer) on the Division's staff. From 1 September 1942, Heike took part in general staff training with 5th *Panzer* Division in the heavy defensive fighting in the sector to the north east of Vyazma. From 1 March 1943 to 30 May 1943, he attended the *Kriegsakademie* in Berlin and from 25 June 1943, served as Ib (Second General Staff Officer) with 122nd Infantry Division in the Staraya Russa sector. On 1 August 1943 he was promoted to the rank of *Major*. Heike was also the recipient of *Sturmabzeichen*, and the *Ostmedaille*. See *Personal-Akte* Wolf Dietrich Heike, *Lebenslauf* and *Personalangaben*, NA, A3343-SSO-76A, and *Soldbuch*, AA.
199. Heike himself describes his position as '1. *Führungsgehilfe des Div.*KDr' – i.e. first assistant to the Divisional commander. His main duties were as Operations Officer. As a major on the General Staff of the German Army, Heike was assigned by the then Chief of Staff of the OKH *Generaloberst* Zeitzler, to temporary service with the Waffen-SS because of the severe shortage within the Waffen-SS of Ia ranks.
200. Freitag's evaluation, which is dated 1 July, 1944, concludes with the statement "H[eike] stands firm on the grounds of National Socialist ideology," although it is hard to see how this could be the case, especially as he was never a member of the Nazi Party. See *Galizische SS-Freiw.* Div., Div. *Gef. St. den* 1. Juli 1944, *Kommandeur, Beurteilung für den SS-Sturmbannführer* Wolf-Dietrich Heike, *Geb. am*: 27.6.13, R.D.A.:1.8.43 1 *Generalstabsoffizier. Personal-Akte* Wolf Dietrich Heike, NA, A3343-SSO-76A.
201. Born 19 April 1914, Zweibrücken, SS-Nr. 422,124. Party member who served in the SA from 5 March 1933 to 1 April 1935. Prior to joining the 14th Gal. Div, Wittenmeyer joined the 4th *Polizei* Div, 30 January 1940, and was later attached to *Kampfgruppe* Fegelein from 1 December 1942, to 1 February 1943. See *Personal-Akte* Friedrich Wittenmeyer, NA, A3343-SSO-002C.
202. Heike, Eng. ed., op.cit. p.6.
203. More than one instance has been recounted to the author whereby German commanding officers, at regimental, battalion, company and platoon level escaped punishment for blunders or mistakes for which they were fully responsible as will be seen in later chapters.
204. Born 17 May 1896, Perevozets, Kalush Oblast, Paliiv was a member of the Polish parliament (*Sejm*) from 1928-30. He enlisted into the Galician Division on 17 July 1943. (Information taken from his service record, AA).
205. Hunczak, op.cit., pp.4 and 6.
206. In his memoirs Heike acknowledges that the Division's command was aware of this problem but unable to take effective preventative action as long as it was based at Heidelager. Heike, Eng. ed., op.cit., p.25.
207. Having a civilian organisation directly attached to the Galician Division was a unique distinction within the German military establishment.
208. A list of Ukrainian candidates for the Propaganda Platoon, *SS-Schützendivision* Galizien dated 13 July 1943, gave the following names:
Wortberichters (journalists): Ivan Martschuk, Ivan Durbak, Stephan Konrad, Lev Schankwskyj. *Filmberichters* (film reporters): Jaroslav Kezalo, Wolodymyr Ratydsch, Wladymyr Dawydok, Roman Pryima, Rabij Ewstachij. *Rundfunksprecher* (radio broadcasters): Stanislav Krawlschyschyn, Wasyl Bavuza, Demijan Lischtschynskyj. Zeichner (illustrators): Myhailo Mychalewytsch, Bohdan makohin, Julian Woljanjuk, Andrij Lepkyj. *Rundfünktechniken* (radio technicians): Lev Tschotyzbak, Mychaijo Tzezkiwnyk, Jurij Holobradskyj. *Bildberichter* (photo-reporters): Eugen Brykowytsch, Iwan Danyschtschuk, Ing. kurylowytsch, Ivan Kowaslskyj. Lemberg den 13.Juli 1943, *Verzeichniss der Kandidaten für den Propaganda-Sug den SS-Schützendivision Galizien*, ABFC.
209. Letter to author, 19 March 1996, from a former *Kriegsberichter* O. Lysiak.
210. Memoirs of M. Ostroverkha, *Visti Kombatanta* nos. 2,3,4,5,6, (1972).
211. A good example of previous successful activities of this nature was the entertainment programme entitled the 'Great Concert of Selected Songs' performed by Ukrainian artists, at the L'viv Opera House on 15 September 1943. Individuals were able to pick their favourite song and dedicate it to friends or family members serving in the Division, in return for a contribution being made to the Welfare Fund for Riflemen of the Galician Division, whereupon those traditional songs attracting the most donations were performed. The largest donations from single Galician families were also announced during the concert when the entire amount raised was presented to the Ukrainian Military Board. Flyer dated 10 August 1943, issued under the names of Dr Kost Pankivskyj and Myhailo Kushnir in his capacity of Head of the Cultural Section of the L'viv branch of the Ukrainian Central Committee. AA.
212. Each parcel contained sugar, honey, baked goods, dry fruits, apples, cigarettes, nuts, shoe polish, toothpaste, shoe laces, a pencil, a Christmas card with greetings, a notebook and 10 postcards.
213. See Message to *SS Ustuf.* Szillat, Liaison Officer of SS Ops HQ. in *Wehrkreis* X, Hamburg, from 14 Galician SS Volunteer Div. *Abtl.* VI, SS Troop Training Area Heidelager, signed pp Zoglauer, *SS-Hauptstuf.*, and Kdr *Abtl*, 6, on 17/12, HW 16/100 Copy No. 13 12/1/44, CX/MSS/Q.32.
PRO. In fact the delivery of the packages to Galicians in the named locations caused those within the British intelligence who were responsible for analysing the decrypted enigma messages to draw this entirely erroneous conclusion in their Top Secret report which read:
Top Secret, covering information received between 0800 hrs. 21/12 and 1800 hrs. 11/1/44.
General.
Three documents, two of 17/12, and one of 29/12, dealing with Christmas comforts for Galician volunteers of the SS appear to throw some interesting light on the internal affairs of Germany. Comforts were being sent to 'volunteers of SS volunteer Division Galizien' in a number of places including: Osnabrueck, Hamm, Verdun, Luebeck, Hilversum, Karlstadt, Radolfzell, Hamburg, Moerchingen and Muenster; moreover this list is not complete. Four points should be noticed: (a) with the exception of Hilversum and Moerchingen, no SS training units are known in these places. (b) In Muenster the information regarding the comforts was sent to [the] Liaison Officer of the SS Ops. HQ in Wehrkreis VI. (c) Most of the named towns are towns with fairly large populations, many of them bombed by the Allies. (d) SS Division Galizien is in training at Heidelager.
It will be remembered that when volunteers for the SS from Galicia were called for, the Germans announced that they had sufficient volunteers for six divisions [sic]: so far as is known to the present, however, only one division and five independent regiments have been formed. Also in the past, there have been several cases of Polish and White Russian Schutzmannschaft battalions being sent in to keep order in Germany after air-raids. It would, therefore, seem that these 'Galizien Volunteers' who received Christmas comforts are attached to the SS Div. Galizien for administrative purposes, but are being used in large towns for police and guard duties: that, in fact, the Master Race is being kept in order by 'sub-men'. See SS Report No. 12. Copy No.12 HW16/83, PRO.
214. The Military Board simultaneously delivered 20 x 100kg of wheat, 4 x 100 kg of poppy seeds and 4 x 100 kg of honey for the preparation of the traditional sweet *Kutya* and spent the sum of 100,000 *Zloty* on Christmas events and entertainment for the recruits.
215. NS 19/1785: *Der Höhere SS-und Polizeiführer Ost* Koppe to Dr Brandt, Cracow 8 Jan. 1944, *Spenden der Bevölkerung des Districts Galizien fur die 'SS-Freiwilligen-Division Galizien*. HFD, H/10/75. The

letter read "I would ask you to inform the *Reichsführer* about this exemplary donation which bears witness to a considerable capacity for sacrifice in the Galician people."

216. The Bandura is a Ukrainian musical instrument similar in construction and appearance to a Lute.
217. Ferkuniak, op.cit., p.17. Ferkuniak ascribes hardship of the families of Division members and the failure of the German authorities to provide the promised relief as the main cause.
218. Ibid.
219. The visits took place in late November to early December 1943. On his return, Dr Makarushka gave a very positive account to the Military Board on the conditions and training of these volunteers in France and their high morale. During the visit to the 4th Regiment, the German training instructors are said to have remarked to Wächter that the Ukrainians should be sent to fight only on the Eastern Front, and warned of a catastrophe if they should deployed anywhere else. On the whole Wächter was pleased with the visit and viewed the Ukrainian soldiers as intelligent and enthusiastic. For details of the report see 'Minutes of the Military Board', 14 December 1943, ABFC.
220. Himmler refers to this report in his letter to Wächter of 31 December 1943, See RF/M, 263, Field command. HFD, H/10/73.
221. To 14th Galician SS. Volunteer Infantry Division, from [*Orpo*] Chief of Staff, signed RODE, *SS-Oberführer*, on 11/12/43, Subject: Disbanding of Galician *Polizei* Regiments 6 and 7. HW16/100, Most Secret, Copy No. 13, CX/MSS/ Q.41, 22/2/44, PRO.
222. Telex, *Der Chef der Ordnungspolizei*, Berlin, den 23 Dezember 1943, Kdo. g I (Org.3) Nr. 282/43 (g). *Betr: Abgabe von 2.000 Freiwilligen der 14. Gal. SS-Freiw. Regiment*. BA-KO, R 19/326. The document specified these soldiers were to only bring with them their uniforms and personal kit and not their weaponry.
223. For further information relating to this unit see *Schnellbrief Chef der Ordnungspolizei/* kdo. I 0 (3) Nr. 455 II/43 v 20.8.1943 *Betr: Aufstellung des Gal. SS-Freiw. Ersatz-Batls*. Heidenheim, R 19/103, BA-KO.
224. Letters to author, I. Sadoveyj, 17 January 1999 and 9 February 1999.
225. Letter to author, I. Sadoveyj, 9 February 1999.
226. On 31 January 1944, a second instruction was issued giving further explicit details of their disbandment. See, *Schnellbrief Der Chef der Ordnungspolizei*, Berlin den 31. Januar 1944, O-Kdo.g I Org. (3) Nr.305/43 (g.). *Betr: Auflösung der Gal. SS-Freiw. Regimenter* 6 u. 7, R 19/304, BA-KO.
227. Letters to author, I. Sadoveyj, 17 January 1999 and 9 February 1999.
228. See NA T175 roll 141, frame 2668945
229. *Feld-kommandostelle*, 22 January 1944: RF/N.36/141/44. HFD H/10/76. *Schützmannschafts-Bataillon* 204 comprised three companies of Ukrainians with a combined strength of around 500 men, predominantly from Galicia
230. *Der Reichsführer-SS, Feldkommandostelle* 5 July 1943, Tgb.Nr 35/88/43g RF/Bn. HFD, H/10/43.
231. It should be noted that a telegram concerning the transfer of the battalion dated 8 February 1944, sent to the *Chef der Ordnungspolizei* indicated that the final arrangements for the transfer had not yet been made when it asked; "Please let us know at what time the Galician SS Volunteer Division will take over the battalion and when we can anticipate the return of the German personnel, who are presently attached to the battalion and also uniforms, equipment and motor-pool which is owned by the *Polizei* ....." See *Der Chef der Ordnungspolizei* Berlin NW7, den 8 Februar 1944, Kdo. g I Org.(11) Nr.96/43 (g). *An SS-Führungshauptamt in Berlin-Wilmersdorf, Betr.,: Übernahme des Schützmannschafts Batl. . 204 in die Galizische SS-Freiwilligen-Division*, R 19/326, BA-KO.
232. Letter to author, Horodyskyj, 26 February 1999.
233. Ibid.

Chapter 5

1. Wilhelm Koppe: *SS-Obergruppenführer und General der Polizei*: born 15 June 1896, SS-Nr. 25,955/Party Nr. 305,584.
2. See *'Personalverfügung der SS-Oberführer Fritz Freitag'. SS-Führungshauptamt Amt V/Abtl.* IIa/Ref 2, Az.:21c 24 Fu.P. PZ, Gren, 29.1.1944. See *Personal-Akte* NA, A3343 SSO-220.
3. Beyersdorff's service record shows his appointment was effective as of 1 January 1944, see *Personalverfügung, SS-Führungshauptamt, Amt* V IIa/Az.: 21c 16 Lg/Ge. 1.12.43. *Personal-Akte* NA, A3343-SSO-066, although M. Dlaboha states that he did not actually arrive at Heidelager until 7 January 1944. *Visti* nr. 5-6 (43-44), May-June 1954.
4. This date for the formation of the original battlegroup is obtained from a decrypted enigma message which refers to a communication dated 13/2 addressed to *Amt* X, from 14th SS *Freiw*. Div, requesting urgent allocation of 45 cbm. 'O' [Otto] (i.e. Petrol) fuel as replacement for fuel consumed in setting up battlegroup on 9/2. See, HW16/100, Most Secret, CX/MSS/ Q.41, 22/2/44. PRO.
5. 'Kovpak's partisans' was the general designation of all Soviet partisans which fought in the north-western districts of Ukraine even though Major-General Sydir Kovpak was only active in this area of Galicia during summer and autumn of 1943. Kovpak, who was an Ukrainian Communist, had previously directed operations in the Sumy region using a mixture of Ukrainian and Russian Communist partisans.
6. Although ordinarily regular Wehrmacht or Waffen-SS combat formations stationed in the *Generalgouvernement* were not subjected to the authority of the HSSPf, in exceptional cases individual frontline units were temporarily seconded for the execution of special assignments.
7. Heike states that Himmler did not issue the order but had merely mentioned the possibility of using elements of the Division to fight the Soviet partisans active in western Ukraine. Koppe then conveyed the order on the basis of these discussions. See Heike, Eng. ed., op.cit., pp. 20 and 21.
8. HW16/100, Most Secret, CX/MSS/ Q.46, 16/3/44. PRO.
9. M. Dlaboha, Visti Nr. 131, 1969, pp. 101-103.
10. HW16/83, CX/MSS/ SS Report 16. 24/2/44 PRO.
11. Ibid., p.21. Roman Dolynskyj, 'Boieva hrupa Bayersdorffa', *Visti*, nos. 3-6 (77-80), pp. 10-11: also nos. 7-10 (78-80), pp. 6-9. There is some discrepancy over the eventual size of the battlegroup. According to Dolynskyj it consisted of two infantry battalions (the second being commanded by *Waffen-Hauptsturmführer* Rembalowych). For his part Heike omits the cavalry reconnaissance unit. Dr M. Maleckyj who took part in the organisation of both groups was originally assigned as the commander of one of the two infantry battalions, but remained in Heidelager when the order was revised omitting the second battalion. Letter to author, R. Kolisnyk, 11 December 1997.
12. Other Ukrainian officers assigned to the artillery were: *Waffen-Untersturmführer* Dlaboha, *Waffen-Untersturmführer* Krajczyk, and *Waffen-Untersturmführer* Roslak.
13. Along with Governor Wächter, Dr Otto Bauer (Deputy Governor of Galicia) had devoted considerable effort to improving the attitude of the German administration towards the local residents, both Ukrainian and Polish, as well as to the organisation of the Galician Division.
14. The chief of the office of the Governor.
15. The Soviet agent Nikolai Kuznetsov was responsible for the assassinations and not the German *Sicherheitsdienst* who were originally suspected and with whom Bauer was unpopular because of his frequent interventions on behalf of interned or arrested Ukrainians. Dr Bauer, who was married to a Swiss national, had also resided in the USA immediately prior to WWII, which was enough in itself to alert the suspicions of the xenophobic German security services and fuel rumours that they were responsible for his death.
16. On this occasion 45 members of the Divisional band travelled to L'viv. In its entirety the band consisted of seventy-eight musicians. Initially it was led by *Kapelmeister* Krawchuk. Later this position was held by *SS-Oberscharführer* Johannes Thiessen. All musicians were trained as front line medics and were pre-assigned to the three infantry regiments. The *Tennermarsch,* a traditional arrangement from the old Austro-Hungarian army, was chosen as the Divisional march.
17. The first public appearance of soldiers of the Division, albeit for entertainment purposes, was on Wednesday 15 September 1943, when the Divisional choir under Vasyl Ostashevskyj made a highly successful public appearance together with other Ukrainian artists, at the *Wünsch Konzert* held in the L'viv Opera House. The 'Great Concert of Selected Songs' was dedicated to the soldiers of the Galician Division and was broadcast on the radio on 21 September 1943 at 19:00. Flyer dated 10 August 1943, issued under the names of Dr Kost Pankivskyj and Myhailo Kushnir in his capacity of Head of the Cultural Section of the L'viv branch of the Ukrainian Central Committee. AA. Also letter from Bohdan Kutny, 27 July 1999, who took part in the event several photographs of which later appeared in the Divisional newspaper *Do Peremohy*.
18. Letters to author, W. Motyka, 15 April 1993, and M. Holowaty, 30 October 1999.
19. Immediately before departure the personnel selected to be part of *KGr.* Beyersdorff were hurriedly issued with armshields and collar patches bearing the Galician lion emblem. In the absence of any instructions to the contrary the soldiers were directed incorrectly to attach the armshield to the lower right sleeve. Later this was changed to the correct position of the upper left sleeve.
20. M. Dlaboha, 'Boiova hrupa Bayersdorffa', *Visti,* No. 131, 1969, pp. 101-103.
21. Letter to author, R. Kolisnyk, 2 January 1998.
22. Altogether some 2000 packages were distributed to the soldiers of *Kampfgruppe* Beyersdorff containing baked goods, meat and cigarettes, and copies of local newspapers and *Do Peremohy* were also distributed.
23. Letter to author, M. Holowaty, 13 July 2000.
24. For further details see M. Dlaboha, op.cit.
25. Ibid.
26. Letter to author, J. Kunyckyj, 10 March 1993.
27. The 'Winter Campaigns' were offensives undertaken by troops of the Army of the Ukrainian National Republic against the White Russian and Bolshevik armies in 1919-20 and 1921, conducted as partisan warfare behind enemy lines.
28. M. Dlaboha, op.cit.
29. 518 *Ortskommandantur* I/524, 518/22 (*Polizei Lagemeldungen*: February 1944) *Der Kommandeur der Ordnungspolizei im Distrikt* Lublin 1a, Lublin, den 25. Februar 1944, *Tägliche Lagemeldung*, (22/133) *Der Kommandeur der Ordnungspolizei im Distrikt* Lublin 1a, Lublin, den 29. Februar 1944, *Tägliche Lagemeldung*, (22/157), Lublin, *Archiwum Panstwowe w Lublinie* (hereafter cited as APL).
30. Ibid., *Der Kommandeur der Ordnungspolizei im Distrikt* Lublin Ia, Lublin, den 5. März 1944, *Tägliche Lagemeldung*, (23/34-35), APL.
31. Ibid.
32. *Der Kommandeur der Ordnungspolizei im Distrikt* Lublin Ia, Lublin, den 7. März, 1944, *Tägliche Lagemeldung*, (23/47), APL.
33. *Waffen-Hauptsturmführer* Roman Dolynskyj who produced a comprehensive report on the activities of the *Kampfgruppe*, wrote that in the third and final stage of the operation, elements of it took part in the assault on the bulk of the partisans which had been surrounded, inflicting significant casualties although a large group of around 150 managed to escape to the north where the terrain was boggy. For further details of the operation see Dolynskyj 'Boieva hrupa Bayersdorffa', *Visti*, nos. 3-6, 7-9, Munich, 1957.
34. Letter to author, Kolisnyk, 2 January 1998. Other elements entrained on 20 March 1944, Dolynskyj, op.cit., nos. 7-10 (78-81), p.8.
35. On the same day II/*Gal.SS-Freiw.* Rgt 5 received the order to return to its parent regiment on foot to Zwierzyniec and then by rail to Biala Podlaska.
36. Letter to author, R. Kolisnyk, 2 January 1998.
37. An unconfirmed figure of 10 killed and 13 wounded is given as the number of casualties by V. Styrkul in *We accuse*, Kyiv, Dnipro Publishers, 1984, p.169.
38. Letter to author, R. Kolisnyk, 2 January 1998.
39. Dolynskyj gives a figure of approximately 150 men who received decorations for their part in the campaign. Germans such as *SS-Hauptsturmführer* Kleinow, *SS-Hauptsturmführer* Bristot and *SS-*

Obersturmführer Schneller, received the *Kriegsverdienstkreuz* (War Service Cross) 1st Class while Ukrainians including *Waffen-Hauptsturmführer* Rembalowych *Waffen-Hauptsturmführer* Palienko and *Waffen-Hauptsturmführer* Dolynskyj received the *Kriegsverdienstkreuz* 2nd Class. See Dolynskyj, op.cit., *Visti*, nos. 3-6, 7-9, 1957.

40. Heike, Eng. ed., op.cit. p.22.
41. Dolynskyj, op.cit., *Visti,* nos. 3-6, 77-80, p.12.
42. Heike, Eng. ed., op.cit., p.22. At least one recorded case of misconduct by Ukrainian personnel within the *Kampfgruppe* has come to light. This concerned the company led by *Waffen-Unterstumführer* Sobolewsky whose soldiers organised some additional meat for their field kitchen. Unaware of this, Sobolewsky denied the report to his German superior. Upon learning from the company cook that livestock had indeed been illegally appropriated by his men he felt his 'officer's honour' to be at stake and consequently shortly before the *Kampfgruppe* returned to the Division, he shot himself. This account as related by M. Maleckyj, letter to author, 12 May 1995.
43. BdO. Stuttgart.
44. *An der Chef der Ordnungspolizei* Berlin, *Geheim*, Kdo I Org (3) I No. 78/44, v 3.2.44 No. 552, Betr. *Marsch und Einsatzfähigkeit des Gal SS-Freiw.* Rgt 4. ABFC.
45. BdO.Dag.No. 154 8/2 0855. *An den RFSS und ChdDtPol. Chef der Ordnungspolizei* in Berlin NW7, *Betr. Einsatzbereitschaft des Gal.SS-Freiw.Rgt.* 5, 3.2.1944. ABFC.
46. *Der Chief der Ordnungspolizei, Abschrift*, Berlin, den 9 Februar, 1944. Kdo.g I-Ia (i) No. 1020 11/43 (g), *Fernschreiben, An die BdO. in* Stuttgart, Danzig, Nimwegen und Cracow, *Betr., Verlegung der Gal. SS-Freiw.Rgtr.* 4 und 5. BA-KO, R 19/326. The 3rd Battalion did not leave from Maastricht, where it had been temporally transferred, until 19 February. See KTB OB West v 1.2.44 to 28.2.1944, RH 19 IV/22 and RH 19 IV/23, BA-MA.
47. At a session of the Governor and Department Chief in Cracow on 16 February, 1944, Wächter explained: "The population, in particular the general farming population, is as yet still anti-Bolshevik in its feelings. Should the Bolsheviks succeed in further pursuing their propaganda and in setting up a liberation army (*Befreiungsarmee*), then it would become impossible to discount the concern that they could make rapid gains in terms of influence. The nationalist youth of Ukraine is ready and willing to march. German propaganda should adopt a unified and consistent approach. Many of those Ukrainians who are friendly towards the Reich and allied to us have turned to the German leadership and declared, 'Give us an opportunity. Show us that you have plans for us; perhaps self-administration as is the case in Estonia.' The situation is ripe and cries out for political measures. A gesture must be made towards the wavering Ukrainians. This would enable us to take the wind out of the sails of the nationalist Ukrainian youth and turn it into an active component of German interests.

    "The German political approach towards the Ukrainians is extraordinarily confused. A German radio station in Königsberg ended each transmission with the cry, 'Hail, free Ukraine'. Should an Ukrainian say this openly in Lemberg then he would be arrested. This utter confusion in the official German approach is intolerable. The drafting of young people from the R.K.U. and their deployment as flak soldiers in the Reich does not make sense in their eyes. It is contrary to the Reich's Ukrainian political policy. If an absolutely consistent and positive position regarding Ukraine is not taken soon, dire consequences will result. The only basis for this is represented by the *SS-Schützendivision Galizien*. This has succeeded in catching for German interests, a section of the active Ukrainian youth who want to march. There are still many Ukrainians who are convinced that while no future could be expected under Stalin, prospects of a future are still being offered by the Germans. It is requested that a decisive emphasis is given to the political factors, when deploying the first formations of the *SS-Freiwilligen-Division Galizien*. The force is initially, to be valued in terms of propaganda rather than militarily, being poorly armed, not possessing heavy weapons or anti-tank guns, etc. Every thing depends upon how it performs in its first active deployment. The political element should not be neglected. It may be a good idea to make among its ranks political arrangements in our direction, by giving it politically well-disposed Ukrainian officers. The volunteers would then receive constant propaganda influence via these officers. Frank, Tagebuch, op.cit., p.800.
48. The detachment from the 12th *MG-Lehrkompanie* and the Divisional band.
49. Wächter suggested that the II/4th Rgt be used.
50. Telex from Berger to Himmler, shas nr. 1049 14/2/44 2130, H/10/77.
51. Himmler to *HSSPf. Ost SS-Obergruppenführer* Koppe, 16 February 1944, H/10/78.
52. The 3rd Battalion travelled to this area from Maastricht in the Nederlands, where it had previously been moved.
53. The entry dated 7 March 1944, in 'Minutes of the Meetings of the Military Board Galicia' *Shevchenko Scientific Society of Canada* Vol. 30: 1993, pp. 91-93, refers to the warm welcome received by 4th Regiment in Galicia.
54. Ivan Franko (born 27 August 1856 in Nahuievychi, today Ivan Franko in western Ukraine) was a writer, scholar, political and civic leader, and was one of Ukraine's greatest creative geniuses.
55. The text of the speech made by Pyndus was quoted verbatim in an article in the *Lemberger Zeitung* of 25 February 1944, entitled 'Marsch in ein neue glückliche Zukunft' ('March to a new, successful future'). AA.
56. Speech of Governor Wächter to 1/4th Regiment. L'viv, 25 February 1944. AA.
57. While the higher German authorities actively opposed any association with the UPA, in at least one instance (i.e. 6/II) contact was instigated by the German company commanders who instructed the Ukrainian soldiers to give the daily password to the local UPA units in order to avoid any unnecessary conflict. Later, this co-operation was further extended when one UPA unit acted as an escort for the company. Verbally Maksymiw, 27 November 1995.
58. Lemberger Zeitung, op.cit.
59. Positive verification of Soviet collaboration with the Poles in Huta Pieniacka can be found in Mieczyslaw Juchniewicz, 'Z dzialalnosci organizacyjno-bojowej gwardii ludowej wobwodzie lwowskim ppr-gl,' in *Wojskowy Przeglad Historyczny*, (Warsaw), No. 4 (48), pp.153-154.
60. The first two casualties were Roman Andriichuk and Oleksa Bobak. Their lavish funerals took place at the *Heldenfriedhof*, Brody, on 2 March 1944, accompanied by a Luftwaffe band. Alfred Bisanz was present, as was Governor Wächter who laid a wreath. The third soldier Yurij Hanusiak, was wounded and died a few days later in hospital in L'viv. He was buried in the city on 7 March. *Gal. SS Freiw.* Regt. 4, O.U., den 3.3.1944, *Regiments Tagesbefehl* No. 10. AA.
61. The other two members of the Military Board were Yurij Krokhmaliuk and Dr Lubomyr Makarushka.
62. For details of the action in which Khronoviat himself took part see the 'Minutes of the Military Board' op.cit., 7 March 1944, pp. 91-92.
63. See for example Antoni B. Szczesniak and Wieslaw Z. Szota, *Droga do nikad* (Warsaw, 1973) p.127. This account, as well as those of other Polish or Soviet authors, is largely based on the report on the action sent less than a month later by the underground Polish *Armia Krajowa* to the Polish Government in exile in London which states: "On February 27, 44 at 5.00am the 14th Division of the Ukrainian SS (sic.) surrounded the village Huta Pieniacka from three sides, shooting from a distance at houses, set some buildings on fire and then entered the village, plundering all the belongings of the inhabitants. The people were gathered in the church or shot in the houses. Those gathered in the church, men women and children were taken outside in groups, children killed in front of their parents. Some men and women were shot in the cemetery, others were gathered in barns, where they were shot. The village was completely burned down. The only people who saved themselves were those who on finding out about the approaching Ukrainian SS, managed to hide in the forests (only men) or those who pretended to be dead or managed to hide in potato holes in the basements. Right now it is difficult to establish how many survived as they spread themselves around the area. Many injured with burned arms and legs are being treated, impossible to say how many since people from surrounding villages took them to their homes after the SS left. Not a single shot was fired on the SS division on the part of the inhabitants since they were considered part of the German army."

    Reported by Uta WSK Huta Pieniacka who survived, badly burned. The action of the SS was to be in revenge for the killing of 4 SS men on February 23. "About 60 entered the village in the evening and began to plunder the houses. Since they wore German uniforms and spoke Ukrainian, they were taken for a disguised group. Thus the local defence action started, killing 2 for sure, and wounding several. Since the Ukrainian SS came to the area such cases may repeat themselves in every Polish village." A copy of this report can be found in the Huta Pieniacka Case files at the Cracow Regional Office of the Polish Main Commission [for the investigation of crimes against the Polish nation]. This version of the events and subsequent witness statements by survivors, relate the event in graphic and dramatic detail but contain several significant discrepancies. Additional convincing evidence that Ukrainians were responsible for the pacification can be found in the Reports of representatives of Ukrainian Aid Committees (subordinated to the Ukrainian Central Committee, currently located in the Michael Chomiak Collection in the Provincial Archives of Alberta (85.191, folder 59)). One report that mentions the incident at HUTA states unequivocally that the 'pacification' was conducted by soldiers of the Galician Division in retaliation for the death of their two comrades on the outskirts of the village. The same report mentions another 'action' of the German gendarmerie and Ukrainian members of the SS-Division in the Polish village of WICEN on 4 March 1944 in retaliation for the killing of 15 Ukrainians in the village of PUKIV by Polish partisans.
64. *Reisebericht u. Bericht über die Besprechung mit dem Kommandeur des Gal. SS-Freiw.Rgt.*4, *Major der Schutzpolizei* Binz, R19/333, Bundesarchiv.
65. Mitscherling held the rank of *Hauptmann der Schutzpolizei*.
66. Gert Frick, *Fester Platz Tarnopol 1944*, Verlag Rombach, Freiberg, 1969, pp.26-27.
67. For details see Vasyl Petrovskyi, *Visti*, nos. 6-7, 1952, Munich.
68. Frick, op.cit., p.31.
69. Ibid., p.44.
70. *Anlagen zum* KTB Pz.AOK 4, RH 21-4/201, BA-MA.
71. Frick, op.cit., p.68.
72. In 'Berezhany' *Visti,* nos. 4-5, Munich, 1952, Yuri Krokhmaliuk states that only two men returned while other sources give a figure of four. For the personal account of one survivor see Vasyl Petrovskyi, *Visti,* nos. 6-7, Munich, 1952.
73. The photographer was Karl Weyer and the reporter was Oleh Lysiak. Two of the Ukrainian recipients were Wasyl Wykluk and Wasyl Bilecky who was recommend for the award after capturing and recovering a Soviet light anti-tank gun during a combat action in the locality. Letter to author, O. Lysiak, 14 June 1996.
74. 518 *Ortskommandantur* I/524, 518/22 (*Polizei-Lagemeldungen*: March 1944) *Der Kommandeur der Ordnungspolizei im Distrikt* Lublin Ia, Lublin, den 28. März 1944, *Tägliche Lagemeldung*, (23/183) 518/24, *Polizei-Lagemeldungen*: April 1944) *Der Kommandeur der Ordnungspolizei im Distrikt* Lublin Ia, Lublin, den 6. April 1944, *Tägliche Lagemeldung*, (24/37) APL.
75. For further details of the activities of the 5th Regiment see unpublished memoirs of Josaphat Konchak, *Visti Kombatanta*, No.3, 1996, pp.83-88.
76. Ukrainian sources give a total figure of around 100 men from the Regiment having successfully deserted to the UPA, while it was stationed in the vicinity of Zamosc, see Shankovskyj 'UPA and the Division', reprinted in *Visti*, July-August 1954, No. 7-8 (45-46), p. 10. In the article the author describes in some detail the UPA units in which former Divisional soldiers excelled.

77. 518 *Ortskommandantur* I/524, 518/23 (*Polizei-Lagemeldungen*: March 1944) *Der Kommandeur der Ordnungspolizei im Distrikt* Lublin Ia, Lublin, den 9. März 1944, *Tägliche Lagemeldung*, (23/59), Lublin, APL.
78. Ibid., *Der Kommandeur der Ordnungspolizei im Distrikt* Lublin Ia, Lublin, den 16. März 1944, *Tägliche Lagemeldung*, (23/109), APL.
79. Ibid., 518/24 (*Polizei-Lagemeldungen*: April 1944) *Der Kommandeur der Ordnungspolizei im Distrikt* Lublin Ia, Lublin, den 20 April, 1944, *Tägliche Lagemeldung*, (24/127), APL.
80. Two such instances have been verified by former members of the Regiment; the first in a squad of about 50 men stationed in the village of Stryzhiv, (Oleksander Kozak, letter to the author, dated 22 March 1993) and the second involving a company stationed in the village of Bila Pidlaska. (Verbally, Reskovitch 27 November 1995). In all probability the plans were discovered by Polish-speaking Germans in the units. Additionally, in his memoirs Josaphat Konchak mentions the desertion of the 1st Platoon, 2nd Company, 1st Battalion to the UPA. ABFC.
81. *Fernschreiben, + kdr* LbL nr 298 16/5/ 1530, *an den höheren SS-u. pol. führer ost – führungsstab roem. eins a – Cracow, Betr: roem.eins a banden meldung. geheim.* AA.
82. *SS-Oberscharführer* Rudolf Baronyay and *SS-Untersturmführer* Emil Weis both members of 3./ *Gal.SS-Freiw*.Regt.5, (*Kriegsverdienstkreuz* 2nd Class with Swords) also took part in defensive actions against partisan attacks in Kosin on 26 April, 1944 and Zabuze on 13 May, 1944. Another example, *SS-Oberwachtmeister d.Sch.* Wilhelm Glück 1/ *Gal.SS-Freiw*.Regt.5, was decorated with the *Kriegsverdienstkreuz* 2nd Class with Swords for bravery under enemy fire during a heavy partisan attack in the forests south of Lublin in Zwierzenie and Susic (district of Bilgoraj); I/*Gal.SS-Freiw*.Rgt.5, Dresden, den 6.12.1944, *An den Höheren SS-und Polizeiführer* in Cracow, *Betr. Anträge auf Verleihung des Kriegsverdienstkreuz II.Klasse mit und ohne Schwerter.* AA.
83. Prag & Jacobmeyer, op.cit., p.828.
84. *Der Chef der Ordnungspolizei* Berlin 22.4.44 Tgb Nr. Ia/1260/44 *geh Betr SS-Freiw*, 4 und 5. *SS-Oberführer* Rode. *Abschrift von Fernschrift* NS 19/ 1785, BA-KO.
85. On one occasion, in a speech in Cracow on 12 May 1944, Wächter declared, "The commander of the 'Galician' division was thoroughly satisfied with his troops." Prag & Jacobmeyer, op.cit., pp.847-848.
86. Notification of the impending move was duly sent to the appropriate authorities such as the Field Equipment Inspectorate in Berlin and the Transport Officer of the SS by various departments of the Division's staff including the Second General Staff Officer. from Section Ib (Quartermaster supply – weapons and ammunitions) *SS-Obersturmführer* Schaaf as early as 13 February. For further details see, HW16/100, Most Secret, CX/MSS/ Q.41, 22/2/ 44, PRO.
87. The 14.*Galiz.SS-Freiw*.Div. is listed as being based at Neuhammer as of 20 February 1944.
88. Large parts of Heidelager were still under construction.
89. See message to SS Ops. HQ II, Org. *Abtl.* from 14 Gal. SS. Volunteer Div., signed pp.. Div. Kdo, Second General Staff Officer SCHAAF, SS *Oberstuf.* CX/MSS/Q.36, HW16/100, PRO.
90. *SS-Sturmbannführer* Sepp Syr, born 18 October 1903, SS-Nr. 283, 029. See *Personal-Akte* NA A3343-SSO-171B.
91. See *Personalverfügung Der SS Sturmbannführer* S. Syr *SS-Führungshauptamt Amt* V /*Abtl.* IIa 25.2.44. Ibid.
92. See *Dienstlaufbahn* des Syr Sepp, Ibid.
93. See message to SS Transport Officer West, UNNA, signed STEIGLITZ on 8 March 1944, HW 16/100, CX/MSS/Q.52, 16/4/44. PRO.
94. I.T, *Visti*, 1984, No.3, p 74.
95. *SS-Sturmbannführer* Serge von Kuester, born 12 December 1896, SS-Nr. 314,013. See *Personal-Akte* NA A3343-SSO-227A.
96. The original cadre for the *SS-Flak Ausb. u. Ers. Btl.* were selected in August 1943 and sent to the SS school in München for appropriate instruction. Unable to fulfil the necessary requirements most were returned to Heidelager where *SS-Sturmbannführer* Viters had begun organising and *Flak-Abteilung* primarily from personnel from the 2nd, 11th and 12th training companies. The largest contingent came from the 2nd Company and comprised mainly of students. On completion of their basic training, in December 1943, those selected for service with the *Flak-Abteilung* command of which had now passed to *SS-Sturmbannführer* von Kuester, were sent to München for a three month training course conducted by SS instructors and which by all accounts did not include any form of 'political' education. Throughout this period, every Sunday the trainees were able to attend Mass that was held for the Ukrainian workers in the area. On completion of the course in March 1944, the soldiers returned to Neuhammer. Letters to author, Roman Hayetsky 1 January 1993, and Myron Pasij 10 January 1994. See also message to 14th Galician SS Volunteer Division, from Ops. H.Q. signed Gutberlet, SS Staf., 18/1, HW16/100, Most Secret, CX/MSS/ Q.37, 31.1.44, PRO.
97. The battery of 2cm guns had a strength of 200 personnel and consisted of four sections each consisting of three guns, plus six MG42 heavy machine guns used in an anti-aircraft role.
98. The battery of 3.7cm guns had a strength of 200 personnel and consisted of three sections each consisting of three guns, plus six MG 42 heavy machine guns used in an anti-aircraft role.
99. One section of four 88mm guns, one squadron of two 2cm anti-aircraft guns.
100. Heike, Eng. ed. op.cit., p.25.
101. See *Abschrift, Meldung vom* 15.3.1943. *Verband: 14. Galizische SS-Frw. Div. Unterstellungsverhaltnis.* AA. A copy of this document can be found in Document N 756/170 (Sammlung Vopersal), BA-MA.
102. Ibid.
103. In his memoirs, Dmytro Ferkuniak, a Ukrainian officer who served in the Division's Ic (intelligence) section described Wiens as "A sadist who despised the Ukrainians, especially the Galician Volunteers." Ferkuniak, op.cit., p.13.
104. Born in 22.3.1906 in Muntau by Halbstadt, Ukraine. SS-Nr. 22,984. Party Nr. 663,222.
105. *Einsatzgruppen* D was an operational task force of the *Sicherheitspolizei* and *Sicherheitsdienst* charged with special missions (i.e. liquidations) in occupied territory of opponents and enemies of the Nazi regime.
106. According to his personal file, in June 1941 Wiens was appointed to serve with *Einsatzgruppen* D as a *Dolmetscher* (interpreter) with *Sonderkommando* 10a under *SS-Sturmbannführer* Heinz Seetzen. Within weeks of the German invasion of the Soviet Union Wiens was appointed a *Teilkommandoführer* (section leader) and together with his group of ten men actively participated in executions. In spring 1942, Wiens transferred to *Einsatzkommando* 12 in the Stalino area and once again personally took part in mass liquidations. All four *Einsatzgruppen* were turned into static *Sicherheitspolizei* command posts and he was still serving with *Einsatzgruppen* D in January 1943, after its conversion to KdS (*Kommandeure*) Simferopol. In March 1944, after attending a short training course, he was appointed to the 14th Division's staff as Ic/a, and in doing so joined his younger brother Jakob who was also serving with the Division in the *Nachschubtruppen* as an *SS-Obersturmführer*.
107. A typical example of an individual targeted by Wiens was *Waffen-Obersturmführer* Myhailo Kaczmar. Born 19 September 1914, prior to the outbreak of the Second World War Kaczmar had studied and graduated from the Berlin Technical University as an aeronautical engineer. As a member of the OUN he was a liaison-messenger charged with various assignments and reporting directly to Riko Jary (an OUN leader based in Berlin). In September 1941 Kaczmar was arrested by the Gestapo because of his affiliation with the OUN-B, but later released on the grounds of ill health. He was directed to join the Division by M. Lebed of the OUN in Ukraine. He served with *Kampfgruppe* Beyersdorff as adjutant to Bristot, and later became adjutant to the commander of WGR 30, Hans-Boto Forstreuter. Wiens sought to arrest him and was only prevented from doing so by the direct intervention of *Waffen-Hauptsturmführer* Dmytro Paliiv. Although he was a first-rate officer, he was subsequently denied the promotions that he deserved. Wounded in the leg and captured at Brody, he was subsequently sent to work in an aircraft plant at Zagorsk. In December 1946 he received Soviet citizenship but remained as a 'Special settler' (with restrictions). In 1954 he was freed from his 'Special settler' status and eventually settled in L'viv in 1966, where he resided until his death on 8 January 1999.
108. In his appraisal of Wiens, Freitag wrote, "With energy and enthusiasm, he carries out his tasks with much success. W [Wiens] is a man whose training and interests are very much one-sided [and therefore] he is not suitable for alternative employment. Neither is he suitable for employment as a representative of Ic. His conduct towards his superiors and within his circle of comrades is appropriate." *Beurteilung fur den SS-Hauptsturmführer* Wiens, Div.St.Qu. 15.11.44 Nr. 1,376
109. According to a statement given to the *Polizei* on 29 December 1961, by one of his brothers, Jakob, who also served with the Division in the *Nachschubtruppen*, Heinrich Wiens was last seen in Steiermark in March 1945 and was presumed to have been killed. (Certificate of presumed death of Heinrich Wiens, 31 December 1945) AA. Notwithstanding this, a relative of Heinrich Wiens informed the author that a family member confirmed that Heinrich had survived the war, gone into hiding and successfully evaded capture. AA.
110. Ferkuniak, op.cit., pp.19-20.
111. The 1st Btl. was comprised of companies 1-4: 2nd Btl. 5-8, 3rd Btl. 9-12.
112. *SS-Gren.-Ausb. und Ersatz-Regiment* 14 (*ukrain. Ausbildungs-Regiment* 1), AA.
113. Ibid. Usually such a regiment would be responsible to a reserve commander in the rear. Its independent status is confirmed by the fact that it was explicitly forbidden to transfer any cadre personnel from it to the Galician Division.
114. Heike, Eng. ed., op.cit., p.26.
115. See 17 April 1944, *Auszug aus der Stärkemeldung des SS-FHA,* 14.*Galiz.SS-Freiw. Div.* The respective strengths given in the table below clearly demonstrate that at this point the Division suffered from a crippling lack of officers and NCOs, with a shortfall of 1765 NCOs alone.

	Regulation strength	*Actual strength*
Officers	458	291
NCOs	2431	666
Men	11110	13042
(of which *Hiwis*)	2092	—
Total	13999	13999

A copy of this document can be found reference document N 756/170 in the Sammlung Vopersal, BA-MA.
116. Personal file – NA, A3343 SSO-220, f 619.
117. These were the first of the younger generation of Ukrainians graduates who arrived at Neuhammer from NCO schools. Hawrylak, op.cit., p.12, also letter to author, Roman Herasymowycz, 1 November 1995.
118. Wächter's attitude towards the Galician Division's first combat deployment is adequately summarised by his comments during a session of the Governor and head department leaders in Cracow on 16 February, 1944; "[....] the troops [those of the Galician division] are primarily more propagandistically than militarily to be valued, [as they are] not in possession of heavy weaponry, anti-tank guns, etc. Everything depends on how they are at the first deployment. The political moment cannot be neglected with them." Prag & Jacobmeyer, op.cit., p.800.
119. By doing so Wächter showed considerable acumen as Model not only had a reputation as an extremely talented military commander but as an inspired improviser, renowned for employing unorthodox methods to get the required results.
120. Heike, Eng. ed., op.cit., p.27.
121. Wächter was probably referring to bestowal of 24 Iron Crosses 2nd Class to members of the 4th Regiment – 4 of them Ukrainian – for their bravery (see section on deployment of 4th Regiment).
122. *Der Gouverneur des Distrikts Galizien*, Lemberg, 3 Mai, 1944, Dr Wa/Ra *An den Reichsführer-SS und Chef der Deutschen Polizei, Reischinnenminister* Heinrich Himmler, H/10/80.

123. Himmler's schedule is set out in his diary of official appointments, AL1862/4 Imperial War Museum.
124. A copy of the audio recording can be found in National Archives Washington DC, Record Group 242- Item 206.
125. The extent to which this admission was influenced by the arguments proffered by Wächter in his letter to Himmler of the previous July remains a matter of conjecture.
126. Himmler clearly did not accept this argument, as is evidenced by his contradictory comments made on 2 October 1944, "If one of these White Russians or Ukrainians belongs to a regiment of his own kind, he's nevertheless a Russian. Otherwise he'd be like some German emigrant who came from Bavaria or Baden and went round saying that he wasn't a German but a Bavarian or Badener and fighting for the freedom of Bavaria or Baden. That's sheer nonsense. Those are fantasies concocted by that idiot Rosenberg". See Jurgen Thorwald, *The Illusion (Soviet Soldiers in Hitler's Armies)*, Harcourt Brace Jovanovich, New York, 1975, p.228.
127. For example, see Himmler's speech on the principles of the SS order to the generals of the SS at Poznan, 4 October, 1943, selected extracts of which appear in translated form in *The Order of the SS*, Frederic Reider, W. Foulsham and Co., 1981, pp.205-215.
128. *Rede des Reichsführer-SS auf dem Appell des Führerkorps der Galizischen SS-Freiw-Infanterie-Division in Neuhammer am* 16. Mai 1944. R 52 III/3c, BA-KO, audio recording, AA.
129. Affidavit of J Temnyk dated 1 August 1989, AA. This account was subsequently corroborated by *Waffen-Obersturmführer* Bohdan Pidhayny.
130. Although there is no record of Himmler's reaction, in the article 'Dmytro Paliiv – Soldier and Patriot', Vasyl Veryha writes, "After the officers had been dismissed, a German staff officer approached Paliiv, shook hands with him and said 'I congratulate you'," See Veryha, *Visti Kombatanta*, 5-6, 1968.
131. *Der Reichsführer-SS*, Field-Command, 28.5.1944, Bra.\H.G.b.No.39\37\44, AA.
132. Several publications such as *Die Woche* and *Signal* published reports and pictures of the visit as recorded by SS- *Kriegsberichters* Markert and Loos.
133. Heike, Eng. ed., op.cit., p.28.
134. Wächter's promotion was effective as of 16 May 1944, which coincided with the date of Himmler's arrival for his inspection of the Division. See *Personalakt* Dr Otto Wächter NA, A3343-SSO-213B.
135. See *Der Reichsführer-SS Feld-kommandostelle, den* 21.5.1944 Tgb.No: 1537/44 Gro/Dr See NA, A3342-SSO-215.
136. For exact times, see Himmler's diary of official appointments 17 May 1944, AL1862/4, IWM.
137. See *Befehl für die Vorbereitung der Operation Schild und Schwert*, Records of the 1st Panzer Army, NA, T313, roll 73, frames 7311019-21.
138. Ibid., frame 7311020.
139. For the original order (effective 11 May) to report to the 3rd *Totenkopf* Division, and subsequently countermanding instruction see *SS-Führungshauptamt* Berlin-Wilmersdorf, Kaiserallee 188, den 15.5.1944, Amt V/Abtl. IIa/Ref. 2 Az.: 21c 16/Fu/31 *Personalverfügung SS-Sturmbannführer* Heike, Wolf. *Personalakt* Wolf Dietrich Heike, and *SS-Führungshauptamt* Berlin-Wilmersdorf, Kaiserallee 188, den 22.5.1944, W II Abtl. 2 z.: 21clc./RS./illegible, Bert.: *Versetzung SS-Stubaf.* Heike, Wolf *Bezug: Pers.-Verfüg.* FHA/IIa V. 15.5.44. *Personal-Akte* NA, A3343-SSO-76A.
140. Heike, Eng. ed., op.cit., p.28, R. Krokhmaliuk, *Zahrava na skhodi: spohady i dokumenty z pratsi u viiskovii upravi 'Halychyna' y 1943-1945 rokakh* ('The Glow in Eastern Europe'), Toronto-New York, Bratstvo kolyshnikh voiakiv I-oi Ukrainskoi dyvizii UNA, 1978, pp.81-82. Members of the MB and UCC were also invited to Neuhammer to inspect the Division during May 1944.
141. Although according to the organisational chart dated 30 July 1943, it was originally intended to have three battalions for each of its infantry regiments, the Galician Division was formed with only two battalions per regiment (see organisational chart dated 22 September 1943). The entry in the publication *Verordnungsblatt der Waffen-SS*, by the *Verbindungsoffizier der SS beim OKH* (SS Liaison Officer to the Army High Command) records the order dated 1st June 1944 for the *SS-Gren.Ausb.u.Ers.* Rgt. 14/*galiz* Nr.1) at Wandern to provide the manpower for the 3rd battalions for the Galician Division. [*Tg.Buch-Nr* VOSS 1606g v.11.6.44]. AA. This document can be found in the BA-MA in document N 756/170 (Sammlung Vopersal). Reference to the same order (SS-FHA, *Amt* II Org.Abtl. Ia/II, Tgb. Nr II/8602/44) is also made in a document issued by the *SS-Führungshauptamt*, dated 5 Sept 1944. Amt II Org. Abtl. Ia/II Tgb. No.2880/44g. Kdos. v. 5.9.1944, *Betr: Neuaufstellung der 14. Waffen-Gren.Div. der SS* (*galizische* Nr. 1). (ABFC). It was not until 5 September 1944 when the completed battalions were actually transferred to the 29, 30 and 31 Regiments.
142. During their stay in southern France, one group of Ukrainians who had formerly belonged to the 6th Regiment, and the *Galizisches SS-Freiwilligen-Ersatz-Bataillon* Tarbes, made plans to desert to the Maquis. During transfer, the train came under attack by Allied aircraft in the vicinity of the city of Tours. In the resulting confusion, the group led by Osyp Krukovskyj deserted to the Maquis taking with them 4 horses, 4 machine guns, 25 rifles, 10 submachine-guns and other matériel. As members of the resistance, the Ukrainians who were ultimately incorporated into the French Foreign Legion, fought with some success against the Germans until the end of the war. For details see Myroslav Nebeliuk, *Under Foreign Flags*, Piuf Editions, SCIP, Paris, 1951, pp.195-201.
143. Letters to author, I. Sadoveyj, 17 January, and 9 February 1999.
144. *Abschrift von Fernschrift* 22.4.1944, Betr.*Galiz.SS-Freiw.Rgt*.4 und 5, *Der RFSS hat gem.*FS Kdo.-Stab RFSS. Nr.570 v. 22.4.1944 -Tgb.Nr.Ia/1269/44*geh.* – *die Abgabe der Gal. SS-Freiw.-Rgt.* 4 *und* 5 *an* 14. *Gal. SS-Freiw – Div befohlen*. AA.
145. See *Überführung der Gal. SS-Freiw. – Rgt. 4 und 5 in die Waffen-SS'. Der Chef der Ordnungspolizei*, Kdo.g.1 Org. (3) Nr.104/44(g), *Schnellbrief.* Berlin, den 9 June 1944, R 19/326, BA-KO.
146. *'Überführung der Gal. SS-Freiw.-Rgt. 4 und 5 in die Waffen-SS'*. Der *Chef der Ordnungspolizei*, Kdo.g.1 Org. (3) Nr.104II/44, Berlin, den 17.June 1944, R 19/105, BA-KO. As of 18 May 1944, the regiment was officially disbanded in Strassburg.
147. The incorporation of soldiers of both units into the Division's three infantry regiments just before they left for the front was confirmed verbally to the author by members of both those regiments: Maksymiw, 27 November 1995, and Reskovitch, 15 January 1996.
148. Verbally to author, Reskovitch, 15 January 1996.
149. *Abschrift! Der Höhere SS-und Polizeiführer im Generalgouvernement Befehlshaber der Ordnungspolizei*, Cracow, den 29. Juni 1944, Akt.Z. Abtl. III b (1) 2795 d – Tgb.Nr. 1441/44 (g.) *-Geheim, Betr: Übernahme des Schützmannschafts-Batl.*.204 *in die Galizische SS-Freiwilligen-Division*. R 19/326, BA-KO.
150. The order for transfer followed a message to the commander of Heidelager from SS Ops H.Q. Amt. II Org. Abtl. I.E., I (1) on 1/3, which reads: 'After the arrival of Guard Bn. 5 or of the men transferred from SS. *Gebirgjäger* Bn. 7 to relive *Schuma* Bn. 204, 200 German-speaking men are to be despatched to the 14. Gal. SS Volunteer Division.' See HW 16/ 101, CX/MSS/ Q.48, 21/3/44, PRO.
151. This battalion was comprised of Ukrainians from eastern Ukraine. The chaplain assigned to it was Reverend Markevych.
152. At a meeting with Dr Fritz Arlt on 17 June 1944, Wächter complained about the command deficiencies in the Division. He stated that he felt as a former *Polizei* general Freitag's psychological leadership qualities for a Ukrainian Division were inadequate, compared to the Division's Ia *Major* Heike who was understanding and sympathetic towards the Ukrainians and a good *Gesprächspartner* (interlocutor). See Fritz Arlt, *Polen Ukrainer Juden Politik*, Wissenschaftlicher Buchdienst, Herbert Taege, 1995, p.105.
153. D'Alquen was the editor of the weekly SS journal *Das Schwarze Corps* ('The Black Corps'), and commander of the SS war correspondent regiment known as *Kurt Eggers*. Once he had converted to opposing the *Untermensch* (sub-human) doctrine, his influence played a pivotal part in ultimately persuading Himmler to revise his views on the utilisation of former Soviet nationals in the service of the German armed forces. See Thorwald, op.cit., pp.196-207.
154. Heike, Eng. ed., op.cit., p.28. Thorwald writes that the results of *Skorpion* exceeded all expectations, encouraging approximately 4,500 desertions in the area in 18 days. Ibid., pp.202-203.
155. By 31 May 1944, the *'Galizische SS-Div.'* was mentioned being used together with one or two Hungarian reserve divisions, to relieve the 1st and 371st infantry divisions. For further details see *Panzerarmee-Oberkommando* 1 *Abtl.* Ia Nr. 17/44 g. *kdos. Chefs. A.H.Qu. den* 31.5.1944. *An Oberkommando H.Gr. Nordukraine, Studie ' Schild und Schwert'*. (Fall a), T313, roll 73, frames 7311028 and 7311030.
156. See *Panzerarmee-Oberkommando* 1 A.H.Qu., den 9.6.1944. *Abtl.* Ia Nr.21/44 g.k. *Chefs. Bez. H.Gr. Nordukraine*, Ia Nr.0802/44 g.*k.Chefs*, *An Oberkommando H.Gr. Nordukraine, Studie 'Schild und Schwert' (Fall b)*, T313, roll 73, frame 7311006. The same document also allowed for the possibility of one or two Hungarian reserve divisions and the *'Galizische SS-Div.'* relieving 1st and 371st infantry divisions. For further details see Ibid., frame 7311003.
157. In all probability, the favourable disposition adopted by General Raus towards the Division, stemmed from his previous experiences with the Ukrainians as a former officer in the Austro-Hungarian Army.
158. Letter to author, R. Wysockyj, 23 May 1996.
159. The details of one such manoeuvre are given by Lubomyr Ortynskyj in his account entitled 'Polkovi Vpravy' ('Regimental Manoeuvres') *Visti*, 1951, June, No. 6 (8).
160. Heike, Eng. ed., op.cit., p.29.
161. Letter to author, R. Drazniowskyj, 11 March 1996.
162. This included anti-tank weaponry, and new automatic weapons. Letter to author, R. Drazniowskyj, 11 March 1996.
163. According to M. Maleckyj, an announcement regarding the Division's destination was made to the officers at a meeting shortly before departure. Letter to author, 7 March 1996. It seems that the soldiers were under the impression that it would either be deployed in Stanyslaviv or Kolomyia. Information given verbally to author by V. Veryha, 19 February 1996.
164. Heike, Eng. ed., op.cit., p.36. In his memoirs, Ferkuniak writes that the explanation for the change as given to him by Dymytro Paliiv was that the orders for the Division's original deployment in the Kolomyia region had been revoked because "it could have led to conflict with the Hungarians". Ferkuniak, op.cit., pp.24-25.
165. The Allied invasion of Europe, codenamed Operation Overlord, was launched on 6 June 1944.
166. The operation was named after Prince Peter Bagration, an Imperial Russian Army officer who had fought Napoleon in 1812.
167. For an account of the collapse of Army Group Centre, see Earl F. Ziemke, *Stalingrad to Berlin: The German Defeat in the East*, Military Heritage Press, New York, 1985, pp.313-325 and Alex Buchner, *Ostfront 1944, The German Defensive Battles On The Eastern Front 1944*, Schiffer Publishing, 1991, pp.143-218. The German armies were in a hopeless position because Hitler's rigid orders to hold ground were depriving them of all strategic latitude, and seriously impeded even their tactical operations.
168. Ziemke, op.cit., p.325. For further details see Buchner, op.cit., p.213.
169. The 47th Rifle Corps was also in front reserve. Further details of the distribution of rifle divisions in the 1st Ukrainian Front can be found in *L'vov – Sandomierz 1944, The Soviet General Staff Study*, (translated and edited by David M. Glantz and Harold S. Orenstein from the Directorate For The Exploitation Of War Experience Of The USSR Armed Forces' General Staff, secret, copy 6191, Collection of War Materials for the Study of War Experience No. 22, January-February 1946) Military Publishing House of the People's Commissariat of Defense, Moscow, 1946, L'vov, pp.26-29.

In addition the 1st Czechoslovak Army Corps was subordinated to this front.

170. Ibid., p.29.
171. The front also had 11 anti-aircraft divisions and 17 anti-aircraft regiments.
172. Ibid., p.33.
173. Ibid., pp.36-37.
174. This figure, which includes rear service and support personnel, is the same as that quoted as the total strength of the 1st Ukrainian Front as of 13 August 1944, Ibid., Appendix 4, table p.192. Appendix 2, p.190, quotes the following strength returns for the 1st Ukrainian Front at the beginning of the operation; 843000 men, 13825 guns and mortars, 2432 anti tank guns, 1222 anti aircraft guns, 2206 self propelled guns. Other figures provided by Konev are 13079 mortar and artillery pieces, 2200 tanks and self-propelled guns, and 3000 planes. See Marshal I Konev. 'Zavershenie osvobozhdenia sovetskoi Ukrainy i vykhod na Vyslu', in *Voienno-istoricheskii zhurnal*, Moscow, July 1964.
175. Harpe took over from Model who was transferred to Army Group Centre 28 June, Buchner, op.cit., p.222.
176. 4th *Panzer* Army (Harpe) consisted of VIII Corps, LVI *Panzerkorps*, XXXXII Corps and XXXXVI *Panzerkorps* (16th, 17th Pz. Divs.) plus a rear reserve corps.
177. 1st *Panzer* Army (Raus) consisted of XIII Corps, XXXXVIII *Panzerkorps*, XXIV *Panzerkorps*, LIX Corps, XIII Reserve Corps (1st, 8th Pz. Divs.).
178. In *The Russo-German War, 1941-45*, Arthur Barker, London, 1971, p.444, Albert Seaton confirms that there were 31 German divisions, of which 4 were *Panzer*, citing as his sources *OKH Kriegsgliederung*, 15 July 1944, whereas the situation map shows 34 formations to be present of which five were *Panzer* divisions (1st, 8th, 16th, 17th Panzer and 5th SS *Panzer Wiking* Division). The latter was, however, moved north to another sector in early July and cannot therefore be counted. Likewise other infantry units may also have been moved, so that Seaton's estimate can be accepted as correct.
179. On p.62 of *The Russo-German War, Summer,* 1944, Valour Publishing, Pa., 1987, V. Madej gives the numbers of tanks available to the *Panzer* divisions as follows: 16th Pz: 22, 17th Pz: 21+ ('+' indicating reinforcements were expected), 1st Pz: 61 and 8th Pz: 77. This information is partly corroborated by Heike who states in his memoirs that the 4th *Panzer* Army (that is, the 16th and 17th Pz.Divs.) had approximately 40-50 tanks in total, Eng. ed., op.cit., p.37.
180. On p.128 of the previously cited *L'vov-Sandomierz* report it states that "opposite 60th Army's sector the enemy had around 230 tanks and self-propelled guns which belonged to the 8th Panzer Division, 506th Separate Panzer Battalion and the 311th Assault Gun Battalion". If the known figures for the 1st Panzer Division (61) and those of the 16th and 17th Pz.Div's (43 in total), are added to this the overall figure is around 334 operational tanks and self-propelled guns.
181. This source states that at the time of the commencement of their offensive, aligned against 1st Ukrainian Front were 32 German infantry divisions, plus 5 *Panzer* and 1 *Panzergrenadier* divisions, which amounted to around 300,000 men, equipped with 800 tanks, 230 self-propelled guns, 3,500 guns of various calibres, 1,900 mortars and supported by 700 aircraft (440 bombers, 150 fighters and 60 assault aircraft and 50 reconnaissance planes). *L'vov Sandomierz 1944*, p.18.

    Confusion over the number of German divisions and consequent total of manpower may have been caused by the late redeployment of some of the German units. However despite this discrepancy, Soviet estimates in respect of the strength of German armour and aircraft are almost certainly exaggerated. For example, contrary to their claims, the number of operational tanks available to the four main *Panzer* divisions involved amounted to approximately 181 (see footnote 170 above). Taking into consideration additional self-propelled guns belonging to smaller units, this would still be significantly short of the Soviet figure of 800, which appears to have been computed on the assumption that five armoured divisions were present (and not four) and that each was at its full authorised strength of 165 tanks per division, which was certainly not the case. Similarly, it is doubtful as to whether their estimate of Luftwaffe strength is accurate, as the numbers of aircraft quoted above are more likely to have represented 'paper authorisations'.
182. For an insight into the concerns of the German command regarding the disturbance of troop and equipment transports to the front see *Bandenlage im Monat April 1944, Bandenlage im Monat Mai 1944, Bandenlage im Monat Juni 1944,* NA, T313, roll 406, frames 8697467-8697477.
183. Ziemke states Army Group North Ukraine had surrendered three *Panzer* and two infantry divisions to Army Group Centre in response to the Soviet offensive in Belorussia, See Ziemke, op.cit., p.330.
184. Heike mentions the failure of the efforts to rescind the new standing orders in his memoirs although he does not specify who made the representations, or to whom they were subsequently made. See Heike, Eng. ed., op.cit., p.36. As Wächter was largely responsible for engineering the Division's deployment in the first place, it is likely that he lead the opposition to the change of plans.
185. Ibid., p 36.
186. *Abschrift, Der Reichsführer-SS Feld-kommandostelle den* 27 Juni, 1944, H/10/81. The redesignation was in accordance with an order issued by Himmler that the racial characteristics of Waffen-SS divisions should be included in their titles. The Galician Ukrainians were given the lowest form of title, that of *Waffen*, indicating non-Germanic. Thus from 27 June 1944, the Division was retitled once again. As a rule, the style of title conferred on any Waffen-SS division fell into three categories and varied depending on its racial composition; Units composed of German volunteers were styled *SS-Division*; Units containing a high percentage of 'racial' Germans and Germanic volunteers, i.e. Scandinavians, Dutch, Flemings, Walloons, and Frenchmen, carried the designation *Freiwilligen*, e.g. 11th *SS-Freiwilligen-Panzergrenadier-Division 'Nordland'*; Units containing a preponderance of 'non-Germanic' personnel, especially members of the Slavic and Baltic peoples, carried the designation *Waffen* as part of their names, and where necessary, a national description was appended in brackets at the end, e.g. 15th *Waffen-Grenadier-Division der SS (Lett. Nr.1)*

    In the same way officers of non-Germanic origin could not become fully-fledged members of the SS corps and were therefore designated accordingly as *Waffen-Führer der SS*. Individual rank was given in the same way, i.e. *Waffen-Untersturmführer*.
187. Among its quota of horses, the Division received several hundred directly from the Eastern Front, a large percentage of which were sick, wounded or had simply been starved to such an extent that they ate everything in sight, even trying to gnaw on the iron chains in the stables and tents. As a result of their generally poor condition many subsequently had to be destroyed. I. Nakonechny, 'From the Veterinary Company into the Bolshevik Camp', *Visti Kombatanta*, Nr. 5-6, 1994, pp.118-120.
188. Details of the first transport to leave Neuhammer were provided by I. Nakonechny, in two letters to the author dated 6 March 1993, and 17 April 1996.
189. 38 transports were required to transport the entire Division to the front.
190. *SS-Grenadier-Ausbildungs-und Ersatz-Regiment* 14 (*ukrain. Ausbildungs-Regiment* 1) AA.
191. Ibid.
192. Verbally to author, V. Tomkiw, 23 December 1996. Within two weeks, about one third of this group had failed the course mainly because of language difficulties.
193. V. Veryha, letter to author, 29 April 1993.
194. For further details of the defence of the Division's disembarkation zone by the *Flak-Abteilung* see B. Nebozhuk, 'Brody', *Visti Kombatanta*, 1992, Nr. 2, p 72.
195. Heike refers to the meeting in his memoirs. (Eng. ed., op.cit., p.38) Although no record of the meeting exists, Heike mentions that upon rejoining the Division at the front, Freitag filed a special request with XIII Army Corps that the Division be committed as a whole and not as individual regiments, and that it should always remain under its own command. It would seem likely that the origins of the request were directly attributable to the discussion between Wächter and Freitag on that occasion.
196. Born 20 December1891 in Wittgendorf, in July 1944 Hauffe was a highly-decorated officer holding both the German Cross in Gold (awarded 25 July 1943) and the *Ritterkreuz* (Knights Cross) conferred on him as commander 46th Infantry Division.
197. Heike, Eng. ed., op.cit., p.37.
198. To cite an example, the Pioneer Battalion was equipped with liberal quantities of close-support weapons such as the formidable 8.1cm mortar, both the *Panzerschreck* and the *Panzerfaust* (infantry weapons similar to a bazooka, designed for anti-tank combat), and flamethrowers. It also had at its disposal some of the very latest weaponry including the most recent models of machine guns and the new *Goliath*, a small radio-controlled device resembling a miniature tank which carried an explosive charge used for the destruction of tanks or defensive structures. (See Schmitt, op.cit., U.7) Personal weaponry was also generally of a higher standard, with a high proportion of automatic and semi automatic weapons being issued.
199. To ensure a rapid advance for their armoured and motorised forces, the capture of the main road to L'viv which ran through Zolochiv was of primary importance.
200. Heike, Eng. ed., op.cit., p.38.
201. For a comprehensive account (with situation maps) of the encirclement of XIII Corps that took place from the end of March until mid-April 1944 and the subsequent piercing of the encirclement by *Panzerverband* Friebe (a unit from 8th Panzer Division) see NA, T313, roll 73, also T315, roll 2152 for an account of the 361st Infantry Division's part, and T315, roll 2147 for the rôle of the 349th Infantry Division.
202. *L'vov-Sandomierz 1944*, p.128.
203. Heike, Eng. ed., op.cit., p.38. See also the secret 27-page after action report by General Lange entitled *Korpsabteilung 'C' in der Kesselschlacht des XIII A.K. sudwestlich Brody vom 13-22 Juli 1944*. IC Nr. 12/44/ Geh, vom 2.11.44, 171/44 Geh, Geheim, p. 2, NA, T78 roll Nr. 139-H 41/2. In his after action report General Lange claims that the *Korpsabteilung* C "had by itself also nearly completed preparation of the Prinz Eugen *Stellung*, including the positions for the artillery and the heavy infantry weapons [and other secondary positions]" (Lange, p 1) – a claim that many Ukrainian veterans angrily refute. They contend that for the most part the trenches largely existed 'on paper' and had to be built from scratch. For example, in a letter to the author dated 3 February 1998, *Waffen-Unterscharführer* Roman Drazniowskyj, a platoon commander serving with 3/I/30, stated unequivocally, "The trenches were only on paper, we had to build those trenches when we arrived".
204. An organisational chart gives the following disposition of the Corps HQ at the beginning of the battle:
    Stab Gen. Kdo XIII Corps
    Korpskartenstelle (mot.) 413
    Feldgen. Trupp (mot.) 413
    Kraftf.Komp. 413
    Kraftf.Inst.Zug 413
    Pi-Regts.Stab 516 (*ko.Pi.Fhr*)
    Art. KDr 413
    Korps Jagd-Kdo. XIII
    Panz. Zerst. Kp. XIII
    Nachr.Abtl. 53 with 1,3,4.*Kp und Versorg.Staffel*
    Feldpostamt 413
    See OKH/*Abwicklungsstab, Sachgebiet*: E XIII, Rudolstadt/Th., den 29.Okt.1944, NA, T78, Roll 139 frame no: 6067693.
205. The following units are listed as being attached to the Army Corps:
    Art. Regt. z.b.V. 617
    s.Art. Abtl. 842
    le.Beob.Abtl. 35
    Sturmgeschütz-Brigade 249
    Pi-Batl. 672
    Heers Art. Abtl. II/70
    Heers Art. Abtl. 841
    Ibid.
206. This figure for *Gesamtstärke des Verbandes* (total number in unit) for K.Tr.XIII Corps, and the subsequent strengths of the Corps' other units

quoted, (with the exception of the Galician Division) are taken from the final report dated 1 March 1945, of the liquidation commission activated to establish the losses of the XIII Corps' army units. (See NA T78 roll 142 frame 6072050). These figures, however, in all probability represent each units' overall total strength and not the respective actual battle strength or *kampfstarke*. A more accurate representation of the number of men each of the Corps' army units could deploy in the field can be calculated by reducing the quoted total strength of each of the army units by around 20%.

207. See the final report dated 1 March 1945, of the liquidation commission activated to establish the losses of the XIII Corps' army units. See NA T78 roll 142 frame 6072050.
208. Ibid.
209. See NA, T78 Roll 142 frame 6072050. By calculating the various figures cited in *Gefechtsbericht der 361. Inf. Div.* the 'battle strength' of this unit is estimated at 9,000. NA T315 roll 2152, frames 000002 – 22.
210. A *Korpsabteilung* was equivalent to one infantry division. It consisted of three weakened divisions each with the approximate strength of one infantry regiment.
211. Figure taken from report dated 1 March 1945, NA T78 roll 142 frame 6072050. Lange, op.cit. pp. 26-27 gives the strength of the unit (i.e. probable 'combat strength') as being 9059.
212. Figure taken from report dated 1 March 1945, NA T78 roll 142 frame 6072050.
213. Lange, op.cit. p 2.
214. According to a strength return dated 30 June 1944, these troops consisted of 725th Battalion (8 officers, 62 NCOs, 338 men; total 408); the 502nd Battalion (5 officers, 34 NCOs and 191 men: total 230) and the 327th Battalion (2 officers, 15 NCOs and 88 men; total 105) See NA T313, roll 73, frames 7310732-73310733.
215. This unit comprised 5 officers, 38 NCOs and 220 men: total 263 men. Ibid.
216. Consisting of 9 officers, 57 NCOs and 251 men plus 29 men of the *Pz.Jag.Zug*: total 346. Ibid.
217. The figure of 55,100 (less 340th Inf. Div.) would be the maximum Corps strength. The actual 'fighting strength' would have been closer to 43,175. It is worth noting that the figures provided by the report of the liquidation commission also includes a further 9,362 men for the 340th Inf. Div, part of which was also later surrounded with XIII Corps. See NA T78 roll 142 frame 6072050. Buchner gives an estimate of XIII Corps strength as 65,000, Buchner, op.cit., p.228.
218. Heike, Eng. ed., op.cit., p.37.
219. Ibid.
220. Bender & Taylor, op.cit., Vol. 4, p.48. The strength return referred to is as of 30 June 1944. It does not include those in the Replacement Regiment, which was in the process of relocation to Neuhammer, or those on leave.
221. Heike, Eng. ed., op.cit., p.53. As has already been noted, the third battalion of each of the three infantry regiments were still in the process of being formed and the personnel assigned to them remained at Neuhammer thus leaving the Division short of approximately 1,600 troops.
222. A document in the author's archive dated 3 July 1944, which lists 136 Ukrainian officers, the vast majority of whom were present at Brody, gives the following breakdown in ranks: 2 *Waffen-Sturmbannführers*, Mykola Palienko, Eugen Pobihushtschyi: 12 *Waffen-Hauptsturmführers* are named as Michael Brygidyr, Roman Dolynskyj, Dr Theodor Mamtschur, Leonid Martyniuk, Arsen Melnytschuk, Eugen v. Nikitin, Dmytro Paliiv, Iwan Rembalowych, Peter Roschanetz, Basil Sajatz, Hennadij Salesskyj and Porfirij Sylenko: 40 *Waffen-Obersturmführers*: Roman Bojcun, Wasyl Budsyllo, Dmytro Danylyschyn, Peter Duda, Roman Dybko, Emil Hermann, Waldemar Horko, Mykola Horodyskyj, Stephan Hulak, Mykola Jurniuk, Zenon Jusyschynskyj, Michael Kaczmar, Michael Karpynec, Jaroslav Kasaniwskyj, Josef Kladotschynj, Alexander Kolominskij, Sosont Komar, Roman Kosak, Wolodymyr Kosak, Alexander Kusminskyj, Swiatoslav Lewytzkyj, Myhailo Lischtschynskyj, Peter Makarevych, Myroslav Maleckyj, Rostislav Markowskyj, Myroslav Martynetz, Petro Mykytiuk, Johann Olinec, Bohdan Pidhayny, Igor Pospilovsky, Serhij Ruditschew, Johann Sandulak, Peter Saudyk, Dr Ostap Schuk, Myhailo Senio, Paul Sumarokiv, Julian Temnyk, Roman Tschaikowskyj, Iwan Wituschynskyj, Sawelij Yaskevych: and 82 *Waffen-Untersturmführers*. In addition to which were Dmytro Ferkuniak and Averkiy Honcharenko, both of whom held the rank of *Waffen-Hauptsturmführer*. Several more officers with the rank of *Waffen-Untersturmführer* (such as six medical doctors) were also known to have been present, bringing the total to around 150 men. SS *Personalhauptamt* II W, II W II – *Abteilung* 3, Az.: 21 a 13/21 c 20 Mü. Berlin-Charlottenburg, den 3. Juli 1944, *Betr. Übernahme und Beförderungen von Offz. und Offz. Anwärtern der* 14. *Gal. SS Freiw.* Division. AA.
223. WGR 31 was under the command of *SS-Obersturmbannführer* Paul Herms.
224. *SS-Obersturmbannführer* Forstreuter commanded WGR 30. *SS-Hauptsturmführer* Siegfried Klocker and *SS-Hauptsturmführer* Friedrich Wittenmeyer commanded the 1st and 2nd battalions respectively.
225. At the time of the Battle of Brody WGR 29 was commanded by *SS-Standartenführer* (as of 1 July 1944) Friedrich Dern. *Waffen-Hauptsturmführer* Myhailo Brygidyr commanded the 1st Battalion and *SS-Hauptsturmführer* Wilhelm Allerkamp the 2nd Battalion.
226. Interview, W. Molodecky, Toronto, 2 June 1993.
227. Commanded by *SS-Hauptsturmführer* Karl Bristot.
228. Stepan Hulak, *'Fiuzylirskyi Kurin'*, *Visti*, February-March 1952, Nos 2-3 (16-17) p.6 and Roman Bojcun, *'Kurin fiuzyliriv' I. UD UNA pid Brodamy*, *Visti*, Nov – Dec 1953, Nos 11-12 (37-38) pp. 5-6.
229. Interview, Julian Wilshynskyj, Toronto, 6 June 1993.
230. Unlike all the other units of the Division, the *14. Feld Ersatz Bataillon* was billeted in public buildings and houses in the villages in which the respective companies were stationed, *The Medical Service of the Field Reserve Battalion of the 1st Ukrainian Division 1944-45*, an unpublished manuscript, Dr W. Krywulak, AA. Also interview, Petro Maslij, Scunthorpe, 8 February 1992, and Yurij Krokhmaliuk, 'Polevyi Zapasnyi Kurin Pid Brodamy' ('Field Replacement Battalion at Brody') *Visti*, 952, Nos. 2-3 p 12.
231. In his article 'The UPA and The Division', Lev Shankovskyj goes as far as to say that the mere presence of strong UPA units was enough to convince the Germans to redeploy the Division:
"Initially the Germans planned to deploy the Division in the regions of Kolomyia and Horodenka. The German command subsequently changed these plans because it seemed inadvisable to place the Division in regions where the UPA had a very strong presence. Therefore the Division was transferred to the region of Brody where only one company of UPA ('Druzhynnyky') was active." See Shankovskyj, op.cit., pp.55-61, Kyiv, 1994. English translation by Ostap Sokolskyj, p.4. While the Germans were undoubtedly concerned about the influence of the UPA on the Ukrainian soldiers in the Division, it would appear that Shankovskyj has exaggerated the extent of the concern.
232. Letter to author, V. Veryha, 10 January 1994.
233. Letter to author, R. Kolisnyk, 7 March 1996.
234. One such instance was related to the author by a former member of the WGR 31, who together with three other Ukrainian soldiers rescued several cows that had been taken by Germans soldiers of another Division from Ukrainian villagers near Brody. Letter to the author, Oleh Ostrowsky 19 January 1997.
235. Heike, Eng. ed., op.cit., p.39.
236. A number of desertions did take place from the Division, for example one soldier from 7/II/WGR 30, deserted to the UPA with a machine gun and ammunition. This was reported to the company commander *Waffen-Obersturmführer* M. Maleckyj who asked the UPA to make arrangements for the return of the soldier to the Division. This subsequently took place and no further action was taken against the soldier. Letter to author, 17 April 1996.
237. An UPA group known as *Druzhynnyky* ('Comrades in arms') operated in the Brody region under the command of Lieutenant Chernyk. See Pobihushtschyi, op.cit., p.165, and Shankovskyj, op.cit.
238. "During the period from 4 to 14 July my unit (3 Plat, 3 Co, 1 Btl, WGR 30) was frequently ordered to conduct reconnaissance missions. I used that opportunity to make contact with the UPA. All meetings with UPA soldiers were reported to the company commander *Waffen-Obersturmführer* Bohdan Pidhayny, as was the transfer of weapons and training of their use." Letter to author, R. Drazniowskyj, 1 April 1996. The training of recruits and the provision of supplies to the UPA was confirmed by former members of the Division in numerous interviews and letters to the author. For example the 3rd Company of the Pioneer Battalion was instrumental in providing the UPA with medical supplies. Interview, Julian Wilshynskyj, Toronto, 6 June 1993.
239. Bohdan Pidhayny refers to the instruction by the OUN to young men to join the Division in the article "UPA- Dyviziia-Halychyna-Nimtsi", *Visti Kombatanta*, 1990, No. 3, p. 65. It is worth noting that the number of men enlisted in this way was limited because the Division did not have the capacity to accommodate them in large numbers.
240. Interview, W. Sirskyj, Toronto, 5 June 1993.
241. Lange, op.cit. p 4.
242. Ibid., p 3.

Chapter 6

1. *L'vov-Sandomierz 1944*, op.cit., pp.63-64.
2. For details of the Soviet strike on XIII Corps' left flank, Ibid., pp.165-168.
3. As part of 4th *Panzer* Army, the 16th and 17th *Panzer* Divisions were known as XXXXVI *Panzerkorps*. Both units had recently been involved in heavy fighting at Cherkassy and Ternopil that accounted for their lack of usable armour. Madeja, op.cit., p.62.
4. Between 13 July and 15 July, 3rd Guards and 13 Armies' shock groups penetrated the German defensive to a depth of between 15-30 kms. In this period, 13th Army alone destroyed 2450 officers and men, 25 guns, 25 tanks and self-propelled guns and 18 armoured transports. *L'vov-Sandomierz 1944*, p.67.
5. Ibid., pp. 70-73.
6. W. Lange *Korpsabteilung 'C' in der Kesselschlacht des XIII.A.K. südwestlich Brody vom 13-22 Juli 1944*. IC Nr. 12/44/Geh, vom 2.11.44, 171/44 *Geheim*, NA T78, roll 139-H 41/2, pp. 4-5.
7. Lange, op.cit., p.4.
8. *L'vov-Sandomierz 1944*, p.68.
9. To give an example of the extent of the losses I.Btl. 913th Regiment was reduced to *Kampfgruppe* Ziegahn, which had a strength of 26 men. See *Überblick uber den Werdegang der Aufstellung bis zum Tag der Auflösung* ('Review of the Development of 349th Infantry Division From the Day of Formation to the Day of Disbandment'), p. 9, NA T315, roll 2152.
10. Ibid., pp. 8-9.
11. Ibid. p10.
12. The total strength of WGR 30 was recorded as being 1903 men (34 Officers, 116 NCOs and 1753 enlisted men). Of this number 54 were German (14 officers, 35 NCOs and 5 men). See 30. *SS Freiw. Gren. Regt. Abwicklungstelle O.U., den* 22.9.1944. ABFC. *SS-Hauptsturmführer* Siegfried Klocker commanded the Regiment's 1st Battalion while its 2nd Battalion was under the command of *SS-Hauptsturmführer* Friedrich Wittenmeyer.
13. Lange states that the Regiment was ordered to occupy the line Huta Verkouzhs'ka-Huta Peniatska-Hutyshche Peniatska. Lange, p.6.
14. In *Pershyi Den' Boiv Pid Brodamy* ('The First Day of the Battle at Brody') Toronto, Kalendar-Almanakh Novoho Shliakhu, 1984, p.103. V. Veryha, a former member of WGR 30, states that it received the order to move into this area in the late evening of 13 July. This is confirmed in the accounts of *Waffen-Untersturmführer* Bohdan Pidhayny 'Dva Shliakhy – Odna Meta', in *Brody: Zbirnyk Stattei i Narysiv*, edited by O. Lysiak, p.115 and Pavlo Sumarokiv, in 'V Otochenni Pid Brodamy. Proryv 2-ho Kurinnia 30-ho Polky UD Halychyna', *Visti*, 1961, No. 103, pp.70-74.

15. Heike, Eng. ed., op.cit., p.43. This order, which was to mark the beginning of the end of the Division, has long been the subject of much controversy. In his memoirs *Major* Heike also states that it was given contrary to a special request by the Division's staff that it be deployed as a whole unit and not as individual regiments as was the usual practice in such engagements, Ibid., p.38.
16. R. Drazniowskyj verbally to the author, 26 February 1996.
17. Letter to author, R. Drazniowskyj, 3 February 1998.
18. *Das Brotbeutel* was a haversack made from cloth for carrying bread and other provisions worn by each soldier (both regular army and Waffen-SS) on the belt at the back. *Brotbeutel* was a derogatory colloquial term by which Waffen-SS men sometimes referred to Wehrmacht soldiers. It implied that they would rather have a full haversack than fighting spirit.
19. Letter to author, O. Slupchynskyj, 1 November 1998.
20. V. Veryha, op.cit., p.106.
21. Heike, Eng. ed., op.cit., p.43.
22. *'Überblick...'* pp.11-12.
23. *L'vov – Sandomierz 1944*, op.cit., p.68.
24. Buchner, states the 8th *Panzer* Division's counterattack was led by the 10th *Panzer* Regiment's 1st *Abteilung* (which had only one full strength *Panzer* company), the 4th and the 301st *Panzer Abteilungen*. Buchner, op.cit., p.224.
25. *L'vov-Sandomierz 1944*, p.69.
26. Ibid.
27. For details see *Panzer Battles*, Major-General F.W von Mellenthin, Futura Publications, London, 1984, pp.340-341.
28. The Soviet General Staff Report states that 60th Army's 23rd, 15th and 28th rifle corps, advancing with a tank and a mechanised brigade (from 3rd Guards Tank Army) continued the offensive on the morning of 15th July supported by artillery fire and massive air strikes, "*Overcoming heavy resistance* and repelling counterattacks by the 8th *Pz* Div and the SS *'Galicia'* Division which were approaching from the depths..." [author's italics] *L'vov-Sandomierz 1944*, p.169.
29. The infantry reached the line Verkouzhs'ka-Iwaczow, Lange, op.cit., p.5.
30. *'Überblick...'* p.10.
31. The 349th Infantry Division had previously been attached to XLVIII *Panzerkorps* of the 4th *Panzer* Army. Thereafter it was subordinated directly to the command of XIII Corps. *'Überblick...'* p.10.
32. *L'vov-Sandomierz 1944*, op.cit., p.70. The Soviet attack on the L'viv axis (i.e. the southern pincer), was more difficult than had been anticipated as 38th Army's attack had faltered on the German tactical defences and 60th Army had opened only a small gap through the main German defences east of the village of Koltiv. Marshall Konev's decisive response was to thoroughly analyse all the circumstances surrounding 38th Army's failure to fulfil the mission assigned to it, following which he ordered Rybalko's 3rd Guards Tank Army and Lelyushenk's 4th Tank Army to thrust their armies successively into the 'Koltiv corridor', on 60th Army's front in order to hold and widen the corridor, accompanied by 31st and 4th Guards tank corps, whose missions were to hold open the shoulders of the penetration. See David M. Glantz and Jonathan M. House, *When Titans Clashed, How the Red Army Stopped Hitler*, University Press of Kansas, 1995, pp.210-211. See also Erickson *The Road to Berlin*, p.235 and pp. 695-697.
33. The first elements of these reinforcements were committed during the night of the 15/16 July.
34. In the latter part of the war the prefix 'Guards' signified a first-rate Soviet unit.
35. The remainder of the Galician Division received its marching orders on the evening of 15 July, Veryha, op.cit., p.113.
36. Heike, Eng. ed., op.cit., p.44.
37. Lange, op.cit., p.6.
38. Ibid. pp. 6-7. These precise instructions as issued to the 361st Infantry Division are confirmed in *Gefechtsbericht der 361 Inf.Div*, NA T315, roll 2152, p 7, frame 000009.
39. Ibid. Its forward units were placed in front of this line. For exact locations see p 12.
40. Ibid. p 8 – frame 000010, Lange, op.cit. p 7.
41. *Kampfgruppe* Haid was commanded by *Obstlt.* Haid *Kdr* Gren.Rgt.953 of the 361st Infantry Division. For its subsequent orders and deployment see Ibid. p 7.
42. Ibid.
43. *'Überblick...'* p.12.
44. Ibid.
45. Heike, Eng. ed., op.cit., p.45.
46. The early withdrawal of German units and the lack of prepared positions were confirmed to the author by several veterans of the battle during interviews conducted between 1989-1996, including former members of the Fusilier Battalion, interview, O. Wawryk, Fakenham, England, 22 March 1990, WGR 29, interview, I. Nyzka, Rushden, England, 6 January 1991, and the supply unit, letter to author, S. Wasylko, 11 March 1998.
47. The estimation of the Regiment's losses was provided by Roman Drazniowskyj, who took command of 3rd Company after its commander was wounded; verbally to the author, 26 February 1996.
48. Pobihushtschyi, op.cit., p.173. All eight of the regiments Ukrainian company commanders were killed, wounded, or missing: *W-Obstuf.* Rozanetz (1st Coy.) killed, *W-Unstuf.* Berezowskyj (2nd Coy.) killed, *W-Obstuf.* Pidhayny (3rd Coy.) wounded, *W-Obstuf.* Pospilovsky (4th Coy.) killed, II/Btl. *W-Obstuf.* Iuryniak (5th Coy.) missing, *W-Obstuf.* Maleckyj (7th Coy.) wounded, *W-Obstuf.* Sumarokiv (6th Coy.) wounded, *W-Obstuf.* Makarevych (8th Coy.) captured. The *Ordonnanz Offizier* of the 1st Battalion, *W-Unstuf.* Andrij Borynetz, also perished.
49. This was III/AR 219.
50. Lange, op.cit., p.8.
51. V. Sirskyj, letters to author, 24 October 1991, 26 January 1992, 22 March 1992, and interview, Toronto 3 June 1993.
52. During the battle V. Molodecky received a field promotion to the rank of *Waffen-Unterscharführer*. Interview, Toronto, 2 June 1993.
53. The company had four platoons – two commanded by Germans and two by Ukrainians. Each platoon was comprised of four sections of eleven men. One section consisted of one gun with a five man crew, one machine-gun (MG42 with two men), a *Panzerschreck* with two men, a driver and the *Geschützführer* or Section/Gun Leader. (The *Panzerschreck*, otherwise known as the *Ofenrohr*, was a rocket launcher, similar to the bazooka, firing a 7-pound hollow-charge rocket projectile.)
54. The *Raupenschlepper Ost* was a fully tracked prime mover developed for use on the Eastern Front.
55. Interview, W. Molodecky, Toronto, 2 June 1993.
56. Felix Korduba, *Brody, Dyvision tiazhkoi artylerii pid Brodamy* ('Detachment of Heavy Artillery at Brody'), pp.96-102.
57. Heike, Eng. ed., op.cit., p.45.
58. The tanks were captured Soviet T-34s.
59. The attack was delayed from the start after the preparatory artillery fire fell short amongst German troops. *'Überblick...'*, pp. 2-13.
60. Lange, op.cit., p.9.
61. Major-General von Mellenthin offers the following account of the failed attack by the 8th *Panzer* Division. "On the evening of 17th [July] I tried to make contact with XIII Army Corps, in order to arrange for them to attack southwards on the 18th, while 8th *Panzer* Division struck north, but communications failed. I assembled the regimental commanders and explained my plan, in particular I stressed the moral significance of the attack on which depended the salvation of 40,000 of our encircled comrades. In order that there should be no confusion over command, I placed the infantry units holding our front line under the command of the *Panzer* regiment for the duration of the night. At dawn on 18th I went to the battle HQ of the *Panzer* regiment...and found to my astonishment that our infantry – due to attack in an hour's time – were withdrawing southwards. The commander of the *Panzer* regiment confessed that he had ordered this withdrawal as he wished to re-group before launching the attack. I immediately relieved him of his command, but once again the disobedience of this division had done irreparable harm. In the circumstances I had no choice but to cancel the attack." Mellenthin, op.cit., pp.342-43.
62. Lange, op.cit., pp.8-9.
63. Ibid., p.9. Heike states that the greatest drawback in fighting in the encirclements was that communication between the Galician Division and its right-hand neighbour, the 349th Infantry Division, was impossible, Heike, Eng. ed., op.cit., p.46.
64. In his report, General Lange seeks to apportion the blame for the failure of this attack squarely on the 14.*SS-Freiwi-Div.Galizien* when he writes "The SS [i.e. 14th Galician Division] had been unable to overcome the stronger enemy resistance it had faced and came flooding back in a state of total disorder. As a result the Fusilier Battalion came under most heavy fire on both flanks. The attack was thus halted." Lange, op.cit., p.9.
65. Heike, Eng ed., op.cit., p.45.
66. Lange, op.cit., p.9.
67. *L'vov-Sandomierz 1944*, p.173.
68. Interview, P. Maslij, Scunthorpe, England, 8 February 1992, and P. Cisarskyj, Norwich, England, 14 November 1999. For an account of the escape of the supply units of the 361st Infantry Division see *Hauptfeldwebel* W.Mehlhorn, *Im Felde*, 10 Febr. 45, *Bezug: Abw-Stab* OKH/361 v.16.11.44, *Betr. Erlebnisbericht*. NA T78, roll 139-H 41/2.
69. This unit was part of the 9th Mechanised Corps. *L'vov-Sandomierz 1944*, p.74.
70. At the time of its encirclement, in addition to the five divisions which made up XIII Corps, the small parts of other formations which had been broken off from their parent formations at the beginning of the Soviet offensive or during the counterattacks, were also surrounded. These included small contingents of the 1st and 8th *Panzer* divisions, the 357th Infantry Division, the 20th *Panzergrenadier* Division, and the garrison forces within Brody itself (725th, 502nd 327th Infantry Battalions).
71. The most recent Soviet sources cite the following formations as having been amongst the surrounded forces: the 361st and 340th infantry divisions, the 454th Security Division, the SS Infantry Division *'Galicia'*, and the remnants of the 349th Infantry Division, along with detachments of the 505th and 507th *Panzer Abteilungen*. *L'vov-Sandomierz 1944*, p.143. In fact, in mid-July 1944, *Panzer Abteilung* 506 was attached to 8th *Panzer* Division (see *Tiger: The History of a Legendary Weapon 1942-45*, Egon Kleine and Volkmar Kühn, J.J. Fedorowicz, Winnipeg, Manitoba, 1989, p.114) However, there is no evidence to suggest that *Pz.Abtl.* 505 was present. Moreover, *Korpsabteilung* 'C' has been omitted, as has *Pz. Abtl.* 509 (it was known to have been deployed around Sokal in mid-July 1944).
72. *L'vov-Sandomierz 1944*, p.74.
73. *Izvestia* Nr. 170, 19 July 1944, p.1, col.6-7.

Chapter 7

1. Konev hoped to outflank and capture L'viv off the march before the Germans had time to bring up their reinforcement.
2. That is 3rd Guards Tank and 4th Tank armies, 60th and 38th armies and General Sokolov's Cavalry Mechanised Group. *L'vov-Sandomierz 1944*, p.76.
3. Ibid., p.175.
4. Communications difficulties was one of the main contributory factors which prevented the Corps from conducting a successful breakout.
5. Thereafter the Corps was forced to rely on airdrops for re-supply. There is some evidence to suggest that the Luftwaffe made a small number of airdrops but at best these were of negligible significance. Letter to author, W. Sirskyj 22 March 1993, p 177. Contemporary Soviet sources state 'the Germans succeeded in dropping only 8 tons of fuel by parachute during the period of encirclement'. *L'vov-Sandomierz 1944*, p.177.
6. Lange, op.cit., p.10
7. Ibid., pp.10-11.
8. This made the Division easily distinguishable from the regular Wehrmacht units operating alongside it and also served to identify individual soldiers as being Waffen-SS personnel.
9. Heike, Eng. ed., op.cit., p.44.
10. Apart from being the only infantry regiment with an Ukrainian battalion commander, in July 1944 all WGR 29's infantry, artillery, and anti-tank companies were commanded by Ukrainians. Of the total

number of 42 officers serving with the regiment, 34 were Ukrainian and 8 were German. See Lubomyr Ortynskyj 'Pikhotnyi polk UD' ('An Infantry Regiment of the Ukrainian Division') *Visti*, pp.13-14.

11. *L'vov-Sandomierz 1944*, p.171. On 18 July, the three divisions which made up the corps, the 162nd, 172nd rifle and 117th Guards Rifle, had reached the line Toporiv, through Razhiv, Zabolottsi, Haii Dubitski.
12. Heike, Eng. ed., op.cit., p.47.
13. 'Überblick', p.13.
14. See the report by the adjutant of the 349.I.D, von Meyerinek, *Div. Gef. St., den 28.7.44, An den Adjutanten des* XLVIII.*Pz.Korps Herrn Major* Prahmann. NA T315, roll 2147, frames 000052-53.
15. In a letter to the author dated 6 September 1996, a former member of the II/WGR 31 confirmed that during the battle his company took several prisoners whom they transferred to the Division's military police unit, which was composed predominantly of Germans. One of the prisoners met his son who was fighting in the Galician Division and together they both tried to escape from the encirclement. The son was killed and the father remained behind. See also LZ 'Remembrances, 38 years', *Visti* 1982, nos. 5-6, pp. 54-55.
16. Interview I. Nyzka, Rushden, England, 6 January 1991.
17. To make up for the high losses suffered by all Red Army units, local commanders mobilised vast numbers of the local male population aged between 18 and 50 years, and sent them into battle as infantry, untrained, and poorly armed and equipped, with the words "Take rifles from fallen comrades". This is confirmed in the previously cited Soviet General Staff Study of the L'vov-Sandomierz Operation which states "During the preparations for the operation, the 1st Ukrainian Front's formations and units received considerable personnel replacements that were drafted from the right bank of the Ukraine region. A great deal of work on combat and political training was done with these men." Op.cit., pp.51-52. In March 1944, 'Booty Ukrainians' are said to have constituted 40% of the 38th Army under General Moskalenko, which was one of the Red Army units that took part in the encirclement and destruction of XIII Corps in July 1944. Zeimke, op.cit., p.279.
18. The good treatment of Red Army prisoners – as long as they remained under the direct supervision of the Division's Ukrainian soldiers – has been verified by several veterans. R. Wysockyj letter to author, 23 May 1996. See also 'SM', 'Spomyny, Horiachi Dni Pid Brodamy' ('Remembrances; The Hot Days at Brody'), *Visti*, 1979, No. 3, pp.43-44. An Ukrainian veteran of the battle told how during the breakout, himself and another member of his company were voluntarily joined by a group of about ten Soviet POWs who were also trying to escape from the encirclement. The entire group rested in a barn overnight. Both men felt uneasy with the prisoners and in the early hours of the morning simply ran away from them. B. Jasinskyj, Letter to author, 6 September 1996.
19. Letter to author, R. Drazniowskyj, 1 April 1996.
20. V. Veryha, 'Breakout of the Encirclement', *Visti Kombatanta*, nos. 3-4, 1971, p.28.
21. Lange, op.cit., pp.11-12. If Lange's evaluation of the Galician Division in the above report is accepted at face value, then the recapture of Pidhirtsi and Khvativ by its forces must by his own reckoning therefore rank as an extraordinary accomplishment.
22. Ibid.
23. To increase its effectiveness, for the breakout attempt a group from the 361st Infantry Division and the 249th *Sturmgeschütz* Brigade were temporarily subordinated to *Korpsabteilung* C. For details of the plan see Lange, op.cit., pp.,12-13.
24. Heike, Eng. ed., op.cit., p.47.
25. Ibid., p.48.
26. According to Lange's testimony, during the briefing, Curt Von-Hammerstein informed the assembled commanders, incorrectly, that not only a successful drive was underway by the 1st and 8th *Panzer* divisions of XLVIII *Panzerkorps*, but that also there were only enemy security forces between its positions and the main L'viv – Zolochiv road, to a depth of five kilometres. Lange, op.cit., pp.12-13.
27. During the battle several of the Division's soldiers encountered females in combatant roles, especially as members of tank crews. In an interview which took place on 6 January, 1991, in Rushden, England, I. Nyzka related to the author how during the breakout he found the body of a young woman in a destroyed Soviet tank. Likewise, W. Molodecky described a similar incident during an interview on 2 June 1993, in Toronto. In a letter to the author dated 23 May, 1996, Roman Wysockyj confirmed that early in the battle his (artillery) unit downed a Soviet biplane which had two crew, one of which was a young woman.
28. To prevent its destruction, on 18 July the Division's medical section was relocated from Potutory to Pochapy. For further details see 'Surgeon Volodymyr Prokopovych', *Visti*, 1981, No.1, pp.65-66.
29. *Gefechtsbericht...* p.10.
30. Interview, V. Molodecky, Toronto, 2 June 1993.
31. Heike, Eng. ed., op.cit., p.47.
32. For a full account of one such occurrence where a group set out on bicycles to contact their regimental HQ only to discover that Soviet tanks and infantry had got there first, see W. Sirskyj; 'The staff Company WGR 29 at Brody', *Visti Kombatanta,* No. 4, pp.7-8, 1953, pp.33-34. Two other such instances were also related to the author. "A member of the Pioneer Battalion returned to the Divisional command post during the battle to find that it had been abandoned in such haste that a great many items and personal effects had been left behind." (Julian Wilshynskyj letter to author, 27 May 1996); an Ukrainian grenadier serving with the II/WGR 29 recounted that two men had been sent to the battalion HQ to get orders but found no one there (interview I. Nyzchka, Rushden, England, 6 January 1991).
33. Heike, Eng. ed., op.cit., p.47. The actual date of Herm's death as stated in his service record is given as being 22 July 1944, and this appeared in the subsequent obituary published in *Das Schwarze Korps* However, this date which is generally taken as the end of organised resistance by the remnants of XIII Corps that were still trapped, is almost certainly approximate. See his service record NA A3343-SSO-091A.
34. See account of Father Levenets, 'Account for the Divisional Archives' *Visti*, 7 (9), 1951, pp.. 5-6. Dern was replaced by the commander of II/29 Regt. *SS-Hauptsturmführer* Wilhelm Allerkamp, who was later killed. In a statement given for the *Deutsches Rotes Kreuz Suchdienst*, dated 11 August, 1962, *SS-Hauptsturmführer* Allerkamp's driver Georg Mackanyn, who was wounded during the breakout and captured on 22 July, 1944, states that the following week in a transit camp in Kiev he learned from a comrade that Allerkamp was killed at the same time by machine gun fire. AA.
35. The *Katyusha* (Little Katie) was one of the most formidable and effective weapons in the Soviet armoury. Christened by the Germans 'Stalin's Organs' because of the peculiar noise of the rocket in flight, the *Katyusha* was an 82mm solid fuel rocket carrying a 6.5lb high explosive warhead with a maximum range of about 6,000 yards. The weapon could be launched from an open frame mounted on the back of a 2.5-ton truck which carried 36 rockets. A heavier model of 132mm calibre and carrying a 40lb warhead was also introduced.
36. Letter to author, I. Nakonechny, 6 March 1993. Interview, I. Nyzka, Rushden, England, 6 January 1991.
37. Ferkuniak, op.cit., p.26. In his memoirs Ferkuniak states that during the battle he met two Ukrainian officers, *Waffen-Untersturmführer* Wolodymyr Kosak and *Waffen-Hauptsturmführer* Myhailo Brygidyr who stated that without their officers in command the Ukrainian units panicked. Heike confirms that German units had also panicked, see Heike, Eng. ed., op.cit., p.47.
38. Ferkuniak, op.cit., p.26.
39. Heike, Eng. ed., op.cit., p.47.
40. Ibid. Heike states that the decision to reject the offer of assistance was based on the fact that the soldiers of the UPA were mainly youths lacking military training and uniforms.
41. Heike, Eng. ed., op.cit., p.48.
42. Lange, op.cit., p.14.
43. For a detailed but somewhat embellished blow-by-blow account of the breakout see Lange, op.cit., pp.14-27.
44. *L'vov-Sandomierz 1944*, p.78.
45. Ferkuniak, op.cit., p.15.
46. Interview, I. Nyzchka, Rushden, England, 6 January 1991. It should be noted that several veterans elaborated on the movement difficulties caused by the effect of the rain on the poor quality roads.
47. In a letter to the author dated 11 March 1998, S. Wasylko, a former member of the Divisional supply unit wrote, "Supply units (horse drawn vehicles) never received the order to withdraw before hand. On the night of 19/20th July the commander of the 1st, unit Roman Dolynskyj, gave the order on his own initiative for the horse drawn vehicles to proceed to Bilyi Kamin', the only available road at that time, under the command of *Waffen-Obersturmführer* Jury Mitzowskyj. He [Mitzowskyj] was lost together with his whole group."
48. Lange, op.cit., p.11.
49. Virtually all the memoirs of the veterans of the battle emphasis the complete Soviet air superiority. Reference to the particularly devastating air attacks which took place on 20 July is made by Ferkuniak, op.cit., p.20.
50. *L'vov-Sandomierz 1944*, p.79.
51. In a letter to author, dated 10 January 1994, V. Veryha, wrote that, "Soviet planes appeared in such profusion that they even shot at individuals and single vehicles".
52. Ferkuniak, op.cit., p.26. In his report General Lange falsely states: "The anti-aircraft guns of the 14. *SS-Freiwi.Div-Galizien* had been abandoned by their crews and no longer took part in the fighting." Lange, op.cit., pp.16-17.
53. To cite an example, I/A.R 217 shot down one enemy aircraft with carbines. Lange, op.cit., pp.16-17.
54. In a letter to the author dated 11 March 1998, S. Wasylko described how he went to assist the injured troops when one of two Soviet aircraft was brought down in Bilyi Kamin', on 20 July, by rifles and flak guns by forces of the Galician Division, crashing amongst the troops.
55. Wolfgang Lange *Korpsabteilung C; Vom Dnjeper bis nach Polen (November 1943 bis Juli 1944)*, Scharnhorst-Buchkameradschaft, Neckargemund, 1961, p.106.
56. See Mykola Fylypowych, 'Z fiuziliramy pid Brodamy', *Visti*, November, 1964, No.115, pp.84-85.
57. *L'vov-Sandomierz 1944*, p.78.
58. Lange *Korpsabteilung 'C' in der Kesselschlacht....*, p.17.
59. Schmitt, op.cit., p.7.
60. In his account, Yurij Kopystansky who was attached to the Galician Division's *Kriegsberichter* unit states that he learned of the event via a special radio bulletin; see *Visti Kombatanta* 1994, No.1. pp.94-95, as did other groups that still had access to working radios.
61. It is difficult to access the full extent of the impact of the news of the attempt on Hitler's life, on the German soldiers, as evidence is often contradictory and conflicting. Some Ukrainian veterans contend German morale collapsed when news reached them. Others assert that they took it very calmly and that any noticeable decline in morale came about as a result of a feeling of utter hopelessness against such overwhelming Soviet superiority; letter to author, Roman Wysockyj 23 May 1996. The truth would seem to lie somewhere in between.
62. R. Drazniowskyj, verbally to author, 4 May 1996.
63. Lange, *Korpsabteilung 'C' in der Kesselschlacht...*, p.18.
64. Heike, Eng. ed., op.cit., p.47.
65. The failure of the relief attempt by elements of 8th *Panzer* Division and an armoured battlegroup from 1st *Panzer* Division, was caused by a combination of factors including a failed radio link between LVIII *Panzerkorps* and XIII Corps, and the disobedience of the commander of the 8th *Panzer* Division's *Panzer* Regiment. For a full explanation see Mellenthin, op.cit., p.342.
66. The first group, which broke out at 4.00am, on 21 July, near Iasenivtsi, consisted of elements of 217th Division reinforced by stragglers and the 249th Assault Gun Brigade (less armour).

67. See GPD (German Police Decrypt) 2874 No. 1 Traffic: 21.7.44, EE, LYZ de SPY 1519 SSD ESG7 No.10 1445 472 DQH 6890, An SS *Führungs-hauptamt* Berlin, *von KDr Felders. Batl.* 14. To SSFHA Berlin, HW 16/70, PRO. Because of the known provenance of this message (that is a decrypted enigma radio transmission), it is exceptionally unlikely that the figures quoted could be wrong. The number quoted as being 'members of the Feld Ersatz Battalion' would still seem to be too high unless, for example, this is a generic term referring to all those from the Division (other than those included in the separate figures for the support and supply units) who had gathered in the Sambir area on that particular day. Alternatively, the reason for the artificial inflation of the strength of this unit could be explained by the rapid influx of personnel who enlisted in July 1944, *en masse*, in preference to being drafted into the Red Army, and who were promptly sent to the FEB.
68. M. A. Polushkin, *Na sandomirskom napravlenii*, pp.73-77 and pp.79-80.
69. *L'vov-Sandomierz 1944*, p.176.
70. These were comprised of the remaining elements of *Korpsabteilung* C and the 349th Infantry Division, along with the attached Divisional *Gruppe* 339.
71. The railway embankment was under heavy and continual machine gun fire and crossing it without suffering massive losses became almost impossible. Luckily many of the survivors of the Galician Division found conduits in the embankment and crawled through them to the other side. Heike, Eng. ed., op.cit., p.58.
72. Lange *Korpsabteilung 'C' in der Kesselschlacht...*, op.cit., pp.23-24.
73. Among the XIII Corps' senior officers, and commanders of break-out units, *Oberstleutnant* Simons (CO, Div.Gr.183), *Major* von Bonin, (CO, Div.Gr.217), *Hauptmann* Zingl (CO, Fusilier Btl., *Korpsabteilung* C) were posted as 'missing'. Lange, op.cit., p.27.
74. Heike, Eng. ed., op.cit., p.50.
75. Yurij Kopystansky, *Visti Kombatanta* 1994, No.1, pp.94-103.
76. Ferkuniak, op.cit., p.27.
77. Several of the wounded were gathered in barracks in Zolochiv. I. Nakonechny, letter to author, 6 March 1993. From the memoirs of survivors it seems that the treatment of Ukrainians who fell into enemy hands varied considerably and was dependent on the individual from the Soviet military counter-intelligence (SMERSH) who conducted the interrogation immediately after capture. Some of those who were captured changed into Wehrmacht uniforms or discarded their Ukrainian/Waffen-SS insignia as quickly as possible to avoid detection. However, it was still possible to identify the Ukrainian soldiers since unlike their Wehrmacht counterparts, each one was indelibly tattooed under his left armpit with his blood group. Most Ukrainian officers were shot immediately. The experiences of Andrij Veremenchuk, a Ukrainian who was captured and witnessed the execution of Division members, were related to the author, in a letter from R. Kolisnyk dated 22 March 1993.
78. "During the breakout from Brody I did not see one single German carrying a weapon. In contrast every Ukrainian (even the mortally wounded) had a weapon of some sort be it a rifle, machine gun or pistol." Verbally to author, S. Vasylko, 19 November 1997.
79. In *The Russian German War, 1941-45*, London, The War Office, 1956, p.99, General A. Guillaume states that by the evening of 22 July some German units were telephoning the Soviet command for instructions as to how to reach the points of assembly for prisoners.
80. Interview, Julian Wilshynskyj, Toronto, 6 June 1993.
81. After his capture on 28 July 1944, Wolodymyr Molodecky spent fourteen months in Soviet prisoner of war camps, in Kiev, Stalino, Makijiwka, and Kadijiwka in the Donbas region of Ukraine, and later near Minsk in Belarus. Throughout this period he was pretending to be a Polish national. In September 1945 he was 'repatriated' back to Poland where he stayed until 1 May 1947. To avoid arrest and certain execution he escaped to Czechoslovakia, which he crossed on foot, before crossing the German border under fire from the border guards. From Germany he went to France where he met up with his parents, before emigrating to Canada in January 1948, where he joined the Canadian Army reserve and served with the rank of Captain.
82. General A. Guillaume quotes from Hauffe's interrogation report as follows, "Knowing that the Soviet air force was engaged in White Russia, we never could have imagined that it could intervene against us with such resources. It has ceaselessly bombed us so that we could not even raise our heads. Even the old officers who had fought in the 1914-1918 war were morally shaken". Guillaume, op.cit., pp.99-100.
83. *Istoriia Velikoi Otechestvennoi Voiny Sovetskogo Soiuza*, Vol.4, p.214, names the Corps commander General Hauffe, as well as generals Lindemann (CO, 361st Infantry Division) and Nettwig (CO, 454th Security Division) as having been captured, Nettwig after having sustained a serious head wound. Other commanders of the 217th *Kampfgruppe* and 183rd *Kampfgruppe* were classified as missing.
84. Heike, Eng. ed., op.cit., p.51.
85. Heike incorrectly states that in one such battle in the town of Holohory the Corps' commander Hauffe was killed. Ibid., p.50. Hauffe was in fact captured and condemned to death by Hitler in *absentia*, see *Istoriia Velikoi Otechestvennoi Voiny Sovetskogo Soiuza*, Vol.4, p.214. See also *L'vov-Sandomierz 194'*, p.79.
86. The meeting with a mechanised infantry group accompanied by tanks was confirmed by several veterans of the battle who took the same route including Heike, Eng. ed., op.cit., p.51, W. Sirskyj, letter to author, 20 October, 1992, B. Jasinskyj verbally to author, 18 June 1996.
87. Ferkuniak, op.cit., p.29. From the moment they reached Staryi Sambir, the survivors of the Galician Division encountered refugees heading west to escape the advancing Red Army, whom they often assisted as best they could.
88. In his memoirs, Heike writes that during an evening meal, given for the surviving commanders of XIII Corps units, Raus expressed his gratification to Freitag for having extricated at least part of the division from the encirclement. The credit should not however have gone to Freitag, as by that time he already resigned command of the Division. Heike, Eng. ed., op.cit., p.52.
89. See *...im Letzten Aufgebot, 1944-45. Die Geschichte der 18.SS-Freiwilligen-Panzergrenadier-Division Horst Wessel*, Wilhelm Tieke and Friedrich Rebstock, pp.18-29.
90. Similarly, survivors from the entrapped German units also frequently encountered UPA groups at this time. For example, in an after-action report dated 15 February 1945, entitled *Gefechtsbericht fur die Zeit vom 22.7.44 – 4.8.44* Lt Domschke, (*Ausb.Komp., Gren.Ers.u.Ausb.Batl.* 58, 361st Inf. Div.) wrote:
    "27.7.44. We marched about 30kms. In the evening we had a short rest in the forester's station near Kopky. Here we encountered a partisan group of 80-100 persons [these must have been UPA]. They wanted us to march with them in the direction of Kiev After the theft of a map and one light machine gun (MG 42), which were seized from us, we managed to disengage from them....", NA, T313, roll 73 frame Nos: 6067671-1- 6067671-2.
91. Drazniowskyj verbally to author, 4 May 1996. For a description of a similar meeting between UPA members and soldiers of the Division from a German perspective see Erich Kern, *Der Grosse Rausch, Russlandfeldzug 1941-1945*, Zurich, 1948, p.148.
92. Heike, Eng. ed., op.cit., p.52.
93. The German members of the Divisional staff who perished during the battle included the commander of WGR 31, *SS-Obersturmbannführer* Herms, together with his staff, *SS-Hauptsturmführer* Wilhelm Allerkamp CO II/WGR 29 (killed), Ustuf. Hans Braun (*Abtl.* 3), Beyersdorff's adjutant *SS-Hauptsturmführer* Hans Wagner, (born 5 August 1914, SS Nr. 422,126) who died as the result of an accident on 9 July 1945 (Kalba, letter 5 August 1996), *SS-Sturmbannführer* Alfred Schützenhofer (CO Art. Rgt., born 16 July 1898, SS Nr. 58,056), Serge von Kuester, *Flak Abtl.* 14 (captured), and *SS-Sturmbannführer* Johann Burkhart, born 18 August 1901, SS Nr. 1,704. From the testimonies of the Ukrainian veterans of the battle, it would appear that many of German officers preferred to attach themselves to groups of German soldiers rather than remain with their commands during the breakout.
94. Erich Kern, *The Dance Of Death*, p.195.
95. Ferkuniak, op.cit., p.26. The Ukrainian officers included; Brygidyr, Ferkuniak, Kosak, Czuczkewycz, Ortynskyj, Chaplain Levenets, Dr Panasiuk, Honcharenko, Bayborak, Sylenko, Bojcun, Dolynskyj, Yaskevych and Karantnyzky.
96. Heike, Eng. ed., op.cit., p.52.
97. For example, a report by *Luftflotte* 6 (Air Fleet 6) to the OKH General Staff Operations Department commander *Generalfeldmarschall* Model (Army Group Centre) dated 15 July 1944, entitled *Beurteilung des Lage am* 15.7.1944 ('Review of the Situation on 15.7.1944'), gives an excellent and accurate analysis of the situation facing the Army Group on this date. It reads:
    "The enemy commenced the expected attack operations in sharply concentrated spearheads, along the lines [directions] expected from this Army Group in accordance with its structure and the regional [geographical] conditions – Northwestwards Ternopil and south-westwards Luzk. At the former point the involvement of the 4th *Pz.* Army has been confirmed and at the latter point the 1st Pz. Army.
    "All indications are that [the enemy] will shortly also attack at Kovel with very considerable forces. It is uncertain whether the enemy will also commence an appropriately timed approach southwards of the Dnestr in order to attack in the direction of Stanislav.
    "The strength of the enemy is unchanged, with 99 infantry divisions and with 3900 tanks and self-propelled guns mostly attached to three tank armies. [The enemy] has the freedom to sharply concentrate their forces at weakening points during the attack along the line/region defined by them.
    "Army Group North Ukraine faces this enemy with 37 divisions (of which 7 are Hungarian) along the front. At the beginning of the attack Army Group North Ukraine had 6 light divisions (of which one was Hungarian), and 4 infantry divisions (of which 3 were Hungarian) in reserve."
    "Decisive is:
    "The allocation of forces for the Army Group at the end of June was tailored to having just sufficient forces to allow a good prospect of success in countering the enemy attack at all points, making use of reserves in particular *Panzer* units. Since that time the Army Group has given away (taking into account the addition of the 17th *Pz.* Div.) 6 *Panzer* divisions, 3 *Panzer Abteilungen*, and 3 infantry divisions. This amounts to nearly all of the reserve, as the Hungarian divisions are of minimal value. The 14th *SS.Freiw.* Div. *'Galizien'* and the newly-arrived combat group of the 18th *SS.Freiw.* Div. are only to a small extent ready for deployment. The consequences of this reduction in forces have been reported by the Army Group in the past two weeks."
    See *Geheime Kommandosache, Fernschreiben.* 15.7.1944, *Zeit: an* O.K.H./GenstdH/Op. Abtl. I. KR *Generalfeldmarschall* Model H.Gr. Mitte, g.Kdos. *nachr: Luftflotte 6, Beurteilung des Lage am* 15.7.1944, RH 19 VI/19, BA-MA.
98. Heike, Eng. ed., op.cit., p.52.
99. *28 Juli, 1944 dzt Kracow, Gouverneur des Distrikts Galizien, An den Reichsführer-SS und Chef der Deutschen Polizei Reichsinnenminister* Heinrich Himmler, NA T175, roll 32.
100. *Fernschreiben* 344/64 *Geheim,* 1 August 1944 *An den Gouverneur SS-Gruppenführer* Wächter, Kracow. NA T175, roll 32.
101. According to Ferkuniak, Freitag actually said, "Your battalion fought bravely. Your only mistake was when the enemy started to encircle your individual companies. Instead of pulling them back you rushed all your reserves into the battle. This was the reason that your battalion collapsed." Ferkuniak, op.cit., p.29.
102. Ibid.
103. 'There could be no mistake,' wrote Ferkuniak. 'In order to hide their misdeeds and inefficiencies in

command, they covered it with an imagined unwillingness to fight'. Ibid.
104. *Waffen-Obersturmführer* Roman Bojcun. Related orally to R. Kolisnyk. Freitag was also known to suffer from a heart condition.
105. Ferkuniak, op.cit., p.29. Among the German officers who exhibited this type of behaviour was the commander of the staff company WGR 29, *SS-Untersturmführer* Weiss, who "upon reaching the safety of Transcarpathia, refused even to stay under the same roof with the seven remaining men from the staff company, calling them cowards." Interview W. Sirskyj, Toronto 5 June 1993.
106. In 1938 Uzhorod was detached from Galicia and incorporated into Hungarian territory.
107. After-action reports by former members of 361st I.D, *Korpsabteilung* C and 349th I.D., and a map showing the locations of the assembly areas of all XIII Corps' units, indicate that for the most part they withdrew along the same route passing through Khodoriv and Stryj, to their designated assembly area of Mukachiv. Further information and extensive post Brody reports for both units can be found in their entirety on NA microfilm Nos T315, roll 2152 (361.I.D.) and T315, roll 2147 (349.I.D.) respectively.
108. Ferkuniak quotes this figure, op.cit., p.29.
109. Verbally to author, R. Drazniowskyj, 4 May 1996. Letter to author, B. Kalba, 24 June 1996.
110. Figure provided by W. Sirskyj who together with Roman Shirko was involved in the registration of survivors. Letter to the author, W. Sirskyj, 20 October 1992.
111. No individual unit escaped without any casualties, either killed or wounded. For example in July 1944 the 3rd Company of 14th *Feld Ersatz Bataillon* had a strength of 250 men of which approximately 80 returned to Neuhammer after Brody. Of the remainder, some deserted to the UPA, some were wounded and sent to German hospitals, around a dozen were killed and the rest deserted and remained in Galicia. As the vast majority of these men had been serving with the Division for less than two months and had not been tattooed with their blood group under their left armpit, they could not be readily identifiable as having served in the Division and their sudden reappearance in their local village did not necessarily arouse suspicion. Letter to author, Ostap Sokolskyj, 9 September 1996. The battalion also lost one of its doctors. Krywulak, op.cit., p.3. From the 780 men who deployed with the Division's supply troops, 78 gathered in Seredne. Verbally to author, S. Vasylko, 19 November 1997.
112. Heike cites that enquiries with the 18th *SS-Freiwilligen-Panzergrenadier* Division *'Horst Wessel'* which was in the Iaslo district revealed that a number of the Division's soldiers had been assigned to it.
113. To give three examples of individual unit losses within the Division; of an initial strength of 275 personnel assigned to the staff company of WGR 29, only seven were accounted for after Brody, (W. Sirskyj, "Molod Druhoii Svitovoi Viyny" ('The Youth of the Second World War'), *Visti Kombatanta* 198, No.1 p.79). Similarly from an original strength of 182 men of the 3rd *schnell* (fast) Company of the Pioneer Battalion, no officers, two NCOs and seven men returned to the Division. (Julian Wilshynskyj Interview Toronto 6 June 1993). In fact none of the Ukrainian officers serving with the 14th Pioneer Battalion returned to the Division, *Pioneer Battalion of the 14 Galician Division*, Bohdan Kutny and Taras Kaczmarchuk, unpublished paper, p.3. Letter to author, B. Kutny, 24 November 1997.
114. Oleh Puszkar, *Lagernyi Tryptykh*, Ukrainskyj Arkhiv, Warszawa, 1994, p.272. Puszkar, who was the commander of the 1st Section, 1st Platoon, 1/I/ WGR 31, was himself taken prisoner, states that in the first camp he read in a Moscow newspaper that 2,000 soldiers of the Galician Division were captured by the Soviets. The officers and the badly wounded were shot on the spot and the majority of the rest given sentences of ten years' hard labour.
115. Schmitt, op.cit., p.8.
116. Letter to author, Kolisnyk, 5 August 1996.
117. Later, when the survivors had returned to Neuhammer a special *Abwicklungstelle* (inquiry centre) was established to verify all the information about returnees. The statistics were forwarded to the Divisional headquarters. In order to certify the death of a soldier in action verification was required by two or more independent witnesses. For the results from WGR 30 see *30 SS Freiw. Gren. Regt. Abwicklungstelle O.U., den 22.9.44* (Appendix XV)

The figures for the Ivano-Frankivsk branch of the Brotherhood of Former Members of the 1st Ukrainian Division as of 15 April 1993, are as follows:

Former members of the Division	190
Were at Brody	141
Successfully broke out of the encirclement	10
Taken prisoner by the Soviets	92
Joined the UPA	33

118. *Waffen-Unterscharführer* Evhen Smyk led one of the larger groups that deserted from the staff company of WGR 29, letter to author, W. Sirskyj 22 March 1993. The figure of 3000 was mentioned at a UPA conference in 1992, but again this is only an approximation. See *America*, 12-16 July 1954, Philadelphia – reprinted in *Ukrainska Dyvisia Halychyna*, pp.55-61, Kyiv, 1994 (English translation by Ostap Sokolskyj, pp.4-6). A more realistic number would have been 1000, given the situation, the circumstances, possibilities and the terrain and its size. The author shares the view of some veterans who feel that it is unlikely that 3000 men could have been absorbed into reliable units of the UPA which had neither the necessary organisational nor technical capacity to accommodate such a large influx in such as short space of time. The UPA operated principally with small mobile units as large groups would have attached too much attention and for those who failed to break out, their chances of reaching a reliable UPA unit were slim.
119. For example, a first rate officer *Waffen-Hauptsturmführer* Ivan Semenovych Rembalowych, the former commander of the 1st Company of the Pioneer Battalion, born 1897 in Horodnia, joined the UPA after having been wounded during the fighting at Brody. Under the alias 'Kropyva' he subsequently went on to organise an officer school in the Carpathian Mountains for the UPA, which held three or four courses, lasting three-four months each. He was eventually captured on 17 May 1950, and convicted by the Carpathian War Zone, according to the Criminal Code of the USSR, 54-1a: 54-11, and subsequently executed on 8 September, 1950. This information is confirmed in a document from the Security Service of Ukraine, No. 13729, dated 14 October 1998 (AA).
120. This figure included the sections of the supply troops who found themselves outside the encirclement and thus escaped almost entirely unharmed. Lange *Korpsabteilung 'C' in der Kesselschlacht...*, p.27.
121. Ibid.
122. 28 officers, 62 NCOs and 199 men were certified as killed, while 112 officers, 18 officials, 1008 NCOs and 4883 men were classified as 'missing'. See *Gefechtsbericht...*, frame 000022.
123. See NA T78 roll 142 frame 6072050.
124. Lange, *Korpsabteilung C*, p.116.
125. The Soviet figures for killed and captured personnel incorporate all those from the 'Brody Grouping', including a force of around 3000 infantry from the 454th Security Division and the 340th Infantry Division that penetrated into the woods east of Kaminka Strumilova. There they were surrounded and liquidated by 112th Rifle Division on 19 July. They are, however, in all probability still exaggerated.
126. *L'vov-Sandomierz 1944*, p.178.
127. *Div Gef. St., den 28.7.44 An den Adjutanten des* XLVIII *Pz.Korps Herrn Major* Prahmann. NA T315, roll 2147 frames 000052-53.
128. During a secretly monitored conversation between three German officers, *Oberst* Reimann, *Gen. Lt.* Elfeldt, and *Oberst* Wilck (commander of the 913th Gren. Rgt. of the 349th I.D.) on 27 October 1944, Wilck made reference to the casualty figures for XIII Corps, and reiterated his previous comments regarding the Galician Division's performance (see his statement cited earlier in relation to the fighting on 15 July in which his unit was involved). The conversation went as follows:
Elfeldt: "Those are all desperate measures because everything else has failed."
Wilck: "Yes. Then there is actually an SS Galicia 'Division', which was perfectly equipped and consisted of Galician volunteers. They were in the so-called 'Rudolf' position, which had been constructed about 10 or 12km behind the front line. That was the last line which should have been held at any cost according to Model's theories. It was lost even before the Russians approached. They made off as soon as they noticed that things were starting. Afterwards we disarmed the remnants of them."
Elfeldt: "How many of your Division got out of the pocket?"
Wilck: "Only about 12000 out of 65000 men in the *Korps* got out. But without – there were assault guns there in great quantities – it was pitiful. All the new artillery, new guns and all the wounded were lost" ... [asked where the 12000 men re-assembled:] "Far behind the lines. I believe only after they'd got beyond the Carpathians. The Russian had learnt all that from us. First of all, they formed an inner circle; there was still plenty of time. Two days later they had strengthened it to such an extent that an actual hard fight was necessary to get through there at all, besides which they had formed an outer circle. We got out 40 or 50km to the south of L'vov. We got through in the neighbourhood of Strij. There was another small position behind the river Strij, which forms a perfect obstacle, as it is marshy, secure against tanks and all that."
See CSDIC (UK) S.R. Report – S.R.G.G. 1068, WO 208-4169, PRO.
129. Ferkuniak writes in his memoirs that the report which was prepared by *SS-Sturmbannführer* Karl Zoglauer was read out at an officers meeting on 2 August and contained proposals to disband the Galician Division and distribute its remaining personnel among German Divisions and as manual workers. Ferkuniak, op.cit., p.30.
130. Ibid.
131. Schmitt, op.cit., p.8.
132. It would seem that the decision to reconstitute the Galician Division had already been made prior to the meeting since on this occasion Himmler displayed none of the reticence which had characterised his involvement the previous year when Wächter had first broached the subject of its formation.
133. Heike, Eng. ed., op.cit., p.55.
134. On 20 July 1944, following the unsuccessful attempt on Hitler's life, *SS-Reichsführer* Heinrich Himmler was appointed Chief of Army Equipment and Commander of the Replacement Army in place of Fromm. He controlled the conscription of the armed forces, the Army training and replacement system, and Army procurement and supply.
135. For an account of the rising, see *The Warsaw Rising*, Günter Deschner, Pan/Ballantine, 1972. Amongst the forces involved in suppressing the rising was a unit of an Ukrainian *Schuma* Battalion which was at that time distinct from the Galician Division.
136. Another contributory factor may have been the Division's closeness to the UPA. Various agencies within the SS establishment were keen to exploit that in the war against the Soviets. The issue of contact between UPA and the Germans is a complex one and therefore deserves some further explanation. It would appear that fundamentally the UPA command continued to regard the Germans as enemies and even though local tactical requirements had resulted in some co-operation with them, such arrangements were rare and strictly forbidden. In three recorded cases when UPA commanders disobeyed these instructions, two were court-martialled, condemned to death and executed. The third escaped while trial proceedings were still pending. The reason for enforcing that policy so severely was the fear that even local co-operation might compromise the UPA in the eyes of the population against whom the Germans used inhuman terror, and in the opinion of the Allies, since at every opportunity the Soviets proclaimed that the UPA was co-operating with the Germans.

For their part, German commanders were forbidden to discuss any political issues or to assist the UPA with weapons. Notwithstanding the seemingly intractable position of both sides, the *Aufnahme einer Verbindung mit den Ukrainischen*

Partisanen of 18 September 1944, stated that with the departure of the German civilian population from Ukrainian territory, no obstacle remained for the establishment of links with the insurgents. Thus the *Reichsführer-SS* gave his permission for such contacts to take place. For details of one instance of mutual co-operation, after that date, which involved a German reconnaissance raid which took place behind Soviet lines from 6 October-7 November 1944, with Ukrainian help, named 'Operation Kirn', see James Lucas's *The Last Year of the German Army, May 1944 to May 1945*, Arms and Armour Press, London, 1996, pp.120-126. According to a former UPA battalion commander, its policy was as follows: "To fight without mercy against the [Nazi] party members, SD, and Gestapo. To be tolerant to the Wehrmacht. Not to attack individual soldiers who were captured and to exchange higher officers for political prisoners. To disarm ordinary soldiers and non-commissioned officers and then to release them allowing them to return home." Maksym Skorupskyj, *U nastupakh i vidstupakh*, Spohady, Chicago, 1961, p.218.

137. Heike, Eng. ed., op.cit., p.55.
138. See *Der Reichsführer-SS, Feld-kommandostelle*, 7.8.1944, RF/M.Tgb.Nr. 111/1294/44 g. Kdos. Point 7 of this document read: "It must be understood that the Division, in spite of all the difficulties, receives a cadre of 1000 German NCOs. I imagine that these 1000 NCOs will come from the Luftwaffe."

    NA T175 roll 141, frames 2669211 – 2669212. ABFC. Heike actually states that Freitag only agreed to remain as commander of the Division if this was done. Heike, Eng. ed., op.cit., p.63. Other measures are outlined in the secret order issued by the SS-FHA some four weeks later, see *SS-Führungshauptamt*, 5 September 1944, AmtII Org.Abtl.Ia/II, Tgb. Nr.2880/44 g.Kdos. NA T175roll141, frames 2669182-2669183.
139. *Der Reichsführer-SS, Feld-kommandostelle*, 7.8.1944, RF/M.Tgb.Nr. 111/1294/44 g.Kdos. NA T175 roll 141, frames 2669211 – 2669212. The relative order was not issued by the SS-FHA until 5 September 1944, NA T175 roll 141, frames 2669182 – 2669183.
140. Ibid.
141. Wächter to the *Wehrausschuss* Galicia, Kracow, 10 August 1944, ABFC. In the letter, Wächter thanked the Military Board for its past co-operation, and asked it to continue to contribute to the numerical strengthening and internal consolidation of the Division over the next few months.
142. A full account of the incident was provided in a letter to author dated 1 August, 1996, by E. Shypailo who was present on that occasion, also R. Herasymowycz 13 September, 1996, and in the unpublished memoirs of Roman Hawrylak, p. 15. Heike also mentions the incident in his memoir, Eng. ed., op. cit., p.53.
143. Ferkuniak, op.cit., p.30.
144. Ibid.
145. Ibid. Interview, V. Veryha, Toronto, 21 June 1999. Letter to author, I. Sadoveyj, 25 December 1998.
146. Ferkuniak, op.cit., pp.30-31.
147. These included standard German awards such as the *Infanterie Sturmabzeichen* (infantry assault badge) and the *Verwundetenabzeichen* (wound badge) in various grades and *Kriegsverdienstkreuz* (War Merit Cross). The author has appropriate citations for all these examples in his possession dated 1 September 1944. For example, *Besitzzeugnis dem W-Sturmmann* Wasyl Sirskyj *stb.Kp./Waffen Gren.Rgt.d.SS Nr.29 (gal.a) Verleihe ich das Infanterie-Sturmabzeichen in Silber*. AA.
148. See aff. *Grenadier Division der SS\gal Nr.I.\Einsatz: Ostfront, Südabschnitt Verleihungsliste Nr.1, fur Eiserne Kreuze 2.Klasse*. ABFC.
149. Wolodymyr Kosak, born 26 May 1917, Peremyshl, Ukraine. From 1935 until 1938 he served in the Red Army attaining the rank of Lieutenant with the 26th Mot. Brig. in Voronesch, before serving with the German Wehrmacht from 7 July 1942 until 25 January 1943 as *3. Deutsch-Ukrainischer Milizchef* the district of Mitrovynowka. He enlisted for service with the Galician Division on 17 July 1943 where, in addition to the Iron Cross 2nd Class, Kosak was awarded the *Infanterie-Sturmabzeichen in Silber* (Infantry Assault Badge in Silver) and the *Verwundetenabzeichen in Schwarz* (wound badge in black) after the Battle of Brody. He went on to become the highest decorated Ukrainian serving with the Division receiving the *Verwundetenabzeichen* in Silver (for three or four wounds) on 6 December 1944 and finally the Iron Cross 1st Class on 20 April 1945.
150. For details of the promotion see his personal file, NA, A3343-550-220.
151. For example Ferkuniak, op.cit., p.25, states that after Freitag had resigned command of the Division, Heike continued to issue orders for all Ukrainian units on the Brody-Krasne highway to be directed to him in Pidhirtsi. In his memoirs, Shandruk writes that upon arriving at the Division's Training and Reserve Regiment in April 1945, the Ukrainian officers who took part in the battle of Brody gave him an account of the battle and was told, "Even at the start of the battle General [sic] Freitag had lost all contact with his regiments and instead of trying to re-establish contact, he left to join the army staff. At that time our experienced officers took over command of individual units and following general directions furnished by staff major Heike who valiantly stood his post at the front, succeeded in leading the remaining men out of the entrapment". *Arms of Valour*, Pavlo Shandruk, New York, Robert Speller and Sons, 1959, p.269.
152. Heike's injury (albeit not a serious one) was confirmed by Bohdan Kalba, who saw him with his left arm bandaged and in a sling after the breakout. Interview B. Kalba, Toronto, 7 June 1993 and letter to author, 6 July 1998.
153. It would appear that, as a rule, *Major* Heike insisted on wearing his regular army uniform instead of that of the equivalent SS rank of *SS-Sturmbannführer*, much to the annoyance of Freitag. (Photographic evidence does exist of Heike dressed in a SS-uniform; Bender & Taylor, Vol. 4, op.cit., p.25) This in turn created a great deal of friction between the two men and was the primary reason that Freitag refused to give Heike the promotions he deserved.
154. The figures for the relative strengths of the various categories as of 4.9.44, were:

	Regulation strength	*Actual strength*
Officers	480	134
NCOs	2587	522
Men	11622	4419

    The breakdown of the figures for the *A.u.E.Rgt.* 14. were: 43 officers, 288 NCOs and 8504 men, total 8835. See *Der Reichsführer-SS Adjutantur, Feldkommandostelle, den* 7. September 1944, *Kdo.Stab RF-SS* Tgb.Nr.Ia/3530/44 *g.Kdos. Stärkemeldungen Stand vom*: 5.9.1944. Unlike the other Waffen-SS units, the figures for the Galician Division are marked as being from 4 September 1944 and not 5 September. SeeT175 roll 141 frame 2668962.
155. See above.
156. *SS-Führungshauptamt*, 5 September 1944, Amt II Org.Abtl.Ia/II Tgb.Nr.2880/44 g.Kdos. Betr. Reformation of the 14.Waffen-Gren.Div. der SS (galician Nr.1). NA T175 roll 141, frames 2669182 – 2669183.
157. Heike, Eng. ed., op. cit., p.63.
158. *SS-Standartenführer und Oberst der Schutzpolizei* Rudolph Pannier: born 10 July 1897, in Gera, Thuringen. SS Nr. 465,891. Not a party member. The son of an electrical engineer, during WWI he volunteered for service in IX Corps and fought on both the Western and Eastern fronts. After the war he was a member of the German *Freikorps*, before joining the *Schutzpolizei* in Hamburg. At the beginning of the German-Soviet war in 1941 Pannier had risen to the rank of *Hauptmann* and was serving as a company commander in the 4th SS *Polizei* Division which was attached to Army Group North, on the Leningrad sector (Novgorod – Tschdovo) of the Eastern Front. On 27 January 1942, he was awarded the Iron Cross 2nd Class and on 5 February Iron Cross 1st Class. He was promoted to the rank of *SS-Sturmbannführer* and *Major der Schutzpolizei* and on 11 May, 1942, as commander of the 1st Battalion of the SS-*Polizeischutzenregiment* 2 he was awarded the *Ritterkreuz* for his bravery in combat. He was promoted again to the rank of *SS-Standartenführer* and while recuperating from his many wounds received the German Cross in Gold. In September 1944 he was transferred to the 14th Galician Division at Neuhammer. (See Ernst-Günter Kratschmer *Der Ritterkreuzträger der Waffen-SS*, Plesse Verlag, Gottingen, 1957, pp.318-321, and Jost W. Schneider *Verleihung Genehmigt!/Their Honour was Loyalty!* R James Bender Publishing, San Jose, CA, 1977, pp.264-265. A former Ukrainian officer who served as a staff officer with WGR 31 suggests that because of his wounds, which had left him with a permanent limp, Pannier often took morphine injections to which he later became addicted. As a result "he often gave foolish and unreasonable orders". Hawrylak, op.cit., p.17.
159. Werner Heinz, born 20 September 1914, SS Nr. 405 814.
160. Wuttig later wrote an account of his experiences, entitled *Auf dem wege in den Ural*, in Soviet captivity, from which he was finally released in October 1955. AA.
161. *SS-Obersturmbannführer* Carl (also spelt Karl) Georg Heinrich Marks, born 17 September 1903, SS Nr. 257,785, Party Nr. 3,601,899. Marks, whose military service had included spells with the *Ersatz* battalion of the 1st SS *Panzer* Division *'Leibstandarte SS Adolf Hitler'* and later with the 24th *Gebirgs (Karstjäger)* Waffen-SS Division, was a much decorated veteran. He held the Iron Cross 1st and 2nd class, and the *Infanterie-Sturmabzeichen* in Bronze, amongst several other awards. He had previously fought in Poland and on both the Western and Eastern fronts. See *Personal-Akte* NA A3343-SSO-299A.
162. *SS-Obersturmbannführer* Karl Wildner, born 17 December 1897, in Königshof, Germany. Affectionately known by the Ukrainians as 'Papa', Wildner was a first-class officer who was very popular with the Ukrainians, partly because he insisted on speaking to the soldiers in his native language rather than in German. Wildner had 30 years of military service behind him prior to joining the 14th Galician Division, his most recent commission as an officer in the Slovak Army. See *Personal-Akte* Karl Wildner NA, A3343-SSO-246B.
163. Ludwig Josef Alexander Kuchta, born 4 August 1909, in Georgenberg. Kuchta was a long serving and combat experienced soldier who transferred to the Galician Division from the Slovak army. He already held the *Tapferkeitsmedaille* 2nd and 3rd classes and the Iron Cross 2nd Class when he was awarded the Iron Cross 1st Class on 14 March 1943, while fighting in the Caucasus with I/21 Battalion. From November to December 1943 he held the post of *Garnisonoffizier* in Odessa. See *Personal-Akte* NA A3343-SSO-223A.
164. *SS-Sturmbannführer* Albert Czermin, born 18 April 1909.
165. *SS-Sturmbannführer* Elemer Scholtz, born 6 June 1909, Michelsdorf. See *Personal-Akte* NA A3343 SSO-097B.
166. Wilhelm Podlesch, born 27 January 1902. Party Nr. 1, 095, 485. Holder of the Iron Cross 2nd Class. See *Personal-Akte* NA A3343-SSO-385A.
167. Alfred Bisanz as head of the *Wehrausschuss* Galicia refers to his concern about the suitability of these NCOs in a letter to Freitag, dated 8 November 1944. ABFC. As was always the case throughout the Division's existence, several of the replacement German cadre personnel who continued to arrive until December 1944, had unsavoury service records.
168. Heike, Eng. ed., op. cit., p.64.
169. The Ukrainians had good reason to feel disgruntled. In his memoirs Heike notes that when the Division was first formed Ukrainian officers had lagged behind because of their age and inexperience. After the battle of Brody the situation was reversed and the German officers and NCOs lagged behind because of their youth, lack of practical experience and rapid rise through the ranks. Ibid., p 66.
170. Palienko was killed at Brody. Brygidyr was removed "for the common good". See Ferkuniak, op.cit., p.31. See footnote 187 below.
171. Born 12 August 1899, Kalush, Galicia. Served briefly in Austrian Army then in the first battalion of the Ukrainian Galician Army. In 1930 he was elected as a candidate to the Polish parliament (Sejm). As a member of the Military Board he was

responsible for the recruitment of officers and later liaison with the Division.

172. Verbally to author, M. Scharko, 4 December 1999.
173. While some Ukrainians were promoted to the rank of *Waffen-Unterscharführer* they almost always held the lowest rank of *Waffen-Rottenführer*.
174. The figures for the relative strengths of the various categories as of 10 September 1944, were:

	Regulation strength	*Actual strength*
Officers	480	148
NCOs	2587	572
Men	11622	5796

The breakdown for the *A.u.E.*Rgt. 14. was 45 officers, 293 NCOs and 7196 men, total 7534. See *Der Reichsführer-SS Adjutantur, Feldkommandostelle, den* 16.9.1944, Kdo.Stab RF-SS Tgb.Nr.Ia/3765/44 g.Kdos. *Stärkemeldungen Stand vom*: 10 September 1944. See T175 roll 141 frame2668956.

175. See above.
176. The figures for the relative strengths of the various categories as of 20 September 1944, were:

	Regulation strength	*Actual strength*
Officers	480	261
NCOs	2587	673
Men	11622	11967

See *Stärkemeldungen Stand vom* 20 September 1944. See T175 roll 141 frame 2668949.

177. *The Formation and History of the 1st Company/I Battalion/30th Regiment/1st Ukrainian Division (14 Galizien)*, Roman Herasymowycz (unpublished paper), p.1.
178. The Training and Reserve Regiment was only officially incorporated into the Division as part of the order to transfer the Division to Slovakia. Even then the transfer of cadre personnel (staff officers, and NCOs) from it to the Division was still expressly forbidden.
179. For example, an estimated 50-60% of the Division's Training and Reserve Regiment, the strength of which stood at around 7000 men, comprised east Ukrainian youths. See V. Gotskyj, 'Na Slovachchyni' *Visti*, Nr.9 (11), p.5, 'Vyprava na partyzan u Slovachchyni', Nos. 2-3 (16-17) p. 11. The Military Board was fully cognisant of the fact that large groups were volunteering for the Division to avoid being drafted into the Red Army as is evident from the discussion that took place on 21 June 1944. It should also be noted that during the same discussion the Military Board stated that it would be willing to agree to a 'general mobilisation' but the Ukrainian Central Committee rejected it, as it was a 'Political matter'. See 'Minutes of the Military Board Galicia', *Shevchenko Scientific Society of Canada*, Vol.30, 1993.
180. See *Abschrift*, 14.*Waffen-Gren. Div. der SS (Ukrain.Nr.*1), VI, Div.St.Qu. d.17.11.44, *Betr: Weltanschauliche*. ABFC.
181. These were taken principally from the counties of Buchach, Pidhaitsi and Rohatyn, where the German frontline had stood. The author's own father was among those taken in this way. Another man from his village taken within days of the author's father wrote, "On 28 June, 1944, Hungarian soldiers rounded us up and took us from our homes to a camp in our village (Koropec). From there we were taken to L'viv and then we were escorted by members of our own Division to Neuhammer." Q12 Sadiwskyj.
182. Other Waffen-SS Divisions in which young Galician Ukrainians were known to have served included 5th SS *Panzer* Division *Wiking*, 18th *SS-Freiwilligen Panzergrenadierdivision 'Horst Wessel'*, 9th SS *Panzer* Division *'Hohenstaufen'*, and 10th SS *Panzer* Division *'Frundsberg'*, all of which had been active (or had elements active) in western Ukraine in the spring and summer of 1944. In July 1944, a further 900 men from the 14th Reserve Regiment were sent to the 22nd *Freiwilligen-Kavalleriedivision der SS 'Maria Theresa'* and subsequently took part in the defence of Budapest in November 1944. The only survivors of this group were those who deserted or had sustained injuries and were sent to hospitals in Hungary. Interview Marian Kohut, Toronto, 1 June 1993. See also Vasyl Horbatyuk, *Visti Kombatanta*, No.3, 1977, pp.54-55. To fill their depleted ranks the Germans evacuated entire villages and took all the young men for service. Letter to author, O. Sokolskyj, 11 September 1992.
183. By way of example, upon arrival at Neuhammer a through physical examination was carried out on those taken from the village of Koropec in June 1944, after which eight were rejected as unfit for service. S. Dmytryk interview, Rushden, England 21 October 1990. Likewise, a number of UPA soldiers were discharged in May/June 1944 because of injury or prolonged periods of sickness and were advised to join the Division. Letter to author, O. Sokolskyj, 9 January 1997.
184. Verbally to author, Drazniowskyj, 4 May 1996. Ferkuniak, op.cit., pp.,30-31.
185. In the Minutes of the Meeting of the Military Board, held in Lüben on 26-27 October, morale in the Division was described as "very bad". It was also noted that "the German NCOs do not respect the Ukrainian officers" and that there was "no common ground between the Germans and the Ukrainians". Two major contributory factors in this respect were identified as the unbearable behaviour of the German officers corps and because there had been no evolution in the German policies towards the Ukraine/Ukrainians, pp. 114-122. ABFC.
186. According to Heike, as a sign of disapproval no message of congratulations was received from Dr Wächter, or the Ukrainian Central Committee. Heike, Eng. ed., op.cit., p.71. A message from the Military Board to this effect was not sent until 8 November 1944. See *Der Leiter des Wehrausschuss Galizien, z.zt. Kracow, 8 November 1944*. ABFC.
187. Freitag was nominated for the award by General Raus on 23 August 1944. The award was approved by Himmler on 16 September and made on 30 September 1944. See *Vorschlag fur die Vorleihung des Ritterkreuzes des Eisernen Kreuzes Verliehen 30.9.44: Nr. 3692. uber SS-Brigadeführer Freitag KDr 14. Waffen-Gren-Div. der SS (galiz.Nr.1). Der Reichsführer-SS, Reichsführer-SS Personl. Stab Verb. Offz.* b.OKH/PA/P5 *Eingang* 16 September 1944 Tgb.Nr.843/449/1. (Proposal for the awarding of the Knight's Cross of the Iron Cross) Also, the accompanying review by *Der Oberbefehlshaber* A.H.Qu. 23.8.1944 *der 3. Panzerarmee* General Raus. NA A3343-SSO-220. Public announcement of the award was made in *Das Schwarze Korps*, Berlin, 28 December 1944.
188. See *SS-Personalhauptamt* II W, II W II – *Abteilung* 3, Pe/P. Berlin January 1945, *Betr. Waffen-Hauptsturmführer* Michajlo Brygidyr (sic.), *geb*.24.9.02; *Bezug.: Dortiges Schreiben* Alc (1) Az. W.-SS Co. *vom* 28.11.44, *An das Reichsicherheitshauptamt, Amt* I A 1, *Personal-Akte*, NA A3343-SSO-112. According to Rev. Dr Ivan Hrynokh, after his discharge from the Division in late 1944, Brygidyr managed to make his way to the western Lemko region of Galicia. There he took over command of a newly formed UPA company which, according to his orders, he led to the Carpathian Mountains in Moravia. See article by Reverend Dr Hrynokh entitled 'Division 'Galicia' and the Ukrainian Underground Movement', in Oleh Lysia, *Brody: Zbirnyk stattei i narysiv* ('Brody: A collection of Articles and sketches'), Munich, Bratstvo kol. Voiakiv Pershoi UD UNA, 1951, p.53. He survived the war and emigrated to Canada where he died, in Toronto, on 14 July 1966.
189. Ferkuniak, op.cit., p.31.
190. Division's *Tagesbefehl*, 19.10.44. An original copy of this document is in the author's possession.
191. *Waffen-Untersturmführer* Yurij Krokhmaliuk who served with the Division's staff suggests that prior to the Battle of Brody, Freitag would never have singled out the Ukrainians for special mention.
192. In a speech to his officers on the same theme, i.e. his receipt of the *Ritterkreuz*, made at Christmas 1944 in Zilina, Slovakia, Freitag also overlooked his previous complaints about the Ukrainians, while at the same time acknowledging their 'heroic bravery' whose sacrifices and valour made possible the distinction [that he now wore]. Hawrylak, op.cit., p.15.
193. *Kommandeur* 14. *Waffen-Gren. Div. der SS (galiz.Nr.*1) Div. St. Qu., 28.10.1944, 1357/44, *Betr: Politische Führung der Truppe*. ABFC.
194. Heike, Eng. ed., op. cit., p.68.
195. Ibid., p.69.
196. The Germans drafted youths from all occupied nations between 14-18 years of age to undergo pre-military training as *Flakhelfer* (Flak auxiliaries) with the Luftwaffe. The programme was administered by the *Hauptstelle* (Main Office) of the Hitler Youth organisation in Berlin. Recruitment and training were the responsibility of *Hauptbannführer* Nickel and the newly formed *Dienstelle Nickel* which had a staff of about 100 officers, 200 NCOs and men, and over 100 boys and girls from the *Hitlerjugend*. This organisation operated through 3 branches: *Kommando Nord* (Baltic), *Kommando Mitte* (Belorus and East Ukraine) and *Kommando Sud (Generalgouvernement)*. *Dienstelle Nickel* delivered the conscripts to the *Oberkommando der Luftwaffe* (OKL) for distribution through *Luftgaukommandos* (LGK) which undertook training as required. Neither the Ukrainian Central Committee nor the Military Board approved of the programme but Alfred Bisanz, acting on his own initiative, issued a poster under the names of members of the Military Board (i.e. Zeleny and Navrotskyj) without their knowledge or consent. For the Military Board's involvement with recruitment of Flak auxiliaries see 'Minutes of the Military Board', entry for 13 June 1944.
197. The two respective groups who were geographically separated, were also distinguished by arm brassards in the Ukrainian national colours of blue and gold, bearing either the Galician lion emblem (for Galician Ukrainians) or Trident emblem (for those from the *Reichkommisariat Ukraine)* and diamond-shaped cap badges in those colours.
198. By way of an inducement the Galician recruits only were promised that their schooling would continue throughout their training and service, although the evidence suggests that this was honoured only in part. 6547 boys and 1121 girls from Galicia were registered although the total number employed was in the region of approximately 14000.
199. For an interesting and detailed account of the personal experiences of a Ukrainian youth who joined the Galician Division having first undergone training at this camp see *Victim of Circumstance*, Michael Paziuk, Bridge Books, Wrexham, Clwyd, 1993. See also P. Pilkiv 'Ukrainian Youths in the Division', *Visti Kombatanta*, No.2, 1995. I would like to express my gratitude to Mr Paziuk for placing his comprehensive photographic collection on this subject at my disposal for the purposes of my research.
200. As the result of an order dated 28 June 1944, all Waffen-SS divisions lost their *Flak Abteilungen*. See Jüttner's circular, *Führungshauptamt Amt* II Org.Abtl.Ia/II Tgb.Nr.1757/44g.Kdos. *Betr: Kriegsgliederungen der 14.Galiz.SS-Freiw. Div. und der Waffen-Gren.Divisionen-SS*. 28 Juni 1944, *Geheime Kommandosache*. NA T175 roll 141, frames 2669258-2669260.
201. Letter to author, 15 March 1994, M. Paslij. *SS-Obersturmführer* Freit commanded the 3.7cm battery. Letter to author, R. Kolisnyk, 10 February 1997.
202. Born 20 March 1909, Party Nr. 8,348, 592. Drapatz was formerly a *Zugführer* with a motorised *Feldgend-Truparneriep* of the 15th *Waffen-Gren.Div.* SS (*Lett.Nr.* 1). For Freitag's favourable appraisal of Drapatz see 14.*Waffen-Gren.Div.der* SS (*gal.Nr.*1) IIa, Div.St.Qu. den 4 November 1944, *Beurteilungsnotiz fur SS-Untersturmführer* Drapatz, See *Personal-Akte* Wilhelm Drapatz, NA A3343-SSO-162.
203. Moroz verbally 21 June 1999, and letter 17 September 1999.
204. Heike, Eng. ed., op. cit., p.69.
205. V. Gotskyj, 'Na Slovachchyni', *Visti*, Nr.9 (11) p.5, 'Vyprava na partyzan u Slovachchyni', nos. 2-3 (16-17), p 11.
206. Letter to author, O. Sokolskyj, 14 July 1992, and verbally to author, M. Sadiwskyj, 24 February 1997.
207. Heike, Eng. ed., op. cit., p.68.
208. The official complement of nurses was 20 for the hospital and a further 10 for the Division's dental unit. See *O.U., den 16 November 1944, Betr. Besprechung des Div. Arztes mit den leitenden Arzt von Ukrainischen-Wehrausschuss D. Bilozor, Wolodymyr*, ABFC.
209. Letter to author, O. Sokolskyj, 20 August 1994.
210. The Military Board had relocated its head quarters in Lüben and established three additional branches in Vienna, Berlin and Cracow. See circular letter issued by Bisanz dated 14 September 1944. ABFC.

211. Prior to Brody a significant number of families of Division members did receive monetary assistance from the German authorities – as is evidenced by an alphabetical list entitled, *Leistungsnachweisung über von der Kreishauptmannschaft Lemberg-Land verauslagten Familienunterhalt für den Monat April 1944, für SS.Schützen Division Galizien*, AA. In his memoirs Heike explains the failure to provide the soldiers' families with the aid to which they were entitled on two main contributory factors. There was sabotage by lower-echelon Polish functionaries in the German local administration, and on the Ukrainian soldiers themselves who "regardless of the constant reminders and published guidelines, did not send the requisite formal requests for assistance or did not complete them properly." Heike, Eng. ed., op.cit., p.18. In any event, by September 1944 sabotage by Polish functionaries was no longer applicable.

Chapter 8

1. For a detailed study of the origins of the uprising, the forces involved and their subsequent military actions, see Wolfgang Venohr, *Aufstand in der Tatra: Der Kampf um die Slowakei 1939-44*, Athenaum, 1979.
2. In a report on the situation in Slovakia, dated 7 November 1944, following the suppression of the uprising, the list of captured or destroyed weaponry included: 2 armoured trains, 267 aircraft (63 of them usable) and 104 tanks. *Der Wehrmachtbevollmächtigte beim Deutschen Staatsminister für Böhmen u. Mähren u. Befehlshaber im Wehrkreis Böhmen u. Mähren* Nr.1878/44 *geheim. Feindlageoffizier*. Prag, *den* 7.11.44, Betr. *Lage in der Slowakei*. Statni ustredni archiv v Praze (hereafter abbreviated SUAP).
3. This brigade was formed by the Soviets, from the Czechs who served in the German army, became prisoners of war and were parachuted into Slovakia in the Zarnovica region. See M. Matchak, 'Z boiv kurenia 'Wildner'' *Visti*, September-October 1951, No.9, pp.3-5.
4. Venohr, op.cit., pp.211-212.
5. This *Kampfgruppe* commanded by *SS-Obersturmbannführer* Klotz, had a strength of 2200 men and was made up of staff and cadets from the *SS-Panzergrenadier-Schule* Kienschlag in the protectorate of Bohemia and Moravia.
6. *Kampfgruppe* Schafer consisted of 1200 troops of the 18th *SS-Freiwillige Panzergrenadierdivision 'Horst Wessel'*, supported by a reinforced battalion of 1200 men from the 86th Infantry Division. For a detailed day-by-day account of the activities of *KGr.* Schafer during the campaign in Slovakia see 'Einsatz der Kampfgruppe Schafer beim Aufstand in der Slowakei 31.August bis 10.Oktober 1944', in Tieke & Rebstock, op.cit., pp.61-80.
7. This unit was made up of 6000 regular Army men from replacement units of the 85th and the 178th infantry divisions. According to Venohr, between them these units had the additional armoured support of 28 tanks and 16 assault guns. Venohr, op.cit., p.212.
8. In all probability, Berger was appointed to deal with uprising on 31 August 1944, because he had been instrumental in the establishment of the collaborationist Hlinka puppet regime in Slovakia in 1939.
9. Born 12 September 1898, in Augsburg, tried and condemned to death. Executed 1948. SS Nr. 463, 093. Former HSSPf – *Wehrkreise* XI (Hanover).
10. The Division's command received formal notification on 22 September 1944, when a telegram from the SS-FHA arrived confirming the *Kampfgruppe* was to be sent to Slovakia at the earliest opportunity. SS-FHA/Amt II Org.Abtl. Ia/II – Tgb.Nr. 3045/44 g.Kdos. v. 22.9.1944 *Betr: Zuführung eines vesrt. Bataillons der* 14. *W.Gren.Div. der SS (galiz. Nr. 1) nach* Pressburg. NA, T175, roll 141, frames 2669159-2669160.
11. Matchak, op.cit., pp.3-5. These men replaced several German officers and NCOs who had volunteered but opted out when they discovered the destination of the battle group. R. Drazniowskyj, verbally to author, 7 December 1996.
12. Interview, M. Klymchuk London, 28 November 1996, and verbally to author, R. Drazniowskyj, 7 December 1996. M. Matchak, op.cit., incorrectly cites the strength of the *Kampfgruppe* as being 900 men.
13. Heike, Eng. ed., op. cit., p.73.
14. Letter to author, W. Popadynec, 11 March 1998.
15. The infantry company commanders were 9th Company: *SS-Untersturmführer* Lilinger (after he was wounded, *SS-Oberscharführer* Mitzinger, and later *Waffen-Untersturmführer* Zeniuk). 10th Company: *Waffen-Hauptsturmführer* Tatarskyj. 11th Company: *Waffen-Oberstführer* Wolodymyr Kosak. 12th Company: *SS-Obersturmführer* Schneller. Artillery commanded by *W. Unstuf.* Michael Dlaboha.
16. The fact that the *Kampfgruppe* was provided with second-rate equipment was confirmed by an officer and a former non-commissioned officer who served with the unit. Letter to author, O. Kulchyskyj, 7 January 1997, verbally R. Drazniowskyj, 7 December 1996. As an example, for the most part the infantry companies were armed with the older MG 34 machine guns. Only the heavy weapons company was equipped with the newer MG 42, however ammunition for the weapon was in such short supply that its usefulness was limited. Verbally to author, M. Prymak, 28 November 1997.
17. Interview, M. Klymchuk, London, 29 April 1997. Heike states that the *Kampfgruppe* was allocated three trains. Heike, Eng. ed., op. cit., p.73.
18. Entries on pp. 4 and 7 in the *Soldbuch* belonging to *SS-Obersturmführer* Wolodymyr Kosak, an Ukrainian company commander who served with the battlegroup, describe the unit as *Einsatz Battalion* Wildner. AA.
19. Interview, M. Klymchuk, London, 29 April 1997. He was replaced by *SS-Oberscharführer* Mitzinger.
20. Verbally to author, O. Kulchyskyj, 24 December 1996. Letter to author, R. Drazniowskyj, 12 March 1997.
21. Letter to author, R. Drazniowskyj, 29 June 1994.
22. *Kampfgruppe Wildner* (an unpublished paper), Roman Drazniowskyj, pp.1-2. See also M. Matchak, op.cit., pp.3-5.
23. Ibid. Letter to the author, O. Kulchyskyj, 9 April 1997.
24. Letter to author, M. Prymak, 6 April 1998.
25. Himmler actually arrived in the Slovakian capital of Bratislava, in person, on 4 October 1944.
26. This Soviet offensive was undertaken by the armies that formed part of the 4th Ukrainian Front.
27. *SS-Sonder Regiment 'Dirlewanger'* arrived in Slovakia from Poland fresh from its participation in the suppression of the Warsaw rising. For details see George H. Stein, *The Waffen-SS: Hitler's Elite Guard at War 1939-1945*, Ithaca, New York, 1966, pp.264-270.
28. The figures for the strength of those two units are quoted in *Der Wehrmachtbevollmächtigte...* No. 207/44 geh. Kdos. Prag, den 12.10.44, *Feindlageoffizier Betr: Eigene Kräftegliederung in der Slowakei*. For further details and comparative strengths of other reserve and security units see Venohr, op.cit., pp.272-273.
29. The order stated that with effect from 1 October 1944, the *SS-Gren.Ausb.u.Ers.Rgt.* 14 was to come directly under the Division's command. The transfer of officers, NCOs, and men of the staff personnel to the Division remained prohibited.
30. Secret telegram from *SS-Standartenführer* Ruoff, FS SS-FHA/Amt II Org.Abtl. Ia/II/ Tgb.Nr.3411/44 g.Kdos. v.28.9.1944 Betr.14. W.Gren. Div. d. SS, NA T175 roll 141, frames 2669143 – 2669144.
31. *Der Wehrmachtbevollmächtigte...* No. 207/44 geh. Kdos. Prag, den 12.10.44.
32. Heike, Eng. ed., op. cit., p.76.
33. The movement of WGR 30 to Slovakia ahead of the remainder of the Division was confirmed to the author verbally by P. Jacyna, 27 January 1997, and V. Veryha, 31 January 1997.
34. Heike, Eng. ed., op. cit., p.75.
35. The Training and Reserve Regiment took a full two weeks to transfer to Slovakia beginning on 1 October until 15 October, 1944, *SS-Grenadier-Ausbildungs-und Ersatz-Regiment* 14 (*ukrain. Ausbildungs-Regiment* 1) AA.
36. *Der Wehrmachtbevollmächtigte...* No. 207/44 geh. Kdos. Prag, den 12.10.44.
37. The command appointments within the Artillery Regiment were as follows:
    CommanderBeyersdorff *SS-Stadtf.*
    Adjutant Muller *SS-Hauptf.*
    Reg.Doctor R. Dziubanowskyj *Waffen-Obstuf.*
    Reg.Vet Kiszko *Waffen-Obstuf.*
    Reg. Chaplain Rev. E. Korduba *Waffen-Obstuf.*
    Abtl. CO:
    I. (HQ: Rajecke Teplice) O. Glaess *SS-Ostuf.*
    II. (HQ: Rajec) Dlaboha *Waffen-Ustuf.*
    III. (HQ: Rajec) Schesinger *SS-Hauptstuf.*
    IV. (HQ: Lietavska Luczka) Sparsam *SS-Hauptstuf.*
    The Structure, Organisation and Command of the 14 Artillery Regiment in Slovakia September/November 1944, A. Hawirko, unpublished paper. AA.
38. In Vrutky the Pioneer Battalion occupied the barracks of the former Slovakian army. Its staff at the time were as follows:
    Commander Remberger, Josef (Sepp) *SS-Stubaf.*
    Adjutant Glockner *SS-Ostuf.*
    z.b.V. Balzarek *SS-Ustuf.*
    1.*Verw. Fhr.* Zaborowski *SS-Ostuf.*
    2. -"- Martyniuk *Waffen-Ustuf.*
    Btl. Doctor Cehelskyj, Myhailo *Waffen-Standartenoberjunker*
    Kp.CO
    1. Coy. Krause, Heinz *SS-Ostuf.*
    2." Dzillum, Wilhelm *SS-Ostuf.*
    3." Dombrowskyi, Alfred von *SS-Ostuf.*
39. 1st Company was stationed in Varin, 2nd Company in Krasniany, 3rd Company in Bela and 4th in Terchova. The Battalion HQ was based in a former Hungarian castle in Krasniany. Letter to author, Dr W. Krywulak, 31 January 1997.
40. *SS-Grenadier-Ausbildungs-und Ersatz-Regiment* 14 (*ukrain.Aus.-Reg.*1). AA. 1st Btl. was quartered in Czerny, 2nd Btl. in Turzovka, 3rd Btl. in Oscadnica and the Reserve *Ersatz* Battalion in Cadca.
41. *Der Wehrmachtbevollmächtigte...* No. 1703/44 *geheim. Feindlageoffizier.* Prag, den 16.10.44, *Betr. Lage in der Slowakei. Abendmeldung des Dtsch. Befehlshabers Slowakei vom* 15.10.44.
42. Ibid., Nr. 207/44 geh. Kdos. Prag, den 12.10.44, *Feindlageoffizier Betr: Eigene Kräftegliederung in der Slowakei.*
43. Herasymowycz, op.cit., pp.1-2.
44. *Der Wehrmachtbevollmächtigte...* No. 1719/44 *geheim. Feindlageoffizier.* Prag, den 18.10.44, *Betr. Lage in der Slowakei. Abendmeldung des Dtsch. Befehlshabers Slowakei vom* 17.10.44. Nr.1725/44 *geheim Feindlageoffizier.* Prag, den 19.10.44, *Abendmeldung des Dtsch. Befehlshabers Slowakei vom* 18.10.44.
45. Ibid. Nr.1759/44 *geheim. Feindlageoffizier.* Prag, den 24.10.44, *Betr. Lage in der Slowakei. Abendmeldung des Dtsch. Befehlshabers Slowakei vom* 23.10.44.
46. In view of the earlier instruction that any additional combat groups and their deployment against partisans was to take place only with the express authorisation of the head of the SS-FHA, it is likely that the order originated from Höfle.
47. Heike, Eng. ed., op. cit., pp.78-79.
48. Letter to author, [Maziar] 24 March 1997.
49. Ibid.
50. *Der Wehrmachtbevollmächtigte,* No. 1766/44 *geheim. Feindlageoffizier.* Prag, den 25.10.44, *Betr. Lage in der Slowakei. Abendmeldung des Dtsch. Befehlshabers Slowakei vom* 24.10.44.
51. Ibid., Nr.1780/44 *geheim. Feindlageoffizier.* Prag, den 27.10.44, *Betr. Lage in der Slowakei. Abendmeldung des Dtsch. Befehlshabers Slowakei vom* 26.10.44.
52. Ibid., Nr.1798/44 *geheim. Feindlageoffizier.* Prag, den 29.10.44, *Betr. Lage in der Slowakei, Abendmeldung des Dtsch. Befehlshabers Slowakei vom* 28.10.44.
53. Heike, Eng. ed., op. cit., p.79.
54. Letter to author, E. Shypailo [Maziar] 24 March 1997.
55. Interview, M. Klymchuk, London 7 October 1990, and Myron Matchak, op.cit., pp.3-5.
56. Letter to author, O. Kulchyskyj, 5 March 1997.
57. A former member of *KGr.* Wittenmeyer serving with the 1st Platoon of the 13./WGR 31, recounted how his platoon took more than one company of Slovak partisans as prisoners, amongst which were two American airmen. Letter to author, E. Shypailo [Maziar], 24 March 1997.
58. Amongst the weaponry obtained in addition to the rifles were the much-prized Soviet-made Finka machine pistols and some Czech-made light machine guns. Letter to author, O. Kulchyck, 7 January 1997, and letter to author, W. Popadynec, 25 March 1998.

59. Letter to author, M. Prymak, 6 April 1998.
60. Letter to author, W. Popadynec, 11 March 1998.
61. Tieke and Rebstock, op.cit., pp.93-94.
62. See *'Grenzbote'* 1 November 1944, ABFC. The article incorrectly refers to the *den verbanden der 14 SS Panzerdivision*.
63. The actual wording of the announcement dated 8 November 1944 was *"Die organisierte Aufstandbewegung in der Slowakei ist zusammengebrochen und zerschlagen..."*
64. Drazniowskyj, op.cit., pp.2-3, letter to author, 6 October 1997, verbally to author, 21 November 1997.
65. During one such engagement a platoon of the 12th Company together with a platoon of pioneers was assigned the task of surrounding the village of Ture, and capturing a group of 200 partisans who were reported to be hiding there. In the early morning hours the Ukrainian group formed a ring around the village and entered it only to discover that most of the partisans had fled the day before. During the subsequent house search around 30 partisans were captured including a Soviet colonel commissar, who subsequently betrayed the hiding places of generals Jan Golian and Rudolph Viest during his interrogation. The Ukrainian commander was awarded the Iron Cross 2nd Class. O. Kulchyskyj, *Visti Kombatanta*, Nr. 4, 1990 and letter to the author, 7 January 1997.
66. Letter to author, O. Kulchyskyj, 3 March 1997 and W. Popadynec, 25 March 1998.
67. Drazniowskyj, op.cit., pp.2-3.
68. Ferkuniak, op.cit., p.15.
69. Letter to author, W. Popadynec, 11 March 1998 and 25 March 1998. During the campaign 20 soldiers were sent as reinforcements to the *Kampfgruppe* to replace losses and a further 11 men were killed outright or seriously wounded as the result of a direct hit on a platoon by a mortar round. Letters to author, O. Kulchyskyj, 7 January 1997, 20 January 1997 and 5 March 1997. A few desertions also occurred amongst the enlisted men who in all probability deserted in the hope of returning to UPA. Interview, M. Klymchuk, 7 October 1990, and R. Drazniowskyj, verbally to author, 7 December 1996.
70. Typical of the other combat awards given on this occasion to both Germans and Ukrainians were the *Infanterie-Sturmabzeichen* (Infantry Assault Badge) and the *Verwundetenabzeichen* (wound badge).
71. Ukrainian officer recipients of the Iron Cross 2nd Class included O. Kulchyskyj, (12th Coy.) *Waffen-Hauptsturmführer* W. Tatarskyj (10th Coy.) and *Waffen-Untersturmführer* E. Korczak.
72. Seven outright, ten for bravery in the field and fifteen for being wounded in battle. Letters to author, W. Popadynec, 11 March 1998 and 25 March 1998.
73. Heike, Eng. ed., op. cit., p.79.
74. Secret telex from *SS-Standartenführer* Ruoff, *SS-Führungshauptamt, Amt* II Org.Abtl.Ia/II, Tgb.Nr.5218/44 g.Kdos. 31.12.44. NA T175 roll 141 frames 2668967-2668968.
75. Heike, Eng. ed., op. cit., p.77. The list of spoils and their distribution to the German units involved stated that 'In the fighting in west and middle of Slovakia, the enemy lost over 4000 counted dead and 15000 prisoners. Taken or destroyed were 2 armoured trains, 267 aircraft (63 of them usable) 104 tanks (almost all destroyed in battle), 309 guns (from this number the SS 13. *Pz.Gren.Div Gal.* Nr. 1's (sic.) heavy artillery *Abteilung* was fully equipped).' See *Der Wehrmachtbevollmächtigte*, Nr.1878/44 *geheim. Feindlageoffizier*. Prag, den 7.11.44, *Betr. Lage in der Slowakei*.
76. Ibid., p.79.
77. Letter to author, O. Sokolskyj, 23 June 1992. WGR 29 received over twenty vehicles of all types.
78. *Der Wehrmachtbevollmächtigte*, No. 1878/44 *geheim. Feindlageoffizier*. Prag, den 7.11.44, *Betr. Lage in der Slowakei*.
79. When he realised that further organised resistance was impossible, on 29th October General Rudolph Viest issued his last order dissolving the 1st Czechoslovak Army and directing that all the remaining units change over to partisan methods.
80. To cite as a typical example, a mobile *Ski-Jagdzug* (ski platoon) comprising three sections, each of 15 men, was formed from the staff company of WGR 31. It was well equipped with automatic weapons for armed reconnaissance patrols. Hawrylak, op.cit., p.17.
81. Letter to author, O. Sokolskyj, 2 April 1997.
82. Verbally to author, M. Scharko, 27 January 2000.
83. The locally raised anti-partisan units did not take part in any resulting engagements. Heike, Eng. ed., op. cit., p.82.
84. 5/II/WGR 30, Zenon Kuk, unpublished memoirs, p 22.
85. Heike blames failure to communicate on one abortive action that took place east of Zilina and north of the Vah valley involving the entrapment of around 200 partisans by the Division's forces. In this instance the partisans managed to escape during the night when the Ukrainian commander of the 7/II/WGR 29 went into a tavern to warm himself. For dereliction of duty he was convicted by a field court and sentenced to 8 years but survived the war and lives in the USA. Ibid., p.82.
86. One amusing incident was told to the author by an Ukrainian platoon commander who found himself in the same room as an Ukrainian radio operator when a message was received from battalion command to which the Ukrainian kept replying *Jawohl! Jawohl!* ('Yes sir! yes sir!') implying that he understood perfectly the instructions that he was being given. When the message had ended the radio operator turned to his comrade and said, "What the hell did he say?" Verbally to author, M. Prymak, 16 October 1997.
87. Heike, Eng. ed., op. cit., p.82.
88. "I was stationed in the village of Bield with the 14th Field Reserve Battalion. We mainly performed guard duties, protecting the village and surrounding area from communist partisan attacks. From time to time expeditions were made into the Carpathian mountains on the Slovak side. On one such occasion, our unit caught a partisan and he was held captive within our unit pending transfer to Divisional HQ. The prisoner asked my brother, who was on duty at the guardhouse (a private house in the village) for permission to go outside the building to the toilet at night. My brother took him outside and allowed him to escape after having fired a few shots into the air to protect himself against further investigation." Letter to author, O. Sokolskyj, 14 July 1992.
89. In a letter to the author, dated 24 May 1994, a former medical practitioner serving with the Division's reserve battalion, Dr W. Krywulak related how in the village of Bela he treated a Soviet partisan for a compound shotgun fracture of the leg by the application of a leg cast.
90. During a routine search of some houses, a few rifles were found in a Roman Catholic pastor's house. Although the penalty for such an offence in German occupied territories was the death sentence the pastor was not reported and therefore escaped punishment. Letter to author, O. Sokolskyj, 14 July 1992.
91. Heike, Eng. ed., op. cit., p.81. The *Ostturkischer Waffenverband* was a Waffen-SS formation formed from Muslim volunteers recruited in the Crimea and Caucasus.
92. Ibid., p 80. Interview, M. Klymchuk, London, 6 October 1990.
93. In his unpublished memoirs, Roman Hawrylak, a former Ukrainian officer serving with WGR 31, relates in detail one occasion during a large-scale operation during which an enlisted man stole a watch while searching a house for partisans. On receipt of a complaint by the owner of the watch, the regimental commander, *SS-Standartenführer* Rudolph Pannier, demanded that the death penalty be meted out for 'plundering'. After the submission of a character reference by the enlisted man's commanding officer and some heated argument, the sentence was commuted to service with a Waffen-SS penal detachment. Hawrylak, op.cit., p.20.
94. For example when it was first deployed in Slovakia 1/I/30 had four German NCOs (all transferred from 4th SS *Polizei* Division), all of whom had been replaced by Ukrainians by the end of 1944. Verbally to author, Roman Herasymowycz, 25 November 1997 and 29 November 1997.
95. S. Vasylko verbally to author, 23 December 1996. Q11 Padyk.
96. Q19 Sokolskyj.
97. Heike, Eng. ed., op. cit., p.86.
98. As an example, in an interview with the author M. Duskursky described in some detail how he helped steal a cartload of ammunition which was exchanged with friendly partisan forces for two pigs and a cow. Interview, M. Duskursky, Norwich, England, 16 February 1991.
99. One such episode of this nature was related to the author by a former member of 12/III/WGR 29. This particular incident occurred in Banska Bystrica and resulted in the discovery of an armed NKVD agent. Verbally to author, M. Prymak, 8 November 1997.
100. Zoglauer was promoted to the rank of *SS-Sturmbannführer* on 9 November 1944.
101. 14.*Waffen-Gren. Div. der SS* (*galiz.Nr.*1) Div.St.Qu. d.6.11.44, *Betr.: Feindliche Propaganda (als Lehrstoff zu verwenden)*, ABFC. See also circular letter from Freitag, to the Ukrainian soldiers about the situation at the front, especially guerrilla activities in Slovakia, the enemy's propaganda and agent provocateurs. 14.*Waffen-Gren. Div. der SS* (*ukrain.Nr.*1) VI; Div.St.Qu. d.7.12.44. ABFC.
102. Figure given by Heike, Eng. ed., op. cit., p.84.
103. Estimate based on entries in *Spysok Polyahlych WII-hiy Svitoviy Viyny v Boyakh proty CCCR*, Obyednannya Buvshykh Voyakiv u Veliki Brytaniyi, London 1953 ('Listing of the Killed Soldiers of the 1st Ukrainian Division and other Military Formations in WWII in the Battles Against the USSR') published the Association of Former Combatants in Great Britain, London, 1953. Each entry lists (wherever possible) name, place and date of birth, unit to which they belonged, location and time of death.
104. Eastern Ukrainians who had formerly served with the Red Army and who came to the '14. *Waffen-Grenadier-Division der SS* (*ukrainische Nr.*1)' from other German formations were prominent among those who deserted. Q1 Dmytryk.
105. *Spysok*.... Several examples of individuals who were shot were given during interviews with veterans of the Division including P. Maslij, Scunthorpe, England, 8 February 1992.
106. M. Hrycyszyn, *Smert Podolav* ('Death Cheated'), unpublished memoirs, p.102, and verbally to author, M. Prosac, 22 November 1991. It should be noted that various estimates ranging from 1000-1300 have been given in post war accounts by Ukrainians who were amongst the group that was assigned to the *'Wiking'* Division.
107. During the summer of 1944, Ukrainians who were enlisted into what was then the 14th *Waffen-Grenadier-Division der SS* (*galizische Nr.* 1) were taken to the Division's Training and Reserve Regiment, which had relocated at a new training ground Gross Kirchbaum near Frankfurt-an-der-Oder shortly after the Division left for Brody. From these men 1,200 were assigned to the *Wiking* for training.
108. After a preliminary medical examination some were transported firstly at the training ground at Gross Kirchbaum before being sent on to Heidelager which acted as an assembly point. Interview, Lev Babij, Toronto, 2 June 1993.
109. In the interim the group received a few weeks' training in the forests near two villages Laizau and Koglan (near Frankfurt-an-der-Oder). They stayed in tents and continued training. Since no supplies were available, local farmers were used to supply food. The remainder had to be begged from the local population.
110. Two officers from each of these regiments selected the men for his unit.
111. In support of the appointment of a chaplain, Bisanz wrote to the *Wiking* Division's HQ, explaining the Ukrainians had volunteered for the Galician Division and not *Wiking*, and that this had created special difficulties. See *An das Kommando der 5-ten SS-Division Wiking', Kracow, den 24.10.1944. Betr. Divisionspfarrer Waffen-Obersturmführer* Julian Habrusevych. ABFC.
112. For Reverend Julian Habrusevych's experiences see 'Bachyv ia bachyv, ranenoho druha...' ('I saw, I saw a wounded friend'), *Visti Kombatanta*, No.2, 1994, pp.88-91.
113. Interview, Lev Babij, Toronto 2 June 1993, See also Ia. D., Vikingy, Surmach, Nos. 1-4 (1983), pp. 20-25.

114. In the unpublished account of his father's experiences while serving with the *Wiking* Division, Michael Hrycyszyn writes:
"During the campaign against the partisans, an Allied airdrop took place. We were very near to Warsaw just after the uprising had taken place, when late one morning Allied aircraft came over at fairly low level and parachutes started to fall. There was great commotion because we thought this might be the start of the invasion. We knew that the western Allies had some Polish military units and we feared that they might even be Polish paratroopers who would pick on us as traitors. Whoever we were it was more dangerous for any Ukrainians in German uniform so we started to rip off our lion insignia". Hrycyszyn, op.cit., p.117.

115. The Division did include Hungarians and Romanians who spoke Ukrainian. It has also been suggested that difficulties with the language were used as an excuse for sending Ukrainians into dangerous situations. Interview, Lev Babij, Toronto, 2 June 1993.

116. See 'The Battles in the Wet Triangle' in Strassner, op.cit., pp.180-191.

117. The figure of 360 returnees from those assigned to the *Wiking* is given Ia. D., Vikingy, Surmach, Nos 1-4 (1983) pp. 20-25.

118. Apart from the heavy fighting, two main contributory factors that led to the heavy casualty rate were the inevitable misunderstandings of orders occurred because of language difficulties that resulted in unnecessary casualties. In addition to which during brief periods of rest and respite some Ukrainians were assigned to dangerous tasks such as burial detail. That involved the recovery of bodies from the battlefield. Interview, Lev Babij, Toronto, 2 June 1993. Regardless of their endeavours the author has found no evidence of any Ukrainian being decorated as a result of his service with the *Wiking* Division.

119. On the initiative of interpreter Yaroslav Deremenda, a petition was written to *Wiking* HQ asking to be removed and returned to the *'Halychyna'* division, threatening hunger strike if the request was not complied with. The German commander threatened disciplinary action for insubordination and said he could not resolve the request and forwarded the letter to higher authorities. Interview, Lev Babij, Toronto, 2 June 1993.

120. *Abschrift*, 5.*SS Panzer Division Wiking Kommandeur, Div.Gef.St.*, 4.11.1944, *Division-Sonderbefehl/anl. der Verabschiedung der gal. Waffen-willigen am* 3.11.44. An original copy of this document is in the author's possession.

121. Half the heavy weapons company (45-60 men) were former *Wiking* members who were very good and well trained. V. Tomkiw, verbally to author, 23 December 1996.

122. Hitler and several of his immediate associates would have preferred to have nothing to do with the idea of outright Russian collaboration in the war against the Soviet Union.

123. For further details concerning the Vlasov movement see Thorwald, op.cit., Andreyev, *Vlasov and the Russian Liberation Movement, Soviet Reality and Émigré Theories*, Cambridge UP, 1987, and Strik-Strikfeldt, *Against Stalin and Hitler*, Macmillan, 1970.

124. Vlasov himself believed in a centralised unified state.

125. The Wehrmacht Propaganda IV section, General Kurt Zeiter, *Hauptmann* Wilfred Strik-Strikfeldt, and the intelligence community were also among those who energetically backed and promoted this initiative.

126. Otto Braentigam, *Major* Wilhelm Kinkelin, Prof. Gerhard von Mende, Friedrich Markull and others had been submitting proposals for the establishment of a Ukrainian committee which was to have far reaching administrative and political authority since as early as February 1943. Hunczak,op.cit., pp.7 and 8.

127. Born 12 April 1912 in Niederkumersdorf, Oberlausitz. A former instructor at Breslau University, Arlt took part in the war against Poland – detailed to the staff of General Blaskowitz. In 1939 he joined Hans Frank's administration in the *Generalgouvernement* and participated in the formation of *Roland* and *Nachtigall*. In August 1943, Arlt transferred to the Eastern Front for service in the *'Das Reich'* Waffen-SS Division, in which he gained practical experience of the real conditions in the east and on 18 February, 1944, he was wounded at Jampoland and sent home. Extensive biographical details can be found in 'Lebenslauf von Dr Fritz Arlt' – Arlt, op.cit., pp.143-145.

128. Himmler approved the formation of the *Leitstelle Ost* in June 1944 to gain formal jurisdiction over the eastern volunteers already fighting on the German side. Berger subsequently appointed Dr Arlt as its head and charged him with the task of raising and organising volunteer formations composed of eastern nationals within SS formations. Arlt accepted the position with the proviso that he was "authorised to concede national autonomy to the same extent to both those formations made up of the outlying nationalities and those made up of Russians". Without the authority to make such far-reaching concessions, Berger nevertheless permitted Arlt to pursue his own course without interference. Arlt promptly created a number of separate bureaux within his organisation for Belorussia, Latvia, Lithuania, Estonia, Russia, and the Caucasian countries (thus upholding the principle of political separateness). See Thorwald, op.cit., p.189.

129. The 'federalists' opposed this concept believing it would splinter rather than unite the forces struggling against Bolshevism.

130. The clandestine founding meetings of the UHVR were held between 11-15 July 1944, near Nedilna in the Sambir region under the protection of UPA forces. There were twenty participants (the majority of which were not OUN members), ten from the north western Ukrainian lands and central Ukraine. For further details see *Encyclopaedia Ukraine...* Vol.5, pp.447-448.

131. As early as 20 August 1944, Army Group North Ukraine reported 'the leadership of the UPA has recognised that it cannot wage the struggle against the Bolsheviks by itself. It has repeatedly asked the Wehrmacht for support in the form of arms', and that since the UPA's operations were directed principally against the Red Army, the Army Group would do all in its power to assist the nationalists. See Alexander Dallin, *German Rule in Russia*, 2nd revised edition, Westview Press, 1981, p.622, and Lucas, op.cit., p.122. For the local success of the new approach, see *Verhandlungen mit der UPA*, 5. Juni 1944, H3/474, BA-MA.

132. For details of a report dated 27 November 1944, about the activities during a five week mission of 'Long Range Reconnaissance Commando 202' led by Captain Kirn, involving airdrops of supplies to UPA units operating behind Soviet lines see Lucas, op.cit., pp. 123-126.

133. It is uncertain who was responsible for securing the release of the nationalist leaders. Reitlinger suggests it was Berger's doing, while Dallin credits Rosenberg. Thorwald discounts both and suggests instead "on [Dr] Arlt's insistence Stephan Bandera was released from a concentration camp and 'turned over' to Arlt". Thorwald, op.cit., p.234.

134. Dallin, op.cit., p.623.

135. To cite an example, Bandera demanded the creation of an independent Ukrainian state and the creation of a Ukrainian armed force. See *Aktion des Generals Wlassow-Regelung der ukrainischen Frage*, Pressburg, 23, Nov. 1944, Bundesarchiv R70 Slowakei 223/2, pp.5 and 8. The meeting between Berger and Bandera took place on 5 October 1944. In a memorandum prepared the following day, Berger concluded that Bandera was a tough and tricky partner, "at present extremely valuable to us, later dangerous". Dallin, op.cit., p.625.

136. The attitude of most of the minority populations towards the KONR is aptly summarised by the leader of the Georgians M. Kediya who, when urged to subordinate his committee to Vlasov responded "I would rather have Stalin in front of me than Vlasov behind me". Shandruk, op.cit., p.205.

137. After his release from Sachsenhausen, on 17 October 1944, Andrij Melnyk received a mandate from the Ukrainians to head a 'working Commission', and conduct negotiations with the Germans with a view to being the head of the future UNC which he agreed to do only if certain preconditions were met. These included (i) full amnesty and release of all Ukrainians from prisons and camps (except criminal cases and those resulting from Bolshevik actions) (ii) a declaration by the Germans which would have pledged the establishment of a sovereign Ukrainian state within its ethnographical borders, (iii) creation of a Ukrainian national army under unified Ukrainian command (iv) withdrawal of all German troops from Ukrainian territory immediately upon the signing of the peace treaty (v) a guarantee that the UNC would be independent of General Vlasov. When the Germans refused his demands, Melnyk refused to accept the leadership of the UNC. Hand written statement by Colonel Andrij Melnyk, Berlin, 18 November 1944, ABFC.

138. The UNR was a five man directorate which had emigrated to Poland under the leadership of Symon Petlura after the collapse in 1921 of the Ukrainian struggle for independence.

139. General Pavlo Shandruk, born 28 February 1889, in Lubny (Poltava Province) Ukraine, died 15 February 1979, Trenton, New Jersey, USA. Served as an officer in the imperial Russian Army in 1914, and was awarded six military decorations and promoted to the rank of captain. In 1917 he joined the Ukrainian armed forces and fought against the Red Army commanding various units earning himself promotion to the rank of Colonel. In 1938 he served as a contract officer in the Polish army and fought against the Germans after their invasion of Poland in September 1939. He was wounded and taken prisoner by the Germans and kept under Gestapo surveillance. See 'General Pavlo Shandruk and the Ukrainian National Army 1945-1985', V. Veryha, pp.35-45, *Visti Kombatanta*, 1985, Nr.2, pp.36-37.

140. Other candidates for chairman considered by the Ukrainians included Prof. Isaac Mazepa and General V. Petriv.

141. Only *Hetman* Skoropadskyj objected on ideological grounds and because he wanted to head the committee himself.

142. For the meeting between Shandruk and Dr Arlt, see Shandruk, op.cit., pp.200-201, and Thorwald, op.cit., pp.190-192.

143. Shandruk, op.cit., p.202.

144. Thorwald, op.cit., p.192.

145. The influence of several factors (and of individuals) contrived to bring about the *Reichsführer's* remarkable turnabout in his eastern policy. Himmler, who had always regarded Vlasov as a 'butcher boy', never fundamentally revised his view. His tactical change came about only after meeting Vlasov on 16 September when he assumed a protectorate over the Vlasov movement that he saw as a means "to accelerate Soviet exhaustion". Himmler believed a united front against Bolshevism to be an "inescapable necessity", and did not favour the creation of a separate Ukrainian National Committee independent of Vlasov, as he thought by doing so it would undermine Vlasov's belief that he had Himmler's support. He never departed from his original concept and refused to differentiate between the Soviet minorities all of whom he regarded as Russians. For a graphic illustration of his view see his comment quoted in Thorwald, op.cit., p.228

146. Shandruk, op.cit., p.203.

147. At first, Berger was inclined towards the separatist view of the *Ostministerium* favouring the non-Russian groups partly because of their preponderance in the Waffen-SS. He installed Arlt who was a specialist in the nationalities of the Soviet Union as head of the Eastern Volunteers Desk, and charged him with the task of raising and organising volunteer formations composed of eastern nationals within SS formations.

148. Shandruk, op.cit., p.208. The salient arguments regarding the Ukrainian position *vis-à-vis* Vlasov are covered in a report to the commander of the German security service in Slovakia Dr Witiska dated 4 January 1945. Interestingly the report contains a revealing comment that gives an insight into the relationship between the UNC and the German government. It reads, "although the Ukrainian national government has strong leanings towards Germany, they do not want to make this too obvious, as they still reckon with an outcome of

the war which is not in Germany's favour. If this comes about, the Ukrainian national government does not want to be considered to be too closely associated with the Reich as this might make them unpopular with their fellow countrymen." R70 Slowakei/223, Bundesarchiv Koblenz, *Der Befehlshaber der Sicherheitspolizei u. d. SD in der Slowakei, Sonderkommando z.b.V.* 15 O.U. 4.1.45, III Tgb. Nr. 197/45, Am./Ha. ABFC.

149. The meeting took place on 30 January 1945. For Shandruk's account of it see Shandruk, op.cit., pp.219-222.
150. Dallin, op.cit., p 646. In his memoirs Shandruk omits any mention of the compromise variants or deals that were discussed. According to his account, Vlasov wanted Shandruk's Ukrainian Committee to merge with his own Ukrainian Committee and emphasised several times that if this were to occur, Shandruk would be his 'first deputy not only in military but also in political matters'. Shandruk declined the offer. However, he did agree that in the interests of the struggle against a common enemy he was prepared to co-ordinate the military activities of the two committees. To that end exchange liaison officers or even delegates with the Russian National Committee and with the other national groups. Shandruk, op.cit., pp.220-221.
151. When informed of it by Ribbentrop, Hitler is said to have retorted "Stop playing games". Dallin, op.cit., p.646.
152. Ibid.
153. It is interesting to note that Jurgen Thorwald credits the efforts of Dr Fritz Arlt with having successfully assured the reorganisation of the Division after Brody, the change of name, the new wording for the oath and the introduction of Ukrainian national flags and the Ukrainian national anthem. See Thorwald, op.cit., pp.233-234.
154. These were *'Deutschland, Deutschland Über alles'* and the *'Horst Wessel Lied', 'Die Fahne Hoch'.*
155. Heike, Eng. ed., op. cit., pp.70-71.
156. From the very outset, the German authorities had actively discouraged the use of the Trident, which signified Ukrainian nationalist aspirations, although in practice it had never been possible to enforce this regulation. See Governor Wächter's secret circular instruction, *Der Gouverneur des Distrikt Galizien Betr:* TGB.N.104\43G *Aufstellung der SS-Schützen Division Galizien.* ABFC.
157. The German text was:
"Ich schwöre bei Gott diesen heiligen Eid, dass ich im Kampf gegen den Bolschewismus, zur Befreiung meines ukrainischen Volkes, meiner ukrainischen Heimat, dem Obersten Befehlshaber der deutschen Wehrmacht und aller Kampfer der jungen europaischen Volker gegen den Bolschewismus, Adolf Hitler, unbedingten Gehorsam leiste und als tapferer Kampfer bereit sein will, jederzeit fur diesen Eid mein Leben einzusetzen". It is known that the oath incorporating the new wording was first sworn by soldiers of the Division in Slovakia. A copy of the oath with this wording was pasted into the back of each soldier's *Soldbuch* in one of three forms, German, Ukrainian or transliterated from the Cyrillic (i.e. Ukrainian) to the Latin alphabet. The author has in his personal archive original examples of all three types. Himmler officially authorised this oath on 16 February 1945, for details see *'An den Reichsführer-SS und Reichsminister des Innern' den* 5.2.1945, NS19/544, BA-KO.
158. The change was officially noted in the publication *Verordnungsblatt der Waffen-SS*, by the *Verbindungsoffizier der SS beim* OKH, [Tg.Buch-Nr VOSS 862g, v. 12.11.44 and VOSS 2470g v, 25.11.44, AA. A copy of this document can be found in the Document N 756/170 (Sammlung Vopersal), BA-MA.
159. *'Beurteilung fur den SS-Hauptsturmführer* Wiens' 1376, Div.St.Qu. 15.11.44. AA.
160. Divisional orders, rubber stamps on citations, and personal documents issued to members of the Division provide ample evidence that in some quarters use of the old title continued until the end of the war.
161. These were given during training courses.
162. *Abschrift,* 14. *Waffen-Gren. Div. der SS* (*Ukrain.*Nr.1), VI, Div. St. Qu., d. 17.11.44, *Betr.: Weltanschauliche.* ABFC.
163. Freitag continued to repeatedly emphasise the importance of the appropriate political leadership and the doctrinal education of the troops, via the so-called *Weltanschaulichen* (political doctrine) lectures, threatening those guilty of 'poor' political leadership with punishment for dereliction of duty. See 14. *Waffen-Gren.Div. der SS (galiz.Nr. 1),* Div.St.Qu. d.28.10.44, commander, 1357/44. Further specific details of the 'New Europe' motif are given in *'14.Waffen-Gren. Div. der SS (ukrain.Nr.1) VI': 7.12.44, Betr: Richtlinien fur die weltanschauliche Erziehung in der 14.Waffen-Gren.Div. der SS (Ukrain.Nr.1) vom 9.9.44. Thema: Das Reich als Führungsmacht in Europa (das neue Europa)'.* ABFC.
164. See Div.St.Qu. d. 14.*Waffen-Gren.* Div der SS (*ukrain.Nr.* 1)VI; Div. St. Qu. d.17.11.44; *Betr.: Weltanschauliche Erziehung.* ABFC.
165. 14.*Waffen-Gren. Div. der SS* (*galiz.Nr.*1) *Kommandeur* Div. St. Qu. d. 10.11.44. An original copy of this document is in the author's possession.
166. The commander of Section VI (Spiritual Care, Education, Entertainment and Information, Recreation) *SS-Sturmbannführer* Karl-Robert Zoglauer gave a similar directive. Heike Eng. ed., op. cit., p.85.
167. Ibid., pp.84-85.
168. Ferkuniak, op.cit., pp.12-13 and verbally to author, M. Scharko, 12 March 2000. Ultimately after strong and continued pressure from the Ukrainians, led by *Waffen-Obersturmführer* Makarushka, in spring of 1945 Bessel was reassigned to another unit.
169. The *Hauptamt SS-Gericht* was the SS-Legal Department administering the special disciplinary and penal code governing all SS and *Polizei* personnel. Its head was *SS-Obergruppenführer* Franz Breithaupt.
170. *14.Waffen-Gren.Div. der SS (ukr.Nr.1), Kommandeur, O.U., den 7. Dezember 1944, An den Richter beim Reichsführer-SS zur Vorlage beim Reichsführer-SS, Kdo.Stelle Reichsführer-SS, Nachrichtlich an 1. Gericht d. deutschen Befehlshabers in der Slowakei, Pressburg, 2. Hauptamt SS-Gericht Prien/ Chiemsee.* Berlin Document Centre, NS 7/75.
171. There was. however. one exception when *Waffen-Obersturmführer* Bohdan Pidhayny, the officer for special assignments with WGR 30, wrote truthfully that when the Division was sent to the front he was afraid that it would not fight for the 'New Order in Europe', which had no meaning for the Ukrainians. When presented with his report, incensed by the content, the regimental commander *SS-Obersturmbannführer* Forstreuter summoned Pidhayny, who enjoyed a high profile within the Division and was very popular amongst his countrymen. Afraid of the consequences if he was to overtly punish him, Forstreuter, according to the testimony of his Ukrainian *Ordonnanz Offizier* who witnessed the event, threatened him verbally saying "You're a lost man". Verbally to author, M. Scharko, 4 December 1999 and 27 January 2000. For details of one of the men required to produce the actual reports see the article by Dmytro Bojko, entitled 'Moye perebuvannia v Dyviziyi i poza neyu', *Visti Kombatanta,* Nr.4, 1999.
172. Schmitt, op.cit.,pp.9-10.
173. For example, within the Pioneer Battalion a fourth platoon was set up for every company, equipped with three mortars, and a SMG. Ibid.
174. Heike, Eng. ed., op. cit., p.89.
175. Drazniowskyj, op.cit., pp.1-2. Verbally to author, 13 March 1994, letter, 29 June 1994.
176. For a German account of this local action see Tieke and Rebstock, op.cit., pp.130-132.
177. Ibid. The Ukrainian battlegroups' *'funker'* (radio operators) were able to assist their colleagues by intercepting Soviet radio communications and feeding them falsified reports confirming that they were surrounded and should withdraw. Letter to author, M. Klymchuk, 7 May 1997.
178. Verbally to author, R. Drazniowskyj, 13 March 1997.
179. Interview, M. Klymchuk, London, 29 April 1997.
180. Reference to the speech is made in the telex from *SS-Obersturmbannführer* Dr Witiska to *SS-Brigadeführer* Bierkamp oViA Kracow, II B L.N. 807, Pressburg, am 17 Januar 1945, R70 Slowakei/223. BA-KO.
181. Letter to author, 19 April 1997, O. Lysiak. Only ten editions of *Do Boyu* ('Zum Kampf') ('To Battle'), appeared before Germany capitulated. At first the paper was published in Vienna but as transport became increasingly difficult it moved its base once again this time to Marburg. The last edition was dated 6 May 1945, two days before Germany signed surrender terms. The former editor of the paper Myhailo Ostroverkha suggests that the publication of an article in *Do Peremohy* against Vlasov's Army had caused problems with its German censor. *SS-Untersturmführer* Kretz which brought about its relaunch under a new name. (See Memoirs of M. Ostroverkha 'Do Peremohy' ('To Victory'), *Visti Kombatanta* No. 2., pp. 39-48, No. 3, pp.27-35 ,nos. 5-6, pp.71-82, 1972.
182. The group was led by Professor Lew Turkewych, the musical director of the L'viv opera and featured two soloist singers from the L'viv opera, Reinarovych and Staryckyi, and the prima ballerina Roma Pryima.
183. See Stephan Wolynetz, 'Report on the Trip to the 3rd Battalion of the 14th Ersatz Regiment during Christmas Holidays 1944/1945'. Berlin den 11 November 1945. ABFC. In his report, Wolynetz relates that Slovak community leaders including the mayor, the notary and senior officials of the Hlinka-Garda, were present at a Mass which was held for the battalion in the local Catholic Church, and later as guests at a special Christmas lunch.
184. Dmytro Ferkuniak writes that these individuals came to Slovakia not to encourage the troops but to purchase commodities that were not available elsewhere. Ferkuniak, op.cit., p.31. The Military Board had continued to maintain regular contact with the Division even after the forced relocation of its head quarters to the as yet unthreatened part of the *Generalgouvernement* in the wake of the Soviet advances of the summer and autumn of 1944, and later to Germany. From this time on, like its sister civilian organisation the UCC, it devoted much of its time to giving assistance and looking after the welfare of Ukrainian refugees who had fled to the west.
185. During the Christmas lunch of the staff company of the 3rd Battalion of the 14th Ersatz Regiment, the question of the Division's relationship with Vlasov's movement arose stimulating heated debate between the West Ukrainians and the east Ukrainian soldiers. The east Ukrainians believed that all the Ukrainians should actively cooperate with and under the overall direction of Vlasov. This view, which was popular amongst the numerous former officers and NCOs of the Soviet Army, was rejected by the west Ukrainians who remained suspicious of the 'Pan-Slavic' concept expounded by Vlasov. Echoing Shandruk's position, they contended that subordination to Vlasov should not be compulsory for Ukrainian units, but those wishing to do so should be allowed to transfer to Vlasov and his command. See Stephan Wolynetz 'Report on the Trip to the 3rd Battalion of the 14th Ersatz Regiment during Christmas Holidays 1944/ 1945'. Berlin den. 11.1.1945. ABFC.
186. Heike, Eng. ed., op. cit., p.84.
187. Born 5 July 1894, SS Nr. 422,296, Party Nr. 6,289, 103. After holding posts within the civilian administration in Bohemia and Moravia, Dr Josef Witiska took up his appointment as KdS (*Kommandeur der Sicherheitspolizei*) in Galicia in early March 1943. With the loss of Galicia in the summer of 1944 to the Soviets, Witiska transferred to Slovakia where he effectively became the BdS (*Befehlshaber der Sicherheitspolizei*) for Slovakia and thus was responsible for all internal security matters within that country. As part of his associated duties he commanded *Einsatzgruppe H* which was involved in the ruthless suppression of the ill-fated Slovak uprising.
188. In his three page report, *SS-Obersturmbannführer* Witiska writes that in his speeches to the officers and men of the Division, Bisanz did not clearly spell out his opinion, while Kubijovych who also spoke, said that he felt 'the Ukrainian question would soon come to a proper solution'. Amongst the most prominent complaints was that the Division lacked heavy weapons especially anti-tank and that there was no training for Ukrainians in administration and other non-combatant duties. With regard to German Ukrainian relations within the formation Witiska noted "even the Ukrainians who

finished the German training courses are looked down upon by the Germans." It goes on to mention that rumours were circulating that the Division would be subordinated to Vlasov, a factor which explained why more of its soldiers were willing to desert to the UPA. See *An das Reichssicherheitshauptamt* – IV N – z.Hd.v. SS-*Gruppenführer und Generalleutnant der Polizei* Muller Berlin, -N- Tgb.Nr.93/44g, *Geheim*, 26.1.1945, *Betrifft: SS-Schützen-Division-Galizien, jetzt* 1.*ukrain. Division,* R70 *Slowakei*/223m, BA-KO.

189. Not all services were this lavish although in Vrutky the whole Pioneer Battalion (including some of its German personnel) took part in a similar church service held beside the river Nitra before a cross fabricated from blocks of ice. Letters to the author, B. Kutny, 25 June 1994 and 30 October 1995. For a German account of Christmas/New Year period see 'Weihnachten 1944 in der Gegend der Hohen Tatra', Ludwig Hummer, *Der Freiwillige* Nr.12, 1993.
190. Letter to author, E. Shypailo, 21 September 1994.
191. On this occasion the support units included the 2nd Company of the Pioneer Battalion which arrived at the Slovakian Hungarian border in January 1945 but encountered no enemy forces and was ordered to return to Vrutky on foot. Schmitt, op.cit., p.9.
192. Interview, M. Klymchuk, London, 29 April 1997, and letter to author, 7 May 1997.
193. Between August and November the reforming was carried out under the Commander in Chief of the replacement Army (Himmler). From December to March 1945 it was supervised directly by the SS-FHA which signified that it was ready for operations.
194. In his memoirs, Heike states that at this time the army group in Cracow expressed an interest in using the Division to fight partisans and maintain security in its rear. Heike, Eng. ed., op. cit., p.87.
195. Ibid.
196. Ibid., p.96. In the same way that Koppe and Hölfe when experiencing difficulties with partisan forces in the *Generalgouvernement* and Slovakia respectively, on request, had been allocated the whole or part of the Galician Division by the *Reichsführer-SS*, Heike states that the Division was moved to Slovenia at the demand of Rösener.
197. SS Erwin Rösener, born 2 February 1902, Westphalia, died 31 August 1946. Joined the NSDAP 1926 SS Nr. 3,575. *SS-Obergruppenführer Generalleutnant der Polizei und Waffen-SS*. HSSPf. Yugoslavia. Ruth Bettina Birn, *Die Höheren SS-und Polizeiführer: Himmler's Vertreter im Reich und in den besetzten Gebieten*, Droste Verlag, Dusseldorf, 1986, p.345. On 17 May 1945, Rösener was arrested by the Field Security Services of the British 78th Division, in hospital, in Spittal, masquerading as a private soldier. For a detailed account of his capture and preliminary interrogation see the War Diary of 5th Corps, WO 170/4241, PRO.
198. Heike, Eng. ed., op. cit., p.91.
199. Ibid., p.91.
200. Ibid., p.92.
201. Some of the clothing was promptly "swapped with the population for food." Q1 Dmytryk.
202. Verbally to author, M. Scharko, 18 October 1997. That comment was directed partly at those who had a mistress (i.e., Wittenmeyer, who he had picked up a Russian émigré who was fleeing to the west in Slovakia. Thereafter he had a difficult time trying to keep her with him).
203. See *SS-Führungshauptamt*, Berlin-Wilmersdorf, den 26.1.45, Amt II Org.Abtl.Ia/II Tgb.Nr 550/45 g.Kdos, *Betr: 'Verlegung der 14.Waffen-Gren-Div.d.SS (ukrainische Nr.1)'*. NA T175, roll 140, frame 266422.
204. Q15 Sokolskyj.
205. Verbally to author, A. Hawirko, 19 May 1997.
206. Heike, Eng. ed., op. cit., p.94, Hawrylak, op.cit., p.21. One veteran of the Division whose father had been a member of the Austro-Hungarian Army, successfully managed to enter the city on a borrowed bicycle. He explained his motives for doing so by stating that he wanted to see the centre of the Austro-Hungarian Empire for which his father had fought, at first hand. Interview, M. Klymchuk, London 29 April 1997.
207. Letter to author, W. Sirskyj, 2 July 1997.
208. In a letter to the author dated 29 August 2000, a former member of the *Jagdzug*, II/WGR29, wrote:
"On the way to Yugoslavia, we were billeted in a building, the ground floor of which was a warehouse and the top floor was our quarters for an overnight rest. I went downstairs to see what kind of warehouse it was. For security purposes two old *Volkssturm* men had been assigned to guard it. When they discovered our presence they assumed that we would be providing security for the night and went home. To my surprise I found 300kgs of butter in 12 barrels each weighting 25kgs. I went upstairs and mentioned to the boys that there was some butter downstairs. The following morning I saw that some Germans were searching our boys but did not find anything. We had three small ammunition wagons with one horse, and some hay for feeding the horses. Nobody suspected that this was the hiding place for 25kg barrels of butter." Letter to author, D. Lishchynsyj, 21 August 2000. Later, the butter was distributed amongst the soldiers who hid it in their gas mask containers. Letter to author, 21 November 1992, O. Sokolskyj. In his memoirs, Heike states that an investigation found no guilty parties within the Division and incorrectly concludes the theft was by the enemy or was a fabrication. Heike, Eng. ed., pp.97-98.
209. Ibid., p.95.
210. R. Drazniowskyj, letter to author, 6 October 1997, and verbally, 21 November 1997.
211. See message to: *Lufigaukdo* Vienna, from: 14. *Waffen Gren Div. SS 'Ukraine'* Nr. 1, HW 16/70, GPD 4034 No. 1 Traffic: 26.2.45, PRO.
212. A secret message from SS-FHA, to the 14. Div. dated 3 March 1945, requests that the Division report when the last marching units were due to arrive at their final destination. See SS-FHA, Abtl. II, i.a Weber to 14 *Waffengrenadier div.d.SS Ukrain*. Nr. 1, *über Kdo Marburg/Drau,* HW/16/43 GPD 4088, Addendum III, 3 March 1945, PRO
213. *14. Waffengrenadier Div an RFSS Feldkommandostelle and HSSPf. Laibach* [Ljubljana] 26 February 1945, HW/16/43 GPD 4034, PRO.
214. *14 Waffengrenadier div. an RFSS Feldkommandostelle and HSSPf. Laibach* [Ljubljana] 27 February 1945, HW/16/43 GPD 4035, PRO.
215. Bender & Taylor, Vol.4, op.cit., p.48. According to the same source, while this chart shows WGR 29 to have three battalions, both WGR 30 and 31 are shown as having only two. Heike, op.cit., p.94. In his memoirs, Heike gives what the author believes to be a greatly inflated figure for the strength of the Division inclusive of the Training and Reserve Regiment as 22000. Heike, Eng. ed., op. cit., p.111.

Chapter 9

1. Letter to author, R. Kolisnyk, 24 April 1997.
2. In place of the Nazi Party in Styria was the *Heimatsbund* headed by Dr Stindl (until his death in March 1945), who was subordinated to *Gauleiter* Uiberreither in Graz.
3. All German outpost and other military and administrative buildings had to be guarded and heavily fortified with barbed wire, protective ditches and machine gun nests. Q19 Sokolskyj. Hawrylak, op.cit., p.23.
4. Companies in Oberhaag, Eibiswald, Arnfels, Leutschan.
5. The Divisional Field Hospital relocated to Celje. Sirskyj, *Visti Kombatanta*, Nr. 3, 1997, and 'Memoirs of a Nurse', Olha Wankevych, *Visti Kombatanta*, Nr.2, pp.81-86, 1998.
6. In a letter to the author dated 7 December 1997, Philip Trotch a former *Waffen-Untersturmführer* who commanded a platoon in 14./WGR 30, wrote: "At one time we caught a 'Royalist' woman partisan (from the army of General D. Mikhailovich). After an interrogation we let her go and offered to return her pistol which she refused to take back."
7. See Joze Marolt, *Šercerjeva brigada na Štajerskem*, Zalocba, Obzorja Maribor, 1993, pp.323-338.
8. Verbally to author, M. Scharko, 18 October 1997.
9. Within the first few days of deployment 1/I/WGR 30 had lost three soldiers in this way. Herasymowycz, op.cit., p.3. Other veterans of the Division reported similar occurrences to the author during interviews.
10. Hawrylak, op.cit., pp.23-26.
11. Heike, Eng. ed., op. cit., p.101.
12. *SS-Führungshauptamt*, 5 Sept 1944, *Amt* II *Org.Abtl.*Ia/II Tgb.Nr.2880/44 g.Kdos. Re: Reformation of the 14.Waffen-Gren.Div. der SS (galician Nr.1). NA T175 roll 141, frames 2669182 – 2669183.
13. This *ipse dixit* is recorded in the unpublished memoirs of *Waffen-Hauptsturmführer* Dmytro Ferkuniak, one of very few Ukrainian officers serving on the Division's general staff, who would have had access to such information. See Ferkuniak, op.cit., p.32. According to Ferkuniak the outcome of this was that "the Division was notified in the second half of March that as it was not yet battle ready, 80% of its armaments should be given to units that were, and that the Division itself should be moved to the region of Salzburg for further training". Ibid. In his memoirs Heike does not mention this episode but does confirm that "it was decided that the Division could keep twenty per cent of its weapons and supplies". Wolf Dietrich Heike, *Sie wollten die Freiheit: Die Geschichte der Ukrainischen Division 1943-1945*, Dorheim, Podzun Verlag, 1973, p.199. Unfortunately, Heike does not elaborate or specify on the exact origins of this directive.
14. Ferkuniak, op.cit., p.32.
15. Several veterans have confirmed receipt of similar orders by their respective units: Ivan Sadoveyj, (1st Coy./Fusilier Battalion) letters to author, 27 February and 21 March 1999. A similar unequivocal directive which read: '*unter dem Niveau stehende Elemente zu entfernen*' ('remove sub-standard elements'), was received by the commander of WGR 30, *SS-Obersturmbannführer* Forstreuter, as confirmed by his former *Ordonnanz Offizier*, a *Waffen-Untersturmführer* who surreptitiously read the instruction. Verbally to author, M. Scharko, 18 October 1997, and letter to author, 13 January 1998. In this instance, the instruction does not appear to have been implemented until later in the month. Based on his diary entry, in a letter to the author, dated 16 August 1997, V. Veryha writes: "On March 25th or close to it, an order came that anybody who wanted to be demobilised to civilian life may do so at this time. As a result of this from 9/II/WGR 30, where I served as *Rechnungsführer*, 10 soldiers volunteered and the next day they were led by the only German NCO in the company named Blume to the regiment. In fact they were not sent to a civilian camp but redirected to an *Arbeitsbataillon*. Some of them were later in the POW camp in Rimini." Veryha estimates 200 soldiers were transferred from WGR 30 in this way. The 10 soldiers from 9/II/WGR 30 were Czuczman, Kramar, Bulysh, Protz, Bocwinok, E. Zastavwnyi, Lewytzkyj, Sawaryn, Kalyniak, Zastrockyj, led by *SS-Untersturmführer* Blume.
16. Of this number over 50 men were from the 3rd Battalion. 'Last days of the War in a Labour Battalion' ('Ostannii dni viyny u robochomu kureni'), *Visti Kombatanta*, Nr. 3, 1968, pp. 23-26.
17. Ibid. In his account Mr Senchyna states that whilst engaged in building work on 7 April 1945, they were attacked by Allied aircraft. 17 were killed (including 1 Ukrainian) and many wounded (6 of which were Ukrainian). Later, about 100 of the Ukrainians were invited to volunteer for the *Volkssturm* (local defence units similar to the British Home Guard) having been promised new uniforms and better food. In mid April they were relocated to the area of Graz where they were accommodated in private houses.
18. As part of the negotiations leading up to the establishment of an 'Ukrainian National Army' a number of possible variations were considered, one of which envisaged the establishment of an Ukrainian Directory headed by Shapovalov, similar to that which had existed from 1917/1919 under Symon Petlura. According to this proposal, which was supported by both the Melnyk and Bandera factions of the OUN, all political rights of this temporary Ukrainian Government would be acknowledged by the Reichsgovernment. The '*SS-Schützendivision Galizien*' would form the basis of a 100,000 strong Ukrainian National Army, which would comprise three or four divisions. Its commander would be an Ukrainian while its chief of staff would be a German. See circular from Dr Witiska to the Heads of Departments III B, (Dr

Ehlich) III B (Dr Buchardt) IV B, VI C (Dr Hengelhaupt), IIIB -Bo./Ot. – LN 1209, Pressburg, 2.Februar 1945. *Betr: 'Angebliche bevorstehende Regelung der ukrainischen Frage'* ABFC.

19. Dallin, op.cit., p.646. Five days later the four Caucasian Committees and the Crimean Tartars also received similar declarations that which accorded them recognition on behalf of the German Government.
20. ABFC.
21. The author has found no evidence to suggest that any other German agency actively supported Rosenberg's declaration.
22. Shandruk made a conscious effort to select individuals who would provide regional representation as well as raise the committee's prestige and increase its chance of success. As representative of western Ukraine Professor Volodymyr Kubijovych was already well experienced in dealing with the Germans and had played a pivotal part in the formation of the Galician Division. He was put in charge of all civilian matters. Oleksander Semenenko, a well-known lawyer from Kharkiv represented eastern Ukraine. Petro Tereshchenko was appointed to the post of Secretary-General. The post of Chairman of the Military Council of the UNC was given to General Omelianovych-Pavlenko a distinguished veteran of the Ukrainian Army from 1917-1921. Shandruk charged Pavlenko with the task of drafting the bylaws and an organisational chart of the Military Council. Col. A. Valiysky was appointed as Army Chief of Staff. Shandruk, op.cit., p.233.
23. To legalise the UNC, following a conference held in Weimar 12-14 March, 1945, attended by 13 representatives, for the sake of appearances Shandruks' appointment was subsequently ratified by the UNR (Livytsky) who issued this order of appointment:
    Order.
    To the Army and Navy (sic.) of the Ukrainian National Republic.
    No.8. 15 March 1945.
    Re General Staff:
    Lieutenant-General of the General Staff Pavlo Shandruk is hereby appointed Commander of the Ukrainian National Army as of 15 March 1945. For further details as well as a complete list of signatories to the order see Shandruk, op.cit., pp.235-237.
24. In the transitionary period immediately prior to obtaining recognition of the Committee, Shandruk's German supporters managed to secure the use of the camp which became a collecting point for all those who wished to join the Ukrainian National Army. Shandruk entrusted the formation of the '2nd Division' which began on 22 February 1945 to Colonel Petro Diachenko. By the end of month the formation of a second company had been initiated and the unit's total strength soon reached 1900 men. These men came from various backgrounds, the majority being former POWs, forced labourers, and those who had transferred from other units. On 28 March 1945, Shandruk visited the unit and formally initiated over the swearing in ceremony. On 3 April it transferred to Glatz (Koldzko) in Silesia. Here the formation of a third company began and on 12 April the unit (which never reached more than regimental strength) transferred to the front in Saxony and engaged the Red Army in battle near the city of Bautzen on 15 April 1945. The brigade was then incorporated into the German corps stationed at the front and given further battle assignments. After German capitulation the Brigade was trapped in the Soviet zone but two-thirds managed to escape only to be promptly handed over to the Soviets by the Americans as they were from eastern Ukraine. The officer staff of the Brigade (2nd Div. UNA) consisted of:

Commander:	Colonel Petro Diachenko
Adjutant:	Lieutenant Iurkiv
1st Coy:	Captain Fursa
2nd Coy:	Lieutenant V. Hladych*
3rd Coy:	Lieutenant Staroviit

(*Shandruk claims that Hladych was Diachenko's Chief of Staff). For details of the formation, organisation and subsequent activities of this unit see: *Visti Kombatanta* Nos. 3-4, 1971, pp. 89-90 (2 letters to the editor from R. Krokhmaliuk and V. Hladych); *Visti Kombatanta* Nr. 5, 1971, p.73, letter of Orest Horodyskyj to the editor; Tytarenko Petro, 'Protypantsyrna brygada 'Vil'na Ukraina' in *Visti* (Munich) Nr.6-7, 1952, pp.3-4: Shandruk, op.cit., p.235. See also *Ternystyi Shlakh 2-1. Dyvizii UNA* ('The Thorny Road of the 2nd Div. of the UNA'), Ivan Burchak. published by United Soldiers and Friends of the 2nd Division of the UNA, New York, 1994, Clifton (Obeyednannia Voyakiv i Pryiateliv 2-1. Dyvisii UNA).

25. One group of 77 volunteered from the *Kriegsgefangenen Lager* (POW camp) at Flossenberg. See HW 16/43 GPD 4037 Addendum I 28 Feb 1945, An den 14.Waffengren.div der SS Ukr Nr. 1, from SSFHA TO SS, signed *SS-Obstubaf.* Ladewig. PRO.
26. One such example is Vitali Bender, a former Ukrainian Red Army prisoner of war, who volunteered for the 'Ukrainian' Division Galicia, believing (as did the rest of his group) that they were volunteering for service in a 'purely Ukrainian unit'. Upon reaching the Division's Reserve Regiment, most were shocked to discover that its Ukrainian soldiers were dressed in German uniforms, whereupon part of the group chose to return to the camp from which they had come. See 'Dyvisia, hey, ridna maty' ('Division, You Dear Mother'), *Visti*, Nos. 45-46, 1954, p.4. Bender himself remained with the Division until the end of the war.
27. Organised on 19 March 1943, near the village of Antonovets in the Kremianets area of Volhynia the unit was formed from a group of approximately 200 men mainly from the Lutsk, Kremenets and Dubno regions to defend the local population against attacks from the Polish and Soviet partisans. As the consequence of a direct and violent confrontation between the 'Legion' and a group from the Bandera faction of the OUN-B in October 1943, the unit was disarmed only to be reformed shortly thereafter under the auspices of the *Sicherheitsdienst*. During 1944 it absorbed the Kholm Self Defence Detachment, commanded by Yuri Lukashchuk, several east Ukrainians from *Schutzmannschaft* 207 and a few former officers of the Galician Division who had been discharged because of insufficient qualifications or because of their age. The legion had its own NCO school at Klay near Cracow and had a number of nurses who served as medical personnel. It was well equipped with several horses, radio equipment and a mixture of German and Soviet weaponry including a light infantry support gun, mortars and heavy machine guns. Its members wore standard pattern German uniforms with no distinguishing insignia. Interview, Fedir Tsymbaliuk, 20 June 1999, Toronto, and Orest Horodyskyj, *The Organisation, Formation and History of 'The Volhynian Self-Defence Legion, 1943-45* (unpublished paper).
28. *Oberst* Woldymyr Herasimenko (Tur) was the legion's senior Ukrainian officer. From mid 1944, *Oberst* Petro Diachenko acted as assistant commander. Other prominent Ukrainian officers (some names are pseudonyms) included: 1st Lt. Lytwyn, Capt. Oksentijiw, Lts. Roman Kyveluk, Charvckyj, Wowk, Kowal, 'Trojan' Nechaj, 'Traktor', Kaschuk, Cobchak, and Popobuz.
29. The Legion's first commander was *SS-Hauptsturmführer* Siegfried Assmuss, who had previously been attached to the SD in Lutsk whose "heroic death" in an ambush by Polish partisans during the retreat before the Red Army south of Lublin, was described in a letter of condolences dated 14 November 1944, from the commander in Posen to his widow. AA. Assmuss was assisted by a *SS-Unterscharführer* named Rawlin who spoke fluent Russian and acted as interpreter.
30. Heinrich Biegelmeyer: Born; 21 July 1911, Parsberg near Regensberg. Party Nr. 482 311, SS Nr. 272 273. Promoted to *SS-Sturmbannführer* 30 January 1944. From July 1942 to July 1943: *SS-Hauptstuf.* and *Abteilungsleiter* with Kds Lublin. From July 1943 to April 1945: *'Ukrainische Selbstschutzlegion Einsatzbatl. in Kracow mit der Führungsbeauftragt und überführt in die 14.Waffen Gren div (1 ukrainische) an der front'*.
31. Apart from Biegelmeyer himself, most of these, such as *SS-Untersturmführer* Schmidt, were polyglots speaking fluent German, Polish, Russian and Ukrainian.
32. Some of the Legion's anti-partisan activities in which it is sometimes referred to as *'der Melnykkampfgruppe'* are partly documented in the reports to Der *Kommandeur der Sicherheitspolizei und des SD für den Distrikt* Lublin, *Grenzpolizeikommissariat* Hrubeshiv, 7 to 30 March, 1944, WAP. Lublin Ortk, I/524/23, – AGR MSW 185, APL.
33. During the fighting in Warsaw at least ten members of the Legion were killed. These have been named in a document signed by *SS-Oberscharführer* Rawlin as *Feldwebel* Filimon Buszanskij, and privates Iwan Dub, Iwan Halaszewskij, Jurij Hajworonskij, Eugen Kolacki, Andrij Melnyk, Andrij Sledz, Gregor Trofimowicz, Teodosij Wosniuk and Archip Wachara. S.M.d.S.-Batl.31- (*Ukr. Selbstschutzlegion*) Targowisko den 12.10.1944, AA. The Legion's political leader, known by the pseudonym 'Soltys', objected to the deployment at Warsaw and in consequence was arrested by the SD and sent to a concentration camp, where he perished.
34. The unit was stationed in the villages of Spielfeld, Oberschwarz and Unterschwarz.
35. Amongst these were *Waffen-Untersturmführers* Lytwyn, Popivskyj and Lychmanenko.
36. During an interview with the author, Fedir Tsymbaliuk, a former NCO who was with the formation throughout its existence, stated that the initial plan had been for a group of around 80 men to join the western Allies, but the rumour spread that it would be returning to Ukraine to fight the Bolsheviks, as a result of which the numbers quickly grew. Interview, Tsymbaliuk, 20 June 1999, Toronto.
37. A full written detailed account of this episode by one of the participants see Fedir Tsymbaliuk, *Visti Kombatanta*, Nr.2, 1996, pp. 73-81.
38. The presence of these individuals was confirmed by M. Scharko, verbally to author, 7 December 1997.
39. The priests were Scakalsky and Dubycky and the doctors were Miroshnychenko and Jurgens (the latter was a Latvian national). Interview, F. Tsymbaliuk, 20 June 1999, Toronto.
40. The largest group was sent to the 14. *Feld Ersatz Bataillon* under *SS-Sturmbannführer* Kleinow.
41. J. Hnatkiv, *The Fusilier Battalion of the Ukrainian Division*, p.2. (unpublished account).
42. Orest Horodyskyj 'Dva dni v partyzantsi', *Samostiina Ukraina* (Chicago-New York), Nr. 7 (161) July 1962 and letters to the author dated 12 February 1993, 25 March 1993, 12 November 1994, 20 June and 13 July 1997. Among the fellow Ukrainian officers serving with the Division who later attested to this was *Waffen-Untersturmführer* Hawrylak who stated in his memoir: "Much later we learned that our Divisional commander had ordered 'Voron' Kyveluk shot. I was sorry to hear that because I knew him to be an outstanding and noble person" Hawrylak, op.cit., p.28. It was Horodyskyj who warned him against going.
43. Information pertaining to Operation *Donnerwetter* was provided verbally to the author by V. Veryha 6 June 1997 and in Herasymowycz, op.cit., p.2.
44. Marolt, op.cit., pp.323-338.
45. Q 23 Herasymowycz, Q 26 Kolisnyk.
46. See Mirko Fajdiga, *Braciceva brigada na Štajerskem, Koroškem in Gorenjskem*, 2. knjiga, Zalocba Obzorja, Maribor, 1994, pp.537-554.
47. Ibid.
48. Marolt, op.cit., pp.323-338.
49. Ibid.
50. It would appear that most of the casualties were suffered during a sharp encounter with partisans in the Bela Pec region on 10 March during which *Waffen-Unterscharführers* Sirskyj and Bekesh together with several grenadiers were wounded. In addition to losing several killed, the partisans were forced to leave behind several rifles and machine guns. Letter to the author, W. Sirskyj, 2 July 1997. Among the prisoners captured by 11/III/WG 29 was a group of four comprising of two Serbs, one Pole and one Ukrainian from the Poltava region. Their British rifles having been taken, they were kept under guard until the morning when the two Serbs and the Pole were handed over to the Battalion HQ for interrogation. Not wanting to surrender their Ukrainian captive for almost certain execution, the

Ukrainian was sent to the company cookhouse where he was successfully concealed and employed until the end of the war. Verbally to author, M. Prymak, 3 November 1997.

51. Verbally to author, R. Drazniowskyj, 13 September 1997.
52. The entire investigation is chronicled in the file AIR 402315, PRO. The secret report from Provost Marshal R.A.F, M.A.A.F, C.M.F to Provost Marshal R.A.F., Air Ministry, Ref PM/2072/1/4 German War Crimes, Death of No O.A427416 F/ SGT. Calder, L.W. No. 148 Squadron, which formed the basis of the subsequent inquiry reads:

"1. The following information concerning the death of the above named N.C.O., received by G.2. (P/W) Section, A.F.H.Q., has been passed on to the Provost Marshal R.A.F, M.A.A.F., for action:

Information dated 22 April, from an Allied Mission in N.E. Slovenia, reports that Sgt. Calder, 148 Squadron, R.A.F., a member of the crew of the Halifax which crashed over Slovenia last October and for whom several attempts at evacuation were made, has been killed by the Germans.

2. The story is as follows: Last October Calder's aircraft crashed, he was injured in the leg that subsequently had to be amputated. He was cared for very well by the doctors of 4 Zone in a hidden hospital.

3. The Germans found the hospital, the location of which had been betrayed to them, set fire to it and burned alive all the patients including Calder, who were unable to move.

4. The units which carried out this atrocity were from 14 SS-Division, who had committed similar atrocities before in the Marburg area."

The report continues by asking for exact information regarding (i) the exact location of the hospital alleged to have been burnt by 14th SS Division, (ii) Names of officers and other ranks of 14th SS Division taking part in the burning of the hospital, (iii) Name of the officer who ordered the burning of the hospital, (iv) Names of other service personnel who were burned to death, and details of other patients in the hospital, (v) details of other atrocities committed by 14th SS Division, giving names of victims and persons responsible, (vi) names of witnesses. AIR 402315, PRO.

Document WO 108/107, AIR 402315, PRO contains the statement of Flight Sergeant Parker in which he states: "[....] On the morning of 10 March 1945, we received another alarm. I was moved from the hospital to the hills, on 11 March. I was hiding under a cliff with partisans when I was captured by German troops of the Ukrainian Division that would be about 07.00 hours. With the party captured were three Slovacs [sic.], one a man of 45 years of age, and two boys about 16 years of age. The man and one of the boys had been in the same hidden hospital as F/Sgt. Calder. They told me in broken English that they had left the hidden hospital on 8 March and my friend Calder was doing fine. They could not tell me the location of this hospital. I was marched with the Slovak [sic] man and the two boys for about 2 hours, the man could not march very well because of his injury. The officer in charge of the guard ordered him out of the group and with two guards they went into the trees. Then I heard rifle fire. I suspect he was shot but I did not see the atrocity. The two boys were beaten up by the guards. I suspected that was to gain information from them. I myself never witnessed any atrocities committed by the Ukrainian Division or the 14 SS Division.

"The only building I saw burning was the last hospital that I was in, and that was when I was being marched from the hills on the morning of me being captured. I could not say if any partisan patients were in the building at the time and I could not say who ordered the hospital to be burned down."

In summary, the Provost Marshal PM/2072/1/4 dated 3 September 1945 concludes:

"[...] 7. Whilst it cannot be precluded that Sgt Calder's hospital was, in fact burnt down, it will be observed that the statement of F/Sgt. Parker does conflict with the original report upon which this enquiry has been based, since, though the hospital which he vacated was burnt, Sgt. Calder was certainly not therein at the time.

8. In view of this and the difficulties involved in obtaining permission for entry into Yugoslavia, it is not proposed to make further enquiries which can only take place in Yugoslavia."

On the basis of the above evidence the matter was not pursued.

53. See Dr Miroslav Stiplovsek, *Šlandrova brigada, NOV in POS 10*, Ljubljana, Maribor, 1971, pp.646-650.
54. Ibid.
55. Throughout March 1945, the partisan units within the '4th Partisan Operative Zone' received air dropped supplies from the Allies. For example the Bracic Brigade received supplies on 14 March near the village of Zavodnje (see Fajdiga, op.cit., pp.537-554) as did the Šercer Brigade on 14 March near Razbor and again on the 23 March in the vicinity of the villages of Dolic and Paka, (see Marolt, op.cit., pp.323-338)
56. For an account of the operation by the German commander of the 2nd Company of the Pioneer Battalion *SS-Obersturmführer* Wilhelm Dzillum see Schmitt, op.cit., pp.10-11.
57. Heike, Eng. ed., op. cit., p.102.
58. The co-ordination of forces during these actions was sometimes poor. Support for this statement is evidenced by the account of a *Waffen-Untersturmführer* whose company 5/II/WGR unexpectedly encountered a unit led by *Waffen-Sturmbannführer* Evhen Pobihushtschyi from the Division's Reserve Regiment, during one action. Catching sight of each other, from a distance, neither had been notified of the possible presence of the other and as some members of Pobihushtschyi's unit were wearing short fur jackets over their uniforms, they were almost mistaken for partisans. A potential disaster was only averted because somebody heard the Ukrainian language being spoken and was therefore able to identify the unit as being 'friendly'. 5/II/WGR 30, Zenon Kuk, unpublished memoirs, p.30.
59. For example a platoon of Volhynians from 3/I/ WGR 31, were responsible for the discovery of a military radio station which was subsequently dismantled and brought down from the mountains intact. Q 26 Kolisnyk.
60. Letters to author, W. Sirskyj, 2 July 1997, B. Kutny, 7 November 1997.
61. In the chapter on Slovenia in his unpublished memoirs entitled *Masheruyut' Dobrovoltsi* ('The Volunteers Are Marching'), M. Fylypowych, a NCO serving with the 4th company of the Fusilier Battalion writes:

"While combing the area, the advanced troop noticed smoke rising from the snow covered ground. They surrounded the area, found the entrance and entered what turned out to be an underground bunker used as a field hospital. One wounded solider was lying on a bed. He wore a cap with a red star and a rifle was lying next to him. In the bunker were about 30 beds and a supply of medicine. The partisan was interrogated – he turned out to be a fanatical communist – and later was turned over to the battalion staff".

62. Several veterans have described ambushes taking place, for example a former member of 14/WGR 30 recounted the following incident in a letter to the author, dated 7 December, 1997:

"The partisans set up an ambush but were afraid to attack our marching column. However they grabbed the company cook, a *Waffen-grenadier* named Husak who had stayed behind for a couple of minutes to relieve himself. When it was reported to the platoon commander that a soldier was missing, he stopped the marching column and sent a group to look for the missing soldier. The group encountered heavy machine-gun fire and all six were killed except the group leader who jumped into a nearby stream and retreated back to his unit under cover of the forest undergrowth. During the combing of that area we captured a wounded partisan who was turned over to the military police with the appropriate report. During an intensive interrogation he revealed the partisan hide-out. [Later] Five partisans were captured, three of which were sentenced to be shot in front of the prison wall, and two were sent to higher authorities for further interrogation." See Schmitt, op.cit., p.11.

63. One individual killed by a booby trap was *Waffen-Untersturmführer* Terlecky.
64. Letter to author, E. Shypailo, 5 August 1997.
65. In one action in the mountains near Celje, a medical doctor, together with his orderly, was brutally killed while they were sleeping in a hamlet. The enraged Ukrainians subsequently burnt down the house in which the two men had been sleeping. Q 24 Kulchyskyj. Verbally to author, M. Prymak, 16 October 1997. In his memoirs *The Trials of the Ukrainian Division* ('Dyvisiynymy stezhkamy'), p.185, Stephan Medynsky, describes how on the afternoon of Friday 23 March his unit (6/II/WGR 29), found the body of a Divisional soldier murdered by partisans.
66. Of this number at least twenty-eight were known to have been convicted by a field court and sentenced to death by firing squad mostly for desertions and other infractions such as petty theft and disobeying orders. See 'Spysok Polyahlych...'.
67. Local truces were recorded as having been made by a number of veterans; Interview, Dmytryk, Rushden (Pioneer Battalion), 21 October 1990, Interview, M. Klymchuk (III/WGR 29) London, 29 April 1997 and letter to the author dated 2 July 1997, W. Sirskyj, (13/WGR 29). *Waffen-Obersturmführer* Bohdan Pidhayny, one of the prominent OUN-B operatives serving with WGR 30 also played a significant part in negotiating a cease-fire in the vicinity of Velenje where it was based. At Pidhayny's instigation, a meeting was set up with representatives through a Ukrainian intermediary at which an agreement was reached that neither party would interfere with the other. Verbally to author, M. Scharko, 18 October 1997.
68. Two such incidents of soldiers of the Division being released by partisans have been recorded. In one case an Ukrainian grenadier was visiting a family with a young girl during when five partisans emerged from hiding but did not harm him. For another documented case see V. Veryha 'Zustrich z Titovskymy partyzanam,' *Visti Kombatanta* 1977, Nr.3, pp.45-50. A former member of 6/II/WGR 29 deserted from the Division and was subsequently captured by Tito's partisans whom he joined, fighting with them until the end of the war and receiving a decoration in the process. He returned to western Ukraine at the end of the war and was not punished by the Soviets. Letters to author, O. Sokolskyj 23 June 1992, 12 August 1997.
69. In a letter to the author, dated 2 July 1997, W. Sirskyj relates an episode during which seven cart drivers from 13/WGR 29 wished to dance with local girls. The partisans seized them, disarmed them and undressed them to their underwear, put them on a truck and transported them a few kilometres and staged a mock execution. The Ukrainian soldiers jumped off the wagon and ran barefoot for their lives back to the castle at Gonobitz, where they were quartered.
70. Letter to the author, V. Veryha, 16 August 1997.
71. Verbally to author, V. Tomkiw, 23 December 1996. Since the Division's soldiers carried the Death's Head insignia pinned to their cap, the local population often assumed that they were non-Christian 'unbelievers' and were both relieved and amazed when confronted with evidence to the contrary.
72. Heike, Eng. ed., op. cit., p.106. One recorded instance of the desertion of a German was referred to in a letter to the author from Roman Kolisnyk dated 4 June 1997 and Q26 Kolisnyk.
73. Ibid.
74. Volodymyr Bohdan Mykula – platoon commander 2/I/WGR 31, (unpublished memoirs) p.182.
75. Interview, M. Bihus, Toronto, 30 June 1999.
76. Code named Operation 'Spring Awakening' (*Frühlingserwachen*), the German offensive which took place in the vicinity of lake Balaton began on 6 March 1945 with the strategic objective of recapturing the Hungarian capital of Budapest and the Hungarian oil fields. For details see *1945: Kriegsende in der Südoststeiermark*, Feldbach 1989, pp.8-9.
77. *Generaloberst* Alexander Löhr commanded Army Group E, and as of 15 March 1945, the commander of all German forces in south-east Europe (OB Südost).
78. *Fernschreiben, Geheime Kommandosache, Generalleutnant* v. Grolman, 24.3.1945. RH 19 V/63, BA-MA.
79. Victor Madej, *The Russo-German War, 25 January to 8 May 1945*, Valor Publishing, 1987, p.67.

80. Heike, *Sie Wollen...*, p.199. Also see intercepted radio communication from Rösener to the *SS-Gauleiter* Dr Uberreither, HW/ 16/43, GPD 4077 Addendum II, 31 March 1945, to *Gauleiter* in Graz, PRO.
81. Heike, *Sie Wollen...*, pp.194-195. Elements of the 14th Waffen-SS Grenadier Division *'Galizien'*, are also reported to have arrived at Gorenjska (north west of Ljubljana) on 19 March 1945, to take part in the first phase of an offensive (code-named *'Frühlingsanfang'* ('Beginning of Spring'), aimed at defeating the 9th Corps NOVJ. Together with the 13th SS *Polizei* Regiment, 17th SS *Polizei* Regiment and the 28th SS *Polizei* Regiment they became part of an 'assault group' operating under Rösener's command. The offensive is reported to have started on 19 March 1945, when elements of the 14th SS Division *'Galizien'* moved from its positions in the valley of the Sava river in order to sweep the Jelovica plateau. On 22 March, troops of 14th Waffen-SS Division *'Galizien'* are stated to have advanced to the Selska Valley and then during the night of 22/23 March arrived at the hamlet of Prtovc on the southeast slopes of Ratitovec mountain. The account states that the last units of 14th SS Division *'Galizien'* departed from Jelovica plateau, two days after *'Frühlingsanfang'* ended on 5 April 1945. For further details see Zdravko Klanjscek, *Deveti korpus slovenske narodnoosvobodilne vojske 1943-1945*, Drustvo piscev zgodovine NOB Slovenije, Ljubljana, 1999,pp.386-394.
82. The confusion prompted Hitler to remark "What is the 'Galician Division' anyway? Is it the same thing as the Ukrainian Division? There's always a Galician Division floating around. Is that the same as the Ukrainian Division? Because if it is made up of Austrian Ruthenians, the only thing to do is to take away their weapons immediately. The Austrian Ruthenians were pacifists. They were lambs not wolves. They were miserable even in the Austrian Army." Felix Gilbert, *Hitler Directs His War (The Secret Records of his Daily Military Conferences)*, Oxford University Press, 1950, p.149.
83. The 30th *Waffen-Grenadier-Division der SS* (*russische Nr.* 2) comprised a German cadre with White Russian (*weissruthenische*) and Ukrainian soldiers.
84. The fact that the Division had a T/O (table of organisation) strength of 11000, but an actual strength of 14000 surprised Hitler. In all probability the figure of 14000 included its Training and Reserve Regiment (*SS-Ausb.u.Ers.Rgt*.14) which uniquely, was deployed in the Division's area of operations. As a rule, under the German system, a Division's Training and Reserve Regiment remained garrisoned in Germany and did not accompany its parent formation into the field.
85. As has already been seen, by this time the Division had undertaken extensive anti-partisan operations in both Slovakia and Slovenia.
86. *SS-Sturmbannführer* Göhler gave the following itinerary of the Division's weaponry: 2100 pistols, 6100 sub machine-guns, 9000 rifles, 70 rifles with telescopic sights, 65 automatic rifles (M-34), 434 light machine-guns, 96 heavy machine-guns, 58 light mortars, 4 heavy mortars [at this point the divisions horses and vehicles are omitted] ...22 flame-throwers, 1 medium AT (anti-tank) gun, 11 7.5cm AT guns, 17 light infantry howitzers, 3 heavy infantry howitzers M-33, 9 3.7cm AA guns, 37 light field howitzers and 6 heavy field howitzers. Gilbert, op.cit., p.150.
87. Ibid. pp.147-150. Hitler's comments at this time indicate that he never officially sanctioned the formation of the Ukrainian National Committee.
88. Himmler's standing with Hitler had already begun to slip a few days earlier, as recorded in Goebbels' diary entry for 15 March 1945, in which he refers to Himmler having received an extraordinarily severe dressing down from Hitler; see *The Goebbels Diaries: The Last Days*, Secker and Warburg, London, 1978, p.145. Seven days later and only two days before the disarmament order was issued Hitler had relieved Himmler as the commander of Army Group Vistula because of his incompetence.
89. Heike is not specific about the date that the order was received. In his memoirs he writes: "This order arrived at the Division around 20 March 1945." *Sie Wollten...*, p.195. Referring to this incident, Dmytro Ferkuniak, one of very few Ukrainian officers serving on the Division's general staff, writes that the order was prompted by a report by Division's command at the beginning of the month to higher authorities that it was still not yet ready to be committed at the front. Ferkuniak, op.cit., p.32.
90. Heike, *Sie Wollten...*, p.195.
91. Verbally to author, R. Kobryn, 10 April 1998. During the march that took place during the day, the column was attacked by aircraft, resulting in casualties.
92. Letters to author, [Niniowsky], 24 June 1997, 17 September 1997, and 16 February 1998. The presence of the Pioneer Battalion was confirmed in a letter to the author by Bohdan Kutny 14 January 1998, and in Schmitt, pp. 10-11.
93. Heike, *Sie Wollten...*, op.cit., p.197.
94. Ibid., pp.197-198.
95. Among the units which did have their weapons taken away were parts of WGR 29, Klymchuk, verbally to author, 7 June 1997; 13/WGR 30, letter to author, Jacyna 10 December 1997. Several units including the artillery do not appear to have received the order at this time, Q 24: Kulchyskyj, Q 26: Kolisnyk, Q 2: Havrych, Q 3: Humeniuk.
96. One rumour circulating at this time was that once disarmed, the Ukrainian soldiers would be interned in concentration camps by the Germans, a prospect that for some individuals provided sufficient impetus for them to desert. Letter to author, O. Sokolskyj, 23 June 1992.
97. The idea of mass mutiny by the Ukrainians soldiers was discussed within the Division at all levels. Two prominent men who had connections with the Ukrainian underground circles, *Waffen-Obersturmführer* Bohdan Pidhayny and Father Laba are known to have conferred on the subject. Verbally to author, M. Scharko, 18 October 1997. Other local clandestine discussions also took place at which it was agreed to "resist the disarming and disarm – by force if necessary – the German personnel and then head towards the advancing western Allies or join the local partisans".. Letters to the author, W. Sirskyj, 13./WGR 29, 2 July 1997, and R. Kolisnyk (3/I/WGR 31) June 24 1997. However attractive this solution may have seemed to be, the reality was fraught with difficulties, mainly because the co-ordination of all sub-units for any such action was almost impossible: "Our horizontal connections and communication with other units was almost non-existent. We had good vertical connections, but for the most part this was in German hands." Hawrylak, op.cit., p.26. In addition to which, individual units were reluctant to desert for fear of reprisals against those who remained.
98. Letter to author, V. Veryha, 10 January 1998. It appears that most units were disarmed for a day as confirmed by Q1 Dmytryk, interview, M. Klymchuk, London, 6 June 1997. On this issue, a *Waffen-Untersturmführer* who was commander of the heavy mortar platoon of the 4th company of the Fusilier Battalion wrote: "Shortly before noon we were told to surrender our weapons. The first heavy machine gun platoon and the light mortar platoon placed their rifles on the ground across the road from where they were billeted and went back to their quarters. The rifles lay on the ground until evening with no one guarding them. The machine guns and mortars remained with the soldiers. The heavy mortar platoon, which was billeted a few kilometres away from the rest of the fourth company, received no such orders. We were anxious, not knowing what would come next. Late in the afternoon before dark, we were told to retrieve our weapons." Letter to author W. Kudla, 11 September 2000.
99. Heike, *Sie Wollen...*, p.200.
100. Ibid. p.201.
101. Ibid.
102. Letter to author, R. Kolisnyk, 24 June 1997. The movement of WGR 31 was possibly a precursor to a third large-scale operation planned by Rösener designed to advance of the centre of Tito's forces. The Division which was to have been the backbone of the advance was to cover an area from the outskirts of Ljubljana south-west, all the way to Trieste. Heike mentions this operation in his memoirs, Eng. ed., op.cit., pp.103-104.
103. Heike, *Sie Wollen...*, p.203.
104. Ibid., p.201.
105. The short-term objective of this manoeuvre was intended to get behind 6th and 2nd *Panzer* armies and link up with Soviet forces coming out of Yugoslavia. The Soviet breakthrough in this sector was largely attributable to the collapse of the Hungarian infantry units several of which according to the war diary of Army Group South had begun deserting in droves, see Ziemke, op.cit., p.455. For details of the German counterattack see *Oberstleutnant* Josef-Paul Puntigam, *Vom Plattensee Bis Zur Mur: Die Kämpfe 1945 im Dreilandereck*, Hannes Krois, Feldbach, pp.146-149.
106. Heike, *Sie Wollten...*, op.cit., p.207.
107. Gustav Harteneck: (commander I *Kavallerie* Corps.) *Das Deutsche Kavallerie-Korps*, February 1963 (unpublished manuscript) p.14 (21), RH 24-202/23, BA-MA. For a complete list of all units assigned to I *Kavallerie* Corps see Ibid., p.26.
108. Madej, op.cit., p.67. The chart dated 24 March 1945, reveals that I *Kavallerie* Corps had the highest ratio of low combat effectiveness according to a system developed by the German high command which gave a numerical value for the estimate fighting capabilities of every fighting unit; 1 = a unit capable of offensive actions, 2 = limited attack capability, 3 = full defensive capabilities, 4 = limited defensive capability, 5= unreliable. The following breakdown is given for I *Kavallerie* Corps:
10th *Fallschirmjäger* – forming
117 J[äger] Div. – none given
3.Kav – 4
14.SS.PzG *'Ukrainian'* – unreliable
44 *(Reichs-Gren. Div. Hoch-u.Deutschmeister)* – 4
23.*Pz*. – 4
9.SS.*PzK* (*Kampfgruppe*) – unreliable
109. Heike, Eng. ed., op. cit., p.116.
110. HW/ 16/43, GPD 4077 Addendum II, 31 March 1945, to *Gauleiter* in Graz, PRO.
111. *SS-Gruf.* von Kammerhofer, an *SS-OGruf.* Roesener Laibach. [Ljubljana] *Geheim!* HW 16/49 GPDR 50, 4065, PRO.
112. In his memoirs, *Sie Wollten...*, p.200, Heike states that this was the Fusilier Battalion. If this is the case, it can only have been the HQ, 1st and 4th companies, as in letters to the author dated 11 December 1997, and 30 December 1997, two former members of the 2nd and 3rd companies respectively have confirmed that these units were accompanying the Divisional Artillery Regiment at this time. For the command structure of the Fusilier Battalion in Spring of 1945 see *Visti Kombatanta* Nr.3, 1992, p.90, and (for corrections) *Visti Kombatanta* Nr. 4, 1992, p.96.
113. Verbally to author, Jacyna, 5 November 1997, verbally to author, Prymak, 8 November 1997, verbally to author, E. Shypailo, 20 December 1997.
114. Verbally to author, O. Sokolskyj, 5 November 1997, and 6 December 1997. A former member of 8/II/WGR 29 confirmed that the battalion crossed in this way.
115. Letter to author, O. Sokolskyj, 12 August 1997.
116. The presence of Ukrainian soldiers in the vicinity of the villages of Popendorf and Trautmannsdorf on 2 April 1945, is confirmed by civilians who came into contact with them, see *Kriegsende in der Südoststeiermark*', p.14.
117. See 'Fights of the Castle of Gleichenberg', *Visti*, Nr. 4 (6) April 1951. W. Kosak.
118. Letter to author, O. Sokolskyj, 26 December 1997. This is corroborated by an account that states on "2 April 1945, crowds of Ukrainian SS-men went begging [for food] from house to house." *Kriegsende...*, p.14.
119. Letter to author, O. Sokolskyj, 23 June 1992.
120. "The first patient I had to treat was a 16 years old mildly retarded girl, who was raped by Soviet soldiers a day or two before our arrival." Letter to author, Dr Krywulak, 23 August 1997. Numerous incidents of rape of local women have also been reported. Letter to author, W. Sirskyj, 16 September 1997.
121. Herasymowycz, op.cit., pp.3-4 and letter to the author, 14 July 1997. Letter to author, V. Veryha, 16 August 1997, M. Scharko verbally to author, 7 December 1997.
122. Herasymowycz, op.cit., pp.3-4. Letter to author, 14 July 1997.
123. The movement of the 13/WGR 30 was confirmed verbally to author, Jacyna, 31 August 1997. Letter to author, E. Shypailo, 5 August 1997.

124. Volodymyr Bohdan Mykula – platoon commander 2/I/WGR 31, (unpublished memoirs) pp.181-188.
125. Letter to author, R. Kolisnyk, 4 June 1997.
126. Letter to author, R. Kolisnyk, 24 June 1997. The regiment arrived in Gonobitz on 1 April 1945. Verbally to author, P. Jacyna, 31 August 1997.
127. It was rested for one day before being committed. Letter to author, R. Kolisnyk, 4 June 1997, Q26.
128. Kutny & Kaczmarchuk, op.cit., p.7.
129. Hnatkiv, op.cit., pp.1, 2. Interview, P. Cisarskyj, Norwich, England, 14 November 1998.
130. Heike, *Sie Wollten..*, p.203. Letter to author, W. Sirskyj, 16 September 1997.
131. Letter to author, O. Sokolskyj, 26 December 1997, Q15.
132. Interview, M. Klymchuk London, 7 June 1997. Those Ukrainians who had themselves at this time been temporarily disarmed took revolvers from the Hungarians for self-defence. Letter to author, O. Sokolskyj, 23 June 1992.
133. Letter to author, O. Sokolskyj, 26 December 1997.
134. It is interesting to note that at least on paper the quantities of the weapons listed here exceed the numbers held by the Division at this time as given by *SS-Sturmbannführer* Göhler, the adjutant to the Liaison Officer of the Waffen-SS at the Führer conference a few days earlier (see footnote 13). An additional 500 sub-machine guns, and 10 rifles with telescopic sights would have been required to meet the required quota.
135. HW/16/43, GRD 4053, PRO.
136. Including WGR 30, as confirmed by Herasymowycz, op.cit., p.4, M. Scharko verbally to author, 7 December 1997, V. Veryha letter to author, 10 January 1998, and the elements of both the Pioneer and Fusilier Battalions based in or close to the city. Q 1: Dmytryk, Q 12: Sadiwskyj, Q 13: unknown, Q 14: unknown, Q 4: Jacyna, Q 5: Melnyk. Neither WGR 29, the forward elements of which had by this time already been involved in skirmishes with Red Army units, the Artillery Regiment nor WGR 31, which was still marching through Slovenia appear to have been effected.
137. Letter to author, V. Veryha, 10 January 1998.
138. Heike, *Sie Wollten...*, op.cit., p.202.
139. *Geheime Kommandosache*, Op Abtl/Ia, Nr 4178 g. Kdos., 4.4.45, *notiz nach Führervortrag Nacht 3./* 4.4.45. A reference to this order can be found in the *Verordnungsblatt der Waffen-SS*, where it is recorded thus: 'Führer has decided that the Division is to provide cadre for the 10th *Fallschirmjäger* Div.' [Tg.Buch-Nr Il 1907 gk v.9.4.45.]. AA. See also Document N 756/170 (Sammlung Vopersal), BA-MA, Freiberg.
140. In his memoirs Heike states that the Division received a telegram from the headquarters of *Wehrkreise* XVIII (Salzburg) with which it had no connection, for it to immediately reform as the 10th *Fallschirmjäger* Division, Eng. ed., op. cit., p.113. This order was almost certainly the same order (or a variation of) that quoted above.
141. Heike, *Sie Wollten...*, op.cit., p.208.
142. V. Veryha letter to author, 10 January 1998, Herasymowycz, op.cit., p.4.
143. See GPD 4053 No. 1 Traffic: 3.4.45, HW 16/71, PRO.
144. Dmytro Ferkuniak writes: "[....] At an officers' conference on April 2nd to which Ukrainians were not invited, a decision was taken to return the arms to the Division and send it to the front in southern Styria". Ferkuniak, p.32. The return of the weapons to elements of WGR 30 was confirmed by V. Veryha in a letter to the author dated 10 January 1998 and Herasymowycz, op.cit., p.3.
145. Heike, *Sie Wollten...*, p.208.
146. Heike, Eng. ed., op.cit., pp.115-116.
147. *Kriegsende...*, p.142.
148. For a highly detailed account of the German counter-attack in the Raab valley sector see *Oberstleutnant* Josef-Paul Puntigam, *Vom Plattensee Bis Zur Mur: Die Kampfe 1945 im Dreilandereck*, pp. 146-149 and a second account by the same author containing excellent maps, 'Ortskampf – am Beispiel der Stadt Feldbach im Jahr 1945', *Truppendienst* 1/1989, pp.27-37.
149. Julian Wilshynskyj, letter 2 September 1998. Kutny, op.cit., p.7.
150. Ostap Czuczkewycz (born Romaniv, 2.10.1907) served with the Polish army from 15 July 1928 until 15 January 1930 and then with the Wehrmacht from 1 June 1939 until 1 December 1939. See *Personal-Akte* A3343-SSO-133 (ff. 25-26) NA.
151. The description of these events is given as told to the author by Myhailo Klymchuk, a NCO who prepared the battle maps. According to his testimony, in this period 1/I/WGR 29 lost 50-60 of its strength of 110 in killed and wounded. His account continues, "following the attack on Bad Gleichenberg, maps were submitted to the battalion HQ where Wildner discovered that *Waffen-Obersturmführer* Kosak's company had pulled back without orders. Wildner ordered an immediate counterattack to retake the positions which was scheduled to begin at 4.00am the next day, however this was superseded when at 3.30 the Soviets attacked and suffered heavy casualties. As a result 1st Battalion withdrew approximately ½km to the edge of Bad Gleichenberg". Verbally to author, M. Klymchuk 30 August 1997.
152. The movement of the bulk of WGR 30 was recorded by two of its former members, Herasymowycz, op.cit., p.4, and V. Veryha, letter to the author, 10 January 1998. The commander of 5/II confirmed that it remained behind in Slovenia guarding a brown coalmine which was important for the local industry. 5/II/WGR 30, Zenon Kuk, unpublished memoirs pp.30-32.
153. In his account W. Kosak confirms that on 6 April the Soviets broke through the lines of WGR 30 regiment, 'Fights for the Gleichenberg Castle', *Visti*, Nr. 4 (6), April 1951. W. Kosak.
154. Herasymowycz, op.cit., p.4.
155. These tactical problems were confirmed to the author by the regimental commanders' former *Ordonnanz Offizier* M. Scharko, verbally on 5 and 10 February 2000. It is possible that the actual choice of line was influenced by Freitag or Forstreuter's ambition, or even a combination of both. In support of this contention Myron Scharko related an incident which took place in his presence. While marching to the front in the Gleichenberg sector, Forstreuter and the Divisional commander were studying a map spread out on the bonnet of a car. During the discussion Forstreuter intimated that he was Freitag's youngest officer and wished to win the *Ritterkreuz*, to which Freitag responded by saying, "I'll take care of you", Verbally to author, M. Scharko, 18 October 1999, and 4 December 1999.
156. The combined strength of this disparate force was approximately 2800 men supported by a handful of tanks and self-propelled guns. The German forces involved in this action included *Kampfgruppen* from 10th *Fallschirmjäger* Div., 1st *Panzer* Division, and *Fahr Ersatz und Ausbildung-Abteilung* 18, see Puntigam, 'Ortskampf – am Beispiel der Stadt Feldbach im Jahr 1945', *Truppendienst* 1/198, p.30.
157. Just south of Odet the battalion's medical team established its advanced clearing station, serving and treating the seriously wounded and referring more than a dozen in a short while to the field hospital. Krywulak, op.cit., p.3.
158. See Kurt Mehner, *Die Geheimen Tagesberichte der Deutschen Wehrmachtführung im Zweiten Weltkrieg 1939 – 1945*, Band 12, Biblio Verlag, Osnabrück, 1985, p.354.
159. These men had graduated from Posen Treskau and gone on to attend an advanced weapons training course at Leshany which was completed on 17 March 1945. Returning to the Division, the 82 men split up into small groups that travelled independently by various forms of transport, both military and civilian, which explains why they arrived within a few days of each other at different times. Letter to author, J. Kunyckyj, 19 October 1997. Source for figure of 82 men – *SS-Personalhauptamt Personalamt der Waffen-SS Amt* VII-*Hauptabteilung* 1, *Abteilung* 3 -Fi./P. Weimar, 14 Marz 1945, *Sophienstifischule, Betr.*: 16./17. *Oberjunkerlehrgang an der SS-Pz.Gren.Schule*, AA.
160. This group travelled via Vienna to the Training and Reserve Regiment at Deutschlandsberg and then to Marburg (where they were quartered at the castle of Wittschein) before joining the Division in Austria around 10/12 April. For his part, Wächter was very friendly towards the young Ukrainians and is reported to have said, "Look around you gentlemen," (pointing to the mountainous landscape), "the area resembles our [sic.] beautiful mountains near Stryj" (a provincial town in western Ukrainian at the foot of the Carpathians mountains). Evidently, Wächter considered himself a fellow countryman rather than a representative of an occupying power. Letter to author, W. Motyka, 17 September 1997.
161. Under these extenuating circumstances some (both German and Ukrainian) found it difficult to cope with the demands placed on them and subsequently made errors which cost them their lives. The Ukrainians were said to be emotional. Verbally to author, M. Klymchuk 30 August 1997, and interview, O. Holynsky, Rutherford, USA, 25 June 1999.
162. As early as 8 March 1945, Wächter's immediate superior *SS-Obergruppenführer* Wolff, the HSSPf. in Italy, had already agreed with the Americans with whom he had been negotiating, to a capitulation of all the German armed forces in Italy. Despite this agreement, both German army field commanders, Kesselring and later his replacement Vietinghoff continued to postpone the actual signing as long they could. For additional details see Heinz Höhne, *The Order of the Deaths Head*, Pan, 1972, pp.527-529.
163. Heike, Eng. ed., op.cit., p.120.
164. Consisted of 20th Guards Division, 61st Guards Rifle Division, 113th Rifle Division, 299th Rifle Division, 864th Assault Gun Rgt.
165. 73rd Guards Division, 10th Guards Airborne Division, 104th Rifle Division, 32nd Guards Mech. Brigade, 52nd Tank Rgt.
166. Details of the German and opposing Soviet forces involved and their relative positions in relation to each other see the maps in *Oberstleutnant* Puntigam, *Vom Plattensee...*, p.180 (map 38), map 49, p.251, and *Lagekarte der Heeresgruppe Sud vom 20 April, 1945*, Ausschnitt, BA-MA.
167. Heike, Eng. ed., op.cit., p.118.
168. Ibid., p.119.
169. The Soviet 57th Army which faced 2nd *Panzer* Army had one tank brigade with a total of 65 tanks and one tank corps consisting of 200 tanks (most of which were the ubiquitous T-34) at its disposal. The bulk of the Soviet armour and mechanised forces which faced the German Army Group South in April 1945, were concentrated within the 27th Army, which was deployed north of Feldbach. See *Kriegsende...*, p.29.
170. As the fighting took place day and night, the infantry units were given four or five hours in the rear to rest, eat and attend to basic hygiene before being re-committed at the front. Interview, Klymchuk, London 6 October 1990. Letter to author, J. Kunyckyj, 9 September 1997, and 22 August 1997.
171. Volodymyr Vashkovych 'At Gleichenberg', *Visti Kombatanta*, Nr.1, 1972, pp.41-47.
172. Puntigam, *Vom Plattensee...*, op.cit., p.176.
173. Vashkovych, 'Pid Gleichenbergom: Kviten-traven 1945', *Visti Kombatanta* 1972, Nr.1 (57).
174. Motyka, unpublished memoirs, pp.12-13 and letter to author, 17 September 1997.
175. For a map detailing all the units involved in the counterattack against the Soviet units from 20th Guard Rifle Division in Trautmannsdorf see Puntigam *Vom Plattensee...*, op.cit., pp.175-176.
176. Letter to author, 22 August 1998, from the commander of the *Jagdzug* attached to III/WGR 29, *Waffen-Untersturmführer* Kulchyskyj, whose unit played an active part in the fighting at this location.
177. See 'Fights for the Gleichenberg Castle', *Visti*, Nr. 4 (6), April 1951. W. Kosak.
178. A *Waffen-Untersturmführer* serving with 2nd Company of the Pioneer Battalion wrote, 'one night we had Soviets attack our line and I recall they came within about 10ft of us. In the morning I saw two bodies in front of our positions'. Letter to author, B. Kutny, 20 June 1994.
179. To defend its new line, the Division's tactics involved manning the frontal positions with weak forces whilst keeping a large reserve massed near the front ready to counterattack. This was because the Ukrainian soldiers were more susceptible to artillery fire than Germans and therefore easier to flush out of defensive positions. This idiosyncrasy was however largely negated by the fact that they were superior in counter-attack and typically won back lost territory. Heike, Eng. ed., op.cit., p.117.

180. WGR 31 arrived in Straden on 6/7 April. Letter to author, R. Kolisnyk, 17 September 1997. Hawrylak, op.cit., p.29. Like WGR 30, a token force was left behind in Slovenia by WGR 31 guarding a depot in a town near Marburg. Surrounded by partisans at the end of hostilities this unit refused to surrender and eventually its personnel were escorted under the protection of Australian soldiers to Austria. Verbally to author, P. Jacyna, 31 August 1997.
181. Heike, Eng. ed., op. cit., p.117.
182. Puntigam, *Vom Plattensee...*, op.cit., p.175.
183. P. Trotch, letter to author, 15 March 1998.
184. Ibid.
185. Herasymowycz, op.cit., p.3.
186. Kutny, op.cit., p.7, and Schmitt, op.cit., p.12.
187. Two separate accounts by witnesses of how Pannier received his wound concur that it was due to his arrogance and failing to conduct himself properly when in an exposed position. See Hawrylak, op.cit., p.30, and Mykula, unpublished memoirs, p.197. His place was taken by *SS-Sturmbannführer* Wittenmeyer who commanded III/WGR 30, which was dissolved on this day because of heavy losses. V. Veryha letter to author, 10 January 1998.
188. Puntigam *Vom Plattensee...*,p.158.
189. See Mehner, *Die Geheimen...*, p.363.
190. Ibid. p.366.
191. Puntigam, *Vom Plattensee...*, p.158.
192. Ibid. p.176.
193. For details and personal accounts of the fighting in this area see *Kriegsende...*, pp.126-136 and pp.149-152.
194. Letter to author, I. Sadoveyj, 24 October 1998.
195. Letter to author, W. Kudla, 24 September 2000.
196. Letter to author, W. Kudla, 2 October 2000.
197. Heike, Eng. ed., op. cit., p.118.
198. Puntigam, 'Ortskampf – am Beispiel der Stadt Feldbach im Jahr 1945', *Truppendienst* 1/1989, pp.35-36. A *Kampfgruppe* from 1st *Panzer* Division commanded by *Major* Ritz and *Fahr-Ersatz-und Ausbildung-Abteilung* 18 were also involved in this action.
199. Ferkuniak, op.cit., p.32.
200. All sources are agreed that the Division had a strength of 14000, however there is some debate as to whether this included its Training and Reserve Regiment. At the time of the Führer conference 23/24 March 1945, the Division's table organisation strength was given as 11000, with an actual strength of 14000. Gilbert, op.cit., p.149. In all probability the 14000 included its Training and Reserve Regiment, stated by Shandruk in his memoirs to have had a strength of 3,000 as of April 1945. Shandruk, op.cit., p.264. Heike maintains the Division had 22000 men, which is accurate if his figure of 8000 for the Training and Reserve Regiment is added to the 14000. In either case the maximum combat strength of the Division at the time is unlikely to have exceeded 14000.
201. Kuchta had only recently assumed command of a battalion having graduated from the 26. *Btl. und Abtl. Führer-Lehrgang an der Heeresschule* Güstrow which took place from 3 January-10 February 1945.
202. Heike, Eng. ed., op. cit., p.118.
203. Krywulak, op.cit., p.3.
204. On 9 April 1945, the *Verbindungsoffizier der SS beim* OKH (SS Liaison Officer to the Army High Command) has recorded verbatim in the *Verordnungsblatt der Waffen-SS*, "The 14th *Waffen Gren.Div der SS* (*Ukr Nr.*1) is not to be disarmed. German personnel will be reinforced by inclusion of 3-4000 soldiers (ground crew) of the Luftwaffe. The Division is to remain part of the Waffen-SS." [Tg.Buch-Nr II 1890 gk v.9.4.45.]. AA. See also BA-MA document N 756/170 (Sammlung Vopersal). The order from the SS-FHA which followed the next day was a direct result of this order.
205. 10 April 1945, *Geheim!* an 14.*Waffengren.div.d.SS (Ukr. Nr.* 1), from SSFHA, gez Blume. HW 16/43 GPD 4065, PRO.
206. Heike, Eng. ed., op.cit., p.120. Ex-Luftwaffe personnel were sent to augment other SS formations or units under the command of the SS, for example the 16th *Reichsführer-SS* received four Luftwaffe draft battalions (*Marschbataillone der Luftwaffe*) on 3 April 1945, while in February 1945, plans were afoot to assign the 11th Luftwaffe Field Division to the newly created Cossack Cavalry Corps. Samuel J. Newland, *Cossacks in the German Army*, Frank Cass, London, 1991, p.164.
207. Heike, Eng. ed., op.cit., p.120.
208. Ibid. p.121.
209. Ibid.
210. Interview, M. Klymchuk, 7 October 1990, London.
211. Kolisnyk, letter to author, 17 April 1996.
212. Verbally to author, M. Scharko 18 October 1997. Forstreuter's mistrust of the Ukrainians was so pronounced that he had already taken steps to ensure that all radio and communications operatives with WGR 30 were German.
213. Heike, Eng. ed., op.cit., p.121.
214. In a letter to the author dated 23 June 1992, a former member of 8/II/WGR 29, O. Sokolskyj wrote, "they [the German Luftwaffe personnel] spent their time milling around the command post and playing cards".
215. See Puntigam *Vom Plattensee...*, map 49.
216. Ibid., map 48.
217. Letter to author, M. Pasij, 29 September 1998.
218. Stephan Hulak, 'Easter in the Front in 1945', *Visti*, Nr. 5-5, April-May 1955, pp.18-19.
219. The 2nd Company was the first to be replaced by an infantry company. The two other pioneer companies were withdrawn some days later. Schmitt, op.cit., p.12.
220. While building the bridge one man from 2nd Company was swept away in the strong current and presumably drowned, as his body was never recovered. Letter to author, B. Kutny, 24 November 1997. A considerable amount of material was needed for the construction of both bridges and it was simply not available at that time.
221. Schmitt, op.cit., p.13.
222. Ibid.
223. Heike, Eng. ed., op.cit., p.119.
224. Interview, M. Klymchuk, London, 6 October 1990.
225. For a rather amusing incident during one such raid concerning the theft of two pigs by a group of fusiliers see Paziuk, op.cit., pp.95-97.
226. Shandruk, op.cit., p.264. Although the Regiment may previously have had 8000 men, at the time of capitulation 3000 is a more likely figure.
227. To forward their cause, the partisans frequently resorted to unorthodox methods. One veteran relates in his memoirs how during a patrol in mid April 1945, a young girl exploited her feminine charms on a Divisional soldier, only to pull out a pistol from her undergarments and fire at him. Fortunately the bullet struck the edge of his belt buckle and embedded itself in his leather belt. Paziuk, op.cit., pp.99-100.
228. F. Tsymbaliuk-Obychenko 'Ostannii bii pid Feldbakhom', *Visti Kombatanta* 1971, Nr.5 (55) pp. 33-34.
229. Hawrylak, op.cit., pp.33-34.
230. On this occasion the Germans drank heavily before the raid began and attempted to delegate the difficult task to a unit of Volhynian Ukrainians while they covered the flanks. V. Vashkovych 'At Gleichenberg', *Visti Kombatanta*, Nr.1, 1972, pp.41-47.
231. *Do Boyu*, Nr.6, 28 April 1945. AA.
232. Stephan Hulak, 'Easter at the Front in 1945', *Visti*, Nr.4-5 (18-19), April -May 1955, pp.4-5, op.cit., pp.18-19.
233. For one such example headed *'An alle Generale, Offiziere und Soldaten der deutschen Wehrmacht am Südabschnitt der Ostfront'*, and circulated under the name of Marshal F. Tolbuhkin see Appendix XVIII.
234. Letter to author, J. Kunyckyj, 9 September 1997.
235. Motyka, unpublished memoirs, p 14. Letter to author, 13 May 1993.
236. For example, no desertions were recorded from the Pioneer Battalion, Schmitt, op.cit. p12. Verbally to author, B. Kutny, 26 September 1997.
237. Klymchuk verbally to author, 30 August 1997.
238. Bohdan Pidhayny, 'The End of the war 1945 and the Beginning as a Prisoner of War in Italy'. *Visti Kombatanta*, 1979, Nr.1, p.66.
239. Heike, Eng. ed., op. cit., p.119.
240. Verbally to author, M. Scharko – 18 October 1997. Within the Division disciplinary cases were dealt with by *SS-Sturmbannführer* Hans Ziegler. (see HW 16/43, GPD 4040 Addendum III, 2 March 1945, An 14.*Waffengren.div.d.SS.Ukr.Nr* 1, Marburg/Drau, zHd.SS-Stbaf Ziegler, PRO). Cases have been recorded of Ukrainians receiving a reprieve, Verbally to author, M. Scharko, 18 October 1997. Vashkovych – *Ordonnanz Offizier* to Wildner – opened secret telegram mail in Feldbach asking why had no one been shot in his battalion as an example to maintain discipline. Volodymyr Vashkovych 'At Gleichenberg', *Visti Kombatanta*, Nr.1, 1972, pp.41-47.
241. Several veterans witnessed executions by firing squad for desertion: Q8 Melnyk. Q1 Dmytryk. Q2 Havrych.
242. Letter to author, J. Kunyckyj, 9 September 1997.
243. Two men were hanged from a railway bridge. Letter to author, O. Sokolskyj 23 June 1992, and two by a main road, Hawrylak, op.cit., pp.32-33.
244. Isolated instances of Red Army desertion were recorded in Austria. For example, four Red Army soldiers are reported to have deserted to *Waffen-Untersturmführer* Orest Yarymovych (1/I/WGR 29) – Pidhayny & Kinets, 'Viiny 1945 r.i Pochatok Taboru Polonenykh v Italii' ('The End of the War in 1945 and the Beginning of Being a Prisoner of War in Italy'), *Visti*, 1979, Nr.1, p.66. Interview, M. Mochnaty, 17 January 1990.
245. The front page of the penultimate edition of the Divisional newspaper *Do Boyu* of 28 April 1945, carried the following short article headed 'The First Iron Crosses 1st Class for Poruchnyks' [Ukrainian rank equivalent to 1st Lieutenant], which described the awards as follows: "1st Ukrainian Division Wolodymyr Kosak and Ostap Czuczkewycz. 1st Lt Wolodymyr Kosak, who received the Iron Cross 2nd Class for bravery in the Battle of Brody, excelled again in fighting of the Division. On April 15th at the head of his soldiers in a frontal attack on the castle Gleichenberg, he cleared a path in hand to hand fighting and freed the surrounded troops in the castle, and at the same time re-established the previous front line. 1st Lieutenant Ostap Czuczkewycz excelled in fighting on April 6th and 8th for the village of Gleichenberg. Disregarding the dangers he went at the head of his company into the attack against the fortified Bolshevik positions. Giving an example to his soldiers they were successful." *Do Boyu*, Nr.6, 28 April 1945. AA.
246. The list of recipients as given in *Do Boyu*, 6 May 1945, is as follows: *W-Grenadiers* and *W-Oberschütze* Ivan Ivashko, V. Slivinskyj, M. Zarichnyi, V. Soroka, A. Shevchuk, H. Severa, M. Kerd, S. Hutnyk, I. Kosak, Z. Dankiv, I. Kochetov, M. Andrukhiv, I. Ivanchechko, V. Volia, I. Kovalj. *W-Sturmanns*: Mykola Kobak, Osyp Novosad: *W-Unterscharführers*: V. Stasiv, I. Shapoval, M. Shevchenko, B. Bilynskyj, M. Sichko, P. Vardalj. *W-Untersturmführers*: V. Mykula, Yurij Kostiv, Osyp Holynskyj, M. Pronchak, R. Kovalskyj, I. Havryliv, Evhen Khmilovskyi, V. Handziuk, I. Skira, Andrij Komorowskyj, Taras Kaczmarchuk, Bohdan Spivak. The list was not complete and the editor noted that a further list would be published in the next issue. Other known recipients of the Iron Cross 2nd Class included *W-Untersturmführers*: Oleksa Horbatsch, Roman Herasymowycz, Phylyp Trotch, Roman Tymkevych, Orest Yarymovych, Roman Drazniowskyj, Myhailo Prymak and Volodymyr Malynovych. It should be noted that because of acute shortages that prevailed, most of the awards given at this time were the cloth and not metal varieties, as would have usually been the case.
247. *Do Boyu*, 6 May 1945.
248. *Lagekarte der Heeresgruppe Sud vom* 20 April 1945, Ausschnitt, BA-MA.
249. 6th Army, III *Panzerkorps*, 117th *Jäger* Division, *KGr.* Semmering/9th *Gebirgsjäger* Div., 1st *Gebirgsjäger* Div., SS-*Polizei* Rgt 13, 1st *Panzer* Div, *Arko* 3, 3rd *Panzer* Div. IV SS *Panzerkorps* comprised: 5th SS *Pz.* Div *'Wiking'*, 1 Hung. SS-Ski-Btl, 14th *SS-Waffen-Grenadier* Div. *'Ukraine'*, SS-Rgt. *'Ney'*, CO Rear Area 593, *KGr.* Wolf, *KGr.* Kunz, II Abtl. Fallsch. Art. Rgt 10, *Sperrverband* Motschmann, *KGr.* Gottwald, *KGr.* Siegers (with *Geb. Ers.u.Ausb Btl* 138), *sPzAbt* 509.

Chapter 10

1. Shandruk, op.cit., p.263.
2. Eventually Freitag issued Marks with a sharp written reprimand and urged Shandruk not to pursue the matter any further. Ibid. p.272.

3. Ibid. Some of the new ranks are shown on p.257.
4. The situation *vis-à-vis* Krat's proposed appointment as Divisional commander, in many ways typified the unfortunate Ukrainian position in respect of the securing the services of Ukrainian officers with recent tactical training in modern warfare. Born 6 August 1892, in Hadiache Poltava, Myhailo Krat had served in the Imperial Russian Army and later the UNR in 1917, where he attained the rank of Colonel. After holding various staff appointments, in 1919 he was given command of the 'Black Sea Regiment'. He served as Chief of Staff of the 'Third Iron Rifle Division' and then the 'Zaporozhian Division' in 1920. He had not seen active service since, yet had he been appointed he would have immediately have been given control of a Division which was for the greater part staffed by Germans and was actively engaged in combat on the Eastern Front. Krat had previously had no connection whatsoever with the Division and only took command of it during its internment in Italy. See Y. Krokhmaliuk, 'In Service of a Nation. The 80th Anniversary of General Myhailo Krat', *Visti Kombatanta* 1972, Nr.5-6, pp. 67-70 and L. Romaniuk, 'General Myhailo Krat', *Visti Kombatanta*, 1980, Nr.1, pp.68-73.
5. Shandruk, op.cit., p.267.
6. For his demands in this respect, see Ibid., p.270.
7. Shandruk, 'It was Like That', *Visti*, Nr.3-4 (53-54), March-April 1955, pp.2-6. No mention is made of the possibility of appointing the popular *Major* Heike as Divisional commander even on a temporary basis.
8. Another Ukrainian-born General who was fighting with the Germans, Sergei Buniachenko adopted a completely different attitude towards his German superiors. In mid-April 1945, Buniachenko, in flagrant disregard of his orders, marched the 1st 'Vlasov Division' away from the front towards the safety of Bohemia, and refused to put his troops at the disposal of Army Group Centre, commanded by Field Marshal Schörner, regardless of Schörner's threats that if he failed to do so he would have the 17000 men machine-gunned from the air by a fighter squadron. For an account of his enterprise see Reitlinger, op.cit., pp.379-304.
9. Shandruk, op.cit., p.271, in his capacity as 'Commander of the army and fleet of the Ukrainian Republic' (sic).
10. Herasymowycz, op.cit., pp.4-5.
11. O. Sokolskyj, letter to author, 23 June 1992.
12. ABFC. This was not however the wording agreed by Himmler on 16 February 1945, when Shandruk had proposed a new oath to the German authorities which read:
Neuer Vorschlag 'Ich schwöre bei Gott diesen heiligen Eid, das ich im Kampf gegen den Bolschewismus, zur Befreiung meines ukrainischen Volkes, meiner ukrainischen Heimat, dem Obersten Befehlshaber der Deutschen Wehrmacht und aller Kämpfer der jungen europaischen Völker gegen den Bolschewismus, Adolf Hitler, unbedingten Gehorsam leiste und als tapferer Kämpfer bereit sein will jederzeit fur diesen Eid mein Leben einzusetzen'. For details see *'An den Reichsführer-SS und Reichsminister des Innern'* den 5.2.1945, NS19/544, BA-KO.
13. In various post-war accounts, many veterans of the Division have described the oath and the effect it had on them. Two typical accounts can be found in Roman Prypkhan 'My Prysiahaly Ukraini' ('We Swore Ukrainian Allegiance'), *Visti*, 1951, Nr.7 (9), p.4, Roman Lazurko, *On Europe's Crossroads*, The Brotherhood of Former Soldiers of the 1st Ukrainian Division of the Ukrainian National Army, Chicago, 1971, pp.242-249.
14. A few lower-ranking German officers were present – *Hauptsturmführer* Klocker (CO I/WGR 30), *SS-Hauptsturmführer* Vorkörper (CO 13/WGR 30) were both present and affixed the trident badge to their officers caps. In the case of the latter this was exceptional, as he, according to a member of his company, was an ardent Nazi.
15. Letters to author, former *Kriegsberichter Waffen-Sturmann* Oleh Lysiak, 11 and 14 June 1996.
16. A copy of the paper that was published in Marburg is in the author's possession.
17. See *An: 14 Gren. Div. der SS 'Ukraine' 1, Marburg/Drau: 29.4.45, 'SS-Hauptstuf. Streithorst ist fur Sonderauftrag vorgesehen und hat sich Sofort mit marschgepack hier, melden...zu melden.' Von Pers.d.W-SS, SS-Brig. u. Genmaj. Dr Katz*, HW/16 (43) GPD/ – 4 – 4056, 29.4.45, OEU de DPM.1948/SSD/ DQH Nr 86/1245/193/LYV/3595. PRO.
18. ABFC.
19. According to the testimony of Shandruk, he despatched Colonel K. Smowsky, a former Polish army officer, with a letter to General Anders personally requesting that he or the Polish Liaison Officers intercede with the appropriate military authorities in getting the Division moved to rear of the British lines. See Shandruk, op.cit., pp.279-280. In a letter to the author dated 26 February 1999, Orest Horodyskyj, who saw the letter, stated that Colonel Smowsky never reached Anders. In his memoir, Heike states that a short while previously, Wächter had expressed the opinion that it would be prudent to change name of the Division back to 'Galicia' to emphasise its territorial origins, thereby its possible merger with General Anders Polish Corps. Heike, Eng. ed., op.cit., p.120.
20. The document stated that "The inclusion of Luftwaffe personnel, which would mean the raising of German personnel to 3600, is for the aforementioned political reasons not viable and a decision regarding their use has been requested."
21. Two Ukrainian veterans of the Division related instances to the author during interviews in which individual Germans who were vehemently hated by the Ukrainians were shot by them in the combat zone: one, a German *SS-Unterscharführer* from WGR 29, who always goaded the Ukrainians and forced them into the front without letting them rest, was shot during the fighting at Gleichenberg Casle (verbally to author, M. Prymak, 16 October 1997), and the second, a *Volksdeutsch SS-Obersturmführer* who was universally disliked after demonstrating more concern for his Alsatian dog than for the Ukrainian troops under his command. According to a former member of his company he was shot in the back with a *Panzerfaust* during the fighting around Stradner Kogel. Interview, S. Ryszkowycz, 3 March 1991, Bedford.
22. Heike, Eng. ed., op.cit., pp.131-132.
23. Shandruk, op.cit., p.273. On this issue Shandruk goes on to say "General Shkuro came to see me on 2 May, but during our talks he did not display any desire to put himself under my command or join me."
24. Letter to author, O. Wankevych, 28 October 1998.
25. Heike, Eng. ed., op. cit., p.128.
26. The Germans celebrated Easter by the Gregorian Calendar (Pope Gregory the Great) according to which Good Friday fell on 31 March 1945. The Eastern Rite or Orthodox celebrated according to the Julian Calendar (Julius Caesar).
27. In one instance the soldiers were able to hunt down a wild boar. Letter to author, A. Komorowskyj 30 September 1998. Others found domestic livestock.
28. Letter to author, J. Kunyckyj, 10 October 1998.
29. Letter to author, M. Pasij, 29 September 1998.
30. The same company also arranged to send a representative to the Soviets to give them an Easter basket after the necessary security measures had been taken. Stephan Hulak, 'Easter in the Front April/May, 1945', *Visti*, Nr.5-5 (18-19), April/May 1955.
31. W. Motyka, letter to author, 24 May 1993.
32. Although no official announcement was made, many of the 1st Ukrainian Division's units that had access to a radio learned of Hitler's death in this way. Verbally to author, M. Nykolyshyn, 23 February 1992, Hawrylak, op.cit., p.34, R. Herasymowycz verbally to author, 27 September 1998, letter to author, J. Kunyckyj 10 October 1998.
33. Motyka, unpublished memoirs, p.14.
34. General Rendulic's orders specified that the cease-fire on the Western Front, (against the Americans) would become effective on 08.00 on 7 May 1945. In his unpublished post war account the commander of I *Kavallerie* Corps, *General der Kavallerie* Gustav von Harteneck, confirms that to avoid falling into Russian [Soviet] hands the 'Ukrainian Division' marched in the direction of Italy but makes no mention of any special provision having been made to facilitate its escape. See *Das Deutsche Kavallerie-Korps*, February 1963, unpublished manuscript, p.14 (21), RH 24-202/23, p 16, BA-MA.
35. There is a discrepancy between the dates given in the two primary accounts of Makarushka's mission. Heike states that Makarushka made contact with the British on 5 or 6 May 1945 (Heike, Eng. ed., op.cit., p.129), while Shandruk gives the date of his departure as 9 May, 1945 (Shandruk, op.cit., p.279. There is no record in the war diary of 5th Corps of the meeting).
36. *SS-Grenadier-Ausbildungs-und-Ersatz-Regt.* 14 *(ukrainian Ausbildungs-Regiment* 1) AA.
37. Letter to author, R. Drazniowskyj, 6 October 1997.
38. Myron Maslovsky, 'My Last Shot', *Visti Kombatanta*, No.3, 1997, pp.99-100.
39. Volodymyr Gotskyj, 'Ostannii dni viiny v Zapasnomu polka 1 UD', *Visti*, 1952, pp. 17-18. According to a former member of his company, *Waffen-Untersturmführer* Stephan Shuhan addressed his soldiers in an informal manner:
"Well boys, as all of you have already realised by the very unusual conditions around us, the war is over. It is true. I am sure that every one of you is glad but there will be no cheers, no shouts of delight or warm embrace on our part. Just the sadness in our hearts as we remember all our friends who laid down their lives for an abominable dream which each one of us was led to believe was possible – the freedom of our country. It was the wrong time and the wrong place and most of all the odds were far, far too great. Now we have an even bigger fight on our hands and will have to try and prove to the British and American forces that we had no quarrel with them and we never fought against them. So maybe, just maybe they will understand. As you will now realise we will all have to pay the price rightly or wrongly as being soldiers we will become prisoners of war – hopefully under British protection. For they are a great democracy and have freedom of speech. We will have to pay the price of no freedom for a few years but for our countrymen it will be much harder.
"On no account must we surrender to either the partisans or the Red Army. We will stay together and in this way protect ourselves from anyone who might try and change our minds or prevent us from reaching our goal. I guess it will be a couple of days before we reach the British.
"In the meantime I ask everyone to conduct themselves sensibly and do not let anyone provoke you into doing something which we all may regret. There will be some abuse shouted at you now and later on. Just be patient and the truth will eventually surface."
Paziuk, op.cit., pp.102-103; verbally to author, 7 August 1997.
40. Divisional Order Number 71, issued on 27 April 1945, gave explicit instructions that files, war diaries and Divisional staff papers were to be destroyed, presumably to prevent them from falling into the hands of the Soviets. This is the principal reason that so little documentary material from this period has survived.
41. Although both the Germans and Soviets developed a number of gases for chemical warfare, neither side ever used them. Consequently unbeknown to unit commanders, the gas mask canisters that were issued to every soldier were put to a variety of uses and frequently contained foodstuffs, playing cards or other personal items.
42. Letter to author, W. Sirskyj, 27 September 1998.
43. According to Heike, on the day of general surrender every gun had a standard allotment of 10-15 rounds, and in this regard was in a better position than any other units in 6th Army. Heike, Eng. ed., op.cit., p.122.
44. This figure of 729 is the number of known dead, including those killed in Slovenia, as taken from a list compiled by the Brotherhood 'Brody-Lev' which cares for the graves of the former soldiers of the Ukrainian Division. An estimate of 1500 killed in action in Austria, given in 'Pamiatnyk Ukrainskym Heroiam', ('Memorial to the Ukrainian Heroes'), *Visti*, 1961, No.3, p.47, may come close to the truth.
45. M. Prymak, verbally to author, 28 November 1997.
46. Shandruk, op.cit., p.281.
47. Heike, Eng. ed., op.cit., p.132.
48. Letter to author, A. Komorowskyj, 30 September 1998. The rearguard forces are likely to have had a strength of approximately one company per battalion.

49. F. Tsymbaliuk-Obychenko 'Ostannii bii pid Feldbakhom', *Visti Kombatanta* 1971, No.5 (55), pp.33-34. Letter to author, 30 September 1998.
50. Motyka, unpublished memoirs, pp.15-16.
51. Interview, T. Kaczmarchuk, Etobicoke, Canada, 20 June 1999.
52. For example *Waffen-Hauptsturmführer** Wolodymyr Kosak, whose company was given the responsibility for the rearguard of I/1st Regiment, did not destroy all the bridges over the Mur in the 1st Ukrainian Division's sector. See *Erklärung, Major (SS-Sturmbannführer)* Elemer Scholtz, 4 April 1973, *Erklärung Major* Wolf Dietrich Heike, 14 May 1973, *Eidesstattliche-Erklärung Oberst (SS-Obersturmbannführer)* Karl Wildner 7 April 1957, AA. On 28 February 1984, Maria Berghold, an Austrian civilian, swore an affidavit that stated that Kosak intervened to save her property from destruction by over zealous German military personnel. Maria Berghold, *Eidesstattliche Erklärung*, AA. *Kosak's *Soldbuch* indicates that he was promoted to the rank of *Waffen-Hauptsturmführer* on 1 May 1945. AA
53. Heike, Eng. ed., op. cit., p.133.
54. Krywulak, op.cit., p.4.
55. Letter to author, A. Komorowskyj, 30 September 1998.
56. Motyka, unpublished memoirs, p.16.
57. Letter to author, A. Komorowskyj, 30 September 1998.
58. Several veterans recounted instances of casualties caused by attacks from Soviet aircraft, Q4 Jacyna, Dmytryk Q1.
59. Dmytryk Q1.
60. Shandruk, op.cit., p.283.
61. Verbally to author, M. Nykolyshyn, Leicester, England, 23 February 1992.
62. Q8, and Letter to author, I. Melnyk, 12 June 1991.
63. *Himmler's Bosnian Division, The Waffen-SS Handschar Division 1943-1945*, George Lepre, Schiffer Publishing, 1997, p.310.
64. Heike, Eng. ed., op. cit., p.135.
65. His body was interned in the cemetery at St. Andrae. See WO 170-7127 See Secret Security Intelligence Report No.1 (covering period 1-15 June 1945) from OC 313 Field Security Section CMF to GSI(b) HQ 78 Division, CMF: PRO. Had he lived, Freitag would certainly have stood trial for his activities prior to his appointment with the Galician Division.
66. Britain at that time had no comparable significant ethnic Ukrainian community.
67. Shandruk survived the war and emigrated to the USA with his wife in the early 1950s, where he obtained manual work. He remained active in the Ukrainian community in the USA and politically involved with the national RADA and the Ukrainian government in exile, holding the post of Minister of Military Affairs. He died on 15 February 1979, and is buried in the Ukrainian St Andrews Orthodox cemetery in South Bound, New Jersey, USA. See 'General Pavlo Shandruk and the Ukrainian National Army 1945-1985', V. Veryha, *Visti Kombatanta*, 1985, No.2, pp.42-45. His companions, Dr Fritz Arlt and Dr Makarushka both survived the war. Ultimately, Arlt remained in Germany where he continues to write, publish, and give interviews. Makarushka lived in the city of Bonn, in Germany, until his death.
68. During his tenure as Governor of Galicia, Wächter had also signed death warrants for Polish and Ukrainian citizens for alleged partisan activities and for those convicted of OUN/UPA membership and participated in the criminal practice of taking hostages. For further information on the latter issue see the oral testimony of defence witness Dr Joseph Buehler, State Secretary to Government General, in the case for Frank, *Trial of the Major War Criminals before the International Military Tribunal*, Vol. XII, p.168.
69. From the end of the war until his death on 10 September 1949, he lived in hiding in Rome's Maria dell'Anima monastery. See *Morality and Reality*, p.142, footnote 42.
70. Heike was interned from August 1945, to May 1947, on the suspicion that he had been a SS company commander. During his captivity he wrote his memoirs. From 1950 until his retirement he enjoyed a successful career with the automotive firm Audi, eventually becoming company director. He attended several veterans gatherings in Austria and maintained regular contact with the Ukrainian veterans up until his death in his home of Lenting, in Bavaria, Germany on 30 November 1994. Heike was the only German, of any rank, who responded to any of the author's numerous letters.
71. The author has in his possession two examples of identity cards issued to known former members of the Division who had registered themselves as 'stateless persons'.
72. See various entries in the war diary of 5th Corps, WO 170/ 4241, PRO.
73. Bisanz remained with the Ukrainians for a short period, whereupon believing his work with them had come to an end, he travelled to Innsbruck before returning to Vienna a few weeks later for his wife. There, he was taken prisoner, by the Soviets, extradited to Poland and executed. Interview, M. Dobrianskyj, 25 August 1990, London.
74. Letter to author, V. Veryha, 14 February 1999.
75. Personal account prepared for the author covering capitulation and internment by Roman Cholkan 26 April 1999, pp.1-2.
76. Ferkuniak, op.cit., pp.36-37.
77. Letter to author, R. Kolisnyk, 21 February 1999. Those interned by the Americans were however released sooner than those held by the British.
78. Ferkuniak, op.cit., p.35.
79. Ibid.
80. O. Horbatsch, *Visti Kombatanta*, No.4, 1961, and No.1, 1962.
81. This group of Ukrainians was transferred in succession to camps at Bad Aibling, Murnau, Regensberg, Auerbach, Ludwigsburg and Darmstadt.
82. Hawrylak, op.cit., p.37.
83. Up to this point the British did not bother the Ukrainians beyond the legal request to lay down their weapons which at times they returned to them to facilitate defending themselves against Tito's partisans see V. Veryha, *Pid sontsem Italii: voiaky dyvizii 'Halychyna'-pershoi ukrainskoi dyvizii Ukrainskoi Natsionalnoi Armii v brytiiskomu tabori polonenykh '5ts' u Belliarii, Italiia, cherven-zhovten 1945*, Toronto, Shevchenko Society, 1984, p.180. *SS-Obersturmführer* Dzillum: "[....] Having arrived in Spittal we bivouacked the unit in a big meadow, fully armed, as POWs guarded by Americans. Eight days later the NCOs and men had to surrender their arms. The Americans took us to Udine in Italy by truck. There we were handed over to the English. Now the officers had to give up their weapons and binoculars etc." Schmitt, op.cit., pp.12–13. (Author's note: Dzillum's account appears to be incorrect, as it was British and not Americans who guarded the POWs and moved them to Udine.)
84. WO 170/4241, 26, 1630 B. PRO. Most significantly, this is contrary to the conclusions pertaining to the Ukrainian Division reached in the report prepared by Anthony Cowgill, Lord Brimelow and Christopher Booker entitled, *The Repatriations From Austria in 1945, The Report of an Inquiry*, Sinclair-Stevenson Ltd, London, 1990, 2 vols. Although it incorporates the actual reports from which these verbatim quotes are taken, astonishingly and in flagrant disregard of their content goes on to state: "What we know about the Ukrainian Division is that it was not retained by 5th Corps in Austria, and that by the end of May it had turned up in Italy. It has been something of a mystery as to how this move came about". On page 94 it goes on to say "*there is no mention of them [the Ukrainians] in any movement order*". (Author's emphasis)
85. Motyka, unpublished memoirs, p.20.
86. Ibid.
87 At the 8th Plenary Meeting at the Potsdam Conference 'Terminal' on 22 July 1945, Stalin specifically singled out the 'Ukrainian (i.e. Galician) Division' for repatriation. During the sixth sitting (Stalin, Truman and Churchill) on this date, the Soviet delegation read a communication on the Soviet POW camp in Italy. It said that this was Camp No. 5 in the vicinity of the town of Celsinatica, (sic.) under the control of the British authorities, in which mainly Ukrainians were kept. The Soviet delegation stated that initially the British authorities said that the camp contained 150 men, but when a Soviet representative visited the camp it proved to contain 10,000 Ukrainians of whom the British command had formed a whole division. Twelve regiments were organised, including a signals regiment and a battalion of engineers. The officer corps was made up chiefly of Petlyura (sic.) men, who previously had commands in the German army. The Soviet delegation stated in conclusion that when the Soviet officer made his appearance at the camp 625 men at once declared their desire to return to the Soviet Union. The verbatim exchange was recorded as follows:
Churchill: "We welcome every manner of observation on your part. I shall demand a report by telegraph. There may be many Poles. "
Stalin: "No, there were only Ukrainians, Soviet citizens."
Churchill: "When approximately did all this happen?"
Stalin: "We got the telegram today, and it happened over the last few months."
Churchill: "I've not heard anything of this until now."
See Robert Beitzell, *Tehran Yalta Potsdam, The Soviet Protocols*, Academic International, 1970, pp.222-223.
88. In this respect three main theories have gained currency in recent years. The first and 'official' explanation is that the Ukrainians were *de jure* Polish citizens (i.e. they came from territory which prior to 1939 had belonged to Poland and not the Soviet Union) and hence as Polish citizens they were not eligible for repatriation. The second is that Papal intervention played a decisive part, whilst the third and most probable theory is that the Division was held by the British in Austria and later in Italy as a kind of 'insurance policy' in the event of an outbreak of hostilities with Tito's forces (especially in the area of Trieste) or between the Allies and the Soviet Union. The author is currently collecting evidence on this important issue, which will be subjected to close examination at a later date. For a contemporary observer's account of how the Division's members were rescued see G.R.B. Panchuk, *Heroes of Their Day: The Memoirs of Bohdan* Panchuk (Toronto, Multicultural History Society, 1983) and the interpretation offered by L.Y. Luciuk, *Searching For Place: Ukrainian Displaced Persons, Canada, and the Migration of Memory* (Toronto, University of Toronto Press, 2000).
89. The vast majority of the allegations against the 14th Galician Division were subjected to due legal process by the Canadian legal authorities by virtue of a lengthy and exhaustive 'Commission of Inquiry on War Criminals' led by the Right Honourable Jules Deschênes, the findings of which were published on 30 December 1986. The conclusion of the report states:
"The commission accordingly finds that:
56. The Galicia Division (14.*Waffengrenadierdivision der SS* [*gal.Nr.*1]) should not be indicted as a group.
[....]
58. Charges of war crimes against members of the Galicia Division have never been substantiated, either in 1950 when they were first preferred, or in 1984 when they were renewed before this commission."
The conclusion of the Deschênes report, issued in 1986 was later ratified by another judicial investigation by the Minister of Justice in Canada, Anne McLellan, in 1998.

Glossary of German Military Terms

See also Notes on Sources and Style for abbreviations relating to source material.

Abteilung/Abt.	Battalion/department/section, dependent upon context
Abwehr	Military intelligence service
Ausbildungs	Training
Ausbildings-und-Ersatz/ Ausb.u.E.	Training and Replacement
Auskunftstelle für Kriegsverluste der Waffen-SS	Office for War Casualties of the Waffen-SS
Chef	lit. 'chief', CO
Dolmetscher	Interpreter
Fallschirmjäger	Paratroop
Feldkommandostelle	Field command post/HQ
Feldlazarett	Field hospital
Freiwillige/Freiw.	Volunteer
Galizische	Galician
Gauleiter	High-ranking Nazi Party official responsible for a *Gau*, or Nazi administrative district
Gebirgsdivision	Mountain division
General der Panzertruppen	General of Armoured Troops
Generalfeldmarschall	Field Marshall
Generalgouvernement	German-occupied Poland
Generalleutnant	Lieutenant-General
Generalmajor	Major-General
Generaloberst	General
Hauptamt	Head office
Hauptausschuss	Central committee
Heeresgruppe	Army group
Hilfpolizei	Auxiliary police
Hilfswiger/Hiwis	Auxiliaries or 'helpers'
Höhere SS-und Polizeiführer/ HSSPf.	Senior SS and Police Commander
Ia	First General Staff Officer (operations)
Jagdzug	lit. 'hunting platoon', the prefix *Jagd-* was attached to a myriad of terms used to refer to combat units during the final phase of the war
Junkerschule	Officer school
Kampfgruppe/KGr.	Battlegroup
Kavallerie	Cavalry
Korps	Corps
Korpsabteilung	Corps detachment
Kriegsberichter	War correspondent
Kriegsverdienstkreuz/KVK	War Service Cross
Nachrichten	Signals
Oberst	Colonel
Oberstleutnant	Lieutenant-Colonel
Oberwachtmeister	Sergeant-Major
1. Ordonannzoffizier	Assistant to Ia
Panzeraufklärungsabteilung	Armoured reconnaissance battalion
Panzerjäger	Tank hunter
Polizei	Police
Panzerspähwagen	lit. Armoured reconnaissance vehicles, frequently refers to either half-tracks or armoured cars
Reichsarbeitsdienst/RAD	National Labour Service
Regimentsartz	Regimental Doctor
Reiterregiment	Cavalry regiment
Ritterkreuz	Knight's Cross
Rittmeister	Captain
SS-Artillerie-Schule	SS Artillery School
SS-Brigadeführer	SS Major-General
SS-Ergänzungsstelle	SS Replacements Bureau
SS-Führungshauptamt	SS Main Operations Office
SS-Gruppenführer	SS Lieutenant-General
SS-Hauptsturmführer/ SS-Hauptstuf.	SS Captain
SS-Oberführer	SS Brigadier
SS-Obergruppenführer/ SS-Obergruf.	SS General
SS-Oberscharführer	SS Senior Sergeant
SS-Obersturmbannführer	SS Lieutenant-Colonel
SS-Obersturmführer/SS-Ostuf.	SS Lieutenant
SS-Stabsscharführer	SS Staff Sergeant
SS-Standartenführer	SS Colonel
SS-Sturmbannführer/SS-Stubaf.	SS Major
SS-Sturmscharführer	SS Staff Sergeant
SS Untersturmführer/SS-Ustuf.	SS Second Lieutenant
Schutzmannschaft/Schuma	Police units, usually referring to formations composed of troops of non German origin.
Schützen	lit. 'Rifleman', in this book's context usually translates as 'Rifle division'
Sicherheitsdienst/SD	Security Service
Sicherheitspolizei	Security Police
Soldbuch	Soldier's paybook/identity papers
Stellung	lit. 'position', usually referring to a series of defences or defensive line, e.g. 'Prinz Eugen *Stellung*'
Sturmgeschütz/StuG	Assault gun
ukrainische	Ukrainian
Volksdeutsch	Ethnic German
Wachbataillon	Guard battalion
Waffen-Hauptsturmführer	Captain
Waffen-Oberschütze	Private 1st Class
Waffen-Obersturmführer	Lieutenant
Waffen-Sturmmann	Lance-Corporal
Waffen-Sturmbannführer	Major
Waffen-Unterscharführer	Corporal
Waffen-Untersturmführer	2nd Lieutenant
Wehrausschuss	Military board
Werbekommission	Recruitment commission
Werkschutz	Units formed to protect specific locations or premises
Werwolf	Nazi guerrilla movement
z.b.V.	For Special Purposes (repr. *zur besonderen Verwendung*)
Zug	Platoon

Select Bibliography

Unpublished papers, manuscripts and memoirs

Drazniowskyj, Roman *Kampfgruppe Wildner* – unpublished paper

Ferkuniak, Dmytro *Spomyny z Zhyttia Dywiziji Halychyna* ('Memoirs from Life in the Division 'Galicia') – unpublished manuscript

Fylypowych, Mykola *Masheruyut' Dobrovoltsi* ('The Volunteers Are Marching') – unpublished manuscript

Harteneck, Gustav [commander, I *Kav.* Corps] *Das Deutsche Kavallerie-Korps* (Bundesarchiv-Militärarchiv, February 1963) – unpublished manuscript

Hawirko, Andrij *The Structure-Organisation and Command of the 14 Artillery Regiment of 1st Ukrainian Division UNA in Slovakia September–November 1944* – unpublished paper

Hawrylak, Roman *Memoirs of Bygone* Years – unpublished manuscript

Herasymowycz, Roman *A History of the 1st Company, I Battalion, 30th Regiment/1st Ukrainian Division 14 Galizien* – unpublished paper

Hills, Dennis *Bellaria/Moscow Mission/Repatriation Problems [in connection with the Ukrainian Division]* – unpublished paper

Hnatkiv, Jaroslav *The Fusilier Battalion of the Ukrainian Division* – unpublished paper

Hrycyszyn, Michael *Smert Podolav* ('I Overcame Death') – unpublished memoirs of Ukrainian who served with the 5th *'Wiking'* Division

Krywulak, Dr W. *The Medical Service of the Field Reserve Battalion of the 1st Ukrainian Division 1944–45* – unpublished paper

Kuk, Zenon *The 5/II/WGR 30* – unpublished memoir

Kutny, Bohdan & Kaczmarchuk, Taras *The Pioneer Battalion of the 14. Galician Division* (Eng. transl.) – unpublished paper. Originally published in edited form in *Visti Kombatanta*

Luciuk, Lubomyr Y. *Divisia Halychyna* – unpublished manuscript

Mykula, Volodymyr Bohdan – unpublished memoirs

Nostitz, *Graf* Eberhard von *Die 2. Pz. Armee (Von der Monatswande April/May 1945 bis zu Kapitulation)* – unpublished paper

Schmitt, Dr Helmut *Pioniereinheiten Der 14. Waffen-Grenadier-Division, (ukrainische Nr. 1)* (April 1987) – unpublished manuscript

Veryha, Vasyl *Ukrainian Division 'Galicia'* – unpublished manuscript

Newspapers and periodicals

Do Boyu [Zum Kampf] ('To Battle') January-May 1945. Divisional newspaper.

Der Freiwillige – Kameradschaftsblatt der Hilfsgemeinschaft der Soldaten der ehemaligen Waffen-SS (Osnabrück, 1955–1977)

Do Peremohy ('To Victory'). The weekly newspaper published by the Military Board for the soldiers of the Division.

Krakivski visti ('Cracow News')

Lemberger Zeitung

Das Schwarze Korps ('The Black Corps') 1935–45. The official newspaper of the SS.

The Spectator

Visti ('Veterans News'), published in Munich

Visti Kombatanta ('Veterans News'), published in Toronto

Books and Articles

Andreyev, Catherine *Vlasov and the Russian Liberation Movement: Soviet Reality and Émigré Theories* (Cambridge: Cambridge University Press, 1987)

Anon. *Druzhyny ukrainskykh natsionalistiv u 1941 1942 rokakh* (München: Nasha knyhozbirnia, 1953)

Anon. *Istoriia Velikoi Otechestvennoi Voiny Sovetskogo Soiuza 1941–1945* (Moscow: 1960–1963, Vol.4)

Anon. 'The Mysterious Death of Lieutenant Hezner' in *World War II Investigator*, Vol. 1, nos. 1 & 2, May 1988

Anon. *Reichsrangliste der Offiziere der Schutzpolizei und Gendarmerie. 1. Teil, Generale und Stabsoffiziere* (Berlin: Reichsdruckerei, 1941)

Anon. *Reichsrangliste der Offiziere der Schutzpolizei und Gendarmerie. 2. Teil, Hauptleute* (Berlin: Reichsdruckerei, 1941)

Anon. *Reichsrangliste der Offiziere der Schutzpolizei und Gendarmerie. 3. Teil, Oberleutnante und Leutnante* (Berlin: Reichsdruckerei, 1941)

Anon. *Unsere Ehre Heisst Treue, Kriegstagebuch des Kommandostabes Reichsführer SS. Tätigkeitsberichte der 1. und 2. SS-Inf.Brigade, der 1. SS-Kav-Brigade und von Sonderkommandos der SS* (Vienna/Frankfurt a.M./Zurich: Europa, 1965)

Arlt, Fritz *Polen Ukrainer Juden Politik* (Lindhorst: Wissenschaftlicher Buchdienst Herbert Taege, 1995)

Armstrong, John A. *Ukrainian Nationalism 1939–45* (Littleton, CO: Ukrainian Academic Press, 1980, 2nd revised ed.)

Association of Former Combatants in Great Britain (Eds.) *Spysok Polyahlych v WII-hiy Svitoviy Viyny v Boyakh proty CCCR* ('Listing of the killed soldiers of the '1st Ukrainian Division' and other Military Formations in WWII in the Battles Against the USSR') (London: Association of Former Combatants in Great Britain, 1953)

Barger, Charles & Bowman, J.A. *Personnel Documents of the SS* (Imperial Publications, 1991)

Beitzell, Robert *Tehran Yalta Potsdam. The Soviet Protocols* (Academic International, 1970)

Bethell, Nicholas *The Last Secret* (London: Coronet Books, 1987)

Bender, Roger J. & Taylor, Hugh Page *Uniforms, Organisation and History of the Waffen SS* volumes 1–5 (San Jose, CA: R. James Bender Publishing, 1986)

Bihl, Wolfdieter 'Ukrainer als Teil der Streitkräfte des Deutschen Reiches im Zweiten Weltkrieg' in *Osterreichisches Ost- und Südosteuropainstitut*, Jahrgang 29, Wien, 1987

Birn, Ruth Bettina *Die Höheren SS-und Polizeiführer: Himmlers Vertreter im Reich und in den besetzten Gebieten* (Dusseldorf: Droste Verlag, 1986)

Boshyk, Yuri *Ukraine During World War Two: History and Aftermath.* (Canadian Institute for Ukrainian Studies, University of Alberta, 1986)

Broszat, Martin 'Nationalsozialistische Polen Politik 1939–45' in *Schriftenreihe Der Vierteljahrshefte für Zeitgeschichte* No.2, Stuttgart, 1961

Buchheit, Gert *Der Deutsche Geheim Dienst (Abwehr)* (München, 1966)

Buchner, Alex *Ostfront 1944, The German Defensive Battles on the Eastern Front, 1944* (Schiffer Publishing, 1991)

Budnyi, Vsevelod B. *Rimini 1945–47. Symposium 1, Persha Ukrainska Dyviziia Ukrainskoi Natsionalnoi Armii u britanskomu poloni v Italii* ('Ukrainian National Army, First Ukrainian Division in British Interment in Italy') (Toronto: Veterans of the Ukrainian National Army, First Ukrainian Division, 1979)

Bulba-Borovets, Taras *An Army Without a State. (Glory and Tragedy of the Ukrainian Insurrection Movement) Memoirs of Otaman T. Bulba-Borovets* (Winnipeg: Research Institute of Volyn No. 45, Society of Volyn, 1981)

Burleigh, Michael *Ethnics and Extermination. Reflections on Nazi Genocide* (Cambridge: Cambridge University Press, 1997)

Burtyk, Ivan *Ternystyi Shlakh 2-i Dyvizii UNA* ('The Thorny Road of the 2nd Division of the UNA') (New York: United Soldiers and Friends of the 2nd Division of the UNA – Obcyednannia Voyakiv i Pryiateliv 2-i Dyvisii UNA, 1994)

Child, Cliffton J. 'The Ukraine under German Occupation 1941–44' in T. & V. Toynbee (eds.) *Survey of international affairs 39–46, Hitler's Europe*, Oxford University Press, 1954
Chirovsky, Nicholas L. *An Introduction To Ukrainian History Vol. 3.* (New York: Philosophical Library, 1986)
Cowgill, Anthony, Lord Brimelow & Booker, Christopher *The Repatriations From Austria in 1945. The Report of an Inquiry* (London: Sinclair-Stevenson, 1990, 2 vols)
Dallin, Alexander *German Rule in Russia, 1941–1945: A Study of Occupation Policies* (London: Macmillan, 1957/Boulder, CO: Westview Press, 1981, 2nd revised ed.)
Dmytryshyn, Basil 'The Nazis and the SS Volunteer Division Galicia' in *American Slavic and East European Review* 15, No.1 (February 1956), pp.1–10
Dmytryshyn, Basil 'The SS Division Galicia: Its Genesis, Training, Deployment' in *Nationalities Papers* Vol. XXI, No.2, Fall 1993
Dorner, D. *1945: Kriegsende in der Südoststeiermark* (Feldbach: Feldbacher Beitrage zur Heimatkunde der Südoststeiermark, Heft 4, 1989)
Erickson, John *The Road to Berlin. Stalin's War with Germany* volume 2 (London: Weidenfield and Nicholson, 1983)
Fajdiga, Mirko *Braciceva brigada na Štajerskem, Koroškem in Gorenjskem* (Zalocba Obzorja Maribor, 1994, 2. knjiga)
Fischer, George *Soviet Opposition to Stalin* (Cambridge, Mass.: Harvard University Press, 1952)
Fricke, Gert *Fester Platz Tarnopol 1944* (Freiburg: Verlag Rombach, 1969)
Gilbert, Felix *Hitler Directs His War. The secret records of his daily military conferences, selected and annotated by ...* (Oxford: Oxford University Press, 1950)
Glantz, David M. & House, Jonathan M. *When Titans Clashed. How the Red Army Stopped Hitler* (University Press of Kansas, 1995)
Glantz, David M. & Orenstein, Harold S. (transl. & eds.) *L'vov-Sandomierz 1944, The Soviet General Staff Study* (David M. Glantz, n.d.) (Translated and edited from The Directorate For The Exploitation Of War Experience Of The USSR Armed Forces' General Staff, secret, copy 6191. *Collection of War Materials for the Study of War Experience* No 22, January-February, 1946. Military Publishing House of the People's Commissariat of Defense, Moscow, 1946)
Guillaume, General A. *The German Russian War 1941–1945* (London: War Office, 1956)
Heiber, Helmut *Reichsführer: Briefe an und von Himmler* (Stuttgart: Deutsch Verlags Anstalt, 1968)
Heike, Wolf Dietrich (transl. Roman Kolisnyk) *Ukrainaka dyviziia "Halychyna": Istoriia formuvannia i boiovykh dii u 1943–45 rokakh – The Ukrainian Division Galicia, the History of its Formation and Military Operations 1941–45* (Toronto: Bratstvo Kolyshnikh voiakiv 1-oi ukrainskoi dyvizii UNA, 1970)
Heike, Wolf Dietrich *Sie Wollten die Freiheit: Die Geschichte der Ukrainischen Division 1943–1945* (Dorheim: Podzun Verlag, 1973)
Heike, Wolf Dietrich *The Ukrainian Division 'Galicia', 1943–45, A Memoir* (Toronto/Paris/Munich: Shevchenko Scientific Society, 1988)
Hills, Dennis *Tyrants and Mountains: A Reckless Life* (London: John Murray, 1992)
Hirniak, Kost *Ukrainskyj legion samooborony: prychynky do istorii.* ('Ukrainian Self Defence Legion') (Toronto: Nakladom starshyn i voiakiv legionu, 1977)
Hitler, Adolf *Mein Kampf* (München: Zentralverlag der NSDAP, Franz Eher I, 1942. Eng. ed. translated by James Murphy, London: Hurst & Blackett, 1938)
Höhne, Heinz *The Order of the Death's Head* (London: Pan Books, 1972)
Höhne, Heinz & Zolling, Hermann *The General Was A Spy* (London: Pan Books, 1972)
Horodyskyj, Orest 'Dva dni v partyzantsi' ('Two Days among Partisans') in *Samostiina Ukraina* (Chicago/New York) No.7 (161) July 1962
Hrytsak, Pavlo *Vezhi i Kulemety (Spohady z Dyvizii bolshevytskoho polonu)* ('Towers and Machine-guns, Memoirs from the Division and Bolshevik prisons') (Munich: Brotherhood of Veterans of the 1st Ukrainian Division of the UNA, 1959)
Hunczak, Taras *In Enemy Uniforms* (Kiev: Time of Ukraine (Chas Ukrainy) 1993)
Hunczak, Taras *On the Horns of a Dilemma. The Story of the Ukrainian Division Halychyna* (Lanham, MD: University Press of America, 2000)
Il'nytskyj, Roman *Deutschland und die Ukraine, 1934–45: Tatsachen europaischer Ostpolitik, ein Vorbericht* (Munich: Osteuropa Institut, 1955, 2 vols)
Kalba, Myroslav *U lavakh Druzhynnykiv* (Denver, CO: 1982)
Kalba, Myroslav *'Nachtigall' A Battalion of the Ukrainian Nationalists (Facts and Documents)* (Denver, CO: 1984)
Kalba, Myroslav *Druzhyny Ukrainskych Nationalistiv u 1941–1942, rocac* (München, 1953)
Kamenetskyj, Ihor *Hitler's Occupation of Ukraine (1941–44) A Study of Totalitarian Imperialism* (Marquette Slavic Studies II, 1956)
Kern, Erich *Der Grosse Rausch, Russlandfeldzug, 1941–1945* (Zurich, 1948)
Kern, Erich *The Dance of Death* (London: Collins Clear-Type Press, 1951)
Kern, Erich *The Third Reich and the Ukrainian Question. Documents 1934–1944* (London: Ukrainian Central Information Service, 1991)
Kern, Erich *L'Allemagne national-socialiste et L'Ukraine* (Paris: Publications de l'est Européen, 1986)
Klanjscek, Zdravko *Deveti korpus slovenske narodnoosvobodilne vojske 1943–1945* (Ljubljana: Drustvo piscev zgodovine NOB Slovenije, 1999)
Klein, Egon & Kühn, Volkmar (transl. David Johnston) *Tiger, The History of a Legendary Weapon 1942–45* (Winnipeg: J.J. Fedorowicz, 1989)
Klietman, K.G. *Die Waffen SS. Eine Dokumentation* (Osnabrück: Verlag 'Der Freiwillige', 1965)
Knobelsdorff, Otto von *Geschichte der niedersachsischen 19.Panzer-Division (Bis 31.10.1940, 19 Infanterie-Division)* (Bad Nauheim: Verlag Hans Henning Podzun, 1958)
Kolisnyk, Roman 'Military Board and the Ukrainian Division' in *Shevchenko Scientific Society of Canada*, Vol. 30, 1990 and supplement 'Minutes of the Meetings of the Military Board 'Galicia' in *Shevchenko Scientific Society of Canada*, Vol. 30, 1993
Kovac, A. *Ukrainska vyzvol'na borot'bai 'Vlasovscyna'* (Germany, 1948)
Krätschmer, Ernst-Günther *Der Ritterkreuzträger der Waffen-SS* (Göttingen: Plesse Verlag, 1957)
Krokhmaliuk, Roman *Zahrava na skhodi: spohady i dokumenty z pratsi u viiskovii upravi "Halychyna" y 1943–1945 rokakh.* ('The Glow in Eastern Europe') (Toronto/New York: Bratstvo kolyshnikh voiakiv I-oi Ukrainskoi dyvizii UNA, 1978)
Krokhmaliuk, Yury-Tys *Guerra Y Liberatd. Historia De La Division "Halychyna" (D.U.I) Del Ejercito Nacional Ucranio (43–45)* (Buenos Aires: Biblioteca del Instituto informativo, 1961)
Kubijovych, Volodymyr *Meni 70* ('I am 70') (Paris/Munich: Naukove tovarystvo im Shevchenka, 1970)
Kubijovych, Volodymyr *Meni 85* ('I am 85') (Paris/Munich: Molode zhyttia, 1985)
Kubijovych, Volodymyr (Ed.) *Encyclopedia of Ukraine* volumes 1–5 (Toronto: University of Toronto Press, 1985)
Lange, Wolfgang *Korpsabteilung C; Vom Dnjeper bis nach Polen. (November 1943 bis Juli 1944)* (Neckargemund, 1961)
Lazurko, Roman *On Europe's Crossroads. Memoirs.* (Chicago: Brotherhood of Former Soldiers of the 1st Ukrainian Division of the Ukrainian National Army, 1971)
Lederrey, Colonel E. *Germany's Defeat in the East (The Soviet Armies at War 1941–45)* (London: War Office, 1955)
Lepre, George *Himmler's Bosnian Division, The Waffen-SS Handschar Division 1943–1945* (Schiffer Publishing, 1997)
Lewyckyj, Bohdan 'Ukraincy a likwidacja Powstania Warszawskiego' in *Kultura* No.6, Paris, 1952
Littlejohn, David *The Patriotic Traitors* (London: William Heinemann, 1972)
Littlejohn, David *Foreign Legions of the Third Reich* volume 4 (San Jose, CA: R. James Bender Publishing, 1987)
Lucas, James *The Last Year of the German Army, May 1944-May 1945* (London: Arms and Armour Press, 1996)
Lucas, James: *Alpine Elite. German Mountain Troops of World War Two* (London: Jane's Publishing Co., 1980)
Luciuk, Lubomyr Y. *Searching For Place: Ukrainian Displaced Persons, Canada, and the Migration of Memory* (Toronto: University of Toronto Press, 2000)

Lysiak, Oleh *Brody: Zbirnyk stattei i narysiv.* ('Brody: A Collection of Articles and Sketches') (Munich: Bratstvo kol. Voiakiv Pershoi UD UNA, 1951)
Madej, Victor *The Russo-German War, 25 January to 8 May 1945* (Valor Publishing Co., 1987)
Magocsi, Paul Robert *Morality and Reality, The Life and Times of Andrei Sheptytskyj* (Edmonton: Canadian Institute of Ukrainian Studies, University of Alberta, 1989)
Marolt, Joze *Šercerjeva brigada na Štajerskem* (Zalocba Obzorja Maribor, 1993)
Matla, Zynovii *Pivdenna pokhidna hrupa* (München: Nasha knyhozbirnia, 1952)
Medynsky, Stephan *The Trials of the Ukrainian Division (Dyvisiynymy stezhkamy)* (Toronto: Privately published, 1991)
Mehner, Kurt *Die Waffen-SS und Polizei 1939–45 (Führung und Truppe)* Norderstedt: Militär-Verlag Klaus D. Patzwall, 1995)
Mehner, Kurt *Die Geheimen Tagesberichte der Deutschen Wehrmachtführung im Zweiten Weltkrieg 1939 – 1945* (Osnabrück: Biblio Verlag, 1985, 12 vols)
Mellenthin, F.W. *Panzer Battles* (London: Futura, 1984)
Melnyk, Michael James *Alphabetical Listing of Former Officers from the '14. Waffen-Grenadier-Division der SS (galizische Nr. 1)* (Privately published, 2001)
Meyer, Brun (Ed.) *Dienstaltersliste der Waffen-SS: (SS-Obergruppenführer – SS-Hauptsturmführer) Stand vom 1.July, 1944* (Osnabrück: Biblio Verlag, 1987)
Michaelis, Rolf *Die Grenadier Division der Waffen-SS Teil 1* (Michaelis Verlag, 1994)
Molau, Andreas *Alfred Rosenberg – Der Ideologe des Nationalsozialismus – Eine politische Biografie* (Koblenz: Verlag Siegfried Bublies, 1993)
Moore, John P. *Offiziereliste Der Waffen-SS* (J.P. Moore Publishing, 2001)
Nahayevskyj, Reverend Isidor *Spohady poliovoho dukhovnyka* (Toronto: Ukrainian Book Co, 1985)
Nebeliuk, Myroslav *Under Foreign Flags* (Paris: Piuf Editions, SCIP, 1951)
Neufeldt, H.J., Huck, J. & Tessin, G. *Zur Geschichte der Ordnungspolizei 1936–1945* (Koblenz: 1957)
Neulen, Hans Werner *An deutscher Seite, Internationale Freiwillige von Wehrmacht und Waffen-SS* (München, 1985)
Newland, Samuel J. *Cossacks in the German Army* (London: Frank Cass, 1991)
Ortynskyj, Lubomyr 'Prawda o Ukrainskiej Dywizji' in *Kultura*, Nr.11, Paris, 1952, pp.109–116
Ostrowsky, Oleh *Vodyla molodistj.* ('Led by Youth') (L'viv: R.V.O., Osnova Foundation, 1996)
Paziuk, Michael *Victim of Circumstance. (A Ukrainian in the Army of the Third Reich)* (Wrexham: Bridge Books, 1995)
Panchuk, Gordon & Bohdan, R. *Heroes of Their Day: The Memoirs of Bohdan Panchuk* (Toronto, Multicultural History Society, 1983)
Pankivskyj, Kost *Roky nimetskoi okupatsii* ('Years of the German Occupation') (New York: Kliuchi, 1965/2nd ed. Naukove tovarystvo im Shevchenka, New York, 1983)
Pidhayny, Bohdan 'Two Paths One Aim' (article translated from the Ukrainian by J. Hnatkiv)
Prag, Werner & Jacobmeyer, Wolfgang *Das Diensttagebuch des deutschen Generalgouverneurs in Polen 1939–1945* (Stuttgart: Deutsche Verlags-Anstalt, 1975)
Pobihushtchyi-ren, Evhen *My Life's Mosaic* (Association of Ukrainians in Great Britain, 1982)
Pohl, Dieter *Nationalsozialistische Judenverfolgung in Ostgalizien 1941–1944. Organisation und Durchführung eines staatlichen Massenverbrechens* (München: R. Oldenbourg Verlag, Publikation des Instituts für Zeitgeschichte, 1997)
Polushkin, M. *Na Sandomirskom napravlenii Lvovsko-Sandomirskaya Operatsiya (July-August 1944)* (Moscow: Voenizdat, 1969)
Puntigam, Oberstleutnant Josef-Paul 'Ortskampf – am Beispiel der Stadt Feldbach im Jahr 1945' in *Truppendienst* 1/1989
Puntigam, Oberstleutnant Josef-Paul *Vom Plattensee Bis Zur Mur. Die Kampfe 1945 im Dreilandereck* (Feldbach: Hannes Krois Verlag)
Puszkar, Oleh *Lagernyi Tryptykh* (Warsaw: Ukrainskyj Arkhiv, 1994)
Rebet, Lev *Svitla I tini OUN* (München: Ukrainskyj samostiinyk, 1964)
Reider, Frederic *The Order Of The SS* (W. Foulsham & Co., 1981)
Reitlinger, Gerald *The House Built On Sand. The Conflicts of German Occupation Policy in Russia 1939–1945* (New York: Viking Press, 1960) Reitlinger, Gerald *The SS: Alibi of a Nation, 1922–1945* (New York: Viking Press, 1968)
Schellenberg, Walter *The Schellenberg Memoirs* (London: Andre Deutsch, 1956)
Schneider, Jost W. *Verleihung Genehmigt! Eine Bild und Dokumentargeschichte der Ritterkreuzträger der Waffen-SS und Polizei 1940–1945* (San Jose, CA: R. James Bender Publishing, 1977)
Seaton, Albert *The Russo-German War 1941–45* (London: Arthur Barker, 1971)
Semotiuk, Jaroslav *Ukrainian Military Medals* (Toronto: Shevchenko Scientific Society in Canada, 1991)
Semchyshyn, Myroslav *From the Book of Lev. Ukrainian L'viv, 20th–40th years, Memoirs* (L'viv: Schevchenko Scientific Society Memoir Library of SSS, No.4, 1998)
Shandruk, Pavlo (Transl. O. Olesnyckyj) *Arms of Valour* (New York: Robert Speller & Sons, 1959)
Shankovskyj, Lev 'UPA and the Division Halychyna' in *America*, July 12–16, 1954
Shankovskyj, Lev *Pokhidni hrupy OUN; prychynky do istorii pokhidnykh hrup OUN na tsentralnykh I skhidnikh zemliakh Ukrainy v 1941–1943 rr.* (München: Ukrainskyj samostiinyk, 1958)
Skorupskyj, Maksym *U nastupakh i vidstupakh: Spohady* (Chicago, 1961)
Slaboshpytskyi, Myhailo & Stetsenko, Valerii *Ukrainian Division Galicia* (Kiev/Toronto: Association 'Negociant–Plus', Brotherhood of Former Soldiers of the 1st Ukrainian Division on the UNA, Editorial Board of the newspaper *News from Ukraine*, 1994)
SS-Personalhauptamt (Eds.) *Dienstaltersliste der Schutzstaffel der NSDAP: (SS-Obersturmbannführer und SS-Sturmbannführer) Stand vom 1.Oktober 1944* (Berlin, 1944)
SS-Personalhauptamt (Eds.) *Dienstaltersliste der Schutzstaffel der NSDAP: (SS-Obersturmbannführer und SS-Sturmbannführer) Stand vom 9.November 1944* (Berlin, 1944)
Stein, George H. *The Waffen SS: Hitler's Elite Guard at War 1939–1945* (New York: Ithaca, 1966)
Steiner, Felix *Die Armee der Geachteten* (Göttingen: Plesse Verlag, 1963)
Stercho, Petro *Karpato-ukrainska derzhava: do istorii vyzvolnoi borotby karpatskykh ukraintsiv u 1919–1939 rokakh* (Toronto, 1965)
Stiplovsek, Dr Miroslav *Šlandrova brigada. Knji nica NOV in POS 10* (Ljubljana: Maribor, 1971)
Strik-Strikfeldt, Wilfred *Against Stalin and Hitler* (London: Macmillan, 1970)
Strle, Franci *Veliki finale na Koroškem* (Ljubljana, 1976)
Sydnor, Charles W. *Soldiers of Destruction. The SS Death's Head Division 1933–1945* (Guild Publishing, 1989 reprint)
Szezesniak, Antoni B. & Wieslaw, Z. *Szota, Droga do nikad* (Warsaw, 1973)
Tessin, Georg & Neufeldt, H.J. *Zur Geschichte Der Ordunungspolizei 1936–1945* (Koblenz: Schriften des Bundesarchivs Vol. 3, 1957)
Thomas, N. & Mikulan, K. *Axis Forces in Yugoslavia 1941–45* (London: Osprey, 1995)
Thorwald, Jurgen *The Illusion (Soviet Soldiers in Hitler's Armies)* (New York: Harcourt Brace Jovanovich, 1975)
Tieke, Wilhelm & Rebstock, Friedrich *Im Letzten Aufgebot, 1944–45. Die Geschichte der 18.SS-Freiwilligen-Panzergrenadier-Division Horst Wessel* (Regensberg: Truppenkameradschaft 18/33, 1995)
Tolstoy, Nikolai *Victims of Yalta* (London: Corgi Books, 1971)
Tolstoy, Nikolai *The Minister and the Massacres* (London: Century Hutchinson, 1986)

Torke, Hans-Joachim & Himka, John-Paul *German-Ukrainian Relations in Historical Perspective* (Edmonton: Canadian Institute of Ukrainian Studies Press, 1994)

Trevor-Roper, Hugh *Hitler's War Directives 1939–1945* (London: Pan Books, 1964)

Trevor-Roper, Hugh (Ed.) *The Goebbels Diaries: The Last Days* (London: Secker and Warburg, 1978)

United States War Department *Handbook on German Military Forces* (Washington, D.C.: 15 March 1943, technical manual TM-E 30–451)

Vashkovych, Vasyl 'The First Ukrainian Division at Gleichenberg, Styria' (*Visti Kombatanta* No.1, 1972, pp.41–47)

Vashkovych, Vasyl, article in *The Ukrainian Independent*, 1972, pp.567–568

Venohr, Wolfgang *Aufstand in der Tatra (Der Kampf um die Slowakei) 1939–44* (Athenaum, 1979)

Veryha, Vasyl: *Dorohamy druhoii svitovoi viiny: legendy pro uchast ukraintsiv u zdushuvanni varshavskoho povstannia v 1944r.ta pro ukrainsku dyviziiu "Halychyna"* (Toronto: New Pathway, 1980/2nd revised ed. – Toronto: Bratstvo kolyshnikh voiakiv 1-oi ukrainskoi dyvizii UNA, 1984)

Veryha, Vasyl *Pid sontsem Italii: voiaky dyvizii "Halychyna"-pershoi ukrainskoi dyvizii Ukrainskoi Natsionalnoi Armii v brytiiskomu tabori polonenykh '5ts' u Belliarii, Italiia, cherven-zhovten 1945* (Toronto: Shevchenko Society, 1984)

Veryha, Vasyl 'General Pavlo Shandruk and the Ukrainian National Army 1945–1985' in *Visti Kombatanta*, 1985, No.2. pp.42–45

Witte, P. et al *Der Dienstkalender Heinrich Himmler 1941/42* (Hamburg: Christians, 1999)

Zahachevskyi, Evstakhii *Beliariia, Rimini, Anhliia* (Chicago/München, 1968)

Zelenko, Constantine 'Shche pro dyviziiu Halychyna' in *Ukrainskyj samostiinyk* (Munich) 23, nos.11–12 (November-December 1972) 26–32; 24, No.1 (January 1973) 25–32; 24. No.2 (February 1973) 30–41

Zeleny, Zenon *Ukrainske iunatstvo v vyri druhoii svitovoi vinny* ('Ukrainian Youth in the Turmoil of WWII') (Toronto: Bratstvo kolyshnikh voiakiv 1-oi ukrainskoi dyvizii UNA, 1965)

Zentral Stelle der Landesjustizverwaltungen *Das Sonderkommando 4a der Einsatzgruppe C und die mit diesem Kommando eingestzten Einheiten während des Russland – Feldzuges in der Zeit vom 22.6.1941 bis zum Sommer 1943* (Ludwigsburg: Zentrale Stelle der Landesjustizverwaltungen, 30 December 1964)

Ziemke, Earl F. & Bauer, Magna E. *Moscow to Stalingrad: Decision in the East* (New York: Military Heritage Press, 1988)

Ziemke, Earl F. *Stalingrad to Berlin: The German Defeat in the East* (New York: Military Heritage Press, 1985)

A selection of forthcoming titles

IN THE FIRE OF THE EASTERN FRONT
The Experiences of a Dutch Waffen-SS Volunteer on the Eastern Front 1941–45
Hendrick C. Verton
ISBN 978-1-874622-54-3

THE KNIGHT'S CROSS: HOLDER'S OF PANZERKORPS GROSSDEUTSCHLAND
Including its Sister Units: Panzer-Führer-Begleit Division/Panzer-Führer-Grenadier-Division/ Panzer-Grenadier-Division Brandenburg/Panzer-Grenadier-Division Kurmark
Ralph Tegethoff
ISBN 978-1-874622-93-2

OPERATION GOODWOOD, JULY 1944
A Corridor of Death
Perry Moore
ISBN 978-1-874622-73-4

SOME ADDITIONAL SERVICES FROM HELION & COMPANY

BOOKSELLERS

- over 20,000 military books available
- four 100-page catalogues issued every year
- unrivalled stock of foreign language material, particularly German

BOOKSEARCH

- free professional booksearch service. No search fees, no obligation to buy

Want to find out more?
Visit our website

Our website is the best place to learn more about Helion & Co.
It features online book catalogues, special offers, complete information about our own books (including features on in-print and forthcoming titles, sample extracts and reviews), a shopping cart system and a secure server for credit card transactions, plus much more besides!

HELION & COMPANY

26 Willow Road, Solihull, West Midlands, B91 1UE, England
Tel: 0121 705 3393 Fax: 0121 711 4075
Email: publishing@helion.co.uk Website: http://www.helion.co.uk